The absurd
in literature

Manchester University Press

The absurd in literature

Neil Cornwell

Manchester University Press
Manchester and New York

distributed exclusively in the USA by Palgrave

Published by Manchester University Press
Oxford Road, Manchester M13 9NR, UK
and Room 400, 175 Fifth Avenue, New York, NY 10010, USA
www.manchesteruniversitypress.co.uk

Distributed exclusively in the USA by
Palgrave, 175 Fifth Avenue, New York,
NY 10010, USA

Distributed exclusively in Canada by
UBC Press, University of British Columbia, 2029 West Mall,
Vancouver, BC, Canada V6T 1Z2

British Library Cataloguing-in-Publication Data
A catalogue record for this book is available from the British Library

Library of Congress Cataloging-in-Publication Data applied for

ISBN 0 7190 7409 6   *hardback*
EAN   978 0 7190 7409 7

ISBN 0 7190 7410 X   *paperback*
EAN   978 0 7190 7410 3

First published 2006

15 14 13 12 11 10 09 08 07 06   10 9 8 7 6 5 4 3 2 1

Typeset in Sabon with Gill Sans display
by Action Publishing Technology Ltd, Gloucester
Printed in Great Britain
by CPI, Bath

We are overwhelmed by a flood of words, by polemics, by the assault of the virtual, which today can create a kind of opaque zone ... The question of sin has been displaced from the centre by a question that is perhaps more serious – the question of meaning and meaninglessness, of the absurd.

(Paul Ricoeur)

You may not be interested in absurdity, ... but absurdity is interested in *you*. (Donald Barthelme)

> But I sometimes picture my poor soul
> As a translator locked up by a madman,
> Forced to decipher an absurd text,
> Struggling to find meaning.
> (José Carlos Somoza, *The Athenian Murders*
> [*La caverna de las ideas*], 2000)

Contents

Preface   *page* ix
Abbreviations   xiii

PART I   Introductory

1 The theoretical absurd: an introduction   2
  The philosophical absurd   2
  Jokes, humour, nonsense and the absurd   14
  The socio-linguistic absurd   23

2 Antecedents to the absurd   33
  From the ancients ...   33
  Madness: mysteries to Shakespeare   36
  Nonsense, Swift and Sterne   41
  Romantic grotesque to 'higher' realism and pre-Surrealist
  nonsense   43

PART II   Growth of the absurd

3 The twentieth century: towards the absurd   66
  Introductory pointers   66
  'Post-Impressionists' in England   69
  Avant-garde theory and practice   74
  Disparate European prose: Western and Eastern
  proto-absurdism   86

4 Around the absurd I: twentieth-century absurdist practice   99
  Fernando Pessoa and the 'pessimistic absurd'   100
  Antonin Artaud and the 'cruelty' of the absurd   107
  Camus and the Dostoevsky connection   114

5 Around the absurd II: the Theatre of the Absurd   126
    Ionesco and others: the French-language scene   128
    Pinter and others: the English-language scene   133
    The East European scene   143
    (Soviet) Russia: the OBERIU   143
    (Cold-War) Poland and Czechoslovakia   147

PART III   Special authors

6 Daniil Kharms as minimalist-absurdist   158
    A Kharms sketch   158
    The Kharmsian canon   160
    A poetics of extremism   163
    Logic of the black miniature   166
    Pursuing the red-haired man   169
    Kharmsian others?   175

7 Franz Kafka: otherness in the labyrinth of absurdity   184
    Kafka and the other(s)   185
    Kafka in the other(s)   189
    Falling and cawing in the labyrinth   198

8 Samuel Beckett's vessels, voices and shades of the absurd   215
    In the wake of Kafka?   215
    The prose   220
    The drama   226
    Further shades of the absurd   232

9 Flann O'Brien and the purloined absurd   251
    The hydra-headed man   251
    At Swim-Two-Birds: *juvenile scrivenry as metafictional absurd?*   259
    The Third Policeman: *questions, mysteries, answers*   264

PART IV   In conclusion

10 Beyond the absurd?   280
    The prosaic absurd   280
    Beyond the 'Theatre of the Absurd'?   291
    Popular culture   299
    That miscellaneous and ubiquitous absurd   301

    Conclusion   309
    Bibliography   314
    Index   337

Preface

> A distinguished bishop, a priest and a peasant are in a great cathedral. In turn the priest and the bishop approach the altar rail, beat their chests and declare, 'I am nothing. I am nothing.' The humble peasant, moved to imitate, shuffles to the altar and says the same thing. The bishop turns furiously and hisses in the priest's ear: 'Who the hell does he think he is?'

This 'apocryphal', or anyway anonymous, anecdote has been said to be somewhat akin to contemporary theology, 'with theologians competing verbosely as to who can say the most about saying the least about God, thus abasing human reason, and showing all the more their awareness of the glory and otherness of the Creator'.[1] This brief narrative obviously represents a satire on the hierarchical attitudes to be found within institutionalised religion: church officialdom, class and education. Reason is indeed abased, as the peasant's claim to being 'nothing', while slavishly following supposedly superior example, is preposterously denounced as arrogance. Humour is added by the mildly unbecoming phraseology of the bishop: with regard to his own position, and to the other circumstances of the incident. 'Hell' may seem an inappropriate concept to introduce, and irony comes from the perception of pretentiousness in what is apparently an act of extreme servility, or even genuine self-abasement. These comments are fairly obvious. However, what else, if anything, might tip this text into the category of 'the absurd'?

Satire, humour and incongruity are always potential ingredients of the absurd. The abasement of reason, particularly within a disparate setting of humility, 'glory' and 'otherness', also goes some way in the direction of the absurd. The clinching element, however, may be seen to lie in the controversy aroused by the assertion of a condition of being 'nothing': the negation, or at least the indignant questioning, of a claim for negative ontology in the implicit light, or reflected glory, of a metaphysical cosmology, with associated ritual, that may itself be illusory – or, in other words, based on 'nothing'.

It may be time already, though, for a lighter piece, and a lighter approach.

PECKLE AND BRACES (GRANARTHUR)
How many body peoble wash 'Peotle and Plaices'? In a recent
Doddipottidy Poll, a roaming retorter intervined asking –
    '*Do you like Big Grunty better more than Gray Burk*'?
To these questiump many people answered
    '*On the other hand who are we to judge? I mean who are we?*'

In this rather contrasting piece by John Lennon (from *In His Own Write*,
1964), one of a group of short skits of television reviewing, the linguistic
register puts the text well towards the nonsense end of the humour spec-
trum. Almost seeming to cry out for translation ('People and Places
[Granada]'), the discourse (as well as being anyway not untypical of
Lennon's 'style') in this case owes something to the Liverpool comedian
Ken Dodd. However, the existential (or identity) question posed (or
lapsed into) at the end, bearing at least some comparison with that (or
those) raised in the first anecdote, nudges it firmly in the direction of the
absurd.
    Many of the same, or similar, points will be seen to recur in the discus-
sions which follow – discussions of absurdists writing in English, as
indeed of many others who certainly *have* demanded translation. There
will be a stream of questions and answers (and questions that won't be
answered – ever!); perceptions of 'nothingness', or 'the void'; and tremors
from extremes of identity crisis (or multiple identity). Chaos will abound,
and the 'abyss' will loom; but there will be profusions of stories – old and
new, linear or circular, tall stories, non-stories or stories destroyed. The
Inferno may lurk, along with such timeless motifs as 'the ship of fools', or
'the dance of death'. Absurdist moments and startling notions will burst
forth: 'man wakes up one morning as gigantic insect' (courtesy of Kafka's
Metamorphosis). Or they may prompt amused perplexity, like the idea of
'a 53 year-old architect with a tragic sense of brick' (Donald Barthelme,
Paradise). Through a variety of devices, we shall need to attune to what
Gary Adelman (167) has termed (in relation to Kafka and Beckett) 'that
cannonade effect of exaggeration rumbling to absurdity'. Occasionally
even just a title might provide sufficient indication: try *There Is No
Such Place as America* (by Peter Bichsel), or *The Bus Driver Who Wanted
to be God* (Etgar Keret).

The present book, while endeavouring to present, to a degree at least, a
historical survey of absurdist writing and its forebears, does not aspire to
being a comprehensive history of absurdism. Rather, it pauses on certain
historical moments, artistic movements, literary figures and works, before
moving on to discuss aspects of the *oeuvres* of a small and select number

of 'special authors' – Daniil Kharms, Franz Kafka, Samuel Beckett and Flann O'Brien – perceived, in the author's view, as key (and, to an extent, as we shall see, inter-relating) figures within the designation 'the absurd'. The concluding chapter endeavours to extend discussion up to, and in to, the twenty-first century.

Given that Martin Esslin's classic study *The Theatre of the Absurd* (first published in 1961; third edition, 1980, reprinted by Penguin Books as a Peregrine, 1987, and reprinted again by Methuen, 2001), focuses explicitly on drama, I am here concentrating mainly, though not exclusively – as absurd theatre can absolutely not be ignored – on prose fiction.[2] Following an opening theoretical chapter, and then a summary of what are seen as the antecedents of the absurd, and attempts to identify absurdist elements within authors who may normally be thought of as belonging to 'mainstream' fiction, the stress will, naturally enough, fall heavily on the twentieth century. The study is largely Euro-centric (both Western and, to an extent at least, Eastern), with a limited stress on works and writers from the British Isles and (if only really in the final chapter) from North America.

Acknowledgements

I wish to express my gratitude to the University of Bristol for granting me a University Research Fellowship (in the academic year 2000–1) which, together with periods of departmental study leave, accompanied with an AHRB 'top-up' (in 2003), were essential to the working through of this project. The support of Matthew Frost, at MUP, is also greatly appreciated. On a personal level, I am grateful to the following friends and colleagues for bringing particular thoughts, works or writers to my attention, or for assisting me with information or with secondary materials: Birgit Beumers, Leon Burnett, Paul Cartledge, Robert Chandler, Adrian Clarke, Sally Dalton-Brown, Carla de Petris, George Donaldson, Charles Ellis, David Gillespie, Brian Hulme, Mark Jones, Ron Knowles, John Lyon, Bill Mc Cormack, Sheelagh McCormack, Robin Milner-Gulland, John Parkin, Robert Porter, Mike Pushkin, Robert Reid, Vittorio Strada, Dennis Tate – with apologies to anyone undeservedly omitted.

I feel I must mention too, as an erstwhile mentor in things absurd (in Paris, in the Iberian peninsula and in Dublin in the mid-1960s), the late Justin O'Mahony – author of elegies such as 'On the Banks of the Grand Canaille', as well as *The* (I assume never completed or published) *Blue Book of Nicodemus O'Rahilly*, which began memorably, as I recall: 'Lapidation was the talk of the turn of the century'.

Special thanks, not least for her capacity to tolerate absurdity, go to Maggie Malone.

Pill and Campo Soriano
Winter/Spring 2005

Notes

1 Christopher Insole, 'Kant for Christmas', *TLS* (17 December 2004, 4–5).
2 Lesser surveys, following in the wake of Esslin, include those by Arnold P. Hinchliffe (1969) and John Killinger (1971).

Abbreviations

BH	Dickens, *Bleak House*
CS	Kafka, *The Complete Stories*
CSP	Beckett, *The Complete Short Prose*
CDW	Beckett, *The Complete Dramatic Works*
En. Phil.	Edwards, Paul, ed., *The Encyclopedia of Philosophy*, 8 vols
GE	Dickens, *Great Expectations*
GS	Ford, *The Good Soldier*
GWC	Kafka, *The Great Wall of China and Other Short Works*
FM	Apollonio, *Futurist Manifestos*
F O'B	Brooker, *Flann O'Brien*
KD	Bennett, *Kafka's Dick*
2 K Plays	Bennett, *Two Kafka Plays*
LF	Kafka, *Letters to Felice*
LFFE	Kafka, *Letters to Friends, Family, and Editors*
LM	Kafka, *letters to Milena*
NED	Simpson, in *New English Dramatists, 2*
OED	*The Oxford English Dictionary*
P 1 (to *P 4*)	Pinter, *Plays* (vols 1–4)
PSS 2	Kharms, *Polnoe sobranie sochinenii*, vol. 2
RF	Lawton, *Russian Futurism through its Manifestos*
SF	James, *The Sacred Fount*
SW	Artaud, *Selected Writings*
TL	Borges, *The Total Library*
TP	O'Brien, *The Third Policeman*
Th. Abs.	Esslin, *Theatre of the Absurd*
Trilogy	Beckett, *Molloy Malone Dies The Unnamable*
Webster	Webster's *New Collegiate Dictionary* (1975)

1

Introductory

1

The theoretical absurd: an introduction

> Now I knew that Jean-Paul Sartre and Mr Camus were right when they
> claimed it is the Absurd that matters. The Absurd with a most capital A ...
> (Jeanette Winterson, 'Holy Matrimony', in *The World and Other Places*,
> 1998)

The philosophical absurd

The 'Absurd' (which henceforth will normally be spelt without the capital
letter and mostly without quotation marks) appears not to be, as such, a
fully accredited philosophical category. That is to say, at least, that it is
not accorded its own entry in the major philosophical encyclopedias (for
instance the multi-volumed works edited by Paul Edwards [*En. Phil.*] in
1967, and by Edward Craig in 1998). It does receive a brief entry in *The
Oxford Companion to Philosophy*, as the 'term used by existentialists to
describe that which one might have thought to be amenable to reason but
which turns out to be beyond the limits of rationality', the thought of
Sartre being cited as the prime (if 'mistaken') example (TRB, in
Honderich, 1995, 3). It enjoys, though, far more currency in literature, or
comprises 'an important aspect of the broader cultural context of existentialism' (ibid.), where it has become the subject (in either a general or
a particular sense) of a number of monographs and has given the name to
the now widely familiar 'theatre of the absurd' – this phrase itself having
been coined by Martin Esslin in his book of that title, the first edition of
which was published in 1961.

Chris Baldick, in *The Concise Oxford Dictionary of Literary Terms*
(1990), explains the absurd as 'a term derived from the existentialism of
Albert Camus, and often applied to the modern sense of human purposelessness in a universe without meaning or value'; he goes on to single out
the works of Kafka, 'in which the characters face alarmingly incomprehensible predicaments', and to stress the 'theatre of the absurd'

phenomenon, highlighting Beckett's *Waiting for Godot* (originally written in French as *En attendant Godot*, 1952). Already we gather that existentialism and purposelessness feature strongly as key concepts, while Sartre, Camus and Beckett are seen as leading exponents in thought and literature.

Webster's New Collegiate Dictionary confirms the noun 'absurd' as 'the state or condition in which man exists in an irrational and meaningless universe and in which man's life has no meaning outside his own existence', while 'absurdism' is defined as a philosophy based on this, and on the belief that '[man's] search for order brings him into conflict with his universe' (adding 'compare EXISTENTIALISM'). The *Oxford English Dictionary* gives the original meaning of absurd as 'out of harmony' – initially in a musical sense, but subsequently and more generally out of harmony 'with reason or propriety; incongruous, unreasonable, illogical', or in modern everyday parlance 'ridiculous, silly'. Peter L. Berger (175) chooses to stress the Latin derivation: *absurdum* 'literally means out of deafness'.[1] All of these qualities may well contribute to a literary understanding of the absurd.

Ionesco's conception of the absurd is 'that which is devoid of purpose ... Cut off from his religious, metaphysical, and transcendental roots, man is lost; all his actions become senseless, absurd, useless' (quoted from Esslin, *Th. Abs.*, 23). For Sartre, absurdity is not 'silly', but 'contingent' (Danto, 24), while, with the thought of Hume in mind, Terry Eagleton (in his study of tragedy, *Sweet Violence*, 223) comments that 'The price we pay for our liberty is contingency, which is never very far from absurdity'. William Lane Craig refers to 'the hopeless absurdities of the Megaric school'; these pre-Socratics (who were dismissed as of 'no particulars' by Erasmus in his *Praise of Folly* (23) 'had denied all becoming and change in the world' (W.L. Craig, 27; 20). The seeds of irrationality, therefore, are lurking throughout the history of western thought; a sense of paradox and ambiguity, and the decline of religious faith are all of the essence. And *Existenz*, 'the existence of a human being', Kierkegaard argued, 'is prior to "essence"' (Passmore, 468); Sartre, in consequence, holds too that existence 'precedes' essence (Danto, 24). For Camus, in his key treatise for an understanding of the absurd, *The Myth of Sisyphus* (ostensibly written as an enquiry into suicide), 'the absurd is sin without God' (Camus, *Myth*, 42); it is also 'the revolt of the flesh' (ibid., 20) – what John Macquarrie (*Existentialism*, 77) terms 'heroic absurdity in Camus'. There have always been constraints imposed on the posing of the most difficult questions, from Aristotle's injunction, 'one must stop', to Kant's caution over those 'absurd' questions that 'not only [bring] shame on the propounder of the question, but may betray an incautious listener into absurd answers' (*Critique of Pure Reason*: cited Fotiade, 197). The shame of absurdity can therefore call forth moderation!

Ontology, Nihilism, Existentialism

> Logic is doubtless unshakeable, but it cannot withstand a man who wants
> to go on living. (Franz Kafka, *The Trial*, 1914–15)

As good a starting point as any, perhaps, is the ontological conundrum.
Heidegger's question, 'why is there anything at all and not rather
nothing?' (Sartre's protagonist Roquentin also wishes to wonder 'how it
was that a world should exist rather than nothing': *Nausea*, 192),[2] was
earlier put in the same or similar form by Leibniz and by Schelling,
Unamuno (in his *The Tragic Sense of Life*, 105), and probably many
others: Donald A. Crosby (131) calls it 'that favorite question of Western
philosophers'.[3] The question was later to pass from Heidegger to Ionesco.
A negative answer, or even uncertainty, would appear to be but a short
step from 'nihilism' and, for most commentators, absurdity is to be
equated with nihilism. The objection to, for instance, the cosmological
argument of Leibniz, that 'there is no sufficient reason for the universe,
that it is simply unintelligible ... raises serious existential questions',
writes W.L. Craig (287), 'since it implies that man and the universe are
ultimately meaningless': again nihilism. 'The wonder of Greek metaphysics', Michael Weston (96) stresses, 'is directed toward this: that
reality is intelligible'. Referring to 'negative doctrines in religion or
morals', or 'an extreme form of scepticism' (*OED*), nihilism is a term
commonly held to have been popularised by Turgenev's novel *Fathers and
Sons* (or *Fathers and Children*: *Ottsy i deti*, 1862), through his protagonist Bazarov – although the *OED* cites a number of earlier usages of the
word.

Possibly the first nihilist thinker was Gorgias of Leontini (a contemporary of Socrates), whose treatise *On Nature* propounded the tripartite
reasoning, according to which: firstly, 'that nothing is'; secondly, 'that
even if it is, it cannot be comprehended'; and thirdly 'that even if it can be
comprehended, it cannot be communicated' (G.B. Keferd, *En. Phil.*,
3:374–5). Gorgias maintains that 'we cannot say of a thing either that it
is or is not, without absurd results'. Appropriately enough too, for a
precursor of the absurdists, this treatise has sometimes been taken as a
parody or philosophical joke, or purely as a rhetorical exercise. As we
shall see, it may have had a formative impact on Beckett, among others.
Metaphysics, from the Greeks onwards, assumes or determines (or
presumes to determine) 'a *ground* for our ways of thinking and relating to
what is'; this ground, which 'must lie beyond language', is undercut,
denied or deconstructed by more recent thinkers (from Nietzsche to
Derrida) in 'the death of God' or the lack of a 'transcendental signified'
(see Weston, 116–17). Nietzsche's criticism of knowledge, or 'secret
history of philosophers', according to Roberto Calasso (*The Forty-Nine
Steps*, 17–18), amounted to a 'history of nihilism'.

The absurd, then, is born of nihilism, out of existentialism, fuelled by the certainty of death (anxiety, dread and death being the scourge of the existentialist). Eagleton (9) reminds us that 'for a certain strain of existentialist philosophy death is tragic as such, regardless of its cause, mode, subject or effect'. So too is life; Crosby (30–1), in the spirit of Schopenhauer, puts it thus:

> The existential nihilist judges human existence to be pointless and absurd.
> ...
> ... The only feasible goal for anyone who understands the human condition is the abandonment of all goals and the cultivation of a spirit of detached resignation while awaiting life's last and greatest absurdity, an annihilating death that wipes us so cleanly from the slate of existence as to make it appear that we had never lived.

'If consciousness is, as some inhuman thinker has said,' writes the Spanish 'philosopher of life' Miguel de Unamuno, in his treatise on *The Tragic Sense of Life* (13), 'nothing more than a flash of light between two eternities of darkness, then there is nothing more execrable than existence'. '[T]he real discovery of death', made independently by the Jews and the Greeks, he affirms (62), had constituted 'the entrance into spiritual puberty'. Death for Sartre 'is just the final absurdity, neither more nor less absurd than life itself' (Macquarrie, 198). Macquarrie conjectures (195): 'Is it not absurd even to imagine that one could arrive at an existential understanding of death?' As for notions of immortality through living on in one's descendants, in one's created works, or 'in the universal consciousness' – all of this 'is but vague verbiage which satisfies only those who suffer from affective stupidity' (Unamuno, 16). Even the notion of posthumous survival (were it believable) would not necessarily help very much; for absurdist existential nihilists, Crosby avers (172), indeed 'the very prospect of a perfect afterlife can make our existence on this earth seem scandalous and absurd' (for similar thoughts, see, for instance, the theoretical physicist Paul Davies, 111; 154). For Nietzsche, indeed, 'the compensatory belief in heaven ("the Land of Back and Beyond")' merely 'reduces the value and dignity of physical existence' (Stern, 93).[4] Without it, and in the teeth of the suffering of this world, 'to live is to teeter for a few brief moments over an abyss, and then to be hurled indifferently into its depths' (Crosby, 57). Nevertheless, Leszek Kołakowski suggests (in his *Metaphysical Horror*, 58): 'It is perhaps better for us to totter insecurely on the edge of an unknown abyss than simply to close our eyes and deny its existence'. And time, of course, is the 'worst enemy' (Camus, *Myth*, 20).

Existentialism concerns itself first and foremost with the subject, rather than the object. The personal pronoun – 'I' – represents 'an existent who *stands out* (the basic meaning of 'existing': my emphasis.) as this existent and no other' (Macquarrie, 73). 'Existentialism has its roots in German Romanticism', affirms John Passmore (467), although Pascal, St Augustine and Socrates are often credited as precursors. Arthur C. Danto (20) confirms that Sartre, for instance, 'has worked always ... within the dry array of distinctions of a largely scholastic metaphysics'. Kierkegaard, though, is commonly held to be the father of existentialism in its modern form,[5] with strong elements of pessimism coming from Schopenhauer[6] and of negation from Nietzsche; Lesley Chamberlain (90), indeed, affirms that Nietzsche might be called 'the First Existentialist'. For Nietzsche, human orders in any guise were 'vain attempts to draw a veil over the "ghastly absurdity of existence"' and his thinking, Catherine Bates affirms, had an immense effect thereafter on theory and philosophy: 'Dismantling the presupposition that order and meaning might inhere within the world, Nietzsche pulled the rug from under every theorist's feet, orbiting himself and those who follow him into deconstructive free fall' (Bates, v). Put in a not dissimilar way by Chamberlain (7–8): 'He questioned whether Western philosophy since Plato had any meaning in the face of the absurd and irrational forces underlying human life, symbolized by Dionysus'.

Although a number of thinkers have contributed to existentialism as we now think of it (Berdyaev, Shestov, Unamuno and Karl Jaspers,[7] for instance; and – more recently and more significantly – Heidegger, Camus and Sartre), there is, in Macquarrie's view, 'no common body of doctrine to which all existentialists subscribe'; it is therefore to be regarded not so much as a 'philosophy' but rather as a 'style of philosophizing' (Macquarrie, 14). Ramona Fotiade distinguishes between 'the "existential" line of thought' (as developed in particular by Lev Shestov and Benjamin Fondane) and 'the emerging "Existentialism" of the 1930s' (Fotiade, 7). Alasdair Macintyre declares that 'any formula sufficiently broad to embrace all the major existentialist tendencies would necessarily be so general and so vague as to be vacuous'; for that matter, he avers, 'as in theology so in politics existentialism appears to be compatible with almost every possible standpoint' (in *En. Phil.*, 3:147; 151).

Part of the paradoxical nature of existentialist thought involves 'a kind of love-hate relationship in which elements of belief and disbelief are intertwined' (Macquarrie, 19). Dostoevsky has provided perhaps the finest novelistic illustrations of this contradiction, while in a famous epistolary comment he proclaimed that, were Christ ever proved to lie outside the truth, he would himself prefer to remain with Christ.[8] Within the tradition of mysticism, Meister Eckhart, 'in a surprising fit of heresy' (according to Camus: *Rebel*, 25), declared that 'he prefers Hell with Jesus to Heaven without Him'. Camus, however, states that, for 'the absurd man', 'seeking what is true is not seeking what is desirable' (*Myth*, 43); we shall look in Chapter 4 at Dostoevsky's impact on Camus.

'Signification', Gilles Deleuze extrapolates from Descartes, 'does not establish the truth without also establishing the possibility of error. For this reason', he continues, 'the condition of truth is not opposed to the false, but to the absurd' – defined as 'that which is without signification or that which may be neither true nor false' (Deleuze, 14–15). Kierkegaard places his notion of 'repetition' (belonging to a different dimension of thought and analogous in part to Nietzsche's 'eternal return') within the sphere of the absurd, or 'the level at which religious faith defies logical reasoning, ... at which individual, exceptional, unique occurrences disrupt the "chrono-logical" discourse, the homogeneous flux of historical continuity' (Fotiade, 160).

Kierkegaard, having – even before Nietzsche – deconstructed the tenets of Christianity, nevertheless chooses (like Dostoevsky) a blind leap into Christian faith – which may be compared to Pascal's famous wager.[9] Bates, however, raises the question as to whether God would necessarily have kept his side of the Pascalian bargain and sees the logic of this as having been, in any case, philosophically 'first and most rigorously blown apart' by Nietzsche's insistence that 'the assumption of a logical world was ... no more than a presupposition' (Bates, 40; 55; 69). Nietzsche's own leap, therefore, is into negation and despair (or 'the bottomless abyss': Deleuze, 108). Nietzsche believed himself to be living in 'the age of the death of God', within a 'morality of decadence' (Stern, 88); for him, 'Christian theology is replaced by the penitential theology of a God-less universe' (ibid., 90); indeed, he presents a confrontation between 'faith' and 'the *absurdissimum*' (Nietzsche, 1998, 44). Berger (211) admits that '[God's] absence is a central feature of our existence'. Macquarrie (251) qualifies the theistic/atheistic existential distinction as follows:

> By its very approach to the problem, existentialism lives in a tension between belief and doubt. Kierkegaard's faith involves risk and fragility, while the unfaith of Camus has elements of belief, for if everything were totally absurd and meaningless, it would make no sense to rebel against being treated as an object.

Crosby poses a similar question in relation to Nietzsche: if the conclusion to be drawn from his philosophy is that 'there is no truth', how reliable, then, is the latter thinker's own analysis? This point may analogously be raised with regard to art and literature (just as it frequently is with regard to deconstructionist writings): if the world, or indeed the universe, is an absurdity, why should its existentialist or absurdist proponents trouble themselves to offer coherent artistic or philosophical accounts of this phenomenon (although some at least, it may be claimed, at times do not)?[10] Even what Esslin (*Th. Abs.*, 24) terms 'the open abandonment of rational devices and discursive thought' by absurdist writers does not go – normally – or, at least, with any great artistic recognition – beyond a certain point.[11] Ionesco, for example, in his celebrated exchange with Kenneth Tynan, showed himself to be fully aware of this point (see his *Notes*, 90; and Esslin, *Th. Abs.*, 129).

Rationality, or the irrational, clearly assumes here a key importance. The philosophical crux, or reduction to absurdity, would appear to arise along with any possibility of the denial of the axiom 'nothing is without a sufficient reason' (W.L. Craig, 267), or be incurred in blind-alley deductions resulting in such propositions as '*Therefore, we do not now exist, which is absurd*' (Saadia: quoted ibid., 130). Existentialists hold that 'no rationally provable metaphysical system can be constructed' (Macquarrie, 250), while, for French existentialism in particular, 'the thesis that existence is absurd ... turns out to be a denial of sufficient reason' (Macintyre, 148). Fondane, indeed, 'introduces a crucial distinction between irrationality and the absurd, the former being reducible, more or less, to rational categories, while the latter expresses the irreducible residuum of any rational analysis'; at the same time, he insists on an incompatibility of poetic and philosophical intuition (Fotiade, 47). The absurd, to Camus, is born of the encounter between the irrational and human nostalgia: 'the three characters in the drama that must necessarily end with all the logic of which an existence is capable' (*Myth*, 32). This logic, to an absurd mind, means that 'reason is useless and there is nothing beyond reason', while, at the same time, even in creative mode, 'an absurd attitude, if it is to remain so, must remain aware of its gratuitousness'.[12] Existentialist disciples of Nietzsche, in the words of J.P. Stern (77), thus argue that 'the choice of a gratuitous object or of an absurd task is better than no choice at all'. Or they take refuge in a posture of defiance, assuming the qualities and finally even the persona of the 'more or less invented' god Dionysus; for Nietzsche, 'Dionysian life positively celebrates human capacity by looking absurd existence in the eye' (Chamberlain, 7; 104).

In another sense, the absurd arises from 'confrontation between the human need and the unreasonable silence of the world' (Camus, *Myth*, 32): 'several of the existentialists speak appreciatively of silence', remarks Macquarrie (144). The 'self-evident limitations of language' may be subverted by silence or by madness; indeed, Fotiade (51–2) informs us, with particular reference to Shestov and Antonin Artaud, 'the existential investigation of "the absurd" ... led to a re-evaluation of the interconnected issues of silence and madness'. When silence gives way to speech, however, an artistic effect may be realised, in an authentic spirit of gratuitousness (as dramatists such as first Chekhov, and later Beckett, well knew), amid either linguistic disintegration or even a meticulous reproduction of reality (as often found in Pinter): 'In a world that has become absurd, transcribing reality with meticulous care is enough to create the impression of extravagant irrationality' (Esslin, *Th. Abs.*, 301).

A further vital concept is that of freedom (of will, or of action). The crux of the problem is put by Crosby (333), in that 'it is assumed that the only alternative to actions that are completely causal is actions performed in total independence of causes'. This constant dichotomous view is an age-old problem likened by Galen Strawson to 'a carousel', or a 'meta-physical merry-go-round' (Strawson, *TLS*): 'the Pessimists' argument that we can't possibly have strong free will keeps bumping into the fact that we can't help believing that we do'. Macintyre (147) dubs existentialists 'disappointed rationalists'. Sartre, 'a more recent proponent of the primacy of the will' (Crosby, 333–4), holds out for there being 'a sense in which we are condemned to freedom, not free not to be free' (Strawson, *TLS*). Douglas Hofstadter (54) considers the deterministic universe to be 'an open question'. Strawson aptly cites André Gide: 'Everything has been said before, but since nobody listens we have to keep going back and beginning all over again.' Such a situation would seem also to chime with, for instance, A.J. Ayer's assessment of the views of Heidegger and Merleau-Ponty on time: 'it is obvious that any such attempt to extract temporal predicates out of psychological or metaphysical ones must be circular at best if it is not wholly beside the mark' (Ayer, 228).

An arguably tangential strand of philosophical thought (although he is not normally found numbered among the existentialist-nihilists), conceivably analogous to the activity of existentialist-absurdist artistic production, is Hans Vaihinger's 'philosophy of fictions' (expounded in particular in his *The Philosophy of 'As If'*, 1911: translated 1924).[13] Vaihinger, following Schopenhauer's views on irrationality, embraced a 'rational pessimism', involving a recognition of the necessity and utility of acting on the basis of 'fictions' known to be false: 'something can work *as if* true, even though false and recognized as false' (Handy, *En. Phil.*, 8:222). False but expedient fictions can be utilised as a tactic to cope with a world which, in the last analysis, may be absurd, posing 'senseless problems', such as the relation of mind to matter or the purpose of existence. In Vaihinger's terms, 'true' religion, for instance, would be 'not the belief in the kingdom of God but the attempt to make it come about while recognizing its impossibility' (ibid., 224). Unamuno (263) seizes eagerly on the words of Etienne Sénancour's eponymous Obermann (in the epistolary novel of 1804): 'Man is perishable. That may be; but let us perish resisting, and if it is nothingness that awaits us, do not let us so act that it shall be a just fate' – otherwise glossed (259), in terms yet closer to Unamuno's contemporary Vaihinger, 'we must feel and act *as if* an endless continuation of our earthly life awaited us after death' (my emphasis).

While existentialist-absurdists may not admit to embracing such a theory, some of them at least appear to put it into (creative) practice. Roger Caillois (himself, in his early days, a Surrealist), in his comprehensive study of games – another field of study clearly of tangential relevance to the absurd – points up the significance of 'as if' (*comme si*) in the philosophy of play and games (Caillois, 40–1). Catherine Bates, in her revisionist-deconstructionist study of the topic, finds the origins of play theory in Plato, who saw life 'as a play of the gods' (Bates, 28–9). Plato, she argues, suggested that (even holy) 'ritual treated reality *as if* it were play' (emphasis in the original: Bates, 31), while the first modern writer to discuss play as significant in the development of civilisation is said to be Schiller (ibid., 15–18).

Negative theology

Logic is always wrong. (Tristan Tzara, 'Dada Manifesto', 1918)

A further concept of potential or actual relevance to some practitioners of the absurd is that known as 'negative theology' (or the *via negativa*). Tertullian (c.160–c.220) expounded the paradox that the incarnation of Christ is 'certain' because 'impossible' (*certum est quia impossibile*: apparently based on an assertion contained in Aristotle's *Rhetoric*, on the likelihood of the unlikely). '*Credo quia absurdum*': 'I believe because it is absurd', said Tertullian; the world is absurd, and therefore faith is possible (see Berger, 182–3). Unamuno considers Tertullian's comments in this vein to be 'superb' and 'sublime'; 'Spanish, too at heart' (although he in fact flourished in Carthage), Tertullian had operated as 'a kind of Don Quixote in the world of Christian thought in the second century' (Unamuno, 74; 313); the Aristotelian God (or 'God-Idea') is in any event wrought in contradiction (as demonstrated by Unamuno, e.g. 162–3).[14] Kierkegaard in his *Fear and Trembling* had taken up this notion with alacrity, venturing so far as to claim that a life of infinite resignation is transformed by living 'joyfully and happily every instant by virtue of the absurd' (Weston, 88). Shestov and Fondane, too, utilised this same paradoxical type of thinking (see Fotiade, 69; 78).

Borges draws attention to 'the unknown author of the *Corpus Dionysiacum*' at the end of the fifth century, who 'declares that no affirmative predicate is fitting for God' (Borges, *Total Library*, 341).[15] The twelfth-century Jewish, but Muslim-Spanish based, philosopher Maimonides too sets forth in his *Guide of the Perplexed* a doctrine according to which nothing positive can be known about God and the only admissible 'statements concerning God considered in himself should, if they are to be regarded as true, be interpreted as providing an indication of what God is *not*' – applying 'even to the statement that God exists' (Pines, *En. Phil.*, 5:131; see also W.L. Craig, 152).[16] Maimonides may, in this respect, have taken his lead from Avicenna (the Muslim philosopher of a century earlier), whose 'third state of essence is essence as sense' is 'indifferent to affirmation and negation, ... indifferent to all opposites'; this, according to Deleuze (34–5), leads to 'the paradox of the absurd, or

of the impossible objects' (see also W.L. Craig's account of these philosophers). René Daumal talks of a paradoxical 'absurd evidence',
nevertheless bearing meaning, but a meaning 'irreducible to rational
analysis' (Fotiade, 211; 34–5). Eagleton (260) points out, with particular
regard to the foibles of post-structuralism, that 'it is never easy to distinguish the claim that no meaning is absolute from the suggestion that there
is no meaning at all'.

Elaborating such a doctrine (in relation to 'the One'; and the 'principle'
of 'Nothingness' – though at two levels) back in the sixth century was the
Neoplatonist philosopher Damascius.[17] Kołakowski affirms (51) that
Damascius, 'in the laboriously constructed chaos of his work', had
produced the idea much later summed up by Hegel as: 'Pure Being and
pure non-Being are the same'. That 'God is' and 'God is not' must have
the same sense constituted the 'fantastic paradox' of the fourteenth-
century anti-Aristotelian philosopher Nicolas d'Autrecourt and was to be
reinvented at the end of the nineteenth century by Alexius Meinong; this
alleged validity of impossible objects is therefore termed 'Meinong's
paradox' by Deleuze (33; 35), who relates the problem (and much else
besides) back to the Stoics. Even earlier, in Eleatic thought, Parmenides,
in 'the first recorded stretch of sustained philosophical argument', had
purported to apply logos ('reason') to the opposition between esti ('is')
and ouk esti ('is not') as objects of thought (M.R. Wright, 21–2). A critic
of Stoic epistemology, Arcesilaus of Pitane (third century BC), rejected the
claim of Socrates 'to know that he knows nothing'; according to
Arcesilaus, 'we cannot even know that' (Ricken, 224). In any case, with
the notion that God 'is necessarily not-something, or no-thing', according
to Kołakowski, 'language breaks down' and with the collapse of 'the
Absolute' into Nothing ('its name, if there is one') comes what is styled
'the horror metaphysicus' (Kołakowski, 55; 58).[18] We are now well and
truly into the realm of the 'inexprimable'.[19]

Erasmus (of whose Folly the Stoics were singled out as her chief oppo-
nents) too conjured with such deliberations as to 'whether the assertion
God cannot do the impossible is more appropriate to God than the assertion that The impossible cannot be done by God' (Screech, 180–1).[20] One
apparent Eastern variant has it that the answer to the question 'What is
the higher Buddhism?' would be 'It is not Buddha' (Hofstadter, 255).[21] In
a more modern Western vein, Hegel believed the 'divine power' of negation to be the source of progress (Wilden, 245). More in tune with
psychoanalytical thought, however, such false consciousness of God is
seen as being transferred to the unconscious; in this process, according to
Michael Epstein (348), 'all positive sources of knowledge are extinguished
and dispersed in its dark abysses'. Fotiade (86) observes that, 'on the
boundary of Surrealism, the aquatic figuration of the unconscious signals
a process of dissolution and death: it is the topos of the void and of the

creation from the void'; the existential rejectionist line of thought (Daumal and Gilbert-Lecomte) leads to 'a paradoxical notion of revolt, defined as negative progression towards the void', resistant to rational analysis, but leaving an opening for 'the human aspiration towards the divine' (ibid., 105; 193). Jean-Jacques Lecercle, however, noting the occurrence of the word 'nonsense' in the language of philosophers, reminds us of A.J. Ayer's proposition (in *Language, Truth and Logic*, 1936) that 'all utterances about the nature of God are nonsensical' (Lecercle, 85).

Negative (or 'apophatic') theology employed 'ablative' and 'negative' language to circumvent the difficulty – indeed the impossibility – of giving full and effective expression to the mystery of divinity: as Neil Carrick (77) puts it, 'the inadequacy of human expression and language was thus paradoxically used to assert precisely that which, by its very deficiency, it appeared unable to affirm'. Such a precept was introduced to the Russian absurdists (the *Oberiuty*: Kharms and Vvedensky), almost certainly by their associate Yakov Druskin, who expressly linked the work of Aleksandr Vvedensky to this tradition: 'If one does not fear the words, then in Greek one calls this paradox (Kierkegaard); in Latin, absurd (Tertullian); in Russian, nonsense [*bessmyslitsa*] (Vvedenskii)' (quoted by Carrick, 77).[22] It has also been argued that Gogol was close to the tradition of negative theology (see Spieker, 9–10; and various contributions to his collection). It should also be remembered that, as has been pointed out by Kenneth Burke and others, in any event 'the negative is a peculiarly linguistic resource' (see Wilden, 245–54, at 245), as are other forms of contrastive imagery, such as the assertion by the alleged or 'pseudo-Dionysius (the Areopagite)' that: 'The divine darkness is the inaccessible light in which God is said to dwell' (Unamuno, 160).[23] 'In the final analysis', however – at least according to Epstein (353) – 'negative theology negates itself as theology, becoming atheism'.

The Jesuit commentator William F. Lynch relates the artistic struggle between 'the men of the finite and the men of the infinite' to 'the first battle between the gnostic and the Hebraic imaginations' (Lynch, 3), with the absurdist tendencies of 'the tragic finite' representing a rebirth of 'the old heresies of Manicheanism and Pelagianism' (ibid., 76–7). The former, in its modern manifestation epitomised by Sartre, who 'gave a definitive formulation, in theory and on the stage, to the principle of the absurd', indeed 'has attached a very dubious quality of worthlessness, threat, evil, absurdity, to the whole world of situation and existence' (77); the latter, for its part, has 'corrupted the idea of the infinite, making it crazy, guilty and absurd' (78). Sartre's thesis, in Lynch's view, is representative of 'the idea of disgust', constituting 'only a sleight-of-hand, a brilliantly dialectical summary of the wave of nausea that has plagued the poets since the latter part of the nineteenth century' (103). To be numbered among the 'poets' here too is Nietzsche. 'In fact, Nietzsche claims', as Raymond Geuss summarises, 'full, undiluted knowledge of the metaphysical truth about the world would be strictly intolerable to humans; it would produce in us a nausea in the face of existence that would literally kill us' (Nietzsche, 1999, xix). Art, for Nietzsche, is the sole palliative, with the capacity to 're-direct those repulsive thoughts about the terrible or absurd nature of existence into representations with which man can live': those of 'the *sublime*' and 'the *comical*' (ibid., 40).

Where does that get us?

Logic's hell! (Bertrand Russell, in Wittgenstein's notebook, 1937)

What does emerge from the foregoing would seem to be two (frequently – though not necessarily inherently – interrelated?) predicaments. Firstly there is the concern deriving from a perception of inherent absurdity in the human condition and perhaps in the state, or the very existence, of the universe as a whole – at least, in so far as it is perceivable from a human and Earth-centred standpoint (from which we are limited by certain modes of perception).[24] Secondly, there is the situation that any (verbal) philosophical system can be – or so it would seem – (verbally and logically) deconstructed into a stream of contradiction, non-sense (or frequently nonsense) and absurdity.

The lives of philosophers and social scientists, Lecercle tells us, are spent among 'linguistic monsters', while 'As Nietzsche said, how can we hope to get rid of God, so long as we insist on believing in grammar?' (Lecercle, 43).[25] And telling ourselves that God created the world, says Unamuno (161), is in any case 'a merely verbal solution'. Further confusion can only be caused by conjuring, as Shestov did, with the hypothesis of a 'Malign Creator' (Fotiade, 30) or, as Ionesco did, the 'inept demiurge' or 'a clumsy demon who created this universe' (Dobrez, 184). Ludwig Wittgenstein, it is considered, did not necessarily reject the metaphysical as such; 'rather, he rejected the possibility of *stating* the metaphysical' (Norman Malcolm, *En. Phil.*, 8:331), holding that 'all metaphysical doctrines ... are distortions of the structure of our language, projected on to the world' (Hyman, 7).[26] Or, to put it yet another way, perhaps indeed 'Institutionalized religion may hardly survive a prescription of the sad truth that prime movers are logical absurdities' (Shoham, 108). Ancient theories may fare no better: the Egyptian and early Greek enthusiasm for a cosmology of 'creative masturbation' (Zeus swallowing the severed genitals of Uranus, and therewith the entire creation, ready for re-creation into our world) seems unlikely to appeal greatly to modern taste. Debates on the 'First Cause' and related (as well as unrelated) matters are duly conducted in Tom Stoppard's philosophical satire *Jumpers* (1972).

The waters are muddied still further by the impact of modern scientific and cosmological thinking, which in the twentieth century found itself having to respond first to Einstein's theories of relativity and then to the principles of quantum mechanics, Heisenberg's uncertainty principle and probability theory. Hofstadter (699) would add 'the mixing of subject and object in metamathematics', beginning with Gödel's Incompleteness Theorem (of 1931) and seen as closely linked to the symbol–object dichotomy explored by Wittgenstein. More recently we are blessed with the benefits of chaos theory (see Gleick) and now so-called quantum evolution (or 'quantum biology'). All of this, then, ushered in the modern period when, as Merleau-Ponty and Morando (xv) put it, 'cosmology returns by entirely new paths to the domain of science'. In their view (179), 'a cosmology consistent with the principles of general relativity', strongly suggested by twentieth-century advances, 'is almost impossible to interpret in classical terms' (see also 201; 264). The rediscovery of the Greeks had displaced the cosmogony of the book of Genesis, as well as classical physics. The cosmology of the ancient world had been mainly cyclical; and that of the classical world static.[27]

Hofstadter ingeniously reads Gödel's Theorem (paraphrased as: 'All consistent axiomatic formulations of number theory include undecidable propositions': Hofstadter, 17) as a 'metaphorical analogue' of the human condition (in terms of the certainty of personal non-existence) and juxtaposes this with the Zen attitude of revelling in the irreconcilable, the contradictory and the 'MU' – the 'unasking' of questions (ibid., 233; 698). We shall later see how these various philosophical points play out in varieties of absurdist writing, as well as examining the devices used in their presentation. It may be no accident that, as Macintyre proposes (149), 'dramatic dialogue, whether in plays or in the novel, is probably a form of expression more consistent with the author's intentions than deductive argument would be'. 'Play' comes into play in all its senses; play and illusion (*in ludere*: meaning, originally, 'in play' or 'in mockery') – and is there anything behind or beyond (Bates, iv; 51)? We shall also, however, need to look at further ways of approach, including those of nonsense and humour theory, into the realms of the absurd.

Jokes, humour, nonsense and the absurd

Joking indeed is a paradoxical affair, being at once the toughest and the frailest form of human intercourse. (Edith Welsford, *The Fool: His Social and Literary History*, 1935)

Jokes and humour

'Most joke-books make dreary reading', admits one at least momentarily rueful commentator (Galligan, 19), and the same could be said for many of the books written on humour theory. Long ago Cicero opined: 'One may write with more wit upon any subject than upon Wit itself' (quoted by Michelson, 153, n. 18). Another modern critic alludes to 'certain themes which, like bad pennies and bad jokes, have a way of cropping up again and again' (Hill, 9). One of the main instigators of modern humour analysis, no less a figure than Sigmund Freud (263), is himself, I have to assume, not joking when referring to his own efforts at 'scientific insight into the nature of jokes' as 'this laborious investigation'. To Samuel Weber, for one, Freud remains 'ensnared in this shaggy-dog story which he cannot bring to a satisfactory conclusion' (Hill, 224), while for Bates (who has her own angle of approach to Freud), 'as it strains towards clarity and explication, Freud's theory comes to look increasingly like the jokes it so scrupulously records' (Bates, v).[28] As early as the beginning of the nineteenth century, for that matter, the Romantic writer and aestheticist Jean Paul Richter was warning his readers that 'the more often the words "laughing", "ridiculous", or "humorous" appear in a comic work, the less it will be any of these' (Richter, 119).

Richter (or 'Jean Paul', as he is commonly known) wrote at some length on 'the ridiculous' and must count as one of the earliest (and is very far from being the least acute) of modern humour theorists. Perceived superiority was the cause of the 'sudden glory' of laughter, arising, for Hobbes in the seventeenth century, from the 'conception of some eminency in ourselves, by comparison with the infirmity of others, or with our own formerly' (quoted by Bates, 103).[29] Kierkegaard, as noted by Weston, felt able to detect, or insert, unexpected elements of comedy within the ethical critique of philosophical discourse (he, for instance, 'notoriously, found Hegel *comic*': Weston, 28; 52–3). The Romantic-Symbolist concern with 'the essence of laughter', however, was pursued in an essay of 1855 under such a title by Charles Baudelaire, who discussed the 'profoundly human' quality of satanic laughter, based on superiority through pride ('De l'essence du rire': Baudelaire, *Curiosités*, 240).[30] Both Richter and Baudelaire provide their own categorisations of comedy. Richter seeks to differentiate between 'satire, humor, irony and whimsy', while adopting the Aristotelian proposition that the ridiculous 'stems from harmful incongruity' (Richter, 81, 71). Baudelaire takes his examples from works by Charles Maturin and E.T.A. Hoffmann, broaching also such questions as madness and the grotesque.

M.A. Screech, in his survey of Christian laughter and responses thereto (*Laughter at the Foot of the Cross*, 56), which concentrates on Erasmus and Rabelais, reports that, back in AD 96, 'Quintilian held that laughter was never far from derision'. Even earlier, according to Aristotle's *Poetics* (Chapter 3), those ancient philosophical absurdists the Megarians had claimed the invention of comedy. Umberto Eco's novel *The Name of the Rose* (1980) motivates its medieval monkish murder plot on the determination of the fundamentalist librarian Jorge of Burgos (a play on Jorge Luis Borges) to ensure that Aristotle's second 'hidden' book on the poetics of comedy remains lost; every book by 'the Philosopher' has destroyed a part of purist Christianity, and should the missing treatise elevate the subversive force of laughter into an art form, 'we would have crossed the last boundary' (Eco, *Name*, 473). There could result, according to Jorge, a drive 'to destroy death through redemption from fear' (475), and fear of death, according to Erasmus (36), 'by Jove, is no piddling evil!'. God's people 'would be transformed into an assembly of monsters belched forth from the abysses of the terra incognita' (Eco, *Name*, 475). It is this potential power of comedy and 'the truth of signs' that leads William of Baskerville (Eco's admittedly fictional, derivative and postmodern medieval investigator) to the declaration that 'there is no order in the universe'; even if such an imagined order 'was useful, it was meaningless' (492).

W.D. Howarth (1978, 12–13) traces a stress on the incongruous as a basic element of comedy to an essay of 1776 by the Scottish common-sense philosopher James Beattie – although this can be dated even earlier to the moral-sense theorist Francis Hutcheson (Berger, 22). Howarth observes a dichotomy between 'incongruity' and 'superiority' theories of comedy, or the joke (established too, as we have just seen, in writings by Richter and Baudelaire respectively). This division has been restated more recently by Susan Purdie, who names Plato, Sidney, Hobbes and Bergson as 'prominent examples of superiority theorists', while 'Beattie, Kant, Schopenhauer, R.W. Emerson, Arthur Koestler and Jonathan Miller all offer incongruity approaches' (Purdie, 9, n. 3).[31] Berger (x), who argues that, 'From its simplest to its most sophisticated expressions, the comic is experienced as *incongruence*', provides a further review of 'philosophers of the comic' (including some not referred to here: see Berger, 15–37). Grotesque incongruity and 'strained expectation' had also been highlighted in the aesthetic writings of Kant (ibid., 24).

Henri Bergson's once celebrated essay on 'Laughter' (*Le rire*, 1900) fails to differentiate between laughter and humour and, in so doing, in the view of one recent commentator, John Parkin (in his *Humour Theorists of the Twentieth Century*, 26), analyses 'only one type of humour, satire, and one type of laughter, the corrective type'.[32] For Bergson, humour has a largely aggressive function, in support of 'responsibly held values' (Parkin, 95). 'Laughter is above all, a corrective', claims Bergson (187), 'intended to humiliate'; he also, re-emphasising the time-honoured link between laughter and cruelty, formulated the (still celebrated, by Erich

Segal for one) statement that, to produce its full effect (the appeal of which 'is to intelligence, pure and simple'), 'the comic demands something like a momentary anesthesia of the heart' (Bergson, 63–4; see Segal, 276 and passim). Peter Conrad (427) epigrammatically graces Chaplin's fascination with Hitler and Napoleon: 'Comedy is aggression by other means'. 'There is something funny as well as menacing about absurdity', however, we are reminded by Eagleton (68).

For Freud, on the other hand, in his *Jokes and their Relation to the Unconscious* (of 1905), 'it was a vital principle that the comic reside in things inappropriate to an adult' (Parkin, 95): 'the subversion of inhibition' (Palmer, 34), or 'release'. Freud misses out on incongruity, an essential ingredient later recouped by Koestler (principally in his *The Act of Creation*, 1964), which may be glossed as a clash of value systems, or 'the application of a secondary value system', although there remains a deficiency in Koestler's approach, in that 'comic art' is a concept which he 'is reluctant to admit into his framework' (Parkin, 151). Parkin considers too the potential for humour theory in writings by Mikhail Bakhtin, Northrop Frye and Hélène Cixous.[33] As a further development he explores the concept of 'incongruity resolution' as against jokes depending on 'nonsense'.

Bruce Michelson (20–30) considers the humour speculations of such 'elder[s] in literary theorizing' as Bergson, Freud and Bakhtin to be buried in outmoded paradigms of the past, lacking in the necessary distinctions and owing their (inflated) reputations, in this regard at least, mainly to their originators' prowess in other fields.[34] Wishing to reclaim the concept of 'literary wit' for modern critical currency, Michelson seeks to extend and refresh conventional descriptions of '*wit*', which he promotes as 'in fact a discourse with the power to transgress and overthrow limits', and 'like the mythical acid that no crucible can contain' (ibid., 12). 'As social discourse in Western English-speaking societies, modern *wit* is distinguished by brevity, eloquence, and surprise', he claims; 'It favors incongruous congruity: quick verbal performances of insight or insights as verbal performance' (4).

The performance skills side of comic art (or 'negotiation', in more senses than one) is, naturally enough, given his concentration on film and television comedy, accorded due weight by Jerry Palmer (in his *The Logic of the Absurd*, 21–2 and passim). For Palmer (34), it is 'the balance between plausibility and implausibility' that is the key element (along with a number of more mechanical factors and devices) in the potential success, in comic terms, of a range of types of verbal-visual humour, extending from the one-liner, or the comic gag, to sitcom or the comic feature film. At the same time, comic performance, and particularly, as we may see, theatrical dialogue, may lean heavily on the triangular 'joke' (or 'smut') relationship identified by Freud (143): 'Generally speaking, a tendentious joke calls for three people: in addition to the one who makes the joke, there must be a second who is taken as the object of the hostile or sexual aggressiveness, and a third in whom the joke's aim of producing pleasure is fulfilled.'

Nonsense

'Nonsense' is widely thought to be a largely English phenomenon and is traditionally held to centre on, or indeed to have started with, the body of work created in the Victorian period by Lewis Carroll and Edward Lear. Moreover, these writers (and Carroll in particular) have effectively dominated serious philosophical studies by, in particular, Gilles Deleuze (*The Logic of Sense*, published in French in 1969, English translation 1990) and Jean-Jacques Lecercle (*Philosophy of Nonsense*, 1994). Carroll's Alice books have also inspired an accessible allegory of modern physics (Robert Gilmore's *Alice in Quantumland*). However, nonsense clearly does extend, or at least have its counterparts, geographically beyond the shores of the British Isles and chronologically posterior to (and, for that matter, anterior to) Victorian England. Sir Edmund Strachey's pioneering review article of 1888, dedicated to a new posthumous edition of the works of Lear, adopting a liberal interpretation of nonsense, claims affiliations going back, through theology, to Chaucer and Shakespeare. Noel Malcolm's more recent anthology establishes the genuine earlier English tradition (from Shakespearean times) and there were even older European analogues. Clearly, there have to be at least some affinities between nonsense and the absurd.

According to one near-comprehensive explorer of the field of nonsense, Wim Tigges, nonsense is essentially 'a narrative genre in which the seeming presence of one or more "sensible" meanings is kept in balance by a simultaneous absence of such a meaning' (Tigges, 1988, 255). In the view of Deleuze (68), 'a word which says its own sense' represents nonsense. The essential point for Lecercle in nonsense is 'the dialectic of excess and lack', with the proviso that 'excess always compensates for lack' (Lecercle, 3; 6); nonsense is furthermore 'an *a contrario* reflexion on the tradition of hermeneutics' and it 'deals not in symbolism but in paradox' (ibid., 5; 20).[35] However, Lecercle also designates it '*la philosophie en riant*' (164). Susan Stewart sees nonsense as 'humour without a context' and as 'a mistake on purpose' (Stewart, 38, 206), but as, at the same time, requiring a concomitant element of sense: 'without sense there is no nonsense' (4). Palmer (34–5) refers us back to the sense and nonsense mix to be found in Freud. For Malcolm, though (83), 'fantasy which makes sense, however fantastic, is not nonsense'. Stewart additionally points to a lack within nonsense of any concern with 'the ontological status of the "real" world prior to members' interpretations' (12). This would seem to indicate a major potential point of division from our understanding of the absurd. For Leonid Geller, however, '"nonsense" least of all signifies the absence of sense', its task (analogous to that of the 'trans-sense', or *zaum*´, language of the Russian Futurists) consisting in 'the generation of [a presumably new] sense' (Geller, 110).

Far from always being completely divorced from any semblance of surrounding reality, as may be commonly thought, nonsense does tend to interact with society or civilisation, whether as an expression of cultural or political alienation, or of other forms of oblique comment. Stewart (209) claims nonsense as a force that divides and rearranges and, in any event, 'It refuses the uplifting note by which the world assumes a happy ending'. Lecercle stresses the pedagogic function of Carroll's Alice books, in that eventually 'she becomes a philosophical figure' (163), going on to remark the overall connection between Victorian narratives (nonsense included) and the Victorian educational system (of both schools and governesses), which he terms for short 'the School' – itself seen as containing 'an absurdity which nonsense barely exaggerates' (Lecercle, 214–15). This tradition – literary, educational and nonsensical – continued well into the twentieth century, culminating perhaps with the Molesworth books of Geoffrey Willans and Ronald Searle (first appearing as 'The Diaries of Molesworth' in *Punch* in the early 1950s, and achieving a timely reprint as *Molesworth* in Penguin Twentieth-Century Classics, 1999). Indeed, the continued health of this phenomenon, right up into the twenty-first century, has been manifested by the years of exaggerated media and high-profile political attention paid, both in general and in bizarre detail, to all aspects of schooling.[36] Not necessarily totally unrelated to the foregoing, more will have to be said at a later juncture with regard to madness and the grotesque, as well as to 'black' or 'sick' humour.

Nonsensical returns to the absurd?

> The stupidity of wisdom can only be accessed through the absurdities in the path of thinking: sophisms, jokes, paradoxes. (Matthijs van Boxsel, *The Encyclopaedia of Stupidity*, 2003)

There are of course many points of contact between theories of humour or nonsense and the absurd. Richter (71) restates Aristotle's old definition that 'the ridiculous stems from harmless incongruity', but also his caution that not all forms of incongruity or absurdity are comic. For Richter, too, humour is the great leveller, in that 'before infinity everything is equal and nothing' (89). Bergson (177) reminds us of Théophile Gautier's belief that 'the comic in its extreme form [is] the logic of the absurd'. Such philosophical implications are pointed up too by Tigges (1988, 259), for whom: 'Nonsense is indeed one possible reflection of life in that it is at

once both *and* neither meaningful and meaningless. An utterly meaningful life can only exist in a world of dogma, an unfree world'. Malcolm
(114) relates certain types of 'Fool's foolery' to nonsense literature, as well
as to the 'deliberate cultivation of absurdity' – 'the bathetically absurd,
the inconsequential and the mock-gnomic', identified as 'characteristics of
Foolish humour'. Parkin, in his critique of Bergson, updates this lineage
(which he will subsequently ascribe to the Bakhtinian carnivalesque: on
which see also Lecercle, 194–5):

> The whole tradition of *sotie* and *mascarade* focused both in the great clowns
> of history, the numskull figures of folklore and the mystique of the local
> village idiot, culminates for us in the theatre of the absurd, Milligan and the
> Goons and *Monty Python's Flying Circus*, and it represents the depth and
> breadth of this strain of humour wherein the bitter surface froth of satiric
> humour is replaced by a deep and rich visceral laughter with which in fact
> Bergson has not the apparatus to deal. (Parkin, 32)

Stewart comments on slapstick as 'an infinite action that never arrives,
never gets anywhere' as a part of her discussion on the quality of 'circularity' frequently to be found in nonsense (Stewart, 129–33; see also
Gruner, 69–73, who sees slapstick as 'virtually *nothing but* mock aggression'). This 'begin again' tendency is reminiscent (within the realm of the
philosophical absurd) of the myth of Sisyphus: a constant uphill struggle
which must eternally begin again as the stone inevitably rolls downhill
again. Tigges contends that 'Sisyphus' labour is sensible when viewed as
a punishment, but nonsensical from the point of view of an expected
result' (Tigges, 1988, 56; a comment originating with Walter Blumenfield,
in 1933). Since the myth is presented as the former, however, it is not to
be regarded as a nonsense story. In modern cosmological terms, the
Sisyphus myth may be seen as a metaphor for the concertina model of the
universe (the theory according to which a cyclic universe will alternately
expand and collapse inward on itself: see Davies, 141–2), analogous, as
well, to Nietzsche's theory of eternal recurrence (or Zarathustra's 'Ring of
Recurrence': *Thus Spake Zarathustra*, 244–7).[37] Elsewhere (at the end of
The Birth of Tragedy: Nietzsche, 1999, 114) Nietzsche metaphorises the
creative spirit through the eternal building, knocking down and rebuild-
ing of a child's sandcastle – an image purloined from the pre-Socratic
philosopher Heraclitus (see Bates, 52), while the Stoics had postulated
'cycles of eternal recurrence for the cosmos and individual, with far-reach-
ing results' (M.R. Wright, 144).
   Merleau-Ponty and Morando (203) admit that 'the myth of the
"eternal return", often associated with the truism of "becoming"', now
has 'an unexpected counterpart in contemporary cosmology'. It may not
be accidental that Walter Benjamin (writing in 1934: Benjamin, 145)
could find 'in all of literature ... no passage which has the Kafka stamp

to the same extent' as two paragraphs from Eddington's *The Nature of the Physical World* (1929). Much later cosmological thinking, however, appears to favour rather the principle of an ever-expanding universe, leading to ever-increasing isolation for all heavenly galaxies.[38] Either way, many might find such a cosmic system meaningless, or absurd: the prospect of a dying universe, in accordance with the laws of thermodynamics, was of itself quite sufficient a depressant for Bertrand Russell (see Davies, 12–13). Michelson (145), revitalising his conception of 'wit' in the light of twentieth-century science, posits 'a universe of universes where possibilities seem endless, where absolutes crumble, and where all theoretical bets, as it were, are off'. Merleau-Ponty and Morando (210) recognise, mildly enough, at least the possibility of such questionings and ponderings being regarded as 'totally futile', or of their giving rise to 'a state of philosophical insecurity'.

As we have seen, Kierkegaard and Dostoevsky, for instance, preferred to obviate the meaningless by leaping into faith (into 'that unthinkable paradox known to Kierkegaard as faith': Eagleton, 44; 'the leap to faith' is satirised by Donald Barthelme's story 'The Leap': *Sixty Stories*, 374–80). Such a choice approximates to Lynch's third gnostic attitude toward images of limitation: 'the imagination of the "double vacuum", which confronts the finite only long enough to generate some emotion such as disgust and then recoils into an unsubstantial world of infinite bliss'; however, a further (or fourth) alternative is 'the absurdist imagination, which holds that the finite world is indeed empty and disgusting but proudly refuses to recoil into visions of infinite, heavenly glory' (as summarised by Galligan, 25). The opposite of this, once again, must be, as Unamuno puts it, 'the absurd of Tertullian', which 'can only base itself on the most absolute uncertainty'; from a scepticism, 'produced by the clash between reason and desire', and the consequent 'embrace between despair and scepticism, is born that holy, that sweet, that saving incertitude, which is our supreme consolation' (Unamuno, 104; 118). The 'faint humming' of the voice of uncertainty, of course, is revealed as a double-edged sword, acting on believer and unbeliever alike (118).

Berger's concluding musings (205–15) on the comic as 'signal of transcendence' are also of relevance here. Underlying the nonsense verse of the German poet Christian Morgenstern is a feeling of the 'absurdity of existence, pointing to God as the only solution'; Tigges glosses this as 'a Chestertonian attitude', in that '"absurd" here means inexplicable and wonderful' (Tigges, 1988, 16; 126, n. 50).[39] G.K. Chesterton (subsequently himself a Catholic convert), in his essay 'A Defence of Nonsense' (1901), had written of the 'new literature' (Lear and Carroll): 'it has its own version of the Cosmos to offer, namely that the world is not only tragic, romantic, religious, but also nonsensical, in as much as Creation is itself nonsensical rather than logical' (quoted by Tigges, 1988, 8).

Creation, a theologically gratuitous act, 'is that which might just as well never have been, and is thus the final refutation of an instrumental rationality' (Eagleton, 128).

Lecercle sees the limericks of Lear, particularly when read as a corpus, to be anticipatory of Heideggerrian existentialism, with their 'omnipresent reference to an aggressive "they"' (Lecercle, 2; 108). Carroll's *The Hunting of the Snark* too, in his view, is open to interpretation 'as the lyrical expression of existential *angst*' (194), while nonsense as a whole, Lecercle feels, may be read as 'the mythical repetition of the literature of carnival' (195). We need to bear in mind throughout, however, M.R. Haight's word of caution that 'absurdity' (in many instances at least) is 'not to be equated with The Absurd, a term that suggests one particular school' (Haight, 255). Palmer's appropriation of the phrase 'the logic of the absurd' clearly derives from the Gautier–Bergson tradition of 'the comic in its extreme form' (see above), rather than Haight's 'particular school'.

Tigges, commenting on 'Absurdity and Absurdism' in relation to nonsense, concludes that 'in nonsense, language *creates* a reality, in the absurd, language *represents* a senseless reality' (Tigges, 1988, 125–31; at 128). There is in any case a sense in which 'all discussions of the theory of linguistic types' must be said to be 'meaningless' (Hofstadter, 22). Pointlessness and arbitrariness are singled out as building blocks of both nonsense and the absurd. The basic difference may be that pointlessness as the point of nonsense is essentially non-serious; pointlessness as the point of the absurd, however, is (potentially, at least) altogether more serious.

Lecercle's comment on nonsense, noted above, that it 'deals not in symbolism but in paradox' is important here, in that a 'symbolic', rather than a straight or 'naive', reading of comedy may tip it from nonsense-humour into serious intent, or into the absurd (or indeed both). Let us take Plato's joke, attributed to Socrates, or rather, ultimately, to a 'clever witty Thracian handmaid' (and apparently appropriated anyway from Aesop) in the dialogue *Theaetetus*, about (the pre-Socratic astronomical sage) Thales, who fell into a well while looking up at the stars: 'She said that he was so eager to know what was going on in heaven that he could not see what was before his feet'. 'The history of western philosophy begins with a joke': so potent with import is the handmaid's quip, that Berger (15) considers such commentary to be 'only a slight exaggeration'. Joke or nonsense? – philosophy, in any case, according to an aside by Unamuno (30), frequently converts itself 'into a kind of art of spiritual pimping'.

Even more apposite, perhaps, is the following 'joke' cited by Freud (190): '"Life is a suspension bridge", said one man. – "Why is that?" asked the other. – "How should *I* know?" was the reply.' Freud can find here no 'concealed sense behind the nonsense'. Uproariously funny this apology for an anecdote may not be. Nevertheless, once placed within an absurd universe (that of 'the absurdist view of language as a net over a void': John Stokes, in Raby, 33) its symbolic significance may perhaps be rather more portentously glossed as: puzzlement at the apparent meaninglessness of a brief means of transition, threatened even then by an abyss, from one state of existence (?) to another. It is also reminiscent of Nietzsche's image of the tightrope walker and man as 'a rope over an abyss' (*Zarathustra*, 47; 43). Much more recently, the Italian novelist Gesualdo Bufalino has his protagonist constantly 'walking a catwalk half a metre wide between two yawning chasms of nothingness' (Bufalino, 82).

Considerable stress has been laid, by older theorists and more recent commentators alike, on the quality of incongruity (or incongruence). Only Berger (208), however, has posed the question: '*Incongruence between what* and what?' (his emphasis). He suggests two answers. The first tends to the anthropological, 'the built-in incongruence of being human', the 'ongoing balancing act between *being* a body and *having* a body', or the traditional philosophical mind/body split; the second he sees as ontological, Pascal's location of humanity 'between the nothing and the infinite' (209). This brings us back again to the absurdist perception of the universe, the answer to which has to be that much-advocated blind leap of religious faith, 'unless we are prepared to resign ourselves with stoic fortitude to the ultimate hopelessness of the world' (214) – or, indeed, we are content to take refuge in Unamuno's supreme consolation of incertitude. The final remaining option, for what it may be worth, could be that favoured by Andy in Harold Pinter's *Moonlight*: to follow the advice of Dylan Thomas, and 'rage against the dying of the light'.

The socio-linguistic absurd

'In the beginning was the Word' (John, 1:1);[40] words form a language and, Unamuno affirms (310), 'a language, in effect, is a potential philosophy'. Furthermore: 'All philosophy is ... at bottom philology. And philology, with its great and fruitful law of analogical formations, opens wide the door to chance, to the irrational, to the absolutely incommensurable' (Unamuno, 311). Puns, for instance (and as James Joyce insisted, 'the Holy Roman Catholic Apostolic Church was built on a pun'), may represent a realm of uncanny semantic foresight, or, for that matter, in Michael Wood's words, a 'withering or etiolation of chance, the sense of secret if insane orders behind the ostensibly arbitrary world of signs' (Wood, 52). The possibilities of being misled by what Borges terms 'the rough, homespun metaphysics – or rather ametaphysics – that lurks in the very origins of language' must be unlimited (Borges, *TL*, 8). The philosophy behind philology may even be malign. All language, as far as the more deconstructive of modern writers are concerned – 'including their own' – is in any event 'the father of lies, the sinister origin of ideology's whole bamboozling exercise' (Bates, 75). Thus may we proceed, in customary circular fashion (in thrall in any case to what Kołakowski [10] terms the inescapable 'infernal circle of epistemology'), from the utterance to the absurd, and back again.

In sociological terms, the absurd has been defined as 'a breaking down of norms, or a series of grave disharmonies within them, as perceived by the individual' and 'a disengagement both resulting from and leading to a breakdown in human interaction' (Shoham, xi; xvii). The incongruous here too resurfaces in renewed tension with the congruous. In an exploration of what is termed 'the no-man's land between sociology and existentialism', S. Giora Shoham deploys arguments extending from absurdist existential philosophy to a social-psychological analysis of the absurd embracing criminality and madness, to arrive at what is construed as 'a sociology of the absurd' (185). Utilising the term 'accidia' (here distinguished from the sociological usages of 'anomie' and 'alienation'), signifying disjunction from an originally normative situation, and through 'newly transmitted normative expectations', leading to an 'absurd breakdown', or 'a breakdown of congruity-motivated involvement' (26–7), Shoham reformulates Camus's approach to the absurd as 'a state of mind; a breakdown of value-involvement; a disengagement' (25). In this sociological approach, therefore, Shoham ventures 'to integrate social deviance, alienation, crime and madness into the wider matrix of the ontological crisis of accidia and the absurd' (185). Although all of these issues may prove to have a recurrent relevance, here the main thrust clearly falls on the side of society and social behaviour, rather than the cosmic-philosophical import of an absurdist analysis of the universe and the human condition therein.

In their manual of communication and cognition (*Relevance*, 1986, 49), Dan Sperber and Deirdre Wilson assert that 'all human beings automatically aim at the most efficient information processing possible'. Their approach to communication theory derives from 'principles of relevance', by way of 'pragmatics', or contextual factors in verbal communication (vii). The building, presentation and perception of a context will involve a process of coding and decoding, along with such factors as inference, implication (or 'implicature'), intention, recognition, deduction and questions of what may be 'manifest' or consist only of 'triviality'. In texts of the absurd such factors and processes are likely to be subverted to a greater or lesser extent, or to be subjected to excessive 'redundancy' (when 'more signals are sent than are strictly necessary to transmit the information in the message': Wilden, 188). In addition, we are reminded, 'cognition and memory superimpose differences even on common experiences', and, owing to various possible causes, 'a mismatch between the context envisaged by the speaker and the one actually used by the hearer may result in a misunderstanding' (Sperber and Wilson, 16). We are now close again to questions of (perceived) congruity and incongruity, already seen to be a frequent staple of humour, nonsense and the absurd.

Another, perhaps more straightforward but not over dissimilar, model of verbal communication had been supplied by Roman Jakobson in his essay 'Linguistics and Poetics' (first published 1960). In essence, the addresser sends a message to an addressee, in a certain context and involving contact and code:

CONTEXT

ADDRESSER   MESSAGE   ADDRESSEE

CONTACT

CODE

(Jakobson, 66)

Again, it is clear that tampering in practice with the normal conventions of such a theoretical model could lead to the generation of text that may degenerate into, or at least approximate to, the absurd. Indeed, Jakobson's model has frequently been used to such illustrative purpose as an analytical tool, for instance by Ann Shukman (in relation to the short prose of Daniil Kharms) and by David Lodge (applied to a short dramatic sketch by Harold Pinter). Isaak and Olga Revzin, adherents of the (then Soviet) Tartu school of semiotics, developing Jakobson's system by adding further axioms of their own, demonstrated absurdness in plays by Ionesco (*The Bald Prima Donna* and *The Lesson*) on the grounds of 'their frequent infringement of certain presuppositions which lie behind every normal act of communication' (Shukman 1989a, 65). Jakobson complemented his model with a scheme of functions:

REFERENTIAL

EMOTIVE   POETIC   CONATIVE

PHATIC

METALINGUAL

(Jakobson, 71)

Lodge makes particularly telling use of the 'poetic' and 'phatic' functions in his analysis of the Pinter text (*Last to Go*). As early as the 1830s, Gogol was engaged, by employing the alogicality of plot structure as a narrative device in addition to his verbal quirks, in shattering the 'customary realistic relationship of words and events'.[41]

In another essay ('Two Aspects of Language and Two Types of Aphasic Disturbances', dating from 1956), Jakobson turns his attention more specifically towards breakdown in communications:

> The addressee perceives that the given utterance (message) is a *combination* of constant parts (sentences, words, phonemes) *selected* from the repository of all possible constituent parts (the code). The constituents of a context are in a state of *contiguity*, while in a substitution set signs are linked by various degrees of *similarity* which fluctuate between the equivalence of synonyms and the common core of antonyms. (Jakobson, 99; emphasis in the original)

Furthermore, 'there must be some kind of contiguity between the participants of any speech event to assure the transmission of the message', and 'there must be a certain equivalence between the symbols used by the addresser and those known and interpreted by the addressee' (100). Without such equivalence, or, once again, if the process is infringed by whatever cause (physical or mental), the message is fruitless or distorted. One (potentially medical) cause is the condition of aphasia. In the semiotic-structuralist tradition, stemming from Peirce and Saussure (and ultimately, it would seem, from St Augustine), Jakobson presents a binary scheme of 'similarity' or 'contiguity' disorders, linking these polarities in literary-poetic terms with metaphor and metonymy, Romanticism and realism, and poetry and prose respectively.[42] Again, the potential application here for the absurd is plain to see.

A somewhat kindred approach comes through the concept of 'language games', associated primarily with the later philosophy (or 'linguistic naturalism': Pears, 35) of Wittgenstein and, in some estimations at least, now an overused or abused influence on postmodern hermeneutics. From Wittgenstein's original, one may say relatively tentative and banal, illustrations in the *Philosophical Investigations*, 'the idea of a language game came to be seen as a paradigm of the complex patterns of social behaviour ... which exist on every scale in human societies' (Hyman, 7).[43] In any event, if the totality is an illusion,[44] then the language games within which 'the variety of reason-giving and appeal to the real is played out have themselves ... no reason: they are there "like our life"' (Weston, 8). The conceit of the language game may now best be seen as a genuflexion to the practicalities of an existence to be endured, perforce, in the absence of a Derridean 'transcendental signified'.[45] Wittgenstein deliberately refrained from explaining his terminology to avoid generating 'philosophical disorders': for him, in any case, 'philosophy ... explains nothing, analyses nothing – it just describes' (Passmore, 426).[46] The notion of the language game, then, which seems largely to represent the context in which the words are uttered (ibid., 432), is ripe for exploitation, and it will come as no surprise when we see that this is already under way in critical analysis of the absurd in literature.

The much-vaunted inadequacy or deception of language (meandering from the Greeks to the esoterics; from the Romantics to the 'post-meta-physical' thought of Nietzsche, through to Heidegger and Derrida) may manifest itself in the inexorable processes of logic, in theories of communication, or language game. David Pears comments that 'it would be strange to argue that, because language is a creation of the human mind, it cannot be a guide to the general features of reality' (Pears, 32). Nevertheless, this would appear to be one implication to be drawn from the bulk of the arguments summarised through the present discussion.

Notes

1 The original Latin *surdus* should also here be noted (an adjective, meaning deaf; silent; stupid), giving rise to 'surd' – lacking sense; also used mathematically (an irrational root or quantity) or phonetically (a voiceless speech sound): *Webster*; *OED*.

2 Colin Wilson's once precocious study *The Outsider* (1956), stronger in its scope than in its detail, covers some of the same ground, asserting that 'the Outsider tends to express himself in Existentialist terms' (27). Sartre's Roquentin is one of the starting points (21–5). Wilson went on in subsequent books to propagate his own form of 'new existentialism' (summarised in his 1967 'Postscript': 309–24).

3 The 'ontological argument' is not to be confused with the 'cosmological argument', although, in one way or another, it frequently is – the two occasionally being combined or merged by philosophers themselves. The cosmological variant is 'an *a posteriori* argument for a cause or reason for the cosmos' (W.L. Craig, x). '*A posteriori*', rather than '*a priori*' (arguing from effect back to cause, or from cause on to effect), is the key distinction; see also the respective cosmological and ontological argument entries in *En. Phil.* (2:232–7; 5:538–42). William Lane Craig provides a full historical-philosophical account, including analyses of the vital contributions of the Arabic and Jewish philosophers; the burning questions to emerge are those of infinite regress, a 'prime mover', determination, causality and 'sufficient reason' (W.L. Craig, 282–3).

4 Nietzsche, however, Lesley Chamberlain reminds us, 'had a horror of what he called nihilism' ('"Nihilist" rhymes with "Christian" – in German at least – he mused frivolously in *The Antichristian*'), associating the term with a combination of loathing and pity, a 'will to nothingness', illness and decay (Chamberlain, 155–6); see *The Anti-Christ* (Nietzsche, 1990, 129–30), and *Twilight of the Idols* (ibid., 96).

5 'The problem of existence Kierkegaard deals with is one faced by the individual in relation to his own existence' (Weston, 36), involving 'at the existentiell [*sic*] level ... an understanding ... of existentiality' or the 'Dasein' ('Da-sein,

to be there': ibid., 37; all emphases in quotations from Weston are present in the original). According to Heidegger, Kierkegaard had 'seized upon the problem of existence as an existentiell problem, and thought it through in penetrating fashion' (ibid., 104).

6 'Philosophical pessimism in its modern form dates back to Schopenhauer, who interpreted human history as an anarchic and absurd struggle for existence among beings doomed by death' (Aileen M. Kelly, 346); Kelly (passim) also points to Aleksandr Herzen as a thinker of interest in this tradition. However, for Kierkegaard too, what could give significance must have 'for us an essentially *negative* form' (Weston, 50).

7 Jaspers, who adopted what he called 'philosophical faith', is seen as providing a bridge between metaphysics and anti-metaphysics.

8 'Even if somebody proved to me that Christ was outside the truth, and it really were true that the truth was outside Christ, then I would rather prefer to remain with Christ than with the truth' (F.M. Dostoevskii, *Polnoe sobranie sochinenii*, vol. 28, 1, p. 176). Nietzsche's comment, in *The Anti-Christ*, that 'If this God of the Christians were *proved* to exist, we should know even less how to believe in him' (Nietzsche, 1990, 175) seems almost to be a retort to this sentiment of Dostoevsky's; Nietzsche came late to Dostoevsky, a novelist whom he in many ways admired. The Russian religious existential thinker Nicholas (Nikolai) Berdyaev examines such aspects of Dostoevsky's 'worldview'; for Dostoevsky, 'the existence of evil is a proof of the existence of God' (Berdyaev, 87).

9 Shestov (or Léon Chestov, in the French spelling under which he became known as his works reappeared in French: see Fotiade, passim) ultimately took a similar leap of faith, but into a non-specifically Christian theism. For selections of Shestov's writings in English translation see Lev Shestov, *Potestas Clavium*, translated by Bernard Martin, Athens, OH: Ohio University Press, 1968; and the same translator's *A Shestov Anthology* (Ohio University Press, 1970). Fondane, incidentally, published originally in Romania as B. Fundoianu.

10 'Incoherence, however, seems unavoidable once genuinely philosophical questions are asked' (Kołakowski, 12). Conversely, absurdist philosophy may itself be appreciated rather as art; for Chamberlain (6): 'The tension between meaning and non-meaning, between picture and painter and perceiver, holds Nietzsche's work together like an experimental novel.' Art, in any case, for Nietzsche himself was 'the saving sorceress with the power to heal' (Nietzsche, 1999, 40).

11 As Richard Sheppard puts it (341): 'To affirm the absurd spontaneity of life by concatenating meaningless words and phrases may be philosophically defensible, but over several pages it becomes an empty exercise'.

12 'To Chestov, reason is useless but there is something beyond reason. To an absurd mind reason is useless and there is nothing beyond reason' (Camus, *Myth*, 38; 93).

13 See Hans Vaihinger, *The Philosophy of 'As If'* [translated by C.K. Ogden], reprinted (London: Routledge) 2001.

14 According to Umberto Eco, 'Leibniz was convinced that [his] calculus had a metaphysical foundation because it reflects the dialectic between God and

Nothingness', suggesting too that the inventor of calculus was Hermes Trismegistus (Eco, 1999, 70; 74).

15 See Borges, 'From Someone to Nobody' (*TL*, 341–3): 'Nothing should be affirmed of Him, everything can be denied. Schopenhauer notes drily: "That theology is the only true one, but it has no content"' (341–2). Borges then proceeds to cite John Scotus Erigena, who, in the ninth century, holds that God 'does not know what He is, because He is not a what, and is incomprehensible to himself and to all intelligence' (342).

16 A kind of half-way house toward negative theology had seemingly been reached by Xenophanes of Colophon (sixth century BC), to whom is attributed the statement: 'God is spherical, because that form is the best, or least inadequate, to represent the Divinity' (quoted from Borges, 'The Fearful Sphere of Pascal', *Labyrinths*, 224). Moreover, the (then new) concept of a single god was, according to Xenophanes, 'gained via a negative path'; at the same time, however, such a deity 'can only be conceived with the help of superlatives' (Ricken, 19).

17 'And indeed "impenetrable darkness" was the name by which the Egyptian sages, from whose secret teachings Damascius claims ... to have drawn his wisdom, referred to the single principle, or beginning, of the universe' (Kołakowski, 51).

18 '"God" becomes a sobriquet for the supreme Nothingness of the Absolute' (Kołakowski, 97).

19 Some 'existential' thinkers, imposing a positive take on such 'absurd evidence' will see an 'absurd possibility' of awakening 'the lost sources of life' in order 'to express the "inexprimable"' (Fotiade, 57).

20 One is reminded here of the classic paradoxical conundrum: 'Can God make a stone so heavy that he can't lift it?' (cited by Hofstadter, 478). However, were we to follow Leibniz, it would appear that 'the principle of non-contradiction is no less binding for God than it is for us' (Kołakowski, 83).

21 Negative theology found particular expression in Eastern Christianity while, in any case, 'the Orient has been the cradle of religions embodying a negative infinity' (Epstein, 353). See also Borges, 'Personality and the Buddha' (*TL*, 347–50): 'Negation is not enough and one arrives at the negation of negations; the world is emptiness and emptiness is also empty' (349).

22 Cf. Graham Roberts ('Aleksandr Vvedenskii, 1904–1941', *Reference Guide to Russian Literature*, edited by Neil Cornwell, London and Chicago: Fitzroy Dearborn, 1998, 893–4): 'Vvedenskii's extant opus is united by one tripartite theme, namely that of time, death and God, and the impossibility of expressing these concepts satisfactorily using conventional human language, with its basis in rational thought'. 'The absurd [*bessmyslitsa*] was understood by Kharms (Vvedensky and other *Chinari*) as a rich characteristic of the world of eternity – the only real and authentic one, as opposed to the earthly world' (V.N. Sazhin, in Kharms, *PSS*, 2, 472).

23 'Alleged' and 'Pseudo' in that this figure, whose writings were first cited at the beginning of the sixth century, has been wrongly identified with Dionysius the Areopagite, a first-century Athenian, converted by St Paul (and also with Denis, patron saint of France).

24 Unamuno reminds us (104): 'It is conceivable that the universe, as it exists in

itself, outside of our consciousness, may be quite other than it appears to us, although this is a supposition that has no meaning for reason'. See also Bates (47), glossing Nietzsche: 'The human mind ... surveyed the surface of things and gave the name reality to what was no more than its own particular way of seeing'.

25 'I fear we are not getting rid of God because we still believe in grammar ...' (*Twilight of the Idols*: Nietzsche, 1990, 48). According to Joseph Brodsky (287), 'the presence of the absurd in grammar says something not about a particular linguistic drama but about the human race as a whole'.

26 For that matter, Wittgenstein's first period is dismissed by some as philosophy, only to be described as 'philosophic poetry of the highest order', while, in his second period, he was elaborating an 'anti-philosophy' (Strathern, 40; 51).

27 M.R. Wright, in her study *Cosmology in Antiquity*, points out that in fact precursors of both the 'big bang' and 'steady state' theories, as of much else current in modern (i.e. twentieth-century) science, had their precursors in ancient Greek cosmology (and cosmogony).

28 'It's not at first obvious to Freud that his own book is a joke, that his theoretical presentation itself shores up the same civilized and repressive constraints – above all, the intellectual constraints of reason and logic – from which he argues jokes to be a longed-for liberation and blessed relief' (Bates, 77). By the end, Bates argues, he does at least have a slight inkling of this; however, it would take Lacan to 'open the door out onto absurdity and alienation where all the lures of order and coherence went up in illusory smoke' (122).

29 Quoted also by Gruner (13), who offers a long-winded insistence on the 'superiority' theory of laughter. Nietzsche, in *Beyond Good and Evil*, quotes (in German) Hobbes, 'as a true Englishman': 'Laughter is a nasty infirmity of human nature that any thinking person will endeavour to overcome'; Nietzsche himself would 'actually go so far as to rank philosophers according to the level of their laughter – right up to the ones who are capable of *golden* laughter', while, for that matter, even 'Gods like to jeer' (Nietzsche, 1998, 175).

30 Translated as 'Of the Essence of Laughter, and generally of the Comic in the Plastic Arts', in Baudelaire, *Selected Writings*, 140–61.

31 Gruner (14), however, firmly claims Koestler for superiority theory.

32 'Satire', according to Wyndham Lewis, 'refers to an "expressionist" universe which is receding a little, a little drunken with an overdose of the "ridiculous" – where everything is ... *steeped* in a philosophic solution of the material, not of mirth, but of the intense and even painful sense of the absurd' (Lewis, *Men Without Art*, 1934), quoted from T. Miller, 54 (on Lewis's view of laughter satire and 'smut' see ibid., 46–58).

33 For a discussion of Bakhtin and Russian attitudes to 'impermissible' laughter see Averintsev, 1993.

34 '[A]uthorities on literary wit and humor are venerated usually because they reshaped our culture's thinking about matters very different from literary wit and humor, or because they talked about wit, *Witz*, jokes or laughter in ways that conveniently blur literary situations and intentions with much else – pratfalls, playground ridicule, the Medieval carnival, funny faces, physical deformities, locker-room bawdy and so on. Addison, Frederick Schiller, Leigh

Hunt, George Meredith, Freud, Bergson, Mikhail Bakhtin, Johan Huizinga –
it's hard to imagine that we would privilege these commentators on the subject
of wit if they hadn't written so effectively about a great deal more' (Michelson,
12). Hilary L. Fink, however, detects an impact from Bergson's ideas on the
absurdism of Daniil Kharms (Fink, 89–100) and reports that Kharms
borrowed library copies of Bergson's main works, including *Le Rire* (95–6;
136, n. 26).

35 The phenomenon of 'paradox' clearly emerges as an important element in
connection with the absurd. In addition to its interest in 'nonsense', it has been
suggested, Surrealism 'can also be defined as the structural use of paradox'
(Bohn, 126).

36 Not least by the farcical inability of prominent late twentieth-century educational ministers and functionaries to furnish correct answers to elementary
mathematical questions while simultaneously demanding that schools and
educational authorities put their houses in order.

37 Chamberlain (126–7) puts the following gloss on this concept: 'The most
important aspect of Eternal Recurrence, after the acceptance of a kind of
cosmological monotony, is the notion that there can be no end or goal or final
purpose for mankind. Life is an endlessly self-repeating process, in which the
individual can only wait for a release from consciousness.' Borges outlines a
refutation of 'the doctrine of the Eternal Return' in his 'The Doctrine of
Cycles' (*TL*, 115–22); on a similar tack, in 'Circular Time', he affirms that this
doctrine, 'attributed to Plato', was formulated rather by an 'unknown
astrologer, who had not read the *Timaeus* in vain' (*TL*, 225). The 'return'
aspect apart, the concept of 'eternity' is frequently seen as a disturbing one:
Woody Allen has said 'eternity is very long, especially toward the end' (quoted
by Rees, 3). Terry Eagleton (243–4) opines: 'Like the smaller Greek islands,
Eden is alluring, but there is not enough to do', while Beckett refers to a
'promise of God knows what fatuous eternity' (Beckett, *CSP*, 62).

38 Paul Davies provides an accessible account of such ideas in his book *The Last
Three Minutes* (1994); more recent developments in cosmological thinking
may be accessed from, for instance, the 1999 BBC series *The Universe*
(repeated 2001) and Channel 4's *Edge of the Universe* (2002). See also Rees
(2001); and his book: Martin Rees, *Our Cosmic Habitat*, London: Weidenfeld,
2002.

39 On the 'verbal grotesque' in Morgenstern see Kayser, 150–7.

40 Nevertheless, it may be noted: 'In one Greco-Egyptian myth, in the beginning
was not the Word, but the Laugh – and the Laugh was God' (Segal, 24).

41 According to the Formalist critic, Viktor Vinogradov, writing in 1921 (quoted
in R.E. Jones, 408).

42 Tzvetan Todorov, in his *Theories of the Symbol* (Chapter 1, 'The Birth of
Western Semiotics'), traces semiotics and hermeneutics back to Augustine and,
before that, to Aristotle and the Stoics. Augustine can seemingly be credited
too with the founding of communication theory (Todorov, 1982, 36–7) and
with being the holder of strong views on the issue of play (Bates, 32–5).

43 For an extensive examination and typology of games in society, see Caillois,
1967; for a recent 'alternative theory of play', though, see Bates.

44 The 'questioning by the individual of their *own* life', in Kierkegaardian terms,

can only be posed 'in the appropriate existential form, that of the despair of the I over the significance of his life in its *totality*' (Weston, 83–4)

45 Peter Conrad (117) sees 'another desolating image of divine absenteeism' in Wittgenstein's 'beetle' in the box model (see *Philosophical Investigations*, no. 293).

46 Given the constraints of restrictive relativism, maintains Kołakowski (6), 'the validity of any question, whether it concerns Fermat's last theorem or the Eucharist, can only be determined by an appeal to the rules of a particular game', however these may have been established.

2

Antecedents to the absurd

only the finite being cannot think the thought of annihilation (*The Night Watches of Bonaventura*, 1804)

Long before his existentialist followers, the man from the underground proclaimed the majesty of the absurd. (George Steiner, *Tolstoy or Dostoevsky*, 1959)

From the ancients ...

It has become a commonplace to trace the antecedents of the absurd back to the older stages of Greek theatre (the so-called Old Comedy), or indeed beyond that. Roberto Calasso, in his *Literature and the Gods*, would trace the roots of 'absolute literature' back to, and indeed before, the era of the gods.[1] For Martin Esslin (*Th. Abs.*, 327), 'the Theatre of the Absurd is a return to old, even archaic, traditions'. According to Lois Gordon, Cain and Abel are 'the Old Testament's first innocent victims in a gratuitously capricious, unfathomable universe'; in 'the first example of dialogue in the Bible ... language avoids or obscures communication' (Gordon, 84; 93). While the theatre of Aristophanes, in particular, laid a strong emphasis on intellectual or literate repartee, it would none the less be misleading not to argue that elements of performance remained paramount. These derived from the oldest ritual, fertility rites, or rustic revels (the *komos*) and other forms of pre-dramatic mumming, as well as from a primitive popular theatre known as *mimus* (mime) that paralleled classical tragedy and comedy. The absurd, in fact, as we shall see, has taken from tragedy as well as from comedy – perhaps in equal measure. In any event, as M.R Wright has stressed: '"The world's a stage" was an ancient as well as a Shakespearean concept'.[2]

'The *mimus* was a spectacle containing dancing, singing, and juggling, but based largely on the broadly realistic representations of character types in semi-improvised spontaneous clowning' (Esslin, *Th. Abs.*, 330). 'Comedy', as explained by Erich Segal opening his *The Death of Comedy*, has been assumed to derive from the similar Greek words for sleep (*koma*), village (*kome*) and revel (*komos*), with the latter supplying the most important element, along with the quality of song (*oide*: Segal, 1–4), amounting to something like 'a dreamsong of a revel in the country', or 'nightsong country revel' (ibid., 9; 23). Sexuality, fertility and growth, imbued with the spirit of Dionysian cults and cyclical festivals, became very much a part of the Old Comedy: not for nothing does Segal entitle one of his chapters 'The Lyre and the Phallus'.[3] Indeed, 'two original elements of the ancient *komos* [were] Chaos and Eros'; as Segal observes (16–17), these 'vibrant feelings' are still to be sensed 'in the most sophisticated comic authors: Shakespeare, Molière, Gilbert and Sullivan, and even parodistically in absurdist authors like Ionesco'. The wearing of masks, symbolising changes of personality, a practice of multi-levelled cross-dressing, the presence of a chorus (giving out its commentary, plus an argument in the form of *parabasis* – a pronouncement of advice, often seemingly unrelated to the rest of the play), a widespread tone of vulgarity (evident both in stage-props and dialogue), and various metatheatrical devices were all prominent features.

The more unusual the combination of such elements contained in a particular play or performance, the closer such a drama (the Greek *drama*, meaning 'something done') might approximate to our modern understanding of Theatre of the Absurd. And we have yet to mention the pivotal absurdist ingredient of laughter. 'All Comedy aspires to laughter – although not all laughter is related to Comedy' is Segal's judgment (23). In addition to laughter, key constituents of the Old Comedy, and of course beyond, were invective, cruelty and misogyny: Segal (30) points out that the 'comedy of cruelty is found in all cultures, but has been most aptly named by the Germans – *Schadenfreude*'.

Greek tragedy (or 'goat's song'[4]), which returned to the European consciousness at the time of the Italian Renaissance, contains within it, as Maurice Valency has pointed out, the absurd, 'chthonic poetry' and darkness; the grandeur that was tragic in classical drama may have dissipated in our modern bourgeois settings, but there does remain 'the sadness of existence, a deep and poignant pathos' (Valency, 1; 6). The caprices of fate, or the justice of the gods, left much to be desired throughout Greek tragedy: 'Zeus rules the world. But he does not love it' (ibid., 79).As Ramona Fotiade (97) points out:

> Sophocles' tragedy *Oedipus Rex* brings man and God together in the same violent, passionate confrontation recounted in the book of Job from the absurd perspective of faith, which rejects any ethical consolations (relating to the injustice of human destiny) as well as any rational appeals to moderation ... Sophocles, no less than 'Job's scribe', conveys this revelation in its absurd clarity.

As the Odysseus of Sophocles puts it, amid this cosmic tyranny: 'We are no more than dim shapes and weightless shadows' (*Ajax*; quoted from Valency, 96). Indeed, Valency asserts: 'Sophocles ... could account for much that is mysterious in the plays of Ibsen or Chekhov or Beckett' (ibid., 91). Greek tragedy was reconsidered by Artaud in his 'Theatre of Cruelty' and by Shestov and Fondane in their 'philosophy of tragedy' (Fotiade, 68). Jan Kott, *à propos* of Shakespeare and Beckett ('"King Lear", or Endgame'), links tragedy with the grotesque and the absurd in the following formula (Kott, 108): 'The tragic situation becomes grotesque when both alternatives of the choice imposed are absurd, irrelevant or compromising. The hero has to play, even if there is no game.' A wide-ranging summary of definitions – and both theoretical and practical manifestations – of tragedy is offered in Terry Eagleton's study *Sweet Violence* (2003).

Aristophanes, in a vast succession of comic dramas, of which eleven have survived intact, combined the foregoing traditional constituents with a highly satirical treatment of social, political and philosophical themes. Segal (34) characterises his *oeuvre* as 'episodic vaudeville'. The theatrical pieces of Aristophanes were presented (as was the requirement) in competitions for the award of prizes at Dionysia; such a system was, as always in such competitive proceedings, ever open to question, to arbitrary judgment or indeed and inherently to potential farce. His plays include 'aerial flights of absurdist fantasy' and what have been termed 'if-only' types of fantasy (Cartledge, 55; 56), as well as the immortal nonsense-setting of 'Cloudcuckooland' (*Nephelokokkugia*, or 'Cuckoonebulopolis', in *Birds*). In addition to such what might well be considered absurdist trappings, Aristophanes also includes occasional flashes of more philosophically absurdist discourse, such as his birds'-eye view of the human condition:

> Dim creatures of earth, who attain unto birth like leaves, in blind fecundation,
> Ye men of a day, frail figures of clay, mere phantoms in wild agitation,
> Ungifted with wings, poor suffering things whose life is a vision diurnal.
> (*Birds*, in R.H. Webb's translation: Aristophanes, 255)

Paul Cartledge characterises the Aristophanic drama as (admittedly in anachronistic terms) 'something like burlesque, ... broad farce, comic opera, circus, pantomime, variety, revue, music hall, television and movie satire, the political cartoon, the political journal, the literary review, and the party pamphlet', the whole denigrating the powers that be (or were), perhaps to advocate fairer shares for all, or perhaps just to delude through 'carnival dreams of inverted looking-glass worlds' (Cartledge, 73; 78).

The Old Comedy was succeeded by a 'Middle' and then the New Comedy which, with its stock character types, from Menander through to Plautus and Terence, was to form the basis of 'classic' comedy into the modern age; according to Segal (108), 'every definition of comedy, from antiquity to our own day, refers exclusively to the Menandrian form'. Moreover, Segal goes on to affirm (154), 'from the point of view of influence, Menander is arguably the single most important figure in the history of Western comedy'.

Mention of the spirit of carnival, though, evokes Mikhail Bakhtin's theory of the novel, and especially his seminal study *Problems of Dostoevsky's Poetics* (published in 1963, as a much expanded version of his 1929 book, *Problems of Dostoevsky's Art*), in which he describes the phenomenon of Menippean satire and its influence on the development of European novelistic prose (Bakhtin, 1984, 112–22). Menippus of Gadara was a Cynic of the third century BC whose works have not survived, but whose style was taken up in the first century BC by Varro (the genre being occasionally known also as Varronian satire), from whose prolific hand a large number of fragments at least have come down. This form of writing was developed in the early centuries AD in Greek by Lucian, and in Latin by Petronius and Apuleius.[5] The tradition may go back further even than Menippus, to 'the logistoricus (a combination of the Socratic dialogue with fantastic histories)', it is thought (Bakhtin, 1984, 113). During the Roman Saturnalia ('the symbolic return of the deposed Saturnus, father of Jupiter and king of golden-age Italy'), 'slaves were kings for a day, while their masters served them a feast' (Segal, 15). As well as linking what he calls 'menippea' to carnival and 'a world upside down', Bakhtin (133) lists the basic ingredients as: a comic element, a spirit of the unfettered, fantasticality, 'slum naturalism', the posing of ultimate questions, the depiction of psychic states, eccentricity (often of a scandalous nature), incongruities and mésalliances, varieties of utopianism and a satirical topicality – all within a stylistic and generic mix. Northrop Frye, who (in his celebrated *Anatomy of Criticism* of 1957) likened the genre of Menippean/Varronian satire to his conception of the 'anatomy' (drawn from Burton's *Anatomy of Melancholy*), points in particular to the element of what he terms 'encyclopaedic farrago', later 'clearly marked in Rabelais', and involving parodic displays of erudition (Frye, 311).

Madness: mysteries to Shakespeare

Between the proto-novels of the late classical period and the inventive and fantastical compositions of Rabelais, on which Bakhtin went on to expatiate in the later *Rabelais and His World* (Bakhtin, 1968), came the presentations of medieval drama, in both their serious and their more subverted forms. The dramatised allegory of morality plays seemingly arose in England, probably from about the end of the fourteenth century, and developed in France and elsewhere. Mystery and miracle plays began

to appear as early as the ninth century and flourished until the late
sixteenth century (or later in some corners of Europe), liturgically based,
but with the miracle plays enjoying a much greater range of plot and situation, affecting in their turn the development of secular drama in its
higher and lower forms. For that matter, according to Bakhtin at least
(1984, 129), 'in the realm of carnivalistic folk culture there was no break
in tradition between antiquity and the Middle Ages'; indeed, there was a
sense in which 'the entire theatrical life of the Middle Ages was carnivalistic'. Menippean components lived on in miracle and morality plays and
their parodic variants, surfacing for instance in the 'infernal buffoonery'
of the mystery play – itself 'a modified medieval dramatic variant of the
menippea' (ibid., 138; 147). Bakhtin sees what he terms 'carnival-mystery
play' space-time (177) as a prominent 'chronotope' in the fiction of
Dostoevsky, which he regards as a true modern development of the
Menippean tradition within medieval mystery and morality drama.[6] Frye
links the morality play to the 'archetypal masque', detached in setting
from time and space, often in 'a sinister limbo' or 'the interior of the
human mind', inhabited by 'abstract entities' or 'the stock types of the
commedia dell' arte' and leading to more modern forms of 'myth-play'
(Frye, 282; 290–1).

The *commedia dell'arte* was a form of professional, or travelling,
improvised comic performance art, popular in particular from the
sixteenth to the eighteenth centuries in Italy, but also in France and elsewhere in Europe, involving standardised situations and plot intrigues,
acted out by a series of stock characters, including Harlequin
('Arlecchino', or 'Hellequin'), Columbine, Pantaloon, Pierrot, extraneous
'zany' (*zanni*) or subsidiary clowns, and indeed the 'Zany Harlequin'.
Such comic fools may descend from the *mimus* of antiquity, as does the
phenomenon of the court jester (Esslin, *Th. Abs.*, 332–3), and they
indulged too in multifarious forms of incongruous semantic speculation
and verbal misunderstanding.[7] Jung links the figure of the 'trickster' to the
medieval description of the devil as *simia dei* (the ape of God) and earlier
representations as 'a forerunner of the saviour', down to 'the carnival
figures of Pulcinella and the clown' and what he sees as 'a collective
shadow figure' (see Jung, 255–72). Harlequin, according to Edith
Welsford, was 'an odd hybrid creature, in part a devil created by popular
fancy, in part a wandering mountebank from Italy', at times represented
as a 'diabolical acrobat' (Welsford, 289–90); he was also descended or
transformed from the 'devil Erl-King' (Bakhtin, 1968, 267). In its various
facets, this form of performance art was absorbed into legitimate theatrical drama, as well as into other forms of European popular theatre, plus
pantomime, music hall and vaudeville, and thence into the twentieth-
century popular artistic form of the silent movie. The latter was to become
'without doubt one of the decisive influences on the Theatre of the

Absurd' (Esslin, *Th. Abs.*, 335), as well as on certain other avant-garde artistic movements.

From the 'parasites' of ancient Greece to the 'buffoons' of medieval Italy (including those based at the Vatican) and France and beyond, among those doubling as laughter-makers and 'ridiculous men of the court' were poets (including the occasional 'absurd extempore poet'), painters, friars and academics, arranging 'triumphs, comedies and morescoes during the Carnival season' and improvising or indulging in 'caprices' (Welsford, 16–17).[8] The ranks of medieval court fools, operating as amateur 'fool-societies', as strolling minstrels or itinerant professional troupes, were further swollen, in accordance with the particular whim of individual potentates, by clairvoyants, the deformed (and other 'grotesques'), the insane (actual or purported), pedants and the occasional disgraced courtier. The phenomenon, at court and subsequently in the big houses, historically documented from the twelfth century, of course, features in legend (Till Eulenspiegel being a famous example) and is widely and variously presented in literature (from Erasmus and Rabelais to Shakespeare). Essentially a medieval figure, although attaining his (or occasionally *her*, for there were female fools) greatest prominence in the Renaissance, the 'sage-fool' whose function lay in 'reversing the judgments of the world' belonged to an age when 'all worldly distinctions, theoretically at least, were regarded as unreal and transitory' (Welsford, 248). This attitude also pertains, however, though in a somewhat different sense and with an added intuition of pointlessness, through into the modern age.

For many of their contemporaries, according to M.A. Screech (150), Erasmus and Rabelais were models 'of reborn Lucianic laughter': 'they were both mocking atheists, masquerading as priests!'. Among the basic ingredients of Rabelais's massively hyperbolic parodic novels, *Gargantua* and *Pantagruel*, may be numbered (in no particular order of prominence): gluttony, obscenity (with particular emphasis on bodily parts and evacuations), the grotesque, abuse (in various senses), degradation and sacrilege; all of this is carried out in a style of travesty and a spirit of 'glee' (Parkin, 101).[9] Rabelais is seen to have operated, on several levels, at a crucial cultural crossroads. For Bakhtin, Rabelais, along with Cervantes and Shakespeare, represents 'an important turning point in the history of laughter' – at a line dividing the Renaissance from the seventeenth century and beyond (Bakhtin, 1968, 66). In his own time, Rabelais was a mouthpiece for popular profanity, in a fight back against 'the old, gloomy truth of medieval philosophy, of "Gothic darkness", the somberly hypocritical and serious, the messengers of darkness' (ibid., 172), challenging the hierarchical character of the medieval cosmos in both a physical, or socio-historical, and a symbolic, or semiotic, sense (400ff). The sounds of the world were now being heard 'in a new key', approached 'not as a

somber mystery play but as a satyrical drama' (233). According to Frye
(235), moreover, 'in the riotous chaos of Rabelais, Petronius and Apuleius
satire [my emphasis] plunges through to its final victory over common
sense', linking Lucian to Swift.

Rabelais, who 'has a greater vocabulary than any other French author'
(Screech, 224), at a clear linguistic turning point, fervently indulged in
(though he was far from being dominated by) 'billingsgate', or abusive
language. He is also considered 'perhaps the greatest of the masters of
nonsense prose and verse' (Esslin, *Th. Abs.*, 341), or the 'absurdities and
alogisms' of *coq-à-l'âne* (see Bakhtin, 1968, 422–6). While Rabelais, like
other Renaissance masters, was extremely well versed in ancient sources,
in particular those of 'a carnivalized antiquity', any slight impact on the
Rabelaisian treatment of the comic from Aristophanes 'should not be
exaggerated' (ibid., 98); much more significantly, 'Rabelais inherited and
brought to fulfillment thousands of years of folk humor' (473). Parody of
form seems to have been an on-going tradition in itself since time (or
form) immemorial, from a jaunty mixing of prose and verse to what has
been seen as 'the jerky [early] cinematic changes of scene in Rabelais'
(Frye, 234). Further areas of quirk and effect transmitted from or through
Rabelais to progeny within modernity will be indicated shortly.

The works of Shakespeare, of course, include plentiful instances of
fools or foolery, absurdities of one kind and another, and symptoms of the
carnivalesque. These qualities occur not only in the comedies, such as *As
You Like It* and *Twelfth Night* (in which play the Clown observes:
'Foolery, sir, does walk about the orb like the sun, it shines everywhere').
'It is probable', according to T. McAlindon, that Kyd and Marlow, like
the author of *A Midsummer Night's Dream*, were deeply impressed by the
superbly contrarious art of *The Knight's Tale*'; Chaucer's first Canterbury
Tale has been interpreted 'not only as an affirmation of Boethian provi-
dentialism but also as an absurdist vision of a world in which men are the
deluded instruments of powers who care little for them'.[10] Metaphors
such as 'Romeo being stabbed with a white wench's black eye or Heaven
stopping its nose at the crime attributed to Desdemona', 'clearly ridiculous' on a literal level but possessed of a quality of *le merveilleux*, were to
prove irresistible to the Surrealists (Bohn, 145). Fools and absurdity too,
of course, are to be found in what are considered the serious
Shakespearean dramas. The obvious figure of Falstaff apart, just one
example from the histories would be the antics surrounding Jack Cade in
King Henry VI, Part 2.[11] At the same time, Shakespeare's tragedies, naturally enough, encompass what is 'a very strong sense of the futility and
absurdity of the human condition' (Esslin, *Th. Abs.*, 333). The tragedies,
indeed, according to Duncan Salkeld (155) 'make futility a theme'.
Furthermore, Welsford (270) has emphasised that 'when Shakespeare
desired to communicate his reflections on the human tragedy he could

make use of figures who were already partially stylized and invested with symbolical significance in everyday life'.

Macbeth, on hearing of the death of the Queen, articulates one of the great Shakespearean plaints:

> To-morrow, and to-morrow, and to-morrow,
> Creeps in this petty pace from day to day,
> To the last syllable of recorded time;
> And all our yesterdays have lighted fools
> The way to dusty death. Out, out, brief candle!
> Life's but a walking shadow; a poor player,
> That struts and frets his hour upon the stage,
> And then is heard no more: it is a tale
> Told by an idiot, full of sound and fury,
> Signifying nothing.
>
> (*Macbeth*, Act V, Sc. v)

Here futility, or lack of meaning, in what is an overwhelmingly historical as well as a personal situation, strikes on levels of time, reason, performance, narrative, tone and language. For Macbeth, 'every choice is absurd' in a world of absurdity (Kott, 99).

In the case of *King Lear*, Frye (239) refers to 'the ironic parody of the tragic situation'. Shakespeare's apparent conception of life is famously expressed by the recently blinded Gloucester:

> As flies to wanton boys, are we to th'Gods;
> They kill us for their sport.
>
> (*King Lear*, Act IV, Sc. i)

As for Lear himself, as Welsford (269) expresses it, 'Lear's tragedy is the investing of the King with motley: it is also the crowning and the apotheosis of the Fool'. Terence Hawkes (34) puts it slightly more starkly: 'When the king shows himself to be a fool, then the Fool has a good claim to be a king.' Whether the Fool's disappearance from the play be explicable by his 'replacement' by Lear himself, or some kind of 'doubling' with the role of Cordelia (Hawkes, 35), his relationship with Lear, or rather Lear's relationship with the Fool, is to be seen as a big part of the play's tragic movement: 'the movement downwards towards that ultimate exposure and defeat' – degradation, the stripping away of power and dignity, resulting in nakedness, madness and death (Welsford, 262).[12] Welsford sees this as 'an amazingly daring version of the culminating moment of the sottie: the great reversal when the highest dignitaries appear as fools' (262–3). It might also be seen as a slow-motion, but irreversible, charade of the carnivalesque.

The nature of Shakespearean laughter, on occasion however – for instance that surrounding Jack Cade – was, in the view of Paola Pugliatti, 'not the liberating and festive laughter of the carnival tradition; it was the grim, bitter, moralistic laughter that comes from the grotesque, a laughter that proclaims some kind of disease' (quoted in Knowles, 1998, 17). The language of madness, for that matter, is never quite what would normally be understood by 'language', it has been argued: 'it is a language without syntax, without logic; difference without identity; a mass of signifiers struggling for all too few signifieds' (Salkeld, 45). The great irony of *King Lear*, in Salkeld's view (105), is that 'in madness, Lear engages with philosophical issues'; indeed, even, '*King Lear* reads as an exact corollary to Descartes' (see further, ibid., 107–9). Kott affirms (120) that in Shakespeare 'clowns often ape the gestures of kings and heroes, but only in *King Lear* are great tragic scenes shown through clowning'. These aspects, among others, place Shakespeare's theatre firmly among the precursors of modern developments in the absurd. This has indeed been accorded full recognition in the case of Shakespeare, as also (and as already noted) of Sophocles: 'Most of us are too familiar with Shakespeare to notice how rich his plays are in precisely the same type of inverted logical reasoning, false syllogism, free association, and the poetry of real or feigned madness that we find in the plays of Ionesco, Beckett, and Pinter' (Esslin, *Th. Abs.*, 332).

Nonsense, Swift and Sterne

As we move out of the Elizabethan period and towards the eighteenth century, we find, for instance, that, in the words of Nicholas Brooke, English tragedy 'springs from violent farce', in which a balance is perceived between 'the grandeur and the grotesquerie', with 'tears and laughter equally projected' (Brooke, 8–9). Death has the last laugh and absurdity abounds. 'Wild laughter resists order' and 'sardonic humour' outlasts 'the statements of order-restored'; order is attacked, anarchy celebrated and chaos generated; the plays of Jacobean tragedy 'are properly known as tragedies, but only if their horrid laughter is realised as essential to their tragic form' (ibid., 130). In Spain, Quevedo produced satrirical works which included *La hora de todos y la Fortuna con seso* (*Everyone's Hour, and Fortune with Brains*, 1635–45), a Stoic–Christian allegory in which chaos is caused by Fortune releasing her wheel; every object is undermined by its own opposite; clichés are played off against each other; the world is paradoxical, and yet (or thus) this situation frees humankind to endow an ambivalent existence with meaning (see van Boxsel, 95–100). Over the same period, too, English nonsense poetry was raising its eccentric head (see Malcolm, 1998).

In the course of the following century, the work of Sterne could itself be seen as 'nonsense prose' (Esslin, 347), while Swift's 'gloomy world' (as discerned by Bakhtin, 1968, 308), in prose and poetry, descended from medieval forebears, especially in its 'affinity with the *danse macabre* tradition' (Frye, 235) – the latter being a well-trodden metaphor in grotesque carnivalesque form (widely displayed as iconographic allegory) for the human condition – analogous, no doubt, to *The Ship of Fools*.[13] As Ronald Knowles reminds us, too, in the early modern period (that is to say, roughly 1500–1750), 'there was no absolute distinction between the fantastic and the real' and reading was conditioned by 'the balance between credulity and scepticism' (Knowles, 1996, 4; 6).

Swift, whose satirical strength descended from the neoclassical tradition of Menippus, Varro and Lucian (reprised by the early moderns Erasmus and More), with more than a touch of Rabelaisian scatology (ibid., 17; 58–9; 104–5), contrived, or recreated, generic mixes of the Menippean (or Frye's anatomy) type – so much so, that he was later extolled by the Surrealists. For Borges, 'Jonathan Swift acted like a corrosive acid on the elation of human hope' (Borges, *TL* 12). Among the 'multiple possibilities of signification in the textuality' of *Gulliver's Travels* is an absurdist reading, conceivably stretching as far as 'ultimate nihilism'.[14] This reading may be considered predictable in the era of postmodernism; however, still within the eighteenth century, the practical moralist James Beattie had attacked the fourth voyage of Gulliver ('A Voyage to the Country of the Houyhnhnms') as 'an absurd and abominable fiction' (Knowles, 1996, 35). 'Swift's usual satirical techniques include', Knowles affirms, 'the literalization of the metaphorical and the logic of absurdity' (64; 111–12). These extend, within the world(s) visited by Gulliver, to huge reversals that may evoke the 'popular satiric tradition of *mundus inversus*, or "The World Upside Down"', reversing natural and social order or hierarchy in what may be interpreted in reactionary or radical ways: 'Does obvious absurdity buttress the status quo or suggest that the status quo itself is absurd?' (121–2).

Beyond the nonsense element in the work of Laurence Sterne, that is to say in his eccentric saga *The Life and Opinions of Tristram Shandy* (termed by Christopher Ricks 'the greatest shaggy-dog story in the language': Sterne, 7), Sterne was an author – not surprisingly – of considerable interest to the Russian Formalists.[15] In addition, though, as 'the disciple of Burton and Rabelais', Sterne was the outstanding figure to combine the 'anatomy' with the 'novel' (Frye, 312). As an exponent of satire and ironic fiction, or 'the new subjective grotesque' (Bakhtin, 1968, 36), Sterne employed self-parody, digressions, bathos, dislocations of narrative and 'devices turning on the difficulty of communication' (Frye, 234). Bakhtin saw at the heart of *Tristram Shandy* 'the intervalic chronotope of the puppet theater, in disguised form', though, in the work of Sterne (along with Swift, Voltaire and Dickens) 'a relative softening of

Rabelaisian laughter' (Bakhtin, 1981, 166; 237). Especially in Sterne, he noted 'a parody of the logical and expressive structure of any ideological discourse as such' that was almost as radical as the parody found in Rabelais (ibid., 308). This brings us close again to Esslin's 'nonsense prose' and other absurdist features, and indeed Ricks, for one (in Sterne, 16–17; 26), links Sterne forward to Beckett.

Romantic grotesque to 'higher' realism and pre-Surrealist nonsense

'Bonaventura' and Foscolo

What Bakhtin terms 'the Romantic grotesque' relied chiefly on Renaissance traditions, 'especially on the rediscovered Shakespeare and Cervantes' (Bakhtin, 1968, 37). A key work of this category at the turn of the nineteenth century, and one with equally clear affinities to the fantastic and the Gothic, was *The Night Watches of Bonaventura* (published anonymously in German in 1804). In a work as extraordinary for its generic and narrative mix (with its perceived debt to Sterne: Kayser, 197–8, n. 15) as for the mystery of its authorship, 'Bonaventura' furnishes the reader with a striking admixture of apocalyptic vision, the grotesque and the gruesome, underpinned by a stratum of cemetery nihilism. In the Romantic grotesque, as opposed to its medieval and Renaissance counterparts, the emphasis is on terror, alienation and a form of madness laced with 'a somber, tragic aspect of individual isolation' (Bakhtin, 1968, 39). As Wolfgang Kayser has stressed in his study of the grotesque, 'behind Bonaventura's satire is the void' (Kayser, 60).[16] 'A terrible vacuum, a nothingness lurks behind [the Romantic mask]' of Bonaventura too for Bakhtin (1968, 40).

The principal narrator (nightwatchman and sleepwalker) of *The Night Watches*, who purports to be a son of the devil by a canonised saint (or perhaps the offspring of an alchemist and a fortune-teller), is prone to laughter in church and tears in the bordello: the earlier popular tradition of derision of divinity thus becomes 'the sardonic laughter in church of the lonely eccentric' (ibid., 41). The demonic laughter in 'Bonaventura' is seen as 'a mask over an abyss', invented by the devil and 'given to mankind as a reaction of doubt in the face of absurd facts' (Gillespie, in 'Bonaventura', 7; 26). In 'Bonaventura' man remains 'inevitably and hopelessly the dupe of godless nature'; tragedy melds with comedy and metamorphoses into farce, substituting for the old tragedy 'a modern existential anguish' (ibid., 22; 25). Tragedy is to be laughed at; farce to be wept at; 'I find everything rational absurd, just as vice versa' ('Bonaventura', 73; 155). The marionette is promoted as a modern successor to the ancient forms of masked drama, as 'Bonaventura' plays on puppet theatre, the *commedia dell' arte* and the metaphor of the world as a stage (hissing at 'this great tragicomedy, world history': 73), invoking puppet-master, insane poet and further 'mad Creator' variants. Centrepieces are the interpolated 'The Clown's Prologue to the Tragedy: Man' (137–43) and the 'Monolog of the Insane World Creator' (149–53). Further striking features include the disquisition on laughter (219–21); the plan for a 'pseudo-Last Judgement' (109; 233); the introduction of masks, skulls and death's-heads;[17] and the 'contradictions' of loving life for the sake of death (85) or fearing death 'on account of immortality' (211).

In its retreat into isolation and chaos, *The Night Watches of Bonaventura* comprises 'a manifesto of an art of despair deserved by decadence' (Gillespie: 'Bonaventura', 4). A pivotal work among the antecedents to the absurd that anticipates much that is later found in nineteenth-century absurdist precursors, as indeed in the twentieth-century actuality, *The Night Watches* equally looks back to (or may for that matter be seen as a culmination of) the ancient and early modern traditions outlined hitherto. There are references to, or ludic variations on, Greek drama, the *commedia*, Shakespeare (including correspondence conducted in an asylum between Hamlet and Ophelia – or rather actors who played their roles),[18] Cervantes, Don Juan, clowns and fools aplenty, and the (Basel) dance of death.[19] All in all, it seems astonishing that 'Bonaventura' is not in general better known and, in particular, does not feature more prominently in the annals of absurdism.

As the pre-Romantic (or Sentimentalist) movement merged into Romanticism, absurdist elements, of one variety or another, surfaced within a range of genres and writers. Beyond such maverick works as *The Nightwatches of Bonaventura* and the idiosyncratic prose of Jean Paul Richter, these might be said to include the philosophical and ethical disputations of the Marquis de Sade, the Gothic novel (in its varied manifestations) and the fiction of E.T.A. Hoffmann (especially the latter's *The Life and Opinions of the Tomcat Murr*, 1820–22 – half the biography of an eccentric musician and half the memoirs of a cat) – all of which were immensely influential across Europe. The protagonist of Ugo Foscolo's *Last Letters of Jacopo Ortis* (1802), another turn-of-the-century work on the cusp of this Sentimentalism–Romanticism development, includes his own (by no means untypical) existential *cri de coeur*:

> Human life? A dream, a deceptive dream which we value so very highly, just as foolish women entrust their future to superstitions and presentiments! ...
> I don't know, but I suspect that Nature made our species just about the tiniest ineffectual link in her incomprehensible system, giving us so much self-love to ensure that the great fear and hope which fill our imaginations

with an infinite series of ills and blessings, keep us always troubled about this short, uncertain, unhappy existence of ours. And while we blindly serve her ends, she laughs at our pride that makes us consider that the universe was made for us alone, and that we alone are worthy and capable of giving laws to creation. (Foscolo, 31–2)

Gogol

In Russia, Nikolai Gogol was influenced by a number of these trends, as well as by medieval folkloric and religious traditions.[20] However, almost the most important Gogolian feature for present purposes lies in his being an exponent *par excellence* of stylistic absurdism, with Sternean quirks, digressions, inflated similes, snatches of zany dialogue, hyperbole, narrative and syntactic non sequiturs, superfluous detail and irrelevancies, non-appearing characters and other forms of redundancy – or what Cathy Popkin aptly terms 'verbal clutter'.[21]

We also find in Gogol Ukrainian (as well as European and purely Gogolian) folklore and demonology, applications of myth and legend, and a frequently carnivalised atmosphere, whether the setting purports to be the Ukraine, the Russian provinces or the fantastic-modern city of St Petersburg.[22] His most famous major (or better known) works build on an anecdotal incident serving an apparently satirical purpose (social or moral), before eventually veering into elemental, mythic or symbolic realms. The comedy *The Government Inspector*, which hilariously exposes the venality of provincial Russian officialdom, bases itself on the time-honoured ploy of misidentification, rapidly turned to opportunistic imposturing, and culminates in a pseudo-apocalyptic tableau heralding a mock last judgment. The novel *Dead Souls*, conceived as a trilogy of *Divine Comedy* aims and scope (of which only Part One survived complete), and classed by Bakhtin (1981, 28) as a Menippean satire and (1975, 488) 'a most interesting parallel to Rabelais's fourth book', is founded on a confidence trick to obtain a government mortgage for a putative estate to be populated by in fact deceased serfs (or 'souls') – still registered, but accordingly purchasable at rock-bottom prices. The Dantean undertones give way to an extravagantly lyrical apostrophic lucubration on the future of Russia.[23] In *The Overcoat*, a poor clerk's obsession with first the acquisition and then promptly the loss of his most precious possession provokes an exercise in spectral revenge.

Even in these examples the story resides largely within the techniques employed in its own discourse (see Popkin, 156–7), or, as Bakhtin has it (1975, 487–8), elements of popular comic culture are found 'above all in the very style'. Linguistic performance is therefore of the essence in Gogol; as has been said, though with his later didactic writings foremost in mind, '[his] works were examples of *parole*, not of *langue*' (Maguire, 338). In other fictional instances presenting a lesser degree of narrative clarity, this situation tends to pertain all the more. *Notes of a Madman*, more usually translated as 'Diary of a Madman' (the Russian *zapiski* of the title means 'notes') as it comprises 'entries', the headings (and content) of which descend into ever greater incoherence, may also be seen as an excursion into absurd autobiography.[24] Absurdity resides in the self-identification of the protagonist (a minor clerk named Poprishchin – the name having to do with both 'pimple' and 'career') with 'Ferdinand VIII' of Spain. In what Michael Holquist calls 'a bravura exercise in perspective by incongruity', Poprishchin's self-recognition entry, in his view, 'reads very much like a parody of Augustine' (Holquist, 1990, 137). The final apparent inconsequentiality regarding a wart under the nose of the Dey of Algiers,[25] for Holquist (140), 'marks an ultimate rupture between the temporal, spatial, and linguistic parameters of his self and the time, space, and language coordinates of others'. 'Once the possibility of "others" ceases to exist', according to Robert Maguire (66), there is an inward shift, the diary is no longer needed, and 'the story must come to an end'. Whether for that reason, or for another, the diarist-autobiographist may be presumed incapable – mentally, physically or both – of continuing. Maguire, in addition, raises the question of the provenance of the 'notes' (though apparently assuming, in his turn, a probably unwarranted indistinguishability between Gogol himself and the narrator-editor of the notes): 'Gogol never tells us how this document fell into his hands, or how it acquired a title that was obviously not supplied by Poprishchin himself' (ibid.).[26]

What has been identified as 'the hidden absurd' in *Notes of a Madman* becomes open absurdity later in that story, and overwhelmingly so in another of the Petersburg tales.[27] *The Nose* (the Russian *nos* happening also to be 'dream' [*son*] backwards), generally considered Gogol's most nonsensical narrative, is seen (by Iurii Mann and others) – for all their respective stylistic differences – as anticipating Kafka with its theme of unmotivated metamorphosis (or 'an absurd parody of a supernatural transformation': Meyer, 1999, 207).[28] For Renate Lachmann, 'the empty spot left by the nose functions as a circumscription of the void in a tale whose title stems from a palindromic reading of *son* (dream)' (in Spieker, 22: a collection that concentrates heavily on 'absence' and 'negativity' in Gogol). Wolfgang Kayser (125) accepts it as 'genuine grotesque'. Robert Reid (150–1), attempting to supply Gogol with 'a stoic reading', comments that in this situation of nasal removal 'the intelligible chain of cause and effect which in stoic metaphysics underpins the universe and provides semiotic confirmation of a pervasive Logos is here ruptured'; what ensues is 'absurd in stoic terms'.

In this tale, then, a Petersburg upstart awakes one morning to the loss of the eponymous organ (with its connotations of an even more precious organ) which takes on a life of its own as man about town. What Efraim Sicher terms 'the runaway carnival nose' eventually resumes its proper place, as if nothing had happened, but the accounts of these events offered by the incompetent (*skaz*) narrator appear meaningless and incompatible.[29] Gogol goes out of his way in *The Nose* to infringe what narratologists would call 'the decorum of the text' – or a transgression of the rules of textual status as created within a given work. Here, then, as Popkin would have it (208), it is not so much that Gogol is 'plotless' as that 'the story line is inaccessible'. Gogol is likely to go in for doubles or doubling, in story as in character,[30] for dual stories (as in *Nevsky Prospect*), for doubled (or pairs of) stories (see Priscilla Meyer's [1999] reading of *The Nose* against the earlier Ukrainian tale *Vii*), or for concealing the 'real' story behind an incoherent narrative presentation: the *fabula* or 'fable' of *The Nose* is, to most intents and purposes, 'lost' behind the *siuzhet* or surface plot – the story behind the discourse.[31] Put in other words, 'the devil of disintegration is at work in this story at all levels', and/or 'the only consistency lies in the principle of non-consistency' (Shukman, 1989b, 76; 78).

The 'nose' motif itself (with its attendant phallic associations) is traceable back to Sterne and further (with a consequent 'oblique influence of Rabelais': Bakhtin, 1975, 488).[32] One asylum inmate in 'Bonaventura' (155), for that matter, 'has become absorbed over his own nose'. The puppet theatre, as we have seen, claimed as the disguised 'intervalic chronotope' of *Tristram Shandy*, is also the 'hidden chronotope' of *The Nose* (Bakhtin, 1981, 166). Similar remarks have been made on marionette-like speech (Boris Eikhenbaum's view of Akakii Akakievich's diction in *The Overcoat*) and mechanised movement (Vasilii Rozanov on *Dead Souls*).[33] In a similar vein, Meyer (1999, 191) stresses that: 'Gogol's peculiar synthesis of high German and popular Ukrainian *dvoemirie* (two-world system) is analogous to the sacred/profane (Christian) opposition in the Ukrainian *vertep* (puppet theatre) that so informs Gogol's stories' (such plays being staged in 'two-level puppet theatres with the divine story placed physically above the secular').

For all his religiosity, Gogol rooted his supposed Christianity in foklore, paganism and what Konstantin Mochulsky termed 'the experience of cosmic horror and an elemental fear of death' (quoted by Holquist, 2000, 78; and Maguire, 84). Holquist considers that Gogol's 'anxiety' has 'roots deeper than religion', being based on a nostalgia for the sacred amid a growing secularism (ibid., 78; 83). Ann Shukman (1989b, 78) suggests the possibility of the story as 'an iconic sign of the world where the devil holds sway'.[34] What Bakhtin terms Gogol's 'high-spirited absurd' (*veselyi absurd*: Bakhtin, 1975, 493–4), in addition to its 'popular sources' and its linguistic surface, therefore, has darker depths. Meyer detects a 'profound uncanniness' in the 'apparently whimsical

Nose', rather than the more usual 'absolute nonsense' (or other well worn interpretations).[35] Not only did Gogol's peculiar development from German Romanticism, according to Holquist (2000, 75), contain 'a kind of existential set toward things'; it also led him subsequently to be 'perceived as a precursor of the Dadaists, a master of the grotesque', and eventually as 'curiously post-modern', with his 'self-conscious parables allegorizing the pitfalls and absurdities of the arbitrariness of language' (77). For that matter, Gogol's apprehension of a legal system as 'a communal resource that produces failed communication as its most spectacular product' (ibid., 96) surely calls forth Kafka (see also Mann on bureaucracy in both writers). Indeed, Holquist (99) ventures even to pose the question in these striking terms: 'Is the figure of Gogol not the secret legislator of the twentieth-century avant-garde's contempt for the present, and its impatience to break through to a higher reality?'

Dickens

The ubiquitous fog of the celebrated opening paragraphs of Dickens's *Bleak House*, conceivably reminiscent of the fog in which all is enveloped at certain narrative *caesurae* of Gogol's *The Nose* (see Shukman, 1989b, 69–70), bears a significance that spreads considerably beyond the London atmosphere. As the supreme representative in his own time of 'popular literature',[36] Dickens blends his stylistic verve with an individualised eccentricity and grotesquerie, plus a melding of the carnivalised in the sentimental, in works that many, like Bakhtin (1981, 127), have none the less – or even expressly thereby – come to regard as 'classic English realism'. 'Realism of grand style', in Dickens and other nineteenth-century stalwarts (Stendhal, Balzac, Hugo), 'was always linked directly or indirectly with the Renaissance tradition', the grotesque imagery and 'folk carnival culture' of Rabelais, Cervantes and Shakespeare, we are reminded (Bakhtin, 1968, 52). Bakhtin sees what he calls 'the English comic novel' (culminating in Dickens) as 'permeated through and through with the spirit of Cervantes', and indeed that of Sterne; Dickens's variations on the 'classic scheme' of Fielding and Smollett, moreover, 'make his novels the highest achievement of the European family novel' (Bakhtin, 1981, 310; 232). As is customary in listing the originators of the modern novel (in most of its aspects, including, we might add, a proto-absurdism), Bakhtin adds in the name of Diderot (ibid., 125; 126).

For all their classic 'realist', 'comic' and 'family' qualities, the novels of Dickens include in addition features that may be construed as at least conducive to the absurd. If Gogol's perception of bureaucratic and legal systems (notably in *The Story of How Ivan Ivanovich Quarrelled with Ivan Nikiforovich*, one of the *Mirgorod* tales, as well as in the ramifications of the St Petersburg civil service) are suggestive of what was to receive supreme amplification through Kafka, then this must be even more the case as we come to Dickens.[37] Labyrinthine and endless legal processes may take on, from a base in actuality, at least a hint of cosmic metaphor. What are *aficionados* of the absurd to make of the activities of the Circumlocution Office in *Little Dorrit*?

J. Hillis Miller affirms that '*Bleak House* is a document about the inter-pretation of documents' (Dickens, *BH*, 11). Writing his Preface to that novel in 1853, Dickens mentions a 'well-known suit in Chancery, not yet decided, which was commenced before the close of the last century' (*BH*, 42). The case, suit, or 'cause', of 'Jarndyce and Jarndyce', therefore, scarcely required excessive authorial hyperbole. John Jarndyce himself has only the most tenuous notion of the affair, explaining to heroine and part-narrator of the novel, Esther:

> The Lawyers have twisted it into such a state of bedevilment that the origi-nal merits of the case have long disappeared from the face of the earth. It's about a Will, and the trusts under a Will – or it was, once. It's about nothing but Costs now. We are always appearing, and disappearing, and swearing, and interrogating, and filing, and cross-filing, and arguing, and sealing, and motioning, and referring, and reporting, and revolving about the Lord Chancellor and all his satellites, and equitably waltzing ourselves off to dusty death, about costs. That's the great question. All the rest, by some extraordinary means, has melted away. (*BH*, 145)

While Dickens's imagery and capitalisation here and elsewhere accentuate the mystique of Byzantine legal process, the whole edifice has already been parodied in the figure of Krook, 'called among the neighbours the Lord Chancellor' and his shop 'the Court of Chancery' (*BH*, 100). Governed inexorably by what Gridley, the defeated 'man from Shropshire' hopelessly berates as 'the system' (ibid., 266; 268), the Jarndyce case in Chancery is bemoaned as 'the horrible phantom that has haunted us so many years'. 'Better to borrow, better to beg, better to die!' than to 'found a hope of expectation on the family curse!' (393). Esther herself refers to 'the dead sea of the Chancery suit' (592). The Court of Chancery theme, in the words of Vladimir Nabokov (1980, 69), is 'emblemized by London's foul fog and Miss Flite's caged birds'.[38]

Such affairs are endless and insoluble, we are led to believe. Even one of the less malignant lawyers, Mr Kenge (dubbed 'Conversation Kenge'), a firm believer in this 'great system', gesticulates with his right hand 'as if it were a trowel, with which to spread the cement of his words on the structure of the system, and consolidate it for a thousand ages' (*BH*, 901). Certainly, the Chancery suit, as in any case a system of signs, 'can never end except in its consumption in costs' (Hillis Miller, *BH*, 27–8). Miss Flite expects 'a Judgment. On the day of Judgment' (251). Yet a day of judgment for Jarndyce and Jarndyce ('termed, not inaptly, a Monument of Chancery practice': 923), by an almost miraculous fluke, does dawn –

and to something approaching universal hilarity: 'And so the fantastic fog of Chancery is dispersed – and only the dead do not laugh' (Nabokov, 1980, 83). The dance of death, though, textually alluded to above, has, by a diversity of means, directly or indirectly claimed a full range of further participants (including the exhausted supposed main co-beneficiary and 'ward of Jarndyce', Richard Carstone: see Chapter 65, ironically called 'Beginning the World', *BH* 920–7). One of these, Lady Dedlock, is analogously signified through the motif of 'Death and the Lady' (817; 928).[39] The whole thus concludes, as John Jarndyce predicts, 'through such an infernal country-dance of costs and fees and nonsense and corruption, as was never dreamed of in the wildest visions of a Witch's Sabbath' (145–6).

Miss Havisham, in the later *Great Expectations*, having reduced herself to an extremity (or an absurdity), 'has frozen time, but she personifies the processes of mortality' (Bradbury, 1990, 83); as such she assumes, for decades on end, a grotesquely protracted embodiment of the 'Death and the Lady' theme and is surrounded, on her introduction in Chapter 8, with appropriate imagery.[40] In the words of Peter Brooks, 'The craziness and morbidity of Satis House repose on desire fixated, become fetishistic and sadistic, on a deviated eroticism that has literally shut out the light, stopped the clocks, and made the forward movement of plot impossible' (Brooks, 119); such 'repetition without variation' and 'a collapsed metonymy where cause and effect have become identical' (ibid.) were, of course, to become essential signs of a later (twentieth-century) absurd.

Other peculiarities pointing toward the absurd, it need hardly be stressed, abound in Dickens. The lines of reasoning adopted by the middle-aged 'child', Harold Skimpole of *Bleak House* (a malignant variation on Mr Dick from the earlier *David Copperfield*), are seized upon by their originator himself as 'Absurd!' (*BH*, 883). In addition to the situation as depicted of Miss Havisham in *Great Expectations*, one might point in that novel to the divided existence (professional and personal) of Wemmick; Mr Wopsle and 'Denmark'; or even 'the infinitely repeatable palindrome' (Brooks, 142) of Pip's self-assigned name. John Sutherland (135–42) has drawn attention to the ludicrously superhuman swimming powers enjoyed by both Magwitch and Compeyson.[41]

Dickens and Gogol have much in common as writers of intrusive description and speech idiom, vivid style and imagery, fleeting and eccentric characters, and of deceptive plotting. In particular, both are indisputable masters of the unnecessary detail. Further to the anxiety and the darker depths detected within Gogol, we can find in Dickens, too, for instance the 'nihilistic' description (Hillis Miller, *BH*, 33) of Tom-all-Alone's in *Bleak House* (682–3):

> Darkness rests upon Tom-all-Alone's. Dilating and dilating since the sun went down last night, it has gradually swelled until it swells every void in the place. For a time there were some dungeon lights burning as the lamp of

Life burns in Tom-all-Alone's, heavily, heavily, in the nauseus air, and winking – as that lamp, too, winks in Tom-all-Alone's – at many horrible things. But they are blotted out. The moon has eyed Tom with a dull cold stare, as admitting some puny emulation of herself in his desert region unfit for life and blasted by volcanic fires; but she has passed on, and is gone. The blackest nightmare in the infernal stables grazes on Tom-all-Alone's, and Tom is fast asleep.

Hillis Miller points to a tension in *Bleak House* (in addition to that caused by the dual narrative system employed in that novel), as in all Dickens's work, between 'belief in some extra-human source of value, a stable centre outside the shadows of the human game' and, at the same time, 'the shade of a suspicion that there may be no such centre, that all systems of interpretation may be fictions' (*BH*, 32). As Brooks puts it, in a similar style and with reference to the Magwitch trial scene in *Great Expectations*, ultimately, even to the great would-be reassuring Victorian novelist and 'great Christian' (as Dostoevsky saw him: MacPike, 4): 'The greater Judgment makes human plots mere shadows. . . . If there is a divine masterplot for human existence, it is radically unknowable' (Brooks, 141).

Dostoevsky

While Dostoevsky may never have uttered the fabled words 'we all came out from under Gogol's overcoat', there is no doubt that Gogol was a paramount influence, at least on the first half of his career. In addition to Gogol and the carnivalised tradition of the Middle Ages (see Bakhtin, 1984), Dostoevsky – who, like a number of figures among the antecedents to the absurd, occupies a Janus-like posture – also recognised a strong affinity with Dickens. Indeed, Nabokov (who, as a commentator, consistently set out to debunk Dostoevsky's reputation, while making idiosyncratic use of him as a novelist) rather mischievously would have liked to see a reverse impact, noting in his *Bleak House* lecture: 'Lady Dedlock is redeemed by suffering, and Dostoevski is wildly gesticulating in the background' (Nabokov, 1980, 68); the topic of Dostoevsky and Dickens has thus far produced two book-length studies in English (by N.M. Lary and Lorelee MacPike).[42]

Absurdity, and existential perplexity, can be found throughout Dostoevsky's *oeuvre*, and can be readily illustrated by reference to works from his early, middle and late periods. The early, or 'Gogolian' period, saw the epistolary novel *Poor Folk*, in which an overt polemic is carried on with humanistic and social issues perceived in *The Overcoat*. Of greater absurdist interest is the short novel *The Double* (subtitled *A Poem of St Petersburg*) of 1846 (revised 1866)[43] and nominated by Nabokov (1981, 104) as 'the very best thing he ever wrote'. Gogol's St Petersburg tales are instantly evoked and *The Double* can be seen to represent, within the bureaucratic ethos established by *The Overcoat*, an extended reworking of a combination of *Notes of a Madman* and *The Nose*.[44] The mental breakdown of a 'titular councillor' (one Mr Goliadkin, holder of the same minor rank as Poprishchin) takes the form of the usurpation of his identity by an overbearing upstart – his supposedly self-created, or 'autoscopic', double (Mr Goliadkin 'junior').[45] It is Dostoevsky's use here of the (if only at first glance) neutral or objective, and ostensibly third-person, narrative form (as opposed to the diary or more overtly *skaz* narratives favoured by Gogol) that allows *The Double* to be read as a story of the fantastic – or of the absurd.[46] According to John Jones, 'Mr Golyadkin is *King Lear's* "poor, bare, forked animal", ... with the featureless heath of the play transposed into the novel's banal urban wasteland of St Petersburg' – a Gogolian and Dostoevskian ghostly and abstract 'St Anytown', akin indeed to 'Kafka's Prague' (John Jones, 51; 72) – subsequently he considers that 'Mr Golyadkin's Petersburg is more Kafkaesque than Gogolian' (157). In the early stages of this process, we are told: 'The reality of the thing spoke for itself. It was strange, hideous, absurd' (Dostoevsky, 1968, 48). The end takes on what may seem a Kafkaesque tone, as the hapless Goliadkin lands firmly in the hands of his now fiendish German doctor: 'Not the earlier Dr. Rutenspitz, but another, a terrible Dr. Rutenspitz!' (ibid., 144). W.J. Dodd, for that matter (as we shall note in Chapter 7), has something to say on St Petersburg within Kafka.

Peter Conradi (26) has observed: 'As with the blankly sinister yet oddly taken-for-granted world of Kafka's fiction, Golyadkin's fellow clerks express not the smallest surprise at Junior's arrival.' Despite, or perhaps because of, the supposed artistic failings of *The Double*, Malcolm Jones (54) is able to see it as 'a quite remarkable *tour de force* anticipating post-modernist texts'. In any event, as Karl Miller (132) affirms (and we may certainly agree, with reference back to 'Bonaventura' and Gogol, as well as to Dostoevsky): 'The diary, and noctuary, of the madman is still being compiled.'[47] In his essay 'On the Essence of Laughter', Baudelaire had referred to 'the existence in the human being of a permanent dualism, the capacity of being both himself and someone else at one and the same time' (Baudelaire, 1992, 160).[48] Any overt sense of what should be the comic gives way here to an advancing instability that is both psychological and narrative.

Dostoevsky may, in one sense at least, have exorcised the spirit of Gogol by lampooning him (with his pomposities in the late *Selected Passages from a Correspondence with Friends*) in one of his first post-exile publications, *The Village of Stepanchikovo and its Inhabitants* (1859), the parodistic, carnivalised and absurd short novel of a country estate under the temporary sway of a Tartuffe-like 'former *hanger-on* and *buffoon*', turned '*unlimited despot*' and '*carnival king*' (Bakhtin, 1984, 163; his emphases). By 1863–64, the butt of Dostoevsky's spleen was the radical critic Chernyshevsky, his 'rational egoism' (or 'enlightened self-interest': *razumnyi egoizm*), nineteenth-century rationalism in general, and the Crystal Palace as emblem of a misplaced faith in progress. Nevertheless, there is a sense in which *The Double* and *Notes from Underground*, the paramount middle-period work as far as absurdity (and much else) is concerned, are to be seen as 'twin texts (as doubles)' (M. Jones, 72); both are 'anatomies of unreason' (Conradi, 29).[49] The 'Underground Man' is an 1860s version of Goliadkin, and of the pulp-literary 'dreamer' figure of other Dostoevskian works of the 1840s – but with ideology, and very much with attitude. In the estimation of Joseph Frank, writing in 1961, this anti-hero of Dostoevsky's has taken on 'the symbolic stature of one of the great archetypal literary creations', a figure of immense importance to twentieth-century culture, whether 'as a prophetic anticipation', or 'as a luridly repulsive warning'.[50]

In what Bakhtin (1984, 154) categorises as the 'diatribe' of Part I (in the sense of 'a conversation with an absent interlocutor'),[51] the Underground Man (who remains nameless, and to whom everyone else is 'the other') carries on his constant 'polemic with the other' (ibid., 228). He hammers away at points he himself acknowledges as 'patent absurdities' (David Magarshack's translation: Dostoevsky, 1968, 288), to the effect that 'any sort of consciousness is a disease' (ibid., 267), or expressing 'the pleasure of despair' (268) to be experienced in having one's face slapped, or in toothache, and railing in favour of the freedom to act against one's self-interest, or against the tyranny of mathematical tables: 'twice-two-makes-four is not life, gentlemen. It is the beginning of death' (290).[52] Part II (the rather more nineteenth-century counterpart to 'the [first] twentieth-century part': John Jones, 187) is an illustrative memoir of the joys of degradation, chronicling the Underground Man's eccentric forays into the 'real world', and his disastrous interaction with representatives of 'the other', some sixteen years earlier. Just as the Underground Man is an opponent of logic, the plot in which he functions is itself an aberrant one; according to Holquist (1986, 55), it is his 'twisted formula of $2 \times 2 = 5$ expressed in archetectonics'.[53]

If Dostoevsky occupies a Janus position in the development of absurdism (or 'prospect and retrospect' as John Jones puts it: 74), so within his particular *oeuvre* does *Notes from Underground* and its protagonist, seen not only as an anticipatory notable of later fiction but as an embodying, perhaps in tone and pose, of features of 'the trickster figure, whose appearance predates even Homeric references' (R. Anderson, 30ff, following Bakhtin); in any event, 'this modern anti-hero wears an old, grimacing mask' (ibid., 47). For George Steiner (1967, 197) 'he is as old as Cain'. At the same time, it is argued, his self-posturing within a 'philosophical

parable ... has the effect of turning him into an Existentialist hero'
(Holquist, 1986, 57).[54] Dostoevsky's further development in such directions can be seen in particular episodes, monologues or dialogues within
the major novels that followed (the narrative tone adopted by the 'fool
narrator' in much of *The Devils*,[55] the metaphysical wranglings of Kirillov
in that novel; or the cosmic agitations and mental collapse of Ivan
Karamazov in Dostoevsky's last work). There is also a resurgence in two
stories published in the 1870s: the feuilleton, turned macabre graveyard
extravaganza, *Bobok*, and the quixotic-nihilist fable of solipsism, turned
utopian/anti-utopian fantasy, *The Dream of a Ridiculous Man*;[56] both of
which works have, in their different ways, been seen as exemplifying
'Dostoevsky's almost classical menippea' (Bakhtin, 1984, 141), or 'tales
in the pure Gothic manner' (Steiner, 1967, 185).

Dostoevsky's impact has already been noted in the introductory philosophical chapter to this book. It will reccur again and again as we move
through the twentieth century. Angus Wilson, writing in 1970, coupling
Dostoevsky with Dickens, lauded 'their extraordinary mixture of black
and comic vision which allowed them to see how profound absurdity can
be and how utterly ridiculous most of the profound things often are, to
see that profound things and absurd things are totally mixed together'
(quoted by MacPike, 200).

Lautréamont

A noteworthy successor to *The Night Watches of Bonaventura* is
Maldoror (*Les chants de Maldoror*, 1868) by the precocious and short-
lived so-called Comte de Lautréamont[57] – affirmed by Calasso to be 'the
first book ... written on the principle that *anything and everything* must
be the object of sarcasm' (Calasso, 2001, 80: his emphasis). These (prose)
'songs', presented through the intermediate authorial pose of a sensation-
alist aristocratic French writer, purport to celebrate the fantastically evil
maraudings of a supernatural Byronic figure through time and space
(largely in contemporary France, but with time off for periodic joustings
with the Creator). Lautréamont adopts a Dostoevskian diatribe style of
delivery as he cavorts through tales, fables or fantasies of extreme manifestations of sadism, nihilism and cosmic revolt, 'attacking humanity,
which thought itself invulnerable, through the breach of absurd philosophical tirades' (Lautréamont, 1978, 65–6). In addition to Bonaventura
(an episode with a gravedigger features) and Dostoevskian elements (child
sexuality and speculation on two times two, as well as the Underground
apostrophe style), the figure of Lautréamont's fallen angel Maldoror is
reminiscent of, among others, Maturin's Melmoth and Lermontov's
Demon.[58]

Having been forgotten for half a century, Lautréamont was resurrected by the Surrealists, who intuited (indeed 'fanatically revered': Lomas, 149) a kindred spirit of decadence, ironic self-awareness and surreal imagery. André Breton frquently coupled Lautréamont with the equally precocious Rimbaud and included him in his *Anthology of Black Humour*, discerning in his work 'the limits with which words can enter into rapport with words, and things with things' (Breton, 1989, 194). In the colourful phrasing of Aimé Césaire, 'Lautréamont was the first to understand that poetry begins with excess, immoderation, the breaking down of taboos, in the great unreasoning tom-tom, up to the incomprehensible rain of stars' (quoted from Breton, 236). Both Dalí and André Masson supplied illustrations to *Maldoror*. It now, indeed, may seem inevitable that the Surrealists should have ardently promoted the reputation of perhaps their most vibrant predecessor in the realm of surreal-absurd imagery:

> Oh that mad philosopher who burst into laughter when he saw an ass eating a fig! ... Now I have witnessed something even more outrageous: I have seen a fig eating an ass! And yet I did not laugh; ... 'Nature! Nature!' I cried, sobbing. 'The hawk tears the sparrow to pieces, the fig eats the ass, and the tapeworm devours man.' (Lautréamont, 1978, 151)

Also greatly to the taste of the Surrealists was Lautréamont's 'explosive encounter of the sewing machine – female – and his umbrella – male – on the bed of the dissection table' (Caws, 236).[59] 'The pounding of naked fists against the gates of heaven', ... 'In lyrical and pale scatterings, like the fingers of a tropical pear tree falling into the gangrene of the evening, [Lautréamont] piles up the trumpets of death of a comical philosophy' (Césaire, quoted from Breton, 235–6); in the *Poems*, the 'true' author, Isidore Ducasse, ostensibly derides the bleak literary tradition of evil that gave rise to the cruelty (that was to be an inspiration too for Artaud), blasphemy and bestiality of the metamorphoses of Maldoror. According to Breton, however, 'in *Poésies* [Maldororian revolt] necessarily assumes its own dialectical position'; the underlying unifying element here, however, 'rests principally on humour' (195).

Carroll

Hillis Miller (*BH* 22) speaks of Dickensian names shimmering with multiple meanings, 'like the portmanteau words of "Jabberwocky"' (the same is frequently said of Gogol), while John Jones (77) observes that pairs of words in *The Double* are manipulated as 'language facets of the doubling theme, Tweedledum and Tweedledee, lexical enantiomorphs without Carroll's story and Tenniel's illustrations to hang on to'. And, indeed, we should not consider exiting from the nineteenth century without at least brief further reference to Lewis Carroll. Carroll's 'interest in mirror reflections' (Gardner, in Carroll, 10) may be compared to that of Mr Goliadkin, while, as for the Underground Man, for Alice 'the Multiplication Table doesn't signify' (38). 'The last level of metaphor in the ALICE books', according to Martin Gardner (himself a science writer – ibid., 15), is that 'life, viewed rationally and without illusion, appears to be a nonsense tale told by an idiot mathematician, ... a mad, never-ending quadrille of Mock Turtle Waves and Gryphon Particles', dancing 'in grotesque, inconceivably complex patterns capable of reflecting on their own absurdity'. Kafka's Castle looms into view, as does Joe Orton's modern rendering of Carroll, with more than a touch of Swift, in his grotesque fantasy novel *Head to Toe* (or a 'Gombold in giant-land', published posthumously in 1971). Wonderland and Looking-Glass Land may be perceived as parallel universes, as by Edmund Little (53), who also reminds us that Carroll 'was a professional mathematician and logician whose absurdities are seen to be quite rational once the basic point (usually the dramatisation of classical problems in logic) has been grasped' (ibid., 89). A modern-day physicist, Robert Gilmore, is able to use the Alice adventures as a template for his 'allegory of quantum physics', *Alice in Quantumland* (1995).[60] At the same time, in the view of Frye (310) – and Bakhtin, for once, remains silent – 'the Alice books are perfect Menippean satires'.

The issue of names in Carroll is thrown into sharp relief by the highlighting of the lack of connection between things and their appellation in 'Looking Glass Insects' (Chapter III of *Through the Looking Glass*, Carroll, 215–28): 'the realization that the world by itself contains no signs' (Gardner, 227, ibid., n. 7). This is followed up later by the often-quoted exchange between Alice and the White Knight over the classic statement that 'The name of the song is called "*Haddock's Eyes*"' (306), involving 'what logicians now call a "metalanguage"' (or degrees of names of names).[61] The taking of phrases literally and the splitting of hairs in a Carrollian manner have become a staple of absurdism, as of nonsense; for that matter, the concept of backwards memory, or 'living backwards' (247) – sentence, before trial, before crime – has provided inspiration for many an absurdist plot and, more recently, has developed into a fictional plotting device in itself (*Time's Arrow*, by Martin Amis, being the leading example). As Tweedledee affirms (231), however, when it comes to dreams and inverted looking-glass worlds: 'That's logic.' Carroll's narrative nonsense poem *The Hunting of the Snark*, moreover, has been seen as 'about being and non-being, ... a poem of existential agony'.[62]

Notes

1 By 'absolute literature', Calasso means 'literature at its most piercing, its most intolerant of any social trappings' (Calasso, 2001, 21).

2 She points out that this macrocosmic-microcosmic concept is 'highlighted by human conflicts acted out in the ancient theatre, which was built on a circular plane on the earth, beneath the bright open sky and in view of the distant sea' (M.R. Wright, 56–7).

3 The Dionysian spirit is strongly and idiosyncratically stressed by Nietzsche in *The Birth of Tragedy* and 'The Dionysiac World View' (see Nietzsche, 1999). For Nietzsche, indeed, 'knowledge is primarily *a comedy of knowledge*' (Calasso, 2002, 16: his emphasis). For a cultural assessment of the Dionysian phenomenon and its impact thereafter see R.D. Stock, *The Flutes of Dionysus: Daemonic Enthrallment in Literature*, Lincoln and London University of Nebraska Press, 1989.

4 'Goat [or goat's] song' is the generally accepted original meaning of 'tragedy'; Eagleton, however, would prefer the translation 'scapegoat song' (Eagleton, 277–8).

5 Although, for instance, the *Satyricon* had long been regarded as a Menippean satire, it may rather stem from an older Greek tradition of comic-realistic narrative; in any event it presents 'a caricature' and 'a *monde à l'envers*' (Holzberg, 62–3; 72). The heyday of 'the ancient novel' stretches from the first century BC to the third or fourth AD (ibid., 27).

6 Loosely construed as an intersection between temporal and spatial aspects in fiction, the term 'chronotope' was apparently acquired by Bakhtin at a lecture on physiology (Holquist, 1990, 127).

7 One of the standard studies of foolery, from the 'parasite' at the Hellenic banquet tables of antiquity to the cinematic clown, remains that by Enid Welsford, first published in 1935.

8 'Buffoonery is a philosophy and a profession at the same time'; moreover, 'it is also a kind of theatre' (Kott, 133; 134). According to Welsford (7), 'as late as the eighteenth century the professors of German Universities could augment their incomes by playing the fool at court'. I make no comment here on the like activities of their modern counterparts (in Germany or elsewhere).

9 A serviceable modern translation from the complex period French of Rabelais is François Rabelais, *Gargantua and Pantagruel*, translated by Burton Raffel, New York: Norton, 1990. The commentaries consulted here are Bakhtin, 1968 and Screech, 1999; the paramount authoritative overall study of the author remains Screech's *Rabelais* (London: Duckworth, 1979).

10 T. McAlindon, *English Renaissance Tragedy*, Vancouver: The University of British Columbia Press, 1986, pp. 7–8.

11 See the 'Introduction' to The Arden Shakespeare, Third Series, *King Henry VI, Part 2*, edited by Ronald Knowles, Walton-on-Thames: Nelson, 1999; and Stephen Longstaffe, '"A short report and not otherwise": Jack Cade in 2 *Henry VI*', in Knowles, 1998 (a collection featuring the application of Bakhtin's theory of carnival to Shakespeare's drama). Jack Cade's paradox, 'But then are we in order when we are most out of order' (2 *Henry VI*, IV.ii), is quoted by the Polish experimental dramatist Witkiewicz in his play *They* (*Oni*, 1920): Witkiewicz, 1993, 148.

12 George Steiner (1967, 115), with the Russian sage's last days in mind, sees Tolstoy's attacks on *King Lear* as motivated by 'the anger of a man who finds his own shadow cast for him through some black art of foresight'.

13 The *danse macabre*, or 'the Dance of Death, a tradition familiar all over
   Europe since at least the early fifteenth century', particularly through the
   woodcuts of Hans Holbein the Younger: 'In the oldest versions of the Dance,
   emaciated corpses, who draw a succession of reluctant figures into the ring,
   make no distinction between wealth and poverty. They seize representative
   types from the Emperor to the Fool and coax them into the Dance': Belsey, 142
   (see also 140–56; and the application of this to *Hamlet*, 166). The idea of
   Death as a dancer, or a fiddler, is apparently very ancient, a dance of skeletons
   having been found in an Etruscan tomb (c.500 BC). According to Michael
   Ferber (55), the 'dance of death' became a popular theme during the Middle
   Ages, 'probably in response to the bubonic plague . . .; in it Death leads a dance
   of people of all ranks to the grave'. On the other hand, 'to "dance the beginning of the world" was an Elizabethan euphemism for the sexual act' (Segal,
   327). *The Ship of Fools* (or *Stultifera navis*: originally *Das Narrenschiff*, 1494)
   was a vernacular satire by the German poet Sebastian Brant (widely dissemi-
   nated in the European languages, including Alexander Barclay's English
   version of 1509); it was famously depicted in a panel by Hieronymous Bosch
   (middle period: Musée National du Louvre) and in the original woodcuts of
   1494 by Albrecht Dürer. These manifestations probably parodied the medieval
   metaphor of 'the Ship of the Church', manned by prelates, which in popular
   imagery brought its freight of Christian souls safely to the port of heaven. On
   'Ship' as metaphor see Ferber, 193–5.

14 Knowles, 1996, 42; 131. See also Downie (262–87), who attributes the
   phenomenon of 'so many diverse interpretations' of *Gulliver's Travels* to
   'Swift's reticence' in leaving so much up to 'the judicious Reader' (273).

15 See Victor Shklovsky, 'Sterne's *Tristram Shandy*: Stylistic Commentary' (first
   published in Russian, 1921), in *Russian Formalist Criticism: Four Essays*,
   translated with an Introduction by Lee T. Lemon and Marion J. Reis, Lincoln:
   University of Nebraska Press, 1965, 25–57.

16 '"The void", which is the final word of the book, is used with growing intensity at the end of its last three sentences': Kayser, 60 (in Gerald Gillespie's
   translation, the word *Nichts!* is translated as 'Nothing!': 'Bonaventura', 247).
   Kayser's theories of the grotesque, incidentally, at least in the view of Bakhtin
   (1968, 46), cannot be effectively applied to the pre-Romantic era.

17 'The death's-head is never missing behind the ogling mask and life is only the
   cap and bells which the Nothing [*das Nichts*] has draped around to tinkle with
   and finally to tear up fiercely and hurl from itself' ('Bonaventura', 141).

18 'Man is a facetious animal by birth, and he merely acts on a larger stage than
   do the actors on the small one inserted into this big one as in *Hamlet*; however
   importantly he may want to take things, in the wings he must still put off
   crown, sceptre and theatrical dagger and creep into his little dark chamber as
   an exited comedian, until it pleases the director to announce a new comedy':
   'Bonaventura', 139.

19 As for the possibility of life on other worlds – that would mean 'the Basel
   dance of death merely grows all the merrier and wilder thereby and the ball-
   room grander' ('Bonaventura', 245).

20 On the latter see Shapiro's study of Gogol and the Baroque cultural heritage;
   on Gogol's attitude to Jean Paul see Popkin, 178; on Gogol's *Nevsky Prospect*

and Hoffmann see Meyer, 2000; on the impact of German Romanticism and the *Kunstmärchen* see Holquist, 2000.

21 Popkin, passim. On the possible impact on Gogol of Sterne see Szulkin. For an expanded version of this section, Cornwell, 2004.

22 Although a Ukrainian by birth, Gogol, of course, wrote in Russian. According to Bakhtin (1981, 28), however, 'Gogol lost Russia, that is, he lost his blueprint for perceiving and representing her; he got muddled somewhere between memory and familiar contact – to put it bluntly, he could not find the proper focus on his binoculars.' On Gogol and the tradition of popular laughter see Bakhtin, 1975 ('Rabelais and Gogol', his most sustained piece of writing on Gogol: English translation published in 1976).

23 This novel was to undergo 'very effective' dramatisation for the French stage in 1959 by the absurdist Arthur Adamov (Esslin, *Th. Abs.*, 120).

24 See Holquist, 1990 (122–40), who, following Bakhtin, examines in this Petersburg tale 'vestiges of the [Greek] encomium' (131). According to Holquist (128), '[Bakhtin's] historical poetics is intertextual, relative, and comparative in all its findings'. On this story see also Maguire, 49–66. A near contemporary 'autobiographical' work is Flaubert's precociously nihilistic *Les Mémoirs d'un fou* (1838; first published 1900–1).

25 Gogol originally wrote 'King of France', but this was changed to 'Dey of Algiers', probably for reasons of political censorship; most editions and translations use the latter, but the former may also be found, e.g. Christopher English's 'World's Classics' translation: Gogol, *Plays and Petersburg Tales*, 1995 ('But did you know that the King of France has a wart right under his nose?', 178).

26 Paul M. Waszink (82) supplies a metafictional slant: 'The final sentence indicates that the text swallows the main person involved, i.e. the protagonist, who is doomed to stay not so much within the walls of the lunatic asylum as in the grip of the text where he has to remain. ... Thus the question-mark of the last sentence introduces the void into which both the text and the represented reality dissolve.'

27 See Liz Trott, '*Diary of a Madman*: The Hidden Absurd', in Grayson and Wigzell, 50–63.

28 In terms of definitions of the fantastic, loosely *à la* Todorov, both *The Nose* and *Metamorphosis* may be placed in a sub-category of 'the marvellous' (as *What if?* stories), 'set in what seems to be "our" world, but with a single ... element of the manifestly impossible' (as opposed to pure fairy story or fantasy romance with their multiple transformations): see Neil Cornwell, *The Literary Fantastic: From Gothic to Postmodernism*, New York and London: Harvester Wheatsheaf, 1990, 40. Borges, incidentally, regrets the omission, from an anthology of fantastic literature he had compiled, of 'the unsuspected major masters of the genre: Parmenides, Plato, John Scotus Erigena, Alberto Magnus, Spinoza, Leibniz, Kant, Francis Bradley' and asks: 'What, in fact, are the wonders of Wells or Edgar Allan Poe ... in comparison to the invention of God, the labored theory of a being who in some way is three and who endures alone *outside of time*?' (*TL*, 255).

29 Sicher, 223. *Skaz* narration (a term favoured by the Russian Formalists) denotes substandard narrated discourse (employing a pose of uneducated or

'unintelligent' speech, regional dialect etc.), apparently at odds with the historical author's natural mode of expression. For a list of 'explanations' for the events of *The Nose* (posited both within the text and outside it) see Shukman, 1989b.

30 See Meyer, 2000, for this phenomenon in Gogol and Hoffmann.

31 This effect, appropriately enough, anticipates that of Theatre of the Absurd, seen as '*bare* drama, the drama behind drama' (Killinger, 161). On Gogol and French absurd drama see also R.E. Jones. It may also be seen as anticipatory of the position ascribed in the theory of OBERIU theatre to 'dramatic plot', which 'glimmers, so to speak, behind the action [and] is replaced by a scenic plot which arises spontaneously from all the elements of our spectacle' (Gibian, 254); rather than 'scenic plot' here, for Gogol's prose, we might understand 'discursive plot' (or, again, Popkin's 'verbal clutter').

32 Noses also feature in Shakespeare. The Fool asks Lear: 'Thou canst tell why one's nose stands i'th'middle on's face?' (*King Lear*, I.v). Cloten, in *Cymbeline* (III.i), declares: 'we will nothing pay for wearing our own noses'. Of course, nosology continued beyond Gogol too; cf. the following description of a newshound in Joseph Roth's undated story 'The Cartel' (which may well owe something to Gogol and his predecessors): 'One day, a new reporter suddenly turned up: Mr. John Baker from Chicago. He was as long and lean as a greyhound. His nose had left his face, practically declared independence from it. It could steer to the left and right, up and down, without Mr. Baker having to move a muscle in his face. This nose was an autonomous independent creature, positively skittish in its vivacity. It was never dormant. It sniffed out events. It attracted sensations the way a magnet attracts iron filings. It could smell out human flesh, scalpings, sex attacks, robberies. It was a very distinguished nose' (Roth, 2001, 65). In Ionesco's play *Jacques ou la soumission* (1955), the eponymous hero is offered fiancées with two and three noses.

33 Quoted by Graffy, 2000b, 256; 275, n. 65. On parody and the impact of Sterne in *The Nose* see Sicher. Gogol's tale of an obsessive copying clerk (*The Overcoat*) has also been compared to Melville's story of the reluctant scrivener (*Bartleby*, 1853): see G.M. Hyde (1976).

34 Compare Sicher (223): 'As in *Nevsky Prospekt*, the normalized absurdity of social behavior can be explained only by the Devil'.

35 For further comments on sense and nonsense in Gogol see Graffy, 2000b, 266–8; the standard – and still richly rewarding – study of Gogolian quirkiness remains Vladimir Nabokov's *Nikolai Gogol*, New York: New Directions, 1961 (first published in 1944); see also his 'Nikolay Gogol' (Nabokov, 1981, 15–61).

36 Frye (116) can 'almost define popular literature ... as literature which affords an unobstructed view of archetypes'; for him, the inclusive way in which Dickens uses irony is 'a mark of a relatively popular mode', leading to the inference that 'the gap between serious and popular fiction is narrower in low mimetic than in ironic writing' (Frye, 49).

37 On Dickens and Kafka see the study by Mark Spilka, to which reference will be made in Chapter 7; likewise W.J. Dodd, whose study *Kafka and Dostoyevsky* includes comments too on Gogol and Dickens.

38 Compare also the lawyers Dodson and Fogg in the earlier *Pickwick Papers*.

The law, of course, asserts a strong formal presence throughout Dickens; one need only consider too the persona of Jaggers, his 'suspicious legal catechisms' (Bradbury, 1990, 64) and all that surrounds him as the fabled Attorney of Little Britain, in *Great Expectations*. According to Steiner (1967, 34), 'Kafka's principal symbol [the Castle] is related to Dickens's Chancery'.

39 '*Death and the Lady*. A common Renaissance graphic motif. There is a famous example by Albrecht Dürer. A monument in Westminster Abbey by the sculptor Roubiliac shows a skeleton and a female figure' (*BH*, 965, n.).

40 A 'withered' bride, a 'ghastly waxwork', 'a skeleton in the ashes of a rich dress' (*GE*, 87); 'grave clothes', 'the long veil so like a shroud', 'she sat, corpse-like', 'as if the admission of the natural light of day would have struck her to dust' (90); it is another ten years or so before her predicted 'lying in state' comes to pass, when she succumbs to the shock of catching fire.

41 Or perhaps this, along with certain other phenomena, belongs in what has been variously labelled (in relation to the work of Dickens, Dostoevsky and others) 'fantastic fidelity', 'higher realism', 'fantastic realism', 'romantic realism', 'tragico-fantastic realism' – or what John Jones (302) refers to as 'Dostoevsky's high-level fooling and his deeper realism', going 'hand in hand'.

42 Dickens had a volume of Gogol (in French) in his library, along with several volumes of Turgenev; he couldn't have read Dostoevsky (MacPike, 202–3, n. 7). Dostoevsky, like most educated Russians of his day, is known to have been reading Dickens from the 1840s. Nevertheless, in a certain sense, MacPike (2) claims to have produced 'a reverse influence study'. See also Donald Fanger, *Dostoevsky and Romantic Realism: A Study of Dostoevsky in Relation to Balzac, Dickens and Gogol*, Cambridge, MA: Harvard University Press, 1965.

43 The 1846 subtitle was 'The Adventures of Mr Goliadkin'. *Dead Souls*, it should perhaps be remembered, was also subtitled *A Poem*. It is the revised version that is now almost universally printed, both in the original and in translation (as in the rendition by George Bird: Dostoevsky, 1968). However, both redactions are provided in *The Double. Two Versions*, translated by Evelyn Harden, Ann Arbor: Ardis, 1984 (reprinted 2003). John Jones (47–104) constantly compares the two versions, as well as reading *The Double* against *Poor Folk* (or *Poor People*), considering these texts 'complementary and contrasting studies' (110), and employing both – especially *The Double* – as benchmarks for much of the remaining Dostoevskian *oeuvre*.

44 K. Miller (132) states: 'The three stories, and their paranoid-bureaucratic ambience, may be said to haunt *The Double*, where the hero's coat is prominent, along with his poor galoshes.'

45 Freud and Otto Rank associate the 'double' with primary narcissism in the mind of the child or primitive man; 'probably the "immortal" soul was the first "double" of the body'; subsequently, 'he becomes the ghastly harbinger of death' (K. Miller, 135). Bakhtin (1984, 117) points to its presence in Menippean satire (Varro) and as a feature of carnival (127–8). In any event, according to John Jones (74): 'It is a non-temporal *long time* since Humanity *first met* its Double' (his emphases). 'Doubles', of one sort or another, are identified by most critics throughout Dostoevsky's works. MacPike (151–68) offers a generous – possibly an excessive – survey of the phenomenon in Dostoevsky and Dickens, concentrating in particular on Stavrogin and

Steerforth as 'doubles of decomposition'.

46 On narrative form and voice in *The Double* see Bakhtin, 1984, 211–27; M. Jones, 35–58, who (58) is careful to distinguish the narrator 'from what Wayne Booth and others call the Implied Author, the consciousness which apparently organizes the text including the narrator's inconstant voice'. Steiner, on the other hand, makes but two fleeting references to the work he calls *Goliadkin*.

47 Rado Pribic (in his *Bonaventura's 'Nachtwachen' and Dostoevsky's 'Notes from the Underground': A Comparison in Nihilsm*, Munich, 1974), while pointing to extensive parallels, is unable to produce any evidence that Dostoevsky even knew of 'Bonaventura', although the possibility is not excluded.

48 Earlier in the same essay, Baudelaire made essentially the same point in direct relation to laughter: 'It is not the man who falls down that laughs at his own fall, unless he is a philosopher, a man who has acquired, by force of habit, the power of getting outside himself quickly and watching, as a disinterested spectator, the phenomenon of his ego' (Baudelaire, 1992, 148). Baudelaire himself, incidentally, is credited (see Wanner, 2003, 17–18) with originating the 'prose poem' – a building block of the future absurd miniature: 'The moralizing didacticism of fairy tales turns in Baudelaire's prose poems into a logic of the absurd' (ibid., 74).

49 See also John Jones, 56. Nabokov (1981, 115) points out that the title of this work should be 'Memoirs from Under the Floor' ('Notes' would again be more literal: cf. *Zapiski iz podpol'ia*), while himself preferring an arguably more absurdist version still: 'Memoirs from a Mousehole'. His consequent designation of the protagonist as 'the mouseman', though, does not seem entirely fitting. Colin Wilson, rather bizarrely, insists on calling him 'beetle-man' (the 'Floorboards' title suggesting to him 'that its hero is not a man, but a beetle': Wilson, 171–2).

50 Joseph Frank, 'Nihilism and *Notes from Underground*', *Sewanee Review*, 69 (1961), 1–33 (quoted by M. Jones, 63). Wilson (171) stresses that '*Notes from Underground* is the first major treatment of the Outsider theme in modern literature'.

51 Tzvetan Todorov, however, points out that 'the image of the "you" does not remain stable' (Todorov, 1990, 78).

52 Shestov and Fondane later took up Dostoevsky's concern over the $2 \times 2 = 4$ formula (see Fotiade, 227–8 and passim).

53 For the fullest exposition of the arguments of the Underground Man, commentary thereupon and a survey of the critical reception of this text (including a critical glance at Bakhtin's approach: 94–6) see the monograph by Richard Peace.

54 Walter Kaufmann, editor of *Existentialism from Dostoevsky to Sartre* (1956), calls *Notes from Underground* 'the best overture to existentialism ever written' (quoted by Holquist, 1986, 73); Conradi, also citing this comment, however cautions that, be this so, 'it is also a most cogent rebuke' (38; 41). See also Steiner (1967, 197, for whom the Underground Man is '*l'étranger, l'homme révolté, der unbehauste Mensch*, the outcast, the outsider'); Hoyles, 15–20; Peace, 101–2; and a range of comments by John Jones (who sees, for example,

'proleptic French Existentialism' in *The Double*: 73). A discordant tone is struck, though, by Nabokov (1981, 117): 'Dostoevski's mediocre imitators such as Sartre, a French journalist, have continued the trend today.' It should be mentioned in addition that the Underground Man's supposedly Christian antidote to his own malady, suppressed by the censorship, was never subsequently restored, and is presumed lost (see John Jones, 184–5, for a sceptical comment on this). Nabokov (1981, 101; 104), incidentally, deplores Dostoevsky's 'neurotic Christianity' having 'to [his own] regret no ear for Dostoevski the Prophet'; a sympathetic outline of such aspects of Dostoevsky's thought is provided in the study by Berdyaev (dating from 1923). Even before Berdyaev, another Russian existentialist thinker, Lev Shestov (in his *Dostoevskii i Nitche*, 1903) had championed the Underground Man as the first Dostoevskian protagonist to take up a new, existential and rebellious stance against common sense and rationalism.

55 John Jones's term (277). The work in question is *Besy*: also known in translation as *The Possessed* and as *The Demons* (described by Jones, 278, as 'a novel scatty yet dense'). Brodsky (289) suggests that 'Dostoevsky, for his Captain Lebyadkin poem about the cockroach in *The Possessed*, can be considered the first writer of the absurd.'

56 *Son smeshnogo cheloveka*: the adjective *smeshnoi*, the primary meaning of which is 'funny', can equally mean 'ridiculous' or 'absurd'. Other renditions of this title in translation have included 'queer' or 'strange' man; but David Magarshack, Constance Garnett and Alan Myers, to name but three, use 'ridiculous'. The opening of the story accordingly suggests a certain common ground between the epithets 'ridiculous man', 'madman' and 'utterly absurd person' (*ia smeshon*: Magarshack, in Dostoevsky, 1968, 717); *smeshnoi* (occasionally) apart, Magarshack (726) also renders *nelepost'* as 'absurdity'. According to Conradi (69): 'To have a good will in a bad world – as the hero of Dostoevsky's "The Dream of a Ridiculous Man" discovers – is to be necessarily absurd.'

57 'Le Comte de Lautréamont' was the pseudonym of Isidore Ducasse (1846–70), a Frenchman born in Montevideo of whom very little appears to be known. His only other work was *Poems* (*Poésies*, 1870), published under his own name, in which he affects a diametrically opposite pose utilising plagiarism and inversion (giving rise to 'the suspicion that every word he wrote is a spoof': Calasso, 2001, 85). The name 'Lautréamont' is assumed to have been taken from the title of a novel by Eugène Sue.

58 Neither Bonaventura nor (his contemporary) Dostoevsky is directly alluded to by Lautréamont (Dostoevsky's *Notes from Underground*, indeed, was not translated into French until 1886) but, in the *Poems*, Ducasse mentions, among others, Ann Radcliffe ('the Spectre-Crazed'), Poe ('the Marmeluke of Alcoholic Dreams'), Maturin ('the Crony of Darkness'), Byron ('the Hippopotamus of Infernal Jungles'), and Lermontov ('the Roaring Tiger'): Lautréamont, 1978, 265–6. Lermontov's narrative poem *Demon* was first translated into French in 1858.

59 For a discussion of Dalí's *Maldoror* illustrations, through the prism of Millet's *Angelus*, see Lomas, 149–71; in a preface written in 1934, Dalí refers to: 'The *Angelus* of Millet, beautiful as the chance meeting on a dissecting table of a

sewing machine and an umbrella' (ibid., 155). According to Lomas, Breton in particular, and to an extent even Dalí, collude with 'the surrealists' most flagrant suppression of homoerotic content in *Les Chants de Maldoror*' (168).

60 'The Quantumland in which Alice travels is rather like a theme park in which Alice is sometimes an observer, while sometimes she behaves as a sort of particle with varying electric charge' (Gilmore, vi).

61 Doubt has nevertheless been thrown on the final consistency of this celebrated routine (Gardner, in Carroll, 1970, 306–7, n. 8).

62 See Martin Gardner's apparatus to Lewis Carroll, *The Annotated Snark*, Harmondsworth: Penguin, 1974; Gardner compares this work in spirit to that of Unamuno (27) and considers that the Boojum 'is the void' (28); a claim also made by Esslin, *Th. Abs.*, 344.

II

Growth of the absurd

3

The twentieth century: towards the absurd

'... Why do you sigh in this beastly way, somebody? Absurd? Well, absurd. Good Lord! mustn't a man ever – ...'

'Absurd!' he cried. 'This is the worst of trying to tell. ... And you say, Absurd! Absurd be – exploded! Absurd! My dear boys, what can you expect from a man who out of sheer nervousness had just flung overboard a new pair of shoes!'

(Joseph Conrad, *Heart of Darkness*, 1899/1902)

Twenty years ago there were swarms of manifestos. Those authoritarian documents rehabilitated art, abolished punctuation, avoided spelling, and often achieved solecism. If issued by writers, they delighted in slandering rhyme and exculpating metaphor; if by painters, they defended (or attacked) pure color; if by composers, they worshiped cacophony; if by architects, they preferred the humble gas meter to the cathedral of Milan. Each, nevertheless, had its moment.

(Jorge Luis Borges, 'A Grandiose Manifesto from Breton', 1938)

Introductory pointers

The end of the world began, by common consent, in Vienna.
(Peter Conrad, *Modern Times, Modern Places*, 1998)

The hundred years from 1798 (the publication in Germany of the review *Athenaeum*) to 1898 (the death of Mallarmé) are called by Roberto Calasso 'the heroic age' of what he terms 'absolute literature'; this is 'A century to the year, during which all the decisive traits of absolute literature had occasion to manifest themselves', stretching from 'the early days of German Romanticism' (or, at least, aspects thereof) up to what was to be, as he puts it, 'embarrassingly labelled "modernism" or "the avant-garde" – ... so fond of aggressive, disruptive forms, first and foremost of which was the manifesto' (Calasso, 2001, 171). This century included the fleeting contribution of Lautréamont (highlighted here by Calasso,

79–100, along with writings by Novalis, Hölderlin, Baudelaire, Nietzsche *et al.*) and, we might now suggest, those of Bonaventura and certain of the others outlined in the last chapter. Absurdist tendencies must have had something to offer to 'a whole world – and in particular every literary form of whatever level – [that is] inevitably cloaked in a poisonous blanket of parody' (ibid., 84).

As the nineteenth century turns to the twentieth, a strong impression may be gleaned – and by no means inappropriately either, it may be thought – that absurdist, or pre-absurdist, elements are most prominently on display in theatrical works. Chekhov's four major plays (produced from 1896 to 1904) are renowned for their peculiar combination of vaudeville with tragedy and their presentation of both blurring and breakdown in communication. Terry Eagleton (236) compares Chekhov to Beckett (though 'with the thickness of social texture restored'), with the infectious 'atmosphere of tedium' of a world 'just this side of surrealism'. Earlier, for that matter, Ibsen had included absurdist elements in *Peer Gynt* (1867), particularly in the Cairo madhouse scene of Act IV in which, we are told, 'Absolute Reason / Dropped dead last night at eleven o'clock' and one inmate is convinced he is a pen.[1] The more Expressionist turn-of-the-century plays by Strindberg (*To Damascus*, *A Dream Play*, *Dance of Death* and *The Ghost Sonata*[2]) are regarded as 'masterly transcriptions of dreams and obsessions, and direct sources of the Theatre of the Absurd' (Esslin, *Th. Abs.*, 352), while Antonin Artaud was to direct the first French production of *A Dream Play* in 1928. Plays by Wedekind (the Lulu cycle) and Maeterlinck are also seen in a similar light.[3] In Paris, the Théâtre du Grand Guignol opened in 1897, with its unique blend of degeneracy, monstrosity and melodrama: a 'Punch and Judy for grown-ups', using actors, not puppets, to create a stark *théâtre de la peur*.[4] A little later, in the early 1920s, Pirandello was staging near-absurdist dramatic works that played on the tensions between theatricality and life, or performance and 'reality', and playacting and madness, dramatising discrete layers of (ir)reality in the theatrical metafiction *Six Characters in Search of an Author*, and his masterpiece of masquerade and madness, *Henry IV*. Ramón del Valle-Inclán, in the Spain of the same decade, was developing a discordant style and an aesthetic of systematic distortion in his novels and plays (indeed, terming the latter *esperpentos*, or 'frightful absurdities'). It may thus appear equally pertinent that Joyce presented his most absurdist piece of writing (at least, in advance of *Finnegans Wake* in which, incidentally, much else apart, he coined the word 'quark') – the Nighttown (or 'Circe') episode of *Ulysses* – in dream-play dramatic form.

Esslin, however, dates the beginning of the 'movement' that was to lead to the Theatre of the Absurd to the scandalous opening in December 1896 of Alfred Jarry's groundbreaking 'monstrous puppet-play' *Ubu Roi*, with the actors cavorting 'as dolls, toys, marionettes', with 'brushstrokes in the manner of Shakespeare' (*Th. Abs.*, 356–60; see also Styan, 45–51; Segal, 406–12).[5] Erich Segal (407), too, sees *Ubu Roi* as a 'deranged travesty of *Macbeth*'. Jarry (who had, strangely enough, been taught by Bergson) also invented the concept of 'pataphysics', later taken up by the absurdists: 'the science of imaginary solutions', exploring 'the world beyond metaphysics' (Styan, 50).[6] Segal (402–3) tends to agree with the view of Jarry as 'first theatrical offender' in 'the disintegration of classical forms' in comic drama – who thus exploded a tradition which had begun with Menander and reached its 'ultimate perfection' in Beaumarchais. Pointing the way to Theatre of the Absurd, as a prime characteristic of post-classical comedy, 'is the annihilation of logical discourse and coherent plot' (403); nevertheless, Segal considers it 'remarkable that so many of the seminal pieces of the Theater of Absurd deal with the same material as Menander – family matters – albeit from a radically different perspective' (416).

Before he wrote plays, Chekhov (in the 1880s) was engaged in the wholesale production of comic short stories and miniatures. A little later, a prose work of the Austrian poet and dramatist (and Richard Strauss's librettist) Hugo von Hofmannsthal, *The Lord Chandos Letter* (*Ein Brief*, 1902) – 'a text that is generally seen as central to modernism and whose author has even been called the first postmodernist' – conveys a spirit of disintegration in language and reality.[7] This short work takes the form of a fictional letter of personal crisis (an 'inexplicable condition', or an outbreak of insanity), supposedly of 1603, from Phillip, Lord Chandos to Francis Bacon, which can be said to fall into three parts: the nostalgic past; the origins and course of the crisis; and Chandos's resultant state of mind. Richard Sheppard (90) deems it 'an analysis of the sublimated illusions with which Western, humanist civilization has sustained itself' and 'an investigation into the relative power of [Freudian] Eros and Thanatos'. In terms of its proto-absurdist interest, it reveals 'a gap between the illusory security afforded by language and the fluid complexity of reality'; the scrutiny which Chandos undertakes of language strikes him as 'uncanny' (*unheimlich*), leading to disintegration over and above fragmentation. 'Single words floated round me; they congealed into eyes which stared at me and into which I was forced to stare back – whirlpools which gave me vertigo and, reeling incessantly, led into the void'; subsequently, writing and thinking occurs only in 'a language none of whose words is known to me, ... in which inanimate things speak to me and wherein I may one day have to justify myself before an unknown judge' (Hofmannsthal, 134–5; 141). The 'Letter' was discussed by Kafka and Max Brod on the night they met (Adler, 60). For Sheppard (99), 'Chandos's crisis encapsulates the crisis of modernism as a whole', while 'his positive appreciation of folly and the absurd point forward to Dada and to Leopold Bloom'.

'Post-Impressionists' in England

At much the same time as von Hofmannsthal was undergoing a creative crisis from lyric verse to prose, prose fiction from what might be seen as the edges of the supposed realist mainstream or, alternatively, produced by certain other exponents of the early generation of modernism, did have, along with a welter of narrative and stylistic experimentation, at the very least its own proto-absurdist moments. We might note this propensity within the epistemological searches of the turn-of-the-century fiction of, for instance, Conrad and Henry James – at first sight by no means prime candidates to be perceived as cultivators of the absurd.

Conrad's *Heart of Darkness* (first published in 1899) has given rise, in recent years in particular, to a multitude of variant readings, many of which go beyond the complexities of the most obvious issue – that of Conrad's (Polish-English, at any rate, European) presentation of colonialism. Eagleton (29) notes that Conrad 'famously portrays a ship firing its guns pointlessly into an African river bank, as though imperialism were merely some grotesque aberration or absurdist theatre rather than the hard-headed, systematic, sordidly explicable business that it is'. Tzvetan Todorov indicates a series of binary oppositions within the text (light and darkness; white and black; clarity and obscurity; presence and absence; inside and outside), rendering the work 'a narrative in which the interpretation of symbols predominates'.[8] Just as any real knowledge of Kurtz is impossible from Marlow's account, 'so too is any construction on the basis of words, any attempt to grasp things through language'; the heart of the story remains 'inaccessible'; furthermore, in *Heart of Darkness* 'there is no interior and the heart is empty' (Todorov, 1990, 111–12). For Peter Brooks too, 'What stands at the heart of darkness – at the journey's end and at the core of this tale – is unsayable, extralinguistic' (Brooks, 251), while the narrative transmission (a process in fact of retelling: Kurtz and others to Marlow; Marlow to his narratees; the primary narrator to his readership) 'is potentially infinite, any closure or termination merely provisional' (ibid., 260).

If Kurtz's final observation of '"The horror! The horror!" [Conrad, 90] stands on the verge of non-language, of non-sense', this is not to say that it should be characterised as 'the Romantic ineffable'; should Marlow appear to affirm any such thing, then 'the suggestion that the ineffable may simply be an emptiness is present throughout the story' (Brooks, 252; 350, n. 6, quoting too James Guetti). If such a void be (in whatever sense) the destination, then the absurd is also textually present throughout the story. In addition to the cluster of usages in the central passage quoted as an epigraph above, the words 'absurd' or 'absurdity' are to be found a number of times, both before and after, in Marlow's sardonic and circuitous narrative. If 'darkness' is far and away the principal metaphor

utilised in Conrad's novella, then the motif of absurdity, or futility, is of
strong secondary prominence. The quality of absurdity appears attachable
to almost anything: the antics of the natives and of the traders alike; the
dreamlike incredibility of events; instances of utterance ('bits of absurd
sentences', 'the pestiferous absurdity of his talk' – reflecting, indeed, 'the
worst of trying to tell': Conrad, 36; 38; 57); the danger, muddle, or
mystery in the purposelessness or the incomprehensibility of the situation.
Such phraseology abounds as 'lugubrious drollery' and 'the merry dance
of death and trade' (ibid., 15), 'the gloomy circle of some Inferno' (18),
and 'a flabby, pretending, weak-eyed devil of a rapacious and pitiless
folly' (17). Foolery surfaces in the persona of the eccentric Russian 'harlequin' (63). A single sentence may evoke a sudden feeling of the 'hopeless',
the 'dark', the 'impenetrable' and the 'pitiless' (66–7).[9]

In some sense the traders, exploiters and, presumably, the mysterious
'pilgrims' are in thrall to 'They above – the Council in Europe'; at the
same time, however, they remain prey to the claims or assaults of the
'powers of darkness' (58; 59). The droll destiny of life amounts to 'that
mysterious arrangement of merciless logic for a futile purpose' (85). The
dualities – of world, power and setting – in the Europe–Africa opposition
provide, much else apart, a structure for Nabokov later to play on in his
story *Terra Incognita* (1931; English version 1963).[10] For that matter, the
barest bones of the plot of *Heart of Darkness*, or of isolated incidents
there within (the Fresleven episode, for one: Conrad, 8–9), could almost
suggest even the violent plotlines (in so far as they may be so described)
of certain of the mini-stories (or 'incidents') of Daniil Kharms.[11]

The expansive external (and internal) worlds of Conrad may seem a far
cry from those of Henry James, yet jungles of irrationality are explored in
both, whether sought or feared, actual or metaphorical (in *Heart of
Darkness* and *The Beast in the Jungle* respectively).[12] More interesting,
perhaps, in proto-absurdist terms, is the – at first glance – even less likely
comparison to be made with *The Sacred Fount* (1901), a text considered
'an obscure presence at the very margins of James's work', whether it be
viewed as 'a Jamesian joke or a Jamesian nightmare' (John Lyon,
'Introduction' to James, *SF*, vii–viii).[13] *Heart of Darkness* and *The Sacred
Fount* were written, within a year of each other, at a time when the two
writers were on terms of friendly acquaintance in Sussex. An ocean
voyage from London and a river journey of months into the darkest heart
of Africa become a train journey of an hour or so from Paddington, into
the heart of English country-house society (or the rural seat of darkest
Newmarch); the search for an obsessive ivory trader becomes an obsessive
quest for the supposed upper-crust trade in sexual mores (itself 'a finite
and closed system of exchange': ibid., xix). The disposition of the
Jamesian first-person narrator is emphatically the more manic; and the
pre-eminence of dialogue in James is a determining structural factor. At

the same time, the enigmatic qualities of the two works are equally impenetrable and there is, too, a discernible parallel of underlying futility and perhaps even despair.

The process of the 'sacred fount', as theorised by the nameless narrator (and deriving from the story of Egeria: Ovid's *Metamorphoses*, Book 15), has been lucidly encapsulated as 'the continuous acquisition by one lover of the precious substance his or her partner possesses' (Susanne Kappeler, 194). This 'substance' (a literal connotation of bodily fluids apart) can extend to the transference of intelligence, wit and even (at least apparent) age. The narrator's tenacity is focused on (and he is 'on the scent of something ultimate': James, 15) the behaviour of members, or couples, of the Newmarch weekend house-party set, in order 'to interpret the texts of their conduct in the context of their society, where the laws of the sacred fount are in operation' (Kappeler, 157). 'Society' is here limited to 'the deindividualised collective of Newmarch', for such purposes as the peculiar allocation of guest-room accommodation and the table settings for dinner 'following its own secret laws' (ibid., 150; 148). Apparently 'disembodied means' (Lyon, *SF*, xiv) or avowedly 'unseen powers' preside over 'the liberal ease at Newmarch' (James, 120–1). The host and hostess, who presumably are pulling at least the organisational strings, remain all but unseen presences: neither introduced as characters nor named, they receive just one passing mention apiece (ibid., 98; 112).

In common with *Heart of Darkness* (even should we not wish to go so far as to claim these as Conradian echoes, some at least being not so very uncommon elsewhere in James) we find in *The Sacred Fount* multiple uses of the word 'absurd(ly)' (ten instances, by my count); a striking use of 'horrors' in the last chapter (176); the sentence 'Light or darkness, my imagination rides me' (162), followed soon afterwards by a Roman allusion;[14] vampirism, or cannibalism ('she was only eating poor Briss up inch by inch': 43); the dance of death is transposed to 'the Mask of Death' (or is it not 'much rather the Mask of Life?': 34); instead of a harlequin we have a likeness to 'some whitened old-world clown' (34) and the narrator posturing as 'a pantaloon' (66).

The narrator talks of having 'to pay, vicariously, the tax on being absurd' (109), a price incurred from a situation in which, allegedly, *he* 'alone was magnificently and absurdly aware – everyone else was benightedly out of it' (105). Absurdist features may surely be intuited in what has been described as 'non-conversation' proceeding to inordinate lengths and 'pantomimic clowning with infuriatingly cryptic insignificancies – ... elevated to a kind of cerebral slapstick in the Jamesian drawing room' (Lyon, *SF*, xxvii). Of similar note are 'the possibilities for expression through silence' (Bradbury, 1979, 34). The text itself exalts as 'prodigious' what can be passed 'in the way of suppressed communication' (James, 82), while contortions in the telling (or the non-telling) can give rise to such a sentence as: 'It was not the unnamed, in short, who were to be named' (178). The telling (in narrative and dialogue), dressed in precious articulation, is thus immersed in plausible misconception or evasion, amid a flood of negatives, qualifications or diminutions: 'She became vivid in the light of the so limited vision of her that I already possessed – try positively as I would not further to extend it' (54). 'Suppressed communication' is as likely to be effected, or assumed, through silence, looks, a wink or other facial expression, gesture, pose or posture as through any telling, the difficulty of which is evinced by the narrator's admission of being (and retrospectivley at that) 'at a loss to put my enigma itself into words' (15).

As Adeline Tintner (189) has argued, it is 'the details in the *lack* of connection' that weigh as much, or indeed more, than those of the connections (between persons and events) which *are* related, shown or suggested. Undecidability (as with certain other Jamesian texts) has become the quality of *The Sacred Fount* generally favoured by modern criticism.[15] Lyon refers to 'stories which are *fully* consistent only in their refusal to cohere into a single narrative', catching all concerned, 'narrator, novelist and readers alike ... in a vicious hermeneutic circle' (*SF*, xii; xxv). For that matter, 'the narrator's position is unverifiable' and 'all other positions are equally unverifiable'; indeed, the 'fact' that these couples are at all engaged in fashionable love-games remains 'precisely one we cannot verify' (Kappeler, 192; 200). According to Barbara Hardy, 'this novel is a perfect illustration, in its action and its effect', of Heisenberg's uncertainty principle.[16]

A link, in both a biographical and a literary sense, between Conrad and James is Ford Madox Ford and his later, supremely modernist novel, *The Good Soldier* (1915). Ford lived for a while near Conrad, with whom he collaborated on a number of projects, and James, with whom his relationship was more chequered.[17] Ford considered himself a 'literary impressionist', developing a theory of Impressionism himself, and in conjunction with Conrad (see Ford, 257–85); fellow members of the impressionist school, in his view, were Conrad and James.[18] Comparisons have more than once been made between Marlow and Dowell as narrators,[19] while Leon Edel even considers that Ford might himself have been inserted into *Heart of Darkness*, as the 'mysterious ... man dressed in motley' and 'a kind of patchwork European': indeed, the Russian 'harlequin' referred to above (Edel, 42). It scarcely needs pointing out, moreover, that the three writers considered in this section boasted, in their different ways and backgrounds, cosmopolitan credentials.

In addition to its development of some of their modernist styles and structures, *The Good Soldier* can almost be seen as, in a certain sense at least, a synthesis of *Heart of Darkness* and *The Sacred Fount*. Ford, in *The Good Soldier*, takes up the 'international theme' (of Americans in

Europe) that James had dropped in the 1890s to concentrate on the finer points of English society – only to return to immediately on completion of *The Sacred Fount*. In addition to Dowell's inner 'search and re-creation of his memory' (Lynn: Ford, 393), he undertakes a physical journey to 'a darkened room' in Ceylon to rescue a deranged expatriot (the outcast Nancy), while his social quest culminates in what he (whether ingenuously or disingenuously) calls 'just a pleasant country house-party' (*GS*, 149; 156) – and eventually in mastery of the seat in question, which he now occupies in the company of his near-catatonic charge. Allusions within *The Good Soldier* to *Heart of Darkness* have been identified (Martin Stannard's editorial notes: *GS*, 34; 131), while further possible ones could be suggested: a minor character from the novel's prehistory is 'a darky servant, called Julius' (*GS*, 66); there is a mention of 'the Belgian Congo' (*GS*, 88), a recurrent play on 'darkness'; and multiple references to 'horrors' and 'hell'.[20] The nature of Dowell's narration and its temporal structure are key factors in any analysis of Ford's novel and of prime importance in a detailed comparison with the preceding works by Conrad and James.

For present purposes, however, we shall merely point to absurdist elements that pertain within Ford's text. Samuel Hynes, discussing the epistemology of *The Good Soldier* in 1961, considered it 'a narrative which raises uncertainty about the nature of truth and reality to the level of a structural principle' (reprinted *GS*, 310–17: at 311). In similar vein, for Eugene Goodheart, '[Ashburnham's] character, like every other issue in the novel, is undecidable' (ibid., 381). Pluralities of meaning and omnipresent levels of irony leap from the pages of *The Good Soldier*: 'in a world of liars irony goes wild and rival meanings undercut each other infinitely' (Ann Barr Snitow: *GS* 373). Frank Kermode discerns 'between the text and its reader' what he terms 'the hermeneutic gap' in the fiction of Ford, Conrad and James (*GS*, 330–1). The problematics of communication were accentuated by Ford and Conrad (in their 'theory of impressionism') by an insistence that 'no speech of one character should ever answer the speech that goes before it' (279). An aura of pointless pessimism pervades the narrative of Dowell, 'that absurd figure, an American millionaire, who has bought one of the ancient haunts of English peace' (*GS*, 161): 'The Saddest Story' had been intended as the book's title; 'the record of humanity is a record of sorrows' in 'a queer and fantastic world' in which people are mere 'shuttlecocks' (*GS*, 133; 151; 160).[21] Sympathetic to the visionary qualities of 'Post-Impressionists', Futurists and other footsoldiers of the avant-garde, the author of *The Good Soldier* offered much to budding absurdists, while the complexities of his delineation of relations between the sexes anticipate (post)modern texts such as Pinter's *Betrayal* (in which the plot of adultery is presented not only retrospectively, but backwards).

Avant-garde theory and practice

Futurism

> Time and Space died yesterday. (F.T. Marinetti, *First Futurist Manifesto*,
> Paris, 20 February 1909)

The development of the avant-garde from the early part of the twentieth century, as a series of movements or schools in art and literature that sought to experiment in form and content and stood for revolt against tradition, may be seen as, among other things, an aspect of modernity and modernism – the latter itself deemed 'a deeply and multiply fissured movement' (Sheppard, 5–6).[22] The avant-garde also functioned as a forge for the building blocks of the absurd (especially, of course, the Theatre of the Absurd), as it was to be fashioned towards the middle of the century.

'Post-impressionism', as a literary term, enjoys little currency beyond the critical writings of Ford Madox Ford. For that matter, Impressionism in literature (as opposed to French painting) was more subjective tendency than school or movement. The same largely goes for Expressionism – a label that tends to have been applied retrospectively and is perhaps now best remembered for its cinematic productions and its concern with 'the eruption of irrational and chaotic forces from beneath the surface of a mechanized modern world' (Baldick, 78).[23] Of greater overall significance to absurdism, the consensus would probably run, were the Futurist movements (Italian and Russian), Dada, and then Surrealism. George Steiner (2001, 272), indeed, singles out Dada as the originator of all subsequent significant developments in Western art. Also of considerable tangential importance, at least, to the absurd were other artistic movements, such as Cubism; according to Esslin (*Th. Abs.*, 364), 'the Theatre of the Absurd is as much indebted to the collages of Picasso or Juan Gris and the paintings of Klee ... as to the work of its literary forebears'.

Futurism, in its Italian and Russian forms, may be said to have been, predominantly at least, an aggressive celebration of modernity, glorying in the future and in technological progress. Representatives of the avant-garde, at least from Apollinaire onwards, were taken with notions of 'the fourth dimension' and non-Euclidean geometry (see Bohn, 7–27). Kafka and Brod visited an impressionable Paris under the influence of modernism and Futurism in 1910 (see Adler, 69–71). At the same time, in its iconoclasm and verbal (at times even physical) vandalism, Futurism proclaimed an at least equal hostility to the past. The founder of Italian Futurism, Filippo Tommaso Marinetti, emerged from an essentially French Symbolist background to create an Italian Futurist movement perhaps more notable for the scope of its (anti)aesthetic spread than its artistic achievements.[24] Marinetti (in Paris, 1909) staged his *Roi Bombance*, 'a boisterous plagiarism of Jarry's *Ubu Roi*, ... greeted with a small but satisfactory riot'; at the same time (philosophically at least), 'Nietzsche clearly hovers in the background', though turned as ever by Marinetti into 'optimistic Milanese enterprise' or 'failing that, into genial farce' (R.W. Flint, 'Introduction' to Marinetti, 10; 6–7).[25] Indeed, it is considered, Futurism's colourful manifestos, many of them penned by Marinetti, were written with 'a bristling charm and bravura that may often be a more than adequate substitute for the works that followed' (ibid., 4).[26]

Futurism propelled artistic forms towards the limits of the aesthetic possibilities of science as then conceived and of the dynamism of machine technology.[27] This it sought to do by deploying its forces in as many areas as possible. 'Force', 'power', 'will', 'speed', 'youth', 'noise' and 'lust' were among its watchwords and war was proclaimed 'the world's only hygiene' (Marinetti, 42). 'The Art of Noises' and the 'Futurist Manifesto of Lust' (both of 1913) figured among the multifarious programmatic statements issued. Militarism, misogyny and synaesthesia were other prominent features, with a paramount stress on performance throughout the numerous fields of Futurist activity, which included literature, theatre, sculpture, architecture, painting, music, photography, cinema, dance, fashion and typography. Moreover, it is Italian Futurist theatre itself, in the view of Bert Cardullo, that 'represents nothing less than the birth of the twentieth-century avant-garde' (Cardullo, 10). 'The Futurist Synthetic Theatre 1915' manifesto attacked '*passéiste*' theatre, seeking to abolish traditional dramatic genres and techniques, and to promote interaction between *auteurs*, actors and audience through brief theatrical pieces which would be 'dynamic', 'simultaneous', 'autonomous', 'alogical' and 'unreal'.[28]

While poetry (written mainly for performance purposes, and declaimed in a roaring voice) was the favoured Futurist literary form, prose and other printed forms were also a vivid part of the output. Marinetti also produced novels and 'Futurist memoirs'. His 'African novel', *Mafarka the Futurist* (prosecuted for obscenity in 1910), was a tale of a black Futurist Superman, 'warrior-magus-founder of a new religion of "daily Heroism and the Will made extrinsic"' (Shankland, 73). A later extraordinary narrative mix of myth and science fiction is the purported parable-novel *The Untamables* (1922: translated in Marinetti's *Selected Writings*, 163–248), and reputedly Marinetti's favourite – a 'free-word book' preferring to narrative sequence what its author terms 'the simultaneous polyexpression of the world' (164). Centring on the eponymous group of men chained in a pit in what seems an African desert (Marinetti was born in Egypt), *The Untamables* contains strident images of violence and noise, moving (whether in 'actuality' or fantasy) to an allegorical urban setting of revolutionary Futurism, not unlike Fritz Lang's *Metropolis* ('The great book of Futurism teaches us to make up everything, even God!': 234), and back again to the pit, in illustration of a cyclical theory of history and 'the superhuman, cool Distraction of Art' (245).

Marinetti's 'The Founding and Manifesto of Futurism' (1909) initiated, apart from anything else, a sloganising struggle for vigour and against Death: 'Let's give ourselves utterly to the Unknown, not in desperation but only to replenish the deep wells of the Absurd!' (*FM*, 20). However, museums, for instance, were seen as 'absurd abattoirs of painters and scupltors ferociously slaughtering each other with colour-blows and line-blows' (*FM*, 22). Futurism also advocated the abolition of grammar, syntax and punctuation – at least in literary works, while allowing exceptions for philosophy, the exact sciences, politics, journalism and other forms of social discourse: Marinetti adds, 'I am obliged, for that matter, to use them myself in order to make myself clear to you' (*FM*, 96). Literature, though, should follow the principles of 'Words-in-freedom' (*Parole in libertà*) and 'imagination without strings', with sound, weight and smell contributing to 'the instinctive deformation of words' (see Marinetti's 'Destruction of Syntax': *FM*, 95–106).

A number of these manifestos read, particularly today, as fully blown absurdist scenarios: see, to quote just two examples, 'Some Episodes from the Film *Futurist Life*' and 'Manifesto of the Futurist Dance' (Marinetti, 135–41). Politically, by and large, the Italian Futurists, having gloried in the First World War, threw in their lot with the new Fascism; 'Aesthetic Futurism' deteriorated into a 'Mussolinian aesthetics that caused only laughter and dismay in much of the rest of the world' (Flint: Marinetti, 5). According to Umbro Apollonio, 'from magniloquent and extremist revo-lutionism, they progressed to the most extreme variety of nihilism, as manifested in Dada' – itself a point of attraction for certain of the Futurists and their ideas (*FM*, 13). Flint (in Marinetti, 5–6) thus assesses the essence of their contribution:

> Someone had to be the first to carry things to ridiculous lengths and to do so on principle. Someone had to explore the hopeless paradox of unanimity in the arts, to dramatize in the loudest, plainest, most blatant manner possi-ble the joys and absurdities of organized movements in art, to furnish a protocol for Dada, Surrealism, each later attempt at solidarity.

The explosion of old conventions and attitudes was, it goes without saying, massively accelerated by the political and cultural impact of the First World War and the Russian Revolution of 1917. Peter Conrad, in his chapter entitled 'The End of the World in Vienna' (41–57), illustrates the ushering in of the political and cultural 'dance of death' over the years up to 1914; he furthermore stresses that this was 'a war which had insti-tutionalized absurdity' (211). The ensuing couple of decades consequently saw what has been termed 'the desperately heightened incongruities in the social experience of artists between the wars' (T. Miller, 57).

While being a prominent artistic force only in Italy and Russia,

Futurism (the term, allegedly, was invented by a Spanish writer named Gabriel Alomar in 1905) did enjoy a certain, if modest, spread around the world (see Lawton: *RF*, 1–11). Futurist aesthetics generally, according to Anna Lawton (ibid., 8), 'with its emphasis on speed, dynamism, and simultaneity, reflected the poetic perception of a chaotic universe' – but with chaos perceived as a natural condition, rather than a negative disruption. Overall, the movement's most lasting impact was probably on theatre (anticipating Theatre of the Absurd) and cinema. The Russian Futurists, who began in sharp reaction to Russian Symbolism, rather than emerging therefrom, enjoyed an almost parallel existence to their Italian counterparts: arising around 1910, they fragmented, and then embraced the October Revolution of 1917, before fading through the Stalinist imposition of uniformity over the arts and a crushing hostility to the avant-garde in the Soviet Union of the second half of the 1920s. The association of the Italian Futurists with Fascism was, obviously, at this stage no help to Russian Futurism in a Bolshevik climate.

Again closely allied to representatives from the other arts (particularly the painters Malevich, Larionov and Goncharova; David Burliuk was a painter, as well as a Futurist poet), they had flourished, like their Italian counterparts, during the run-up to the First World War (to which, though, their attitude was rather more ambivalent) and they did at least produce two major poets: Velimir Khlebnikov and Vladimir Maiakovsky. Accordingly, from their original designation as 'Hylaea', the principal group renamed themselves 'Cubo-Futurists' in 1913. Notorious for their public performance antics and clowning, the group issued the expected clutch of manifestos and statements in their strivings to *épater les bourgeois*, beginning with 'A Slap in the Face of Public Taste' (1912: *RF*, 51–2); almost the entire European artistic heritage (in these early days, at least) was to have been heaved overboard from 'the Steamship of Modernity'.

By and large, the Russians refused serious recognition to their Italian contemporaries. Aleksei Kruchenykh (along with Khlebnikov, their chief innovator and theorist) dismissed the Italians as 'amateurish' in his 'New Ways of the Word' (1913), while Marinetti's visit to Russia in 1914 met with a mixed response. He was ignored by the main Cubo-Futurist group; the only Russian Futurist to greet him with any enthusiasm was the somewhat lesser figure of Vadim Shershenevich, who was soon to translate a number of his works.[29] Nevertheless, there were obvious and undeniable similarities: regarding enthusiasm for the technological future and antagonism to the art of the past, as well as a concentration on the authentic roots and usage of language – in the Russian case pursued to the limits as *zaum´* ('beyond the mind' or 'transrational' language) by Kruchenykh and Khlebnikov. The latter poet contrived to combine a Slavic primitivism with his 'Martian' Futurism, in pursuit of a future linguistic (and interplanetary) Golden Age; Kruchenykh, however, aimed rather at 'a spontaneous, noncodified language' (Lawton: *RF*, 13; 18).[30]

In addition to the Cubo-Futurists, the 'enemy' groups of this period were the Ego-Futurists (of which the dandified poet Igor Severianin was the principal figure); 'The Mezzanine of Poetry' (to which Shershenevich belonged); and 'Centrifuge' (with which Boris Pasternak was associated in the early years of his career). Of greater interest as proto-absurdists, though, was the later manifestation known as 'Company 41°' (on which, see Lawton: *RF*, 33–9), which flourished for a while in the pre-Soviet Georgian capital (and then Menshevik haven) of Tiflis, coinciding with, among a profusion of artists (visiting and native), the Georgian avant-garde Futurist group, the Blue Horns. The former Cubo-Futurists Kruchenykh and Vasilii Kamensky (a leading exponent of 'ferro-concrete poetry') combined with Igor Terent´ev, Il´ia Zdanevich and others to launch 41° – supposedly the maximum temperature at which the human body could function (Rayfield, 269n; but see also Lawton, *RF*, 36). Here *zaum´* aspired to become 'a grandiose abomination', as the integration of art into life 'was pushed into the realm of the absurd' (*RF*, 36). Kruchenykh concentrated on onamatopoeic harangue, Terent´ev propounded *zaum´* as 'anal', while Zdanevich invented the transrational *dra* (a *zaum´* coinage for 'play': combining lowbrow features of the folk theatre with the musical effects of opera). The latter works are described by Lawton (*RF*, 37) as 'masterpieces of transreason, where incoherent transrational language comes across as absurdly coherent'. In his own absurdist 'study' of Kruchenykh (*Kruchenykh the Grandiosaire*: Tiflis, 1919), Terent´ev terms Kruchenykh's work 'this extreme irrationality, this theater of the absurd', applauds his establishment of 'the unquestionable anal nature of the protoroots of the Russian language, where "*ka*" is the most significant sound' and his 'solemn "kakatruth" [*kakistina*] that the Italians are the Russian Futurists' hirelings' (*RF*, 178–81).[31] Not for nothing is he, together with Kruchenykh, described as 'the most militant advocate of the absurd' (*RF*, 178). While in part at least agreeing with Herbert Eagle's comment that 'What lay behind the bold and inflammatory language of the Cubo-Futurist manifestoes was not absurdity or inconsistency but a radical semiotic program' ('Afterword': *RF*, 288), one might suspect that absurdity dominates by the time of 41°.

Dada

... my art belongs to Dada 'cos Dada 'e treats me so
(Tom Stoppard, *Travesties*, 1975)

If the Georgian innovative Blue Horns, founded in 1915–16, could be described as a 'part-Futurist, part-Symbolist, part-Dadaist group'

(Rayfield, 268), Dada was by now succeeding Futurism as the main European avant-garde force, a position it was to hold until, with the break away of Breton, Eluard and Aragon, it faded or dissolved into Surrealism over the first half of the 1920s. Indeed, Dadaism had ceased to exist as an organised movement (in so far as it ever was one) by the end of 1923. Just as technology had fuelled Futurism, modernism in general, of which Dada was its most experimental wing, was responding to the new developments in science with new thinking. Richard Sheppard (45) in this summary of the argument contained in one section of his already seminal study ('The Changing Sense of Reality': Sheppard, 35–45) effectively links the avant-garde with a preceding or contemporary modernism and the postmodernism that was to follow:

> Most modernists sought to compel their audiences to confront alternative, noncommonsensical metaworlds that they would rather ignore and thereby challenge them to rethink their epistemological *and* their ontological categories. Or to put it another way, the modernist sense that a once stable reality is running or beginning to run out of control generates texts that, through both form and content, aim to shock people into facing that realization with all its attendant consequences.

This trend was particularly manifested in Dadaism and subsequently, of course, in Theatre of the Absurd. Dada has frequently been dismissed as 'childishness', or 'a purely nihilistic forerunner' of Surrealism (Sheppard, 171).[32] Preferring the ideas of Bergson to those of Kant (whose idea of 'the thing in itself' was regarded as an object of mirth: ibid., 176), the Dadaists, in full accordance with the above sentiments, developed, in Sheppard's view (181), 'their awareness of the limitations of reason in a universe characterized by flux, incoherence, and absurdity'. Not surprisingly, in a movement in which anarchic tendencies were the *raison d'être*, Dadaism was a divided aesthetic and artistic force. One type of Dada (mainly the French Dadaists of 1920 to 1922) was, in Sheppard's words (193), 'like a zany version of Sartrean existentialism', proclaiming 'the Dada state of mind *against* a background of absurdity and chaos'; another (including assorted figures or groupings in Zurich and Berlin) was 'more akin to a Westernized, secularized Taoism', declaring that 'the Dada notion of subjectivity makes sense only *within* an environment ... at one and the same time chaotic and yet secretly ordered'.[33] Chaos is indeed an essence of Dada: in one *Dada Almanach* Richard Huelsenbeck proclaims that 'Dada is the chaos out of which a thousand orders arise which in turn entangle to form the chaos of Dada' (quoted by Sheppard, 195).

The geographical divisions of Dada were equally wide: Zurich, Paris and Berlin, with smaller groups or individuals in Barcelona, Cologne, the Netherlands, New York and elsewhere. Continuing the antics and the experimentation of Futurism, but without the militarism (on the contrary, a largely pacifist posture was stressed), or quite the manic technological fervour, Dada embraced poetry (particularly 'sound poetry'),[34] theatre (see Esslin, *Th. Abs.*, 364–70) and theatricality, art (collage pictures and sculptures), film and various forms of extravagant performance and visual art (dance, cabaret, music hall and circus served as outlets and/or inspiration).[35] Avant-garde drama, for instance, 'playfully calls attention to itself as drama, ... and exuberantly combines esoteric art with popular culture' (Cardullo, 29). Linguistic play, satire, versatility, self-irony, carnivalesque laughter and androgyny were notable as standard Dadaist features.[36] Dada continued the Futurist erosion of the distinctions between 'Art' and 'art', art and anti-art, and between art and life. For that matter, 'the Dada artifact has a deeply ambiguous relationship with modernity, the machine, and mass-produced kitsch' (Sheppard, 202). Just as the features of high art brushed shoulders with objects of the utmost banality, the shock tactics and the (anti)aestheticism of Dada, its 'violently exuberant affirmation' of a Schillerian ludic drive, have caused it to be viewed as 'at best like radical cheek or the anus-face of "high modernism"' (206) – an image which at least keeps Dada in step with 41°.[37] Indeed, Dada would appear generally to have been closer to the more anarchic strands of Russian Futurism than to the Italian branch of that movement.

Other prominent Dadaist personalities included the founding poet and dramatist, Tristan Tzara (who makes a reappearance in *dramatis persona* form in Tom Stoppard's post-absurdist play, *Travesties*); the artist and photographer Man Ray; artists Marcel Duchamp (seen as a key modern figure by Steiner: 2001, 273–7 and others) and Max Ernst; the poets and artists Hans (Jean) Arp and Francis Picabia; and the all-round performer Hugo Ball. The latter, who emerged as the movement's diarist as well as one of its higher-profile public figures, before deserting Dada for Catholicism, also wrote a 'fantastical' tripartite novel, *Tenderenda der Phantast* (written 1915–20; published 1967). In part at least of potential absurdist interest, it deals with what is said to be a crazy but essentially comic world, 'absurd, acausal, and moderately apocalyptic', with a final section describing a time 'of collapse and chaos' (Sheppard, 270; 289). Tzara's short play *The Gas Heart* (*Le Coeur à gaz*, 1923), in displaying many absurdist qualities through its 'characters' (or facial parts: 'Mouth', 'Eye', 'Neck' etc.), 'elevates the realm of pointless verbiage', with only Mouth endeavouring 'to counteract and combat the convoluted surrounding inanity'.[38]

A fringe figure of Dada (at least, in the view of Sheppard) was Kurt Schwitters, according to whom 'Dadaists existed at all times', Euripides being 'the classic Dadaist'.[39] Schwitters was the originator of what he called '*Merz* poetry', issuing his own statements on poetics, and was concerned to produce 'total Merz art work, which combines all genres (Schwitters, 218) – in particular verse, sound (or performance) poetry, painting and prose; and collage constructions called *Merzbau*.[40] He was well known in the 1920s for the poem 'An Anna Blume' (Schwitters, 15–17; *Dada Market*, 192–5) and the wordless 35–minute performance poem, 'Ur-Sonata'. However, of more interest for present purposes are his prose works, such as *The Onion*, a grotesque tale of ritual slaughter and its reverse (Schwitters, 121–7); and the particularly noteworthy *Augusta Bolte* (137–64), in which repetition, the relentless pursuit of logic and the self-destruction of story seem to give it Kharmsian and Beckettian qualities.

Surrealism

> Surrealism is no less crazed than the dream which we mistake for reality.
> (Peter Conrad, *Modern Times, Modern Places*, 1998)

The word 'Surrealism' (originally a hyphenated *'sur-réalisme'*) was seemingly coined by Guillaume Apollinaire, labelling his grotesque vaudeville *Les Mamelles de Tirésias* (1917) 'a surrealist drama'; however, his use of the word to express essence rather than appearance, differs from the connotations ascribed to it by André Breton, launching the Surrealist movement with his first Manifesto (text in Cardullo and Knopf, 365–72; Dukore and Gerould, 563–72), and in the so-called 'collective action' review *La Révolution surréaliste* of 1924 (Esslin, *Th. Abs.*, 361–2; Breton, 1978, 120).[41] Breton's 'once and for all' definition reads as follows:

> *Surrealism*, noun, masc. Pure psychic automatism, by which it is intended to express, either verbally or in writing, [or by other means,] the true function of thought. Thought dictated in the absence of all control exerted by reason, and outside all aesthetic or moral preoccupations. (Cardullo and Knopf, 371; Breton, 1978, 122)

Surrealism, the term, though, was expressly chosen 'in homage to Guillaume Apollinaire' (Cardullo and Knopf, 370; Bohn, 130); the concentration was on dream and automatic writing, the resulting elements of which, 'poetically speaking' moreover, were said to be 'especially endowed with a very high degree of *immediate absurdity*' (Cardullo and Knopf, 370; Bohn, 150; italics in the original). The Dadaists and the Surrealists 'built their movements in large part on [Apollinaire's] foundations', in particular on the two principles of 'surprise and analogical parallels', with the former element now 'bifurcating into the twin concepts of *le scandale* and *le merveilleux*' (Bohn, 125–6).[42]

Back even in 1919, Breton and Philippe Soupault had published in the journal *Littérature* what has been called 'the overture to the surrealist drama', *Les Champs magnétiques*, under 'dictation' from the unconscious (Brée, 172). In 1922 Breton stated his belief that, rather than constituting three distinct movements, 'cubism, futurism and dada … belong to a more general movement whose exact scope and significance we do not yet understand' (Brée, 167). Breton's emphasis in Surrealism was placed firmly upon the liberation of the mind, in order to express the authentic functioning of thought through a unification of exterior and interior realities (Breton, 1978, 116); as such, Surrealism became perhaps the main poetic as well as artistic current of the first half of the twentieth century. As already noted, many of the former adherents of Dada became enthusiasts or associates of Surrealism (Tzara and Picabia, for instance, joining the Parisian Dadaists); in the nature of such movements, though, some in their turn defected (Antonin Artaud, Raymond Queneau, Georges Bataille, Louis Aragon and eventually Max Ernst); other figures, however, were to join, including Joan Miró, Salvador Dalí and Luis Buñuel, and the movement became even more international (and considerably longer lived) than its predecessors.[43]

While, of course, spreading through the arts, Surrealism retained a strong literary base – a number of its major figures being primarily poets. 'Automatic writing' (and drawing) became an emblematic technique, privileging the imagination in a spontaneous transcription of words deriving from dream, delirium or wherever in the unconscious. Incongruity, contrast and shock (verbal and visual) remained the avant-gardist stock in trade: 'the poetic spark that illuminates the "hidden reality" is struck by a juxtaposition of unlikely images' (Brée, 176). Man was to be inspired to free himself from the universal fetters:

> The horror of death, the pantomime of the beyond, the shipwreck of the most beautiful reason in sleep, the overpowering curtain of the future, the towers of Babel, the mirrors of inconstancy, the insuperable silver wall splashed with brains, all these startling images of human catastrophe are perhaps, after all, no more than images. (Breton, 1978, 129)

The poetic achievements of a number of the leading figures were real and substantial, although the proclamation that poetry is inherent in all human behaviour, it has been said, inevitably 'opened wide the floodgates on a wave of formless and mediocre texts' (Brée, 175). Automatic writing, according to the Surrealists, 'practised with some fervour, leads directly to hallucination' (Breton, 108; Cardinal, 32); the resulting texts might include 'here and there, a few pieces of out-and-out buffoonery', while as poetry, and as already indicated, 'they are distinguished chiefly by a very high degree of *immediate absurdity*', the peculiar quality of which being 'their yielding to whatever is most admissible and legitimate in the world' (Breton, 1978, 121).

The principles of Surrealism were also demonstrated in prose, as hybrid fictional-journal, or in other more extreme erasures of accepted literary form. Breton's *Nadja* (1928) and *L'Amour fou* (1937) made an impact in the former category. Aragon, in 1928, published anonymously a novel

entitled *Le Con d'Irène*, purportedly exploring the torment of a man's
fixation upon an imaginary woman's genitalia. In the same year, Bataille
published his *Histoire de l'oeuil*. These Surrealist explosions of the literary conventions in prose form 'reaffirmed the ties linking eroticism,
madness and creative writing' (Brée, 146) – the Surrealists anyway developing their own 'aestheticization of madness' (Fotiade, 20). Jonathan
Jones (43) terms it sheer bad taste (in Victorian terms, at least), or 'that
principle of disjunction that can still make surrealist art queasy'. Peter
Conrad (272) writes of 'an upsurge of jesting terrorism', regarded by
Breton as 'lyrical behaviour'.

Nadja, dubbed 'the quintessential Surrealist romance' (Mark
Polizzotti's 'Introduction', *Nadja*, x), is an apparent memoir (integrally
illustrated with photographs for visual documentation) of its author's
brief relationship with an 'enigmatic waif' (ibid., xvi) whose uncannily
Surrealist turn of mind (and pencil) is explored along the margins of love,
'petrifying coincidence' (*Nadja*, 19) and mental disturbance.[44] Breton's
opening question, 'Who am I?' (ibid., 11) is seen by Roger Cardinal as 'no
idle query, but a metaphysical wail' (Cardinal, 29). Nadja is replaced by
a new nameless lover after the ending of the short-lived affair, her ability
to read the Surrealist pattern of signs (and the book's title) notwithstanding; her successor may be seen not so much as 'a guide to the surreal, but
as a literal embodiment thereof' (ibid., 52); at this stage 'the beloved is
transfigured into the nameless Eternal Feminine' (72).[45] The text is a
deceptive and problematic one, purportedly extending beyond its verbal
limits into the real life of Paris in 1926 (as attested by the photographs
and drawings); yet, at the same time, it remains essentially confined
within its own wording.

In the words of Mary Ann Caws (159):

> Surrealism rarely lets us lose the consciousness of the all-importance of
> language: a thing in itself, a substance as untreatable as a person ... the
> whole narration, whether of presence or lack, is based on this splitting of
> elements, on this disquieting symmetry, baroque to a fault. Through such a
> love of doubling, of enigma, and of contraries ..., the baroque spirit and its
> techniques of repetition, anaphora, chiasmic and reversible structures enter
> into the very heart of surrealist vision.

Language, in all its aspects, was, therefore, as important an element for
the Surrealists as it had been for their predecessors.[46] 'Does not the mediocrity of our universe depend essentially on the power of enunciation?' is
the rhetorical question posed in 1924 by Breton; language has been
debased by a hackneyed subordination to the vulgarities of state, bureaucracy and finance, plus 'these constraining fears' and 'this horror of our
destiny' (Breton, 1978, 25). The revolt on behalf of language, as of much
else, involves 'resistance and experiment' (86); the required liberation is

social, sexual and political, as well as psychic, spiritual and intellectual: 'liberation of the mind' necessitates 'the liberation of man' (115).

It will further extend, moreover, to the metaphysical: 'Not only must there be an end to the exploitation of man by man, but also to the exploitation of man by the alleged "God", of absurd and revolting memory' (211). A penchant for a discourse of negatives is also notice-able:

> surrealism is not at all interested in taking into account what passes along-side it under the guise of art or even antiart; of philosophy or antiphilosophy; of anything, in a word, that has not for its ultimate end the conversion of being into a jewel, internal and unseeing, with a soul that is neither of ice nor of fire. (Breton, 1978, 129)[47]

The principal guidelines are an amalgam of Freudian psychoanalysis and Marxian dialectical materialism; the politics, though, are steadfastly anarcho-libertarian.[48] In similarly pivotal synthetic vein, a vital impetus to Surrealist thought is the reconciliation (or union) of opposites (dream with reality; fiction, or imagination, with life; madness with non-madness; detail with collage; subjective with objective; negative with positive; the static with the dynamic; construction with destruction; life with death), which may be traced back through German Romantic philosophy via Giordano Bruno to the alchemists. 'We are the tail of romanticism', Breton would say, 'but now [or 'how'] prehensile!' (Caws, 23; 236). It is indeed their attitude to cultural history that most marks the Surrealists off from their avant-garde forebears: rather than rejected, this cultural legacy should be turned towards 'the overthrow of capitalist society' (Breton, 1978, 143). The admired antecedents of Surrealism stretch from Heraclitus ('surrealist in dialectic'), through Swift ('surrealist in malice'), Carroll ('surrealist in nonsense') to the contemporary or near-contempo-rary Picasso, Jacques Vaché and Raymond Roussel (122–3). The Surrealists also drew inspiration from the occult, the Gothic novel (Walpole, Radcliffe and Lewis), elements of Romanticism and Symbolism, and the works of such key personalities as de Sade, Baudelaire, Lautréamont, Rimbaud, Huysmans, Jarry and Apollinaire.[49]

A vital style to be cultivated, linking Surrealism with what is, or becomes, absurdism, was 'black humour', a term said to have been coined by Breton, who published an *Anthology of Black Humour* in 1940 – an 'extreme, violent humour', observed by Conroy Maddox to be 'a deliber-ate critical attitude in surrealism', challenging 'all forms of accepted belief' (quoted in Breton, 1978, 188).[50] Black humour, of which Swift is designated 'the veritable initiator' (190), according to Breton, 'at a certain temperature, can alone play the role of a safety valve' (246). This 'psychic apparatus of *black humour*' (ibid.) reached such a temperature in the Leningrad of the late 1920s and through the 1930s, as evidenced by the activities of the OBERIU movement (a near acronym of the 'Association of Real Art' – '*Ob"edinenie real'nogo iskusstva*'.

OBERIU

The so-called 'oberiuty' (frequently referred to as the very last of the Soviet-Russian avant-garde), emerged in 1927 out of preliminary groupings – of young experimental writer-performers and minor remnants of Futurism – that included such formulations as 'Radiks', the 'Chinari' and the 'Left Flank' (see Cornwell, 1991, 5–7; Nakhimovsky, 5–24; Roberts, 1997, 1–17). The principal members were Daniil Kharms (who is considered in detail in Chapter 6), Aleksandr Vvedensky and Nikolai Zabolotsky. The *zaum'* poet Aleksandr Tufanov had been an early influence, while Vvedensky had worked with Terent'ev (formerly of 41° fame). Hostile journalistic and political attention (denouncing them in terms that extended from 'Dadaists' to 'class enemy') precipitated the breakup of the OBERIU movement as such by 1930, but individual members were able, at least rather more surreptitiously, to continue their unorthodox literary pursuits until Stalinist repression struck (either in the purges, or following the outbreak of war, upon the Nazi invasion of Soviet Russia).

The group's declaration, published in 1928, sets out the artistic credo in rather more restrained terms than had been found in most of the documents produced by its European and Russian predecessors and feels the need to make at least minimal genuflexions to the proletarian ethos then dominating Soviet culture.[51] Aimed at 'all forms of art', it addresses itself principally to four areas: literature, fine arts, theatre and cinema (with a music section under formation) and includes notes on the styles of its principal participants. Mention is made too in support of such fringe associates, or fellow spirits, as Terent'ev and the painters Filonov and Malevich.[52] The literary side, at this stage concerned with poetry, perhaps surprisingly disassociates the movement from *zaum'*, although an 'appearance of nonsense' is acknowledged (Gibian, 249). In poetry, film and theatre, 'collisions of verbal meanings' are of the essence, while 'dramatic plot' in the latter is played down, in preference to 'scenic plot', arising from disparate constituents of the spectacle – 'seemingly extraneous and clearly ridiculous elements' (ibid., 253). The OBERIU practice of semi-scandalous performance art was, for its time and setting – and while it lasted – rather more daring and provocative than the printed declaration might have suggested. This was to be perhaps even more the case with much of their (mainly unpublishable) literary work of the 1930s.

The exact period of OBERIU's meaningful existence, and the precise composition of its membership, susceptive as ever to squabble and fragmentation, has been the subject of some disagreement. However, literary works of a clearly absurdist nature certainly emerged from Kharms,

Vvedensky and, some at least would say, Konstantin Vaginov (who was also a member of the Bakhtin circle). Vaginov's novels, which incorporate strong elements of metafiction and carnivalisation along with wide cultural and intertextual reference and the creation of alternative worlds, evince both a ludic and a theatrical concern with the relationship of art, life and 'play'. In his novel *The Goat's Song* (*Kozlinaia pesn´*: actually published, 1928), a figure called 'the unknown poet' ruminates on the necessity for art of an Orpheus-like descent to the underworld, albeit in his case an artificial one ('goat's song', we recall, being in any event the meaning of 'tragedy'), stressing 'the need to shape the world anew by means of the word', and in consequence 'the descent into the hell of the absurd, into a hell full of wild noises and wild howling, in order to find a new melody for the world' (quoted from Roberts, 1997, 66).[53]

Vvedensky employs an even more overt use of the grotesque and indeed of black humour, especially in his provocative play *Christmas at the Ivanovs'* (*Elka u Ivanovykh*, written 1938), to which – as with Kharms's *Yelizaveta Bam* – we shall subsequently return when surveying Theatre of the Absurd. In his prose pieces (fictional or non-fictional, in so far as these categories can be differentiated), Vvedensky indulges 'obsessive interest in the tripartite theme of time, death, and God', displaying 'a deep sense of dislocation and incoherence' at both a linguistic and a metaphysical level (ibid., 147; 153). His preoccupations here have been likened to those of Wittgenstein and, in particular, of Heidegger; language (here more than merely 'inadequate' or 'unsayable') leads through madness and death to the eventual desired realm of God and the transcendence of silence (see ibid., 154–6).[54]

Disparate European prose: Western and Eastern proto-absurdism

With regard to what has emerged from Futurism, Dada and Surrealism, as elsewhere and as we proceed towards 'absurdism', it is greatly to our purpose to heed Cardullo's reminder (8) that:

> Both within and outside these movements, however, the specific genius of individual and avant-garde writers and artists flourished, the distinctive trace left by such individuals serving to remind us that historical categories and groupings are often suspect, reductive, or artificial.

As well as being a leading experimental poet and art critic, and something of a godfather figure to various avant-garde groupings over the first two decades of the twentieth century, the cosmopolitan Guillaume Apollinaire wrote a number of fantastical prose works. His earlier erotic – many would say pornographic – novellas, *Les Onze Milles Verges* and *Les Mémoires d'un jeune Don Juan* (both published in 1907) must have been one inspiration for Surrealist eroticism.[55] A bizarre, and more interesting, later example of Apollinaire's prose is *Le Poète assassiné* (1916), following the 'career' of a poet from conception to assassination. This work mixes verse and dramatic dialogue into a text which is constructed from elements of, or resembling, fairy story, the grotesque, erotica, autobiography and allegory, culminating in a symbolic international massacre of poets. The innovative poet-protagonist, named Croniamantal, is also a playwright, and he insists on roaring out a plot synopsis of a composition named *Ieximal Jelimite*:

> A man buys a newspaper on the seashore. From a house on the prompt-side comes a soldier whose hands are light bulbs. A ten-foot-tall giant jumps down from a tree. He shakes the newsboy, who is plaster and falls down and breaks. Just then a judge pops in. He kills everyone with a razor, while a leg comes hopping along and brains the judge by kicking him under the nose, and sings a pretty little song. (Apollinaire, *Poet*, 31)

The Surrealist and absurdist elements here need no emphasis. Among the stories originally intended to accompany this novella is a two-page miniature, entitled 'The Deified Invalid' (Apollinaire, *Poet*, 109–11), which could stand as a minor classic of absurdist parabolic prose. The invalid in question, deprived of the limbs and faculties of his left side following an explosion in the motor car he was chauffeuring, acquires an amnesic and timeless cast of mind, 'communicated to his intelligence' as a result of the hopping gait by which means he now perambulates. Nicknamed 'The Eternal', through his 'divine' infirmity and his 'mental resemblance' to the deity, he effects a God's-eye perception of human existence (past, present and future): 'The whole world and all of time were thus for him a well-tuned instrument which his one hand played perfectly'. Appropriately enough, following his sudden subsequent disappearance, 'those who had met him do not believe The Eternal is dead and they never will'.

The Flemish poet and satirical story writer Paul Van Ostaijen was an admirer of Apollinaire and an associate of the Berlin Dadaists at the beginning of the 1920s. Styling his stories 'grotesques', Van Ostaijen wrote a Dadaist film script entitled *Bankruptcy Jazz*, employed Dadaist 'bruitism' (from the French *bruit*, 'noise') in his poetry and, following idiosyncratic lines of logic, frequently ended in what his translator terms 'a fearful realm of absurdity' (E.M. Beekman, 'Introduction' to Van Ostaijen, xiv). Also to be located in his work is an 'almost unbearable frustration', a 'seething hatred' and a 'demonic presence of violence' (ibid., x). Like many of the writers discussed here, Van Ostaijen is obsessed by time (and timelessness) and by the motif of prison (deemed *per se* 'a function of the state and of religion'). Masquerading as a 'galley slave', an ex-prisoner known as 'no. 200' so hankers after the prison life that he murders an annoying priest to ensure his return to it; contriving to have himself perceived guilty of treason, and facing the axe, he then aspires to 'prison in heaven' ('The Prison in Heaven', Van Ostaijen, 54–66). Van Ostaijen anticipates the casuistic logic of the development of the military-industrial complex (*Patriotism, Inc.*); a madam with no sexual feelings rules her bawdy house on pseudo-Freudian principles ('Ika Loch's Brothel'); and an inebriated retired Peruvian general fantasises in depth on the subject of regiments based on sexual preference ('The General'). In one miniature ('Convictions', 77–8), an accordion player, having pulled his instrument so far open as to tear his arm from his body, undergoes the rejoining of the accordion to his body instead of the arm; the arm is then tied by string to the accordion, thus sustaining the physician's 'conviction' that arm–accordion causality has been preserved. Emblematic, perhaps, of many a stock figure in this type of prose is an image conjured by the general: 'And so you stand at five o'clock in the morning in a Harlequin costume, realizing that there is no carnival' (114).

Joseph Roth's short novel *Rebellion* (1924) covers the career of Andreas Pum – night watchman, one-legged war invalid, hurdy-gurdy man and prisoner, turned lavatory attendant – in his journey, governed by 'mysterious chance' (Roth, 2000, 143), through the misfortunes of life into existential revolt and a desire for 'Hell'. 'We are all of us prisoners anyway, Andreas Pum!', reads the free indirect discourse of the narrative; 'Only if we are extremely fortunate do we manage to stay out of prison. But we are fated to cause revulsion, and to find ourselves ensnared in the luxuriant undergrowth of the laws' (ibid., 94; 108). Roth's translator, Michael Hofmann, calls this starkly grotesque novel 'Brechtian' (Roth, viii), but comparisons with Kafka are also apparent, along with Gogol, while a story by Kharms ('The Knight', from the mid-1930s: see *Incidences*, 105–8) reads almost as a Russified condensed version.[56]

A novel having nothing whatever in common with Ford Madox Ford's *The Good Soldier* is Jaroslav Hašek's anarchic *The Good Soldier Švejk and his Fortunes in the World War* (1921–23), an unfinished 700–page saga of unremitting military farce, in which alcohol, gluttony, carnivalised foolery, uniformed lunacy, scatology and dismemberment are all prominent features.[57] Again, certain of the multiplicity of anecdotes embedded within a deliberately rambling text, mostly recounted by Švejk and amounting in totality to a vast shaggy-dog story (it even extends to embracing what Švejk *would* have said: e.g. Hašek, 682; and, moreover, by the time the manuscript breaks off, Švejk and his 'march company' have still not reached the front), bear an individual resemblance (as we shall see in Chapter 6) to the Kharmsian miniature. The whole takes place during the final (wartime) years of the Austro-Hungarian Empire, an example *par excellence* of what Sheppard (15) characterises (although in a context of 'the modern megalopolis') as ''institutionalized insanity masquerading as order'.

Poland provides the fantasy setting of Jarry's *Ubu Roi*, and it may therefore not be inappropriate that Poland should later supply a number of fascinating practitioners of the surreal and the absurd. Stanisław Witkiewicz (or 'Witkacy'), who also operated as a painter, art critic and novelist, produced dramatic works which independently 'explored the worlds of dream, madness, parody and political satire' (Esslin, 393) and, with his 'Pure Form', sought to transpose reality into a new dimension (see Cardullo and Knopf, 321–6; Witkiewicz, 1993, 233–9).[58] Employing a frantically surreal and self-conscious theatricality, Witkiewicz approaches, and then if anything outdoes in such respects, for instance, the drama of Pirandello and Maiakovsky. With his own plays, another significant Polish literary figure, Witold Gombrowicz, is also to be regarded 'as a precursor and at the same time as a mature master of the Theatre of the Absurd' (see Esslin, *Th. Abs.*, 393–5). Also crying out for at least a brief consideration at this point is the fiction of Bruno Schulz and of the early Gombrowicz.

One of the most extraordinary European writers of the twentieth century's interwar years, Bruno Schulz produced in the 1930s just two slim volumes of what are commonly referred to as stories but which, in the main and taken together, read more as a strangely poetic episodic autobiographical novel, tussling fantastically – and often absurdly – with family life in a Polish-Jewish provincial town. A master of surreal metaphor and imagery (vividly transforming the natural, domestic, urban and commercial worlds of his milieu), Schulz expands or collapses time and space, oscillating and transposing memory with imagination, the inanimate and the organic, in a veritable splurge of perception. In first *The Street of Crocodiles*, and then perhaps more profoundly in *Sanatorium Under the Sign of the Hourglass*, Schulz plays on illusion and materiality to spark (Nabokov-like) 'that vibration of reality which, in metaphysical moments, we experience as the glimmer of revelation' (*Street*, 57). At the same time, he appears to remain, as John Updike puts it, and resembling Borges, 'a cosmogonist without a theology' (*Sanatorium*, xiv).

The most striking figure from the sequence as a whole is the father of Joseph (the narrator's name is revealed only in the second volume). At most seemingly 'half real', and much earlier 'that incorrigible improviser, that fencing master of imagination' (*Sanatorium*, 121; *Street*, 31), this astonishing and near-fabulous object of paternal obsession metamorphoses several times (into cockroach, horsefly and crab: Schulz, incidentally, was long thought to have translated Kafka's *The Trial* into Polish: see Ficowski, 112) and undergoes innumerable stages and states of death, half-death and revival, having at an early point been predicted finally to 'disappear one day, as unremarked as the grey heap of rubbish swept into a corner, waiting to be taken by [the maid] Adela to the

rubbish dump' (*Street*, 25).[59] In the title story of the second volume, a
fierce watchdog turns into 'a dog in human shape' who 'might have been
Dr Gotard's unsuccessful brother' (*Sanatorium*, 137).[60] It is this 'story'
that most effectively displays Schulz's sense of 'the quick decomposition
of time', or 'a shabby time full of holes, like a sieve' (127; 131). Joseph
ends up (in this chapter, at least) singing for alms on a perpetual train
journey, while the eponymous Dodo (whose mind is restricted to the
present) and crippled Eddie of other instalments are close relatives of
personages to be found in works by Apollinaire, Roth and Kharms.
Another, seemingly unconnected, episode (which might stand as an independent story) is 'The Old Age Pensioner', in which the mature citizen in
question returns to repeat his schooling, before being 'swept away' by a
violent wind into 'the unexplored yellow space' (170–1).

'Maturity' is also of the essence in Gombrowicz's bizarre novel
Ferdydurke (1937) in which the (presumably eponymous, though called
only 'Johnnie' [or 'Joey'] within the text) thirty-year-old protagonist
regresses to adolescence to suffer at the hands of, to satirise and then to
reduce to a chaotic state of moral and physical *mêlée*, the stereotyped
ethos first of school, then of liberal 'modernism', and finally of rural
'feudal' family life. An alternative title of '*Memoirs of a Time of
Immaturity*' is in fact provided early in the first chapter (Gombrowicz,
15), while notions of 'childishness' and 'rejuvenescence' occur within
chapter titles. These 'authentic memoirs' (ibid., 70) appear to comprise a
mélange of dream, nightmare, fantasy and absurdity, with a 'juvenile'
emphasis on 'face' and 'faces' ('hollow verbiage' and 'absurd facial
contortions': ibid.), 'thighs' and 'pretty little backsides'; by the end there
emerges in the night sky 'not a moon, but a bum, a great bum spreading
itself over the top of the trees', followed at dawn by 'another huge bum,
red this time and a hundred times more dazzling' (264–5). In the
(melo)dramatic action of the narrative, speechlessness can be as eloquent
as garrulity and tumult; at one key moment, we are indeed informed:
'Absurdity suffocated in the silence' (180). This is a universe in which
ignorance of age is to be 'free of the absurd contingencies of life!' (217),
'the normal is a tightrope over the abyss of the abnormal' (251–2), and,
'tramping through the void', one can encounter a profusion of 'yokels
who were pretending to be their own dogs' (202–4), while both
Dostoevsky and the Russian Futurists would have hearkened to resounding perpetrations of 'the magic of the slap in the face' (229).

Originally from a point still further east, Vladimir Nabokov, having
been brought up in St Petersburg, conducted the greater part of his literary career of the interwar years (during which he wrote predominantly in
Russian) as an émigré in Berlin. Of the works of this period, those most
closely approaching the absurd arguably are the novella *The Eye*
(*Sogliadatai*, 1930), comprising the impressions of a protagonist who,

having allegedly committed suicide, dedicates his posthumous existence to spying on a group of characters that includes one who, it may be surmised, is none other than the narrator himself;[61] and the novel *Invitation to a Beheading* (*Priglashenie na kazn'*, first published in journal form, 1935–36). The latter work, dubbed by its author, in the Foreword to the English edition first appearing in 1959, 'a violin in a void' (Nabokov, *Invitation*, 9) and subsequently 'the only prose poem I have composed' (Connolly, 172), features a man condemned to death by a timeless dictatorship for 'the most terrible of crimes, gnostical turpitude', or 'opacity' in a world of transparent beings (*Invitation*, 61) – a situation calling to mind the predicaments confronting Kafka's Joseph K. and Kharms's Yelizaveta Bam.

Cincinnatus C., as Nabokov's hero is named, is another immature thirty-year-old, like his antithetical double, false friend and executioner to be, M'sieur Pierre (as is, for that matter, Kafka's Joseph K.), who has posed as a fellow prisoner.[62] Nabokov's possibly over-strenuous denials of any knowledge of Kafka at the time he composed this novel (which he squeezed into the lengthy process of writing his major Russian novel, *The Gift* – itself not completely devoid of absurdist features) have not convinced all critics; a parallel with the collapse of an artificial or toy-town world at the end of *Alice in Wonderland* has also been noted (Nabokov had translated this work into Russian in 1923).[63] Nabokov certainly knew and admired Kafka later, lecturing on *Metamorphosis* during his years at Cornell (see Nabokov, 1980, 250–83; and Chapter 7 below). Cincinnatus certainly has his existential preoccupations; indeed, he deconstructs himself – apparently literally (*Invitation*, 29)[64] – and subsequently refers to this 'sensation' in his own written account, as reaching 'the final, indivisible, firm, radiant point, and this point says: I am!'; at the same time, he is also 'perhaps simply a carnival freak in a gaping, hopelessly festive world' (76) that is essentially a hastily assembled theatrical set. This novel has been read metaphysically, socio-politically and metaliterally; more particularly, it has been termed: 'the most overtly "modernist" and antirealistic of Nabokov's works'; a novel whose depicted world falls 'within the perimeter of surrealist art'; a spectacle of 'Chaplinesque pratfall comedy'; and, not least, 'a classic work of absurdist literature'.[65] However, as D. Barton Johnson affirms (in Connolly, 123), Cincinattus's prison is 'double': not only a 'prison fortress' of the 'Communazist state' (ibid., 152), but also (and this expression derives from Nietzsche, via Fredric Jameson) 'the prison-house of language'.

In such novels and stories, or fragments thereof – and another candidate for any such list is the assortment of texts involving Henri Michaux's Plume – the stress consistently falls on the essential Camusian divorce between humanity and the world, with a protagonist (though it is often scarcely possible to speak of such figures as 'characters') in some way crushed by his setting, in the face of a hostile world or malevolent chance, reduced to amnesia, an incoherence that mirrors the nature of his surroundings, or to silence, and the loss of any identity, in a narrative in which incompletion (raised in itself to an art form) is, as a rule and whatever the scale, a basic structural principle.[66] In his stories, prose poems and poems, 'relating the a-logical in a logical manner, Michaux reduces to absurdity verbal constructions that supposedly "adhere" to some kind of reality' (Brée, 216–17), conveying 'that impression of the *absurd* that I find everywhere' (Michaux, 33: his emphasis). Breton's recipe for the future Surrealist fiction is arguably already met in a number of such texts, perhaps especially in the prose of Kharms in the 1930s, while it clearly anticipates common trends in future absurdist productions:

> When, however, will we have the novel in which the characters, having been abundantly defined with a minimum of particularities, will act in an altogether foreseeable way in view of an unforeseen result? And, inversely, the novel in which psychology will not hastily perform its great but futile duties at the expense of the characters and events but will really *hold* between two blades a fraction of a second, to surprise there the germs of incidents? (Breton, 1978, 135)

Notes

1 Henrik Ibsen, *Peer Gynt*, translated by Christopher Fry and Johan Fillinger, Oxford: Oxford University Press, 'Oxford World's Classics', 1998, 112–21 (113).

2 *The Ghost Sonata* is included in Cardullo and Knopf's anthology (134–60).

3 J.L. Styan (29) suggests that some of Maeterlinck's ideas were only fully realised much later in work by Artaud and Beckett, 'or in surrealistic films like Alain Resnais's haunting *Last Year in Marienbad* (1961)'.

4 Muriel Zagha, 'Stars of the big scream', *TLS*, 10 January 2003, 18. On this phenomenon, which ran effectively until the early 1930s, closing finally only in 1963, see Richard J. Hand and Michael Wilson, *Grand-Guignol: The French Theatre of Horror*, Exeter: University of Exeter Press, 2002.

5 Styan (50) calls the effects of *Ubu Roi* 'the beginning of a counter-culture which would display many manifestations of artistic anarchy, and preach a variety of loosely related philosophies, or antiphilosophies, of life and art'. More recently, *Ubu Roi* has been termed 'a round dance prefiguring the century of the Absurd that was to follow' (Fotiade, 5). An English version (translated as *King Ubu*) is included in Cardullo and Knopf (84–122). A 'remake' of *Ubu Roi*, transported to Africa (satirising General Abacha of Nigeria), is Wole Soyinka's *King Baabu* (London: Methuen, 2002).

6 Coined by Jarry in 1890, who developed it through the 1890s, intending to incorporate it into an unfinished and posthumously published story, *Les Gestes et opinions du Docteur Faustroll, Pataphysicien* (1911), a symbolic

journey through 'Ethernity' (Styan, 50); see also Cardullo and Knopf, 77–8. 'La Pataphysique' was taken up by Daumal in the 1930s (see Fotiade, 39–40). The so-called 'Collège de Pataphysique' was founded in 1949 by Ionesco and others. 'Pataphysicians, who are the disciples of Jarry (the prophet of Faustroll), believe that we are all, consciously or not, pataphysicians' (Ionesco, *Notes*, 200, n.). The 'concept' is looked at again by van Boxsel (195–9). According to Peter Conrad (81), for that matter too, 'Duchamp invented his own ludic physics'.

7 On this work see Sheppard, 89–100 (90); see also Steiner, 2001, 220–2, who links it both to Shakespeare and to the twentieth-century 'crisis of language'; and Peter Conrad, passim. It is translated as 'The Letter of Lord Chandos' in Hofmannsthal, 129–41.

8 See Todorov, 1990, 103–12; further oppositions can be pointed to, such as somewhere–nowhere; something–nothing; and no doubt the list is still not exhaustive.

9 In his *A Personal Record*, Conrad wrote: 'The ethical view of the universe involves us at least in so many cruel and absurd contradictions, where the last vestiges of faith, hope and charity, and even of reason itself, seem ready to perish, that I have come to suspect that the aim of creation cannot be ethical at all. I would fondly believe that its object is purely spectacular: a spectacle for awe, love, adoration, or hate, if you like, but in this view – and this view alone – never for despair!' (quoted by Kott, 215, in relation to the 'mature wisdom' of Prospero in *The Tempest*, and mentioning Marlow, but as narrator of *Lord Jim*).

10 A comparison *en passant* between this story and *Heart of Darkness* is made by Maxim D. Shrayer, *The World of Nabokov's Stories*, Austin: University of Texas Press, 1999, 51.

11 For instance 'The Hunters' (Kharms, *Incidences*, 74–6).

12 The comparison is made by Leon Edel, 51. Edel also notes 'the quiet circle, the atmosphere of mystery and gloom, with the hint of terrible evil, the reflective narrator, the retrospective method, the recall of crucial episodes' common to *Heart of Darkness* and *The Turn of the Screw* (54).

13 Nicola Bradbury makes a brief comparison of the narrators of *Heart of Darkness* and *The Sacred Fount* (Bradbury, 1979, 33). James himself remained strangely reticent about *The Sacred Fount* and omitted it from his New York Edition (consequently, he wrote no Preface to it).

14 'She watched me now as a Roman lady at the circus may have watched an exemplary Christian' (James, 163); cf. the extended Roman allusion at the beginning of Marlow's narrative and the play therein on light and darkness (Conrad, 4–5).

15 A notable recent exception, however, is Tintner, who argues plausibly for 'a gay reading', based on evidence from both inside and outside the text of the novel (see Tintner, 176–96).

16 In particular, of 'the idea that observation affects the object observed', rendering the narrator of *The Sacred Fount* 'the observer trapped in observation': Hardy, 23–4. In the words of Hofstadter (699), the uncertainty principle 'says that measuring one quantity renders impossible the simultaneous measurement of a related quantity'.

17 See Edel, 40–8. Fred Kaplan (*Henry James: The Imagination of Genius*, London: Sceptre, 1993, 460–1) puts a more congenial complexion on their contacts. Ford was, until 1919, known (and published) under his original name of Ford Madox Hueffer.

18 See John A. Meixner (Ford, 250); for a more detailed discussion of these three authors as 'impressionists' see Paul B. Armstrong, 1–25.

19 See Thomas C. Moser (352–8), P.B. Armstrong (390), and David H. Lynn (395): all in Ford (the Norton Critical Edition of *The Good Soldier*). P.B. Armstrong's contribution in the apparatus to *GS* is excerpted from a chapter of his *The Challenge of Bewilderment* (189–224), which also includes one on *The Sacred Fount* (29–62).

20 According to Eugene Goodheart (Ford, 383), 'images of paradise, hell and limbo that permeate the novel suggest a vision of a failed Divine Comedy'.

21 Maisie, in James's *What Maisie Knew* (a work much admired by Ford), is also metaphorically termed a 'shuttlecock'. Nancy Rufford may therefore be taken, in part and for all her apparent lack of sophistication, as a development, or older counterpart, of Maisie.

22 On the progress of the term 'avant-garde', from military to political to cultural usage see Cardullo, 12–13.

23 Esslin sees Georg Büchner (1813–37) as 'the germ of Brecht, German Expressionism, and of the dark strain of the Theatre of the Absurd', while counting Yvan Goll (1891–1950) 'the only major writer among the Expressionists who definitely belongs to the antecedents of The Theatre of the Absurd' (*Th. Abs.*, 339; 370). Dobrez (188) maintains that the 'expressionist' area 'marks the transition from the Romantic to the existential'.

24 'The Futurists, before 1910, were still bound up with Symbolism, and even metaphysics and occultism, as well as with Art Nouveau, Pointillism and a cultural climate dominated by the works of Munch' (and others): Apollonio, *Futurist Manifestos*, 15 (hereafter referred to as *FM*). Arguably, Futurist painting was more successful than the movement's other products.

25 According to Hugh Shankland, in *Futurismo* (70), see below, the first night of *Roi Bombance* was 'a full-scale riot, touched off, it is said, by the thunderous sound effects of a priest's digestive system in the second act'.

26 Many of these are to be found in Marinetti, *Selected Writings*; and (authored also by other figures) in Apollonio's edition of *FM*. Another useful source is the exhibition catalogue *Futurismo 1909–1919*, 1972 (for details in Bibliography, see Shankland).

27 Borges, however (*TL*, 251), asserts that 'the Italian Futurists forget that [Kipling] was the first European poet to celebrate the superb and blind activity of machines'.

28 For text see Apollonio, 183–96; reprinted by Cardullo and Knopf, 201–6, who include sample fragmentary works by Franceso Cangiullo and Marinetti.

29 Dubbed 'Stranger' by Khlebnikov on his 1914 visit (see *RF*, 252), Marinetti was, however, in 1916 'invited' by the now self-styled 'King of Time, Velimir I' (Khlebnikov thus paralleled the Dadaist penchant for self-styled 'presidencies') to join, along with H.G. Wells, 'the parliament of Martians, as guests with the right to a consultative vote' (ibid., 106).

30 'Kruchenykh, without formal training in poetics, had no aesthetic inhibitions

and was able to carry the idea of the self-sufficient word to extravagant lengths, reaching a level of abstraction that bordered on the absurd' (Lawton: *RF*, 13). According to Hilary Fink, 'Russian modernists treat words in much the same way' as in Bergson's linguistic approach: 'Bely's magical word (*Magiia slov*), Khlebnikov's transrational language, and Kharmsian words that ostensibly mean nothing, and thus bear [*sic*] their absurd meaning'; however a distinction is drawn between the absurd in Kharms and the effects that result from Kruchenykh's poetry (Fink, 9; 93). The practice of 'forced etymologies', however, goes back at least as far as the Stoics, according to whom 'words picture the nature of the things. The sounds imitate the quality of the object that the names constructed out of them signify' (Ricken, 193). On imagined, proto- and burlesque languages see also Eco, 1999 (especially 'The Language of the Austral Land', pp. 77–95).

31 Robert Musil had Habsburg empire 'Kakanie' (from the abbreviated motto '*K. und K.*' (*The Man Without Qualities*); Peter Conrad quips (114): 'Deconstruction begins in Kakanie.' Not to be confused with this tendency, however, is Khlebnikov's mythological story *Ka* (1916), in which 'Ka' (the Egyptian word for soul) is the soul's 'shadow', transmigrating through time and space; included in Velimir Khlebnikov, *Snake Train: Poetry and Prose*, edited by Gary Kern, Ann Arbor: Ardis, 1976 ('Ka', translated by Richard Sheldon, 159–82).

32 The designation 'Dada', seen by traditional criticism as deliberately meaningless, is the French word for 'hobby horse'. See, however, Tristan Tzara's comments on the word in his 'Dada Manifesto' of 1918 (Cardullo and Knopf, 283–9, see particularly the beginning of the section 'Dada Means Nothing', p. 284).

33 Again (198), Sheppard refers to Dadaist tendencies either 'to absurdism or a more or less secularized mysticism'. Furthermore, Dadaist political dabblings, such as they were, took place despite a 'conviction that reality is "irremediably absurd"' (305).

34 For a selection of Dada poetry, in dual-text (English and the original six other languages), see *The Dada Market: An Anthology of Poetry*, translated with an Introduction by Willard Bohn, Carbondale: Southern Illinois University Press, 1993.

35 On 'performance art' see Henry Sayre, 'Performance', in Lentricchia and McLaughlin, pp. 91–104.

36 Sheppard (292) calls at least some variants of Dada 'the celebration of a cosmic carnival' and the Dadaists themselves 'descendents of . . . fool figures of older, popular culture'. Parallel with C.G. Jung's theory of psychological androgyny and Adler's critique of hypermasculinity, 'Dada was doing likewise: attempting to say "yes" to an androgynous human nature and "no" to fixed gender identities and roles'. Barry Humphries (of Dame Edna Everage fame) is said to have been 'a passionate devotee of Dada' (ibid., 191). One wonders whether The League of Gentlemen (see Chapter 10) have been similarly inspired.

37 In addition to early and mainstream modernism and 'high modernism', and preceding 'postmodernism', Tyrus Miller (see 9–12) emphasises a category of 'late modernism' (epitomised by certain of the works of Wyndham Lewis,

Djuna Barnes, Beckett and Mina Loy).

38 Robert A. Varisco, excerpted in Cardullo and Knopf, 266–71 (270); the text of the play is included on pp. 272–82.

39 *Profane Words over the Eternal City*, in Schwitters, *PPPPPP*, 182.

40 'And when Schwitters built rubbish into his collages, he was simultaneously commenting on the aesthetic potential of the detritus of modernity and the tendency of modernity to generate huge amounts of waste' (Sheppard, 204).

41 Segal (416) sees 'the baton [of 'Absurd Comedy'] passing in turn from Jarry to Apollinaire to Cocteau, who saw himself as their logical heir'; on Cocteau's plays (*Parade* and *The Wedding on the Eiffel Tower*) in this light, see 417–20; Cocteau himself speaks of 'the *absurde organisé*, anticipating the adjective that would come to describe the genre to which he was contributing' (418). This is also noted by Carlson (344).

42 For a cogent discussion of the progression of Surrealism from Apollinaire to Breton, indeed, see Bohn, 121–39. 'Surprise' and 'analogical parallel' correspond to 'the traditional opposition between form and content' (126). Apollinaire had fully developed his 'doctrine of surprise' by 1914 (123).

43 Arguably, Surrealism stretched from 1919 (or 1924) until the death of Breton (1966). However, the English painter and collagist Conroy Maddox (1912–2005) was still exhibiting in London in 2001 – 'the world's oldest practising surrealist painter': see Jonathan Jones, 'Me, Dali and the Deep-sea Diving Suit', *The Guardian* (G 2, 1 March 2001, pp. 12–13). For recent examinations of Surrealist visual art see Caws (*The Surrealist Look*, 1997) and Bohn (*The Rise of Surrealism*, 2002).

44 The English translation is from the 1928 edition. The revised version of 1963 has, textual adjustments (including deletions) apart, additional photographs, while – even in the cheap Folio paperback edition – the quality of the illustrations is superior to those provided in its Penguin counterpart: André Breton, *Nadja*, 'edition completely revised by the author', Paris: Gallimard, 1972 (1987 printing). Page numbers here in the text are from the Penguin edition.

45 This particular survival from Symbolism into Surrealism is reminiscent of the Russian Symbolist tendency to discern the incarnation of such a metaphysical quality in an actual female associate.

46 'Among the things in which surrealism has faith, language ranks highest, as the agent of transformation, including all the techniques worked out so laboriously and with such comings, goings, steps false and true. The proximity to the language of the baroque enables it to traverse and to transgress the boundaries between times and spaces' (Caws, 303).

47 One may be reminded here of the (alternative) 'existential' line of thought, with its 'negative progression towards the void', occasioned though by 'the existential rejection of ethical determinations and of social/political militancy [leading] to a defiant valuation of powerlessness, defeat, resignation and disengagement' (Fotiade, 193).

48 Peter Conrad (494) writes of 'an unholy merger of sadism and socialism'. Cardinal (61; 57) reads *Nadja* as 'a persuasive libertarian manifesto' which 'admits of an *anarchist* rather than a communist reading'.

49 As we have seen, their rediscovery of Lautréamont assumed a particular importance for the Surrealists as a 'foundational surrealist text' (Lomas, 156);

indeed, 'the aspiring surrealist writer had only to follow where Lautréamont had dared to pass' (ibid., 149). According to the existential thinker Roger Gilbert-Lecomte, a 'new morality of perpetual negation emerges after the "death of art" heralded by Rimbaud' (Fotiade, 192). J.-K. Huysmans, in his *À Rebours* (1884; translated as *Against Nature*) displays the *mal du siècle* absurdity and decadence of the archetypal dandy, accompanied by a regime of ascetic *ennui*.

50 Breton's idea of black humour may have been inspired by Jacques Vaché (1896–1919); according to Fotiade (5), Vaché's idea of humour, '"the sense of the theatrical (and joyless) futility of everything", played a crucial part in the initial formulation of the Surrealist conception of the absurd'.

51 Published simply as 'OBERIU', it is translated as 'The Oberiu Manifesto' in an appendix to Gibian (pp. 245–54; reprinted in Cardullo and Knopf, 415–20).

52 Kharms wrote an elegy on the death of Malevich in 1935. Comparison has also been made between the mini-stories of Kharms and prose poems by Kandinsky (see Wanner, 2003, 140).

53 On Vaginov's novels see Roberts, 1997, passim; also David Shepherd, *Beyond Metafiction: Self-Consciousness in Soviet Literature*, Oxford: Clarendon Press, 1992, 90–121.

54 The text mainly considered here (Roberts, 151–6) is *A Certain Quantity of Conversations* (*Nekotoroe kolichestvo razgovorov*, dated 1936–37); similarly relevant for Vvedensky's thought is *All Around Maybe God* (*Krugom vozmozhno Bog*; see ibid., 149–50). As with Kharms, the works of Vvedensky were collected only decades after his death: Aleksandr Vvedenskii, *Polnoe sobranie sochinenii*, edited by Mikhail Meilakh, 2 vols (Ann Arbor: Ardis, 1980–84).

55 These have been translated under a joint title by Alexis Lykiard; Guillaume Apollinaire, *Flesh Unlimited: Two Erotic Novellas* (London: Velvet, 1995).

56 Another Roth story with an arguably Kharmsian feel to it is the undated 'Sick People': see Roth, 2001, 42–54.

57 A rather more extreme example of military debauchery is contained in the concluding Russo-Japanese War episodes of Apollinaire's *Les Onze Mille Verges* (death eventually being administered to the reprehensible protagonist by means of the eponymous 'eleven thousand rods'): see Apollinaire, *Flesh Unlimited*. The closest parallel to Švejk, however, is perhaps (the then Soviet dissident) Vladimir Voinovich's comic novels of a Russian soldier in the Second World War: *The Life and Extraordinary Adventures of Private Ivan Chonkin* and *Pretender to the Throne: The Further Adventures of Private Ivan Chonkin* (1975 and 1979; both translated by Richard Lourie, 1977 and 1981 respectively). Incidentally, there is a Woinowic who makes a fleeting appearance in *The Good Soldier Švejk*.

58 In one play (*The Independence of Triangles*, written 1921), Witkiewicz posits an agency called 'the Department of Metaphysical Absurdity' (noted in Witkiewicz, 1993, 106). One of his contemporaries (the writer and critic Boy-Zelenski) characterised Witkiewicz's theatre as 'metaphysical buffoonery and supercabaret, presenting the sadness, boredom and despair of modern civilization with a spasmodic laugh' (ibid., 35).

59 This may be compared to the fate of a character in the Kharms miniature, 'The

Dream', who 'was folded in two and thrown out as rubbish' (*Incidences*, 59). In Kafka's *Metamorphosis*, the charwoman similarly takes it upon herself 'to get rid of the thing next door': i.e. the remains of the metamorphosed Gregor (Kafka, *CS*, 138). See also Klíma's play *Games* (*Hry*, 1973), in which a girl student has reportedly been strangled and taken away by refuse collectors: see Day, *Czech Plays*, 27–93 (32; 49; 67). Eagleton (69–70) remarks that the people in the Nazi death camps were 'treated more like garbage than like animals' – a horror involving 'the deliberate conversion of meaning to absurdity'.

60 Imaginary or bizarre brothers are also to be located in the work of, for instance, Kharms and Flann O'Brien.

61 Fernando Pessoa, in *The Book of Disquiet*, claims: 'Living isn't worth while. Only seeing is. To be able to see without living would bring happiness, but this impossible, like virtually everything we dream' (Pessoa, 2001, 388).

62 M'sieur Pierre, his odiously obsequious role and characteristics apart, has a line of his own in absurd patter, as he exclaims to Cincinnatus: '"You bear an extraordinary resemblance to your mother. I myself never had the chance of seeing her, but Rodrig Ivanovich kindly promised to show me her photograph' (*Invitation*, 69).

63 Just one such denial is explicitly made in the Foreword: *Invitation*, 7. On Kafka and Nabokov see Margaret Byrd Boegeman, '*Invitation to a Beheading* and the Many Shades of Kafka', in J.E. Rivers and Charles Nicols, editors, *Nabokov's Fifth Arc: Nabokov and Others on His Life's Work* (Austin: University of Texas Press, 1982), 105–21; she also comments on the Carroll parallel, 107; 109. Penner (34) sees affinities with Camus (the end of *The Myth of Sisyphus*) and Ionesco. See also John Burt Foster, Jr, 'Nabokov and Kafka', in Alexandrov, 444–51.

64 This passage is quoted below, in Chapter 6.

65 D. Barton Johnson (in Connolly, 134); Sergei Davydov (in Alexandrov, 189), who explores equally metaphysics (Gnostic and otherwise) and metafiction (ibid., 188–203); Dale Peterson (in Connolly, 73); and Penner (33).

66 Michaux's at very least occasional similarity to Kharms is noted by Jaccard (51); see the dual-text selection in Michaux, *Selected Writings* (including items from *Un Certain Plume*, 1930), and in particular the short story 'Plume at the Restaurant', 82–8. Other particularly Kharmsian stories may be said to include 'The Night of the Bulgarians' (92–103) and the later 'The Heroic Age' (from *La Nuit remue*, 1934, 120–5), while 'The Executioner' (from *Lointain intérieur*, 1938, 199–200) is a miniature that may recall Nabokov's *Invitation to a Beheading*, as well as Van Ostaijen's parabolic 'The Prison in Heaven'.

4

Around the absurd I: twentieth-century absurdist practice

Absurdity is divine.

. . .

Let's absurdify life, from east to west. (Fernando Pessoa, *The Book of Disquiet*, c.1912–35)

IN SLEEP, nerves tensed the whole length of my legs. Sleep came from a shifting of belief, the pressure eased, absurdity stepped on my toes. (Antonin Artaud, *Le Pèse-Nerfs*, 1925)

But an absurd attitude, if it is to remain so, must remain aware of its gratuitousness. (Albert Camus, *Le Mythe de Sisyphe*, 1942)

Given that 'absurdism' is a term that, generally speaking at least, has been applied retrospectively, it may not be surprising if we find something of a chronological jumble, as we approach what might be called the mid-century high point of the absurd, between writers and works whom we may now, in our wisdom, choose to regard as absurdist (if, indeed, any such there be in pure form); proto-absurdist; or something else, but at times embracing absurdist qualities.[1] We are, in the main, talking about a disposition rather than anything approaching an overall concrete twentieth-century movement. We are thereby also dealing with what Yuri Lotman considers an organic interaction, or dialogue, between works arising from 'tradition' (defined as 'a *system of texts* preserved in the memory of the given culture or subculture or personality') and those coming into being, in the context of 'contemporaneity' and therefore 'oriented towards the future'; the resulting clash of what Lotman would call cultural codes leads beyond 'passive transmission' to 'the lively generation of new messages' (Lotman, 70–1). At the same time, what Lotman terms the 'semiosphere' (being 'that synchronic semiotic space which fills the border of culture': ibid., 3) somehow directs ideas in the air to those (or, at any rate, to some) not otherwise in cultural contact. The Futurists, and after them the Dadaists and Surrealists, had effectively 'abolished the distinction between art and life' (Bohn, 125). Similarly, of potential relevance to the absurd, one way or another, is the stress Lotman places on 'theatricality' (and '"theatricality" of gesture') as a concept invading life, as well as influencing art; moreover, Surrealist painting, for example, is seen by him as 'the transfer into a purely pictorial sphere of verbal metaphor and purely verbal principles of fantasy', creating a 'rhetorical situation which holds a powerful source for elaborating new meanings' (62).[2] Of course, Surrealist (and, by extension, absurdist) prose writing leaves verbal metaphor and fantasy within a prose form or, as the case may be, repossesses these from the pictorial (or other) sphere.

Textual inclusion of the word 'absurd' ('absurdly', 'absurdity' etc.), even when repeatedly employed, may not constitute any guarantee that a work is to be regarded with justification as fully, or solely, belonging to what we may choose to consider 'literature of the absurd'. Paul Celan 'defined true poetry as an "absurdity"' (Steiner, 2001, 165–6); he would not normally be categorised, though, as an absurdist poet. However, as we have already seen, such usage is likely to provide some indication of that possibility – or, at the very least, of the presence, or the consciousness at some level – of some sort of an absurdist element therein. One text in which the word frequently recurs is the principal prose work composed by Fernando Pessoa.

Fernando Pessoa and the 'pessimistic absurd'

Commonly, at least in recent decades, considered the greatest Portuguese poet since Camões, Pessoa (1888–1935), though born in Lisbon, was educated in South Africa until 1905, when he returned to his native city. He wrote at first in English and French, was involved in several modernistic literary projects, eked out an existence as a freelance commercial translator, and published very little – leaving behind a vast archive (indeed, a huge trunk) of unpublished works which, subsequently edited, have established his reputation. Both the editing and Pessoa's reputation remain an ongoing process. Whether or not in any way stemming from his mixed background, Pessoa developed personal anxieties: over his sanity, his sexuality and his individuality (both personal and literary). The upshot of this lifelong crisis was the creation of a plurality – indeed a plenitude (reaching as many as seventy-five) – of distinct identities, or 'heteronyms' (each accorded an individual biography, personal philosophy and literary style – including one operating as a Futurist poet and another as a classicist).[3] Of immediate concern here, however, is the persona of Bernardo Soares, termed by Pessoa only 'a semi-heteronym', not so much different from, as a 'mere mutilation' of his own personality: 'He's me without my rationalism and emotions' (Pessoa, 2001, 474); 'Soares had irony but not much of a sense of humour' (Zenith: ibid., xi). Under the name of Soares, whom he introduces as a solitary clerk of an unexpected literary bent, and whom he purportedly encountered at a modest Lisbon restaurant, he wrote (from about 1912 until his death) an extraordinarily fragmented yet extensive prose work, published in book-form selection only in 1982 as *Livro do desassossego por Bernardo Soares* (and translated, in edited form, as *The Book of Disquiet*).[4] The question of the degree of association to be made between Pessoa and Soares remains a moot point that need be taken no further here. A lyrical, aphoristic, compelling and sometimes gruelling work, *The Book of Disquiet* may read as a plotless and jumbled autobiographical (or, at least, autodiegetic) novel, and/or as an intimate existential journal. Soares makes his own assessment of his efforts as follows: 'In these random impressions, and with no desire to be other than random, I indifferently narrate my factless autobiography, my lifeless history. These are my Confessions, and if in them I say nothing, it's because I have nothing to say' (Pessoa, 2001, 20–1). Elsewhere he refers to this purported book (of which incompletion is a fundamental principle) as 'a lament' which will stand as 'the saddest book in Portugal' (ibid., 341).

Soares (Pessoa's 'semi-heteronymic' memoirist), perpetually ruminating from the Rua dos Douradores in the Baixa quarter of Lisbon, is capable of coming to what he recognises as 'absurd' conclusions, such as the realisation that 'I'm nobody, absolutely nobody. ... I am the outskirts of some non-existent town, the long-winded prologue to an unwritten book' (Pessoa, 1991, 8). Real people of 'flesh and blood', on the other hand, are a 'metaphysical absurdity' (ibid., 47). 'Everything is absurd', for that matter (112); at least, when thinking, 'everything seems absurd to me' (133) – if that represents any qualification. Nevertheless, or consequently, one may still contrive to aspire to: 'Absurdity, confusion, extinction – anything but life' (47). A deeper aspiration still, and one which 'of course, cannot be', an ambition 'which outdoes in negativity even the void itself', is the desire 'never to have existed at all'; this 'irremediable feeling' is held to be both an original formulation and a 'sinister absurdity' (136). This merely scratches the surface of Soares–Pessoan notions of absurdity.

From the foregoing, it would indeed be a surprise were questions of identity not to feature in 'the created truth' of Pessoa's 'great narrative', plausibly expressed (virtually in a Bakhtinian sense) in 'someone else's literary style' (133). In the first place, there is a proclaimed (at least intellectual, or spiritual) immaturity: 'God created me to be a child and left me to be a child forever' (140). Identity can be multiple, confused, or lacking: 'I created various personalities within myself. I create them constantly'

(62). At the same time, 'no one knew I had been switched at birth'; no one 'recognized me beneath the mask of equality', or 'imagined that there was always another by my side, the real me' (131). Theatrical metaphor underlies what passes for social interaction: the outer world appears one of 'characters constantly rehearsing their roles' – and in 'a drama consisting only of scenery' that is 'facing the wrong way' (15); at an inner level, though: 'I did not act the part. It acted me. I was merely the gestures, never the actor' (99); yet, 'Every day I put on plays inside myself' (203). As a generality, humankind is 'a transient myth, a mannequin wearing the bright costumes of vanity and oblivion' (213); our life is a masked ball, for which 'we're content to put on the lovely clothes that are, after all, what matters in the dance' (being 'like children playing earnest games') – perhaps the 'invisible garment' of philosophy, or the 'mask' of religion (237).

Creating identities and roles, whether in his own or someone else's script, Soares–Pessoa is, as he might well put it himself, nothing if not a dreamer: 'I live the most sordid and ordinary of real lives and the most intense and constant of dream lives' (15); furthermore, 'I'm not merely a dreamer, I am exclusively a dreamer' (203). Dream is a dynamic part of the identity-role creation process:

> Every dream, as soon as it is dreamed, is immediately embodied by another person who dreams it instead of me.
>   In order to create, I destroyed myself; I have externalized so much of my inner life that even inside I now exist only externally. I am the living stage across which various actors pass acting out different plays. (Pessoa, 1991, 62)

Logically from this it might well follow that 'it's the dreamer who is the true man of action' (188). 'We are asleep', we might now not be surprised to hear, 'and this life is a dream, not in any metaphorical or poetic sense, but really a dream' (182). Such glorification of the figure of the dreamer ('I never tried to be anything other than a dreamer': 194) would certainly have struck a chord with Dostoevsky (especially the early Dostoevsky of *White Nights* and the late Dostoevsky of *The Dream of a Ridiculous Man*), while the suggested ontological status of the dream recalls Lewis Carroll. Detail from nature, weather, and landscape will enter a dreamed poem ('faultless until I try to write it down'), as the whole creative process, by extension, embraces or identifies with God (who is, as we shall see, alternately denied, credited, or doubted) as the 'supreme dreamer' (256).

Pessoa (or the Pessoa of *The Book of Disquiet*, at least) is to be regarded as the supreme (prose) poet of insomnia, and the poet of tedium. Monotony ('just the monotony of being me': 10), banality and sadness are among his watchwords, in an overall ambience of disquiet or anguish.

Existence has to be monotonized 'in order to rid it of monotony'; indeed: 'One must make the everyday so anodyne that the slightest incident proves entertaining' (20). With living reduced to being 'a metaphysical mistake on the part of matter, an oversight on the part of inaction' (114), the consequence is insomnia and 'periods of great stagnation': 'I stagnate in my very soul', and 'I suffer a suspension of will, emotion and thought that lasts for days at a time' (68). Feeling 'no desire to sleep, only the memory of that desire, ... no nostalgia, only disquiet', eventually 'I recover from an illness I never had' (117). Then follows the exhaustion of tedium ('thinking without thinking': 118), which is 'like being possessed by a negative demon, bewitched by nothing at all' (119); this will lead such a dreamer as Bernardo Soares to what he calls 'an aesthetics of indifference' (186–7). Whence this tedium? Perhaps, basically, it's 'an expression of a dissatisfaction in our innermost soul not to have been given something to believe in' (120): a sense of loss and absence, stemming from 'the destructive work of previous generations' which had deprived us of religious security, any anchor of morality, and political stability, leaving just 'uncertainty and the pain of that uncertainty' (206).

Such existential and aesthetic contemplation thus appears to be imbued with an out and out pessimism, but a pessimism of the absurd, in that it is expressly differentiated from that of Vigny, whose reasoned view of 'life as a tragedy ... is an exaggerated, uncomfortable attitude to take' (209); moreover, this narrator can declare: 'I'm not a pessimist. I'm sad' (Pessoa, 2001, 116). Far more comforting, then, one has to assume, is his nihilism: 'For me life is an inn where I must stay until the carriage from the abyss calls to collect me' (Pessoa, 1991, 209). At the same time, exercising the full aplomb of absurdist contradiction, he can equally express the following aspiration: 'To create at least a new pessimism, a new negativity, so that we can have the illusion that something of us – albeit something bad – will remain!' (Pessoa, 2001, 388). Sadness or pessimism: one takes one's choice.

The logic of the foregoing points to an uncompromising sense of insignificance: 'nothing is of any importance' (Pessoa, 1991, 24). In a universe of 'nothing but lightly mixed shadow and dust', 'the dresses run up by seamstresses have as much value as whole kingdoms; the blonde plaits of children are swept up in the same mortal jig as sceptres that once symbolized empires' (65). The individual (epitomised by his image in the office photograph: 'I look like a rather dull Jesuit') suffers a 'final relegation to the rubbish heap' (7–8); his life, imagined as 'some brightly coloured scrap of litter', is destined for 'the dustpan, amongst the crumbs and crusts of reality itself'; the gods, who alone know the ultimate aim of the pointless activity of life or office, 'continue their conversations above the sweeping, indifferent to these incidents in the world below' (12). 'Perhaps there are supreme forces, the gods or devils of the Truth in whose shadows we wander, for whom I am just a lustrous fly resting for a moment before their gaze.' This Shakespearean speculation ('A clichéd remark?') prompts transmutation into a fly and a glance at the ceiling, 'to check there was no supreme being wielding a ruler to squash me' (43–4).

The gods, the Gods and God make various appearances, or non-appearances, in *The Book of Disquiet*. At an early point comes what must be one of the most overwhelmingly nihilistic passages in twentieth-century prose, following a protracted dismissal of the self as a 'nothing ... surrounded by the great nothing':

> And it is as if hell itself were laughing within me but, instead of the human touch of diabolical laughter, there's the mad croak of the dead universe, the circling cadaver of physical space, the end of all worlds drifting blackly in the wind, misshapen, anachronistic, without the God who created it, without God himself who spins in the dark of darks, impossible, unique, everything. (Pessoa, 1991, 9)

Similarly: 'The absence of a true God is become the empty corpse of the vast sky and the closed soul' (74), while the soul itself is dubbed 'an abyss of viscous darkness' (236). Research, or 'futile meditation', however, might yet throw up alternatives:

> Perhaps they'll discover that what we call God, and which is clearly on another level from that of logic and spatial and temporal reality, is just one of our ways of being, one of the ways we experience ourselves in another dimension of existence. (Pessoa, 1991, 172)

On the other hand (and there are shades here almost of Tertullian!), at one stage anyway, 'I considered that God, because unlikely, just might exist and might therefore deserve to be adored' (207). Expression, however, is liable to depend on emotion. 'If it is a clear, irrevocable emotion, I speak of the Gods' ('a consciousness of the multiple world'). On the other hand, in the case of a deep emotion, 'I speak, naturally, of God' ('a consciousness of the singleness of the world'); the emotion as thought bespeaks 'Fate'; in the end, though, 'the actual rhythm of the phrase' will govern the polytheistic or monotheistic choice (247): 'The Gods are simply a function of style' (248). The masquerade of human life, however, continues, 'dancing to the sound of the great orchestra of the stars, beneath the scornful, distant gaze of the organizers of the show'. But as for the reason behind 'the illusion they created for us', and why it should exist: 'That, of course, even they do not know' (238). No wonder, we might now say, that Soares 'always thought of metaphysics as a prolonged form of latent madness' (247).

'We are death' (182) – we, 'the grandchildren of Destiny and the stepchildren of God, who married Eternal Night when she was left a widow by Chaos, our true father' (104).[5] 'Death ennobles and clothes the poor absurd cadaver in unaccustomed finery' (200), bringing an 'admit-

tedly' unsought freedom (here defined as 'the possibility of isolation').
Slavery–freedom is one of the oppositions set up in this text (e.g. 10; 200).
The human condition, in the desperate universe as it is conceived by
Soares–Pessoa, constitutes 'a prison sentence' (15) in an escape-proof
'infinite prison' (74; 122). The prisoner of futility, afflicted by tedium
(here 'the physical sensation of chaos'), cannot anticipate any of the possible alleviations conceivable to the normal prisoner, for 'the walls of an
infinite cell cannot crumble and bury us, since they do not exist, nor can
we claim as proof of our existence the pain caused by handcuffs no one
has placed round our wrists' (123). The jailer, as ever, is time ('the banal
fact of the existence of time': 28) and the presence of a perpetual present
tense ('I live always in the present. I know nothing of the future and no
longer have a past': 60–1), accompanied by 'a nostalgia for the anonymous, prolix, unfathomable present' (177), and even 'nostalgia for the
possibility of one day feeling nostalgia, regardless of how absurd that
nostalgia may seem' (226). The early morning stirrings of life in the city
give rise to the kind of disquiet that would be occasioned by invitations
'to an examination or an execution', for: 'Each day that dawns I will be
judged. And the eternal condemned man in me clings to the bed as if to
the lost mother' (86). Subject to prison sentence and death sentence, 'we
will live out the brief interlude that the absentmindedness of our executioners commutes into a temporary stay of execution' (217).

Negativity as a motif in Pessoa may scarcely need further stressing. 'All
is nothing and in the atrium of the Invisible, whose door swings open only
to reveal another closed door beyond' (65) is a statement that provides a
fair illustration of Soares–Pessoan philosophy. If possible, there are
sentences that seem even bleaker: 'All around me is the abstract, naked
universe, composed of nothing but the negation of night' (47). The
conclusion (at least, of the de Lancastre–Costa version), meditating on the
possible contingency of existence, ends:

> I think this because this is all nothing. Nothing, nothing, just part of the
> night and the silence and of whatever emptiness, negativity and inconstancy
> I share with them, the space that exists between me and me, a thing mislaid
> by some god ... (Pessoa, 1991, 262)

And yet even *The Book of Disquiet* includes the very occasional crumb of
something approaching if not exactly positivity, then a slight variation on
all but ubiquitous gloom. The inconsistency of the divided self is one
natural part of the Pessoan persona. Relegation to the rubbish bin ('along
with the crumbs of what remains of Christ's body') involves an inability
'even to imagine what will come after, under what stars; but I know there
will be an "after"' (12). There is, at least once, a hint of resignation: 'We
should be content with the incomprehensibility of the universe'; this
comes, however, by way of the bizarre dialectic that 'the desire to under-

stand makes us less than human, for to be human is to know that one does not understand' (247).

Soares–Pessoa is, then, a master of paradox (the contemplation of 'a deserted street with people in it': 181; 'Life is as full of paradoxes as roses are of thorns': 256) and a tactician of self-contradiction. He is also an astute practitioner of the metafictional:

> Some days are like whole philosophies in themselves that suggest to us new interpretations of life, marginal notes full of the acutest criticism in the book of our universal destiny. I feel that this is one such day. The foolish thought strikes me that my heavy eyes and my empty head are the absurd pencil shaping the letters of that futile and profound statement. (Pessoa, 1991, 97)

The universe is normally to be construed as absurd in its incoherence: 'The vast unconscious network that lies behind all actions seems an absurd illusion, with no plausible coherence, nothing' (203). The sad and icy moonlight 'seems to reveal everything and that everything is just shadows intermingled with dim light, false intervals, erratically absurd, the incoherent mutterings of the visible world' (250). This is not, however, Soares's last word on the subject, as he declares: 'What I would like to create is the apotheosis of a new incoherence that could become the negative constitution of the new anarchy of souls' (256). Absurdist statements do not come much plainer than that! At the same time, though, Soares can insist on precision in definition of the spiral ('a circle that rises upwards but never closes upon itself'; or 'a virtual circle which repeats itself as it rises but never reaches fulfilment': 257–8).

> To say things! To know how to say things! To know how to exist through the written voice and the intellectual image! That's what life is about: the rest is just men and women, imagined loves and fictitious vanities, excuses born of poor digestion and forgetting, people squirming beneath the great abstract boulder of a meaningless blue sky, the way insects do when you lift a stone. (Pessoa, 1991, 258)

It would be difficult to find a more vivid illustration of the absurdist paradox in discursive practice.

We have already noted a Dostoevskian (and a Carrollian) chime with the stress on dream and dreamer figure; the implicit conservatism of reform of the inner being as the only worthwhile political (or a-political) tactic (199) is also a Dostoevskian trait. Among other affinities that may be remarked are the compassion evinced for 'the unreality of the humble figures' and 'minor characters' of dreamworld (195), which is close to Gogol; the metaphor of human rubbish is to be found in Van Ostaijen and in Kharms (who also used 'turning a corner' as a metaphor for death);[6] and a number of details in the Soares narrative could bracket Pessoa with Nabokov (not, of course, that there can be any suggestion that Nabokov would have known Pessoa).[7]

As a coda to this section on Pessoa, mention should be made first of the Italian novelist and literary scholar Antonio Tabucchi. Tabucchi has done much to promote Pessoa in Italy, having translated him and written profusely on him.[8] In addition, however, and far more unusually, Tabucchi is the author of a surreal novel written in Portuguese, entitled *Requiem* (1991), which may be considered, in part at least, a kind of homage to Pessoa. Pessoa (himself, by name), Bernardo Soares and *The Book of Disquiet* are alluded to in the first chapter ('the Lame Lottery Seller who was always bothering Bernardo Soares'), while in the final chapter the ghost of Pessoa appears as the narrator's 'Guest' for dinner.[9] Secondly, the Portuguese novelist José Saramago's *The Year of the Death of Ricardo Reis* (*O Ano da Morte de Ricardo Reis*, 1984) features the return to Lisbon from Brazil of the eponymous Reis (one of Pessoa's main poetic identities) shortly after the death of Pessoa, and includes ghostly interchanges between the two.[10]

Antonin Artaud and the 'cruelty' of the absurd

In the early 1920s Antonin Artaud (1896–1948), as a budding poet and actor from Marseilles, immersed himself (a bout of mental disturbance already behind him) in the Paris of Dada and Surrealism. In addition to making himself known in the literary magazines, he worked as a stage and film actor, and then as a director in the forefront of the theatrical avant-garde, becoming widely known for his criticism and publicism, and subsequently too for his broadcasts and drawings. He was the sometime friend, or close acquaintance, of Breton, Cocteau, Gide, Picasso, Adamov and many another prominent cultural figure (he claimed once to have brawled with Hitler in a Berlin café: Barber, 51). His collected works and fragmentary writings amount to twenty-five volumes. He wrote poetry, prose poems, film scenarios, plays, essays and a plenitude of vibrant letters (forming a remarkably large part of his *oeuvre*, in the view of Todorov: 1977, 208).[11] He briefly directed the Surrealist Research Centre; he founded the Alfred Jarry Theatre; and he subsequently launched a 'Theatre of Cruelty' project which was to prove immensely influential in the development of drama through the second half of the twentieth century. In Esslin's view, Artaud 'forms the bridge between the pioneers and [the] Theatre of the Absurd', for which he was 'one of the main inspi-rations' (Esslin, *Th. Abs.*, 385; 433).[12] His arguments on the issue of drugs and his polemics against psychiatry are as relevant today as at the time they were made (as with 'cruelty', and indeed a whole range of concepts and issues, the parallel here is with Witkiewicz).

Susan Sontag dubs Artaud 'one of the last great exemplars of the heroic period of literary modernism'; and yet it is difficult to disagree with her bald assessment that 'Both in his work and in his life, Artaud failed' (Sontag, 'Artaud', in Artaud *SW*, xix). It would be hard to point to anything that Artaud did as an unqualified success. Socially and professionally 'difficult', he fell out with almost all friends and associates; he soon split, or was 'expelled', from the Surrealists;[13] his cinematic and theatrical projects either never materialised or met with critical and commercial failure; he required regular sessions of drug detoxification in order to work at all (while at the same time needing regular drug intoxication, principally opium, to even think about working: for him, both the absence and the presence of opium are equally necessary: see *SW*, 339); he disastrously acted out the role of an avenging harlequin (Fool, or 'Enraged One') on his visit to Ireland[14] and, as a consequence, spent nearly nine years of his creative prime (from 1937 to 1946) interned in asylums; his final grand gesture of cultural protest (provocatively entitled *To Have Done with the Judgment of God*) was banned by the chief of French radio the day before it was due to be broadcast; a month later he was dead.[15] Accounts of Artaud incarcerated sound at times almost like a rerun of the experiences of the madman-poet protagonist of Witkiewicz's quintessential absurdist drama, *The Madman and the Nun* (*Wariat i zakonnica*, 1923: see Witkiewicz, 1989).

Undoubtedly, in general terms, Artaud's theory had a greater impact than his practice. Sontag calls him 'one of the great, daring mapmakers of consciousness *in extremis*', one of those 'exceptional cases at the limit of "writing"' – Sade being another (*SW*, lvii). Derrida (234) declares that Theatre of Cruelty 'announces the limit of representation'. Certainly, in terms of anguished poetic extremism and theatricality of life, Artaud seems to belong to a category beyond earlier Romantic and decadent stereotypes, beyond the Futurist-Dadaists who immediately preceded him, and beyond such of his contemporaries in absurdism as Pessoa and Kharms. More than with almost any other figure one can think of, Artaud's work and his life seem indistinguishable, as do his periods of apparent sanity and alleged insanity. Artaud was quite aware within his own writing of this phenomenon. In his historical-biographical novel on the Roman emperor *Heliogabalus* (or Marcus Aurelius Antoninus, AD 204–22), to which subject he was drawn by its qualities of 'murder, incest, debauchery and an anarchic ridicule for the powers of government' (Barber, 60), Artaud paralleled 'the imminent danger of assassination throughout Heliogabalus's short reign ... with his own permanent sense of coming catastrophe'; in addition, Stephen Barber tells us (61), he 'inserted himself into his own narrative of sexual excess', for: 'Theatre in Heliogabalus's time takes place in life, not on the stage'. 'The life of Heliogabalus is theatrical', wrote Artaud, 'But his theatrical way of conceiving existence strives to create a true magic of the real. Indeed, I do not conceive of theater as separate from existence' (*SW*, 348). As far as

Artaud was concerned (in one of his last letters: *SW*, 582–3), the duty of the poet and the writer 'is not to shut himself up like a coward in a text, … but on the contrary to go into the world to jolt, to attack the mind of the public'.

Nevertheless, we are here largely concerned with the ideas, and the writings, that brought Artaud into at least some sort of proximity with absurdism. 'Ideas are the voids of the body', he would write in 1946 (Barber, 26). With reference to the Balinese theatre (which, along with the early Marx Brothers films and Lucas van den Leyden's painting *The Daughters of Lot* in the Louvre, was a strong influence on Artaud's development in the early 1930s), he wrote:

> This intellectual space, this psychic interplay, this silence ridden with thoughts which exists between the elements of a written sentence, is here traced in the space of the stage, between the parts of the body, the air, and the perspectives of a certain number of cries, colors, and movements. (Artaud, *SW* 223)

Here in a single sentence, Artaud contrives to encapsulate many of his principal preoccupations: with the mind, with the body (for the substances and orifices of which he had a strongly Rabelaisian obsession), with the textual semiotic, with theatrical space, sound and gesture – or what has more recently come to be known as 'body language'.[16] The same Artaud, though, could proclaim (in capital letters, or by manifesto) that 'all writing is garbage' (*SW*, 85), or 'pigshit' ('*Toute l'écriture est de la cochonnerie*'), moving towards 'a furious silence that could still be utterly expressive' (Barber, 27). Such an apparent (and an absurd) contradiction persists throughout Artaud's career. Early on, he could write: 'Well, it is my peculiar weakness and my *absurdity* to want to write no matter what the cost, and to express myself' (*SW*, 36; the emphasis is Artaud's). In the final period (now himself prematurely aged and toothless), he would declare: 'All true language / is incomprehensible, / like the chatter / of a beggar's teeth' (*SW*, 549).[17] By this time, he was expressing himself, in part at least, in a diction not far removed from the *zaum´* of the Russian Futurists.[18]

As may be observed with many an absurdist or proto-absurdist, Artaud propagates a series of dualities in persistent opposition: body with mind; art with either anti-art or with life; silence with language (and flesh with language); representation with reality; and rational with irrational – to list but a few. And yet he was to strive, briefly by adopting the Surrealist mentality, and then through the agency of art, and more specifically taking the model of theatre, somehow to achieve a 'unified, non-dualistic consciousness' (Sontag, in *SW*, xxxv). Dichotomies may also be (or become) contiguities. This process might be effected through performance and meditation, through the medium or the exploitation of fire and blood, sound or blows (silence, scream or incantation), movement and dance, or by a sense of magic and stylisation. Characters in Artaud's theatre are 'signs' (Brée, 225), or 'hieroglyphs', utilising the rediscovered notion of 'a kind of unique language halfway between gesture and thought' (SW, 242), there being, in any case, 'no more than a gesture still separating us from chaos' (224). Indeed, in his view, 'the highest art is the one which brings us closest to Chaos' (cited by Todorov, 1977, 217).

Artaud was beset, at least at certain times, with a by now familiar identity problem. Between asylums, in 1943, it was noted that 'he spoke of Antonin Artaud as though he were a stranger'; having insisted for some years that he was 'Antonin Nalpas' (the name of a distant cousin: 'Nalpas' being his mother's maiden name), he reverted to 'Artaud' only after heavy electric shock treatment (which struck him as 'a multitude of little deaths': Barber, 112; 161), in a period that was 'probably that of the deepest fluctuation and loss of identity in Artaud's life' (ibid., 105; 110). In an asylum text called 'Surrealism and the End of the Christian Era' (of 1945, but which has survived only in part), he 'writes of his realization, at the age of eight, that his identity was to be threatened by malicious powers, illness and cacophony all through his life' (Barber, 115). The phenomenon of the double affects or afflicts Artaud on levels of psychology and of art. His best-known book (published in 1938) is entitled *The Theatre and Its Double*, which, in the view of John Killinger, 'anticipated and enunciated practically every essential characteristic in the theory and repertoire of the later writers of the absurd' (Killinger, 7). Again it is the oriental theatre which supplies 'metaphysicians of natural disorder' (SW, 225) who effect 'a mental alchemy' (226), and amid 'the very pantomime of combat ... is the Double, who struts about, indulging the childishness of his schoolboy sarcasms' (227).[19] Beset by the torments of demons and *daimons*, the 'hideous image' of 'forces in the Void' (427), Artaud was diagnosed as a 'former drug addict, suffering from chronic hallucinatory psychosis, with luxuriant, polymorphous, delirious ideas (doubling of the personality, bizarre metaphysical system ...)'.[20]

Artaud's own diagnosis is revealed in a letter he wrote in 1945 to his then psychiatrist, accusing his predecessors of 'treating me like a madman and abusing me on account of a gesture, an attitude, a manner of talking and thinking which were in life proper to the man of the theater, the poet and the writer I used to be' (SW, 437). He then and subsequently installed himself in a pantheon of kindred artistic spirits suppressed (directly or indirectly) at the hands of, as the case may be, bourgeois society, religion, the police or the state – for fear that their art would escape 'and overthrow reality' (SW, 471): this list would include Baudelaire, Lautréamont, Nerval, Nietzsche, Poe, Villon and van Gogh.[21] Throughout the prose of Lautréamont, Artaud discerned 'an epileptic tremor of the Word' (quoted from Calasso, 2001, 92).

As Sontag puts it, 'Artaud's criterion of spectacle is sensory violence'; he wants a theatre of 'emotional violence' employing an 'aesthetics of shock' (*SW*, xxxii; xxxiv). Consistently, Artaud's 'new concept of cruelty' would proclaim: 'The theatre is the scaffold, the gallows, the trenches, the crematorium oven or the lunatic asylum'; 'cruelty' equals 'massacred bodies' (Barber, 132). Inspired in part by the painting of Lucas van Leyden, the title of Artaud's theoretical opus 'will account for all the theatre's doubles which I believe I have found over the years: metaphysics, the plague, cruelty' (Todorov, 1977, 213). Contemporary theatre, apart from all its other failings, has 'lost the sense of true humor and of the physical and anarchic, dissociative power of comedy' (*SW*, 235). Theatre of Cruelty, Artaud writes, 'means a theater that is difficult and cruel first of all for myself' and a theatre of that 'terrible and necessary cruelty which things can practice on us. We are not free', he declares: 'And the sky can still fall on our heads' (*SW*, 256).[22] In his final phase, he was planning a so-called 'theater of blood' (585).[23] The aim is absolutely not, however, for the audience 'to indulge outside the theater in ideas of war, rioting, or random murders', although Artaud admits that there exists a risk; given the right 'style and the purity with which things are done', however, the violent theatrical gesture should serve to produce 'sublimation' (259). This hint of moralistic intent is seized on by Sontag, who insists on 'the purity of his moral purpose' (*SW* xxiv); similarly, Killinger (161–2) talks of 'the therapeutic cruelty of making people face up to their existential situation'. Nevertheless, Artaud has a metaphysical agenda, even a cosmology, to advance as well. In a letter of 1932 he writes (*SW*, 303):

> I use the word cruelty in the cosmic sense of rigor, implacable necessity, in the gnostic sense of the vortex of life which devours the shadows, in the sense of that pain outside of whose implacable necessity life could not go on. Good is willed, it is the result of an action; evil is permanent. The hidden god, when he creates, is obeying the cruel necessity of creation which is imposed even on him, and he has no choice but to create, and hence to accept, at the center of the willed vortex of good, a nucleus of evil which is more and more reduced, more and more *devoured*. And the theater in the sense of continuous creation, the entire magical action submits to this necessity.

In terms of theatrical practice, cruelty 'inhabits or rather *produces* a nontheological space' (Derrida, 235). A Nietzschean negative theology and a Gnostic sensibility are here seen to be of the essence: 'Founded on an exacerbation of dualisms (body-mind, matter-spirit, evil-good, dark-light), Gnosticism promises the abolition of all dualisms' (Sontag, *SW*, xlvi).[24] No wonder Sontag calls Artaud 'a shaman' (lviii).

Artaud would stress (shades again of the Tertullian tradition) that 'it's the Unbelievable which is the truth' (Barber, 94). In a written text, he could proclaim: 'I never use words and I never even use letters'; his language now would be expressed 'by blows and by screams' ('Beat and Hammer', 1946: quoted by Barber, 133). He could also put on his one-man theatrical performance (*The Story Lived by Artaud-Mômo*, 1947, of which accounts, but no recording, survive), delivered to a somewhat stunned audience as a combination of poetry reading, personal rant, unexpected silences, 'wild improvisation', denial of theatre (notwith-standing the fact of its theatrical presentation), and 'denial of death'.[25] In similar vein to Pessoa, Artaud speculates on what he calls 'anterior suicide':

> a suicide which made us retrace our steps, but to the other side of existence, not to the side of death. This is the only suicide that would have value for me. I have no appetite for death, I have an appetite *for not existing*, for never having fallen into this interlude of imbecilities, abdications, renuncia-tions, and obtuse encounters which is the self of Antonin Artaud (*SW*, 103)

Dating from his days in Surrealism, Artaud refers to 'we who aspire to a certain surreal eternity', we, 'the real shadows of ourselves', whose 'atti-tude of absurdity and death is the attitude of greatest receptivity' (*SW*, 103–4). In a 'Manifesto in Clear Language' (also of 1925), he upholds 'the logic of Illogic' and 'the signification of chaos': 'My lucid unreason is not afraid of chaos' (108). Artaud admits 'total pessimism': 'But a certain form of pessimism', he argues, 'carries with it its own form of lucidity'; this is 'the lucidity of despair, the lucidity of senses that are exacerbated and as if on the edge of the abyss' (*SW* 145). 'Chaos', 'abyss', 'the void' and 'zero' are terms frequently to be found among the expressions of Artaud. '[T]he great secret of Indian culture / is to bring the world back to zero', writes the late Artaud (545). As for the deity, to whom Artaud customarily referred with a small letter (as in his banned broadcast, *Pour en finir avec le jugement de dieu*) – a temporary bout of ardent Catholicism in the asylum notwithstanding:

> Is God a being?
> If he is one, he is shit.
> If he is not one
> he does not exist.
> But he does not exist,
> except as the void that approaches with all its forms
> whose most perfect image
> is the advance of an incalculable group of crab lice.
> (*SW*, 561–2)

An early and representative indication of Artaud's elemental and absur-dist proclivities is provided by his short play, or scenario, *The Spurt of Blood* (*Le Jet de sang*), included in an amalgam of disparate materials entitled *The Umbilicus of Limbo* (*L'Ombilic des Limbes*, 1925). This brief dramatic work (performed in London in 1963 by an experimental company under Peter Brook and Charles Marowitz) is thought to be a parody of Armand Salacrou's *La Boule de verre*, and/or of Apollinaire's *Les Mamelles de Tirésias* (*SW*, 604). Its inane dialogue and anachronistic jumble of characters pale into insignificance against wild stage effects and extremist ingredients of blasphemy and obscenity. The London production 'was played with writhing actors on a simple platform and a flight of steps, and a huge "hand of God" descended from above and gushed blood' (Styan, 112). The scenario (see *SW*, 72–6; also in Cardullo and Knopf, 378–81) calls for: cosmic disturbances ('Heaven has gone mad': 73); living flesh, masonry and various creatures to fall; an interchangeability between the dead and the living; extravagant noise, movement and shape-shifting. In the train of an illogical sequence of violent actions, the surreal 'hand of God' is bitten by a 'Bawd' (*La Maquerelle*), and a great jet of 'blood' shoots across the stage. Here already, and in outrageous form, are what Barber (163) summarises as the essentials of Artaud, 'the burning facts of existence: the body, the gesture, death, sexuality, and language'. Artaud was already the prophet of 'a wild and ruthless theatre' (Esslin, *Th. Abs.*, 356) that was to be created in his wake.[26] It was, for instance, now but a short step for Brook to Peter Weiss's *Marat/Sade* (London performance, 1965), a play apparently written and produced according to a combination of the theories (appropriately enough) of Artaud, but also of Brecht (Styan, 112–13).[27] Within his own lifetime, it was rather 'the testing of Artaud's existence' that 'became his creation' (Barber, 163).

As a coda, there remain two further particularities of Artaud's life and creativity that deserve, from our present perspective, brief comment. The first is his bizarre entanglement with the work of Lewis Carroll. While in the asylum at Rodez, Artaud was given, by his electroshock specialist Dr Gaston Ferdière, Carroll to translate as 'therapy' and worked on the Humpty Dumpty chapter of *Through the Looking Glass*; since his knowledge of English was poor, Artaud availed himself of literal translations from the asylum chaplain to make his eventual 'free adaptations' (Barber, 109). This work was revised for publication in 1947, bearing the subtitle 'An Anti-Grammatical Attempt Against Lewis Carroll', whom he claimed to have 'always detested' (*SW*, 647). By this time, he had arrived at the conclusion that 'Jabberwocky' was 'nothing but a sugar-coated and lifeless plagiarism of a work written by me, which has been spirited away so successfully that I myself hardly know what is in it' (*SW*, 451) – pillaged by Carroll across time. Artaud's 'dislike' of Carroll, and of 'Jabberwocky' in particular ('the work of a eunuch'), is stressed in his letters of 1945 to Henri Parisot (see *SW*, 446–51), in which Carroll is accused of 'anal infantilism' and 'wanting to penetrate a void which did not want to be possessed'. Carroll is a mere 'opportunist' who produced 'the fecality of an English snob who forces the obscene in himself into curls and corkscrews as if with hot tongs'. Why this antagonism, and especially to 'Jabberwocky'? Deleuze, who devoted a chapter of his *The Logic of Sense* to the matter, sees the contrast between Carroll and Artaud as one of surface against depth.[28] In the fragment of 'Jabberwocky' which he did translate, may be recognised, 'with horror, ... the language of schizophrenia' (Deleuze, 84). For his part, Deleuze 'would not give a page of Antonin Artaud for all of Carroll; Artaud is the only person to have experienced absolute depth in literature, and to have discovered a "vital" body and its prodigious language, as he says, through suffering'.[29]

One antecedent, or proto-absurdist, with whom Artaud has what at first sight might seem unexpected affinities (for all the obvious differences between them in temperament and milieu) is Nikolai Gogol.[30] A great believer in devils and a fearer of demons (especially those of sexuality), Gogol lived his own peculiar version of a theatricalised life, adopted and pursued wide cultural (and indeed theatrical) activities, and came to a not entirely dissimilar premature end. Gogol's fictional depiction of a disturbed mental state (which may at some level have prefigured his own subsequent development) in *Notes of a Madman* (regarded as bearing psychological authenticity by later specialists) seems almost uncannily close to Artaud's more extreme asylum torments. Artaud's writings to his mother (a letter of 1941 is quoted by Barber, 104) are reminiscent of the appeals to his mother of Gogol's protagonist near the increasingly incoherent end of his 'diary'; the statement 'all the children of France are eating in my own belly', for instance, has a similar ring to Poprishchin's assertion that only noses live on the moon. Poprishchin was subjected to forced cold baths, Artaud to electroshocks; the former (believing himself in Spain) suffered the torments of 'Inquisitors', the latter withstood the torments of psychiatrists (including Jacques Lacan); a demented Gogol, years later in life, was driven in effect to suicide by a malevolent 'confessor' and killed off by blood-sucking leaches. Gogol (his in many ways obscurantist perspectives notwithstanding) was, at least in Artaud's terms, 'suicided by society' and fully entitled therefore to a place in Artaud's pantheon of suppressed artistic paragons.

Camus and the Dostoevsky connection

We have already, of course (in Chapter 1), encountered Camus's *The Myth of Sisyphus* (1942) as a fundamental treatise of the absurd. In the same year he published his short novel *L'Étranger* (translated as *The Outsider* or, in North America, as *The Stranger*). In one view at least, although Camus 'thought of himself as a philosopher of the absurd', his more significant contribution was artistic: 'to have created a fictional image of it' (Showalter, 5).[31] His 'absurd' perception of existence as meaninglessness was ostensibly similar to that of the existentialists; however, in denying that he was an existentialist, as he did in 1945 (Thody, 54), Camus had in mind in particular the Christian existentialism (of Tertullian, Pascal, Kierkegaard, Dostoevsky and Shestov) – the leap into religious faith that entailed 'philosophical suicide' (ibid., 31). In the face of 'the impasse in our secularized modern world that any philosophy of the absolute, or the whole, will come up against', Camus wishes to turn, paradoxically as it may seem, towards happiness, rather than out-and-out nihilism (Brée, 274): living within, or in reconciliation to, the absurd.

Sisyphus eventually 'concludes that all is well' (Myth, 111), while even Mersault, 'the outsider', under sentence of death, recognises a kind of happiness, having dispatched the chaplain and 'laid myself open for the first time to the benign indifference of the world' (Outsider, 117).[32] Sartre in 1943 linked these two works of the previous year by Camus, saying that The Outsider was 'composed about the absurd and against the absurd' (quoted by Showalter, 13; see also Thody, 29–32). The later Camus's pseudonymous Jean-Baptiste Clamence, the 'judge-penitent' discourser of The Fall (La Chute, 1956), too has 'found the happiness that suits [him]' (Fall, 103): 'I am happy unto death!', he declares (105).

Even before The Outsider, in his first novel, A Happy Death (La Mort heureuse, written 1936–38 and published posthumously in 1971), which – featuring Mersault as its protagonist – may be seen as a kind of dry run for The Outsider, Camus proffers a scene in which the death of the crippled murder victim Zagreus is prefigured – or rather, indeed, implicitly invited. Zagreus, when depressed, was wont to fondle his revolver, in anticipation of 'discovering the absurd feasibility of death, ... sticking his tongue into [the gun barrel] and sucking out an impossible happiness' (Happy Death, 51). Later, having fled to Prague, Mersault chances to witness a striking epiphany of the absurd that of itself seems a somehow Dostoevskian moment. Approaching a restaurant, he is halted by a man lying, 'arms folded, head fallen on the left cheek'; bystanders are waiting and speaking in hushed tones:

> But one man in shirtsleeves, his jacket over his arm, hat pushed back on his head, was performing a kind of wild dance around the body, his gestures emphatic and disturbing. Overhead, the faint glow from the nearby restaurant. The man tirelessly dancing, the body with its folded arms, the calm spectators, the ironic contrast and the inexplicable silence – here at last, combining contemplation and innocence, among the rather oppressive interplay of light and shadow, was a moment of equilibrium past which it seemed to Mersault that everything would collapse into madness. (Camus, Happy Death, 77)

A volunteered explanation for this bizarre and solitary dance of death (its dramatic combination of image, sound, light, movement and emotion, surely deserving of Artaud's approbation – and, for that matter, that of Nietzsche[33]), which is omitted from the revised text, may be found in the novel's 'Notes and Variants' (ibid., 192–3).

Camus himself wrote of composing a 'cycle of the Absurd' in his note-books (Brée, 273), his following novel The Plague (La Peste, 1947) being 'also a novel about the absurd' (Thody, 45). Leaving aside The Myth of Sisyphus ('described in a subtitle as an "essay on the absurd"': Thody, 29), Camus's fiction certainly illustrates his celebrated confrontation between an absence of meaning (in the natural world) and a desire for meaning (on the part of a human being). It thus fits, for instance, Edward Albee's definition of the absurd as 'man's attempts to make sense for himself out of his senseless position in a world which makes no sense' (quoted by Killinger, 2–3). One might, in any case, wish to add to Albee's formula an additional essential ingredient of grim humour. This last, however, is a property seldom discerned in the work of Camus (to his displeasure: Thody, 87), and especially not in the cases of the earlier novels (The Fall is perhaps another matter); however, the quality of irony, which Camus also chose to stress, may well offer more promising ground for investigation. The trial and sentencing procedure of The Outsider (inviting comparison with a range of treatments from Dostoevsky and Carroll, to Kafka and Nabokov[34]) has been seen as 'a symbolic distortion' (Showalter, 47); incidentally, The Myth of Sisyphus contains an Appendix entitled 'Hope and The Absurd in the Work of Franz Kafka' (Myth, 112–24). The Outsider may also be read to involve 'spiritual problems raised by the scapegoat' (Showalter, 56) and to prompt serious questions of colonial and racial attitude.[35]

In Caligula, his play written in 1938, Camus follows, in the footsteps of Artaud, into the cruel and absurd extremities of Imperial Rome. The protagonist, aspiring beyond a Dostoevskian policy of 'all is permitted', endeavours to prosecute 'a desire for the impossible' and is consequently frustrated by his inability, total political omnipotence notwithstanding, 'to tamper with the scheme of things' (Caligula, 40; 48). '[W]hat use is the amazing power that's mine', he asks, 'if I can't have the sun set in the east, if I can't reduce the sum of suffering and make an end of death?' (ibid., 48). Caligula literally wants the moon. An archetypal exponent of the theatricality of life, he dresses as Venus or performs a grotesque ballet between giving the orders for executions; his atrocities and debaucheries constitute his own unique poem: 'I don't need to make a work of art; I live it', he declares (95).[36]

The opposition to Caligula's completely manic Caesarism[37] comes less from any moral objection to drastic excess than from indignation at the derisive treatment he metes out to his entourage. The arch-conspirator

Cherea, however, is driven by a 'very reasonable fear of that inhuman vision in which my life means no more than a speck of dust' (54) – in other words, a dread of the absurd. At least a semblance of order and predictability in the world order is required to window-dress a senseless universe. Caligula, 'converting his [albeit logical] philosophy into corpses' (53), is fuelled by a 'devastating scorn' (102) as he provokes his own violent overthrow to reach 'Beyond the frontier of pain [where there] lies a splendid, sterile happiness' (101), the ultimate attainment of 'that emptiness beyond all understanding, in which the heart has rest' (103). Caligula has usurped 'the part of Fate' (75). In the face of any irksome divine rivals, he announces: 'Well, I've proved to these imaginary gods that any man, without previous training, if he applies his mind to it, can play their absurd parts to perfection' (74). For Cherea, however (who may be taken here as Camus's spokesman), most people 'resent living in a world where the most preposterous fancy may at any moment become a reality, and the absurd transfix their lives, like a dagger in the heart' (82), which is what happens once 'one pushes the absurd to its logical conclusions' (82–3).

Camus would go on in *The Rebel* (*L'Homme révolté*, 1951) to make a vital distinction between the negativity (and the totality) of nihilism and the at least potential positivity (despite historical events) of rebellion. 'One cannot be a part-time nihilist' (*Rebel*, 15). However, absurdist logic incorporates a final turn against killing and against suicide, in that human life must be recognised as 'the single necessary good', for 'without life the absurdist wager could not go on' – that is to say, 'persistence in that hopeless encounter between human questioning and the silence of the universe' (see *Rebel*, 13–14). This must override, in Camusian absurdist logic at least, the (nihilistic) conclusion that 'it is a matter of indifference to kill when the victim is in any case already condemned to death' (ibid., 247).[38] Rebellion *per se*, on the contrary, is 'a first step in defiance of an absurd world' (245), a refusal to legitimise murder (and suicide), because (genuine) 'rebellion, in principle, is a protest against death' (249).

The (in relative terms) late novella (or *récit*) *The Fall* is a diatribe (in what we have seen earlier to be the Bakhtinian sense, of a discourse delivered to an absent or undramatised interlocutor[39]). This first-person confession (a monologue, but by no means an entirely monological one) is of an ironic, a sardonic and a misanthropic nature – at the very least verging, at times, on black humour in its vagaries. The narrative tone is one reminiscent of Dostoevsky's *Notes from Underground*, with its spite, declared 'scorn' (*Fall*, 64) and propensity for 'bursting with vanity' (ibid., 37). At times, too, certain of the narrative voices of Kharms come to mind. The foibles of bourgeois professional, social, and political life and mores are pilloried against a backdrop of cosmic absurdity, in which 'the only reasonable divinity' is 'chance' (58), and 'the lyricism of the prison cell' (91) – actual or potential. Collective guilt provides the common ground and slavery the one anticipated comfort (100). Nevertheless, the imagery employed remains ostentatiously biblical (or at least within the Judaeo-Christian tradition), with Clamence invoking Dante (13; 62), the Last Judgment (105) and the 'fall' of the title ('for the fall occurs at dawn': ibid.).[40]

The Fall, according to Ray Davison, in his study of the two writers, 'must unquestionably be seen as Camus's most Dostoevskian work, both in formal and thematic terms' (Davison, 161).[41] While it would be excessive to claim that Clamence was a copy of any Dostoevskian figure, his monologue, in addition to its tone and form, includes a number of undoubtedly Dostoevskian motifs. The most traumatic moment for Clamence, with (of course) hindsight, seems to have been his callous decision not to intervene in the episode of what he believes to have been a young woman drowning herself in the Seine; this echoes Raskolnikov's looking on, 'with a strange feeling of indifference and detachment' while a would-be drowning woman is rescued from the Neva (*Crime and Punishment*, Part II, Chapter VI).[42] Another occasion that plagues his memory is the 'road rage' incident with a motorcyclist – reminiscent of certain street altercations of both Raskolnikov and the Underground Man. From outside Dostoevsky's fiction, in addition, Camus has Clamence 'express, to whoever would listen, [his] regret that it was no longer possible to act like a certain Russian landowner whose character [he] admired' – one who would have beatings administered 'both to his peasants who bowed to him and to those who didn't . . . in order to punish a boldness he considered equally impudent in both cases' (*Fall*, 68). The landowner in question, Davison has pointed out, is none other than Dostoevsky's father.[43]

Camus's interest in Dostoevsky extended from his school days in Algiers, to his own dramatisation of *The Devils*, as *The Possessed* (*Les Possédés*, 1959),[44] and beyond, to his unfinished last work *The First Man* (*Le Premier Homme*, posthumously published, 1994) – a note on Dostoevsky even being found among his preparatory papers for that work following his fatal road accident (Ernest Sturm, Preface to Dunwoodie, 11–12). Camus dated his reading of Dostoevsky to 1933 and in 1938 directed a stage adaptation of *The Brothers Karamazov*, himself playing the role of Ivan (Davison, 3–4). Eventually Ivan Karamazov, the 'metaphysical rebel', came to haunt *The Rebel*, as Kirilov (and suicide) had done *The Myth of Sisyphus*.[45] Camus wrote a short article entitled 'Pour Dostoïevski' (1955), while both *The Myth of Sisyphus* and *The Rebel* include prominent sections deriving from the thought and work of Dostoevsky ('Kirilov' in *Myth*, 95–102; 'The Rejection of Salvation', largely on Ivan Karamazov and the Grand Inquisitor, and 'The Path of Chigalev': *Rebel*, 50–6 and 142–6).

Notwithstanding an obviously high regard for other works by

Dostoevsky, especially *The Brothers Karamazov*,[46] Camus reserved his supreme accolade for *The Devils*. Not only did he dramatise it, but, according to a note he wrote for the Paris opening, '*Les Possédés* is one of the four or five works that I rank above all others' (cited by Davison, 5). Dostoevsky, however, as a Christian existentialist, for Camus betrayed 'philosophically' an absurd that he had portrayed so convincingly, by his insistence on 'using it as a "tremplin d'éternité", a spring-board to faith' (ibid., 14–15; 17). This phenomenon nevertheless (or perhaps in conse-quence) represents what Davison considers 'the epicentre of Camus's interest in Dostoevsky', inciting Camus's philosophical and fictional replies to Dostoevsky's 'challenge' and to his world; Camus's response leads, rather, 'first towards a positive hedonistic individualism and then towards the community of humanistic revolt' (Davison, 8).

Camus's dialogue with Dostoevsky may thus be seen to develop through three phases (see ibid., 190–4). The first phase concentrates on the (meta-physical) absurd, featuring Kirilov and his (optimistic) theory of becoming God through suicide – a theme responded to in *The Myth of Sisyphus*. The second moves from metaphysical to nihilistic revolt and political murder: through the ('all is permitted') thought of Ivan Karamazov to the fiendish praxis of Peter Verkhovensky and the prophetic theories of the Grand Inquisitor and Shchigalev ('Chigalev' in the French transliteration) – tackled in *The Rebel*. The third phase, a developing synthesis, was still in process, extending from *The Fall* into *The First Man*.

A character of pivotal fascination for Camus throughout is the enig-matic figure of Stavrogin (as 'a tzar of indifference': Davison, 8; 87) – a far cry though he may seem to be from *l'homme absurde* of Camus's opti-mistic ideal. The early Camus uses Kirilov's explanation of Stavrogin ('If Stavrogin believes, he does not think he believes. If he does not believe, he does not think he does not believe' – *The Possessed*)[47] as the epigraph to his section 'The Absurd Man' (*Myth*, 64); in the same work, attention is drawn to Stavrogin leading 'an "ironic" life' (*Myth*, 99: qualifying this less than usual use of that adjective by: 'it is well known in what regard'), a phrase he has Stavrogin utter in *The Possessed* ('I led an ironic life': *Caligula*, 344). Indifference, irony, debauchery, detachment and inertia: Stavrogin, a potential hero of the absurd who 'fails' (apart from anything else, by ultimately hanging himself) has, as we have noted earlier, been linked with Dickens's Steerforth; Davison (91–2) reminds us that Dostoevsky himself links him with Don Juan and takes the comparison on to Camus's Clamence; Peter Dunwoodie (168) sees Stavrogin as a haunt-ing figure for Camus, 'as a malevolent being, an object of fascination, an enticement in sterility from the void'. Stavrogin thus joins a number of other key Dostoevskian figures in giving rise to what is seen (Davison, 2) as Camus's 'pervasive preoccupation with the Russian writer as a pene-trating analyst and prophet of twentieth-century "absurd" sensibility'.

Notes

1 The title of the present chapter is borrowed from the collection of essays on absurdist drama edited by Brater and Cohn (1990).
2 Rhetoric is here defined as 'the transfer into one semiotic sphere of the structural principles of another' (Lotman, 62).
3 See Richard Zenith's 'Introduction' to Pessoa, 2001. Harold Bloom, praising him highly as a poet, and as 'Whitman reborn', does not allude to Pessoa's prose magnum opus, though claiming that he, just of himself, 'as a fantastic invention surpasses any creation by Borges' (Bloom, 485).
4 Soares appears to have 'taken over' as author of *The Book of Disquiet* from an earlier persona, named Vicente Guedes (see Zenith: Pessoa, 2001, xvi–xx). Zenith (ibid., 505–9) supplies a 'Table of Heteronyms', briefly outlining eighteen of the more important or bizarre members of this species. The publishing history of *The Book of Disquiet*, both in the original and in English translation, is as extraordinary as its content, its 'authorship' and the history of its composition. Pessoa published a dozen fragments during his lifetime (one as early as 1913) and further fragments appeared posthumously. In keeping with 'the book's general spirit of fragmentation and disconnectedness' (Zenith: Pessoa, 2001, xxx) and the fact that Pessoa left what Zenith terms an 'invented' book 'which never existed, strictly speaking, and can never exist', or 'the ingredients of a book, whose recipe is to keep sifting' (ix), there can be no definitive edition: indeed, the contents are still being deciphered, sifted, edited, argued over, reinterpreted, assigned to (or removed from) the book. Only a minority of the fragments are dated and an attempted chronological ordering, in any case, is not only impossible but inappropriate. All editions (the more so, of course, all translations) are 'automatically guilty' of 'tampering with the original non-order'; the impractical ideal would be a loose-leaf edition to be arranged and re-arranged by each reader (xxix). To cite just one instance, the fragment numbered 208 in Pessoa, 1991 (207–9), which was number 192 in the 1982 'original', now appears as entry number 1 in the 1998 Portuguese edition, the basis for the latest English version (Pessoa, 2001, 11–13).
    The first edition in book form was published in Lisbon in 1982. An augmented edition in two volumes appeared in 1990–1 (an extensively revised version of volume one appearing in 1997). In 1998 Richard Zenith published his own revised Portuguese edition (Lisbon: Assírio & Alvim).
    In 1991, no fewer than four English versions were published. The Serpent's Tail edition (here 'Pessoa, 1991') followed the selection of material that had been made for the Feltrinelli Italian edition of 1986. Richard Zenith's first English version was published by Carcanet in association with the Calouste Gulbenkian Foundation, under the title *The Book of Disquietude* (reprinted with revisions in 1996). The two further versions (both as *The Book of Disquiet*) were from Quartet Books (translated by Iain Watson and subtitled *A Selection*: London, 1991); and Pantheon (translated by Alfred MacAdam: New York, 1991; reprinted Boston: Exact Change, 1998). Finally, what Zenith calls his 'revised, reorganized and expanded English edition' was published by Allen Lane, The Penguin Press (here 'Pessoa, 2001'); the work, in this edition, bears an internal subtitle 'by Bernardo Soares, assistant book-

keeper in the city of Lisbon' (which appears neither on the title page, nor on the book's cover or spine). For general purposes, this version is surely now destined to be regarded as the 'standard' English edition for a considerable time to come. For present purposes, however, I am retaining Margaret Jull Costa's translation (Pessoa, 1991) as my basic text, while making additional and 'controlling' use of Zenith's final version and its apparatus.

5 Cf. the somewhat Nietzschean exhortation: 'go forward into glory or into the abyss, son of Chaos and of Night, always remembering in some corner of your being that the Gods came later, and that the Gods too pass away' (Pessoa, 1991, 194).

6 Cf. Pessoa, 220: 'Those who died simply turned a corner and are out of sight'; and *Incidences*, 85: 'Rakukin's soul, leaping and stumbling, disappeared into space beyond the turning-point.'

7 The references to prison, execution and judgment suggest comparison with Nabokov (as with Kafka, as well as recalling the stories by Van Ostaijen and Michaux mentioned earlier). Sleep as 'a little death from which one wakes feeling fresh and revived, a yielding of the fibres of the soul to fit the raiments of oblivion' (Pessoa, 1991, 86) recalls passages in Nabokov's autobiographical work, *Speak, Memory* (1967), as does a concern with spirals. Soares being 'simultaneously in each person's soul' (referring to passers-by on the street: Pessoa, 1991, 205) is reminiscent of a technique of entering the consciousness of others claimed by the protagonist of Nabokov's *The Gift* (first published in truncated form in Russian, 1937–38). Furthermore, the metaphor of life as a text is frequently to be found in Nabokov.

8 See, for instance, Tabucchi's essay 'Bernardo Soares, uomo inquieto e insonne', in Fernando Pessoa, *Il Libro dell'Inquietudine*, Milan: Feltrinelli, 1986; Maria José de Lancastre and Antonio Tabucchi, *Fernando Pessoa*, translated by Simon Pleasance, Paris: Hazan, 1997 (a pictorial biography, which includes Tabucchi's essay 'A Trunkful of People', 7–44); Antonio Tabucchi, *Dreams of Dreams* and *The Last Three Days of Fernando Pessoa*, translated by Nancy J. Peters, San Francisco: City Lights, 1999 (in the latter piece, the dying Pessoa is visited in hospital by his principal heteronyms: 87–128).

9 See Antonio Tabucchi, *Requiem*, translated by Margaret Jull Costa, London: Harvill, 1994, 13–14; 97–107; Soares refers to the 'crippled seller of lottery tickets who would pester me in vain' (Pessoa, 2001, 392).

10 José Saramago, *The Year of the Death of Ricardo Reis*, translated by Giovanni Pontiero, London: Harvill, 1999.

11 Tzvetan Todorov, 'Art according to Artaud', in Todorov, 1977, 205–17. The same is, of course, said of Kafka.

12 Arnold Hinchliffe, however, points out that 'Absurd dramatists (with the possible exception of the later Beckett) have ignored his ideas about eliminating the author and his text' (Hinchliffe, 53). On the 'unfaithfulness' of the modern theatre (including that of the absurd) to Artaud, see also Jacques Derrida, 'The Theater of Cruelty and the Closure of Representation' (Derrida, 232–50, especially 243–6).

13 'Surrealism has died of the idiotic sectarianism of its adepts', wrote Artaud in 1927, following his split with the movement (*SW*, 144). Ostensibly occasioned by the Surrealists' alliance with the French Communist Party, disagreements

over the understanding of 'revolution', and Artaud's perceived commitment to a 'commercial' theatre, the real cause of the break, in Sontag's view, was the 'fundamental difference of temperament': of despair (Artaud) versus optimism (Sontag, in *SW*, xxvi). On the philosophical differences between Artaud and Surrealism see Fotiade, passim.

14 Artaud was arrested in Dublin and deported for laying about him with a staff or cane – plausibly, as Deane has it (see below), 'a long knobbly shillelagh' – that had been presented to him in Paris, supposedly handed down from St Patrick: on Artaud's visit to Ireland see Barber, 91–6. An exchange of diplomatic letters and memoranda, written in consequence of Artaud's Irish affair, concerned largely with attempts to secure payment of a lodging debt of £1 17s 6d run up by Artaud in the Aran Islands (with the whereabouts of a cherished 'walking stick' a prominent side issue), has been published: '"An absent-minded person of the student type": Extracts from the Artaud file', *Dublin Review*, 1 (Winter 2000–1), 55–80; as the editorial commentary suggests, these texts could of themselves constitute a viable sketch for the theatre of the absurd. The Irish composer Raymond Deane conflated the Irish visits of Shelley (in 1812) and Artaud (1937) in his short opera *The Poet and his Double*, performed in Dublin and Wexford in 1991; the libretto was published in *The Keats–Shelley Review* (6, 1991, 37–48). The title is presumably a play on Artaud's *The Theatre and its Double*. In addition to their common Irish adventures, Artaud had staged his play *The Cenci*, drawn in part from Shelley's tragedy of 1819 – the only spectacle that Artaud succeeded in putting on for the Theatre of Cruelty (the play closed after seventeen performances in 1935).

15 Mary Ann Caws claims to 'have never heard anything to equal', among 'provocative tones', the voice of Artaud in the recording of this broadcast (apparently put out on French radio posthumously in 1952 and much later made available on compact disk): 'it was the voice of an elderly grandmother, it was the voice of a maniac' and it was the voice – since it was the voice of Artaud – of a genius' (Caws, 327, n. 15). This work, under the title *For an End to the Judgement of God*, was revived as a protest in the run-up to the Iraq war (in February 2003) by the American director Peter Sellars and presented at the Tate Modern, London.

16 'Body language', according to Steiner (2001, 128), 'is a shorthand whereby to circumscribe the multitudinous components of physical stance, gesture, motion which accompany, qualify, often undermine or contradict utterance'.

17 According to Deleuze (91), 'Artaud says that Being, which is nonsense, has teeth', indicative of a slide from surface to depth, 'signifying series' toward 'signified series', and words toward bodies.

18 There is a comparison to be made in terms of certain ideas (though not of temperament) between Artaud and Khlebnikov: the pursuit of transrational language; a strong interest in primitivism and orientalism; and a predilection for the Egyptian Ka ('a Double, ... a perpetual specter illuminated by the forces of emotionality': Artaud, *SW*, 261); and, in Artaud's case at least, for its scatological homonym ('the abyss of Kah-Kah, Kah the corporeal breath of shit, which is the opium of eternal survival': 453).

19 There are shades here too, if from another cultural sphere, of *William Wilson*

and Mr Goliadkin; Poe was a major figure in Artaud's cultural pantheon, while Dostoevsky is mentioned by him in connection with his 'change' of identity (see Barber, 102).

20 Jacques Latrémolière (at Rodez), quoted by Barber, 107. The head of one clinic in which Artaud was confined (in 1938–39, the Saint-Anne asylum) was Jacques Lacan; the only diagnosis made there of Artaud was that he was 'chronically and incurably insane' (see ibid., 99–100); subsequently, Artaud was to refer to Lacan as a 'filthy vile bastard' (140).

21 For instance: 'One day the executioners came for van Gogh, just as they came for Gérard de Nerval, Baudelaire, Poe and Lautréamont', in *Van Gogh, the Man Suicided by Society*, 1947 (*SW*, 510).

22 'An End to Masterpieces' (*SW*, 252–9: 'En finir avec les chefs-d'oeuvre', 1933) appeared in *Le Théâtre et son double* (1938) and is also translated as 'No More Masterpieces' (Artaud, *The Theatre and Its Double*, New York: Grove, 1958), reprinted in Cardullo and Knopf, 382–8.

23 'Artaud's [much earlier] project for a Surrealist cinema is irreparably lost'; it was, however, envisaged as 'the collision of blood and chance' (Barber, 37).

24 'Nietzsche insists in *The Birth of Tragedy* that high culture is a spiritualization of cruelty' (Eagleton, 70).

25 See Barber, 136–7. With regard to the last aspect: 'For Artaud, death was always an invented state, imposed by society so that the inert body would become vulnerable raw material for malicious robberies and attacks as it entered a state of limbo, such as he claimed to have experienced during an electroshock coma at Rodez. With a strong enough will to live, and sufficient resistance to social compromise, an independent human body could live forever, powered by anger' (ibid., 137). Artaud's subsequent fate did not, however, bear out this thesis.

26 Sontag (xliv), writing in 1976, lists theatrical developments deriving from Artaud (including 'Happenings, the Theater of the Ridiculous' and various plays and productions); this list could now obviously be considerably lengthened. Another legacy comprises parodies of Artaudian theatre; just one such (in probability) is the Parisian 'Théatre des Vampires', in Anne Rice's *Interview With the Vampire* (1978).

27 Sade was a figure of some importance to Artaud, with whom his asylum performance of 'The Persecution and Assassination of Jean-Paul Marat' struck an obvious chord – all the more so as Artaud had played Marat in Abel Gance's film *Napoleon* (1926–27).

28 Deleuze, 82–93; a variant of this chapter appears as 'The Schizophrenic and Language: Surface and Depth in Lewis Carroll and Antonin Artaud', in *Textual Strategies: Perspectives in Post-Structuralist Criticism*, edited by Josué V. Harari, London: Methuen, 1980, 277–95.

29 For this quotation, I have slightly adapted the translations to be found in Deleuze (93) and Harari (294–5). However, Deleuze adds that Carroll, none the less, 'remains the master or the surveyor of surfaces we thought we knew so well that we never explored them. Yet it is on these surfaces that the entire logic of sense is located' (Deleuze, 93; Harari, 295).

30 Sven Spieker also, however, alludes in Gogol to 'a kind of proto-Artaudian, negative "littérature de la cruauté" in which soul and personality have no place' (Spieker, 13).

31 This may be compared to Camus's own comment on Dostoevsky's *The Brothers Karamazov*: 'It is not an absurd work that is involved here but a work that propounds the absurd problem' (*Myth*, 101).

32 In a later phase too, Camus writes: 'One morning, after many dark nights of despair, an irrepressible longing to live will announce to us the fact that all is finished and that suffering has no more meaning than happiness' (*Rebel*, 227).

33 An association between dance (literal or metaphorical) and death (actual or imminent) has been pointed to several times in this study; Camus elsewhere cites Nietzsche's assertion that 'Damocles never danced better than beneath the sword' (*Rebel*, 63).

34 Nabokov, incidentally, classed Camus (along with 'Lorca, Kazantzakis, D.H. Lawrence, Thomas Mann, Thomas Wolfe, and literally hundreds of other "great" second-raters') among 'a number of puffed up writers': Vladimir Nabokov, *Strong Opinions*, London: Weidenfeld and Nicolson, 1974, 54). Elsewhere he made similar comments on Dostoevsky, Henry James, Faulkner and others.

35 Edward Said (*Culture and Imperialism*, London: Vintage, 1994), in his discussion of Camus (204–24), considers that Camus covers 'the interrelationship between geography and the political contest … with a superstructure celebrated by Sartre as providing "a climate of the absurd"' (219); the absurd therefore serves as a façade, or an imputation by readers and critics, masking the contradictions of the French-Algerian colonial situation (224). According to Colin Wilson, however, for whose concept of 'the Outsider' Camus's novel must have been significant (although Barbusse is his declared starting point), 'Mersault is an Algerian', while, rather than being 'disillusioned or world-weary … His type of light-headedness bears more relation to P.G. Wodehouse's "Young men in spats"' (Wilson, 27–8).

36 This may be compared to the declaration by Witkiewicz's protagonist in *The Cuttlefish* (1922; performed 1933): 'Together we'll create pure nonsense in life, not in Art' (*The Cuttlefish, or The Hyrcanian Worldview*, in Cardullo and Knopf, 297–320, at 319). At a somewhat different level, their contemporaries, Aleksandr Vvedensky and Yakov Druskin, said of another exponent of 'cruelty', Daniil Kharms: 'Kharms does not create art, but is himself art. … This was not aestheticism: "the creation of life like art" was, for Kharms, a category not of an aesthetic order but what would now be called an existential one' (quoted from Cornwell, 1991, 6).

37 Camus later wrote of 'the very day when the Caesarian revolution triumphed over the syndicalist and libertarian spirit' (*Rebel*, 262), having highlighted Dostoevsky's (to Camus) prophetic 'undertaking of the Inquisitors and the Caesars' in *The Brothers Karamazov*.

38 Ivan Karamazov 'hates the death penalty [namely] because it is the image of the human condition' (*Rebel*, 56).

39 See earlier remarks on Dostoevsky and Lautréamont. The interlocutor of Clamence in *The Fall* can be said to be present to the extent that his [her?] replies and reactions are anticipated (presumed or even implied) in the text; this interlocutor, however, ostensibly another visiting Parisian lawyer (*Fall*, 107), may also be understood as an alter ego of Clamence – even his literal mirror image – or as the implied [or indeed, any] reader.

40 Clamence's name ironically evokes John the Baptist ('the voice of one crying in the wilderness'), as noted by Thody (90), who comments that 'Camus had to present his ideas in Christian terms because there is still, in the late twentieth century, no equally accessible world view available'. Indeed, in any event, according to Thody (ibid.): 'The idea that the world has no transcendent purpose has to be couched in Christian terms because only the Christians say it has such a purpose'.

41 See also the equally detailed and rather more Bakhtinian study written in French on this topic by Peter Dunwoodie (1996); and E.P. Kushkin, 'Dostoevskii i Kamiu', in *Dostoevskii v zarubezhnykh literaturakh*, edited by B.G. Reizov, Leningrad: Nauka, 1978, 81–116.

42 Fyodor Dostoevsky, *Crime and Punishment*, translated by Jessie Coulson, Oxford: Oxford University Press, 1995, 164. Earlier, Camus had referred to 'the wine of the absurd and the bread of indifference' (*Myth*, 52). Ionesco includes a reference to a similar incident of leaving a woman to drown in his play *Amédée ou Comment s'en débarrasser* (1954).

43 Davison, 196–7, n. 21; Camus's source for this information (ibid.) may have been Henri Troyat's biography (*Dostoïevski*, Paris, 1948). Dostoevsky *père* was eventually murdered by his peasants.

44 Ionesco also engaged with this novel in theatrical form, acting the part of Stepan Trofimovich (by whom he felt himself 'possessed' or 'dispossessed') in 1951, and furnishing the adaptation with a preface on its publication (Dostoevski, *Les Possédés*, adapted by Akakia Viala and Nicolas Bataille, Paris: Éditions Émile-Paul, 1959): see Esslin, *Th. Abs.*, 144–5.

45 Beyond questions of suicide, and Dostoevsky, *The Myth of Sisyphus* has been seen as 'a barely disguised polemical reply to Chestov's [in the French spelling of Shestov] arguments on the absurd' and 'indirectly pay[ing] homage to most of the recurrent themes in [that] Russian philosopher's writing' (Fotiade, 4).

46 In *The Myth of Sisyphus*, Camus writes that, in general, 'to be sure, nobody, like Dostoevsky, has managed to give the world of absurdity such close and tormented brilliance' (see *Myth*, 100; I have here, however, preferred the translation provided by Davison, 7).

47 Stavrogin is thus 'a sceptic in the philosophical, Pyrrhonian sense: he doubts the existence and the non-existence of God' (Davison, 90): the reference here being to Pyrrhus of Elis (c.360–c.270 BC) who 'left no writings but was, rather, the model of the skeptical way of life' (Richard H. Popkin, 'Skepticism', in *En. Phil.* 7:450). This explanation of Stavrogin, it is thought, may have inspired the narrator of *The Old Woman* by Kharms: 'in my view there are no believers or non-believers. There are only those who wish to believe and those who wish not to believe' (Kharms, *Incidences*, 32).

5

Around the absurd II: the Theatre of the Absurd

> I have been called a writer of the absurd; this is one of those terms that go the rounds periodically, it is a term that is in fashion at the moment and will soon be out of fashion. It is vague enough now, in any case, to mean nothing any more and to be an easy definition of anything. (Eugène Ionesco, 'Notes on the Theatre', 1953)

> You can't be a rationalist in an irrational world. It isn't rational. (Joe Orton, *What the Butler Saw*, 1967)

In his lecture on 'The Theatre of Cruelty' delivered in 1966, Jacques Derrida inserted a list of theatrical categories, or 'themes of infidelity' to Artaud, that rendered just about all subsequent theatrical development 'foreign to the theatre of cruelty'; these comprise 'all non-sacred theatre', 'all abstract theatre', 'all theatre of alienation', 'all nonpolitical theatre', 'all ideological theatre' (in other words, just about all theatre) and – of more immediate concern here and perhaps a little more controversially – theatre of the absurd (Derrida, 243–6). Derrida thus amplifies this particular denomination of the general 'infidelity' (243–4):

> All theater that privileges speech or rather the verb, all theater of words, even if this privilege becomes that of a speech which is self-destructive, which once more becomes gesture of hopeless reoccurrence, a *negative* relation of speech to itself, theatrical nihilism, what is still called the theater of the absurd. Such a theater would not only be consumed by speech, and would not destroy the functioning of the classical stage, but it also would not be, in the sense understood by Artaud (and doubtless by Nietzsche), an *affirmation*.

One can certainly recognise here key elements from Theatre of the Absurd, and the question of the word is clearly fundamental. One can well doubt both the aesthetic and indeed the commercial viability of a theatre basing itself uncompromisingly on Artaud's precepts. Nevertheless, as pointed out previously, Martin Esslin (*Th. Abs.*, 385) saw Artaud as 'the bridge between the pioneers and today's Theatre of the Absurd'. At the same time too, as Ionesco maintained, everything is changed 'if one looks on the word as only *one* member of the shock troops the theatre can marshal' (Ionesco, *Notes*, 28). The one thing that is left from Artaud's theatre, according to J.L. Styan (128), is 'the general notion of exposing the audience to horror'. Tzvetan Todorov stresses that language in the theatre is essentially 'symbolic language' with, as Artaud had indicated, 'a multiplicity of signifiers', amounting potentially at least to an *'overflow off the signifier, a superabundance* (and an overdetermination) of what signifies in relation to what is signified' (Todorov, 1977, 210). In contrast to the more traditional theatrical semantic network of 'repetition, psychology, verbality', we find (a more Artaudian) 'difference, metaphysics, nonverbality' (ibid., 211–12). It might well be thought that this approach may seem fundamentally closer to absurdist drama than to most other theatrical forms.

Esslin, in his seminal study *The Theatre of the Absurd* (third edition, 1982), devotes chapters to five major dramatists of the absurd: Beckett, Adamov, Ionesco, Genet and Pinter (the examination of Pinter here concludes with *Betrayal*, 1978).[1] In addition to treatments of 'Tradition' and 'Significance' thereof, Esslin includes one further (sixty-page) chapter which deals briefly with seventeen writers, ranging from Edward Albee and Arthur Kopit in America; through N.F. Simpson, Fernando Arrabal, Boris Vian and other West Europeans; to Mrożek, Różewicz and Havel in Eastern Europe. Esslin points out the French, indeed Parisian avant-garde, base of his Theatre of the Absurd, but stresses its cosmopolitan nature and spread, and the fact that, for that matter, 'its leading practitioners who live in Paris and write in French are not themselves Frenchmen' (*Th. Abs.*, 26: Adamov, Arrabal, Beckett and Ionesco, for a start, being respectively by origin Russo-Armenian, Spanish, Irish and Romanian). First performances took place across a range of theatres, in the hands of a variety of directors. A term such as 'Theatre of the Absurd' (or *anti-théâtre*, as it was also called) is seen as just 'a working hypothesis'; not denoting any movement as such (given, indeed, that there never was one), it is to be regarded as no more than 'a device to make certain fundamental traits which seem to be present in the works of a number of dramatists accessible to discussion by tracing the features they have in common' (*Th. Abs.*, 12).

'Absurdist plays', according to Styan, 'fall within the symbolist tradition' in their lack of conventional plot and characterisation. Moreover, as he elucidates it (126):

Camus's existentialist use of the term 'absurd' in *The Myth of Sisyphus* was ten years later vastly narrowed to connote man trapped in a hostile universe that was totally subjective, and made to describe the nightmare that could follow when purposelessness, solitude and silence were taken to the ultimate degree. . . .

> As plays, [absurdist dramatic works] do not discuss the human condition,
> but simply portray it at its worst in outrageous images chosen to undeceive
> the innocent and shock the complacent.

Similarly, Esslin (*Th. Abs.*, 25) contends that Theatre of the Absurd 'has renounced arguing *about* the absurdity of the human condition; it merely *presents* it in being – that is, in terms of concrete stage images'. Elements from mime, the music hall, circus and *commedia dell'arte* were drawn upon, particularly in the early plays of Beckett; monotony and repetition are emphasised, along with the methods of farce and laughter, with dialogue 'commonly no more than a series of inconsequential clichés' (Styan, 126).

Ionesco and others: the French-language scene

These qualities are especially evident in the dramas of Ionesco, and these same ideas are reinforced in his theoretical commentaries.[2] In a piece written in 1953, he thus explicates the dramatic projections of his 'tattered and disjointed inner world [that] is in some way a reflection or a symbol of universal disruption':

> So there is no plot, no architectural construction, no puzzles to be solved,
> only the inscrutable enigma of the unknown; no real characters, just people
> without identity (at any moment they may contradict their own nature or
> perhaps one will change places with another), simply a sequence of events
> without sequence, a series of fortuitous incidents unlinked by cause and
> effect, inexplicable adventures, emotional states, an indescribable tangle,
> but alive with intentions, impulses and discordant passions, steeped in
> contradiction. (Ionesco, *Notes*, 159)

'There is only one true way of demystifying', he proclaims in 1959: 'by means of humor, especially if it is "black"; logic is revealed by our awareness of the illogicality of the absurd; ... the comic alone is able to give us the strength to bear the tragedy of existence' (*Notes* 144). Time and space can dissolve for an absurdist, it would appear, just as they could for the mystics of Romanticism:

> Each of us has surely felt at moments that the substance of the world is
> dreamlike, that the walls are no longer solid, that we seem to be able to see
> through everything into a spaceless universe made up of pure light and
> color; at such a moment the whole of life, the whole of history of the world,
> becomes useless, senseless and impossible. (*Notes*, 162–3)

This 'awakening' is one of amazement but, unlike the more religious brands of existential thought (found in Shestov, Fondane and others), such an epiphany does not result as such in a positive spiritual impulse towards 'faith':

the fact of being astonishes us, in a world that now seems all illusion and pretense, in which all human behavior tells of absurdity and all history of absolute futility; all reality and all language appear to lose their articulation, to disintegrate and collapse, so what possible reaction is there left, when everything has ceased to matter, but to laugh at it all?

In these circumstances, Ionesco continues (*Notes*, 163): 'I could do anything I wished with the language and the people of a world that no longer seemed to me anything but a baseless and ridiculous sham.' As Erich Segal points out: 'Ironically, he uses language to present the radical devaluation of language' (Segal, 571, n. 35).

While Ionesco finds the bulk of (all-time and modern) mainstream theatre unbearable, 'he does see himself as part of a tradition including Sophocles and Aeschylus, Shakespeare, Kleist, and Büchner'; and this is 'precisely because these authors are concerned with the human condition in all its brutal absurdity' (Esslin, *Th. Abs.*, 199). Ionesco may have found Strindberg 'clumsy' (ibid.), but L.A.C. Dobrez discerns, particularly in the later plays, the echo of Strindberg's late-Romantic, or more expressionist, work – in the self-projection of both dramatists and 'in their common dramatic use of the dream for confessional purposes' (Dobrez, 187). For Ionesco, in any event, the aim of the avant-garde is 'to rediscover and make known a forgotten truth', or 'the discovery of forgotten archetypes, changeless but expressed in a new way'; in this sense at least, he affirms, 'any true creative artist is classical' (*Notes*, 57; 131). An important means by which this process is effected is the time-honoured technique of making strange (or defamiliarisation): a reflection of 'the strangeness of reality when seen as if for the first time', an incarnation of 'the vision of *angst*, with its radical rearrangement of the everyday' (Dobrez, 298).

Ionesco's first play, *The Bald Soprano* (*La Cantatrice chauve*, 1950: also translated as *The Bald Prima Donna*), apparently owes its inspiration to an Asimil textbook of conversational English. Ionesco himself spoke of the ingredients of parody, banality and 'the hollowest clichés' (*Notes*, 28): 'the idea of making dialogue by stringing together the most commonplace phrases consisting of the most meaningless words and the most wornout clichés I could find in my own and my friends' vocabulary – and to a lesser extent in foreign conversation manuals' (*Notes*, 83). To this are added the pointless, the bizarre as well as the glaringly obvious, and the repetitious – amounting to what Dobrez (163) calls 'tormented puppetry'. Conversation primer provides truisms and clichés, leading to pseudo-truisms and caricature, resulting in eventual disintegration into disjointed verbal fragmentation – the whole 'to be acted in deadly seriousness, like a play by Ibsen or Sardou' (Esslin, 138; 139). As Segal (428) graphically puts it, '*The Bald Soprano* ends with an atomic nuclear meltdown of meaning'. In addition came the chance qualities (in rehearsal) of the accidental stumbling upon the title, and the inspired (though pragmatic) decision to end the play by starting it over again from the beginning, but with the secondary couple, the Martins, assuming the roles of the Smiths (ibid., 140). One commentator has isolated some thirty-six 'recipes of the comic' in this play alone, amounting to something approaching a full gamut of comic devices (see ibid., 195–6). Not least of these is the use of the Fire Chief's shaggy-dog story of 'The Headcold' (Ionesco, 1982, 32–4), in which the irrelevancies and the inconsequential stream of redundant personages mentioned not only matches the earlier 'Bobby Watson' sequence but perhaps even surpasses the previous acknowledged master of such superfluous detail, Nikolai Gogol. Segal (427) emphasises the shattering here of *cognatio*, following the earlier destruction of *cognitio*.

In a brief mention of three more of the earlier Ionesco plays, we may note that *The Chairs* (*Les Chaises*, 1952) has a theme of 'the ontological void, or *absence*' (*Notes*, 190). Absence is embodied, one might say, by 'the chairs themselves', representing the absent, or at least invisible, audience invited to the old couple's apocalyptic non-*soirée*, 'the theme of the play [being] *nothingness*' – an absence of people, emperor, God and matter (cited by Esslin, *Th. Abs.*, 152). There is absence too of the message promised for the end of the play, or at least of any meaningful means to deliver it.[3] Ionesco found it 'difficult to say whether some of the characters exist or not'; at the same time, he can affirm, 'the tightly-packed crowd of non-existent beings should acquire an entirely objective existence of their own' (*Notes*, 136; 190).[4] Segal (430) suggests of the Orator's incoherent appearance at the end: 'Perhaps this babbling infant is their lost child'. *The Lesson* (*La Leçon*, 1951) presents what purports to be a manically repetitive and literally murderous system of pseudo-academic discourse, developing through routines of arithmetical confusion and phoney philology.[5] In *Amédée or How to Get Rid of it* (*Amédée ou Comment s'en débarrasser*, 1954) an enormous corpse that has been growing for fifteen years in a married couple's bedroom may symbolise 'the couple's dead love' (Esslin, *Th. Abs.*, 162), the power of death, or indeed much else. The eponymous hero's career as a writer (two lines written in fifteen years) rivals quantitatively that of the narrator of Kharms's story *The Old Woman* (one line: see Kharms, *Incidences*, 20). Amédée is writing a play 'in which I am on the side of the living against the dead' (*Absurd Drama*, 95). Madeleine's assertion that 'the dead are terribly vindictive' (ibid., 43), in the context of the active corpse, is reminiscent both of Kharms's *The Old Woman* and of remarks in Gogol's St Petersburg story *Nevsky Prospect*. The question of the status and identity of the corpse bears a certain alogical comparison too, as we shall indicate below, with the purported situation in Kharms's absurdist play *Yelizaveta Bam*.

Ionesco claimed to be aiming for 'the extreme exaggeration of parody', in order 'to push everything to paroxysm, to the point where the sources of the tragic lie'; what was needed was 'a theatre of violence: violently comic, violently dramatic' (Esslin, *Th. Abs.*, 142; *Notes*, 26). At least vestiges of Artaud would seem to survive into Ionesco's absurd dramatic conception. However, Ionesco also argued that 'to attack the absurdity (of the human condition) is a way of stating the possibility of non-absurdity'; catharsis or liberation may yet lie at the end of the tunnel (quoted *Th. Abs.*, 198). Psychology is to be avoided – 'or rather give it a metaphysical dimension' (*Notes* 26). According to Dobrez (149), 'the sense of wonder in the plays parallels the disintegrating vision of the Uncanny', in a 'polarity of euphoria and claustrophobia' – seen as 'the major tension in Ionesco' (ibid., 191). Dobrez sees a resemblance, in the later plays in particular, to 'the Heideggerian discovery of Being' in that 'what is involved is first a strangeness of things with a heightened awareness of them, then a luminous insight into the very heart of the existential even as it vanishes into nothingness' (175). Ultimately, Ionesco may prefer the concept of 'unbelievability' to that of the absurd (*Notes*, 216–17), or, as Marvin Carlson (411) paraphrases his position, the world is 'not absurd but incredible', and leading Dobrez (190) to categorise Ionesco as 'a Romantic Idealist in an existential world'.

Arthur Adamov (later the translator of Chekhov, Gogol, Dostoevsky and Strindberg, among others) produced a short prose work called *The Confession* (*L'Aveu*, 1946) before writing the plays for which he subsequently became known; in this and other pieces of that period he broaches a philosophy of the absurd, but 'presupposes the conviction that the world *has* a meaning, although it is of necessity outside the reach of human consciousness'; and therein, unlike a world of total absurdity, lies the tragic element (*Th. Abs.*, 97). His first two plays, *The Parody* and *The Invasion* (*La Parodie* and *L'Invasion*, written in the late 1940s), were published in 1950, successfully provoking a first performance. While perhaps lacking the overtly comic qualities found in Ionesco, *The Invasion* presents a similarly 'hopeless search for meaning' (*Th. Abs.*, 102) and for message amid a disintegrating language – in this case located (or rather not located) in unreadable and fading (and in any event probably meaningless or incomprehensible) manuscripts. Again in common with Ionesco's theory, Adamov, who at first thought he was innovating an indirect dialogue of oblique reference, subsequently realised that he had really just reinvented an already established technique (from the repertoire of Chekhov, among others).

Another early play, *Professor Taranne* (*Le Professeur Taranne*, 1953), based on an actual dream of Adamov's, features a protagonist accused of indecent exposure, plagiarism and other heinous offences, who may appear to be simultaneously an exposed fraud and/or an innocent victim.[6] More ambitious is *Le Ping-Pong* (1955), regarded by Esslin (*Th. Abs.*, 113) as 'one of the masterpieces of the Theatre of the Absurd', depicting two men over a lifetime of obsession with pinball machines, in which technology invades and takes over their entire existence in a display of corporate and machine domination that must retain a prescient significance. Segal (421) says of this depiction of existence as an arcade game: 'This is life. You are born. You play. You die, having accomplished nothing. A grim view indeed.' From *Paolo Paoli* (1957), Adamov moved further away from the absurd to embrace a more Brechtian type of epic theatre. His resolve by now was to reveal in equal measure 'the incurable aspect of things' – which is to say 'the inevitability of death' – and 'the curable ... (the social one)' (cited *Th. Abs.*, 122). Like Ionesco, Adamov disliked the term Theatre of the Absurd. 'Life is not absurd', he claimed, 'only difficult, very difficult' (quoted by Carlson, 411). The French, indeed, appeared to prefer Ionesco's alternative expression, '*théâtre de dérision*' (ibid., 411–12).

There is no shortage of 'cruelty', or brutality, in the 'Panic theatre' (*Théâtre Panique*: a combination of 'panic' and the god Pan) of Fernando Arrabal, a form of theatre designed to administer shock-treatment to the senses of the audience. In *The Two Executioners* (*Les Deux Bourreaux*, 1958: see *Absurd Drama*, 139–55) a woman delivers her husband to a torture chamber and literally proceeds to rub salt in his wounds. *The Architect and the Emperor of Assyria* (*L'Architecte et l'empereur d'Assyrie*, 1967) is directly inspired by Artaud's comments on the cruelty of 'Assyrian emperors' with a *penchant* for mutilation.

Ritual, erotic fantasy, violence, betrayal, the sacramental and the excremental – though this time with a more explicit concentration on the French homosexual and criminal outcasts and underclasses – pervade too the works of Jean Genet. Equally well known (as with Arrabal for his novels) for, in this case, his prose narratives written in the 1940s, Genet made his name publicly first as a dramatist of the absurd (or of the so-called 'theatre of the possessed'). His artistic reputation was also boosted by his being the subject of a monograph by Sartre.[7] 'Genet's theatre', like his prose, 'in a very real sense, is a Dance of Death' (*Th. Abs.*, 211). Tortuous visions of mirror reflection and the switching of identities (of role, sex or race), and play within the play within dreamlike fantasies of power and sex, Genet's more absurdist dramas – notably *The Maids* (*Les Bonnes*, 1947), *The Balcony* (*Le Balcon*, 1956) and *The Blacks* (*Les Nègres*, 1958) – turn to grotesque ritual, violent abuse and ceremonial death.

In *The Maids*, the eponymous duo alternate in playing power games, assuming the role of their mistress and of each other, to the extent of one taking poisoned tea intended for the hated and feared lady. Genet's original intention that the parts should be acted by men was fulfilled in a Berlin production in 1965. In *The Blacks*, featuring the ritual murder of a white woman, some of the cast of black actors masquerade as whites, as do (in intention at least) members of the play's supposedly black audience. The illusion of *The Balcony* is to transform the auditorium into a virtual brothel, doubling as a sacristy, amid an environment of violent revolution. Genet has been taken by some as the true heir to Artaud; but Styan (147), sees him as closer to the 'Pirandellian theatre-game'. 'Pure absurdism', in Styan's view (145), 'was like private poetry: even when it had expressed itself as fully as it could, it had little future'. Perhaps, though, there is no such thing as 'pure absurdism'? In Esslin's view, regardless, 'in the last resort, the Theatre of the Absurd does not provoke tears of despair but the laughter of liberation' (*Absurd Drama*, 23).

Pinter and others: the English-language scene

European playwrights of the absurd apart, this brand of theatrical writing was having its effect by the late 1950s in America and in the British Isles (we refrain, until Chapter 8, from any discussion of Beckett). In Edward Albee's *The Zoo Story* (1958), a chance conversation between two men in Central Park leads to the self-impalement of one, an apparent schizophrenic, on the knife he has provoked the other into picking up. Similar on a smaller scale to Albee's later full-length *Who's Afraid of Virginia Woolf?* (1962), termed by Esslin 'a savage dance of death reminiscent of Strindberg' (*Absurd Drama*, 22), *The Zoo Story* comprises a lengthy dialogue of non-communication and also includes the nearest thing we are likely to find to a literal shaggy-dog story: a rambling monologue announced as 'The Story of Jerry and the Dog!' (ibid., 170–6). Another shorter piece, *The American Dream* (1961), is reminiscent of Ionesco in its forceful exposure of hollowness behind the cliché.

In England, N.F. Simpson's *A Resounding Tinkle* was first produced, in its shortened form, in 1957.[8] This play is closer to the Ionesco of *The Bald Soprano* than to the theatrical cruelty of violence of other examples noted above of Theatre of the Absurd and actually, of course, *is* deriding the mores of the English middle classes. In addition to its suburban social satire, it represents a farrago of nonsense, paradox (the married couple featured are named Paradock), wordplay ('the small of my back is too big, Doctor': *NED*, 75) and pedantry. In a theatrical equivalent to the metafiction of prose fiction (or 'metatheatre': see Fletcher, 19–20), in the full-length version the devices of absurd drama are laid bare and commented on by a succession of subsidiary characters ranging from a pair of comedians (engaged for home visits), the supposed author (whose excuse for the uneven production is that most of the play came to him in Portuguese, a language he barely knows: *NED*, 87[9]), a technician, a team of critics, the producer and a sceptical member of the audience. The comedians, who see themselves as 'metaphysically the Marx Brothers, ...

Presenting the custard pie comedy of the abstract' (ibid., 91), discuss Bergson's theory of laughter with the Paradocks. A hilarious mock-service is broadcast over the radio in voices 'of cultured Anglican fatuity' (99); comic theorising, religious debunking and pseudo-science all represent entanglements of illusion and distortion, lunacy and sanity, falsehood and truth. The critical brains-trust (131–7) delivers shattering *aperçus* to such effect that: 'It is, basically, a parody of a skit on satire that [the author] is burlesquing, and the farce is so to speak a by-product of that' (136). The full text of *A Resounding Tinkle* may be theatrically unwieldy, but in its shorter form at least it remains a classic absurdist exercise – as one 'critic' terms it (ibid.): 'The Comedy of Errors rewritten by Lewis Carroll to provide a part for Godot or somebody'.

Harold Pinter has long been known as the supreme master of dialogue of incoherence and silence, especially set among the English lower or criminal classes (*The Birthday Party*, performed 1958; *The Dumb Waiter*, 1959; *The Caretaker*, 1960; *The Homecoming*, 1965). However, like N.F. Simpson, he is equally at home dissecting the foibles and discourse of the middle classes (*A Slight Ache*, 1959; *The Collection*, 1961, *The Lover*, 1963;[10] and so on); or combining these registers in grotesque forms of upward (and downward) mobility (*Night School*, 1960; *The Homecoming*). He is also famed for his explorations of the personal dynamics arising out of territorial conflict in a confined space (*The Room*, 1957; *The Caretaker*; *The Basement*, 1967). Power and sex, both personal and institutional, are vital ingredients from the beginning (witness *The Hothouse*, with its 'staff' and 'understaff', written 1958 but performed only in 1980). Possession, occupation or control of any sanctum invites hostility. Menace and violence (threatened or actual) constitute the other famed Pinteresque hallmarks of so many of his works, from *The Room* up to later parables of political repression (such as *One for the Road*, 1984; *Mountain Language*, 1988; and *The New World Order*, 1991). For Pinter, 'horror and absurdity go together' (interview of 1960; quoted by Esslin, *Th. Abs.*, 242).[11] Betrayal, invasion, invitation, usurpation and role (name or identity)-change or exchange are fundamental themes or mechanisms. An eternally Pinterian triangle, usually sexual in one form or another and present implicitly or explicitly almost throughout, assumes an increasing prominence (see *Old Times*, 1971; *Betrayal*, 1978).[12] What R.D. Laing would term 'ontological insecurity' remains at the forefront as Pinter 'spans the poles of the existential and the empirical' (Dobrez, 317–18; 369)

Early prose works, in fact, contained many of the ingredients of Pinter's subsequent dramatic practice. A short story, *The Examination* (1955; published 1963), explores manipulation and interrogation. The extended prose work *The Dwarfs* (written 1952–56; converted into a short play 1960; revised and published as a novel, 1990), along with its largely autobiographical content, in Michael Billington's words, 'brings together many of the preoccupations that were to become part of Pinter's permanent theatrical landscape: friendship, betrayal, dominance, subservience, sexual rivalry, space invasion, the dream of a secure, paradisal past and the fear of an insecure, provisional present and future' (Billington, 65).

In addition to incoherence and silence, Pinter's dialogue employs an all too natural (and paradigmatically absurd-sounding) recapture of realistic speech patterns, bringing into relief ambiguity, irrelevance, redundancy, non-sequiturs, cross-purpose exchange (whether heard or heeded, unheard or unheeded), mutterings, repartee, rhythm, garrulity and verbose outbursts (often hilariously convoluted, inappropriate or pretentious).[13] One of Pinter's declared aims is 'to get to this recognizable reality of the absurdity of what we do and how we behave and how we speak' (quoted by Esslin, *Th. Abs.*, 242). Much, if not all, depends on memory, which is shown to be at variance, unreliable and, of course, subject to lack of verification; all of this contributes to what Pinter has called 'that tired, grimy phrase: "Failure of communication"' (Pinter 1, xiii); rather, he argues, 'we communicate only too well, in our silence, in what is unsaid', while what *is* said or 'what takes place is a continual evasion'. 'Communication', he insists, 'is too alarming' (ibid.).

Apparent inconsequentiality and other such absurdist trappings are presented against a backdrop of mystification, dreamscape or even, in certain of the early plays at least, a suspicion of the supernatural. Context is depleted, limited or just not provided. At the same time, Dobrez (332) can justifiably argue 'that the author is not withholding anything, that everything is *there*, out in the open, that there is nothing to *add*'. The 'real story', whatever that may be, may seem nevertheless to be going on behind the scenes, or to have been played out elsewhere in the past. 'Reality' may be pure fantasy – amid farce, which becomes tragedy; or it embraces enigma, stemming from contradictions in the present and incompatible versions in the past; and we (and indeed frequently the characters) experience a resultant blurring of the actual with the fictional. 'The point about tragedy', according to Pinter, 'is that it is *no longer funny*' (quoted *Th. Abs.*, 242; emphasis Pinter's). Tragedy and farce, fact and fiction: Ronald Knowles indeed notes the claim that 'Pinter's creative imagination is fundamentally binary' (Knowles, 1995, 112).[14] Any trade in recollections is likely to be indistinguishable from (sexual or some other form of) mind-games. Repetition, or reversal, may occur – whether monological or dialogical – of actions, of utterances, or of scenes, already staged (or shortly to be staged) or merely alluded to. Self-reference is an essential within the plays. It may even occur between plays.[15]

A number of commentators (Knowles, for one) point out that Pinter's work from (approximately) 1957 to 1963 forms the group of plays 'often referred to as "comedies of menace"' (a term apparently coined for early Pinter by the drama critic Irving Wardle as early as 1958), 'or "theater of the absurd"', while from 1968 to 1975 comes a second period, that of 'the "memory plays", from *Landscape* (1968) and *Silence* (1969) to *No Man's Land* (1975)' (Knowles, 1995, 4–5; see also Dobrez, 323).[16] The view suggested here, though, is that absurdity remains a constant factor, representing a strong ingredient of the intervening *The Homecoming* ('arguably Pinter's most substantial and complex achievement': Knowles, 1995, 5) and perhaps even reaching a peak in *No Man's Land* ('by some way, Pinter's harshest vision of the human predicament': Billington, 244; but a play surprisingly downgraded as 'simply whimsical' in its final effect by Dobrez, 362–3), before re-surging again, albeit with differing emphases, in the later political plays and in *Moonlight* (1993). *Ashes to Ashes* (1996) has been seen by Yael Zarhy-Levo 'to conjoin (but not resolve) two contrary, or very different critical images of the playwright in a single play'; two generally recognised phases (by this count, the early to mid-career 'menace' to 'memory' one; followed by the late 'political' one) are now represented dialogically in 'two contradictory discursive modes' by the (early and 'inexplicit') memory-haunted Rebecca and the (late and 'explicit') interrogating Devlin respectively, comprising a 'meta-play' of a deliberately 'indeterminate' or 'doubled' nature (see Zarhy-Levo, in Raby, 221–4).[17]

The early review sketch *Last to Go* (1959), which comprises a late-night coffee-stall conversation between the 'barman' and a newspaper seller (as noted in Chapter 1), has been subjected to a revealing 'structuralist reading' by David Lodge – a reading which apparently occasioned considerable astonishment in Pinter (see Lodge, 270–1).[18] Lodge (275) discerns in this three-page sketch 'a microcosm of Harold Pinter's dramatic universe'. Using Jakobson's model of communication, he argues that an exchange of largely 'phatic' utterances is able to achieve none the less a 'poetic' quality, presenting 'in condensed form the central paradox of [Pinter's] work: how it is that dialogue superficially so banal, repetitive and full of silences, and a story so slight and ambiguous, can interest and entertain us' (ibid.). The binary patterning of presence and absence, speech and silence (or the characteristically Pinteresque 'pause') is represented by the negative presence (rather the absence or non-location) of a figure named George; and by the (erstwhile) 'presence-about-to-be terminated' of the last evening paper to go, 'just before it goes' (Lodge, 285). According to Lodge (ibid.), the sketch's 'semiotic structure' may be summarised as: 'Speech is to Silence as George is to the last newspaper to go'.

Last to Go apart, discussion here is mainly concentrated on a quartet of four plays, dating from 1959 to 1993, which appear to me to present a certain form of absurdism, perhaps of a particularly Beckettian stripe, consistently over a considerable portion of Pinter's career. The growing disconnection between the speakers in *A Slight Ache* is deepened in the later plays – *Landscape*, *Family Voices* and *Moonlight* – into the non-connecting (or barely, or only occasionally, connecting) monologues that make up these succeeding works. This is not, of course, to say that other plays – *The Birthday Party* being just one obvious case – do not have their absurdist qualities, as no shortage of commentaors have indicated elsewhere.

A Slight Ache was written as a radio play, with theatre performances following from two years later (1961). Like certain other Pinter plays, it features a trio of three characters, though this time with a third personage, the 'matchseller', who never speaks. The incidence of an elderly married couple looking back (in this case particularly obliquely) over their lives, inviting into their country residence a third person who remains mute rather than providing any message or explanation, is a configuration somewhat reminiscent of Ionesco's *The Chairs*; and indeed Edward is somewhat obsessed with chairs, seating and furniture in general (of chairs he declares: 'We have a great variety, as you see': P1, 167).[19] In the original radio version, of course, the very existence of the matchseller may be doubted, while his (eventual) presence on the stage reduces at least somewhat the scope for conjecture, at least in this regard.[20] The intrusive matchseller may none the less still be a figure conjured up – into an allegedly metamorphosing form – in the flesh (or otherwise), from the past, or from the imagination, of one or both of the two main characters, posing as, among other things: Flora's supposed rapist-poacher; Edward's cricketing chum Cavendish; 'a haunting image of the 1930s Depression and post-war deprivation' (Knowles, 1995, 41); 'the Other' (Dobrez, 334); some kind of 'latent double' figure or herald of Death (Burkman: Bold, 134–5);[21] 'an embodiment of meaninglessness' (Morrison, 156); or simply Edward's Nemesis.

Before the matchseller is spotted, or at least alluded to, the opening breakfast bickering over garden floral shrubs is diverted by the intrusion of a wasp (and argument as to whether it might 'bite' or 'sting': P1, 157); the disposal of this insect is interrupted by Edward reporting 'a slight ache' in the eyes (P1, 156). His intention to work on an essay 'on space and time' (P1, 161) is submerged by a sudden obsession with the old matchseller, who has apparently been lurking at the back garden gate for two months (hitherto unmentioned by Edward). 'The irritant wasp', as Mark Batty points out, 'is easily blinded and squashed, but any attempt to wipe out that other irritant intruder clearly proves to have the opposite effect' (Batty, 25; similar points are made by Morrison, 159; and Dobrez, 333). As Francesca Coppa observes, though, Edward, in only trapping the wasp in the marmalade rather than immediately getting rid of it, 'has locked in the thing he wanted to expel': and therein we have 'the play in microcosm' (Coppa: in Raby, 50). Indeed, Edward's ocular 'slight ache' is soon aggravated, as Flora observes his eyes to be 'bloodshot' and he cries: 'Aaah my eyes' (P1, 162); a heightened preoccupation with observation and sight (P1, 181;182) signals Edward's rapid visual and physical collapse.

Meanwhile bizarre forms of identity equivalence are suggested or established between the three characters – through, of course, the mental meanderings of just two of them (Edward and Flora), in their separate and peculiar one-way locutions with the matchseller. Edward's largely (and fruitlessly) interrogative monologue laced with a patronising *fausse bonhomie* becomes an increasingly demented survey of his life and times. The matchseller for him may be an 'impostor' (P1, 163) or an old acquaintance. The squire's daughter (of yesteryear), with her 'flaming red hair' ('Sally', or rather 'Fanny. A flower': P1, 166–7), may be Flora (a flower), herself once with 'flaming red hair' (168), and anyway no different 'in essence' from the matchseller (171). For Flora, the matchseller may be a past partner or assailant; he certainly seems to become a present, or future, sexual substitute for her husband (who has to endure his 'vampiric posture': Batty, 27). Apart from the more allegorical possibilities (suggested by Katherine Burkman), the antics of A *Slight Ache* take on something of the air of a geriatric sex-game – a possibility hinted at by Knowles (1995, 40), by his comparison with *The Lover*.

Edward's ocular troubles presage his confidence in discovering everything 'by nightfall' (P1, 172); he induces darkness by closing the curtains (177): 'You look different in darkness', he tells the matchseller, encouraging him to strip off (178). By the end of the play, Edward envisages there to be moonlight (183), although it appears to be shortly after lunch and the (sunshade) canopy has at last been raised in the garden. Edward is still asking the matchseller ('with great final effort'): 'Who are you?'. Flora has named him 'Barnabas' (according to Burkman, meaning summer: in Bold, 137). Flora has 'replaced' Edward with the matchseller. Several times she has stressed that it is the longest day of the year. By the end of the play Edward's slight ache bites, to bring on his premature midsummer night's dream – in the form of sightless nightmare.

The one-act *Landscape* and *Silence* are seen as Beckettian developments into 'cross-cut monologues' (Billington, 197; '*Silence* . . . is the most Beckettian of all Pinter's plays': Knowles, in Raby, 76). The former play, generally considered the more engaging, indeed, 'is often described as two interwoven monologues that only tangentially intersect' (Batty, 49). A middle-aged couple, Duff and Beth, speechify at the kitchen table of a country house which they still (or, at any rate, used to) manage for its absent (or deceased) owner, a Mr Sykes. As the directions make clear, 'Duff refers normally to Beth, but does not appear to hear her voice', while 'Beth never looks at Duff , and does not appear to hear his voice' (P3, 166); nevertheless, as Kristin Morrison observes (130), 'there are ghostly connections between their monologues': to do with love and/or adultery; hotel or pub scenes; and a (presumably common to both) dog.

Beth's lyrical turn of speech – or the (mental) landscape of the title – covers physical tenderness, a beach scene, the desire for reproduction and her aptitude for drawing; this all seems to relate to the fairly distant past. In contrast, Duff, who jumps about chronologically, is more concerned with events of 'yesterday' (P3, 165) and the present, and has something of a penchant for excremental phraseology and macho sex. Beth's former lover may have been (and is variously seen as) one or more of Duff himself, or perhaps Mr Sykes, or even another altogether; Pinter himself was apparently amenable to ascribing the role to Duff.[22] Beth, then, appears to be, to say the least, withdrawn into the world of her past. Duff makes some attempt at least to go through the motions of attempting communication. At the same time, the pertaining situation apparently has certain compensations – for him, anyway: 'We're lucky', or 'the envy of a lot of people' (P3, 175; 180), to have the Sykes house; 'at least now, I can walk down to the pub in peace and up to the pond in peace, with no one to nag the shit out of me'; and, moreover, he affirms: 'We're together. That's what matters' (182).

The explanation for the prevailing stasis in the Beth–Duff kitchen may lie in the former's lament for what is (or is felt to be) lost love or fertility.[23] Or there may have been traumatic consequences from Duff's confession of infidelity, or from whatever may (or may not) have been the basis for the sexual assault on Beth alluded to by Duff, and set in train by the (allegedly unwarranted) banging of the gong (P3, 186–7): taken as 'rape' (Billington, 200), or 'fantasy' (Morrison, 136). This, in the text at least (and that, as ever, is all we have), follows Duff's enthusiastic enunciation of the cellarman's art of penetration ('Spile the bung. Hammer the spile through the centre of the bung. ... Then you hammer the tap in': P3, 183); it may also be compared with Bert's driving outburst at the end of *The Room*, immediately preceding his vicious assault on Riley ('I caned her along', etc.: P1, 110). However, as Dobrez (357) remarks, in Pinter's works 'these questions require no answers, other than *probable* ones' – if we can even stretch as far as probability.

In what, once again, was first performed as a radio play, *Family Voices* (1981) has been described as 'more reminiscent than ever of Beckett yet totally Pinteresque in its handling of the drama' (Dobrez, 364–5).[24] This time we have three self-standing monologues, delivered in what purports to be letter form, from three 'Voices': belonging to an estranged son (1); his mother (2); and an allegedly dead father (3: even the dead 'write') – as Morrison (218) aptly puts it, these are 'dead letters sent from afar'. The utterances possess a typically Pinterian poetic banality and just about everything stated is contradicted or clowned with (the only name ascribed to any of the three principals is 'Bobo', as Voice 1 is dubbed in his new *ersatz* hearth and home: P4, 146). There appears to be no cognisance of these 'epistles' on the part of their supposed addressees (and again Jakobson's communication model could be applied). The exception to this is that Voice 3, from his 'glassy grave' (146) claims to know at least that Voice 2 has reported his death to Voice 1, and his own final speech (and the final words of the play) – 'I have so much to say to you. But I am quite dead. What I have to say to you will never be said' – seems to come in answer to Voice 1's 'What will you say to me?' (148), although this question had been addressed to Voice 2. The lack of meaningful message from the beyond (Steven Gale draws a comparison here with Eliot's Lazarus in *The Love Song of J. Alfred Prufrock*: see Bold, 148)[25] may, once again, remind us of Ionesco's Orator (as well as Pinter's earlier matchseller).[26]

Voice 3 claims (on balance!) to be dead; Voice 2 may be dying, if not dead; Voice 1, if we do not leap at 'realistic' (in so far as such is possible) or purely psychoanalytical interpretations, may be ensconced either with an alternative 'family' of the mind, or himself in some kind of *demi-monde* of pleasure – or guilt-ridden afterlife (a rather more humorous version of Sartre's *Huis Clos*).[27] For Knowles (1995, 148) '*Family Voices*, is almost an epitome of postmodernism'. According to Gale (148), it 'almost takes on the character of a self-parody'; Billington, too (279), sees it as 'a deeply self-referential work'. In the view of Dobrez (365), it 'takes up all the old concerns, returns to all the obsessive images, in a way which appears to review, *da capo*, every phase of Pinter's development, like a symphonic climax'.

To Dobrez, writing in 1986, it *was* Pinter's climax. Such a comment, however, we can now of course see as slightly premature. A more plausible candidate for such an accolade may be the later – though still by no means final – play, *Moonlight* (see the summary along these lines by Knowles, 1995, 205–6) – dubbed by a *Sunday Times* reviewer 'one of Pinter's most haunting minor works' (Billington, 347). The 'haunting' rather than the 'minor' might here be the more justified epithet. 'Darkness and light, moonlight and loss, separation and death, all re-emerge in the creation of *Moonlight*' (Knowles, 1995, 200). 'Moonlight', somewhat akin to 'no man's land', represents a phase between life and death, or a sphere permeated by the still living who are preoccupied with death (or even by the dead who are still preoccupied with the living) – possibly analogous to, or even deriving from, the Yeatsian concept of 'dreaming back' (a suggestion introduced by Anthony Roche in discussion of *Betrayal*, but perhaps more appropriate to *Moonlight*).[28] Or it could, for that matter, be seen to denote the 'dramatic fourth dimension' discerned by Knowles (1995, 131) as the *mise en scène* of *Old Times*. This is made clear (in so far as anything is) by the ghostly Bridget's association with moonlight, and by Andy's (apparently deathbed) conjectures on what follows death: 'And what's the weather like? Is it uncertain with showers or sunny with fogpatches? Or unceasing moonlight with no cloud? Or pitch black for ever and ever?' (P4, 358). Andy's attempted answer may be said to constitute a classic existential-absurdist *cri de coeur*:

> You may say you haven't the faintest fucking idea and you would be right. But personally I don't believe it's going to be pitch black for ever because if it's pitch black for ever what would have been the point of going through all these enervating charades in the first place? There must be a loophole. The only trouble is, I can't find it. If only I could find it I would crawl through it and meet myself coming back. Like screaming with fright at the site of a stranger only to find you're looking into a mirror. (P4, 358)

The 'voices' in *Moonlight* are, at least some of the time, more interlinking than those of *Family Voices* – though separable by such a tragi-comic device as the sons (those virtuosi of comedic patter and catechismic rhythm) answering their mother's distressed telephone call with 'Chinese laundry?' (381). Again the configuration is dominantly that of family – torn apart by death, estrangement and intimations of mortality across generations; yet the central couple (of Bel and Andy) are somehow held together, while emotionally separated, by a shared 'system' of marital and extra-marital sexual experiences.

The frequently foul-mouthed Andy ('I kept my obscene language for the home, where it belongs': 334) is complimented by Bel on his 'lovely use of language' when, wondering whether he will see another spring, he evokes 'all the paraphernalia of flowers' (335). Beneath a 'vicious some would say demented exterior' there yet exists 'a delicate even poetic sensibility' (ibid.), he is advised (as are we). Bel's keenly elucidatory remarks here would seem to epitomise the Pinterian absurd. As John Stokes has stressed, '[Pinter's] imagination has consistently delivered works that may be puzzling, but which are never simply "absurd"'.[29] Nevertheless, as Billington (348) has written of 'the crucial oneness of Pinter's imaginative world', with particular reference to his work on the adaptation of Kafka's *The Trial* (released shortly before the première of *Moonlight*), 'his vision of man's essential solitude in a baffling and hostile universe permeates his being and carries over from one project to the next'. We shall return to *The Trial* (in Kafka and in Pinter) in due course.

Joe Orton, known as 'the master farceur of his age' and 'a connoisseur of chaos',[30] in a meteoric dramatic career that stretched only from 1964 to 1967, produced a total of seven plays that have given him an assured place in what we might by now be considering as 'English absurdism'. Indeed, Zarhy-Levo (2001, 43–65) provides an account of Orton's assimilation into just such a category. Affinities are not hard to spot between Orton's plays (or at least elements therein) and works by Ionesco and Genet on the one hand, and Pinter and Simpson on the other, as well as ploys or motifs recognisable from Greek (and indeed Jacobean) tragedy.

John Lahr (Introduction to Orton, 8) considers that 'Orton's plays are a flamboyant dance with the death he found in life' and Orton himself always insisted on the serious dimension that lay behind his bleak and hilarious brand of black farce – according to Julia Listengarten (17), 'based upon his awareness of life's tragifarcical absurdity'.

'Black comedy can be seen as a kind of antithesis to the comedy of menace', according to Coppa (in Raby, 52) and, in what she sees as a rewriting of 'a number of Pinterian triangles', Orton eschews the mystery, and instead supplies 'the missing plot and character motivations' (ibid.) – by expressing the previously 'unspeakable' in what Lahr calls 'scenes of macabre outrageousness' (Orton, 11). Thus *The Ruffian on the Stair* (1964) is seen, with certain reversals, to match *The Room*; and particularities of *Entertaining Mr Sloane* (1964) correspond with *The Birthday Party* (see Coppa: ibid., 52–5). Corporate suppression, suffocating bureaucracy, institutional repression, universal corruption and Fascistic undertones permeate the world of Orton's plays; Catholicism, state patriotism, 'purity' and psychiatry are among his principal *bêtes noires*. A number of these features offer a parallel to Pinter's *The Hothouse* – the one early Pinter play which Orton, of course, could not have known. On the more microcosmic level, one suspects that Prentice's line from *What the Butler Saw* (1967), 'Oh, if this gets out I'll be reduced to selling matches' (Orton, 426), may be an allusion to *A Slight Ache*, just as the reported placing of 'a deposit on a five-feet-long python' (*Funeral Games*, Orton, 349) must surely be a nod to Simpson's *A Resounding Tinkle*.

Orton, through his 'inspired megalomaniacs', says Lahr (Orton, 7), 'showed man dummying up a destiny in a meaningless world by making panic look like reason'. McLeavy, in *Loot* (1966), asks: 'Is the world mad? Tell me it's not', to which Truscott (the bent policeman posing as a water-board official) retorts, 'I'm not paid to quarrel with accepted facts' (Orton, 258). Just as the world is run by fools, mental institutions are 'for the most part' run by madmen – former students of an academic failed madman (*What the Butler Saw*: Orton, 386) – a tradition Orton picks up from Poe (*The System of Doctor Tarr and Professor Fether*) and Chekhov (*Ward No. 6*) – among others, including no doubt de Sade, and one could regard Kafka (*In the Penal Colony*) as analogous, as well as Pinter.[31] In Orton's plays, the (speakable or unspeakable) colloquial is finely laced with the ironic, the poetic and the epigrammatic, to further his (surely eminently absurdist) declared aesthetic aim of achieving the 'ridiculous' through 'a combination of elegance and crudity' (Orton, 10). Dubbed in his time (by *The Observer*: ibid., 9) 'the Oscar Wilde of Welfare State gentility', Joe Orton was perhaps rather an authentic Oscar Wilde for the iconoclastic kitchen-sink 1960s.

The East European scene

'In its present form the Theatre of the Absurd is a post-war phenomenon', writes Esslin (still in the 1960s: *Absurd Drama*, 17), effectively dating perhaps from the first performance of Genet's *The Maids* in 1947. Taking the broader historical view, as we have seen in Chapter 3, both Esslin and Segal would see the phenomenon as having commenced with Jarry in 1896. The heyday of Theatre of the Absurd, in most estimations, would run from about 1950 (with the key Ionesco and Beckett productions), probably to the 1970s – and we have already paid some attention to a few of Pinter's later works from a decade or so beyond that. Francesca Coppa (in Raby, 52) notes that many writers 'have built their careers filling in Pinterian silences' – amounting to 'a generation of black comedy'. Some of these figures will be mentioned when we eventually come to consider a possible category of 'post-absurdism'.

(Soviet) Russia: the OBERIU

At the other chronological end of the scale, we have earlier briefly noted the pre-war work of Witkiewicz. Even closer to postwar Theatre of the Absurd, arguably, are the main plays of the Russian OBERIU writers Kharms and Vvedensky. The OBERIU movement (or 'Association of Real Art') has already been summarised in general terms (see Chapter 3) and there will follow a separate chapter on the prose writings of Daniil Kharms. However, we here and now turn to Kharms's main dramatic work, *Yelizaveta Bam*.

Written in twelve days at the end of 1927 (when Kharms was still a mere fledgling writer of twenty-two), *Yelizaveta Bam* is a one-act play consisting of nineteen short scenes of uneven length, labelled 'bits' (*kuski*), stretching from 'Realistic melodrama' to 'Operatic ending'.[32] These relatively realistic opening and closing scenes (the latter a near-repeat of the former, but with its sinister, or fateful, conclusion) sandwich seventeen rather more stylised sections, which form a montage resembling music-hall routines, including snatches of song and dance, rhyme and rhythm, nonsense (or *zaum'* language), and elements of the folkloric, pantomime and the mock-epic. These amount to an emphasis on 'scenic plot', rather than 'dramatic plot' which, in so far as it can be discerned at all, as the OBERIU manifesto has it, 'glimmers, so to speak, behind the back of the action' (Gibian, 254). From the opening setting of 'a shallow, simple room' (*Incidences*, 155), the backcloth moves back, allowing the intruders (presumed secret policemen) through the door (ibid., 160), the scenery 'revolves from living room to countryside' (169) and, by the penultimate 'bit', the scene 'is as the beginning' (182). The styles comprise something of 'a parodic retrospection of all possible theatrical genres' (Mikhail Meilakh, 202).

There is thus an emphasis here on elements beyond language, somewhat analogous to the (near-contemporaneous) theory and practice of Artaud (as noted by Graham Roberts, 1994, 46, n. 28); even though discourse may be subject to 'a certain relegation, or devaluation ... within the play's textual economy as a whole', however, language can be said to remain 'paramount' (ibid., 46). The 'violence' done (in the 'Battle of the Two Heroes': *Incidences*, 177–80), or said to have been done, appears to be carried out, in effect, through words. Characteristic of absurdist drama, in Jenny Stelleman's view, is the notion that 'Fatum is ever-present at the end, despite the play-acting at the level of the dialogue'; the concentration here, though, may be, according to some views at least, on alogicality, play and word-play, transformations and metamorphoses, rather than, as in European Theatre of the Absurd, 'the sense that life has no meaning' (Nakhimovsky, 40; Stelleman, 136; 152; see also Roberts, 1997, 142).[33] Jean-Philippe Jaccard, however, sees a common attitude over the inadequacy of language to express the world as one of the main similarities between the theatre of Kharms and that of Ionesco.[34] Listengarten too (166–7) sees a Kharmsian 'meaninglessness' as prefiguring 'the tragigrotesque nature of the universe depicted in post-World War II absurdist drama, primarily in France', while farcical elements ('the transformation of identity, punning, clowning, maniacally speedy action, and averted as well as real cruelty') serve to 'transport the action of *Elizaveta Bam* into the realm of the absurd'. Hazel Grünewald uses a (Bakhtinian) concept of 'generic ambiguity' to further an absurdist reading, while seeking to demonstrate that 'an absurd critical construct recognises the feasibility of other readings'.[35] Two 'other readings' are supplied by Roberts: approaches to the play from the perspective of language games (*à la* Wittgenstein: Roberts, 1994) and sexual politics (Roberts, 1996; both of these fruitful analyses are summarised in Roberts, 1997). Stress is also laid by a number of commentators on the social and political dimension, including the added qualities of bleak absurdity arising out of life in Stalin's Soviet Union.

Language and communication are seen by Jaccard to function, or fail, in Kharms in ways close to the effects achieved by Ionesco; he makes detailed comparisons with passages from *The Bald Soprano*; he also notes a similarity between the predicaments of the eponymous Yelizaveta Bam and Bérenger (as protagonist of *Rhinoceros*, 1960), as well as discerning a 'metaphysical horror' at the root of both writers – as can be witnessed in their respective notebooks (Jaccard, 26). In terms of the terrorising of women, Roberts (1996, 256; 262, n. 40) draws a comparison between the treatment of Yelizaveta and of the student in *The Lesson*, 'in which, after a series of language games played by the male teacher and his female pupil, he kills her with the word "knife"'. We have already mentioned above a similar motif of murder victim identity to that referred to in *Amédée* (see also below). Listengarten (171) compares *Yelizaveta Bam* to *Waiting for Godot* with regard to their respective exploitation of 'the darker side of clowning'.[36] If we turn to Pinter, we can see the same violation of the sanctity of a room (or personal space). We can also note a distinct similarity in the exposition of the dynamics of interrogational dialogue.[37] Finally, Grünewald (92–3) reads *Yelizaveta Bam* as, among other things, both a subversion and a rejuvenation of Greek tragedy.

This brings us now to the crux of the play: Yelizaveta's 'crime'. The first accusation made against her is that, having 'committed a vile crime', she 'has lost all right of reply' (*Incidences*, 159; more literally, she is 'deprived of all voice'). The 'vile crime' is later clarified as the murder of Pyotr Nikolayevich – one of the two men who are attempting to arrest her.[38] He has allegedly been murdered by Yelizaveta in the country setting of the mid-play pastoral frolics, and at some point before the commencement of the action; during the play, at the culmination of these frolics (the 'Battle of the Two Heroes'), he is ostensibly killed by Yelizaveta's father. In the replay of the opening scene, Yelizaveta opens the door, thus delivering herself into the hands of her tormentors, now for some reason dressed as firemen (and one of whom she is alleged to have murdered); in her last speech, as she is about to be taken away into the darkness, she refers to a cockroach from 'the little house on the hill' (mentioned too in preceding references to the little house), now seemingly in the guise of an executioner ('in his shirt with the reddish collar and an axe in his hands': *Incidences*, 184).[39]

The motif of accusation over a crime that has not in fact been committed, or of which the perpetrator is not aware, of course invites comparison with Kafka's *The Trial* (and by extension Pinter's *The Birthday Party*), as well as with the 'gnostic turpitude' alleged of Cincinnatus C., the protagonist of Nabokov's *Invitation to a Beheading* (written ten years later, as noted by Meilakh, 212). The apparent fact that the crime of murder could not have been committed (given that the supposed victim is palpably still alive and all too active) provides an additional twist in the direction of the absurd, bringing it into line, for instance, with the supposedly murdered 'young man' of Ionesco's *Amédée*, on the fate of whom the eponymous protagonist muses: 'Was it really this young Romeo that we ... that I killed? It seems to me, – oh what a memory I've got! ... it seems to me that the young man had already left ... when the crime was committed' (*Absurd Drama*, 63).

According to Alice Stone Nakhimovsky (132), 'Vvedenskii's later works oscillate between two extremes: the rejection of bourgeois patterns and values, and the recognition of a truth which has the appearance of absurdity'. Aleksandr Vvedensky has, perhaps undeservedly, received

considerably less critical attention overall than Kharms, his fellow-
oberiut. However, his remarkable play *Christmas at the Ivanovs'* (*Elka u
Ivanovykh*), written in 1938, may now, aided by its two English translations, be gaining at least some recognition.[40] *Yelizaveta Bam* was
performed at an OBERIU evening in 1928; *Christmas at the Ivanovs'*, ten
years later in the Soviet Union, was utterly unperformable. Indeed, there
may be some doubt as to whether Vvedensky had ever written it for
performance: certainly, it has been described as 'a drama to be read' (see
Roberts, 1997, 104), and stage instructions which shade into authorial
commentary (and include an autopsy-type vision into a corpse) lend
support to this view. For reasons that will soon be apparent, one could
more easily visualise its realisation either in the form of a surrealist film
or as a cartoon. Nevertheless, in the post-Soviet period in Russia, somewhat stylised productions or adaptations have seemingly been attempted
– as reported by Roberts (ibid., 104–5), who himself suggests the possibility of performance resembling 'a gruesome pantomime/circus show
with a narrator figure situated off stage' to read all the stage directions.

Christmas at the Ivanovs' is quite a short play, though structured in
four acts and nine scenes (or *kartiny*, literally 'pictures' or tableaux).
Commonly seen as a parody of Chekhov's theatre (it is ostensibly set in
the 1890s) with touches of German Expressionism, the setting would
purport to be the household of a family of the nobility, called the Ivanovs,
at Christmastide. Christmas is certainly constantly in the air, but not one
among the characters bears the name Ivanov. The parents are called
Puzyrov and their seven 'children', who are aged from one to eighty-two,
are all being bathed by multiple nannies in the opening scene (on
Christmas Eve), and each of them bears a different surname. The bath tub
of this first 'picture' is said to be 'drawn', thus from the outset calling into
question the dimensionality of the world in question (noted by Roberts,
1997, 98–9).[41] Stage right, 'cooks are slaughtering chickens and slaughtering piglets' (Vved., 395). A clock face indicates the hour at the
beginning and the end of all scenes (even in the one set in the forest, and
often with unreasonable jumps forward). As soon as the directions beginning Scene 2, an alternative 'Christmas at the Puzyryovs' is indicated
(397).

Before long Sonya, the 'precocious' thirty-two-year-old girl, is decapi-
tated with an axe by one of the nannies for voicing sexual insinuations.
The parents, on their return from the ballet, although grief-stricken, determine to carry on with the Christmas celebrations and promptly copulate
in front of the coffin; Sonya's head and body exchange a few words (Body,
having no ears, claims to have 'heard nothing', yet answers Head's question: 401). Other scenes involve Vera the verse-talking dog (shades here
of Gogol's *Notes of a Madman*); other talking animals; the police and a
court, and a lunatic asylum (run, of course, by a madman) in which

patients sail into the room in a boat, 'pushing the oars against the floor' (Vved., 404: presumably, a realisation of the 'ship of fools'). Particularly zany moments here include the doctor's shooting first at a mirror (a farcical play on the double theme) and then shooting a rug, to which he has taken a dislike, whereupon an attendant 'falls as though dead', explaining: 'It seemed to me I was a little rug. I was mistaken' (403). Elements of nonsense (at times quite modern-seeming), fairy tale and total lunacy seem to dominate.[42] In the final scene the remaining characters die, one after the other.[43] 'We didn't know any of them, and they all died, in any case'; the events took place 'forty years before us' (410, indicating, for what significance it may have, the year 1898), so we needn't worry about any of it, we are assured by the stage directions-cum-commentary.

All in all, to say that Vvedensky 'questions the Aristotelian notion of drama as mimesis' (Roberts, 1997, 105) is something of an understatement. Listengarten (176) refers to 'a totally perverse world in which slaughtered animals and bathing children occupy the same space'. Nakhimovsky (146) discerns 'a hierarchy of understanding' according to which the apparently most unlikely characters attain the most 'profound absurdity' (the insights of the one-year-old Petya, for example, are sharper than those of his more aged siblings). Listengarten (177–8) sees a stronger semblance of plot causality in *Christmas at the Ivanovs'* than in *Yelizaveta Bam* (thus removing it slightly from the original OBERIU aesthetic). In the view of Nakhimovsky (152), though, 'it is not frightening or metaphysical in the sense of Kafka or even *Elizaveta Bam*'. It has been seen as 'reminiscent of Marinetti's Futurist theatre' (Roberts, 1997, 105), or, with its penetration into subconsciousness, more 'in the tradition of surrealist drama' (Listengarten, 178).[44] The works of these OBERIU dramatists 'create their absurdity from a fusion of the farcical and the tragic' – in a combination of 'spiritual death', 'the notion of life's futility' and the 'grotesque incongruity' of human affairs (ibid., 180). Kharms and Vvedensky were repressed at the beginning of the 1940s, and, as Listengarten stresses (180), a postwar Theatre of the Absurd could have no existence in Soviet Russia; however, she counts their plays 'among the earliest examples of absurdism in the history of the theater'.

(Cold-War) Poland and Czechoslovakia

Towards the later end of the epoch of classic Theatre of the Absurd (if we may employ such an expression), we encounter contributions from Eastern Europe in the shape of the earlier plays of Sławomir Mrożek and Václav Havel. Halina Stephan, who entitles her study of Mrożek *Transcending the Absurd*, writes that 'his early dramas adapted the cabaret humor and the techniques of the Theatre of the Absurd to the cultural and political situation of post-socialist realist Poland' (Stephan, 7). The dominant relevance of 'the specific sociopolitical system', however, is generally thought to render this resemblance somewhat 'superficial' (ibid., 19–20). Mrożek was regarded as 'the continuator of the interwar tradition of the grotesque', represented by, in particular, Witkiewicz and Gombrowicz (66). Initially a satirical prose writer and journalist, Mrożek wrote what is still perhaps his most famous play *Tango* in 1964, just after leaving Poland.[45] This play deals with attempts to re-establish a sense of order within a family 'in a world bereft of standards' (126), employing weapons of (familial, or localised) power politics and fear of death – Mrożek's on-stage world being built, as one Polish commentator has it, as a 'microsociety' rather than a (more genuinely absurdist) microcosm (see ibid., 100). Order is restored through the eventual triumph of the 'heavy-fisted simpleton', whereupon 'the once avant-garde tango' is danced over the corpse of the 'conservative idealist', thus inaugurating 'the dawn of the new era' (127) – a grotesque dance of death now performed 'on the ruins of the civilized world' (*Th. Abs.*, 321).

In his following plays, such as *Vatzlav* (1968), Mrożek 'departs from the absurdist poetics with political undertones and develops as a contemporary *Lehrstück* built on the conventions of eighteenth-century theatre', although *Emigrants* (*Emigranci*, 1974) is seen to contain echoes of *Waiting for Godot* (Stephan, 151; 165). However a return towards earlier patterns is discerned in at least two of the later plays. In *A Summer's Day* (*Letni dzień*, 1984), audiences are brought back to the 'geometrical structures, circular action, and ultimately the metaphysical despair of the Theatre of the Absurd', in an early twentieth-century setting, placing 'existential ennui' amid a parabolic philosophical and socio-political pertinence (ibid., 197–201).[46] Later still, *The Widows* (*Wdowy*, 1992) 'can best be described as a black comedy in which two females and two males try to avoid a confrontation with death, who is personified as a mysterious silent figure sitting at a table in a coffeehouse' (216: see 215–19). Symmetry rules as two widows (in the first act) recover from the funerals of their respective husbands who have perished in a duel (each having been 'the lover of the other woman'), assuming the third one, 'the silent black-clad woman', to have been 'the mistress of both men and the ultimate cause of the duel'; the two men (in the second act) each dance with 'death', the veiled woman, leading to a farcical duel in which both die (216).[47] The dialogue and the actions turn the play into 'an absurd burlesque that the characters act out in their unwillingness to recognize their inevitable mortality' (217), with elements of self-parody and folklore, closer perhaps to the *commedia dell'arte* (218 n.).

The 'Thaw' years in Czechoslovakia, leading up to the Soviet invasion of 1968, also saw an influx of absurdist theatre. Features of the grotesque, farce and dream had earlier pervaded the plays of the Čapek brothers

(Josef and Karel), the science-fiction robot saga *R.U.R.* (1920) and the satirical 'Entomological Review' drama *The Insect Play* (*Ze života hmyzu*, 1921).[48] Elements of absurdism and the Baroque are discerned in Josef Topol's *End of Carnival* (*Konec masopustu*, 1963: Pynsent and Kanikova, 400), while his *Nightingale for Supper* (*Slavík k večeři*, 1967) too is seen as 'absurdist-influenced' (Burian, 99). The Theatre on the Balustrade in Prague put on at this time key plays by Jarry, Ionesco and Beckett, as well as Jan Grossman's adaptation of Kafka's *The Trial*, and the plays of Havel. Ivan Klíma's play *The Castle* (*Zámek*, 1964), as might be guessed, derives its title and its central character (one Josef Kahn) from Kafka (Burian, 105). The absurdist implications located in this Czech theatre of the mid-1960s, as explained by Jarka Burian (104), 'obviously, ... were inspired by life in Czechoslovakia, but they can relate just as clearly to any technocratic society'. The intent is political, but not only, or merely, political. Grossman, the Balustrade's director, said: 'Absurd theatre takes on the function of devil's advocate ... in order to reveal the devil' (ibid., 121). And the devil was not necessarily confined to matters political: Esslin (*Th. Abs.*, 324) discerns 'Kafkaesque depths' in the work of Havel.

Havel himself, apparently, tended to deny that absurdism was part of this theatre's programme, but added: 'I have the feeling that if absurd theatre had not been invented before me, I would have had to invent it' (quoted from Burian, 104–5). In *Audience* (1975), one of his clutch of what are taken to be autobiographical plays from the following decade, featuring a disgraced playwright named Vanek, the hero, in response to the enquiry as to what he used to write plays about anyway, answers: 'Mainly about bureaucrats ...' (Havel, 1993, 188).[49] Insane bureaucracy is certainly the prime target of the first three of Havel's Balustrade plays of the years leading to the Prague Spring. *The Garden Party* (*Zahradní slavnost*, 1963) presents a ridiculous bureaucratic tangle over the possible function of the Inauguration Service, vis à vis the Liquidation Service, in inaugurating the liquidation of the Inauguration Service.[50]

The Memorandum (*Vyrozumění-Protokoly*, 1966), which remains probably Havel's best known play, features the introduction of a new bureaucratic language ('Ptydepe', maximising the difference between words) designed to 'introduce precision and order' into office terminology (Havel, 1993, 58).[51] Ludicrously complex as the new language is (and after all, 'we're no linguists, are we?', observes the Head of the translation Centre: ibid., 70), it cannot function, and soon has to be replaced with another synthetic tongue ('Chorukov', minimising the difference between words), based on opposite philological principles, which of course will have an equally remote prospect of efficacy. 'Rationality, pressed to an extreme parody of itself', as Terry Eagleton (251) would have it, 'becomes full-blown irrationalism'. In the process, sycophancy, ruthless office politics and a constant preoccupation with lunch seem to rule the roost. As in

The Garden Party (and even through the medium of translation), Havel shows himself a master of word-play and repartee, in which inversion and repetition try conclusions with redundancy and other elements seemingly drawn from information and communication theory and Wittgensteinian word-game (noted by Esslin, *Th. Abs.*, 325–6). Tom Stoppard (in his 'Introduction': Vladislav, 278) refers here to 'the absurdities pushed to absurdity compounded by absurdity and yet saved from mere nonsense by their internal logic'; he also notes 'the utter lack of righteousness or petulance or bile' characterising Havel's drama of this period, shared too with the later Vanek plays (ibid.).

A considerably later play, *Largo Desolato* (1984), directed at the Balustrade by Grossman in 1990, dealt with its autobiographical protagonist (clearly established by the use of Havel's voice-over reading the opening and closing stage directions) by means of 'relatively comic treatment' (Burian, 193–4); this play too, while obviously reflecting the still pertaining East European dissident *ambiance*, maintains at the same time a more universal feel.[52] The third play of Havel's early period, *The Increased Difficulty of Concentration* (*Stížená možnost soustředění*, 1968), combines technological satire with domestic banality in a structual *tour de force* which 'present[s] the action in cubistic fashion' (Burian, 104), with what are apparently chronologically juggled scenes deliberately repeating fragments with interchanging characters and climactic Ionesco-like features of mass character participation and a repetition of the play's opening.

Havel claims to have grown up, 'from a bourgeois background ... in a communist state' with the advantage of 'seeing the world "from below"'; if he displayed, as had often been claimed about him, 'a certain sensitivity for the absurd dimensions of the world', then this was partly due to this experience, for, 'as we know, the absurd and comic dimensions of the world are always best seen from below' ('Second Wind': Havel, 1991, 4). In addition to his view 'from below', Havel capitalised on 'the experience of Franz Kafka and the French theatre of the absurd', being also, he adds, 'somewhat obsessed with a tendency to elaborate on things rationally to the point of absurdity' (ibid., 5). In 1988 he wrote (anonymously) a semi-documentary historical comedy about the founding (in 1918) of the Czechoslovak state (*Tomorrow!*); a year later he found himself repeating aspects of the play in real life.[53] In 1990, having in the wake of the Velvet Revolution been elected president of the Czechoslovak – and subsequently the Czech – Republic (surely the most improbable fate ever to befall an absurdist!), Havel could not but admit to 'a sensation of the absurd: what Sisyphus might have felt if one fine day his boulder stopped, rested on the hilltop, and failed to roll back down' (quoted by Burian, 191).[54]

Notes

1 Esslin's monograph on Pinter, however, eventually takes his discussion up to *Party Time* (1991): Martin Esslin, *Pinter the Playwright*, fifth edition, London: Methuen, 1992 (first published as *The People Wound: The Plays of Harold Pinter*, 1970); there is a sixth edition (published 2000).

2 Ionesco labelled his plays variously as 'anti-plays', 'comic dramas', 'pseudo-dramas', 'naturalistic comedies' and 'tragic farces' (noted for instance in *Notes*, 27).

3 As has been aptly said: 'Ionesco's message is that there is no message' (cited by Segal, 430).

4 *The Chairs* may bear comparison with *Vengono* (*They're Coming*, subtitled 'A Drama of Objects'), a Futurist play by Marinetti, as the following description would attest: 'Servants continually move eight chairs and an armchair around the stage as the majordomo receives different orders from his masters. Marinetti intended to give the impression that the chairs gradually acquired a life of their own through these movements. Finally, they are placed diagonally across the stage, and an invisible spotlight is used to project their shadows onto the floor. As the spotlight is moved, so the shadows move, making it appear as though the chairs themselves are going out of the French window.' – Julie Dashwood, 'The Italian Futurist Theatre' (Cardullo and Knopf, 192).

5 Numerical incompetence here (the Young Pupil, while prodigious in multiplication, cannot subtract anything – to save her life!) is reminiscent of Daniil Kharms's story, 'A Sonnet', in which the narrator cannot remember 'which comes first – 7 or 8' (Kharms, *Incidences*, 51). There is, of course, no possibility that Ionesco could have known Kharms's work, which was not published anywhere for a good quarter of a century following his death in 1942 (see Chapter 6 on Kharms).

6 *The Invasion*, in Robert J. Doan's translation, is included in Cardullo and Knopf (472–97). *Professor Taranne*, translated by Peter Meyer, is to be found in *Absurd Drama* (117–37).

7 Jean-Paul Sartre, *Saint Genet, comédien et martyr*, Paris: Gallimard, 1952; Sartre, *Saint Genet: Actor and Martyr*, translated by Bernard Frechtman, London: Heinemann, 1988 (first published 1963).

8 The full version is included in *New English Dramatists 2*, Harmondsworth: Penguin, 1960 (63–140) For the shorter (one-act) version, see N.F. Simpson, *The Hole and Other Plays and Sketches*, London: Faber, 1964.

9 Interestingly, an apparently completely apocryphal legend of Portuguese ('da Pinta') ancestry formerly surrounded the background of Harold Pinter (Billington, 2).

10 Erich Segal (206) relates *The Lover* to *Amphitryon* by Plautus, seeing it as 'an ironic reworking of the myth which stands in a long line of theatrical variations by such diverse authors as Vital de Blois, Camoëns, Molière, Dryden and Kleist'.

11 Esslin has a later essay entitled 'Harold Pinter's Theatre of Cruelty' (in Burkman and Kundert-Gibbs, 27–36); however, he makes no mention here of Artaud, which is curious, given the title of the essay and the fact that Esslin is himself the author of *Artaud* ('Fontana Modern Masters', 1976).

12 On the relationship between 'Pinterian triangles' and Freud's joke theory (involving the triangle of teller, butt and listener: see Freud, 143) see Francesca Coppa, 'The Sacred Joke: Comedy and Politics in Pinter's Early Plays', in Raby, 44–56. While 'Pinteresque' is the more common label derived from Pinter's drama (on the qualities of which see Yael Zarhy-Levo, *Pinter and the Critics*, in Raby, 212–29, especially, 217–18, 222; and Zarhy-Levo, 2001, 21–41), 'Pinterian' is favoured by some (including Coppa). Billington (250), for one, registers a dislike of 'Pinteresque' as 'a vague and sloppy critical term'.

13 Some of these 'shaggy-dog' spectaculars, at least, would be regarded by Ronald Knowles (1995, 136) as examples of the 'mock epiphany'; the Bolsover Street peroration in *No Man's Land* is obviously a prime instance.

14 David Lodge (280) reports Roman Jakobson's contention that verbal works of art are, in general, characterised by various kinds of 'binary patterning'; this principle Lodge then applies to Pinter's sketch *Last to Go* (see below).

15 In *No Man's Land*, Spooner's comment (on witnessing the advent of a telephonic command), 'I have known this before. The voice unheard. A listener. The command from an upper floor' (3, 372) is surely an allusion to *The Dumb Waiter*. Spooner's 'I have known this before', though, repeated three times, has been identified as alluding to Eliot's (Prufrock's) 'For I have known them already, known them all', in *The Love Song of J. Alfred Prufrock*: Ronald Knowles, 'Harold Pinter and T.S. Eliot', *The Pinter Review, Collected Essays 1999 and 2000* (2000), 106–14 (110); this essay suggests an impact of Dante, as well as Eliot, on *No Man's Land*. See also Knowles, 'Pinter and Twentieth-Century Drama', in Raby, 73–86 (82). For that matter, 'at a glance', *No Man's Land* may appear to offer 'an upper-class re-run of *The Caretaker*' (Knowles, 1995, 135).

16 Peter Hall, however, considers it 'misleading' to categorise Pinter 'as part of the Theatre of the Absurd': 'Directing the Plays of Harold Pinter', in Raby, 145–54 (145).

17 Billington (380) later considers that these 'power-roles have been subtly reversed'. He also sees the characters' names (Rebecca and Devlin) as 'neutral'; surely, however, these names suggest a Jewish and an Irish origin, thus representing two prominent strands in Pinter's work (and in his biography). This is clearly confirmed by the casting of Stephen Rea as Devlin in the first production of the play, directed by Pinter.

18 The text is to be found in Pinter 2 (233–6), and is reprinted by Lodge (272–4), as a preliminary to his essay.

19 Apparently, however, at the stage of the writing of *A Slight Ache* (in the summer of 1958), Pinter recorded that the only play of Ionesco's that he then knew was *The New Tenant* (*Le Nouveau Locataire*): see Billington, 93–4. Esslin (*Th. Abs.*, 245), however, sees 'a curious affinity' between 'the silent matchseller ... and Ionesco's Killer' (of *Tuer sans gages*, translated as *The Killer*).

20 On the differing effects of radio and stage production of this play see Batty, 26. Interestingly, Billington (96) notes that the matchseller was (in 1959) 'jokingly billed in *Radio Times* as being played by David Baron' (this being Pinter's stage name for some years in the 1950s).

21 Katherine H. Burkman, in her 'Death and the Double in Three Plays by Harold

Pinter' (Bold, 131–45) sees the matchseller (*A Slight Ache*), Anna (*Old Times*) and Spooner (*No Man's Land*) as 'latent doubles', operating 'partially as independent characters and partially as projections of the protagonists', becoming 'borderline allegorical figures as well' (134).

22 See Esslin, *Pinter the Playwright* (London: Methuen, 1982), 163–4, n. (Pinter arrived at this view *after* writing the play and 'through rehearsals': 164).

23 For (biographical) speculation on the obvious Shakespearean connotation of these names see Billington, 201. For a more 'Shakespearean' comment see Hersh Zeifman, 'A Rose by any other name: Pinter and Shakespeare', in Burkman and Kundert-Gibbs, 129–36 (131–2).

24 Raymond Armstrong (60) refers to 'the Kafkaesque mode of indirect communication at the heart of *Family Voices*. We shall return to Armstrong's study *Kafka and Pinter* in Chapter 7.

25 Steven H. Gale, 'Harold Pinter's *Family Voices* and the Concept of Family' (Bold, 146–65).

26 Riley (of *The Room*) makes an at least nominal reappearance – this time as a homosexual, religious 'secret policeman' (P4, 145). Riley, or 'the life of Riley', is also treated to a burlesqued reprise in *Moonlight* (P4, 361). See also R. Armstrong, 110. Knowles (in Raby, 82; see also his 'Harold Pinter and T.S. Eliot', 107) suggests that 'Pinter's blind Negro, Riley, in *The Room*, is arguably a burlesque of Eliot's Unidentified Guest who sings the music-hall song of the "one-eyed Riley" and turns out to be Sir Henry Harcourt-Reilly' (in *The Cocktail Party*).

27 According to Eagleton (256), however: '*Pace* Sartre, [hell] is precisely not other people. It is the condition of those whose destiny is to be stuck with themselves for all eternity, like some bar-room bore. It has the absurdity of utter solitude, since nothing which could happen to me alone could make any sense.' Milan Kundera, however, would appear to see Kafka, at least, as closer to Sartre on this, observing that 'the *violation of solitude* is Kafka's obsession' (Kundera, 111; emphasis his).

28 Anthony Roche, 'Pinter and Ireland', in Raby, 175–91: in his 'prose philosophy' *A Vision*, Yeats 'envisages people who are forced to relive the details of their life, bathed in the retrospective light of everything that has occurred since and with the moral burden of much greater knowledge than the ignorance they could claim at the time' (186). Pinter himself tends to relate this quality back to a speech by Hirst in *No Man's Land* 'about that sense of death, and ghosts, and the dead who are alive in us' (Gussow, 99; see P3, 383).

29 John Stokes, 'Pinter and the 1950s', in Raby, 28–43 (40). Similarly: 'it is now clear [in 1981] that Pinter is no longer to be regarded as a reductive absurdist' (Styan, 135).

30 John Lahr, 'Introduction' to Orton, *The Complete Plays*, 7–28 (7).

31 This is present in Aston's experience told in *The Caretaker*, quite apart from *The Hothouse*. The exposure of institutional psychiatry in these plays was apparently stimulated by Pinter's visit to a clinic run in the 1950s by Professor Hans Eysenck (see Billington, 366–7); one is also reminded of the case (quoted earlier) of Artaud and Jacques Lacan.

32 See Kharms, *Incidences*, 155–84 and *PSS* 2, 238–69, in which the names of the labelled 'bits' are not printed. For an explanation of such production matters

see Mikhail Meilakh, 'Kharms's Play *Elizaveta Bam*', in Cornwell, 1991, 200–19. Both the 'standard' and the 'scenic' original versions are published by Meilakh, preceded by a lengthy introduction (from which his piece in Cornwell, 1991, is an abridged version), as 'O "Elizavete Bam" Daniila Kharmsa (predystoriia, istoriia postanovki, p′esa, tekst)', *Stanford Slavic Studies*, 1, 1987, 163–246. Another English version, translated by George Gibian as *Elizabeth Bam*, is to be found in Gibian, 155–77.

33 Nakhimovsky (40) argues of *Yelizaveta Bam*: 'There is no moral to it and there is no philosophy beyond a philosophy of alogical art.'

34 Zhan-Filipp Zhakkar, 'Daniil Kharms: teatr absurda – real′nyi teatr. Prochtenie p′esy "Elizaveta Bam"', *Teatr*, 11, 1991, 18–26 (first published in *Russian Literature*, XXVII-1, 1990, 21–40). It might also be noted that in Adamov's *La Parodie* (1952), the clocks have no hands (as in Kharms's *The Old Woman*).

35 Hazel Grünewald, 'Generic Ambiguity in Daniil Kharms's *Elizaveta Bam*', *New Zealand Slavonic Journal*, 2001, 87–99 (87).

36 Listengarten (210, n. 31) goes on to note the 'dangerous clowning' of 'character-puppets' in Jarry's *Ubu Roi*, as well as in Büchner's *Woyzeck* (1837) and Handke's *Kaspar* (1968), concluding that such clowns, with their clowning and cruelty, 'are therefore the "ideal" inhabitants of an absurdist universe'. Once again *Yelizaveta Bam* is seen as occupying a transitional place in such a tradition. Listengarten (172–3) also points to the 'cruelty' of tying a rope to people common to *Yelizaveta Bam* and *Waiting for Godot*.

37 Compare the following sequences, from (1) *Yelizaveta Bam* (*Incidences*, 158) and (2) *Ashes to Ashes* (P4, 398–9):
(1) SECOND [Voice: Ivan Ivanovich] What do you mean, no conscience? Pyotr Nikolayevich, she says that we have no conscience.
ELIZ. BAM You, Ivan Ivanovich, have no conscience whatsoever. You are just a scoundrel.
SECOND [Voice: Ivan Ivanovich] Who's a scoundrel? Me? I am? I am a scoundrel?!
(2) DEVLIN What do you think?
REBECCA I think you're a fuckpig.
DEVLIN Me a fuckpig? Me! You must be joking.
REBECCA *smiles* Me joking? You must be joking.

38 According to Roberts (1994, 51), essentially her offence is that, having herself initiated many of the language games of the text, Yelizaveta 'chooses not to participate in the one really important one – … the language game according to which she has killed Petr Nikolaevich'; and this, indeed, 'is the key to the play's circular – and thereby "absurd" – logic; Elizaveta is "guilty" because she refuses to join in the language game according to which she is guilty'.

39 Cockroach imagery occurs in other works by the OBERIU writers, and is thought to descend from the (absurdist) verses of Captain Lebyadkin in Dostoevsky's *The Devils* (see Meilakh, 219, n. 28), although such a tradiion goes back at least as far as *Peace* by Aristophanes. Kafka's *Metamorphosis* would now come to many minds. An obvious analogue, too, is *The Insect Play* by the brothers Čapek (see below). A later variant on this theme is *The Life of Insects* (*Zhizn′ nasekomykh*, 1993), by the Russian postmodernist prose writer

Victor Pelevin (translated by Andrew Bromfield, London: Harbord, 1996).

40 *Elka* literally means fir (or Christmas) tree, or (colloquially) yuletide; English
versions, both as *Christmas at the Ivanovs'*, are to be found in Gibian (201–29,
translated by George Gibian); and in Cardullo and Knopf (394–413, by Julia
Listengarten and Karin Coonrod); page references quoted here are to the latter
version (as 'Vved.'). For the original see Aleksandr Vvedenskii, *Polnoe
sobranie sochinenii*, 2 volumes, edited by Mikhail Meilakh, Ann Arbor: Ardis,
1980, vol. 1, 157–83. Useful general analyses of Vvedensky's works are
included in Nakhimovsky; and Roberts (1997).

41 '*Na pervoi kartine narisovana vanna*' (Vvedenskii, *PSS*, 1, 157); both English
translations use 'painted bathtub' and perhaps diminish this nuance.

42 The directions say of the murdered Sonya (Vved. 400): 'Does she hear what her
mother is saying to her? No, how could she? She is completely dead. She was
killed' (*Ona sovershenno mertva. Ona ubita*: *PSS*, 1, 162). Compare this to an
exchange in the Pythonesque alternative television comedy, *The Testing of Eric
Olthwaite* (BBC 2, September 1977):
ROBBER: I'm going to have to kill you ... Eric.
ERIC: What ... completely?
ARTHUR: Well, obviously, it wouldn't be killing you if it wasn't completely.
ERIC: Our Dad was always saying he'd *half* kill me.
(Michael Palin and Terry Jones, *Ripping Yarns*, London: Eyre Methuen, 1978,
110). Cf. also the opening of Beckett's *Malone Dies* ('I shall soon be quite dead
at last in spite of all'), as commented by Ricks (129–33).

43 Intentionally or otherwise, though, one of the children, Varya Petrova (seven-
teen-year-old girl), seems to have been forgotten in the succession of sudden
demises.

44 Listengarten (179) goes on to compare *Christmas at the Ivanovs'* with Roger
Vitrac's *Victor, or Children Take Over* (*Victor, ou les enfants au pouvoir*, 'first
staged by Antonin Artaud' in 1928).

45 There are two English translations of *Tango*: by Nicholas Bethel and Tom
Stoppard (first published London: Jonathan Cape, 1968); and by Ralph
Manheim and Teresa Dzieduszycka (New York: Grove Press, 1968). On
Tango see Stephan, 126–31; Esslin, *Th. Abs.*, 319–21.

46 No English translation is listed in Stephan's bibliography of either *A Summer's
Day* or *The Widows*. *A Summer's Day* also includes the (apparently somewhat
absurdist) motif of the non-rescue of a drowning person (see Stephan, 199);
this is found, as we have noted, in Dostoevsky (*Crime and Punishment*) and
Camus (*The Fall*), but also occurs, for instance, in Pinter (*No Man's Land*).
Drowning is also a phenomenon frequently referred to in the writings of
Kafka.

47 This particular 'dance of death' proceeded, in a Russian adaptation of the play
(renamed *A Banana*), to a 'wild dance of life' when, in the final scene, 'Death
reveals under her black coat a striptease outfit' (Stephan, 218–19).

48 The Brothers Čapek, *R.U.R.* and *The Insect Play* [translated by Paul Selver],
Oxford: Oxford University Press, 1975 (first published as separate editions
1923). An adaptation of *The Insect Play*, as we shall see, was subsequently
undertaken by Flann O'Brien.

49 Tom Stoppard calls Vanek 'a *Doppelgänger*' of Havel: 'Introduction (to *The

Memorandum)', in Vladislav, 278–80 (278).

50 The three plays of this period, together with three one-act Vanek plays of the 1970s, are included in Havel, 1993 (*The Garden Party and Other Plays*).

51 In addition to Stoppard's writing an introduction to Vera Blackwell's English translation of *The Memorandum*, we might note that Harold Pinter took part in a radio production of *Audience*.

52 See Stoppard's English version (Havel, 1987).

53 *Tomorrow!*, translated by Barbara Day (*Zítra to spustíme*), is included in Day (1–26).

54 Havel had earlier introduced Sisyphus into *The Memorandum*, when managing director Gross says: 'Like Sisyphus, we roll the boulder of our life up the hill of its illusory meaning, only for it to roll down again into the valley of its own absurdity' (Havel, 1993, 129). Havel occupied the post of President, in which capacity he wrote all his own speeches, from 1989 until 2003.

III

Special authors

6

Daniil Kharms as minimalist-absurdist

Story Without Title
There were about eleven of us in the room amd we all talked an awful lot.
It was a warm May evening.
Suddenly we all fell silent.
– 'Gentlemen, it's time to go!' said one of us.
We stood up and went ...
(anonymous parody of Turgenev's 'Prose Poems', 1883)[1]

A Kharms sketch

The basic facts about Kharms have now become common knowledge, but might still be worth brief recapitulation here.[2] 'Daniil Kharms' was the main, and subsequently the sole, pen-name of Daniil Ivanovich Iuvachev (1905–42). The son of a notable St Petersburg intellectual (I.P. Iuvachev), Daniil was to achieve, within his lifetime, only limited local renown as a Leningrad avant-garde eccentric and children's writer of the 1920s and 1930s. Among other pseudonyms, he had employed 'Daniil Dandan' and 'Kharms-Shardam'.[3] The predilection for 'Kharms' allegedly derives from the tension between the English words 'charms' and 'harms' (plus the German *Charme*; indeed, there is an actual German surname 'Harms'), but probably also owes something to a similarity in sound to Sherlock Holmes (pronounced 'Kholms' in Russian).

From 1925 Kharms began to attend 'left' poetry readings and other avant-garde activities. He gained membership of the Leningrad section of the All-Russian Union of Poets (from 1926), one of the many predecessors to the eventual Union of Soviet Writers, and published two poems in anthologies in 1926 and 1927.[4] Almost unbelievably now, these were the only 'adult' works Kharms was able to publish in his lifetime. In 1927, as already mentioned (in Chapters 3 and 5), Kharms joined together with a number of like-minded experimental writers, including his talented friend and close associate Aleksandr Vvedensky and the major poet Nikolai

Zabolotsky, to form the literary and artistic grouping OBERIU (the near-acronym of the 'Association of Real Art').[5]

This short-lived movement, in effect something resembling a union between Futurist aesthetics and Formalist approaches and considering itself a 'left flank' of the literary avant-garde, caused a minor sensation with a highly unconventional theatrical evening entitled 'Three Left Hours' ('Tri levykh chasa') in 1928. This included a performance of Kharms's Kafkaesque absurdist drama *Elizaveta* (or *Yelizaveta*) *Bam*. The time for propagating experimental modernist art, however, in the aesthetically hardening Stalinist climate of the late 1920s, was past. Hostile journalistic attention ensured the hurried disbandment of the OBERIU group, following a small number of further appearances.[6] Nevertheless, the post-Futurist antics and eccentricities of the Oberiuty were somewhat honed by Kharms, through the 1930s, into a practised art of 'absurd life-creation' (or *zhiznetvorchestvo*), in which he seemingly consciously attempted to turn his life, or aspects thereof, into an art form (on this phenomenon see in particular Ann Komaromi's article of 2002).[7] At the same time the practised art of prose shed any avant-garde stylistic features. 'As in the fiction of Franz Kafka', it has been remarked, 'even the most absurd events are rendered in a "neutral" style of classic economy and simplicity' (Wanner, 2003, 142). In 1936, Kharms even went as far as to declare Mozart and Pushkin to be his artistic models (ibid.).

Kharms and Vvedensky withdrew into the realm of children's literature, writing for the children's publishing house Detgiz, known fondly as the 'Marshak Academy' (run by the redoubtable children's writer, Samuil Marshak, and involving too the playwright Evgenii Shvarts). By 1940 Kharms had published eleven children's books and he contributed regularly to the magazines *Ezh* and *Chizh* ('The Hedgehog' and 'The Siskin' respectively). However, even in this field, anything out of the ordinary was not safe. Kharms, in his playful approach to children's literature, utilised a number of OBERIU-type devices, already denounced earlier in a Leningrad paper as 'reactionary sleight-of-hand' and, at the end of 1931, Kharms and Vvedensky were arrested, imprisoned and exiled, albeit fairly briefly, to Kursk: the times, in a punitive sense, being still then relatively moderate. Little literary employment was to be had thereafter; work at Detgiz was erratic and periods of near-starvation followed. Kharms and Vvedensky (the latter had moved to the Ukraine in 1936) somehow survived the 'great purges' of the 1930s. However, the outbreak of war brought new dangers: Kharms was arrested in Leningrad in August 1941, while Vvedensky's arrest occurred the following month in Kharkov. Vvedensky died in December of that year (of pleurisy, during penal transit) and Kharms (it seems of starvation in prison hospital) in February 1942. Both were subsequently 'rehabilitated' during the Khrushchev

'Thaw', but the great bulk of their adult writings had to await the Gorbachev period for publication in Russia.

Both starvation and arrest were anticipated in a number of Kharms's writings; indeed, Kharms can lay claim to being the poet of hunger (not for nothing did he take strongly to Knut Hamsun's novel of that name). The arrest of Kharms has, in more recent times, been described by his widow, Marina Malich (by now Durnovo), interviewed in Venezuela in 1996: 'There was a ring. And we knew it was the GPU ... Oh, it's as though it was yesterday. My God! Oh, my lord, my lord! ... He said: "I know, it's me they've come for ..." I went to open the door. Three little sort of strange-looking types were looking for him.'[8] He was apparently charged with spreading defeatist propaganda: there is evidence that, even at the time, he managed to clear himself on this charge, possibly by feigning insanity. Kharms had been a marked man since his first arrest in 1931 and was probably fortunate to escape disaster over a children's poem in 1937, about a man who went out to buy tobacco and disappeared: 'Out of a house walked a man' ('Iz doma vyshel chelovek'), later adapted by Aleksandr Galich into a song about Kharms himself, and subsequently used as the title of a threatrical spectacle on Kharms staged at the National Theatre in London by Théâtre de Complicité (December 1994). Of other former 'oberiuty', Oleinikov was shot in 1937 and Zabolotsky imprisoned the following year. In addition, Kharms's first wife, Ester Rusakova (1909–43), was a member of a prominent old émigré revolutionary family, subsequently purged; it is intriguing to recall that Kharms was, for several years, Victor Serge's brother-in-law. A harmless eccentric littérateur Kharms may have been, but in the circumstances prevailing that afforded him no protection – indeed, it was seen as a provocation. The Russians apart, indeed, the fate of many a European absurdist of this period (and, for that matter, earlier) was not a happy one: Bruno Schulz was shot by the Gestapo in 1942; Pessoa perished from cirrhosis of the liver in 1935; Van Ostaijen died of tuberculosis in 1928; Apollinaire had succumbed to the Spanish flu epidemic of 1918; while Hašek, Jacques Vaché (close associate of Breton and an exponent of 'sterile nihilism' [Brée, 251]) and Jarry all died prematurely.

The Kharmsian canon

Concentrating in the 1930s rather more on prose, Kharms evolved, as the Russians of the Soviet period said 'for his draw', his own idiosyncratic brands of short prose and dramatic fragment. A range of non-fictional writings (theoretical, philosophical and even mathematical pieces) were also penned, along with diaries, notebooks and a still sizeable body of poetry.[9] The boundaries between genres are fluid with Kharms, as are distinctions between fragment and whole, and finished and unfinished states. Adrian Wanner (2003, 143) notes the difficulty of classifying Kharms's texts, and of the tendency of modern editors to lift fragments from diaries or notebooks and categorise them as 'artistic literature'. Most of Kharms's manuscripts were preserved after his arrest by his friend the philosopher Iakov Druskin until they could be safely handed on to a new generation of scholars or deposited in libraries.

From 1962 the children's works of Kharms began to be reprinted in the Soviet Union. Isolated items from the more anodyne of his humorous pieces for adults followed slowly thereafter, as did mentions of Kharms in memoirs. Only well into the Gorbachev period of *glasnost*, though (from 1987), did the belated home flood of publications begin; the first major book-length collection appeared in 1988.[10] Abroad, an awareness of Kharms and the 'oberiuty' began in the late 1960s, both in Eastern Europe and in the West. A first collection in Russian appeared in 1974, and in 1978 an annotated, but somewhat discontinuous, collected works began publication in Bremen, edited unofficially from Leningrad.[11] It is presumably now safe to assume that virtually all of Kharms's surviving works are in the public domain, given the appearance of what is claimed as a 'Complete Collected Works' (published in St Petersburg, 1997–2002).[12]

One more recently published 'find' is a selection of rather mild erotica, largely clinically voyeuristic and olfactory in nature, which suitably counterpoints certain tendencies already noticeable in some of Kharms's more mainstream writing.[13] In 1992 his puppet play *The Shardam Circus* (*Tsirk – Shardam*) was published for the first time.[14] In addition to translations (into English, German and Italian, at least), in Russia OBERIU evenings, Kharms shows and 'mono-spectaculars' soon became commonplace. In June 1995 a large-scale Kharms festival was mounted in the then relatively recently renamed St Petersburg.[15]

On the assumption that Kharms's published works *are* indeed more or less complete, overall assessments of his achievement begin to assume greater validity, although a full critical study of his integral work, either in Russian or in English, has yet to appear.[16] Definitive texts from archival sources have, in many instances, replaced dubious variants. The intended order and content of the *Incidents* (*Sluchai*, 1933–39) cycle is now known (the only full cycle or grouping ordered by Kharms himself), while many later examples of Kharms's short prose, written around 1940, have reached publication only in recent years, as have notebooks and letters. All these factors have been important in bringing us to the present situation in Kharms studies.

Russian literature has long been used to the prose miniature in various forms, in both the nineteenth and the twentieth centuries – though rarely enough with quite the minimalism practised by Kharms.[17] Furthermore he developed the cycle of miniatures, of which *Incidents* (described by

Vladimir Glotser as 'perhaps the most outstanding' of his works) is the one completed example.[18] In spirit, Kharms clearly belongs to the tradition of double-edged humour that extends from the word-play and incoherence of Gogol and the jaundiced 'underground' anti-heroes of Dostoevsky to the intertextual parody of Abram Tertz and the satirical absurd of Voinovich. In the case of Kharms, however, the double edge is altogether blacker. Mark Lipovetsky (2003, 127; 150) considers *Incidents* to be the first example in Russian literature of Roland Barthes's conception of 'writing degree zero' – an experiment in the deconstruction of writing by means of writing ('of the text by means of text itself'). There is a similarity here with Richard Kearney's comment, in relation to 'Beckett and Derrida', that: 'The irony which Beckett makes such great play of is, of course, that one is obliged to use language to deconstruct language' (Kearney, 1985, 360).

In a verse and prose sequence entitled *The Sabre* (*Sablia*, of 1929), Kharms singles out for special admiration Goethe, Blake, Lomonsov, Gogol, Kozma Prutkov and Khlebnikov; in a diary entry of 1937, he lists as his 'favourite writers' Gogol, Prutkov, Meyrink, Hamsun, Edward Lear and Lewis Carroll.[19] Such listings are extremely revealing in determining Kharms's pedigree. Kharms had a good reading knowledge of English and an extensive linguistic capacity in German. On a general European level, he had obvious affinities with (if, with the exception of Russian Futurism, little direct knowledge of) the various modernist, Dadaist, Surrealist, absurdist and other avant-garde movements.[20] In Latin America Borges was writing brief masterpieces, if in a generally more elaborate vein. Kafka and Beckett are frequently seen as providing closer parallels (some of which will be considered later, particularly when we come to Beckett), while both Hamsun and Meyrink furnished Kharms with, at very least, vital motifs.[21] Certain postmodernist and minimalist writings of recent decades are perhaps, as we shall see, still closer.

The Old Woman (*Starukha*, 1939), a novella reaching almost epic proportions by Kharms's standards, has, many would argue, the strongest claims to be regarded as his masterpiece. A deceptively multilayered story, this work looks simultaneously back to the Petersburg tradition of Russian story-telling, through an arguably religious subtext, and forward to the metafictional devices of our postwar and postmodernist era.[22] The character-type of the old woman in Kharms (see for instance 'The Plummeting Old Women', the third piece of the *Incidents* cycle) seemingly derives from the St Petersburg tradition in Russian fiction, but it is a known phenomenon too in nonsense literature, as indeed in folklore.[23] *Incidents* signals an important neo-Romantic concern with the relationship between the fragment and the whole (observable too in Kharms's theoretical pieces) and, now in its 'complete' form, it has begun to attract due critical interpretation as an integral entity.[24] Other assorted stories indicate the development of Kharms's idiosyncratic preoccupations over his last decade. *Yelizaveta Bam* stands as Kharms's contribution to the theatre of the absurd and approaches to that particularly fascinating text are discussed, in Chapter 5 above, under that heading. In the view of Alice Stone Nakhimovsky (41), indeed, 'it is Kharms's concept of theater that is behind his happenings and short stories, which pare down the chaos of the plays to a single, outrageous event, developed to a logical extreme'. Not yet sufficiently widely translated and discussed are his children's writings and the substantial body of verse.

A poetics of extremism

And yet Kharms, taken in the round, still seems somewhat different from all the above mentioned models or comparisons – or more startling. One explanation for this is his constant adoption, at various levels, of what may be termed a poetics of extremism. Most striking, it has again to be stressed, is his brevity: not for nothing did he note in his diary: 'Verbosity – is the mother of mediocrity'.[25] If certain stories (especially some from *Incidents*) seem microtexts of concise inconsequentiality, there remain others which incommode the printer even less: consider, for instance, the following 'complete' story (albeit collected 'From a Notebook'):

> An old man was scratching his head with both hands. In places where he couldn't reach with both hands, he scratched himself with one, but very, very, fast. And while he was doing it he blinked rapidly.[26]

No writer offers a greater reaction to what has been described as the 'enormous excess of *narration* over episode' that so characterised modernism (T. Miller, 148). Another frequently noted feature of Kharmsian extremism resides in his uncompromising quest for the means to undermine his own stories, or to facilitate their self-destruction. This is particularly relevant to one text to which we shall shortly be turning our attention.

Kharms turns a starkly surgical glance both on the extraordinary world of Stalin's Russia and on representation itself – past and present – in storytelling and other artistic forms. He operates, most typically, against a precise Leningrad (or, as he liked to think, St Petersburg) background (unlike, for instance, Michaux, who often turns to Swiftian imaginary tribes and lands), passing sardonic and despairing comment on the period in which he lived. It appears that he did write at least one impromptu verse on Stalin himself, but this has not survived and may not have been written down.[27] He also ventures, equally ludically and ludicrously, into historical areas, to parody the ways in which such respected worthies as Pushkin, Gogol and Ivan Susanin were currently being glorified in print.

More than one Kharms miniature seems uncannily anticipatory of more modern trends: 'The Lecture' ('Lektsiia'), in which a man is battered into unconsciousness as he makes a sexist speech, could almost have been set now on a politically correct American campus; 'Myshin's Triumph' ('Pobeda Myshina'), on a man who sleeps in a corridor as there is nowhere else, smacks of London's cardboard city; while an extract entitled 'On an Approach to Immortality' would fascinate Kundera.

The most disturbing feature, for many readers, is the recurrence of Kharms's strange obsessions: with falling, accidents, chance, sudden death, victimisation and virtually all forms of apparently mindless violence (some of which may be compared to writers discussed earlier, such as Michaux, or later, such as Flann O'Brien). These too are frequently carried to extremes, or toyed with in a bizarre manner. Furthermore, as already noted, there appears little or no difference between Kharms's avowedly fictional works and his other writings. In his notebooks can be found such passages as:

> I don't like children, old men, old women, and the reasonable middle aged. To poison children, that would be harsh. But, hell, something needs to be done with them! ...
> I respect only young, robust and splendiferous women. The remaining representatives of the human race I regard suspiciously. Old women who are repositories of reasonable ideas ought to be lassoed ...
> What's so great about flowers? You get a significantly better smell from between women's legs. Both are pure nature, so no one dare be outraged at my words.[28]

How far into the cheek the tongue may go is often far from clear: the degree of identification with narratorial/authorial position in Kharms is always problematic. Obsessions, such as falling, too, carry over into his notebooks and diaries: 'On falling into filth, there is only one thing for a man to do: just fall, without looking round. The important thing is just to do this with style and energy.'[29] The implications can seem particularly sinister, as in the following note from 1940, which could equally be a sketch for a story, or even, as we have seen, count as a 'mini-story' in itself:

> One man was pursuing another when the latter, who was running away, in his turn, pursued a third man who, not sensing the chase behind him, was simply walking at a brisk pace along the pavement.[30]

The following fictional miniature, published only in 1995 (and provisionally dated '[1935–1936?]'), is said to be 'unfinished' (although it is not necessarily clear how one tells the difference):

> Kulakov settled down into a deep armchair and immediately fell asleep sitting. He fell asleep sitting and several hours later he awoke lying in a coffin. Kulakov realised at once that he was lying in a coffin. A wild fear

gripped Kulakov. With dulled eyes he had a look around and everywhere, wherever he directed his gaze, he saw only flowers: flowers in baskets, bouquets of flowers tied round with ribbon, floral wreathes and flowers just scattered about.

'I'm being buried', – thought Kulakov in horror and suddenly felt pride that he, such an insignificant man, was being buried so splendidly, with such a great quantity of flowers.[31]

Occasionally a diary entry is indeed all but indistinguishable from a known Kharms miniature:

I used to know a certain watchman who was interested only in vices. Then his interests narrowed and he began to be interested only in one vice. And so, when he discovered a specialisation of his own within this vice and began to interest himself only in this one specialisation, he felt himself a man again. Confidence sprang up, erudition was required, neighbouring fields had to be looked into and the man started to develop.

This watchman became a genius.[32]

Other entries rather more predictably affirm what might be supposed to be his guiding philosophy: 'I am interested only in "nonsense" [*chush'*]; only in that which makes no practical sense. I am interested in life only in its absurd manifestation.'[33] This last, apparently frivolous, remark was written at the height of the purges, in 1937 (the year in which his close associate Oleinikov was arrested), although many another note of that year is worded in a more desperate vein.

This type of writing (as we have suggested in Chapter 1) may be approached, or even explained, by means of psychology, of communication theory, of theory of humour, or by reference to the surrounding reality: in times of extremity, it is the times themselves that may seem more absurd than any absurd artistic invention. For that matter, these Kharmsian 'incidents' (to use the – or at least *one* – chosen translation for the concept of *sluchai*, a word which connotes at the same time 'instance', 'case' and 'chance') may trace their ancestry to a multitude of genres and models: the fable, the parable, the fairy tale,[34] the prose poem, the children's story, the philosophical or dramatic dialogue, the comic monologue, carnival, caricature and the silent movie (Kharms did have cinematic involvements in the first half of the 1920s). In another medium again, the figures of Giacometti come to mind. All of these seem to be present somewhere in Kharms, in compressed form and devoid of surrounding explanation or context. Kharms, indeed, seems to serve up, transform or abort, as the case may be, the bare bones of the sub-plots, plot segments and timeless authorial devices of world literature. In his study of Dostoevsky and the novel, Michael Holquist writes:

What plots leave out, of course, is various degrees of contingency, the state in which events may occur by chance, accidentally, fortuitously. This is the irrational against which Aristotle inveighs, the messiness of ordinary lived experience with its confusions, its half-finished sentences, its daily eruptions of the absurd.[35]

This, of course, in his way, is exactly what Kharms does give us. In the words of Lotman: 'The essence of plot lies in selecting the events, which are the discrete units of plot, then giving them meaning and a temporal or causal or some other ordering.'[36] The second half of this prescription is exactly what Kharms typically does not give us. In the modern idiom, theatre of the absurd and theatre of cruelty apart, Kharms's fictions anticipate in some primeval way almost everything from the animated screenplay and the strip cartoon to the video-nasty. Kharms offers a (black and white, as it were) skeletal terseness, in stark contrast to the comprehensive (technicoloured) vacuousness which may be perceived as all too plentifully on offer from more conventional literary forms.

It would be difficult to overemphasise the environment in which he wrote as the most striking thing of all. Kharms, the black miniaturist, is an exponent not so much of the modernist 'end of the Word' (in a Joycean sense) as of a postmodernist, minimalist and infantilist 'end of the Story' (in a sense again most analogous to Beckett). Such a trend is usually taken to be a postwar, nuclear-age (pear-shaped) cultural phenomenon, exemplified by fragmentation, breakdown and an impulse for self-destruction. However, it may be understandable that the mood of Holocaust and Hiroshima should have been anticipated in the bleakness of Leningrad in the 1930s.

Logic of the black miniature

An essential approach to the work of Kharms (as already suggested) is by way of humour theory. This may be Freudian in slant; indeed, Kharms makes a rare appearance in general literary studies in Elizabeth Wright's 'New Accents' volume, *Psychoanalytical Criticism* (1984), in which 'Blue Notebook No. 10' (or 'The Red-Haired Man') features as the book's epigraph; moreover, 'Psychological criticism', we are informed, 'explores texts for the "free" associations that tell of the struggle between a body and the society on which it depends' (E. Wright, 179). Gilles Deleuze (of course, without reference to Kharms) talks of 'a new dimension of the schizophrenic body, an organism without parts ... (the superior body or body without organs of Antonin Artaud)'; such a linguistic construct was indeed contrived by Artaud: 'No mouth No tongue No teeth No larynx No esophagus No stomach No intestine No anus I shall reconstruct the man that I am.'[37] One is reminded too of the manager in Conrad's *Heart of Darkness* ('Perhaps there was nothing within him') who 'was heard to say, "Men who come out here should have no entrails"' (Conrad, 24–5).

This particular psychological, or schizophrenic, approach will come into its own in the next section, when we turn to the phenomenon of the red-haired man. One nonsense historian who does make brief mention of Kharms is Wim Tigges (Tigges, 1988, 220–3), but his fundamental denomination of the themes and motifs of nonsense earlier (77–81) all but anatomises the essential Kharmsian qualities: a concern with numbers and letters; cause and effect; space and time; identity and metamorphosis; violence to the body; and games and rituals.

The body also features prominently in Jerry Palmer's *The Logic of the Absurd* (1987), which deals largely with visual comedy. The most common of 'the peripeteias of traditional farce' is here said to be 'the infliction of pain and/or indignity on the human body'.[38] Such a 'peripeteia' (or surprise, in Palmer's use of the term) is the receiving of a pot of paint on the head, say while walking under a ladder, or the more typically Kharmsian brick, for no reason at all. With any intellectual involvement, to avoid or minimise such an occurrence, we are in the realm of the 'gag' (Palmer, 45). Gags, which may be totally unpredictable or indeed totally predictable, when strung together with some degree of linkage, form a narrative. Other factors involved may include the dislocation of natural laws and/or narrative expectations, the exploitation of coincidence, of 'Murphy's law' ('if it can go wrong, it will': ibid., 145) and of aggression, plus a tension, or balance, between plausibility and implausibility: 'the logic of the absurd demands ... that any event – in order to be funny – should be simultaneously surprising, implausible and plausible' (136). Much, of course, depends on the balance between plausible and implausible: excessive implausibility may tip the absurd into nonsense, but there is likely to be a particular stress on all these factors in 'crazy comedy', as opposed to 'realist comedy' (145).

We are, clearly, again very close to the universe of many of Kharms's shorter prose texts and we may well here feel more at home with this kind of theoretical approach than with that of 'traditional literary theory which insists that the defining feature of comedy is its specific narrative rhythm and not its humorous qualities' (143). The OBERIU history of performance art should also not be forgotten. We need, at this point, test the applicability of such an approach on no more than one Kharms text; let us take 'The Carpenter Kushakov' ('Stoliar Kushakov', a page-long story, numbered eight in the *Incidents* cycle).

The Carpenter Kushakov

Once there was a carpenter. He was called Kushakov.

One day he left his house and went off to the shop to buy some carpenter's glue.

There had been a thaw and it was very slippery on the street.

The carpenter took a few steps, slipped, fell down and cracked his forehead open.

– Ugh! – said the carpenter, got up, went off to the chemist's, bought a plaster and stuck it on his forehead.

But when he went out on to the street he again slipped, fell and smashed his nose.

– Huh! – said the carpenter, went off to the chemist's, bought a plaster and stuck the plaster over his nose.

Then he went out on to the street again, again slipped, fell and cracked open his cheek.

Once again he had to go off to the chemist's and stick a plaster over his cheek.

– Well, then – the chemist said to the carpenter – you seem to fall and hurt yourself so often, that I would advise you to buy several plasters while you are at it.

– No – said the carpenter – I'm not going to fall any more!

But when he went out on to the street he slipped again, fell and smashed his chin.

– Poxy icy patches! – exclaimed the carpenter and again ran off to the chemist's.

– There you are, you see – said the chemist. – You've gone and fallen again.

– Not at all! – shouted the carpenter. – I won't hear another word! Give me a plaster, and hurry up!

The chemist handed over a plaster; the carpenter stuck it on his chin and ran off home.

But at home they didn't recognise him and wouldn't let him in to the flat.

– I'm the carpenter Kushakov! – the carpenter shouted.

– Pull the other one! – was the reply from the flat and they fastened the door, both with the key and with the chain.

The carpenter Kushakov stood on the staircase for a bit, spat and went off down the street.[39]

Kushakov thus undergoes a series of falls (and pratfalls) on the icy street (surprise after surprise). The implausibility of coincidence (or repetition) is balanced against the plausibility occasioned by the slippery conditions, while the reader's awareness of repetition yields swiftly to a sense of predictability. The 'gag' of buying multiple bandages, to offset the predictability of falling, as suggested by the chemist, is refused by Kushakov on the grounds that 'I'm not going to fall any more'. Nevertheless, Kushakov becomes so covered in plasters that he is not recognised and faces the further (unexpected) surprise (or more genuine perepeteia) of being refused admittance to his flat.[40] He spits and goes out to the street: we are not told whether or not he falls again, but the previous sequence, at least, seems to have been broken. The plausibility factor here is low enough to make the story clearly absurd, but it is nevertheless sufficient to keep it, in the terms described above, this side of nonsense.

Such a model may be applied to a range of Kharmsian pieces, achieving varying results with regard to comedy, absurdity and nonsense, with appropriate allowance made, along the lines of the Surrealist view of black humour, for contextual and thematic variables – notably the impingement of Stalinist reality – which may be particularly strong in certain texts. George Orwell's view that whatever is funny is subversive may not hold universally, depending on the particular constituents in the communication process, the ambiguities inherent in humour and the variability of context, circumstance and perception. However, there is little doubt that, in Stalin's Russia, the experimental prose of Kharms would have been, and should have been, construed as subversive. Notwithstanding this over-arching factor, Kharms was experimenting too, as even a casual familiarity with his prose will reveal, with contradictions in expectations and mixes of plausibility and implausibility (the 'wrong' mix as well as the right one: the 'over the top' and unfunny, as well as the hilarious), using different brands of discourse (content and context) and such Kharmsian authorial devices as the narrational self-destruct and the non-punchline.

Pursuing the red-haired man

Such are the rudiments of the life and literary career of Daniil Kharms. Certain of the 'ruder' qualities of Kharms's prose have been alluded to above. Some further examples included in Jean-Phillipe Jaccard's erotic compilation[41] are already familiar, as indicated, from long-standing publication: elements of slightly risqué sex in dubious circumstances, such as the story translated as 'The Drawback' ('Pomekha'), in which the snag of the story lies in the arrest of the female character at a time when she is not wearing knickers; or gratuitous nakedness, invariably of females, as in 'An Unexpected Drinking Bout' ('Neozhidannaia popoika').

As rudimentary as any Kharms story, undoubtedly, is the well-known opening number of *Incidents*, entitled 'Blue Notebook No. 10' ('Golubaia tetrad' No. 10') – often referred to as 'The Red-Haired Man' (*ryzhii chelovek*) and dated 1937. In view of its characteristic brevity, there is once again no problem in quoting in full:

> There was a red-haired man who had no eyes or ears. Neither did he have any hair, so he was called red-haired theoretically.
>
> He couldn't speak, since he didn't have a mouth. Neither did he have a nose.
>
> He didn't even have any arms or legs. He had no stomach and he had no back and he had no spine and he had no innards whatsoever. He had nothing at all! Therefore there's no knowing whom we are even talking about.
>
> In fact it's better that we don't say any more about him.[42]

This startling miniature has already attracted considerable critical comment and established itself as perhaps the archetypal Kharmsian mini-, non- or anti-story. Ann Shukman, in her Jakobsonian communication-theory reading, observes that the story is a 'stream of words ..., making sense grammatically and syntactically, but increasingly detached from any reality in any possible world', in that the identity, or reality, of the topic of discourse is broken, in defiance of normal rules of communication (Shukman, 1989a, 61). It can be read as a parody of narration, destroying itself as a story as it goes along, as Jaccard has pointed out.[43] Its motif of losing parts of the body links it to Gogol's *The Nose* (*Nos*); as Robin Aizlewood has noted, 'it can also be read non-parodically if viewed against the situation of the times', which can be seen to be of importance for the *Incidents* cycle as a whole, but also in terms of lack, or absence, and a 'divorce between signifier and signified', which brings us back to Jakobsonian codes of communication and Kharms's breaches thereof. Aizlewood, interestingly enough, goes on to speak of restoring, or even resurrecting, the red-haired man (by a process of reversability in communication codes).[44] Wanner (2003, 139; 144) sees here 'the narrative dilemma of "creating something out of nothing"', as recorded in one of Remizov's 'dream narratives'. Negation is also to be found in Dostoevsky: according to John Jones, for instance, 'a spirit of slippage presides over *The Possessed*', and he picks on the undermining of Stepan Verkhovensky's credibility as a scholar.[45] We have already alluded above to Artaud's concept of 'bodies without organs or words without articulation'; Carroll's exploitation of the Cheshire Cat may also come to mind (see Deleuze, 224; 235).

A number of these, and further similar, points are elaborated and reinforced in a substantial discussion of this text by Neil Carrick.[46] Carrick characterises Kharms's absurdist prose as 'a negative art', yet is able to discern 'spiritual salvation' (Carrick, 622) of a sort in 'Blue Notebook No. 10', as well as a lingering 'uncanny sense of plot' (624).[47] He argues that 'Kharms employs scepticism and negation to reveal the transcendence of the human spirit in the face of existential chaos' (622).[48] Carrick thus sees this text as, in a certain sense at least, 'primarily religious' and relates it to the 'medieval philosophical tradition known as "Negative Theology", which, as we have seen, sought to affirm the existence of God by emphasising his pervasive absence' (623; on negative theology see Chapter 1 above). Carrick also emphasises Kharms's note, which reads 'against Kant' in the margin of the manuscript of this story (see Carrick, 634–6; and 1998, 69–81). The last line of this particular 'story' certainly strikes a chord with the apophatic school of thought. Discussing the contribution of what he sees as the Eastern Christian tradition of negative theology (as noted in Chapter 1) to what he terms 'post-atheism', Mikhail Epstein (who refers neither to Kharms nor to Druskin) comments: 'If in according with the apophatic principle, one cannot say anything about God, then He should not be spoken about at all.'[49]

It may also be remembered that the Russian word *ryzhii*, used as a noun, means 'circus clown' and that the implications of this connotation could give rise to yet another pursuit, as an alternative to what follows, into possible worlds of circus symbolism and carnivalisation. We shall not, however, here and now pursue the red-haired man to the limits of all such realms of meaning, identity and the beyond; we shall, however, partially repeat our pursuit of him intertextually.[50] As it happens, in this last sense at least, he emerges as somewhat less of a rare phenomenon than might commonly have been supposed. For Russian readers, a *ryzhii chelovek* would be reminiscent of the *ryzhen'kii chelovek* ('little red-haired man') who narrates the tale within a tale of Old Believer conversion in Leskov's *The Sealed Angel* (*Zapechatlennyi angel*, 1873) – a work that, stressing the essential spirituality of art and featuring too both a 'miracle worker' and a 'guardian angel', must have had a particular resonance for Kharms.[51] According to memoirists, for that matter, Kharms himself had reddish hair (Komaromi, 420).

Given Kharms's predilection for posing as Sherlock Holmes,[52] an obvious first port of call in any quest for the red-haired man's possible antecedents is the early story from *The Adventures of Sherlock Holmes* (1892), 'The Red-Headed League'.[53] This work does in fact include two characters with 'fiery' red hair (as well as a brief mass appearance of a multitude of claimants to red-headedness); however, the villain of the piece, one John Clay, is anything but red-headed. Red-headedness is a device, a red herring as it were, to lure the red-headed Jabez Wilson away from his business premises while a tunnel is dug, for purposes of bullion robbery. The 'Red-Headed League' is therefore a hoax. The 'vacancy' in the League, itself an absence, is thus a double 'lack' or sham. The possession, or non-possession, of red hair, though, can be of the essence:[54] Jabez Wilson's red hair is even tugged at by the roots, to establish its authenticity. The non-existent League itself undergoes dissolution (a third negation). Holmes and Watson roar with laughter on hearing this, thus confirming an inherent potential (even in the very quality of red-headedness?) for humour. It is difficult to believe that Kharms, the Sherlock Holmes devotee, did not draw from this story certain bizarre rudiments for his own non-saga of red-headedness.

Further back, in the first half of the nineteenth century, we find a satirical story in which its author starts out describing a fine figure of a man, a certain Brevet Brigadier-General John A.B.C. Smith of unparalleled stature in all senses, and then proceeds to reduce him to 'an exceedingly odd looking bundle of something' which the narrator kicks out of the way.[55] The figure of the general is then reconstituted, with the assistance of his negro slave, by the screwing on of cork leg, arm, and shoulders, bosom and a wig, and the insertion of teeth, an eye and finally a palate. This daily resurrection of the general, who had suffered grievously from his wounds at the hands of the Bugaboos and the Kickapoos, reveals him finally to the narrator (himself a man without name who is erroneously called 'Thompson' at one point) as 'The Man That Was Used Up'. The general is not red-haired, but his hair and whiskers are allotted what is termed 'the no color' of a 'jetty black'. We here have a process of dismemberment (akin to Carrick's description of the removal of bits of the body in Kharms as 'a grotesque parody of a striptease': Carrick, 626), followed by reassemblage.[56] Edgar Allan Poe was immensely popular in Russia, and the appeal to Kharms of this story would again need no explanation.

In the first text of comparative interest to the present discussion (by Conan Doyle), the emphasis is (spuriously) on red hair; in the second (by Poe), it is on bodily disintegration and reintegration. Returning again to the late nineteenth century, in 1890, we come to Knut Hamsun's *Hunger*, one of Kharms's favourite novels, along with *Mysteries*. A number of Kharmsian motifs can be identified in both works, but *Hunger* is particularly notable for the brief presence therein (or rather absence therefrom) of a non-existent 'wool buyer', named Kierulf, whom the protagonist purports at one stage to be attempting to trace. A sort of picture of him is built up: Kierulf does not have a light-coloured coat, but he has a 'knobby stick' and, moreover, 'it would be an extremely rare thing if a man like that did *not* have red hair'.[57] Such a flavour of conditionality and negativity (red hair, combined with absences and assumed presences) is certain to have made its mark on Kharms's imagination.[58]

Another work of this period in which red hair may seem singularly obtrusive is *The Turn of the Screw* (1898), by Henry James. Following the governess's second sighting of the apparition of Peter Quint, she attempts a precise description of him to Mrs Grose: precise enough, seemingly, for the latter to identify the intruder as the now dead Quint. The redness of his hair is particularly emphasised (not only 'red', but 'very red'), together with, once again, negative qualities.[59] The wider literary ramifications of red hair have been noted in the voluminous criticism of James's enigmatic story. Stanley Renner has indicated a prejudicial literary attitude towards red hair that dates from as far back as the Bible (among suspected redheads are to be numbered Esau, Judas and Satan himself); Chaucer and Swift maintained such a bias, which was then influentially reinforced in the late eighteenth century by Johann Caspar Lavater's *Physiognomische Fragmente*.[60] Examples of red-headed perfidy are located by Renner in the fiction of Thackeray, Dickens (including Fagin and Uriah Heep), George Eliot and H.G. Wells, and no doubt innumerable further instances could be found. Such hair as Gogol's Akakii Akakievich (of *The Overcoat* [*Shinel'*]), for instance, has is 'reddish' and, as has been frequently noted, traces of devilry abound here too, while Akakii himself, on his introduction to the reader, is virtually 'erased' (as is, in a sense, the very text).[61] Freud provides a tedious account of the supposed joke of the *roter Fadian* and subsequently discusses the propriety of such humour (Freud, 54–6; 148); he also regales us with a joke playing on Rousseau (Jean-Jacques) and *roux sot* (red-haired sot: 63–4; see also Hill, 93; 99). Kharms's choice of specifically red hair (which Carrick finds to be 'a peculiar mnemonic device': 630) may therefore have wider implications of 'otherness' (whether humorous or sinister) than mere chance or incongruity.

As a last step in this particular exercise, let us turn briefly to a contemporary work which Kharms would almost certainly, we assume, not have known: David Lindsay's science fictional romance-cum-ontological fable *A Voyage to Arcturus* of 1920. One aspect of the paradoxical chain of dualities, stretching towards the absolute in the Arcturan system negotiated by the protagonist Maskull, is named by one of his guides as 'Faceny' and is elucidated in a manner again displaying affinities with Kharms: a kinship, in any event, with Kharms's red-haired man, as with other passages in his writing, is very apparent.[62] Kharms, could he have known Lindsay's novel, would have relished the inspirational potential of 'Nothingness', together with the relationships and tensions between inside and outside, self and other, centre and periphery: the everywhere and the nowhere – incorporated in some sort of human, or purportedly animate, form. It is hard to distinguish the philosophical from the metaphorical or figurative in a work that Harold Bloom, from his self-styled stance of 'Gnostic or Kabbalistic criticism' (an approach not inappropriate to Kharms himself) has ranked as 'nothing less than the most Sublime and spiritually terrifying death-march in all of fantastic literature'.[63] Crystalman's world 'is no joke', we are told at the end of *A Voyage to Arcturus*. The same, ultimately, may be said of the world of Kharms.

The common key to these writings, red-haired men present therein or not, apart from the fact or probability of Kharms's aquaintance with at least some of them, would seem to be, in the most general terms, neo-Romanticism. Among Kharms's other writings, the story 'On Phenomena and Existences. No. 2', about Nikolai Ivanovich and his bottle of vodka, and the non-existence of space inside and outside of him, as noted by Graham Roberts, is clearly of the same type.[64] Attention may also be paid to Kharms's theoretical pieces, 'On the Circle' and the relatively lengthy treatise 'On Time, Space and Existence'. The main point here, which brings us back to earlier comments above, is the relationship, on various levels, between the parts and the whole (Carrick claims [1994, 642] that 'The red-haired man is ... greater than the sum and the separation of all his parts'). This is just one of a series of dualities or dichotomies featured in the particular series of romantic concepts that Kharms seems to evoke: time and space; centre and periphery: spirit and object; abstract and material; entity and diversity; form and content; boundless and particular; finite and infinite, and of course absence and presence. These are all aspects in the dialectical expression of a possible theory of cognition within a circular system linking microcosm with macrocosm, and the human soul with the world soul (or other terms and expressions to that effect).[65]

All of this may be said to be reminiscent not only of the original German Romantic philosophical texts of Schelling, Fichte, Oken and others but also of the theoretical writings of the Russian Romantic writer Vladimir Odoevsky, with whom Kharms enjoys a certain degree of affinity. Although his arguably postmodernist style of short story composition is superficially very different from the early Odoevsky's russified Jena Romanticism, there are nevertheless fundamental points in common: in particular, their respective use of the cycle and the fragment. A common concern with a theory or a philosophy of aesthetics, for instance, is expressed by both Odoevsky and Kharms, using, in the pre-Socratic tradition, both music and mathematics.[66] Yet a further common preoccupation is our by now familiar distrust of the effectiveness of language to convey essential knowledge. Just as the origins of modernist and postmodernist aesthetics are to be located within Romanticism, further pursuit of the red-haired man would take us, it is therefore suggested, into, among other places, the deepest realms of Schelling's philosophy of transcendental idealism and transcendental philosophy of identity. For the moment, suffice it to close this section with Borges's concluding remarks, following his own pursuit of the nature of the circle, from Plato to Pascal (and it did not, of course, stop there), in his essay 'Pascal's Sphere': 'Perhaps universal history is the history of the diverse intonation of a few metaphors.'[67]

Except that it might be worth quoting (in full) another miniature, dating from a 1985 collection published by the American prose poet, Russell Edson:

The Matter

In it were the things a man kept, otherwise they were not in the box: a toy person with an arm missing, also a leg.

Actually, both arms were missing. And, as one leg was missing, so was the other; even the torso and the head.

But, no matter, because in it was another toy person. This one was also missing an arm and one of its legs.

Actually, it had no arms at all; the same with the legs, the torso and the head.

But, no matter, the box was full of armless and legless toys without torsos or heads.

But again, no matter, because even the box was missing ... And then even the man ...

In the end, there was only an arrangement of words; and still, no matter ...

(Edson, *The Tunnel: Selected Poems*, 204)

Kharmsian others?

The writing of Kharms can also be closely linked to that of writers both contemporaneous to him, whose work he may be highly unlikely to have seen, and of a later period – without there being any possibility of his work being known to them. As an example of the former, let us take the following passage from Nabokov's *Invitation to a Beheading*:

> 'What a misunderstanding,' said Cincinattus and suddenly burst out laughing. He stood up and took off the dressing-gown, the skullcap, the slippers. He took off the linen trousers and shirt. He took off his head like a toupee, took off his collarbones like shoulder straps, took off his rib cage like a hauberk. He took off his hips and his legs, he took off his arms like gauntlets and threw them in a corner. What was left of him gradually dissolved, hardly colouring the air. At first Cincinnatus simply revelled in the coolness; then, fully immersed in his secret medium, he began freely and happily to . . .
>   The iron thunderclap of the bolt resounded, and Cincinnatus instantly grew all that he had cast off, the skullcap included. [. . .] (Nabokov, *Invitation*, 29)

Once again, we appear to be in the fictional world of Poe's 'The Man That Was Used Up' and of Kharms's red-haired man – particularly of the latter, perhaps, given the totalitarian setting of Nabokov's spiritual and physical penitentiary.

The military ethos of Poe's story is certainly evoked – in an utterly absurdist war-time setting – in the following extract from Hašek's *The Good Soldier Švejk*, written shortly after the experience of the First World War (Švejk's anecdote of the purported press report of the glorious career of 'a one-year volunteer, Dr Josef Vojna'):

> He was in Galicia in the 7th battalion of the Field Rifles, and when it came to a bayonet charge he got a bullet in his head. When they took him away to the first-aid post he shouted at them that he didn't need to be bandaged for a slash like that. And he wanted to advance again immediately with his company, but a shell cut off his ankle. Again they were going to carry him away, but he began to hobble towards the battle line with a stick and defended himself with it against the enemy. But a new shell came flying at him and tore off the arm in which he held the stick. And so he transferred the stick to his other arm and shouted out that he'd never forgive them that. God knows what might have happened to him if, after a short time, a piece of shrapnel hadn't finally murdered him. Perhaps if they hadn't finished him off he too might have got the silver medal for bravery. When his head had been blown off and it was rolling down it still went on shouting: 'Never mind if death is near! Do your job and never fear!'[68]

As a postwar example, from another literature, few pieces could be closer than Robert Coover's story 'The Marker' (from the collection

Pricksongs & Descants, 1969). In terms of the visual arts, Adrian Wanner
has compared certain Kharmsian texts to the 'utter banality, akin to the
stack of bricks or plywood boxes of minimalist sculpture' (Wanner, 2001,
456). At a length of almost four pages, Coover's prose narrative is too
long to quote here. However, although it contains a slightly greater
element of context and of description than we would expect to find in
Kharms, it is indisputably replete with just about all the Kharmsian
features emphasised above. The story reads almost as stage directions, or
a screenplay, opening with: 'Of the seven people (Jason, his wife, the
police officer, and the officer's four assistants), only Jason and his wife are
in the room.'[69] Highlighting, in the title and the text, the seemingly irrelevant object, a book mark, Coover has Jason make what comes over as
the fatal mistake of extinguishing the light before joining (in a rather full
sense) his wife in bed. His mind moves into abstraction, space and time
apparently warp: she has metamorphosed into a corpse. The lights
suddenly come on and the police burst in: 'Jason looks down and finds
that it is indeed his wife beneath him, but that she is rotting' (seemingly,
seconds before, he had heard her laugh in his ear). The nudity of a nameless wife, grotesque sexual olfaction and necrophilic coagulation, shock
incursion and brutality from the forces of higher authority, an incongru-
ously pretentious speech by the law officer, and the exaggerated
significance of the 'marker' (Jason's ultimate concern): any and all of
these features seem somehow to have uncannily escaped from a
Kharmsian universe. As we have seen, and will see again, Coover is not
the only writer of whom this may be said.

Notwithstanding the above discussion, the question of Kharms and the
absurd still retains its complications. Leonid Geller sees in the Kharmsian
absurd 'not the alogicality of merely fortuitous verbiage, but the intersection of two logical series, or the fluctuation between worlds in which
differing logics operate' (Geller, 110). For all his only too obvious absurdist credentials – the incongruity, the linguistic highlighting and the stress
on language games, the logical inversions and the near (or sheer) nonsense
– the Kharmsian *oeuvre* remains in a state of spiritual tension. The
horrific surrounding reality of the epoch in which he lived merges into the
beyond – both of this world and of a further dimension. His interest in
'heralds' or visitors (*vestniki*) from 'beyond the turning point'[70] (or a
possibly divine beyond) and an apparent concern with the practice of
prayer (as evidenced by diary notes and certain of his poems) may seem to
sit at odds with an absurdist view of the cosmos – although Komaromi
(424) calls him 'a saint of the absurd' (at least partly in the sense of the
Russian tradition of hagiography). However, his religious fervour seems
to have manifested itself largely within what we have come to see as the
approach of negative theology, and the extent to which even (or perhaps
especially) his more spiritually serious writings reflect a literary or ludic

pose is still open to question. Carrick, who has particularly concentrated on this aspect of the study of Kharms, concludes that *Incidents* and *The Old Woman*, for instance, are absurd works, in that 'they defy Reason' and that they operate within a world absurd in its essence; he emphasises too the importance in *The Old Woman* of the concept of a 'miracle-worker', suggesting the capriciousness, withdrawal, or 'absence of signs from God': for Carrick, 'Kharms advances a negative *ontology*, but an absurdist *theology*'.[71] Absurdity, once again, seems to dictate a circularity without exit.

However, Kharms may also be seen as the principal example of a particularly 'Russian brand of absurdity', deriving in part at least from the behaviour of the traditional Russian figure of the 'holy fool' (*iurodivyi*); according to Komaromi (429–30): 'He occupied a position poised between laughter and horror, meaninglessness and the search for divine order' – contriving to seem, at one and the same time, 'deeply Russian and truly modern'. Further glances at Kharms will be taken a little later in this book in our discussions of Beckett and O'Brien (Chapters 8 and 9).

Notes

1 *Strekoza*, 3 (1883), 3; quoted by Adrian Wanner, 2003, 136; 187, n. 36 (translation here adapted).

2 This chapter includes, in revised form and with considerable additions, material previously presented in my introduction to Daniil Kharms, *Incidences*, 1993, and in my article 'The Rudiments of Daniil Kharms', 1998; for further contextual detail see my 'Introduction: Daniil Kharms: Black Miniaturist' (in Cornwell, 1991, 3–21), from which material has also been drawn (as well as other contributions to this volume).

3 Kharms, Khorms, Khkharms, Charms, Pul'khirei D.Kh., Daniil Dandan, Shardam, Garmonius, Karl Ivanovich Shuoterling ... – Il'defons, Tsar' Irod, Karakuliambro, Boguslav Iks': this list of Kharms's pseudonyms is given by S.N. Chumakov, 'Galchin'skii i Kharms: o prirode skhodnogo khudozhestvennogo iavleniia', in *Tekst i kontekst: russko-zarubezhnye literaturnye sviazi XIX–XXvv. Sbornik nauchnykh trudov* (Tver': Tverskoi gosudarstvennyi universitet, 1992), 92.

4 For a comprehensive list of Kharms publications, from 1926 to 1994, see Galina Nosova's 'Bibliografiia', in *Kharmsizdat predstavliaet: sbornik materialov* (St Petersburg: M.K. Kharmsizdat/Arsis, 1995), 121–30.

5 On the close association between Kharms and Vvedensky see the essay 'Druz'ia' in Sazhin.

6 Significant publications of and on OBERIU in recent yearss include: the anthologies *Vanna Arkhimeda: Konstantin Vaginov, Nikolai Zabolotskii, Daniil Kharms, Nikolai Oleinikov, Aleksandr Vvedenskii, Igor' Bakhterev*, ed. A.A. Aleksandrov (Leningrad: Khudozhestvennaia literatura, 1991); *Poety gruppy 'OBERIU'*, ed. M.B. Meilakh and V.I. Erl' (St Petersburg: Sovetskii

pisatel', 'Biblioteka poeta. Bol'shaia seriia', 1994); and A. Kobrinskii, *Poetika 'OBERIU' v kontekste russkogo literaturnogo avangarda* (Moscow: Uchenye zapiski Moskovskogo kul'turnogo litseia, 2000, 2 vols, 2nd edition); plus Nikita Zabolotsky, *The Life of Zabolotsky*, ed. R.R. Milner-Gulland, translated by R.R. Milner-Gulland and C.G. Bearne (Cardiff: University of Wales Press, 1994), 44–87 and passim; and Aleksandr Kobrinskii, 'Daniil Kharms i poetika OBERIU (priroda-chelovek-prostrantsvo)', in *Kharmsizdat predstavliaet*, 68–76.

7 See also Tat'iana Nikol'skaia, 'The Oberiuty and the Theatricalisation of Life', in Cornwell, 1991, 195–9.

8 Vladimir Glotser, 'Zhena Kharmsa', *Literaturnaia gazeta*, 52 (5634) (25 December 1996), 6 (translations mine); full version: Vladimir Glotser, *Marina Durnovo: Moi muzh Daniil Kharms* (Moscow: B.S.G.-Press, 2000). On the circumstances surrounding Kharms's death, and controversy thereover, see also: Mikhail Meilakh, 'Daniil Kharms: Anecdota posthuma (Posmertnye anekdoty Daniila Kharmsa)', *Russkaia mysl'*, Literary Supplement 8, 3781 (23 June 1989), x–xi; Anatolii Aleksandrov, 'Mesto smerti Daniila Kharmsa – ?', *Literaturnaia gazeta*, 8 (5282), (21 February 1990), 5; V.I. Glotser, 'K istorii poslednego aresta i gibeli Daniila Kharmsa (pis'ma M.V. Malich k N.B. Shan'ko)', *Russkaia literatura*, 1 (1991), 204–09; E.S. Spitsyna, 'Vy pomnite, Daniil Ivanovich ... khudozhnik Sterligov o smerti Daniila Kharmsa', *Russkaia mysl'*, 3946 (18 September 1992), 13.

9 On the relatively neglected topic of absurdism in Kharms's poetry see Uspenskii and Babaeva; Geller, who also mentions Kharms's interest in Pythagorian mysticism (106–7) and his propensity, at least at times, to cling to precepts of classical logic (112).

10 Daniil Kharms, *Polet v nebesa*, ed. by A.A. Aleksandrov (Leningrad: Sovetskii pisatel', 1988).

11 Daniil Kharms, *Izbrannoe*, ed. by George Gibian (Würzburg: jal Verlag, 1974); *Sobranie proizvedenii*, ed. by M. Meilakh and V. Erl. (Bremen: K-Presse, 1978–88, vols 1–4).

12 Daniil Kharms, *Polnoe sobranie sochinenii v chetyrekh tomakh*, ed. V. Sazhin (St Petersburg: Akademicheskii proekt, 1997–2001) – hereafter *PSS 2* (volume two contains the prose and dramatic works); followed by two volumes of notebooks and diaries: *Zapisnye knizhki, dnevniki*, 2002. For an extensive, annotated and chronologically presented edition see Daniil Kharms, *Tsirk Shardam*, ed. V.N. Sazhin (St Petersburg: Kristall, 1999).

13 Daniil Kharms, 'Erotika', published by Jean-Philippe Jaccard, *Amour et érotisme dans la littérature russe du XXe siècle*, ed. by Leonid Heller (Berne: Peter Lang, 1992), 213; 223–47. A shorter slection of these texts is translated in Kharms, *Incidences* (1993), 216–25.

14 Daniil Kharms, 'Tsirk Shardam: predstavleniie v 2–kh deistviiakh', published by Anatolii Aleksandrov, *Sovremennaia dramaturgiia*, 1 (1992), 227–38 (commentary 222–6).

15 See the invaluable compilation *Kharmsizdat predstavliaet* and accompanying brochures (1995), in honour of this event.

16 The most extensive monograph to date is that by Jean-Philippe Jaccard: *Daniil Harms et la fin de l'avant-garde russe* (Berne: Peter Lang, 1991; Russian

edition, St Petersburg, 1995); this volume also includes a substantial bibliography of Kharms criticism, for which see also that compiled by Neil Cornwell and Julian Graffy (Cornwell, 1991, 271–7). See also M. Iampol'skii, *Bespamiatstvo kak istok (Chitaia Kharmsa)* (Moscow: Novoe literaturnoe obozrenie, 1998).

17 For a full discussion of this tradition, however, in poetry and in prose, from its 'founders' (Baudelaire and Turgenev) on see Wanner, 2003.

18 Glotser, 'Zhena Kharmsa' (1996). Geller (111) also stresses Kharms's 'poetic *minimalism*' [his emphasis] which breaks forth 'as a radical cleansing of the word, a preparation for reform'.

19 *PSS* 2, 304; Daniil Kharms, '"Bozhe, kakaia uzhasnaia zhizn' i kakoe uzhasnoe u menia sostoianie". Zapisnye knizhki. Pis'ma. Dnevniki', published by Vladimir Glotser, *Novyi mir*, 2 (1992), 218. Chumakov ('Galchin'skii i Kharms', 93) informs us that there are surviving examples in Kharms's handwriting of poems by Carroll and A.A. Milne copied in English.

20 See Jean-Philippe Jaccard, 'Daniil Kharms in the Context of Russian and European Literature of the Absurd', in Cornwell, 1991, 49–70; Shenkman; Wanner, 2003. See also passing comments made earlier in the present study.

21 For previous comments on Kharms and Hamsun see Susan D. Scotto, 'Xarms and Hamsun: *Staruxa* Solves a Mystery?', *Comparative Literature Studies*, 23 (1986), 282–96; and Cornwell, 'Daniil Kharms, Black Miniaturist' (in Cornwell, 1991), 15–16; 21 n. 36. On Kharms and Meyrink see A. Gerasimova and A. Nikitaev, 'Kharms i "Golem"', *Teatr*, 11 (1991), 36–50. On Kharms and Kafka see R. Milner-Gulland, 1984 and 1991; Carrick (1998), 21–2; as well as the Theatre of the Absurd and Kafka chapters in the present book. On Kharms and Beckett see D.V. Tokarev (1999); and Tokarev's book on the absurd as a textual category in Kharms and Beckett, to which we shall return (Tokarev, 2002).

22 *PSS* 2, 161–88 (translation: *Incidences*, 17–46). For recent readings of *Starukha* see Milner-Gulland, 1998; and (the most comprehensive analysis) Jussi Heinonen [Iussi Kheinonen], '*Eto i to* v "Starukhe" Daniila Kharmsa, doctoral dissertation, University of Helsinki, 2002 (published as a book by Helsinki University Press, 2003); see also Neil Carrick, 'A Familiar Story: Insurgent Narratives and Generic Refugees in Daniil Kharms's *The Old Woman*', *The Modern Language Review*, 90, 3 (1995), 707–21; and the edition of *Starukha / The Old Woman*, ed. by Robin Aizlewood (London: Bristol Classical Press, 1995). *The Old Woman* also shares with Gogol (*Nevsky Prospect*) and with Michaux ('The Night of the Bulgarians') a paranoid concern with the abilities for animation of the newly dead.

23 Edward Lear is reported to have been inspired by the nursery collection *The History of Sixteen Wonderful Old Women* (1820): Tigges, 1987, 119. Wanner (2003, 94) notes examples too in prose poems by Turgenev and Remizov.

24 See for instance Robin Aizlewood, 'Towards an Interpretation of Kharms's *Sluchai*', in Cornwell, 1991, 97–122; Brandist, who, bringing a Bakhtinian reading to Kharms's prose (165–95), reads *Sluchai* as within the Menippean tradition; Shenkman; and Lipovetsky (2003).

25 *Novyi mir*, 2 (1992), 195. Kharms is perhaps only exceeded in this respect by the Honduran-Guatemalan author Augusto Monterroso, whose story *El*

Dinosaurio is quoted in Chapter 10. See also Wanner, 2003, for other examples of extreme brevity.

26 *PSS* 2, 42 (translation: *Incidences*, 9).

27 See Grigorii Usner, 'Sluchai iz zhizni Kharmsa', in *Kharmsizdat predstavliaet* (1995), 65–6.

28 'Dnevnikovye zapisi Daniila Kharmsa', published by A. Ustinov and A. Kobrinskii, *Minuvshee*, 11 (Paris/Moscow–St Petersburg: Atheneum/Feniks, 1992), 503–4, *PSS* 2, 88–9 (translation: *Incidences*, 10).

29 *Novyi mir*, 2 (1992); translation: *Incidences*, 10.

30 *Minuvshee*, 11 (1992), 583; *PSS* 2, 156 (translation: *Incidences*, 10).

31 'Daniil Kharms: Dva rasskaza. Pis'ma N.I. Khardzhievu', published by Vladimir Erl', *Kharmsizdat predstavliaet* (1995), 34–41 (36, 39): not previously translated.

32 *Novyi mir*, 2 (1992), 215; translation: *Incidences*, 11.

33 *Novyi mir*, 2 (1992), 218; translation: *Incidences*, 11.

34 On Kharms and the fairy (or folk) tale, particularly with regard to the minimalist and proto-absurdist *Anti-Märchen* texts of Fedor Sologub, see Wanner (2001, 461–4; 2003, 68–84; 137–9). See also Wanner (2003, 85–103) on 'Aleksei Remizov's Dreams'.

35 Holquist, 1986, 56–7. Many a Kharms plot is terse, even by comparison with, say, Apollinaire's brief, grotesque (and Kharmsian) absurdist parable, 'The Deified Invalid' (summarised in Chapter 3).

36 Lotman, 170.

37 Deleuze, 88; Artaud, in *84*, 1948 (quoted by Deleuze, 342, n. 8). Lipovetsky (2003, 147–8) makes the comparison of Kharms's use of violence ('the main source of the divine power of the author') and Artaud's notion of 'cruelty', regarding *Incidents* as a programme of 'cruelty' 'realised "on the stage" of writing'.

38 Palmer, 44.

39 *PSS* 2, 334–5; translation: *Incidences*, 54–5.

40 The gag here of non-recognition, or disputed identity (as well as other Kharmsian qualities shared), is reminiscent of the anecdote related near the end of Breton's *Nadja* (155–6), of a Monsieur Delouit who, suffering from short-term memory loss, on arrival at a hotel, asks the desk clerk to call out his room number on sighting him; subsequently, very shortly after one successful return, he again reappears, 'his clothes covered with mud, bleeding, his face almost not a face at all', having fallen out of the window, whereupon his identity is disputed on the grounds that 'Monsieur Delouit has just gone upstairs!'.

41 See note 13 above.

42 Kharms, *Polet v nebesa* (1988), 353; *PSS* 2, 323 and 330 (translation: *Incidences*, 49). As well as opening the cycle *Incidents*, this piece is the tenth numbered item in Kharms's album 'Blue Notebook' (see also below), the full contents of which are printed in *PSS*, 2, 321–9; and in Kharms, *Tsirk Shardam*, 750–7.

43 Jaccard (in Cornwell, 1991), 64–5.

44 Aizlewood, 'Towards an Interpretation . . .', in ibid., 102, 103, 105.

45 '"Nevertheless he was a most intelligent and gifted man, even, so to say, a scholar, though, as far as his scholarship was concerned, well, in a word, his

scholarship didn't amount to much, to nothing at all, I think." A scholar. Not much of a scholar. Really no scholar. Recall Stavrogin's suicide letter. Only negation. Not even negation. Nothing.' (John Jones, 270; Jones is quoting here from the Constance Garnett translation).

46 Neil Carrick, 'Daniil Kharms and the Art of Negation', *The Slavonic and East European Review*, 72, 4 (1994), 622–43 (page numbers from now on are included in the text).

47 Carrick points out (625, n. 7), and as already signalled above, that: 'In the original *Golubaia tetrad'*, the text bears no title and is merely designated by the number ten. All other entries are similarly marked by numbers. Thus when Kharms copied this story into his *Sluchai* notebook, he specifically gave it the (non) title "Golubaia tetrad' No. 10"'. The Carrollian *Haddock's Eyes* routine returns to mind here. No doubt in view of this incongruous sounding non-title, the story has frequently (if, strictly speaking, erroneously) been tagged 'The Red-Haired Man' (e.g. Shukman, 1989a, 61).

48 Leonid Geller examines Kharms's aesthetic theory (and, in particular, a single Kharms poem) in relation to chaos theory, finding at its centre 'redundancy, difference, noise' (Geller, 109).

49 Epstein, 359. One is also reminded of Wittgenstein's final dictum in his *Tractatus*: 'Of what we cannot speak we must be silent' (*Tractatus*, 49); noted too by Wanner (2003, 145). Epstein (as 'Mikhail N. Epshtein') is one of the contributors to Spieker's collection, in which negativity, absence and negative theology are heavily stressed in relation to Gogol; indeed, he discerns an 'aesthetics of negation' in Gogol (Spieker, 57).

50 The discussion here is abbreviated from Cornwell, 1998, in which the characteristics of 'Golubaia tetrad' No. 10' are compared to extracts quoted from the much longer texts by Conan Doyle, Poe, Hamsun, Henry James and David Lindsay (some of which, at least, Kharms would have known).

51 Translated as 'a short ginger-haired little man': 'The Sealed Angel', in Nikolai Leskov, *Lady Macbeth of Mtsensk and Other Stories*, translated by David McDuff (Harmondsworth: Penguin, 1987), 173–254 (176); cf. N.S. Leskov, *Rasskazy* (Moscow: Sovetskaia Rossiia, 1981), 125–86 (126). I am grateful to Catriona Kelly's *Russian Literature: A Very Short Introduction* (Oxford: Oxford University Press, 2001), 146–7, for the reference to Leskov's story.

52 See *Minuvshee*, 11 (1992), 498: 'At one time I did the Indian pose, then Sherlock Holmes, then yoga, and now it's the irritable neurasthenic.' The Holmes pose is born out by various self-portraits and photographs (see, for instance, the illustrations to Kharms, *Polet v nebesa*, 220, 313) and by the recollections of various memoirists.

53 Sir Arthur Conan Doyle, *Sherlock Holmes: The Complete Short Stories* (London: John Murray, 1953), 29–55 (32, 40).

54 Cf. Carrick's comment (1994, 634), in relation to 'Golubaia tetrad' No. 10', that 'Being red-haired is more important than having red hair'.

55 *The Complete Short Stories of Edgar Allan Poe* (Garden City: Doubleday, 1966), 350–7 (351).

56 A century later, this motif was actualised in *La Serrure* (*The Lock*), one of the short plays (or 'action poems') of Jean Tardieu, complete with overtones of Genet: 'In a brothel, a customer is awaiting the fulfilment of his dreams – to

see his beloved girl through an outsize keyhole. In ecstasy, the client describes what he sees as the girl discards one garment after another. Yet even after she has reached s state of complete nudity she goes on undressing, discarding her cheeks, her eyes, and other parts of her body until only the bare skeleton remains. Unable to control himself any more, the customer rushes against the door and falls down dead. The madam appears: "I think ... the gentleman ... is satisfied"' (Esslin, *Th. Abs.*, 268).

57 Knut Hamsun, *Hunger*, translated by Robert Bly (London: Picador, 1974), 129.

58 Cf. here Carrick's comment on the Kharmsian figure (624): 'the man actually loses his one defining feature, his red hair, and thus grows less rather than more familiar'.

59 Henry James, *The Turn of the Screw*, ed. by Peter G. Beidler, 'Case Studies in Contemporary Criticism' (Boston: Bedford Books, 1995), 46–7. On the third sighting, the governess remarks on a non-existent deformity, 'on the villainous back that no hunch could have more disfigured' (ibid., p. 66); David Punter notes 'the hunch that, we are assured, was *not there* (although in what sense it might have been any less there than the rest of Quint's phantomatic body remains opaque)': '"A foot is what fits the shoe": Disability, the Gothic and Prosthesis', *Gothic Studies*, 2, 1 (2000), 39–49 (see 46–7). James may well have taken this negative bodily image of 'invisible deformity' from Balzac; cf. 'his face seemed to belong to a hunchback whose hump was inside his body'; the character in question here, Goupil, also has hair 'reddish in colour' and is later referrred to as 'the failed hunchback': see Honoré de Balzac, *Ursule Mirouët*, translated by Donald Adamson (Harmondsworth: Penguin, 1976), 33; 228.

60 Stanley Renner, '"Red hair, very red, close-curling": Sexual Hysteria, Physiognomical Bogeymen, and the "Ghosts" in *The Turn of the Screw*', in James, *The Turn of the Screw*, ed. Beidler, 223–41 (see 228–32). It may be of interest here that, in his Schiller Theatre (German), and then the San Quentin production, of *Waiting for Godot*, Beckett added the colour 'red' to the question as to whether Mr Godot's beard was (in the original, *CDW*, 86) 'fair or ... or black'.

61 See Graffy, 2000a, 47.

62 David Lindsay, *A Voyage to Arcturus* (London, Sphere Books, 1980), pp. 203–4.

63 Harold Bloom, *Agon: Towards a Theory of Revisionism* (Oxford: Oxford University Press, 1983), 200. Kharms listed the Kabbala among his 'likes': see *Novyi mir*, 2 (1992), 195; and L. Lipavskii, 'Razgovory', *Logos*, 4 (1993), 8. On such matters see also Gerasimov and Nikitaev, 'Kharms i "Golem"' (1991).

64 Graham Roberts, 'A Matter of (Dis)course: Metafiction in the Works of Daniil Kharms', in Sheelagh Duffin Graham, ed., *New Directions in Soviet Literature* (Basingstoke and London: Macmillan, 1992), 138–63.

65 On various aspects of Kharms and idealist thought see Zhan-Filipp Zhakkar [Jean-Philippe Jaccard], 'Vozvyshennoe v tvorchestve Daniila Kharmsa', and Gleb Ershov, 'Sem' dnei tvoreniia Daniila Iuvacheva', both in *Kharmsizdat predstavliaet* (1995), 8–19 and 20–33; the connection between Kharms and

Kant (on which, see also *PSS* 2, 474–5) has already been mentioned above.

66 On these matters in connection with Odoevsky see Neil Cornwell, *The Life, Times and Milieu of V.F. Odoyevsky, 1804–1869* (London: The Athlone Press, 1986).

67 Jorge Luis Borges, *Other Inquisitions 1937–52*, trans. by Ruth L.C. Simms (London: Souvenir Press, 1973), 6–9.

68 Hašek, 235. There is also an anecdote of a mental patient (a professor) who counts constantly up to six (ibid., 686); this may be compared to Kharms's *Incidents* story 'A Sonnet', in which the narrator cannot remember 'which comes first – 7 or 8' (*Incidences*, 51).

69 Coover, 'The Marker', *Pricksongs*, 88–92; also in *Fantastic Worlds: Myths, Tales and Stories*, ed. by Eric S. Rabkin (New York and Oxford: Oxford University Press, 1979), 456–9.

70 See Robin Milner-Gulland's essay, in Cornwell (1991), 243–67. Again it may seem surprising that Epstein does not mention Kharms or Druskin in his discussion of the phenomenon of 'angelism' (Epstein, 372–7), seen as a symptom of postmodernism; if such emissaries are divine, however, they may have 'forgotten' that to be the case: Epstein speaks of 'messengers without a Message' (375).

71 Carrick (1998), 80. Wanner (2003, 187, n. 40) agrees that 'Kharms' religious message amounts to a "negative theology" at best'. Lotman's comment (167) that 'unpredictability and even absurdity in Dostoevsky are a sign not only of scandal but also of miracle' in an 'eschatological moment of instant and final solution to all the tragic contradictions in life' has a particular resonance for Kharms's *The Old Woman*. Heinonen, however (dissertation, 233–4), prefers to see Kharms in terms of 'paradox' rather than 'absurdity'; Dostoevsky's Underground Man is, of course, regarded by his creator as a 'paradoxist', while for comments relating 'paradox' to the absurd see Chapter 1.

7

Franz Kafka: otherness in the labyrinth of absurdity

> There are two ways to miss the point of Kafka's works. One is to interpret them naturally, the other is the supernatural interpretation. (Walter Benjamin, 'Franz Kafka: On the Tenth Anniversary of his Death', 1934)

As we have seen through the earlier chapters of this book, Kafka has commonly, if not universally, been regarded as a staple of absurdism. John Hoyles puts the case forcefully: 'In his three novels Kafka registers the world as absurd, resists it via the absurd, and takes refuge from it in the absurd' (Hoyles, 219). 'There is some coloration of the absurd that permeates every word that Kafka wrote', according to one Russian commentator.[1] His themes or works have been anticipated, it is frequently claimed, by a number of writers seen as precursors of the twentieth-century absurd (bearing in mind, with Borges [*TL*, 365],[2] that 'each writer *creates* his precursors'), such as Gogol, Dostoevsky and Dickens; or, to an extent at least, aspects of his *oeuvre* have been paralleled by certain of his contemporaries, or near-contemporaries, in at least isolated examples of their works (Joseph Roth, Kharms, Nabokov); or his works have clearly served as inspiration for new 'Kafkaesque' original works, or indeed and not least, translations or adaptations of Kafka into another language or medium – from (supposedly) Bruno Schulz, to Orson Welles, to the Czech theatrical productions of the 1960s (clearly an important step in Kafka's native Prague), on to Pinter, Steven Berkoff, Alan Bennett and Philip Glass.[3] Kafka has been written about by, or been important to, thinkers such as Theodor Adorno, Hannah Arendt, Georges Bataille, Walter Benjamin, Maurice Blanchot, Roberto Calasso, Deleuze and Guattari, Jacques Derrida, Jean-François Lyotard, Gillian Rose and Slavoj Žižek, as well as Borges, Malcolm Bradbury, André Brink, Camus, Elias Canetti, Eco, Fuentes, Kundera, Philip Roth,[4] W.G. Sebald and no doubt many another creative author.[5] Milan Kundera, for instance, delineates the 'Kafkan' elements in a 'true story' of totalitarian Prague.[6] As we can see already, amid such a galaxy, a number of proto-absurdists, absurdists and supposed absurdists seem to have

been at the forefront of the anticipation, the promotion and the rein-
vigoration of the spirit of Kafka.

Kafka and the other(s)

When I studied Kafka, the fate of his books in the hands of the Kafkologists
seemed to me to be more grotesque than the fate of Joseph K. (Philip Roth,
The Prague Orgy, 1985)

There is one passing reference to reading Gogol in Kafka's diaries (possibly another if we count a mention of the Russian troika) – 'Gogol, essay
on the lyric' (Kafka, *Diaries*, 333) – and at least two in the letters (Kafka,
LFFE 244; 326–7). Gogol is also named by Max Brod among Kafka's
favourite authors (Brod, 44n.). 'The infinite attraction of Russia' was, in
any event, something that Kafka was much taken with (*Diaries*, 331; and
see W.J. Dodd's chapter 'Kafka's Russia'). The most obvious comparison
made by commentators concerns *The Nose* and *Metamorphosis* (*Der
Verwandlung*, 1912),[7] both being stories of what Iurii Mann terms
'completely unmotivated transformation'; Mann also quotes Camus's
stress on the 'nuance' of the 'slight annoyance' felt by Kafka's protagonists at their absurd predicaments (Mann, 166; 173).[8] In *The Nose* too
can be found this 'effect of the attitude of the real to irreality' (ibid., 173).
For Carlos Fuentes, Gogol 'is the elder brother' to Kafka, and Akakii
Akakievich's overcoat 'is a carapace, like Samsa's in *The Metamorphosis*:
the body is absent, its presence and its pleasure postponed' ('Gogol':
Fuentes, 92; 96). Mann also makes comparisons with (for all their stylistic differences) the respective treatment of space (he calls his essay on
Gogol and Kafka 'A Meeting in the Labyrinth');[9] also identified are what
he sees as a shared attachment to the binary, concerns with the motif of
fear, and a tendency to use, in reduced form, the Romantic 'two worlds'.
In Gogol, 'especially after *The Nose*, the contours of both worlds merged';
in Kafka too 'the other world does not begin somewhere beyond, but is in
the middle of this world ... hiding somewhere in the folds of everyday
being' (Mann, 175–6). Kafka the insomniac wrote of an inner and outer
clock 'not in unison' as 'two worlds [that] split apart' (*Diaries*, 398–9). In
Kafka's artistic world, too, there is a confusion, or an ignoring, of the
legal and the illegal – the precise division of which is traditionally 'at the
foundation of the criminal novel as a genre', as of 'the concept of crime
and its prosecution' (Mann, 176). We therefore arrive at a situation in
which 'the sense of development of a particular quality of the fantastic,
with the absurdist and irrational tendency of Gogol imprinted in it, has
paved the way for Kafka's work' (182).

The observed shared concern with 'doubling' leads Mann, implicitly at
least, to compare Gogol's Bobchinsky and Dobchinsky (of *The*

Government Inspector) with K.'s 'assistants' (in *The Castle*: Mann, 168). Indeed, one could almost see the basic situation of Kafka's third unfinished novel as something of a psychologically contorted and extended distorted-mirror version of Gogol's play (in which dubious outside 'official' visits provincial town, occasioning minor local disruption). On the subject of Gogol and Kafka, we might also observe a shared inclination towards literary pyromania; however, whereas Gogol (on several occasions) burned his own manuscripts, Kafka preferred to delegate this (supposed posthumous) task to Brod. David Schur, indeed, developing an elemental theme traced from Heraclitus to Blanchot, suggests that the very 'already on fire' quality and the non-burning of Kafka's work condemned it to an 'inferno of misunderstanding' (Schur, 167–8; see also Kundera, 1996, 256–9, on Kafka's intentions in this respect).

Camus, to whose appendix to *The Myth of Sisyphus*, entitled 'Hope and the Absurd in the Work of Franz Kafka', we have earlier alluded, considers that Kafka arrives at an eventual 'deification of the absurd' (Camus, *Myth*, 119; also included in Gray, 147–55). In *The Castle* (*Das Schloss*) he makes a jump of almost Kierkegaardian proportions: 'The more truly absurd *The Trial* is, the more moving and illegitimate the impassioned "leap" of *The Castle* seems' (*Myth*, 120). Camus sees Kafka, along with Kierkegaard and Shestov, as among 'those existentialist novelists and philosophers completely oriented towards the absurd and its consequences', leading in the long run to 'that tremendous cry of hope', embracing 'the God that consumes them' – regardless of 'moral nobility, evidence, virtue, coherence' (ibid., 121). There is, it seems, a recognition of the absurd, whereupon 'it has ceased to be the absurd'; ultimately then, for Camus, and because of its universality, Kafka's work 'is probably not absurd' (121–2). By contrast, Nietzsche is seen by Camus (123) as apparently 'the only artist to have derived the extreme consequences of an aesthetic of the absurd', proclaiming 'an obstinate negation of any supernatural consolation'. Mann (184), however, in this regard also cites Friedrich Dürrenmatt (himself sometimes seen as a dramatist of the absurd), according to whom: 'Kafka declines not belief in God, but belief in the possibility of its apprehension. ... Man has to submit to the absurdity of God, or be doomed to the posing of senseless questions to which there is no answer.'

The impact of Dostoevsky on Kafka has also been emphasised, particularly with regard to *The Trial* (*Der Process*); Mann (181) notes the view that this novel represented a 'direct response' to *Crime and Punishment*.[10] At the same time, 'the "accused" in Kafka is not at all a martyr to the idea, like Raskolnikov or Ivan Karamazov', having his own more mundane preoccupations (ibid.). Mark Spilka, in his study *Dickens and Kafka* (1963), also gives Dostoevsky due weight, particularly stressing the challenge posed by *The Double* with regard to *Metamorphosis*, and the intermittent prevalence of insects in Dostoevsky (on which see Spilka, 90–2; Dodd, 85–95). The concept of the 'urban grotesque' (and 'urban nightmares') is developed from Hoffmann, Gogol and Dostoevsky, and in particular also Dickens, to Kafka (Spilka, 39; 92). The most substantial reference to Dostoevsky in Kafka's diaries defends the presence of 'mentally ill persons' in his works, and sees (the father figure) Fedor Karamazov as 'by no means a fool but rather a very clever man, almost the equal of Ivan' (*Diaries*, 323). Hoyles (230), in a study focusing on the literary underground and totalitarianism and again in relation to *The Trial*, talks in avowedly Dostoevskian terms of overcoming 'the ultimately false dualism of grand inquisitor and underground man'.

The most detailed exploration of Kafka's 'creative exploitation' of Dostoevsky, however, is offered in W.J. Dodd's *Kafka and Dostoyevsky: The Shaping of Influence* (1992), in which 'influence' is liable to take second place to 'affinity' in what Dodd takes to be 'a sceptic's reworking of Dostoyevsky' (Dodd, 151–2). The case (possibly at times somewhat overstated, as with Raymond Armstrong's treatment of Pinter: see below) is put forward in respect of *The Judgement* and then *Metamorphosis* ('a travesty of idealist metaphysics': Dodd, 13) in connection with *The Double* and, in the latter instance, also with *The Notes from Underground*. Kafka is seen as taking up from Dostoevsky 'the anti-*Bildungsroman*' (ibid., 66) and as realising the Underground Man's 'metaphor' of trying to turn into an insect (85), in what might fruitfully be seen as 'a kind of anti-*Notes*' (99). By 1914, Dostoevsky is to be regarded, in Dodd's view, as 'perhaps the single most important influence on Kafka's writing' (106–7); however, in *The Trial*, the principal mani-festation of this tendency (in relation of course to *Crime and Punishment*), Kafka makes 'both a sympathetic and an antagonistic response to Dostoyevsky' (13).

In somewhat similar vein, Kafka's *Amerika* has long been seen as a retort to Dickens, especially in the persona of Karl Rossmann – called 'a Dickensian urchin' by R. Armstrong (4). Indeed, Kafka freely admits a debt to Dickens in the make-up of his protagonists in writing, or even imitating, 'a Dickens novel' (Mann, 172; 181; *Diaries*, 388). Spilka connects, in particular, *Amerika* with *David Copperfield* (and, to a lesser extent, *Martin Chuzzlewit*);[11] *The Trial* with the 'legal metaphor' in *Bleak House*; and suggests that '*The Castle* recalls the bureaucracy in *Little Dorrit*' (Spilka, 242).[12] What he calls 'dreamscape' in Kafka is 'released through fantasy, controlled through the infantile perspective, and applied to the ends of grotesque comedy' (96). The 'family idea' is seen as central to both authors (13),[13] while Kafka, it is claimed, 'for all his intellectual sophistication, for all his legalistic sense of contradictions and alterna-tives, was as confined as Dickens by the child's emotional outlook' (ibid., 200). This, coupled with sexual anxieties, forms part of the 'growing up absurd' syndrome outlined by Paul Goodman which 'begins apparently in the nineteenth century, with the violation of childhood peace and its adult extension, the absence of significant life' (263).[14] Kafka, in his later writings, intensifies, in Spilka's view, the religious dimension that had diminished in the later Dickens, achieving (in *The Trial* and *The Castle*) a remarkable capacity for 'negative affirmations' (240). However, it may well follow that 'in an absurd universe, only a baffling God seems appropriate or believable' (252), for 'the objective depiction of absurdity ... is not exactly pleasant, not even when the absurd is taken on faith' (234). However, we should here perhaps not forget the admonition of Walter Benjamin (himself dubbed 'a nomad and a cabalist in disguise': Calasso, *Forty-Nine Steps*, 252), cited above as an epigraph (see Benjamin, 127).[15]

In her study of Nabokov and Kundera, *The Art of Memory in Exile*, Hana Píchová employs Kafka's parabolic shorter story 'The Bridge' – in which a remote personified 'bridge' collapses while 'turning' out of curiosity in response to the unexpected impact of a clumsy wayfarer (Kafka, *CS*, 411–12) – as a metaphor for the exile of emigration (see Píchová, 1–6).[16] Apart from whatever might be suggested by this very brief tale in relation to Kafka's *oeuvre* – the doomed attempt to straddle two worlds, the necessity of responding to intrusion (*The Trial*), the difficulty of turning (Gregor in *Metamorphosis*), the piercing of a body, or a spike in the head (*In the Penal Colony*), the bridge in *The Judgement* (*Das Urteil*: also known as *The Sentence*, or *The Verdict*) as a site of execution – we bear in mind Benjamin's statement that 'it is their misery and their beauty' that Kafka's writings, parables by nature, 'had to become *more* than parables' (Benjamin, 147; emphasis in the original).[17] Píchová (2) quotes a piece from Kundera's *The Unbearable Lightness of Being*, describing exile in similarly Kafkan terms: exile being 'a tight-rope high above the ground without the net afforded a person by the country where he has his family, colleagues, and friends, and where he can easily say what he has to say in a language he has known from childhood'. Nietzsche's tight-rope walker (in *Zarathustra*, referred to above in Chapter 1, a text well known to both Kundera and Kafka), returns to mind.[18] Nabokov and Kundera both switched their language of literary operation in emigration, while Kafka, feeling a spiritual exile very much of his own, was of course a mainly German-speaking Jew, mainly resident, for most of his life, in imperial Austro-Hungarian Prague, and therefore, as he styled himself (*Diaries*, 264), 'an Austrian lawyer'.[19]

In addition to what have been seen (by various commentators and here, in an earlier chapter) as Kafkaesque moments (conscious or otherwise) in his own fiction, whether involving metamorphosis or systems of infinite repression (of which *Bend Sinister*, Nabokov's first novel written in America, provides a further example), Nabokov claimed (unconvincingly, as far as his biographers are concerned) that he saw Kafka on a Berlin tram in 1923 (see Foster, in Alexander, 445). It may not be clear as to exactly when, or in which language, Nabokov first read Kafka, but he subsequently ranked *Metamorphosis* as one of the great masterpieces of twentieth-century prose fiction, and his lecture on it to Cornell undergraduates appeared (posthumously) in his *Lectures on Literature*.[20] Although the lecture consists mostly of commentary, laced with synopsis and quotation, Nabokov (the entomologist) is at some pains to, as it were, pin down the type of beetle that Gregor is, and isn't (emphatically *not* a cockroach!) – even making his own illustrations (contrary, of course, to the instructions of Kafka, who forbade any such thing to his publisher: Nabokov, 1980, 259–60) – absurd in itself as this discussion may be. Gregor would have had wings, Nabokov affirms, and elsewhere notes that 'he could have flown out and escaped and joined the other happy dung beetles rolling the dung balls on rural paths' (see Foster, 448).[21] Another of Nabokov's sketches depicts the Samsa flat 'divided into segments as [Gregor] will be divided himself' (Nabokov, 1980, 256–7); others have preferred to note a segmentation of the story itself, or its opening sentences (see Dodd, 60).

Kafka in the other(s)

> That's the conspiracy. To persuade us all that the whole world is crazy. Formless, meaningless, absurd ... Does that sentence the entire universe to lunacy? (Joseph K. – in Orson Welles's *The Trial*, 1963)

The practice of appropriating the persona or the theme of Kafka for creative writing purposes must have begun with the literary activities of his lifetime friend Max Brod, to whom we owe the preservation (contrary to instruction) of Kafka's unpublished papers and the posthumous publication of, among much else, the three (unfinished) novels. Before his biography of Kafka, published in 1937, Brod had mingled memoir and fiction in his *Zauberreich der Liebe* in 1928 – a work dismissed out of hand by Kundera, for one.[22] A more recent (indeed, a twenty-first-century) example is a long and rambling first novel by Marc Estrin, entitled *Insect Dreams: The Half Life of Gregor Samsa* (New York: Bluehen, 2002). In this fantasy (rather than Kafka himself being taken to America, as had been done by Philip Roth), Gregor escapes being swept into the bin, is sold off to a freak show and experiences a rich afterlife, having flown (by his own wingpower) to America. As a black, insectile, Jewish immigrant from Eastern Europe, he does not find twenty years of American life exactly smooth, but nevertheless penetrates the White House to become an adviser to Roosevelt, is involved (as a 'risk adviser') in the birth of the atomic age at Los Alamos, and engages in a polemic (claw on typewriter) with Hannah Arendt's twentieth-anniversary assessment of Kafka – he himself stressing, indeed, the negative force of Kafka's characters.[23]

More subtly intriguing, perhaps, is the introduction of Kafka into W.G. Sebald's idiosyncratic blend of travelogue, history and (one assumes) fiction, *Vertigo* (1990/1999).[24] Kafka (as 'Dr K.'), in September 1913, anticipates some of the narrator's steps in northern Italy (Trieste, Venice, Verona, Lake Garda) of much later in the century. Of course, Sebald (or rather his narrating persona) must have been retracing Kafka's steps, as Kafka had indeed then been in these places, on a supposed vacation, as his letters and diaries attest (though Sebald seems to suggest an element of business, too). After foretastes of Kafka, notably a gauche encounter with a double-teenage *Doppelgänger* (identical twins, 'bearing the most uncanny resemblance imaginable' to the adolescent Franz: Sebald, *Vertigo*, 88) – misunderstood as a sexual pass – on a bus from Desenzano to Riva, and other Kafkaesque adventures in a minor vein, Sebald inter-calates 'Dr K. Takes the Waters at Riva' – almost an autonomous novella (ibid., 139–67). Here Sebald imaginatively recreates Kafka's journey and his sojourn at the sanatorium of Dr von Hartungen in Riva (where he had enjoyed an earlier stay, with Max Brod and his brother, in 1909). Dr K.'s emotional crisis (over his relationship with Felice), mingles actual details of Kafka's Riva stay (involving two female residents: a Swiss girl for whom he formed a strong attachment and a Russian woman who told fortunes from cards) and the (not invented, as one might have thought) suicide of a retired general who, 'in some incomprehensible way ... had contrived to shoot himself both in the heart and in the head' (162).[25] This all merges into Kafka's own tale *The Hunter Gracchus*, anticipated by the preceding chapter's Desenzano graffiti '*Il cacciatore*', to which the narra-tor added '*nella selva nera*' ('the hunter', 'in the dark wood', or Black Forest: 86–7) – a reference to the homeland of Gracchus.

'The stay in Riva [at the north end of Lake Garda, and at that time in Austria] was very important to me', Kafka recorded soon afterwards (*Diaries*, 232); another week on, and he wrote a fragment that appears to be the germ of *The Hunter Gracchus* (see ibid., 234), a story eventually written only in 1917. 'Over the years that followed ... from these shadows there gradually emerged the silhouette of a barque with masts of an inconceivable height and sails dark and hanging in folds', bringing into the port of Riva the neither dead nor alive corpse of the huntsman Gracchus, doomed through 'a moment of inattention on the part of the helmsman' (*Vertigo*, 163–4) and an uncertain guilt complex to sail for ever the seas of the world – brought ashore here to meet the *podestà* (or Burgomaster) of Riva. 'Sometimes I think I am no longer in the world but am drifting around in some limbo', Kafka had then written to a friend from Riva, beset by a 'sense of guilt ... that is for me the highest form of penitence' (letter to Felix Weltsch: *LFFE*, 102). For Sebald, however, 'the meaning of Gracchus the huntsman's ceaseless journey lies in a penitence for a longing for love, such as invariably besets Dr K. ... precisely at the point where there is seemingly, and in the natural order of things, nothing to be enjoyed' (*Vertigo*, 165). Sebald suggests that this 'illicit emotion' (166), all but admitted, as he observes, by Kafka in one of his many letters to Felice (see that of 23–4 February 1913: *LF*, 203–4), really derives from a repressed homosexual desire.[26] This effect is counterpointed in *Vertigo* through the earlier misunderstood 'advances' of the narrator on the bus from Desenzano (noted above); the ghostly hand of Grillparzer on Dr K.'s knee in Vienna (*Vertigo*, 142); and then the hand of Gracchus 'touching, in a moment of distraction, the knee of the man who was to have been our salvation' (167) – corresponding too with the end of Kafka's *Gracchus* itself, as 'the Hunter with a smile ... laid his hand on the Burgomaster's knee', his ship 'driven by the wind that blows in the undermost regions of death' (*CS* 230). In more than one sense, perhaps, Gracchus is what Calasso (*K.*, 174) calls 'a foreigner to the entire world'. An absurdity of guilt has usurped the helm.

Harold Pinter had discovered and avidly read Kafka at the age of seventeen, so he told Louis Marks (the producer of his cinematic adaptation of *The Trial*.[27] Comparisons between Pinter and Kafka have frequently been made, whether centring on complexities of communication and silence,[28] the fruitless pursuit of meaning, impenetrable bureaucracy or the infliction or recipience of power – with *The Trial* very often at the forefront. *The Birthday Party* has been called 'an avowed "remake" of *The Trial*' and the short radio play *Victoria Station* (1982) has been read (or rather improbably over-read, one might think) as a reworking of 'Before the Law', the purportedly vital 'parable' from *The Trial*.[29] Raymond Armstrong, in his study *Kafka and Pinter: Shadow Boxing* (1999) concentrates, as his extended subtitle ('The Struggle Between Father and Son') indicates, on works embodying paternal–filial conflict. While it is hard to see very close parallels in the respective family backgrounds of the two writers, and Armstrong may tend at times to overstatement, the presence of such familial strife is of course unmistakable, as we may have already seen, in a number of key Pinter works.

The three sons in *The Homecoming* are somewhat tenuously perceived as a representation (indeed, we are told, one that 'could not have been more inspired') of the Kafka family situation – were Kafka's two brothers to have survived infancy (R. Armstrong, 55–6). The very title of this play 'may well be a conscious *hommage*' to Kafka, in view of the short piece 'Home-Coming' of 1920 (*CS*, 445–6) – a '*morceau* [that] could easily have been written by Teddy, arguably the protagonist of Pinter's play' (R. Armstrong, 75–6).[30] A passage from one of the *Letters to Milena*, seeing letter-writing as 'an intercourse with ghosts', is suggested as 'a blueprint for the thematic structure of *Family Voices*' (ibid., 85–6; see *LM*, 182).

Armstrong further suggests that *Moonlight* too may sound 'a subtle titular tribute' to *The Trial*, citing the repeated evocations of 'moonlight' in the last pages of that novel (121).[31] After delineating a rich tapestry of scriptural reference, seen as comparable in Kafka and Pinter, he concludes, however, that 'the imitations of Christ in *Moonlight* are simply the *reductio ad absurdum* of Andy's theomania' (155). As for 'the revolt of the son against the father', this is finally 'Fundamentally absurd and ultimately self-defeating' and, 'as Kafka had concluded, a subject more suited to comedy than tragedy' (171).

The most solid link between Kafka and Pinter incontestably comes in the form of Pinter's screenplay for the BBC Films (and Europanda Entertainment B.V.) version of *The Trial*, shot in 1992 (with an international cast, including Kyle MacLachlan, Jason Robards and Juliet Stevenson) and first shown in 1993 (published as Pinter, *The Trial*, 1993). Pinter had 'had a long-held wish to write and direct a film version of Kafka's *The Trial*', as he told Louis Marks in 1982; the project was activated by a commission in 1989, when Pinter wrote a first draft in two weeks of that summer in Corfu (Marks, in Burkman and Kundert-Gibbs, 22–3).[32] The transformation in the political situation of Eastern Europe allowed the film to be shot in Prague, enabling it to convey, as Pinter had wished, something of the 'normality' of the seedy atmosphere of the late Austro-Hungarian Empire (the back streets of Prague may or may not have appeared as splendidly seedy and faded in Kafka's own day, some three-quarters of a century before). If 'normality' was Pinter's starting point, beyond that 'all that really mattered was Kafka's text' (ibid., 23). By this time, Pinter had decided, after all, not to direct.[33] The film was shot in its entirety, as published in the screenplay; in final editing, however, a number of short scenes were omitted (with Pinter's approval: Author's Note: Pinter, *The Trial*).

Pinter had determined 'to tell the story straight' (ibid., 18). As far as he was concerned, the over-Expressionist and modernistic Welles version had been 'far too melodramatic' and 'an incoherent nightmare of spasmodic half-adjusted lines, images and effects'.[34] Pinter sticks (unlike Welles) to Kafka's chronological order and, a small number of insertions apart, remains extremely close to the rudiments of Kafka's novel.[35] For Pinter, *The Trial* 'describes a potentially universal human predicament' and his (inevitably slimmed-down) adaptation represents 'a masterpiece of clarity, economy and fidelity' (R. Armstrong, 117; 119). Knowles (1995, 178) argues that 'it is even more concrete than Kafka', in the sense that, as Pinter's production notes point out, 'what is not in the script is Kafka's analysis, or K's interior monologue'. 'Actually', Pinter argues, 'I believe that it *is* there, except that it's not expressed in the same way. It's not a novel, it's a film. The thing to do was simply to show what happens, rather than discuss it' (ibid., 178–9). 'Process and procedure are everything', in any case, adds Knowles (ibid.), reminding us of the original German title of the novel. Recognising a distinction between the screenplay and the finished (David Jones) film, Jeanne Connolly considers that, under Jones, 'the inhabitants of *The Trial*'s unstable universe are unquestionably Pinter material'.[36]

'The important thing about it', Pinter apparently said, 'is that [Joseph K.] fights like hell all the way along the line' (Gussow, 89). One might question whether that is indeed the case, right to the very end, both in Kafka himself and in Pinter's version.[37] Francis Gillen (Burkman and Kundert-Gibbs, 139) notes in Pinter a 'repeated emphasis on K.'s assumption of superiority' and his concern with the 'perception' of his arrest and of his case, tying in too with the extra stress in Pinter on communications telephonic (noted by Armstrong, 132). The apparent soliciting of a new summons from the Court 'tends to support the view that at some level K. is indeed seeking this trial' (Gillen, 140). Joseph K. fails to recognise what Pinter terms (in *The Dwarfs*) his own 'territorial limits' (ibid.) – which would lead him to confine his field of (successful) operations to the boarding house and the Bank. With the Court he is, and remains increasingly, for all his bluster, out of his depth. In the screenplay, as in the novel, there is a 'prevalent acceptance of a structure based on hierarchy and power' (ibid., 146), 'one in which K. himself is implicated' – both in his relationships with women, and in his business career at the Bank.

Pinter did not regard *The Trial* 'as a particularly political work'; he recognised 'a very deep religious conundrum in it', as well as 'a worm of anxiety in the very middle' of the ostensibly solid social and business world of moribund empire (Gussow, 136). The 'worm eating away', from which Joseph K. is 'drowning in quicksand', according to Pinter's publicity material, stems from 'religious identity' ('I have to use the term', says Pinter: quoted by Billington, 349), and seems to embody an innate guilt. The source of this guilt is never made clear, either to Joseph K. or to us, and Gillen (143) maintains 'what has gone almost unnoticed ... is that "guilty" loses its meaning if, as Titorelli [the painter] has stated, there is no such thing as innocence except in myth'. Conversely, as Michael Wood puts it: 'If the court is wrong to accuse you without naming the crime, you must be wrong, for the same reason, to proclaim your innocence' (Wood, 2003, 84). For Pinter, as for Kafka, it may well be that 'the only story possible to tell is that of the inability to find meaning' (Gillen, 146). One caption that Pinter 'would put on *The Trial* is simply: "What kind of game is God playing?" That's what Joseph K is really asking. And the only answer he gets is a pretty brutal one' (quoted Billington, 349; and Knowles, 181).[38] One is reminded here of Max Brod's celebrated, if dismal, reported conversation with Kafka, raising the question of there being any possible hope 'outside our world', given the status of humanity as 'nihilistic thoughts that came into God's head': there is 'plenty of hope, for God – no end of hope', was Kafka's reply, '– only not for us' (Brod, 75; a quotation made much of by Wood, passim). For that matter too, 'all hope remains circular and in the end it is no more than a "misunderstanding", as Bruno Schulz, Kafka's Polish translator, put it' (quoted from Sebald, 1972, 30).[39]

Pinter, visiting Samuel Beckett, who was feeling 'pretty gloomy' during his last illness, told him he would send him 'something which is really going to cheer you up' – the adaptation of *The Trial*. 'He guffawed', Pinter told Mel Gussow. 'The thing was he was reading it when he died. So I'll never know what he thought' (Gussow, 144).

When asked whether he had ever considered turning *The Trial* into a play, rather than a screenplay, Pinter the playwright-actor replied: 'No, I can't do that. I never adapted anything to the stage. It's not my thing' (Gussow, 89). No such inhibition, however, had applied to the actor-playwright Steven Berkoff (who, incidentally, had attended the same school as Pinter: Billington, 11). Three graphic theatrical adaptations flowed from Berkoff in successive years: *In the Penal Colony* (1968), *Metamorphosis* (1969) and *The Trial* (1970: main production at The Round House, 1973). Berkoff's *Metamorphosis* subsequently gave rise to his extended *Meditations* on that play, in which, writing in 1992 and preparing a (final) performance of it in Tokyo, he mused over the ten previous productions spanning twenty-three years.[40] Berkoff, styling himself a 'surreal magician' endowed with 'the higher flights of the absurdist imagination', discerned a potential 'Theatre of the Impossible', just as 'Kafka's stories are legends of the impossible'.[41] Indeed, one of Kafka's condemned proto-protagonists (or one of his 'contestants', as Berkoff calls them: *Adaptations*, 71) expostulates, as he is about to be dispatched by an executioner: 'This singular judicial procedure was instituted just because it is impossible' (*Diaries*, 368).

Berkoff's presentations, along with his theatrical ambitions, grew as he tackled progressively longer works: his version of *In the Penal Colony* ran for 45 minutes and has a text of 16 pages; *Metamorphosis*, at 50 pages long, and *The Trial* (60 pages and in two acts) can be considered full-length plays (the former running to 'nearly two hours without an interval' in Tokyo: Berkoff, *Meditations*, 125; the latter, even in its cut version, being longer again). *In the Penal Colony* is closest to the original (though the guard, at the end here, takes over the role of the dead officer, to ensure the continuity of hellish repression) and the staging included a 'suitably frightening' custom-built representation of 'a machine so fiendish and diabolical that its blueprints could have been designed in Hell' (Berkoff, *Adapt.*, 123). The insertion that the old Commandant had been 'buried like a dog', however, points forward to the end of (Kafka's original) *The Trial* (ibid., 141), just as the Chief Clerk's eating of Gregor's breakfast in *Metamorphosis* (*Adapt.*, 86) does to that novel's beginning. Indeed,

Berkoff reverses the chronological order of his three adaptations in the published collection, giving main prominence to *The Trial*. His version of *Metamorphosis* required a climbing ramp on a set that 'resembled a huge insect', a perilously acrobatic performance from Gregor (initially played by Berkoff himself), and a family becoming 'animated marionettes' that moved insect-like, 'so that they as a group, more than Gregor, were the dung beetle in reality'; with music and movement, the production aspired to 'a piece of Total Theatre' (*Adapt.*, 72), remarkable for its ensemble playing, its diction and other effects.[42] One can only assume that Berkoff's concept of 'Total Theatre' must owe at least something to the blueprints of Artaud (confirmed indeed in *Medit.*, 41; 109; 139), while Kafka's 'quarrel with the body' has also been compared to that source (Hoyles, 154).[43]

It may have been Berkoff's personal experience 'as a salesman for Burberry's gentlemen's outfitters' around US military bases in Germany (in one of which, of all places, he had his first encounter with Kafka's fiction) that gave him a particular empathy with Gregor Samsa, the pressurised salesman (*Medit.*, 52–3), and Arthur Miller's protagonist of *Death of a Salesman* (see *Medit.*, 103). From rehearsals for his first production, Berkoff adopted a sculpted and choreographed approach (see ibid., 107–10): 'The steel scaffold started to look like the skeletal frame of a giant insect and all this evolved from the basic need to raise the flattened beetle above the family so he could be seen' (107). The (Japanese) Samsa family 'enact their ceremonies and tell the story' and are seen 'moving as a trio, cutting their food, raising a fork, munching ... like living paintings caught by a strobe' (38), their clockwork lives arrested in 'freezes of action while the actors are speaking' (40) – in fact telling the story with Gregor's lines (54). The whole being and body language of Gregor and family can be seen at the back of theatre, 'but also creates another art form' (137), while the family trio's movements 'become almost dance-like imitations of life and thus comment on and parody an absurd situation' (138).

In contrast to Pinter's policy of telling the story straight, Berkoff, in his version of *The Trial*, not only identified with Joseph K. and with Kafka but 'became' Joseph K. (though he himself played Titorelli), while 'Kafka expressed me as I expressed Kafka' (*Adapt.*, 5). Like many others, Berkoff saw Kafka's work essentially as: 'The labyrinth. The endless puzzle or the myth of Sisyphus, the quest of Theseus through the maze' (ibid.). As for K.'s 'guilt', for Berkoff it is 'the guilt of betrayal: the guilt of betraying his inner spirit to the safety of mediocrity' (ibid.). Frederick R. Karl (in relation to Pinter's screenplay: 76ff) stresses the difficulties, for any adaptor, of trying to deal with Kafka's weird spatial and temporal contortions. The set contained a door frame (the door 'before the Law'), chairs, a rope and ten instantly movable screens ('the structure of the city, ... external and internal worlds', while the rope is K.'s 'route as well as his death: *Adapt.*, 9).[44] In this stylised (almost balletic) ensemble-playing adaptation, Berkoff uses 'voices', a Greek chorus effect, mime, singing and dancing (even a 'choir' in the cathedral scene) and (now and then) a narrator. Costumes are reduced to the bare essentials ('trousers and waistcoat, a stiff collar told all': *Medit*, 109). He adds considerable extra dialogue and changes the order of scenes; the flogging scene, for instance, is brought forward to a point before K. has even had the chance to 'complain' at his 'first interrogation' (which is not depicted as such).[45] The Uncle is replaced by K.'s Father, designated a 'disembodied voice of the past'. A crucial change, though, occurs in a scene called 'K's Trial' (effectively the 'First Interrogation' of chapter two in the novel transposed to near the end), with the narrator declaring that 'the magistrate is now reading out the charges'; however, according to the stage directions, 'K hears silently the worst crimes he is capable of', while 'we [the audience] hear nothing' (*Adapt.*, 63). The accused's condemnation is seemingly made explicit, his protestations notwithstanding (64). His demise then comes, after two brief intervening scenes, in an imposing cathedral climax, when he is trapped in the rope as he tries to leave the dark and labyrinthine building. Questions of textual purity apart, theatrical beauty can but remain in the eye of a beholding audience.[46]

As described by Osman Durrani, this performance was 'a feast of mime and dramatic invention, set among mirrors and door-shaped frames' (Durrani, in Preece, 220). The present writer would certainly agree, at least on the basis of the subsequently videoed recording (made in Tokyo) and 'based on the production that was shown at the National Theatre in London, 1991', which had 'gone through many stages over the years'.[47] Indeed, among the refinements to the text (at least as first published in 1981) are a number of minor alterations and insertions to dialogue and occasional transpositions of speeches. The Titorelli scene is comedically developed to enhance Berkoff's cod-Italian cameo role, taking on something of a Marx Brothers temper. More significantly perhaps, there are a number of cuts from the printed version, including the opening prologue scene (*Adapt.*, 11–13), 'The Interrogators' (ibid., 47–8), chunks from 'Block' (51–8), and the (already questioned) 'K's Trial' scene (63–4).

'The readers or non-readers of *The Trial* remember it wrong', says Alan Bennett ('Introduction', *Two Kafka Plays*, xvi). And, indeed, he can be shown to have a point. Out of some of *The Trial*'s most illustrious readers, Camus seems to think that Joseph K.'s executioners 'slit his throat' (*Myth*, 113); Borges appears to remember that 'the invisible tribunal' that is judging him, 'without a trial, sentences him to the guillotine' (*TL* 502). The particular anatomical detail of Joseph K's dispatch (the thrusting of 'the knife deep into his heart': Kafka, *The Trial*, 229) must surely of itself have had a particular significance. Frederick Karl, for that matter (80), claims that Joseph's 'ritual slaying' takes place 'one year after the cathedral experience' (rather than exactly a year after the initial 'arrest').[48] Bennett's own absurdist comedy, *Kafka's Dick* (1986), concerns itself with dubious perceptions of Kafka – whether on the part of Max Brod, Kafka's parents, or Kafka's readers and critics, and even Kafka himself – from his place in European literature, down to beetles or cockroaches. It also points up the discrepancies between Kafka (the original figure), *Kafka* (the man and his works, as subsequently perceived by the world) and the supposed 'Kafkaesque'.[49] The decorous emphasis of the play's title purportedly derives from a psychological study of Kafka, deducing 'that one of his problems, of which there were many, was a small penis' (*KD* 6).[50] Given his awareness of Nabokov's homilies on Kafka (*2 K Plays*, xiv; xxii), it is hard to imagine that Bennett should have failed to relish the following, less than felicitous (at least to an English ear) sentence by that master: 'Flaubert who loathed pretty-pretty prose would have applauded Kafka's attitude towards his tool' (Nabokov, 1980, 256).[51]

Kafka's Dick opens with a prologue in which Kafka and Max Brod discuss ('around 1919') the famous instruction to the latter to burn the former's papers. It ends with what amounts to an epilogue in Heaven (or attendance at 'that posthumous cocktail party, posterity': *KD*, 46). These scenes frame the main action, set in the middle-England home of a Kafka-mad insurance man and his long-suffering wife (Sydney and Linda). Sydney is preparing an article on Kafka for an insurance journal (called *Small Print*), when the couple, plus aged father, incur a supernatural incursion from Max Brod, soon to be followed by Kafka himself (who has metamorphosed from their tortoise), a policeman who turns out to be Hermann Kafka, and finally Kafka's mother, Julie. The toss is thoroughly argued over Kafka's literary status (of which he is at first unaware) and his parental relations: 'For him whitewash, for me excrement', complains Hermann (*KD*, 32).[52] Disclosure of the comparative size of the Kafkan sexual organs (*père* and *fils*) is threatened, through paternal moral blackmail, until the fact that 'your private parts have long been public property' (*KD*, 44) is revealed to the distraught writer – based on the thesis gleaned from the aforementioned psychological study.[53] When, finally, Heaven turns out to be a perpetual dancing party, hosted by God – who turns out, once again, to be none other than Hermann Kafka – it is small wonder that Bennett's Kafka (supposedly like his prototype in reality, rarely one to look on the bright side) declares: 'Heaven is going to be hell' (*KD*, 49).[54] More like a first circle, perhaps, though with somewhat reduced hope for Kafka – so wickedly 'malign' is this by now luminously clever comedy.

Kafka, on his posthumous visit to an Ionescan (or N.F. Simpson-like) suburban English home (where: 'This is England. .... Gossip is the acceptable face of intellect' – *KD*, 47), is subjected to a mock trial which threatens momentarily to effect 'a breakthrough in Kafka studies' (*KD*, 34); the models of Marx Brothers dialogue and the Jewish joke tradition (foreshadowed in Bennett's introduction: *2 K Plays*, xi–xii) are here skilfully exploited. *À propos* Kafka's most famous novel, however, Sydney, the ersatz Kafka specialist, makes the following gossipy observation:

> Now this is interesting. Kafka had read *Crime and Punishment*, which is a novel by Dostoevsky. In *Crime and Punishment* the student Raskolnikov commits a murder for which another man is wrongly arrested; the man is a house painter. In Kafka's *The Trial*, Joseph K is wrongly arrested. Who has actually committed the crime? A house painter. And someone in whose name millions of people were wrongly arrested was Adolf Hitler. Who is himself wrongly accused of being ... a house painter. (*KD*, 7)

Leaving aside the expansion into Nazi guilt, and any relevance this might have to Kafka studies, Sydney is suggesting a source for the (mis)identification by the Examining Magistrate of Joseph K. as 'a house painter' (Kafka, *The Trial*, 41) and, by this analogy, introducing – or rather reinforcing – the ingredient (of possible crass error) in that novel of bureaucratic mystery and metaphysical guilt.[55] And, of course, Raskolnikov was guilty all along ...

Among the 'absurd things', the 'only' things, that Kafka allowed to claim his attention had been his law studies and 'the job at the office' (*Diaries*, 395). In his television play of the same year, *The Insurance Man*, Bennett depicts Kafka's office job, at the Workers Accident Insurance Institute:[56] 'This kingdom of the absurd where it does not pay to be well, where loss determines gain, limbs become commodities and to be given a clean bill of health is to be sent away empty-handed' (*2 K Plays*, 125; see also xv). This is: 'Our world, where to be deprived is to be endowed, to be disfigured means to be marked out for reward and to limp is to jump every hurdle' (ibid.). Kafka himself had not been averse to affecting a limp or a facial tick (*Diaries*, 350; 405) – though presumably not at the office. Here, in the rather severe *ambiance* of what passed for the Prague compensation culture of 1910, Kafka generously arranges alternative employment for a man (called Franz) who is due no pay-out for a skin disease developed through working in a dyeing factory. The only problem is that – as revealed in the framing scenes set in the Prague of 1945 – the replacement job is in Kafka's brother-in-law's ill-fated asbestos factory.[57]

Falling and cawing in the labyrinth

kavka, *f*: **1** (jack)daw **2** coll., *lehkoverník* dupe, gull(ible person), gudgeon, country bumpkin

(*Comprehensive Czech–English Dictionary*, 3rd edition, 1997)

For Kafka 'the office is a living person who looks at me wherever I am' and 'is strange to me to the point of absurdity' (*LM* 102–3). Nevertheless, as has been pointed out, 'Kafka was organisation man as well as underground man' (Hoyles, 164). Ficowski (101) termed Kafka 'bookkeeper of the all-enveloping abyss'. What Kundera (1988, 113) identifies as, in effect, the 'bureaucratic fantastic' has been perfected by Kafka from a fashion laid down by Dickens, Gogol and Melville's *Bartleby*.[58] This last protagonist has been compared with Gogol's Akakii Akakievich and with Gregor Samsa – 'shut out from language yet a menace to the ordinary running of . . . affairs' (Hyde, 40). G.M. Hyde sees Melville's narrative as 'subsumed by allegory', of a sort that 'stands midway between Bunyan and Kafka, if such a position is conceivable' (ibid., 42).[59] The extraordinary figure of Bartleby himself, though, stands perhaps midway between Akakii Akakievich and Kafka's eponymous Hunger Artist (*CS* 268–77; the same translation is included in *Wedding Preparations in the Country*, though under the title 'A Fasting Showman'). The early Beckett (of *Dream of Fair to Middling Women*, 168), in his more verbose phase, may have had any of these scribal figures in mind when he referred to 'the gentleman scrivener who has no very near or dear or clear ideas on any subject whatsoever and whose talent is not the dense talent of the proselytiser and proxenete but the rarer article in the interests of whose convulsions clouds of words condense to no particular purpose'.

In Kafka's *oeuvre*, this bureaucratic tradition as a general whole is personified, in more elevated form, by the figure of Joseph K. (Chief Assessor, or Senior Clerk professionally, who is personally 'assessed' according to some more 'senior clerical' system); and once again, in the case of the subsequent protagonist K., it is intimated under the apparently infinite auspices of the Castle. It is also present too in the shorter works, in the frustrated bureaucratic deity of *Poseidon* (*GWC*, 116–17; *CS*, 434–5); and in the paranoid sales-pitching rivals of *My Neighbour* – 'I' and 'Harras' (*GWC*, 73–4; *CS*, 424–5: see on this work Gross, in Preece, 85–7).[60] Similar too is the grotesque business conduct in the later and relatively extended salesman narrative, *The Married Couple* (*GWC*, 178–82; *CS*, 451–6). It is but a short jump from bureaucratic fantastic to bureaucratic absurd: perhaps via 'bureaucratic time', which, in the view of Zadie Smith (36), 'absurd, infinite, and without revealed meaning – is for Kafka the true glimpse of reality'.

Kafka's own office routine could include what Brod regarded as its Chaplinesque side (echoed as a 'comic vision of ludic absurdity', and indeed 'of the totalitarian absurd' by Hoyles, 163–4):

> If only you knew how much I have to do! In my four district headquarters – apart from all my other work – people fall, as if they were drunk, off scaffolds and into machines, all the planks tip up, there are landslides everywhere, all the ladders slip, everything one puts up falls down and what

one puts down falls over oneself. All these young girls in china factories who incessantly hurl themselves downstairs with mountains of crockery give one a headache. (Kafka to Brod, 1909: Brod, 87; *LFFE*, 58)

Kafka saw 'the poetic potential contained in the phantasmic nature of offices' (Kundera, 1988, 113). Falling ('I fall insensibly and that is best': *Diaries*, 275; a motif too in *The Bridge*) is frequently alluded to in Kafka's writings and one can only conjecture as to what that masterly exponent of absurdist plummeting Daniil Kharms would have made of such passages, had he known them.[61] Equally Kharmsian is the propensity for contortionism: Kafka's 'imaginary kaleidoscope' can stretch to executing a trick 'I had admired in a contortionist years ago – I bend slowly backwards, ... draw my head and trunk through my legs, and gradually stand erect again' (*Diaries*, 275). In his experimental early work of fiction, *Description of a Struggle* ('the wildest fantasy he ever wrote': Albright, 103), the narrator feels embarrassed at being taller than his acquaintance, on whom he is strangely fixated:

> it occurred to me that perhaps my long body displeased him by making him feel too small. And this thought ... tormented me so much that while walking I bent my back until my hands reached my knees. But in order to prevent my acquaintance from noticing my intentions I changed my position only very gradually, tried to divert his attention from myself ...
>
> But wheeling suddenly around, he looked at me – I hadn't quite finished yet – and said: 'What's this? You're all crooked! What on earth are you up to?' (*CS*, 16)

Subsequently the narrator falls several times, it being icy (ibid., 18; rather like Kharms's 'The Carpenter Kushakov': *Incidences*, 54–5), and one converser tells of his right leg having 'fallen apart completely' and requiring 'manipulation and careful rearrangement' to get it back into shape (*CS*, 36–7). Disastrous falling could be associated by Kafka with writing, as well as with the office: 'When I sit down at the desk I feel no better than someone who falls and breaks both legs in the middle of the traffic of the Place de l'Opéra' (*Diaries*, 29).

Robin Milner-Gulland has written of the 'obvious comparison' between the short prose pieces of Kharms and Kafka: 'there is a similar ability to build out of mundane events an atmosphere of indefinable and ineluctable menace, the same deadpan ability to move from the humdrum into the fantastic and the nightmarish with no faltering in the detached and witty mode of writing'.[62] The same commentator (1991, 264) further comments:

> Both were splendid aphoristic notebook, diary and letter writers; both had an extraordinary, yet unpompous sense of the significance of their work: Kafka would have understood Kharms's sentiment that for every vain word one would answer at the day of Judgement; Kharms would have sympa-

thised with Kafka's uncertainty as to whether his talent was the gift of God or the Devil. Kharms's remark of 1933 that a poem should be such that it would smash the window if thrown at it ... matches Kafka's sense of literature as an ice-axe to unlock the frozen sea within us. Kharms's address to his creations as 'my sons and daughters' echoes Kafka's short piece *Eleven Sons* ...; each end stories ... with the curious motif of an emaciated hero dying and being thrown out with the rubbish; both writers fantasised about opening up their own heads to observe thought processes within.

Another yet further point of comparison between Kafka and Kharms would be their common, and by no means dissimilar, talent for line-drawings – a talent shared too with Bruno Schulz.[63]

'Kafka is always the whole Kafka', wrote Brod, who nevertheless made a division between 'the Kafka of the tales and novels' who 'tends to be the victim of doubts and self-torment' (indeed 'in the narratives, letters and diaries Kafka let himself go, yielded, surrendered without reserve to his angels and demons') and 'the "Kafka of the aphorisms" ... and [of] certain letters', who 'was no longer the sport of the forces of tragedy and absurdity' (Brod, 243). As we have seen, Kafka was an exponent not only of stories and novels, but of diaries, letters, fragments and aphorisms.[64] Writing, of all types (even of the officialese variety), was life's serious business and a veritable torture. 'Metaphors', for instance, while being his stock in trade, 'are one among many things which make me despair of writing' (*Diaries*, 398). Not only the process of writing, but the very texture of his verbal art is permeated by an elliptical quality of 'postponement' (noted by Benjamin, 129), or what Borges (*TL*, 502) calls a 'motif of infinite procrastination'. This seems linked to the phenomenon that Stanley Corngold terms, particularly as found in the later stories (such as in the incomprehensible design of *The Great Wall of China*), 'chiastic recursion'.[65] This may, in part at least, even represent development of a (probably Talmudic) trait reportedly observed within the Kafka family itself: 'their obsession with retailing and analysing every experience' (Adler, 57). Small wonder perhaps that, as Kafka relates to Milena, one reader 'told me recently he thought I must have made extensive studies in a lunatic asylum'. 'Only in my own', Kafka rejoined (*LM*, 119).

'The fictions', according to Hoyles (191), 'are in a continuum with the diaries and letters'. Julian Preece too sees the impossibility of finalising a quest or ascertaining truth in the novels as 'matched by the failure in the letters': therefore 'the letters belong with the fictions, they are works of literary art'.[66] In Harold Bloom's view, 'no particular genre that he attempted holds his essence'; at the same time, 'Kafka is a highly original crossbreed of an aphorist and a teller of parables, oddly akin to Wittgenstein as well as to Schopenhauer and Nietzsche' (Bloom, 448; 454). Kundera, however (1995, 267–71), argues strongly against any presentation of Kafka's work as a single *oeuvre*. Among those stressing the essentiality of Kafka's corpus of stories over the novels are to be numbered Nahum N. Glatzer ('Postscript' to *CS* 459), Borges (*TL*, 503) and Zadie Smith (37–8). Milner-Gulland (1991, 265) too considers both Kafka and Kharms to be 'among the great minimalists of modern literature, to which their concentrated miniature prose pieces may be their most remarkable single contribution'.

Nevertheless, in this particular survey of his work in relation to something resembling a gamut of others, before and since, *The Trial* may well by now have suggested itself as Kafka's key text. Umberto Eco (1995, 85) has observed that in this work 'we must accept that we are moving in a non-Euclidean world, mobile and elastic, as if we were living on an immense piece of chewed chewing gum'. This non-Euclidean quality (in geometry, geography and even telepathy) applies in both space and time, stretching in actuality and potentiality to the metaphysical and the political: 'Clearly K's trial transcends jurisprudence. It is existential' (Hoyles, 232). One is reminded of Niels Bohrs's term 'complementarity', used 'to express the fact that there may be concepts which cannot be precisely defined at the same time: such pairs of concepts as justice and legality, emotion and rationality' (Gilmore, 47). The very concept of recursive Kafkan irony, though, seems to have got through even to the organs of the unlamented late-Communist state of the 1980s; what is claimed to have been 'a perfectly legal' – indeed an officially sponsored – joke of that era is reported as follows:

> Two grave diggers, sent by the Prague government, arrive with a coffin on their shoulders at the house of one of the signers of 'Charter 77', which demands the implementation in Czechoslovakia of the agreements on Human Rights subscribed to in Helsinki by the Husak regime. The police had informed them that the signer had died. The signer says that he hasn't died. But when they leave and he shuts the door, he waits a moment and asks himself if, in effect, he has not died. (Fuentes, 178)

Similarly, it has been described how, somewhat earlier, *The Trial*, 'circulating in *samizdat* typescript in the Soviet Union, was naturally assumed to be a Soviet novel' (Dodd, 29). 'Literature of the absurd', according to Hoyles (145), 'is one of the most powerful strategies of resistance to collectivist conformity and uniformity in twentieth-century life'; the appropriation of its devices by the organs of repression, however, lend it an unexpectedly Kafkan recursive twist.

Such almost boundless perspectives, though, have their counterparts in what was to Kafka much nearer home – indeed, at home: in the unsent *Letter to His Father* he refers to 'this terrible trial that is pending between us and you' (*Wedding Preparations in the Country*, 53). The appearances in Joseph K.'s room of the pairs of sinister duos from respectively the beginning and the end of *The Trial*, for that matter, might seem to emanate from even closer to home, from Kafka's own 'lunatic asylum', taking on the antics perhaps, in aberrant fashion, of the detective bureau he himself has set on to Felice and her family.[67] Although Kafka's mother had a hand in this last operation, the principal anxiety stemmed from his own fear of marriage and the necessity, as he perceived it, of remaining alone: 'The fear of the connexion, of passing into the other. Then I'll never be alone again' (*Diaries*, 225). Earlier the same year (1913) Kafka had seen the German film *The Other* (*Der Andere*), details connected with which he contrived to turn against himself in epistolary argument to Felice (Zischler, 74–5). The tortuous dealings with Felice turned into what Canetti called 'Kafka's Other Trial', while Kafka had himself earlier drawn attention, with regard to 'a book of letters or memoirs, no matter by whom', to what he describes as 'the concentrated otherness of the person writing', the better to remain behind 'in one's own being' (*Diaries*, 134–5).[68]

Although the unfinished (like all three of Kafka's novels, or at least incomplete) *The Trial* was written in 1914 (or until January 1915: Adler, 149), the concept of 'the trial' was at some level, we can readily see, all-pervasive in Kafka's writing and in his thinking as in his life. The late short story *Advocates* (from early 1922, the time of *The Castle* – itself another form of trial: Calasso sees *The Trial* and *The Castle* as sequels: *K.*, 21) appears emblematic in this respect, and could well be imagined as belonging to or with the earlier novel. The narrator here (and indeed 'everywhere') is 'collecting advocates' but is unable to find any 'as yet', meeting only people who, in their otherness, 'looked like fat old women' in an indeterminate labyrinth of 'corridors, narrow and austerely vaulted, turning in gradual curves with high, sparsely decorated doors, [that] seemed in fact to have been designed for profound silence' (*GWC*, 138–40; *CS*, 449–51). Here again 'within the law itself all is accusation, advocacy and verdict', which rests on ubiquitous 'enquiries' in an endless quest through space and time; there are always further doors and further storeys and 'the stairs will never end'. To Michael Wood (2003, 80), the name Kafka indeed 'mainly suggests a kind of rigged labyrinth; a labyrinth inseparable from ideas of oppression and power'. A labyrinth within the labyrinthine burrow is an important feature of the construction of that even later eponymous structure (*The Burrow*, 1923–24) and this takes on mental as well as physical ramifications. *The Trial* wears Joseph K. down by plunging him into a labyrinth of choices leading to alternatives each producing an endless series of pros and cons ('recursive' and 'algorithmic', as emphasised by Kirkwood). As with Nietzsche's *Ecce Homo*, perhaps, 'nothing remains but the labyrinth of the monologue, the sound of inner voices in endless pursuit of each other' (Calasso, *Forty-Nine Steps*, 29).[69]

'Quiet, darkness, creeping into a hiding place' is the need Kafka expresses to Milena, given that 'my life, my existence consists of this [unspecifiable] subterranean threat' (*LM*, 160). The (other) subterranean other, expressed in conventional terms as 'literary sources' ('which do of course exist in a certain sense'), it is suggested by Malcolm Pasley, will however have 'flowed along the most varied and elusive paths into the inner sea from which [Kafka's] story then originated'.[70] For Zadie Smith (39), in any event, Kafka's 'refinements are sketched in absurdist circles that direct themselves inward'.

In relation to the phenomenon of 'hovering dogs' (in *Investigations of a Dog*, 1922), Hoyles states: 'The logic of the absurd is required to cope with a nonsensical world. This is the essence of the rigorous foolery called Kafkaesque' (Hoyles, 214). Such logic is required to deal with much in Kafka, whether it be the transitional anxiety of *An Everyday Occurrence* (*GWC*, 99; known as *A Common Confusion* in *CS*, 429–30) or merely a head-banging aphorism: 'His own frontal bone blocks his way (he bloodies his brow by beating against his own brow)' (*GWC*, 106).

Another seemingly emblematic piece, short enough to quote in full (and which confusingly seems to have appeared under numerous titles: it is included as *Give it Up!*, in *CS*, 456; as *Give Up!*, in *Metamorphosis*, 79; and as *A Comment*, in *GWC*, 183, representing the author's *Ein Kommentar*), is the following:

> It was very early in the morning, the streets clean and deserted, I was going to the station. As I compared my watch with the clock on a tower I saw that it was much later than I had thought, I had to make great haste; in my alarm at this discovery I became unsure of the way, I was still something of a stranger in this town; luckily there was a policeman at hand, I ran up to him and breathlessly asked him the way. He smiled and said: 'Do you expect to discover the way from me?' 'Yes,' I said, 'since I cannot find it myself.' 'Give it up, give it up,' said he, and he turned away with a great flourish, like a man who wants to be alone with his laughter. (*GWC*, 183)

Adler, referring to it as *A Commentary*, observes (109): 'The anecdote revolves around an episode, which, like many of Kafka's best works, involves a metaphysical accident on the borders between space, time and the mind. The world goes awry, authority collapses, communication ceases, and absurdity reigns supreme.' 'Speech with the nomads is impossible', according to the imperial residents in *An Old Manuscript* (*Wedding Preparations in the Country*, 125–7; *CS*, 415–17): 'They communicate with each other much as jackdaws do. A screeching as of jackdaws is always in our ears' (126; 416).[71] Metaphysical accidents, for that matter, can equally sound what Kafka called in 1917 'the alarm trumpets of the void' (*Diaries*, 377). The famous such 'accident' announcing the void, already alluded to and of which *A Comment* is reminiscent, is the 'Before the Law' parable (of *The Trial*, 235–7). It has been pointed out, incidentally, that the word 'law' here is subject to multiple connotations (see

Zima, 127–8; 193–5). Moreover, Calasso (*K.* 307) remarks, noting the many glosses written on this story: 'The longest and most convincing gloss is that written by Kafka himself – and it is *The Castle*'; it is only necessary to substitute, for the word 'Law' the word 'Castle' – 'and then read *The Castle* right through'.

At the beginning of this chapter, we quoted the view of the Soviet critic Dmitri Zatonsky that 'some coloration of the absurd' penetrates every word by Kafka (in Hughes, 221). From a very different perspective, Martin Buber claimed that, in Kafka: 'A broad meaninglessness governs without restraint. . . . Man is called into this world, he is appointed in it, but wherever he turns to fulfill his calling he comes up against the thick vapors of a mist of absurdity.'[72] Finally, we might venture the suggestion that the theatrical metaphors from the last chapter of *The Trial* point not only back to the Nature Theatre of Oklahoma (as noted by Benjamin, 124–5) but forward, at least when viewed through hindsight, to the Theatre of the Absurd:[73]

> Tenth-rate old actors they send for me', said K. to himself, glancing round again to confirm the impression. 'They want to finish me off cheaply'. He turned abruptly toward the men and asked: 'What theater are you playing at?' 'Theater?' said one, the corners of his mouth twitching as he looked for advice to the other, who acted as if he were a dumb man struggling to overcome a stubborn disability. 'They're not prepared to answer questions', said K. to himself and went to fetch his hat.
> . . . 'Perhaps they are tenors', he thought, as he studied their fat double chins. [Their eyebrows looked as if they had been stuck on to their foreheads, and they danced up and down, independent of the movements made in walking. (Deleted passage)] (*The Trial*, 224; 263)

In Kafka's universe, the jackdaws may screech, but we – Kafka himself, Joseph K., and indeed all we bumpkins and gudgeons[74] – will doubtless remain the eternal dupes; and this is a sentiment shared too by Samuel Beckett.

Notes

1 Dmitri Zatonsky, 'Kafka Unretouched', in Hughes, 206–49 (221) – 'an absurdity that precludes even the possibility of understanding anything that is happening and that appears as the basic method of Kafka's derealization of being'.

2 'Kafka and His Precursors' (1951), in Borges, *TL* 363–5; among these precursors, Borges counts Zeno's paradox, a ninth-century Chinese fable, Kierkegaard, a Browning poem ('Fears and Scruples'), a story by Léon Bloy (about people 'who amass globes, atlases, train schedules, and trunks and who die without ever having left the town where they were born'), and 'Carcassonne' by Lord Dunsany (in which 'an invincible army of warriors

departs from an infinite castle, subjugates kingdoms and sees monsters and crosses deserts and mountains, but never reaches Carcassonne, although they once catch a glimpse of it'). See also Borges, 'Franz Kafka, *The Vulture*' (1979), *TL*, 501–3.

3 The adjective 'Kafkaesque' was allegedly coined by C. Day Lewis in 1938 (Preece, 220). Jeremy Adler (who spells it with a small 'k') sees it as 'denoting nightmarish situations, an all-pervasive bureaucracy, looming totalitarianism, infinite hierarchies, and a deep existential *angst*' (Adler, 4). On confusions over the term see also George H. Szanto, 41; 49; 169. Michael Wood (in the final chapter of his 2003 study) discusses Welles's film of *The Trial* (as do Brady and Hughes: in Preece, 231–4), the philosophical contributions of Gillian Rose, and Philip Glass's operatic version of *In the Penal Colony* (2000). The Welles film is characterised as 'a sort of metaphysical *film noir*' (Wood, 2003, 83). The translation of *The Trial* appearing under the name of Bruno Schulz (1936) was apparently made by his then fiancée (Józefina Szelinska), with corrections by Schulz (Ficowski, 112).

4 Philip Roth, the Kafka sections or themes in *The Breast* (1972), *The Professor of Desire* (1977) and *The Prague Orgy* apart, imagined a film version of *The Castle*, with 'Groucho Marx as K., and Chico and Harpo as the two "assistants"' (Philip Roth, *Reading Myself and Others*, London: Jonathan Cape, 1975, 22); he also wrote movingly on Kafka's last year, to which essay he appended his story of Kafka surviving into an American old age ('"I Always Wanted You to Admire My Fasting"; or, Looking at Kafka', in ibid., 247–70). Incidentally, in *The Prague Orgy*, Roth 'borrows' the fate of Bruno Schulz at the hands of the Gestapo (or something very close to it), to put into the mouth of a 'lying' Czech writer who appropriates it as the fate of his father, whom he is attempting to promote as a significant Yiddish writer – rebutted by his ex-wife as: '"He shot my Jew, so I shot his" ... It happened to another writer, who didn't even write in Yiddish' (Philip Roth, *Zuckerman Bound: A Trilogy and Epilogue*, Harmondsworth: Penguin, 1989, 521; 550).

5 To increase the list in this regard see: Osman Durrani, 'Editions, translations, adaptations' (206–25); and Martin Brady and Helen Hughes, 'Kafka adapted to film' (226–41): both in Preece (2002). A more recent addition to such literature has been Calasso's *K.* (Milan: Adephi, 2002).

6 See 'Somewhere Behind': Kundera, 1988, 99–117.

7 This work has been translated as *Metamorphosis* (the formulation normally used here), *The Metamorphosis* and *The Transformation*. On *Metamorphosis* and *The Nose* see also Idris Parry, 'Kafka, Gogol and Nathanael West', in Gray, 85–90; P. Roth (1975), 66–8.

8 Camus (*Myth*, 116; 113) observes the 'distinction' in Kafka between 'the logical and the everyday' joined in 'secret complicity' to the tragic, shown in the failure (in the case of Joseph K. too) to 'show sufficient astonishment at this lack of astonishment'.

9 Such 'labyrinths' are commonly seen seen as both spatial and psychological. Zadie Smith, however, stresses the labyrinthine in Kafka as 'time itself' (Smith, 36). The word 'labyrinth' seems to be employed almost universally by commentators on Kafka's work and its background. Fuentes refers respectively to 'a Petersburg of infinite labyrinths' in Gogol (109) and 'the labyrinthine tribunals of Kafka' (177).

What Kundera sees in Kafka as the bureaucratic fantastic amounts to 'a *boundless labyrinth* from some unknown mythology' (Kundera, 1988, 113; his emphasis; Benjamin, 117, avers that 'even the world of myth … is incomparably younger than Kafka's world'). Malcolm Bradbury (in his *The Modern World: Ten Great Writers*, Harmondsworth: Penguin, 1989, 255) refers to 'the old labyrinthine world of the Austro-Hungarian Empire'. Kafka himself writes to Milena Jesenská of 'simply running around in one's own labyrinth' (*LM* 29).

10 Cited from W.J. Dodd, 'Varieties of Influence: On Kafka's Indebtedness to Dostoevskii', *Journal of European Studies*, 14 (1984); see more particularly though his *Kafka and Dostoyevsky* (1992). On this pairing see also Boris Suchkov, 'Franz Kafka', in Hughes, 125–85 (passim). Kafka, of course, had his other sources; Michael Müller makes a persuasive case for the memoirs of Casanova (see his 'Kafka, Casanova, and *The Trial*', in M. Anderson, 187–98).

11 The *Diaries* apart, this connection goes back at least as far as Klaus Mann's 'Preface', dated 1940 (*Amerika*, xii–xiii). Still mainly known as *Amerika*, this novel (untitled in manuscript, written 1911–14 and published 1927) has also been translated as *The Man who Disappeared (Amerika)* by Michael Hofmann (Harmondsworth: Penguin, 1997); it had been referred to by Kafka as *Der Verschollene*, which happened to be the title of a film he had seen in 1912 (Zischler, 129, n. 59).

12 There is in fact evidence that Kafka knew *Little Dorrit*, as well as *David Copperfield*: he sent a copy to his then fiancée, Felice Bauer, in 1916 (Kafka, *LF*, 538).

13 Benjamin (113), had remarked: 'There is much to indicate that the world of the officials and the world of the fathers are the same to Kafka'. Kundera (1988, 110) writes of 'the link, in Kafka's work, between the family's private "totalitarianism" and that in his great social visions'.

14 Paul Goodman, *Growing Up Absurd: Problems of Youth in the Organized System*, New York: Random House, 1960; this book is essentially a sociological study of delinquency. Goodman's psychological approach, when prefacing Kafka, *The Metamorphosis* (translated by A.L. Lloyd, New York, 1946) was dismissed by Vladimir Nabokov as 'drivel': John Burt Foster, Jr, 'Nabokov and Kafka', in Alexandrov, 444–51 (447). A somewhat similar approach to 'perfect puerility' in Kafka is taken by Georges Bataille, in his *Literature and Evil*, translated by Alastair Hamilton, London: Marion Boyars, 1993 (first published in French 1957), 149–69. The 'ideal goal' of Bruno Schulz was 'to "mature" into childhood' (Ficowski, 186). W.J. Mc Cormack (400) writes of a 'regression towards infancy' in Beckett's later work.

15 Nabokov (1980, 255–6) similarly dismisses both religious and Freudian interpretations.

16 Píchová also draws attention to Kafka's fragment 'The Truth About Sancho Panza' (Kafka, *CS*, 430), in which there is a reversal of roles – Sancho becoming the creator and Quixote 'a demon exorcised from and by Sancho' (Píchová, 108–9); the inference here is of the need for an expulsion of demons by émigré writers 'assisted by a return to the "ancient wisdom" embodied in the history of the novel'. This latter policy, at least, was followed, in relation to Cervantes in particular, by Nabokov and Kundera, as well as Borges, Brink, Fuentes and

other writers, who have all, in one way or another, written on *Don Quixote* (as well as on Kafka).

17 On this story (*Il verdetto* in Italian) see Calasso (*K.*, 155–64), who writes of it: 'on such a sheet would be written, in a progressive palimpsest, Kafka's entire *oeuvre*' (164; translations from *K.* are mine).

18 Kafka had read *Thus Spake Zarathustra* in 1900 (Adler, 29); see also the following aphoristic fragment: 'I err. The true way leads over a tight-rope which is not placed high up, but just above the ground. It seems to be designed to make you stumble rather than to be walked across' (quoted from Adler, 107).

19 Nevertheless, Kafka can confirm: 'I speak fluent Czech' (*Diaries*, 127); indeed he appears to have conversed with Brod in Czech, at least at times (see ibid., 461). He also urged Milena to write to him in Czech ('Czech please': *LM*, 21; see also 26). He referred (*LM*, 63) to his *Letter to His Father* as 'a lawyer's letter'. For a scenic, cultural and linguistic description of Kafka's Prague see Klaus Wagenbach, 'Prague at the Turn of the Century', in M. Anderson, 25–52.

20 Nabokov, 1980, 250–83. It may be indicative that, whereas Nabokov here makes certain comparisons between Gogol (*The Overcoat*, or 'The Carrick' as he prefers to call it) and Kafka (*Metamorphosis*, see pp. 252–5), Kafka does not figure in the index of Nabokov's study *Nikolai Gogol* (first published 1944). 'Ithaca, 1954' appears as a dateline within the Kafka lecture (ibid., 275).

21 According to Nabokov, neither Gregor nor Kafka realised what sort of an insect Gregor was; Gregor's sister thinks, when she can't immediately see him: 'he couldn't just have flown away' (*Metamorphosis*, 24; 'he couldn't have flown away, could he?', *CS*, 107). Marina Warner, in her *Fantastic Metamorphoses, Other Worlds: Ways of Telling the Self* (Oxford: Oxford University Press, 2002, 113–18), compares the use of metamorphosis in works by Kafka and Nabokov.

22 Kundera, 1996, 37–41: 'this simpleminded novel, this garbage, this cartoon-level concoction, which, aesthetically, stands at exactly the opposite pole from Kafka's art' (38). *Franz Kafka, eine Biographie* was translated by G. Humphreys Roberts as *The Biography of Franz Kafka* (New York, 1947); the revised second edition appeared in 1960 (reprinted: Brod, 1995). The earlier work was translated by E. Sutton as *The Kingdom of Love* (1930).

23 Marc Estrin, *Insect Dreams: The Half Life of Gregor Samsa*, New York: Bluehen, 2002. Estrin's hero is emphatically a cockroach; and he makes a big point too of stressing Gregor's Jewishness. However, 'the Samsas in the story are Catholics' (pointed out by Hibberd, 59; see also Dodd, 1992, 100). The Samsa family cross themselves on hearing that Gregor is dead (*CS*, 136); for that matter, Joseph K. also crosses himself in the Cathedral (Kafka, *The Trial*, 207).

24 Although his creative works were written in German, Sebald is, for various reasons, *almost* to be considered an English writer (a tribute, apart from anything else, to his translators). In his capacity as Professor of Literature (at the University of East Anglia), Sebald was, among other things, an authority on Kafka: see for instance Sebald 1972; and his 'The Law of Ignominy:

Authority, Messianism, and Exile in *The Castle*', in Franz Kuna, ed., *On Kafka: Semi-Centenary Perspectives*, London: Elek, 1976, 42–58. For a bibliography of his publications up to 1996 see the *DAAD Directory of University Teachers of German 1997–98*. Among Sebald's many qualities as a writer, absurdism would probably not rank as a main one with most readers; nevertheless, he is still capable of passages such as the following: 'over the years I had puzzled out a good deal in my own mind, but in spite of that, far from becoming clearer, things now appeared to me more incomprehensible than ever. The more images I gathered from the past, I said, the more unlikely it seemed to me that the past had actually happened in this or that way, for nothing about it could be called normal: most of it was absurd, and if not absurd, then appalling' (*Vertigo*, 212).

25 Potentially, one might have thought, a case here for Sherlock Holmes (if still active in 1913), a figure well known to Kafka (see *Diaries*, 167), or for Poirot (if old enough by 1913). There was in fact an old general among the residents (letter to Brod: *LFFE*, 101), though his demise is not here mentioned; however this figure has now been identified, and he indeed shot himself in this manner during Kafka's stay: Anthony Northey, 'Myths and Realities in Kafka Biography', in Preece, 189–205 (196). Referring back to Riva in 1916, Kafka wrote to Brod: 'I was altogether confused and sick in every possible way' (*LFFE*, 117). Suicide, in Kafka's view, although frequently invoked in his writings, was 'a form of egotism raised to the point of absurdity' (quoted by R. Armstrong, 17); however, 'myths surrounding suicide', and the self-slaying of this retired general, as well as the specified Riva location, are taken by Northey as the source for this story. Kafka was later (in 1920) to spend a night in a Hotel Riva in Vienna, after which he complained to Milena of 'bites from the Riva bedbugs' (*LM*, 65). Suchkov (in Hughes, 181) claims that the name 'Gracchus ... represents the latinized form of Kafka's family name': *kavka* in Czech meaning 'jackdaw'; *graik* is Indo-European 'crow'; modern Russian *grach* is 'rook' (perhaps Kafka himself stretched such doubling, and such loose ornithology, even to take in 'vulture': see the story *The Vulture*, *CS*, 442–3); Kempf (42) quotes Wilhelm Emrich making the same literary-biographical point, based on 'the fact that both the Latin *graculus* and Czech *kavka* mean "raven"'. See also Bridgwater (123–4: referred to later on Beckett, Chapter 8). For Schur (180, developing Maurice Blanchot's 1949 analysis), the emphasis in this story is on the opposition between 'the fall' and 'the beyond'.

26 Germane or otherwise to such an issue, a diary entry from 1912 reads: 'I am supposed to pose in the nude for the artist Ascher, as a model for a St Sebastian' (*Diaries*, 172). For references to suggestions of homosexuality in Kafka criticism see Kempf, 1–2; 13. Sexual anxiety was certainly (as ever) a strong factor in Kafka's emotional crisis with Felice: 'Coitus as punishment for the happiness of being together', he muses, shortly before his Italian trip (ibid., 228). By 1922 he is ruminating that 'sex keeps gnawing at me', wryly noting too that 'Sisyphus was a bachelor' (400; 401); Hoyles (152) notes the link here not only between Kafka and Camus but also with 'that archetypal absurdist bachelor', Kierkegaard.

27 Louis Marks, 'Producing Pinter', in Burkman and Kundert-Gibbs, 18–23 (22). One can easily imagine the resonance that even such a statement as 'one might quite easily have suspected that some criminal plan was being discussed here

and no legitimate business' (*Amerika*, 66) might have had on the youthful
Pinter.

28 According to George Steiner (1977, 185): 'A good deal of what is representative in modern literature, from Kafka to Pinter, seems to work deliberately at
the edge of quietness.'

29 John L. Kundert-Gibbs, '"I am powerful ... and I am only the lowest door-
keeper": Power Play in Kafka's *The Trial* and Pinter's *Victoria Station*', in
Burkman and Kundert-Gibbs, 149–60. Interestingly, perhaps, R. Armstrong,
while listing this essay in his bibliography, makes no comment on its main
thesis. A passing reference by Kundert-Gibbs (151) to the early Pinter story
The Examination (1955), which arguably reads rather more like a Kafkan
fragment (and includes the character Kullus, eponymous 'hero' of an even
earlier version of 1949: one need hardly mention that names beginning with
'K' are widespread throughout Kafka's writings: see, for instance, Kullich and
Kaminer, clerks in *The Trial*), might have merited development.

30 More opportunistic, perhaps (albeit hard to refute) is Armstrong's question
(64) as to whether the names 'MacGregor and Sam' allude just coincidentally
to Gregor Samsa of *Metamorphosis*.

31 As might perhaps in any event be expected, the instruction 'moonlight' occurs
three times in the directions of Pinter's screenplay (Pinter, *The Trial*, 65);
however, although considerable attention is paid throughout to light and
darkness, moonlight as such does not figure here in the David Jones film. On
moonlight in Kafka's novel see also Brink, 198; and 345, n. 6.

32 Brady and Hughes (Preece, 240, n. 4), say there have now (published in 2002)
been in total some forty 'Kafka films'.

33 The producer of *The Trial* was Louis Marks and the film was directed by
David Jones (dedicatees of the published screenplay).

34 Gillen, in Burkman and Kundert-Gibbs, 139; Gussow, 88–9. The writing of
both pieces by Marks and Gillen in fact predates the shooting of the film, as
does the conversation with Gussow just quoted (but not the subsequent one:
see Gussow, 136; 140). Frederick R. Karl's comments on the adaptation (*The
Pinter Review*, 1994) were also written without reference to the film itself (and
seem to be based on the first draft). See however the film reviews by Jeanne
Connolly and Ronald Knowles (in ibid., 84–8 and 116–17 respectively). R.
Armstrong's treatment of Pinter's *The Trial* (R. Armstrong, 117–19) is perhaps
surprisingly perfunctory. See also Knowles (1995), 178–82; Billington,
348–51; and Linda Renton, *Pinter and the Object of Desire: An Approach
through the Screenplays* (Oxford: Legenda, 2002), 54–6.

35 For Karl (83), Pinter is 'paradoxically, too honest, too loyal to Kafka', resulting in his giving us Kafka, but not the Kafkaesque. Pinter's insertions include
an increased emphasis on Joseph K.'s birthday – at the bank (Pinter, *The Trial*,
8) and, at the boarding house, Frau Grubach's birthday cake (ibid., 8–9; in
fact, omitted from the final cut) – and what appears as a brief 'signature' to
Mr Kidd of *The Room* (The Second Stairman's 'the fifth floor. ... I haven't
been up there for years': ibid., 18; noted by Knowles, 1995, 180–1). The
'joiner called Lanz' (the name being that of Frau Grubach's nephew: Kafka,
The Trial, 36) has, however, become 'a plumber' called Lanz (Pinter, *The
Trial*, 17; 18). On Pinter's insertions see also Connolly (85).

36 Connolly, 86.

37 Cf. Hoyles (243): 'at least Joseph K goes down fighting'. Dodd (122) suggests that Joseph K.'s 'refusal of the knife' (proposed 'in a coded way' for 'the decent thing' of suicide), rather than 'an act of spiritual weakness' (as presumably 'the Court would see it'), 'could also be seen as an act of ultimate defiance, even as he succumbs to the power of the Court'. One might, however, feel more inclined to agree with Suchkov (in Hughes, 162) that eventually 'he decides to give up the fight'. Kundera (1996: see 203–13) sees Joseph K. rather as implicitly acquiescing throughout.

38 Knowles (*Pinter Review*, 1994, 116–17) considers that 'in Dantesque fashion K has to endure the limbo-like exposure to circles of the juristically damned in a downward spiralling regression' until, in the quarry, 'he submits to a malign, not a divine comedy'.

39 The assumption that Schulz translated Kafka, however, is dismissed by Ficowski (112: see above).

40 Berkoff, *Meditations*. On tour with a revived *Metamorphosis*, Berkoff and company included short works ('The Bucket Rider' and Kafka's 'strange and lovely aphorisms') as a forty-five-minute curtain-raiser (*Medit.*, 73).

41 'Steven Berkoff on *Metamorphosis*' (in his *Three Adaptations*, 1988), 71: Berkoff styles himself 'the surreal magician, Berkoff – actor/writer/director/novelist and ex-menswear salesman from Stepney'.

42 Subsequent Berkoff Gregors (or 'bugs') were to include Tim Roth (London, 1986), Roman Polanski (Paris, 1988) and Mikhail Baryshnikov (New York, 1989); Berkoff himself, in two London revivals, switched to the role of Mr Samsa. Photographs in role of Berkoff's ten Gregors are included in *Medit.* (between 48 and 49). The Tim Roth version was recorded by the BBC for 'Theatre Night' in 1987 and transmitted in 1989 (BBC video: not available commercially; 1 hour and 20 minutes).

43 Deleuze and Guattari make a more linguistic comparison ('cries, gasps') between Kafka and Artaud: 'What is a Minor Literature?', in M. Anderson, 80–94 (93). Daniel Albright (147) observes that 'Antonin Artaud, whose "theater of cruelty" seems a gross literalization of the technique of Kafka's novels, once hired a stage upon which to go insane', in a 'last public monologue' described as 'the theater of the mind's self-combustion'.

44 By the time of the videoed production, at least, 'screens' are in fact metallic rectangles used to novel effect as frames, barriers, doors, windows and mirrors.

45 Brod's ordering of the scenes, and the question of Kafka's intentions over the uncompleted scenes, leave any edition of this unfinished novel controversial. Brod himself, indeed, suggested this very change 'not impossible' (Kafka, *The Trial*, 274). One assumes that Berkoff (like Pinter, who follows the original Brod chronology) worked from Brod's 'definitive edition' (the Muirs' translation, with or without the appendices). Brink (196–7) suggests that the ordering of chapters, and therefore of events may be 'not important', given that '*The Trial* is constructed around the image of gaps and silences'.

46 According to Berkoff (*Adapt.*, 6): '*The Trial* played successfully in Germany to over 1,000 people a night while in London I had to struggle for audiences at the Round House. So *The Trial* was seen in England for only three weeks, in 1973.'

47 Introductory caption to Franz Kafka, *The Trial*, adapted and directed by Steven Berkoff (East Productions, issued 2001, 2 hours and 23 minutes). The cast of this production includes: Alan Perrin, as Joseph K.; Matthew Scurfield, playing the Inspector and Huld; Katrin Cartlidge, as Leni; and Berkoff, as Titorelli.

48 Of course, it may well be that less illustrious readers, such as the present writer, may also be shown not to be immune to such transgressions.

49 The exact supposed meaning and extent of the last term are not made totally explicit, although 'the Kafka-esque intrigues of high fashion' are mentioned; Bennett's Brod maintains: 'Words don't always get used correctly. What matters is that they get used' (*KD* 30).

50 The book in question (see *2 K Plays*, 64; *KD*, 44; quotations from this play itself will be given from the latter revised text) is apparently Calvin S. Hall and Richard E. Lind, *Dreams, Life, and Literature: A Study of Franz Kafka* (Chapel Hill: University of North Carolina Press, 1970). Such preoccupations are not unique to this one study: Reiner Stach, in his compendious *Kafka: Die Jahre der Entscheidungen* (Frankfurt: Fischer, 2002), 'ruminates on how Kafka regarded his genitals' (Jeremy Adler, 'Nothing but Literature', *TLS*, 11 October 2002, 7–8). For whatever reason, Kafka normally did not strip completely when indulging himself in nudist jaunts ('I am called the man in the swimming trunks' – 'Trip to Weimar and Jungborn', summer 1912: *Diaries*, 478). 'The curious mixture of irony and respect' in Kafka's attitude to the 'cults' of nudism and other forms of nature therapy, and his efforts to follow them, according to Brod, 'defy all analysis' (*Diaries*, 501, n. 143).

51 It is likely as well that the revelation (delivered here by Brod) that 'T.S. Eliot is an anagram of toilets' (*KD*, 38) derives from Nabokov's known delight in that observation.

52 'A book is a coffin and in it is your father's body', declares Hermann Kafka (*KD*, 33), a line (added by Bennett in the revised version) that should have held considerable appeal for R. Armstrong.

53 See note 50 above. This opus is just one of some alleged 'fifteen thousand books and articles about Kafka' (*KD* 46) – and this count was made in, if not before, 1986 (cf. *2 K Plays*, ix). Franz R. Kempf (1994) wrote of 'the kaleidoscopic carnival of Kafka criticism'; 'the labyrinth of Kafka literature'; and that, by 1992, 'Kafka criticism has become "Kafkalogy"' (Kempf, 1; 7; 2). Kundera (1996, 42–4) charges Brod with creating 'Kafkology', a phenomenon which has developed 'to the point where the author whom readers know by the name Kafka is no longer Kafka but the Kafkologized Kafka' (42).

54 Dancing was a long-standing dislike of Kafka's. Of heaven and hell in Kafka, Brod waxes lyrically: 'there is nothing he loves so much as the blue unclouded heaven above him. But this heaven begins to pucker like the forehead of a scowling father' (Brod, 134).

55 Noted (in 1992) by Dodd, who regards this strange question, '*Sie sind Zimmermaler?*', which the Investigating Magistrate half asks, half asserts' as 'anomalous' but (strangely?) considers that 'it does not stand out as an intertextual invitation' (Dodd, 153). Dodd's book postdates Bennett's play, but 'this apparently trivial and aberrant remark ... ha[d] already been pointed out' (doubtless in more than one of the 'fifteen thousand books and articles about Kafka').

56 After working for the Austro-Italian company 'Assicurazioni Generali', Kafka 'finally achieved the longed-for job in July 1908, in a semi-Government office, the "Workers' Accident Insurance Institute for the Kingdom of Bohemia in Prague"' (Brod, 79–80; see also Adler, 46–54).

57 'In 1911 [Kafka] had been pressed by his father to become a silent partner in an asbestos factory in Prague that was owned by his brother-in-law, Karl Hermann': Ruth V. Gross, 'Kafka's Short Fiction', in Preece, 80–94 (84–5).

58 Herman Melville, 'Bartleby the Scrivener: A Story of Wall Street', first published in *Putnam's Monthly Magazine* (November–December 1853).

59 G.M. Hyde, 'Melville's *Bartleby* and Gogol's *The Overcoat*' (1976): 'Both writers are casualties of rationality, and use the grotesque and the absurd to displace rational paradigms' (32–3). Bartleby himself enters as 'the incomprehensible and inarticulate gesture of negation' (40), while Melville's narrative is seen as 'a symbolic text of great literary density dependent upon a sub-text of scriptural authority in criticisng which it inevitably runs into a negation of itself' (44–5). Calasso, in an essay entitled 'The Sleep of the Calligrapher' (*Forty-Nine Steps*, 36–51) implicitly compares writing as sleep, 'or rather, death' to Kafka with Bartleby, in whom 'negation thrives' amid an 'equivalence between silence and a certain ornamental use of words' (ibid., 51), bringing in too *Jacob von Gunten* by Robert Walser (himself an influence on Kafka). Schur (211), as a further point of comparison, sees Kafka's 'version of transcendence' as 'Heraclitean' indeed 'primarily because of its paradoxical emphasis on negative aspects of method'.

60 This story of 1917 may be compared to an earlier (1914) diary fragment, or fantasy, of pointless wrestling with a student neighbour (*Diaries*, 272–3).

61 It is generally assumed that Kharms did not know Kafka's work. However, it may be worth noting Jaccard's comment (in Cornwell, 1991, 67, n. 5): 'It is impossible to affirm that Kharms had read this novel, all the more so as it did not then enjoy the readership that it has today, but the close chronological proximity of the two texts [*The Trial*, published in 1925, and *Yelizaveta Bam*, written 1927] remains astonishing. It can moreover be added that Kharms studied at Peterschule … and that he thereby knew German and English.' Neither does it seem likely that Kafka would have penetrated Stalin's Soviet Russia of the 1930s.

62 Milner-Gulland, 1984, 33; he also notes a common 'anti-psychologism'.

63 A number of Kafka's drawings are reproduced in Adler (2001). Assorted drawings, sketchings and scribblings by Kharms are scattered through the two-volume edition of his notebooks (*Zapisnye knizhki*, 2002). Schulz was also an artist and an art teacher; thirty of his illustrations are reproduced in Schulz, 1979. See also the illustrations in Ficowski; *Letters and Drawings of Bruno Schulz:With Selected Prose* (London: HarperCollins, 1988); and *The Drawings of Bruno Schulz* (Evanston, IL: Northwestern University Press, 1990). Beckett, too, had some sketching ability: see the reproduction in Pilling and Bryden, *The Ideal Core of the Onion*, 57.

64 For two groupings of Kafka's aphorisms ('The Collected Aphorisms', 79–98; and 'He: Aphorisms from the 1920 Diary') see Malcolm Pasley's edition of *The Great Wall of China and Other Short Works* (*GWC*).

65 'In such a pattern, each new term, consisting of elements syntactically and conceptually parallel to those of a previous term, arises by means of an inversion of these elements': Corngold, 'Kafka's Later Stories and Aphorisms', in Preece, 95–110 (104). See also Michael Kirkwood (145), according to whom Joseph K. is presented with an 'algorithmic' and 'recursive, step-by-step problem-solving procedure' (compared here to the 'kaleidoscopic' method employed in Alexander Zinoviev's *The Yawning Heights*).

66 Julian Preece, 'The Letters and Diaries', in Preece, 111–30 (129). A similar view is put forward by Mark Anderson: see his 'Unsigned Letters to Milena Jesenská', in M. Anderson, 241–56.

67 This incident is noted by Zischler (94), though he does not link it as such to *The Trial*.

68 See Elias Canetti, 'The Letters to Felice', in M. Anderson, 229–40 (excerpted from Canetti, *Kafka's Other Trial: The Letters to Felice*, translated by Christopher Middleton, New York: Schocken Books, 1974).

69 What Nietzsche called 'monological art' is 'the art of one who speaks with the void in front of him, the art of one who has created the void in front of him' (Calasso, *Forty-Nine Steps*, 28).

70 Malcolm Pasley, 'The Act of Writing and the Text: The Genesis of Kafka's Manuscripts', in M. Anderson, 201–14 (206).

71 According to Gustav Janouch (in his *Conversations with Kafka*, 1971), 'Kafka compared himself to a *kavka*, a jackdaw, hopping bewildered in the cage of existence' and one 'who longs to disappear between the stones' (quoted from Albright, 108; 136). The protagonist of Haruki Murakami's *Kafka on the Shore* (2002), at least in its English translation (2005), has an alter ego called 'Crow'.

72 Buber, 'Kafka and Judaism', in Gray, 157–62 (159), taken from his *Two Types of Faith*, 1951.

73 Berkoff affirms: 'I was compelled to adapt it for the stage since I felt it was a work of extraordinary imagination and depth and at the same time seemed intensely theatrical' (Berkoff, *The Trial*, Video).

74 In addition to being a small fish, 'gudgeon' has the secondary meaning expressed above by the *Comprehensive Czech–English Dictionary*: cf. 'a credulous, gullible person' (*OED*). Even the fish-like sense may, however, be seen to have a Kafkan resonance, given the frequency of drowning imagery in his writings: see the ending of *The Judgement*; and 'the corpse of a drowned man' passage in the 1910 fragment '"You," I said ...' (*Diaries*, 25–6), to mention but two instances. In his Heraclitean reading, Schur (254–5) quotes Kafka on 'my fishy feeling ' concerning the first and last letters of reading and writing: 'Kafka, and in a sense Georg Bendemann [of *The Judgement*], are swimming inside the breathtaking flow of writing that moves between first and last letters. While that flow of writing drowns Kafka in the *lêthê*, that oblivion (a seeming death to the world) is a fishlike afterlife.' Blanchot's reading of Kafka had argued that 'writing is a method that leads beyond life to survival in oblivion' (Schur, 188).

8

Samuel Beckett's vessels, voices and shades of the absurd

Yes, no more denials, all is false, there is no one, it's understood, there is nothing, no more phrases, let us be dupes, dupes of every time and tense, until it's done, all past and done, and the voices cease, it's only voices, only lies. (Samuel Beckett, *Texts for Nothing*, 3, 1945–50)

To move wild laughter in the throat of death?' [*Love's Labour's Lost*, V, 2, 841] precisely sums up the humor of Beckett's plays. (Hersh Zeifman, 1990)

In the wake of Kafka?

W.G. Sebald (in literary critical mode) introduces his article on Kafka's *The Castle* with an epigraph from Beckett's *Molloy*:

And in the end, or almost, to be abroad alone, by unknown ways, in the gathering of the night, with a stick. It was a stout stick, he used it to thrust himself onward, or as a defence, when the time came, against dogs and marauders. Yes, night was gathering, but the man was innocent, greatly innocent, he had nothing to fear, though he went in fear, he had nothing to fear, there was nothing they could do to him, or very little. (Sebald, 1972, 22; Beckett, Trilogy, 10[1])

Sebald implicitly links this situation with Kafka the boy and with K., the wanderer with rucksack and stick, with imagery of death ('the image of a journey or a hike as a symbol of death'), and with the writings on Schubert (the wanderer) by Adorno – himself too, as we shall see, a commentator on both Kafka and Beckett (Sebald, 1972, 22–3). James Knowlson, in his authorised biography, mentions that several of Beckett's forebears 'appear to have been land surveyors' (Knowlson, 3).[2] In an illuminating comparative essay of 1961, Ruby Cohn had considered Beckett's novel '*Watt* in the Light of *The Castle*'. Gary Adelman, in a recent study, takes a close Kafka comparison through from the four French novellas to *The Unnamable*, and on to *The Lost Ones*.

Sebald would also have noticed, one might assume, among many possible traces of Kafka in Beckett, what might be seen as the apparent echoes of Kafka's *The Hunter Gracchus* scattered through Beckett's work. Indeed, it is impossible to imagine that this particular mythic piece by Kafka would not have struck a deep chord in Beckett, given what Christopher Ricks advisedly terms 'Beckett's apprehension of death in life and life in death' (Ricks, 127). A man (originally an itinerant hunter) is lying perpetually between life and death 'on my old boat, still stranded forlornly on some earthly stretch of water' (see this story in Kafka, *Metamorphosis*, 90–3; Kafka, *CS*, 226–30, and 'A Fragment', *CS*, 231–4; *GWC*, 47–55, subtitled 'Four Fragments') – 'driven by the wind that blows in the nethermost regions of death' (*Metamorphosis*, 93).[3] 'He lay there motionless, his eyes closed, apparently without breathing, yet only the surroundings indicated that he was perhaps dead' (ibid., 91); yet, 'to a certain extent I am also alive', affirms the hunter (92). At the same time, he can put into the port of Riva, on Lake Garda. His 'death ship' having gone 'off course', Gracchus's vessel has 'ever since ... been sailing earthly waters', drifting and forever in motion somewhere 'on the great stairway' leading to the 'hereafter', or the 'other world' (93; *CS*, 228). 'I always find I have forgotten everything', he remarks, in what must now seem a strikingly Beckettian mode (92). Gracchus has difficulties too with the minds, and the language, of the masters of the bark, who have the unfortunate habit, as the centuries roll on, of dying on him (*CS*, 231–2). 'The hunter Gracchus', according to Roberto Calasso, is Kafka's ultimate outsider: an outsider in the whole world (or 'a foreigner to the entire world').[4]

'I don't know when I died' is the opening statement of Beckett's novella *The Calmative* (original *Le Calmant*, 1946; English version 1967). The narrator feels drawn to the sea: 'And I might slip unnoticed aboard a freighter outward bound and get far away and spend far away a few good months, perhaps even a year or two, in the sun, in peace, before I died'; then 'seeing still no sign or stir I made ready to go, to turn away sadly from this dead haven' (Beckett, *Complete Short Prose*, 65–6). This watery thematic is developed further in *The End* (*La Fin*, 1946; English version 1954; corrected 1980).[5] The narrator-protagonist dislikes the sea, preferring lakes, and ends up in an 'adopted' shed on the riverside, in which he makes his bed in a derelict boat, lying in the stern and covered by a lid made with stray boards, to keep off the rats (*CSP*, 95–6). The lapping of the river, a nearby sewer and the occasional penetration of rain altogether 'composed a rather liquid world' (ibid., 97), giving rise to visions of the boat 'gliding on the waters' and then 'buffeted by the choppy waters of the bay' (98). Water rises (or seems to rise) through a plughole in the floor and the narrator calmly awaits the end: 'I swallowed my calmative'. What he calls this 'narration of self-abandonment within an apocalyptic scene' reminds Paul Lawley that the young Beckett had translated Rimbaud's *Le*

Bateau ivre (in 1932). And, in Gracchus-like fashion, poised perhaps to go off course: 'The memory came faint and cold of the story I might have told, a story in the likeness of my life, I mean without the courage to end or the strength to go on' (*CSP*, 99). As with that of the neither dead nor alive Gracchus, the story has – at least sort of – nevertheless been told.

Typically of Beckett's fictional practice, such echoes and details from his early French novellas re-emerge in the novels that soon followed. Molloy's 'region' extends to 'this sea too, its reefs and distant islands, and its hidden depths' (Trilogy, 68–9). Immediately before the sucking-stones sequence, he even wonders whether he ever came back from a voyage on it, 'in a sort of oarless skiff': 'For I see myself putting to sea, and the long hours without landfall, I do not see the return, the tossing on the breakers, and I do not hear the frail keel grating on the shore' (ibid., 69). Near the end of *Malone Dies*, just before the protagonist appears finally to drift away into silence (or oblivion), his last 'story' is of a grotesque excursion by boat of a phantasmal group of inmates from the indeterminate institution of 'the House of Saint John of God', led by a malevolent warder named Lemuel and including one Lady Pedal and the narrator (Malone, in the persona of Macmann).[6] After mayhem has broken loose on an island comes the return crossing:

> This tangle of grey bodies is they. Silent, dim, perhaps clinging to one another, their heads buried in their cloaks, they lie together in a heap, in the night. They are far out in the bay. Lemuel has shipped his oars, the oars trail in the water. The night is strewn with absurd
>   absurd lights, the stars, the beacons, the buoys, the lights of earth and in the hills the faint fires of the blazing gorse. Macmann, my last, my possessions, I remember, he is there too, perhaps he sleeps. (Trilogy, 289)

Malone (or Macmann), who commenced his narrative fearing that he may end up 'quite dead' (with 'quite' here readable 'as a compromiser or a diminisher': see Ricks, 131) seems to finish up, Gracchus-like, in a parodic marine setting extended to include too some semblance – if by now, on the return journey, in horizontal posture – of *The Ship of Fools* (which, as we have noted before, may itself be seen, like 'the dance of death', as a medieval icon of the human condition and thereby of the absurd) and the voyages of (Lemuel) Gulliver.[7]

The narrative voice of *The Unnamable* too, in the third volume of the '3 in 1', muses in similar deathly maritime fashion:

> Now it's I the orator, the beleaguerers have departed, I am master on board, after the rats, I no longer crawl between the thwarts, under the moon, in the shadow of the lash, strange this mixture of solid and liquid, ... unusual hell when you come to think of it, perhaps it's paradise, perhaps it's the earth, perhaps it's the shores of a lake beneath the earth, you scarcely breathe, it's not certain, you see nothing, hear nothing, you hear the long kiss of dead

water and mud, aloft at less than a score of fathoms men come and go, you dream of them, in your long dream there's a place for the waking (Trilogy, 396)

In the later *How It Is* we also find a fragment of Gracchus-like water imagery:

sea beneath the moon harbour-mouth after the sun the moon always light day and night little heap in the stern it's me all those I see are me all ages the current carries me out the awaited ebb I'm looking for an isle home at last drop never move again a little turn at evening to the sea-shore seawards then back drop sleep wake in the silence eyes that dare open stay open live old dream on crabs kelp (*How It Is*, 94)

However, there is of course 'confusion', as 'perhaps it's not me ... perhaps it's another voyage' (ibid., 95). *The Unnamable*'s voice, which doubts its own existence, exclaims: 'What a joy it is, to turn and look astern, between two visits to the depths, scan in vain the horizon for a sail, it's a real pleasure, upon my word it is, to be unable to drown, under such conditions' (Trilogy, 395).

A drowning motif, common as we have seen to a number of absurdist fictions, occurs several times in Beckett's mature work, and indeed earlier.[8] An early Beckett poem, 'Calvary by Night', foisted on a Dublin 'homespun poet' in his first novel (*Dream*, 213–14), according to Cohn (*Beckett Canon*, 41), 'relies on the apocryphal legend of Christ's drowning, thereby becoming the prototype of the suffering man, who knows no resurrection but only "re-enwombing" in "the waste of / the water"'. The narrator of *The Calmative* stresses 'the advantage of death by drowning', or one advantage at least, is that 'the crabs never get there too soon' (*CSP*, 63). The narrative voice of the later *Fizzle 4* (*Foirades*, 1972–73; 1976) dwells on the desire of 'he', his animated self, to drown, through the agency of 'deep water and a millstone', as 'he didn't want them to find him' (*CSP*, 235).

Such imagery recurs in Beckett's dramatic works, too. Lawley (40), who notes a number of such instances, refers to 'the recurrent image of a terminal self-abandonment to the ocean'. Hamm, in *Endgame*, wants Clov to build him a raft, on which 'I'll embark alone!' (Beckett, *Complete Dramatic Works*, 109). Moreover, Adorno (269–70) detects in Hamm a fear 'that death could miscarry' – seen explicitly as 'an echo of Kafka's motif in "The Hunter Gracchus"'.[9] Henry, in *Embers*, is obsessed by the sea, in which his father drowned, presumably by suicide, though the body was 'never found' (*CDW*, 253–4); Kristin Morrison (91) connects this with 'Henry's wish for death, to have been washed from the womb and never to have lived'. Somewhat similar events or aspirations appear to be alluded to in *Cascando* (*CDW*, 299 ff), *Eh Joe* (*CDW*, 366) and even, conceivably, *Rockaby*.[10] The water, however, is the setting for erotic activity in *Krapp's Last Tape* (replayed three times: *CDW*, 220; 221; 223) and (at least in fantasy) in *Play* ('A little dinghy, on the river, I resting my oars, they lolling on air-pillows in the stern ... sheets': *CDW*, 316).[11] In *Endgame* the potential of eroticism, comedy and drowning are combined, as Nagg and Nell, the day after their engagement, 'once went rowing on Lake Como'; Nell was 'in such fits' at Nagg's story of the tailor that 'we capsized. By rights we should have been drowned' (*CDW*, 102). It appears too that Beckett equated the creative process with drowning: he told Eyal Amiran 'that he felt while writing exactly as [his friend Bram] van Velde appeared to him to feel when he painted, as a man plunging into deep water without knowing how to swim' (Amiran, 46, n. 20).

Number 5 of the *Texts for Nothing* (*Textes pour rien*, 1950–52; 1967) displays Kafkan motifs of a nebulous juridical nature: hearings, judge and advocate, 'quite a different justice, in the toils of that obscure assize where to be is to be guilty' (*CSP*, 117); this court appears to be in session over the soul and within the skull, beset by phantoms (of the dead, the living and the not yet born). The sky and the earth are known of and the sea too 'belongs to the same family, I have even gone to the bottom more than once, under various assumed names' (*CSP*, 119).[12] In *The Unnamable* too the narrative voice surmises: 'Perhaps one day I'll know, say, what I'm guilty of' (Trilogy, 372). And, similarly:

> we were foolish to accuse one another, the master me, them, himself, they me, the master, themselves, I them, the master, myself, we are all innocent, enough. Innocent of what, no one knows, of wanting to know, wanting to be able, of all this noise about nothing, of this long sin against the silence that enfolds us, we won't ask any more, what it covers, this innocence we have fallen to, it covers everything, all faults, all questions, it puts an end to questions. (Trilogy, 379)

In the at least intermittent company of 'voluble shades' (such as Worm and Mahood), this presiding voice feels caught within a fantastical-absurd narrative hierarchy; above, it would seem, is 'the master', but 'we don't intend, unless absolutely driven to it, to make the mistake of enquiring into him', though even then, of course, it might not end there, as 'he'd turn out to be a mere high official'; so 'we'd end up by needing God' and 'there are still certain depths we prefer not to sink to' (Trilogy, 378). Brian McHale (13) regards *The Unnamable* as 'a grotesque parody of St Anselm's so-called "ontological argument" for the existence of God'. Ultimately (if anything be ultimate) these stories and lies may be fed in by 'the everlasting third party' (Trilogy, 379). *The Unnamable*'s voice, for that matter, also declares at one point: 'I'll sham dead now, whom they couldn't bring to life, and my monster's carapace will rot off me' (Trilogy, 327).[13]

The limbo-like association of water and drowning imagery, and the echoes of a bureaucratic and jurisprudential dimension, would, in particular and taken together, seem to indicate a certain impact on Beckett from Kafka, at least from his middle (or early French)[14] compositional period. Dante's 'dreary fen' (the Styx, of course: *Inferno*, Canto VII), undulates as a common source.[15] In the last canto of *The Inferno*, we find the lines:

> I did not die, nor yet was I alive:
>   think for yourself, if you've a grain of wit,
>   what I became, of both these states deprived.[16]

The Gracchus situation has also been linked to Nietzsche's story of King Midas the hunter and the response made to him by the daemon (see Nietzsche, 1999, 22–3).[17] Deleuze spoke of the 'tortured characters' created by Francis Bacon, Kafka and Beckett (see Mary Bryden, 'Figures of Golgotha': Pilling and Bryden, 60), while Richard Kearney observes that for both Kafka and Beckett 'language is a labyrinth where the path leads on indefinitely without ever reaching sanctuary' (Kearney, 1988, 75). Knowlson attests Beckett's keen reading of Kafka in his late years; but it may naturally be assumed that there was a strong familiarity from much earlier, while John Calder refers to Beckett's 'deep knowledge and understanding of Kafka's major works'.[18] For Adelman, *Texts for Nothing* 'might as well be dedicated to Kafka' (140), and *How It Is* and *The Lost Ones* descend from *In the Penal Colony*, while he eventually names Beckett's Unnamable as, in effect, 'K. beyond the grave' (159), with *The Unnamable* as 'the inverse of *The Castle*' (146).

Something of what can be regarded as the Gracchus spirit, in any event, may long have been present in Beckett's creative consciousness. The poem *Malacoda* (written following the death of his father in 1933), again named from a figure, a 'deceitful demon', in Dante (*Inferno*, Canto XXI; Malacoda had also been the name of the undertaker officiating at the end of *More Pricks Than Kicks*), concludes with the lines: 'all aboard all souls / half-mast aye aye / nay' (*Collected Poems*, 26; 174). Here, as indeed elsewhere, Amiran (136) ventures, 'Beckett imagines a condition where the Yeatsian spirits, dead souls awaiting rebirth, neither fully alive nor extinguished, incarnate and move on in the cycle of being'.

The prose

'The best reason' said the Jesuit 'that can be given for believing is that it is more amusing. Disbelief' said this soldier of Xist, ... 'is a bore. We do not count our change. We simply cannot bear to be bored.' (Samuel Beckett, *Dream of Fair to Middling Women*, 1932)

The prose fiction of Beckett's earlier (prewar) period encompasses principally three works. The linguistically precocious *Dream of Fair to Middling Women* (published only posthumously) was written as an experimental novel in 1932 and then, following publishers' rejections, partially reworked into the slightly less ornate cycle of stories entitled *More Pricks Than Kicks* (1934) – featuring as its protagonist the Beckettian (and Dantesque) alter ego Belacqua.[19] There then followed the novel *Murphy* (1938), in which, as Sinéad Mooney (10) has it, 'the hectic mannerism of *More Pricks* has been refined into an elegant pedantry'. While these works certainly do contain recognisably absurdist elements, contortions and scenes – Tyrus Miller (180) talks of Beckett 'making his own act of writing ridiculous' – they may perhaps be more readily classifiable as examples of what might be termed 'Irish grotesque' (in terms of their setting, style and Dublin tradition), rather than as fully blown fictions of the absurd. Francis Doherty (1971, 105) alludes, though with particular reference to *All That Fall*, to 'the comedy of rich absurdities in the Irish manner'. One notable instance of this is the observational technique applied by the narrator of *Murphy* to the physiognomy of Cooper:

> The skill is really extraordinary with which analphabetes, especially those of Irish education, circumvent their dread of verbal commitments. Now Cooper's face, though it did not seem to move a muscle, brought together and threw off in a single grimace the finest shades of irresolution, revulsion, doglike devotion, catlike discretion, fatigue, hunger, thirst and reserves of strength, in a very small fraction of the time that the finest oratory would require for a greatly inferior evasion, and without exposing its proprietor to misquotation. (*Murphy*, 115)

Declan Kiberd sees *Murphy* as 'a challenge to the stock English image of the stage Irishman', but one that does not totally succeed, in that 'the diagnosis in the end seems but a version of the disease';[20] from the viewpoint of the present book, particularly apt is Kiberd's comment that 'Being a jester at the London court of his master was hardly the proper role for a writer committed to exploring the void' (Kiberd, 1996, 533–4).

In these works, it might be said, the protagonists, and indeed most of the supporting characters, tend to conduct themselves absurdly in a world that has not, as such, been analysed or presented as itself absurd. More typical of absurdism (as found in much of the fiction of Kafka), would be the attempt by protagonists to make their way, or survive, 'sensibly' within what appears, or turns out to be, an absurd universe. Murphy, 'the seedy solipsist' (*Murphy*, 50), seems more concerned with the classification of jokes ('into jokes that had once been good jokes and jokes that had never been good jokes') – even if these may take a cosmological turn ('What but an imperfect sense of humour could have made such a mess of chaos. In the beginning was the pun. And so on': ibid., 41). The narrator of *Murphy* explores 'the [chess] game between Murphy and his stars' (51). Murphy (who remains devoid of a first name, as the first in the series of Beckettian heroes signalled by the surname initial 'M') discovers his element, however, and in more senses than one, in the 'liminal zone' (Amiran, 93) triple-M mental hospital of the Magdalen Mental Mercyseat (the action of the novel switching between London and Dublin), where 'The issue ... lay between nothing less fundamental than the big world and the little world, decided by the patients in favour of the latter, revived by the psychiatrists on behalf of the former' (101).[21] His own case remained 'unresolved', but 'only in fact': 'His vote was cast. "I am not of the big world, I am of the little world" was an old refrain with Murphy' (ibid.). For Murphy, the institutional padded cells represented 'the little world' and he soon met his doom through the element (not of water, but) of fire, in ludicrous circumstances through a gas (or 'chaos') explosion: 'Death by burns' (*Murphy*, 147).[22] In case any doubt remained, cremation follows.

Watt, written during the later war years in English (but not published until 1953), may be seen to represent a turning point in Beckett's prose – though an even bigger one was soon to come.[23] Up to and including *Murphy*, Beckett's prose fiction takes place in a recognisable outer world, with a keen sense of the topography of both Ireland and London. *Murphy* poses an overt dichotomy between the big (or outer) and the little (or inner) world, with the balance tilting, in the protagonist's case, firmly towards the latter pole of introspection and solipsism. From *Watt* onwards, the big world diminishes ever further in importance, gradually becoming unrecognisable and seemingly non-existent. This is part of the process that L.A.C. Dobrez (10) sees as a gradual movement towards 'a negative point' and terms 'the Beckett Reduction', put into practice indeed through Belacqua onwards.[24] Autobiographical elements (places, people, images – as illuminated in detail in the Knowlson critical biography), though perhaps never totally absent, become much less discernible as Beckett's work goes on, or are reduced to a minor key. In *Watt*, although a very recognisable (if 'unidentified': Cohn, *Beckett Canon*, 121) Irish setting remains, the emphasis is very largely (indeed, almost entirely) placed on its protagonist's inner world. There is also introduced, however, a third world (be it intermediate, or higher) – that of the mysterious house and system of Mr Knott, in and under which Watt spends much of the 'action' of the novel; *Watt* is, apart from anything else it may be, a parody of the Anglo-Irish 'big house' novel.[25] Doherty (1991, 187), setting *Watt* in its 'Irish frame', refers to Beckett's 'own territory, the world of the mind confronted with an irrational universe, a world of horror as disturbing in its way as the real world in which the writer was living'. We shall return to *Watt* in greater detail later.

After *Watt*, Beckett soon began to write his prose in French ('from a desire to impoverish myself still further': quoted by Lawley, 38; or 'Just felt like it': Shenker, 1), as well as making another switch – almost as radical – into first-person narrative. *First Love* and the other three novellas of 1946 were 'written before, almost in anticipation of, the "trilogy" of novels' (Gontarski, Introduction: *CSP*, xxii). Indeed, most – if not all – of the ingredients of the subsequent novels are to be found in these shorter works, in condensed and, many would say, more accessible form. The anonymous narrative voice, which may well be considered to be the same throughout,[26] adopts a somewhat flaky tone of at best questionably competent reminiscence, whether dealing with supposed recent events, or those much further back (harking back to 'visions', perhaps from childhood – 'my myth will have it so': *CSP*, 98). There are allusions to a relatively comfortable early life and to an erudite philosophical education. Latterly, however (if not many decades since), all has given way to vagrancy and destitution. Rejection and hitting the road give the hint to a fairly hopeless quest, apparently to get to the end of life, if not beyond ('is it possible that in this story I have come back to life, after my death?': ibid., 61).[27] 'Once on the road it was all downhill' (90). Derelict settings (graves, mud), darkness and abandonment; bodily functions, movements and ailments; squalid sexual acts or references; death and birth; these are related to the outer world through an almost poetic imagery, created amid an unusual stylistic ambience of what might be termed the lyrical grotesque ('the first bats like flying crucifixions': 64). Facts are questioned, names may change, articulacy fails – verbally on the part of the narrator within the narratives and metafictionally in the writing, or both: 'I have enough trouble as it is in trying to say what I think I know' (25). Ultimately the reader is taunted (in the last sentence of *The End*; 99) by the prospect of 'the story I might have told'.[28]

The setting can be physically constricted to the inner world: 'for we are needless to say in a skull' (70). We have by now already, then, in *The Calmative*, in effect leapfrogged *Molloy* and *Malone Dies*, on to *The Unnamable* – or, at any rate, what Gontarski terms 'the skullscapes of the "trilogy"' (Gontarski, *CSP*, xxiv). Dobrez (25) sees 'the voice within a skull' of the Unnamable as, in effect, 'the end of the Reduction'. Anthony Uhlmann (173) terms the Unnamable's narrative 'a narrative of the threshold' ('the undecidable threshold' that is neither, as such, within life nor after death).[29] In *Texts for Nothing*, 'this farrago of silence and words' (*CSP*, 125), the other end of 'the bookends to Beckett's great creative period' (ibid., xxii), we are still, nevertheless, 'panting towards the grand apnoea' (134). Moreover, we could suggest stretching such comments on continuity in Beckett's prose backwards and forwards. His first published story *Assumption* (1929) opens with the assertion: 'He could have shouted and could not' (*CSP*, 3). Gontarski (*CSP*, xix) calls this opening shot 'the sort of paradox that would eventually become

Beckett's literary signature', while Lois Gordon (176, n. 15) considers that in *Assumption* 'the unnamed woman is very much like Breton's mysterious woman, Nadja'. In almost his final written words (*Stirrings Still*, 1988: *CSP*, 259–65), Beckett is still pointing up the repetitiousness of 'patience till the one true end to time and grief and self and second self his own'; and 'Time and grief and self so-called. Oh all to end' (ibid., 261; 265). Gontarski cites the body of short prose in particular as evidence of 'Beckett's own view of his art, that it is all part of a continuous process, a series' (*CSP*, xxx; see also Amiran, 16–17; 78–9).

Perhaps a word should be said at this juncture on the somewhat unusual status of Beckett's French and English 'double-texts'. The now dominant critical view would seem to be that, as argued by Steven Connor (86), it is extremely hard 'to assign an order of composition and priority' given that almost every text has 'a double existence, in two languages and in two different places in Beckett's authorial chronology'. The variations (or, one should often say, alterations) in Beckett's French and English versions, in both directions, often undertaken or completed years apart, thus mean that, in effect, 'the two versions of his text both have an equal claim to be "definitive"' (Connor, 112).[30]

The other 'bookends to Beckett's great creative period' might be said to be the novels *Mercier and Camier* and – albeit at some delay – *How It Is* (*Comment c'est*, not written until 1959–60).[31] The former work, written as *Mercier et Camier* in 1946, slotted into a three-month period between *The End* and the other three novellas of the 'quartet', was not published until 1970 (English version 1974). Later regarding this book as 'an apprentice work', Beckett eventually published it only reluctantly (Knowlson, 360). Having been long surpassed by the novelistic trilogy, Beckett's first French novel is now regarded as primarily of linguistic interest. Mooney (20) points out that 'the stylized absurdity of the dialogue looks ahead to *Godot*'. *How It Is*, in which 'Beckett reached a new level of austerity' (Esslin, *Th. Abs.*, 41) was the product of 'struggling to struggle on from where the Unnamable left me off, that is with the next next to nothing' (Beckett: quoted by Knowlson, 461), and takes on a form of pared down minimalism in apparently fragmentary unpunctuated short (not exactly) paragraphs (variously termed 'units', 'strophes' or 'versets'), restrictive in style and, superficially at least, in new content, though not in length (extending to 160 pages). Stretching the Unnamable's sense of narrative consciousness in the void to even greater lengths of seeming nihilism, *How It Is* has been succinctly summarised by Albright (166) as 'a weary, farfetched, inconsistent, arithmetical fantasy of an infinite sequence of mud crawlers'. For Dobrez (43), in *How It Is*, 'the Reduction is able to operate further and further in the sphere of language'. Doherty (1971, 129) notes, among other things, the particular absurdity of the regular system of deposition (by 'an intelligence somewhere ... according as we need them': *How It Is*, 150) of the requisite sacks.

Even a cursory survey of Beckett's prose fiction must make mention of at least some of the later works. The stark three-page *Imagination Dead Imagine* (written first in French as *Imagination morte imaginez*: both versions 1965) describes from varied angles, in the objective manner of a mobile camera, a skull-like rotunda containing two white bodies inscribed in semicircles, 'back to back head to arse' (*CSP*, 184).[32] The visual intent of Beckett's writing is on view too in the extraordinary longer 'dehumanized dystopic tale' (Gontarski: *CSP*, xxiv), *The Lost Ones* (*CSP*, 202–23: written as *Le Dépeupleur*, almost to completion in 1965–66; published in French 1970; English version 1972). Here Beckett moves to a larger microworld, the enclosed space of a flattened cylinder, inhabited by two hundred people engaged in a hopeless 'quest' for a way out, dividing themselves into 'searchers', 'climbers' (into tunnels and niches), 'carriers' (of ladders), 'watchers', the 'sedentary' and the 'vanquished'. The observation that 'in this old abode all is not yet quite for the best' (223) must stand as one of Beckett's greatest understatements. This horrific and entropic mini-universe, with its bizarre rules and etiquette, looks back to Dante's hellish visions and sideways, perhaps, to the more Gothic-styled technological dystopias of science fiction.[33] A. Alvarez has likened it to 'a report by a Civil Service commission into the conditions of Purgatory' (Connor, 105), while Amiran sees it as, not just the working out of 'a model of the Neoplatonic cycle', but 'a machine-world, a Kafkaesque colony designed to extinguish all life' (Amiran, 167; 180).

'Closed space novels' is a term also applied to Beckett's trio of late relatively extended prose works from the early 1980s.[34] Of these short 'novels', the first, *Company* (1980), and the third, *Worstward Ho* (1983), were written originally in English; the second, *Ill Seen Ill Said*, appearing first as *Mal vu mal dit* (1981).[35] *Company* reverts to the inclusion of a number of recognisable auto-intertextual allusions and more or less autobiographical images or flashbacks, notably that of father and son, but mainly, and familiarly, comprises the cogitations of a figure lying on his back in the dark.[36] The result is the product of 'himself', or perhaps 'another', 'devising it all for company' (*Nohow On*, 18–19; 24). Joseph S. O'Leary observes that the text seems to present itself as 'a hermetically sealed exchange between deviser, voice, and silent hearer'.[37] The inventions, assertions and consolations emanating from the consciousness of a male figure (delivered in the first, second and third person) in *Company* ('company' being 'reduced to a set of consoling fetishes': O'Leary, 100), give way in *Ill Seen Ill Said* to those of an old woman in black: 'This old so dying woman. So dead. In the madhouse of the skull and nowhere else' (ibid., 58). In *Worstward Ho*, to the 'shades' of an old man and child plodding in the dim void, is eventually added that of a bowed old woman.

The sparseness and the poetic intensity of language increase over the three works, as do the wordplay and the incantatory repetition, stretching towards the limits of language, reducing largely to the monosyllabic in *Worstward Ho* – 'skeletal fiction in more ways than one', in the words of Andrew Renton.[38] Just as this trio of mini-novels is a representation of the desolation of the human condition (not for nothing is 'Alone' the final one-word statement of *Company*: 46), it depicts the fate too of the creative writing process, the failure of language ('when anything is said, it must inevitably be missaid': Knowlson, 675) amid a compulsive process of 'regressive continuation' (Gontarski, *Nohow On*, xiv–xv). As Beckett's figments are ever more stripped of the attributes of recognisable life, or the outer world, the more totally they confront the human conditions of loneliness, the urge to communicate, and the descent to death.[39] 'There is never any need to enlarge this situation', argues O'Leary (110), 'for [Beckett's] task is to probe into its recesses through constant innovations in the writing strategy'. Such probing of the recesses had been emblematically marked out in *The Lost Ones*.

The key words of *Worstward Ho* are negatively inclined: 'fail', 'worse', 'void', 'dim', 'less'. The whole aim of Beckett's writing by this stage, and at a level of intensity almost seeming to lie beyond the absurd (and which in itself would appear to go back at least as far as *The Unnamable*[40]) is to achieve failure – but a failure, though, of a certain order: 'All of old. Nothing else ever. Ever tried. Ever failed. No matter. Try again. Fail again. Fail better' (*Nohow On*, 89). And the final words of *Worstward Ho* (which begins with 'On': 89) are indeed: 'Said nohow on.' (116).[41]

The drama

> I have been brooding in my bath for the last hour and have come to the conclusion that the success of *Waiting for Godot* means the end of the theatre as we know it. (Robert Morley, 1955)

Early in 1947, Beckett – by now, at least in achievement if not yet in recognition, an established writer of prose fiction – began, almost suddenly it would seem, to write for the theatre.[42] 'I didn't choose to write a play', he said in a rare interview, 'it just happened like that' (Shenker, 3). His first and longest play, *Eleutheria*, was never published within his lifetime, nor was it translated by Beckett into English.[43] There were prospects of a performance in 1951, whereupon Beckett withdrew it. Had it been put on early in 1948, as might have happened, *Eleutheria* could well have stood as one of the first significant productions in the new post war era of French drama that came to be dubbed 'Theatre of the Absurd'.[44] However, with hindsight one can see why Beckett took the view he did, as the play now comes over as something like an example of over-long and lesser Ionesco with a touch of N.F. Simpson – interventions coming in Act 3 from a 'Spectator', berating the author (one 'Samuel Béké': *Eleutheria*, 136) and a 'Voice from the Box'. Nevertheless, it is in the third act that we get closer to recognisably Beckettian concerns, when the protagonist, one Victor Krap (a close enough relative of Belacqua and Murphy), is coerced into expressing 'an avalanche of absurdities' amounting to a 'negative anthropology' (ibid., 146–7) covering his aspirations towards 'leaving himself' or freedom (hence the title): 'By being the least possible. By not moving, not thinking, not dreaming, not speaking, not listening, not perceiving, not knowing, not wishing, not being able, and so on' (149).

Godot

> *tangent alpha*
> the number of thieves beside us isn't of significance as we die it's the number
> as we live *Pontius Pilate II* (Tymoteusz Karpowicz, *Solving Spaces*)

The jump made by Beckett from *Eleutheria* to *Waiting for Godot* (written as *En attendant Godot* a mere eighteen months or so on, 'between October 1948 and January 1949': Knowlson, 378) would be difficult to over-stress. From the domestic setting of the first play, we are plunged into an almost primeval wasteland; the social misfits of the first become what we can now see as Beckett's near-regulation perpetual vagrants of the second. Paul Davies (not to be confused with the physicist and natural philosopher of that name: see Bibliography) provides this comprehensive categorisation:

> In the prose and plays alike, the same description fits them all: the homeless, wandering, ageing male, with hat; boots; long coat; infected scalp; speech impediments; general sensory confusion; a special fondness for small objects; sensitivity to animals and plants and dawn/dusk twilights; a tendency to aporia (purposiveness without purpose); hatred of sexuality, conception and birth; isolation from relationships with human beings; varying degrees of cripplement; and a rarely failing sense of humour in the midst of these deprivations.[45]

At the time of his involvement, in 1953, with the first production of what has since come to be regarded as perhaps *the* twentieth-century dramatic masterpiece, according to his first director Roger Blin, 'Beckett knew nothing about the theatre' (Fletcher, 155). Later, in the view of Peter Hall, among others, whereas, unlike Harold Pinter, he was 'not finally a theatre worker, great director though he can be' (ibid., 144). Beckett devoted a considerable part of the ensuing thirty-odd years to the theatre – writing, consulting on, and directing his own plays. In parity with the development of his prose fiction, by and large, Beckett's dramatic works too submitted to a process of greater and greater reduction; as abstracted by Gontarski: 'The minimalism and formal simplicity of Beckett's later work makes even *Godot* and *Endgame* seem almost baroque' (quoted by Fletcher, 123). For present purposes, theatrical comment will mainly be confined to these two plays.

Beckett 'has written a play in which nothing happens, twice'. This memorable encapsulation of *Waiting for Godot*, recorded in the *Irish Times* by Vivian Mercier in 1956, has indeed been almost universally reproduced ever since; and it is not, of course, strictly the case, as Mercier himself fully realised, given his prior admission that 'the second act is a subtly different reprise of the first'.[46] Preferable perhaps, as a curt summation, is John Fletcher's appreciation of 'a witty and moving dramatic symbol: that of two tramp-clowns waiting on a country road for someone who fails to keep the appointment' (Fletcher, 22).

The main pair of characters, Vladimir and Estragon, from what we glean of their lifestyle and from the way they are dressed, are (variously or similarly) seen as vagabonds, wayfarers, men of the road, hoboes, drop-outs – Beckett's 'wanderers', seeking to 'go on' (as they put it), as they decline into 'moribunds' (Davies: Pilling, 1994, 62).[47] However, as has frequently been pointed out, 'in fact neither "tramp" nor "clown" is ever mentioned in the text' (Wolfgang Iser, cited in Boxall, 103; see also 174, n. 20). The 'clownishness' of certain of the pair's antics, though, along with snatches of their music-hall-type repartee, is suggestive of 'the carnival effect, which permeates the whole atmosphere and construction of the play' (at least, in the view of Iser: ibid., 107). This effect can only appear enhanced, should we entertain actor Jack McGowran's notion of a role-reversal between Vladimir and Estragon (see Fletcher, 182–3), just as, in the view of Amiran (26), 'The two acts can be read in reverse'. Dobrez (92) suggests that Beckett's tramps, 'alienated from the everyday world of the sane, exist in a no man's land which is precisely this perilous zone of contact with reality' – if indeed there *is* an 'everyday world of the sane' anywhere within Beckett's universe. Kiberd (1996, 538) considers that 'the world in which they live has no overall structure, no formal narrative'. As a variant of no-man's land, some commentators, such as Uhlmann, relate Beckett's work largely to war-torn France. Amiran (22–3) argues that *Waiting for Godot* 'is fundamentally about historical process' and 'the gap between the postwar world and the idealistic society that existed somewhere before the wars'. Kiberd (1996, 537–45) relates Beckett's characters rather to the tramps, masters and servants (or slaves) of the Anglo-Irish tradition.

This last approach may be seen to apply particularly to the other linked pair, Pozzo and Lucky, initially added to the play, according to Beckett, 'to break the monotony' (Fletcher, 82). 'Why did Pozzo leave home, he had a castle and retainers. Insidious question, to remind me I'm in the dock', mused Beckett a little later (*Texts for Nothing*, 5: *CSP*, 118). Pozzo postures as 'the [absentee?] landlord who wears the clothing of English gentry' (Kiberd, 1996, 542).[48] Lucky, in some sense a former mentor to Pozzo ('He even used to think very prettily once, I could listen to him for hours': *CDW*, 39), takes on something of the aspect of a degenerate and enslaved academic, reduced to inglorious porterage.[49] Erich Segal (443–4) writes that 'Lucky is a twentieth-century version of the learned professor *gloriosus*, whose nonsensical pronouncements make a mockery of pompous philosophers'; apparently, Beckett 'had originally envisaged [Lucky] wearing the uniform of a station porter', but allowed Blin to dress him in footman's livery (Fletcher, 149; 154). 'For here is a servant who will not just do your living, but also your dancing and your philosophy for you, and at the same time connive in his own oppression' (Kiberd, 541).

Thus, as has been affirmed by Seamus Deane (189): 'Beckett's novels and plays contain intellectually brilliant practitioners of the Cartesian method of radical doubt who are also stunned depressives, emotionally crippled by the vision of the meaninglessness of a life which must be lived and relived.' This perception can extend to Vladimir and Estragon (the latter claiming to have once been a poet: 'Isn't that obvious': *CDW*, 14): when someone remonstrated with Beckett that his tramps 'at times talked as if they possessed doctorates, he shot back "How do you know they hadn't?"' (Kiberd, 1996, 538; Segal, 448). The other great unknown, of course, is the identity of 'Godot' – played on by Pozzo in the text ('this ... Godet ... Godot ... Godin': *CDW*, 29). Leaving aside facile or coincidental connections with one-time French boxers or cyclists, and, for that matter, 'an authentic "Monsieur Georges Godot"' who emerged in 1969, at Nobel time, to apologise to Beckett for keeping him waiting (Knowlson, 571–2), the author was (famously) never able to shed any light on this. Esslin (*Th. Abs.*, 49–50, citing Eric Bentley, from 1956) recalled Balzac's 'Godeau', of *Le Faiseur* (or *Mercadet*, produced 1851), 'a character much talked about but never seen'. 'Godot' has not infrequently been seen as a diminutive of the deity; Kearney (1988, 80) points to the Gaelic *go deo*, meaning 'forever'; for Fletcher (47), the name represents a 'nullity': 'Godot is only death'; while, for Segal (451), 'Godot can be equated with sexual potency'.

Hugh Kenner (in the 1960s) pointed out that *Waiting for Godot* 'draws on Greek theatre with its limited number of actors, its crises always off stage, and its absent divinity'; the ingredients of Noh theatre, *commedia dell'arte*, twentieth-century experimental theatre, vaudeville, circus and burlesque were also noted by Kenner (in Boxall, 70). Segal, in his culminating chapter 'Beckett: The Death of Comedy' (Segal, 438–52), revives the classical roots, dubbing the play a Terentian '*fabula stataria* – a nonaction play – but here reduced to total immobility', in which 'Aristophanic devices and themes are all inverted, subverted, and perverted' (Segal, 440; 444). Yet Segal discerns in *Godot* echoes or similarities with 'the play that has been deemed its apogee' – Aristophanes' *The Birds* – 'too remarkable to be mere coincidence', given Beckett's status as 'a chimerical post-modern classicist and a supreme ironist' (450).

'Nothing to be done' is the opening shot of Estragon (trying to take off his boot), and of the play (*CDW*, 11); and indeed 'the whole play proceeds to show how appropriate this statement is to man's bewildered position in the universe', affirm Knowlson and Pilling (*Frescoes*, 268–9). The waiting for Godot will continue and 'Vladimir and Estragon, and Pozzo and Lucky and the boy, will go on meeting in increasingly reduced physical and mental circumstances but will never *not* meet again', declares Michael Worton (in Pilling, 1994, 70). The 'result', therefore, is that we (or, at least, the characters) are in 'a world of eternal recurrence: the protagonists wait for the future, but keep returning to the past' (Amiran, 27). 'Death, as a final ending, as a final silence, is absent from the plays' (Worton) – though 'silence' in itself, Beckett once told John Fletcher, 'is pouring into the play like water into a sinking ship' (Fletcher, 49). This endlessness, at 'the far extreme from Aristophanic triumph', Segal concludes (452), 'makes Beckett's work a deliberate *coup de grâce* to the comic genre'.

Endgame

> Nothing is funnier than unhappiness, I grant you that (Nell: *Endgame*)

The setting of *Endgame* (written as *Fin de partie*, 1955–56; English version 1958) is a 'bare interior' with 'grey light', a domicile seemingly surrounded by a bare, it is often assumed devastated, landscape: 'endgame' is often taken here to signify 'end of the world'. However, it may at least equally be taken to be 'stalemate' (or in an 'eternal check': Adorno, 270), in which case a familiar Beckettian stasis would pertain and remain.[50] *Endgame* was eventually confined to one act.[51] This play, as Dobrez (29) puts it, 'is contracted to the room-skull milieu of the novels'. From *Endgame* onwards, and by various means, 'characters are reduced to smaller and smaller spaces' (see Connor, 141). Again we have two pairs of characters: Nagg and Nell (the parents of Hamm) are confined to ashbins ('*Endgame* is true gerontology. . . . Beckett's trashcans are emblems of the culture rebuilt after Auschwitz': Adorno, 266–7); Hamm and Clov are another symbiotic master–slave coupling ('Hamm, the king piece in this stalemate and his mindless pawn, Clov': Kearney, 1988, 81; and Hamm, like Pozzo and Mr Knott, appears to have been some kind of a landlord). Only Clov enjoys (if that is the word) any real mobility. Metatheatrical (or self-referential dramatic) comments by Hamm 'express the awareness that he is no more than a chess piece in the endgame of language' (ibid.). Kott (127) regards *Endgame* as a *King Lear* repeated 'in its skeleton form'.

As usual, the characters' main preoccupations are with the past – there being, it would seem, no future. 'Ah yesterday!', exclaims Nell twice, elegiacally (*CDW*, 99; 101) – yet, 'Yesterday! What does that mean? Yesterday!', Hamm remonstrates to Clov (*CDW*, 113). 'Do you believe in the life to come?', asks Clov; 'Mine was always that', replies Hamm ('Got him that time!', he adds: *CDW*, 116). 'Ah the old questions, the old answers, there's nothing like them!' enthuses Hamm (*CDW*, 110), referring back to Clov's dreary 'All life long the same questions, the same answers' (*CDW*, 94). The same stories (from Nagg and Hamm), the same questions, the same answers: presumably these always lead to the same range of interpretations, as parroted anecdotage drives the protagonists into, and condemns them in, their mental and physical dotage.[52] The attachments to one another of Beckett's characters resemble, as Kiberd (549) graphically puts it, 'a sado-masochistic conspiracy of the wounded'.

Stories (jokes, anecdotes, songs) narrated or recalled within Beckett's texts perform a varied and prominent role (as Morrison's study *Canters and Chronicles* illustrates). These may range from the symbolic to the inane. One such utterance of Hamm's, beginning 'I once knew a madman who thought the end of the world had come' and who, from his asylum window, could see only ashes (*CDW*, 113), functions arguably as a *mise en abyme* in *Endgame*. Nagg's 'story of the tailor' (*CDW*, 102–3), taken by Kenner as 'a vaudeville standby' (in Boxall, 82) and regarded by Adorno (256) as 'the allegedly Jewish metaphysical joke about the trousers and the world', clearly derives, in part at least, from Beckett's own hapless experience with a bespoke suit during his German sojourn in 1937 (see Knowlson, 254–6). 'Shaggy dogs' make parodic appearances, in the form of Hamm's three-legged toy dog of indeterminate colour, and Vladimir's circular (or shaggy) dog song ('A dog came in the kitchen ...': *CDW*, 53–4) – said to be an 'old German students' song' (Esslin, *Th. Abs.*, 76) – which opens Act Two of *Godot*.[53]

Just before Hamm enters upon his 'last soliloquy', for which he had been impatiently 'warming up' (*CDW*, 130), Clov enters, 'dressed for the road' (132); but, '*his eyes fixed on* HAMM, *till the end*' (133) – does he, will he, ever leave? Will the blind Hamm even know? Connor (125) remarks that 'the closure of possibility [and for that matter, one assumes, the possibility of closure] in Hamm's story is contradicted by Clov's continuing presence on stage'; or has 'this little scene ... been played out between them before'? 'Old stancher! [*Pause.*] You ... remain' are Hamm's final words, covering his face with his handkerchief-cum-comfort blanket (or *vieux linge* in the French original: *Théâtre I*, 145; 216). According to Connor, Hamm's affectionate address to his blood-stained rag extends to the continued presence of the audience, observing the '*Brief tableau*' (*CDW*, 134); in another sense again, perhaps Clov too may be included under 'stancher'.

In Esslin's view, *Endgame* resembles the 'monodrama', taking place '*inside a human being*' and showing 'the constituent parts of his ego ... in conflict with each other'.[54] Boxall (40) paraphrases Adorno, suggesting that '*Endgame* is a response to the decline of culture in a period of rampantly triumphant capitalism'. Fletcher (20) points out that *Waiting for Godot* 'is not subtitled "a tragicomedy" [a 'mixed genre'] for nothing',[55] while Segal (451) observes that, in that play, 'Beckett deliberately replaces Aristophanic *kómos* with a tragicomic stasis'. Roger Blin duly recorded that '*Endgame* for me is a tragic play, but Beckett denies this' (quoted: Fletcher, 157). Modernism had raised 'the issue of *metatheatre* in an acute form', defined by Lionel Abel 'as resting upon two basic postulates: (1) that the world is a stage , and (2) that life is a dream'; under modernism, men and women became again, Shakespeare-style, 'mere actors in an absurd play' (Fletcher, 19–20).[56] Segal writes of a regression in *Endgame* 'from Aristophanic *parrhësia*, the licence to say anything, to *aphasia*, the inability to say anything', and of *Godot* as '*anti*-comedy' (Segal, 438; 450). 'Theatre of the Absurd', of course now at least, seen as deriving from Esslin, is regarded by Fletcher (18), when applied to Beckett's plays, as a 'convenient, if somewhat restrictive label'; incidentally, it is a tag which Beckett himself disliked (see Fletcher, 93–4). We shall return to such labelling shortly. Yet another term suggested by Segal (452) is 'Beckett's theatre of inadequacy'.

Further shades of the absurd

The Kharmsian trace

While Kharms's literary career was first suppressed, and then terminated in appalling circumstances, he and (the early) Beckett were close contemporaries. Beckett was born just four months after Kharms; and when Kharms died of malnutrition (in a psychiatric prison hospital, early in 1942), Beckett was active in the French resistance, and beginning to think of engaging, too, with *Watt*. It seems quite safe to assume that neither writer was ever aware of the other.[57] Brief comparisons, on a micro and a macro level, have been made in the past (and have already been briefly alluded to in the present book). A book-length essay on the two was published in Russia in 2002: D.V. Tokarev's *Kurs na khudshee* (or 'a course for the worst': in fact, the Russian translated title of *Worstward Ho*), subtitled 'the absurd as a category of text in Kharms and Beckett'. Both Kharms and Vvedensky, whom we have earlier considered in discussion of Theatre of the Absurd (although the category 'absurd' was not exactly widely used in Russian aesthetic debate within their lifetimes), were both subsequently seen as predecessors of that West European phenomenon by, indeed, their own friend and collaborator, the philosopher Iakov Druskin (who survived them by several decades). Druskin himself makes play with a progression through the terms 'nonsense' (*bessmyslennost'*), 'alogicality' (*alogichnost'*) and 'absurd' (*absurd*): see Tokarev, 2002, 9; and passim).

On the micro level, similarities of exploitation, attitude or obsession can be seen across a range of thematic detail. Interests in falling, rubbish, begging and 'ageist' proclivity (hostile concerns with children and old women) are to be found in works by both – as well as having been observed in the work of other supposedly absurdist authors. Miniature beggar stories are to be found in the prose poem form, Adrian Wanner has pointed out, from the founders of that sub-genre (Baudelaire in French literature, and Turgenev in Russian) through to Kharms.[58] Falling features prominently in, for example, Beckett's 'From an Abandoned Work' (see *CSP*, 162). The Kharmsian trait of it being human destiny to end up as rubbish occurs frequently too in Beckett: Adorno (274) comments on 'dust' and 'filth' in this regard in *Endgame*; Murphy (in the form of his ashes) is famously swept up as rubbish; and Beckett eventually wrote his briefest (and actorless) play *Breath* (1969) – featuring faint cries of 'expiration' and 'stage littered with miscellaneous rubbish' (*CDW*, 371).[59] Tokarev (2002, 108) notes a tendency for text itself to become filth (*griaz'*). Beckett's interest in the techniques of begging can be seen in *Rough for Theatre I*, and in the novella *The End*. For that matter, *The Expelled* includes the Kharmsian motifs of falling, old ladies breaking bones, and the desirability of lynching children, all within a page (*CSP*, 51–2).

Tokarev, as might be expected, makes a wide range of comparisons involving the utilisation of violence, disturbed forms of sexuality; attitudes to language – the word and punctuation; and the treatment of such dualities as beginning–end, birth–life, death–life, and text–world. Time, the search for death and a return to the womb are seen as vital common preoccupations. Interesting, in view of the attention paid above to *The Hunter Gracchus*, is the use noted of marsh and water imagery. Kharms and Beckett are both seen to be responding, in part at least, to avant-garde literary movements (Futurism and Surrealism respectively), as well as to classical art and modernist painting, music and mathematics.[60]

On what might be regarded as a more macro level, Tokarev, following Druskin and other adherents of the Kharms circle, as well as recent Kharms criticism, pursues the concept of negative theology through Kharmsian emanations, 'at three levels: the ontological, the existential and the narratological' (Tokarev, 2002, 295). While Beckett eschewed the active mystical streak to be found in Kharms, negative theology has been brought into discussion of his work and thought by a number of commentators. Kearney (1985, 286) claims that 'Beckett's explorations of negative theology are nowhere more radical and penetrating than in *Watt*'. Günther Anders considers that Beckett uses the intensifying experience of negativity (in *Waiting for Godot*), while not sharing it from conviction – he 'even derides it as absurd'.[61] Of the same play, Dobrez (28) refers to 'the negative existence of a vigil'; he goes on to stress the 'active' quality of nothingness and the *via negativa* bases of Mr Knott and the Unnamable (109; 114–15), which he finds nevertheless to be rather 'tenuous and parodic' (125). Adorno (273) talks of negative ontology as 'the negation of ontology' in *Endgame*. Tokarev (2002, 312) also sees, on the level of intertextuality, texts by both Kharms and Beckett as 'black holes', filled with hidden allusions, in an often unidentifiable deformed and reworked fashion, to the works of others. Both Kharms and Beckett, as already indicated, have a propensity for re-presenting previous works (or something like them) in a skeletal form.

Tokarev (287–8; 310) compares the protagonist of 'Blue Notebook No. 10' (or 'The Red-Haired Man'), and his deprivations – discussed at some length in Chapter 6 on Kharms – with qualities pertaining to (or absent from) both Mr Knott and the Unnamable. He finds that Kharms in the later 1930s approached closer to (the then and subsequent) Beckett. If Beckett really aspired to an impoverished form of painting, 'authentically fruitless, incapable of any image whatsoever' (*Disjecta*, 141),[62] in effect, as Calder (80) has it, 'an art that is purely imaginary, . . . in other words, no art at all', then he appears almost analogous to the narrator's figure of the miracle worker of *The Old Woman*, who will go through life without working any miracles. This may be analogous to the artistic performance of Murphy, 'from whom works should not be expected. For Murphy's art is expressed not *in* works but in not working' (T. Miller, 186). According to Druskin, Kharms went through a creative crisis in about 1933, when he realised that he himself was no miracle worker – following which he worked his own kind of miracles, triumphing in defeat, with literature becoming an 'apotheosis of non-existence' (see Lipovetskii, 2003, 129; 132).[63] Kharms by now (and by a very different path) somewhat downplayed the importance of art, favouring rather life – he wanted to make his own life into a work of art (on 'absurd life-creation' by Kharms see Ann Komaromi); however, the making of life into art, as Druskin at any rate saw it, was not so much an aesthetic programme, as an existential one (Tokarev, 28). One would not suspect that Beckett would ever have given quite such prominence to his lifestyle: he was more inclined to 'slink around in guilt' (Calder, 84). Nevertheless, in the grim way in which Kharms's life was in the event turned into 'art', not least through the device he adopted under arrest of feigning madness, there is, it might be said, an almost uncanny sense of a Beckett character.

Absurdist Watt?

Watt, as has been pointed out above, has frequently been seen as a turning point in Beckett's fiction. It may also be seen as in many ways the epitome of Beckettian absurdism. Much of the surface text provides, one could well argue, ample and obvious material for such an estimation. The pedantry, the repetitions, the permutations and the tangential outpourings (in which 'Cartesian logic is carried to extremes': Calder, 37) are sufficiently absurdist in themselves, it might well be thought, in the sense of illustrating many of the aspects of absurdist discourse that have featured prominently in this book. The name-play and nonsense in Watt have been widely noted (what, Watt; not, Knott; whatnot, 'what'-ness, etc. – and perhaps 'gnot', if the novel is to be seen as 'a gnosiological quest'[64]). Much of the text is as hilarious to many readers as parts of it may seem excessive, maddening or tedious. Highlights may be said to range from minor descriptive passages dealing with Watt's smile (Watt, 23), with repetition here used as differentiation (Connor, 27: see Connor, 26–43 on repetition in Watt), the newsagent's 'aborted genuflexions' (Watt, 24), and Watt's own preposterous gait (or 'funambulistic stagger': 28–9), to the larger scale 'set-piece' sections treating the complications involved in the feeding of Mr Knott's leftovers to a famished dog (and the consequent saga of the Lynch family: part II), or the farrago of the protracted meeting of the College Grants Committee (part III).

The philosophical underpinning of Watt may well be as absurdist, or as apparently nihilistic, as much else in Beckett's oeuvre – regardless of whether 'the absurdity of the cosmos' arises from 'an unpredictable, seemingly indifferent, but ultimately malevolent cosmos' itself, or from Watt's 'solipsism' (Cohn, 1961, 155; 160). John Pilling (1994, 36) remarks that Watt 'could only have emerged from a world gone mad'. Mooney (17) suggests it to be 'a kind of philosophical farce on rationalism'. According to Doherty (1991, 188), in any event, 'what parody Irish realism there is melts into an existential nightmare which seems only accidentally set in Ireland'. For present purposes, it may only be necessary to concentrate briefly on the novel's structure – the narrative provenance and presentation.

'Two, one, four, three', we are told, 'was the order in which Watt told his story' (Watt, 214). The process through which this purportedly reaches the reader, however, is bizarre in the extreme. The novel consists of four parts, plus 'Addenda' (247–55), which is to be considered an integral part of the text and does include some minor gems or pointers (such as the oft-quoted, or 'now notorious', final words, or 'impossible instruction to the hapless reader': 'no symbols where none intended'[65]) – while 'Only fatigue and disgust prevented its incorporation' (247). The four parts are essentially chronological, except that the narrator's explanation

(in III) of his obtaining the essential bulk of this 'precious and illuminating material' (ibid.) reveals that his acquaintance with Watt is subsequent
to the action of the 'plot' (or the conclusion of IV), thus suggesting something closer to a 'I, II, IV, III' chronology (or, indeed, as Cohn, *Beckett
Canon*, 113, has it more exactly: 'I, II, IIIB, IV, IIIA'). The textual 'I, II,
III, IV' presentation, nevertheless, has its logical, or aesthetic, balance – in
terms both of Watt's 'biography' and of 'worldly' symmetry. Watt walks
to the station and takes a train to within distance of Mr Knott's house, in
which he establishes himself – in so far as that can be said (I). He eventually does the reverse (IV). The two central parts are largely taken up with
existence at Mr Knott's. Also included (in III), however, is the extraordinary explanation of the narrative's provenance. Watt leaves the outer
world (in I), later returning to it (in IV), to penetrate – in so far as that can
be said – the world of Mr Knott; and to go ever deeper into his own internal world (II and III). In any event, '"the order in which Watt told his
story" (214) – and the disorder by way of which *Watt* unfolds – cannot',
according at least to Pilling (1997, 184), 'by even the most ingenious of
adjustments, be made to coincide'. Or, in the terms employed by Russian
Formalism, the 'fable' (*fabula*) is hard, if not impossible, to reconstruct
from the 'plot' (*siuzhet*) as textually presented.[66]

It is presumably the interaction of these worlds that necessitates Watt's
eventual entry, beyond the frame of the main 'story', to a fourth world (of
which we hear in III) – that of the asylum (with 'mansions' and 'pavil-
ions'), in which he forms a close (verbal and, to an extent at least,
physical) relationship with the novel's purported narrator, 'Sam'.[67] Watt's
demented descent to (and in) the asylum is presumably caused by his
joustings with the system of Mr Knott's establishment, termed by Cohn
(1961, 162) 'a bastion primarily against rational assault'; or it may be
occasioned by the necessity of leaving it. Sam appears as such (in III),
when the narrative switches consistently (for a while) into the first person,
and the peculiarities of its descent fully emerge. This development can
both clarify and mystify. While we are treated to the manner of Watt's
imparting of his story to Sam, the framing exterior portions of the scarcely
much less absurdly drawn outer world (in and around the railway station:
I and IV) would seem to lie beyond the perspectives, or the earshot, of
either Watt or Sam.

Hitherto, for that matter (as indeed subsequently), the narrative presentation has not been exactly quirk-free. Arsene's valedictory 'short
statement' (twenty-five pages of monologue)[68] – which is indeed duly seen
by Pilling (1997, 232) as Beckett's 'decisive move towards monologue' –
is delivered verbatim, despite Watt's failure to pay attention to it at the
time (as reported: *Watt*, 77) – although, according to the Addenda (248),
'Arsene's declaration gradually came back to Watt'. Such semiotic devices
as gaps in the text, the occasional '?', and 'Hiatus in MS.' or 'MS. illegi-

ble' may or may not fit in with the 'Addenda' policy. If the words that come down to us may not have been the exact words (employed by whomsoever), we are assured, 'they were not far out' (197). This (the last qualification notwithstanding), given the circumstances described (in III), may be considered to be little (if at all) short of miraculous – or, alternatively, totally absurd.

Patricia Waugh has noted (in her study of metafiction, a category which can frequently border on the absurd), that in *Watt* 'the attempt to describe thoroughly a simple act of physical *progression*, of taking a step forward, leads to extreme (and finally absurd) narrative *regression*' (Waugh, 152, n. 7; emphasis hers). Regression, and reversal, in perambulation is matched by the same motion in discourse. The choreography of the joint ambulatory aspect of the intercourse between Watt and Sam (hands mutually on shoulders, paces forward and back, 'turning as one man, ... 'up and down, up and down, we paced between the fences'), Watt backwards and Sam forwards, is precisely elaborated (*Watt*, 150; 161).[69] Matching this bizarre motion, is the regressive mode of Watt's diction. At the better stage, delivered 'as one speaking to dictation, or reciting, parrot-like', much 'was carried away, and lost for ever' (154). Then, 'As Watt walked, so now he talked, back to front' (162; anticipated much earlier by the explanatory phrase: 'Ruse a by', 126; and, introduced now with: 'Not it is, yes', 157). Watt's inversion of words stretches then to the letters in a word, to 'the sentences in the period' and any and all combinations of these practices simultaneously (for these contortions, see *Watt*, 162–7). Jacqueline Hoefer has argued that 'these semi-systematic inversions, which on the surface [when restored] are mostly nonsense, offer the final comment on the absurdity of Watt's combinations' (Esslin, *SB*, 73). Connor, however, discerns a certain ghostly 'meaning from meaninglessness' here (in both the original and the French texts: Connor, 36).

The full extravagance of this sequence of narrative provenance and presentation may be observed, for instance, in merely considering the already mentioned recital (itself an apparently gratuitous digression, or an extended interpolated anecdote) of the College meeting in the aftermath of Ernest Louit's 'research expedition, in the County Clare', involving the claculations of Mr Nackybal (169–96). Told in Mr Knott's garden by Arthur to Mr Graves, this (perhaps mercifully incomplete) narrative is overheard by Watt, and repeated backwards (plus the other reversals of articulation) while in continuous motion to Sam – from whom, one must assume, despite the seemingly insurmountable difficulties, it is conveyed to the page, in a form of words purportedly 'not far out'. The implication of this, as Connor has suggested, is that, for Wattian 'authenticity', the whole book should be read backwards – except that, as he points out (Connor, 36–7), we cannot know precisely what principle or combinations of inversion Watt would have been using at any one time. The only way to what might be considered a 'true' Ur-*Watt*, therefore, would lie through an indefinite series of textual combinations: a prospect at which even Beckett must have balked.

In case, however, anyone should think that Watt was finished by the end, or even the middle, of the novel that bears his name, he makes a surprise reappearance in the final chapter of *Mercier and Camier*, the next (and first French) novel written by Beckett – 'albeit a very different Watt' (Pilling, 1997, 203). Watt appears here 'emerging from nowhere' (Cohn, *Beckett Canon*, 138). He does, though, loom up as 'a figure of towering stature, squalidly clad' (*M and C*, 110; 'un homme de haute stature, fort sordidement mis': *M et C*, 192), somewhat reminiscent of the mysterious 'figure' or 'hallucination' that intrigues him as he arrives at the station at the end of the previous novel (see *Watt*, 224–7). Cohn (*Beckett Canon*, 139) notes certain points of contact between these two novels, not least the fact that 'Quin' (*M and C*, 118; 119), originally an ur-Knott, is incomprehensible without knowledge of the Ur-*Watt*.[70] Watt deems himself 'unrecognizable' (*M and C*, 111; 'méconnaissable, en effet', *M et C*, 193) – unsurprisingly, perhaps, in the sense that *Watt* was unpublished when Beckett wrote *Mercier and Camier*. He is also unrecognisable from his former self in his behaviour, creating disturbances in a bar by yelling 'Bugger life!' and (this proving inadequate) 'Fuck life!' and laying about him with Camier's stick (*M and C*, 114, 118; 'La vie au poteau!', 'La vie aux chiottes!', *M et C*, 200, 204).[71] According to Pilling (1997, 209), 'Beckett's principal purpose in this chapter is to bring back Watt from the dead', through 'the irony of a ghost' to deliver his future narrative direction:

> One shall be born, said Watt, one is born of us, who having nothing will wish for nothing, except to be left the nothing he hath. (*M and C*, 114)

> Il naîtra, il est né de nous, dit Watt, celui qui n'ayant rien ne voudra rien, sinon qu'on lui laisse le rien qu'il a. (*M et C*, 198)

After this novel, Watt recedes once again to take his place in a ghostly series of voices or personae to be occasionally and metafictionally called to mind by subsequent narratorial figures. Moran (in *Molloy*) refers to the 'rabble in my head, what a gallery of moribunds. Murphy, Watt, Yerk, Mercier and all the others' (Trilogy, 138); and subsequently to 'Youdi, Gaber, Molloy, his mother, Yerk, Murphy, Watt, Camier and the rest' (Trilogy, 168). The Unnamable too, apparently in some hellish after-existence, is accompanied by a range of figural shades ('I believe they are all here, at least from Murphy on': Trilogy, 295) – his 'delegates' (299), Watt included (328).[72]

Beckett's absurd

If the absurd in Beckett appears to peak, at least in certain textual senses, in *Watt*, neither the phenomenon itself, nor the occasional overt recognition of it, is going to go away. Watt was himself aware, with regard to possible notions of periodicity entailed in the service of Mr Knott, of 'the absurdity of these constructions':

> But he had hardly felt the absurdity of those things, on the one hand, and the necessity of those others, on the other (for it is rare that the feeling of absurdity is not followed by the feeling of necessity), when he felt the absurdity of those things of which he had just felt the necessity (for it is rare that the feeling of necessity is not followed by the feeling of absurdity). (*Watt*, 131)

The Unnamable is askance at any idea that he should be silent: 'That the impossible be asked of me, good, what else could be asked of me? But the absurd!' (Trilogy, 340). On the intentions of the voices invading his consciousness (Mahood, supplanted by Worm), the Unnamable ponders whether the point may be: 'Or by the absurd prove to me that I am, the absurd of not being able' (349). Absurdity hereabouts is linked with questions of necessity, identity, (in)capability, 'the mad need to speak', and various manifestations of existence as and in 'nothing' (see ibid.).

'Matrix of surds' is a phrase occurring in the chapter of *Murphy* dealing with the attempt made on 'the expression "Murphy's mind"' (*Murphy*, 66; 63); Dobrez (15), following Hugh Kenner, notes Beckett's appeal 'to the image of the Pythagorean "surd"' – 'the "irrational" number or surd ... also termed an *alagon*, that is an "unnamable" by the Greeks'. 'We do not belong here', writes Kenner, 'runs a strain of western thought which became especially articulate in France after the war; we belong nowhere; we are all surds, ab-surd' (in Boxhall, 81). Beckett's work, according to Dobrez, 'is the voice of Cartesian doubt translated into the modern predicament of existential *angst*' – in particular 'something very like Heideggerian *angst* is a natural condition' (Dobrez, 106; 99). Kearney (1985, 289) compares 'the experience of nothingness' in negative theology (giving rise to the 'mystical'), with that of the existentialists ('the anguish or absurdity of Being'), seeing in *Watt* a 'timeless, spaceless void beyond language' which could be 'the portal to a mystical experience ... or simply the nothingness of the absurd' (ibid., 291) – pointing to Beckett's early reading of Schopenhauer and Nietzsche (ibid., 355, n. 81).

Wittgenstein is mentioned, especially in connection with the ladder references in *Watt* (see Hoefer, in Esslin, *SB* 74–6), but this question is approached rather differently by Marjorie Perloff: in particular, she reports that Beckett 'had nothing to say about Wittgenstein but writes the most Wittgensteinian of parables'.[73] Of existentialist philosophers,

Heidegger is accorded particular consideration (see Dobrez, 85–128). Regressing chronologically (Watt-fashion or otherwise), for P.J. Murphy, '*Watt* is a Kantian novel' (in preference to Hoefer's reading of it as a skit on logical positivism).[74] Descartes is regularly identified as a Beckettian prop: Kearney (1985, 271), for instance, sees in *Murphy* a development of 'the Cartesian parody adumbrated in *Whoroscope*'. The Belgian 'Occasionalist', Arnold Guelincx is another frequently noted figure (see Knowlson, 218–19, as well as earlier references). Back-pedalling further, and Amiran (18 and passim) considers that 'Neoplatonic idealism is fundamental to Beckett's project'. Back again, as ever to antiquity: for Calder, 'Beckett is the last of the great stoics' (Calder, 1; 19); and then we come to Beckett's keen interest in the pre-Socratics. Here we hit a rich seam, in the figure of Democritus (the Abderite), whose mantra 'nothing is more real than nothing' proved a fundamental rallying cry for Beckett – iterated in italics in Malone's Saposcat narrative (Trilogy, 193) and alluded to by Murphy (*Murphy*, 138). Heraclitus, Parmenides and the paradoxes of Zeno of Elea were also of some note, but of still greater import may be the figure of the Sicilian rhetorician and sophist Gorgias of Leontini (late fifth century BC). His relevance for Beckett was 'cunningly' claimed by (his close friend from Trinity days) A.J. ('Con') Leventhal.[75]

Gorgias has been noted, in the introductory chapter to this book, as possibly the first known nihilist, whose treatise *On Not-Being, or On the Nature of Things* is said to be an elaborate reversal of the metaphysical argument of Parmenides and, simply stated, it shows: (1) that nothing exists; (2) that if anything exists, it cannot be known; and (3) if anything can be known, it cannot be communicated.[76] Such an argument, regardless of whether it was seriously or parodically intended by Gorgias, contains the first blueprint of absurdist (or inevitably inadequate linguistic) discourse. Beckett's career can therefore be seen as a continual wrestling with the third proposition of Gorgias – turning his 'literary invention' (Leventhal, 48) from poetry and fiction to the theatre, and eventually to mime. The 'French trilogy' and Watt's breakdown in language are cited as prime examples of what Leventhal saw as recreating a situation of archetypal paradox (and, in effect, turning the deconstruction argument on its head): 'Never, in fiction, have so many words been used as by Beckett to underline the inefficiency of language and never, by his very language, has anyone disproved the point so brilliantly' (Leventhal, 46). Hence the phenomenon of Beckett's 'so-called disintegration of semantic expression' (Amiran, 123), or of what has been termed 'decomposition' (Mc Cormack, 400) as a particularity of Beckett's writing over a long career span. In one of his very last interviews, Beckett acknowledged that he had seen his own way 'in impoverishment, ... in taking away, in subtracting rather than [like Joyce] in adding' (Haynes and Knowlson, 37).

We have pointed to certain comparisons with Kharms. Of other recurrent figures from the present book, brief mention might be made too of Artaud, Camus and Pessoa. Beckett's theatrical development gives rise to speculation on the impact of the former, as he sought 'to create, in Artaud's sense, a poetry *of* the theatre rather than poetry *in* the theatre', given his later 'interest in choreographing movement and from his radical mistrust of language' (Knowlson, 246; 672).[77] Beckett had an indirect link with Artaud through Roger Blin (see Fletcher, 36; 150–3), while he had himself read Atraud's *The Theatre and its Double* (Knowlson and Pilling, *Frescoes*, 114). Existentialist connections between Beckett and Sartre have been argued through (see Dobrez, 63–84; Tokarev, passim), those between Beckett and Camus perhaps less so. Nevertheless, Moran compares his pursuit of Molloy to Sisyphus (Trilogy, 133); and Calder (76) records Beckett as saying 'repeatedly that all he ever wanted to do was to put his head against the cliff-rock and push until he had moved it a fraction of a millimetre away' ('determination', in the face of 'determinism': ibid.). The preference for never having been born brings Beckett close to Pessoa (as would his presumed pessimism), and is frequently thought of as acquired from Schopenhauer. Segal (452) cites precedents in Nietzsche (who took it from Aristotle: see *Birth of Tragedy*, 23), Heine and Sophocles. As for the question of pessimism, 'part of Beckett's "message", if we may be so bold as to call it that, is that there is *no* message' (Segal, 445). However, Beckett could still respond (in 1976) to his future authorised biographer's designating Saul Bellow 'another Nobel prize-winning pessimist': 'Where did you get the idea I was a pessimist?' (Knowlson, 822, 77). In Knowlson's view, 'even some of his blackest, bleakest sentences possess a shape, energy and dynamism that serve to negate nihilism' (Haynes and Knowlson, 20). Apart too from Beckett's well-known insistence that the key word in all his works was 'perhaps' (Abbott, 84; Fletcher, 67), it is worth noting (with Uhlmann, 116), that Beckett has often been accused of being too dark, depressing, distressing and perverse – 'when all he has ever attempted has been to show *how it is*'.

Ruby Cohn had written as early as 1961 (presumably even before Esslin's *Theatre of the Absurd* had appeared) that 'Absurdity today is an overworked catchall', needing justification by detailed examination (Cohn, 1961, 154). Forty years later, Lois Gordon (7) refers to playwrights of the mid twentieth century as 'practitioners of the then-labeled Theatre of the Absurd'. Nevertheless, for her (ibid., 126–7), space in *Godot* 'becomes a manifestation and microcosm of the randomness of the Absurd world, as well as the disarray of the fragmented, internal world'. For Adorno (241), the term – in Beckett, at least – 'is relieved of the doctrinal universality' which is existentialism; and this stage had been 'reached through the immanent dialectic of form', via the 'pan-symbolism' of late Ibsen and Strindberg'. 'Meaning nothing becomes the only meaning' by now (ibid., 261). In any event, though, one should not lose sight of the warning issued by Dobrez (51) that, indeed for any given time, 'Beckett's work is far more than a statement of fashionable clichés'.

Notes

1 Beckett, *Molloy, Malone Dies, The Unnamable* (1973): hereafter 'Trilogy'; this designation (rejected by Beckett) is nevertheless commonly used for convenience. Beckett would though eventually and reluctantly refer to the '3 in 1' (which he always insisted should be printed under their three titles) as the 'so-called trilogy': see S.E. Gontarski, 'Introduction' to Beckett, *Nohow On*, xi–xii). He had also referred to a 'pseudo-trilogy' in a letter to Con Leventhal (Ruby Cohn, *A Beckett Canon*, 185).

2 Beckett's own father, Bill, 'was to become a busy and respected quantity surveyor' (Knowlson, 7).

3 The most recent translation, under the title 'Gracchus the Huntsman', is to be found in *The Dedalus Book of Austrian Fantasy: 1890–2000*, edited and translated by Mike Mitchell (Sawtry, Cambs.: Dedalus, 2003), 152–6.

4 Calasso, *K.*, 174 (noted already in Chapter 7): Gracchus '*è straniero al mondo intero*' because he journeys unceasingly in the intermediate zone between land and the world of the dead ('*fra la terra e il mondo dei morti*').

5 In the Penguin edition, Gerry Dukes purports to follow the now established compositional order in which the novellas were written (in French, during 1946): *The End, The Expelled, The Calmative, First Love*, with the title work printed last (Beckett, *First Love and Other Novellas*) – following Knowlson (chapter 15), although Knowlson (362) in fact dates *First Love* as written third, with *The Calmative* last in line. See also Cohn, *Beckett Canon*, 150. However, the order in which these works are printed by S.E. Gontarski (in *CSP*: *First Love*, followed by the three 'stories', with *The End* bringing up the rear) suggests, at least to the present writer, a more satisfying artistic unit (on the assumption too that these four works might profit from consideration as an integral group or cycle). John Pilling (1997, 212–27), however, presents a logic for a reading in compositional order; and, for another alternative, see Adelman (21–37).

6 On the Beckettian 'identities' of Macmann's associates see Amiran, 114 (who also links Lady Pedal with 'Beckett's bicycle': 209). The metaphor of the ship in Beckett (signifying 'body', with the passenger as 'mind') is also suggested by the *Ethics* of Arnold Geulincx, in which 'the subject ... is a passenger free to walk east on the deck of a ship sailing west' (Dobrez, 74; Uhlmann, 53–4); and, Beckett affirmed, by 'Ulysses' relation in Dante (Inf., 26) of his second voyage' (Uhlmann, 54); cf. 'I who had loved the image of old Geulincx, dead young, who left me free, on the black boat of Ulysses, to crawl towards the East, along the deck' (*Molloy*: Trilogy, 51); and earlier: 'black cruiser of Ulysses' (from 1932: Pilling, ed., *Beckett's 'Dream' Notebook*, 103).

7 Beckett, a great connoisseur of art, would of course have been familiar with

Bosch's painting of *The Ship of Fools* (in the Louvre), along with associated versions, such as the woodcuts of Albrecht Dürer, one of his most admired great masters (on art in Beckett see Haynes and Knowlson, 57–61; and, on the use of it in his works, the rest of their chapter 'Images of Beckett', in the book of that title). He was also a fervent admirer of Swift, whom he counted among his 'old chestnuts' (Knowlson, 653). See Doherty (1991, 190–5) for suggestions of Swift in *Watt*.

8 Watt suffered from a diving nightmare (*Watt*, 221: noted by Cohn, *Beckett Canon*, 396–7, n. 12); this occurs too in his first play, *Eleutheria*, where (as in instances dotted throughout Beckett's writing) it is connected with the boyhood reminiscence (and recurring dream) of high diving into a rocky pool: 'I was afraid of hurting myself. I was afraid of the rocks. I was afraid of drowning. I couldn't swim' (*Eleutheria*, 154). It also features in Beckett's earliest surviving verse, 'For Future Reference' (Cohn, *Beckett Canon*, 7–8). 'The pretty vaulting sea refused to drown me', conjured Beckett (when Jean-Louis Barrault was preparing a version of Shakespeare's *Henry VI*): 'French me that', he commented (Knowlson, 544).

9 Adorno's essay 'Trying to Understand *Endgame*', first published in 1961, also links Hamm to Hamlet (Adorno, 267; see also Mc Cormack, 410–11) – a notion strongly denied by Beckett (see Knowlson, 479). There would appear to be no record, though, of Beckett objecting on this occasion to the Kafka suggestion.

10 Christopher Ricks (52) traces the terminal rocking of *Rockaby* ('rocks itself') back to Shakespeare's 'That rots it selfe in ease, on Lethe Wharfe' (*Hamlet*, I.v), via a misquotation in Beckett's essay on Joyce (*Disjecta*, 28) and 'rocks itself softly' ('Enueg I', in *Collected Poems*, 10). Cf. too Amiran (92): 'The swilling motion of waters ebbing to the rim and flowing back to the center in Belacqua's cup is like the swing of Murphy's chair.'

11 The association is there in *Embers* too: 'In Henry's mind copulation is associated with the sea – "Where we did it at last for the first time" [*CDW*, 261] – and the sea for him is the antithesis of life' (Morrison, 91–2). The sea is observed by Morrison (110) to be a 'thematic image Beckett has used often in his work' as a 'mixed image of life and death'.

12 Knowlson and Pilling (*Frescoes of the Skull*, 49) sound a note of caution here; seeing *Text 5* as 'an examination ... of the image-making faculty that has been at the root of Beckett's enterprise in the previous texts', they stress: 'We need not, in other words, seek analogues in Kafka, from whom Beckett has been careful to distinguish himself'. Adorno (259), too, talks of Beckett turning Kafka 'upside down'; see also Cohn, *Beckett Canon*, 198. See too Beckett's own words of self-differentiation from Kafka (Shenker, 1956; Uhlmann, 47; Fletcher, 69): 'In my work there is consternation behind the form, not in the form'. According to Daniel Albright (*Representation and Imagination*, 179), Moran's description of 'the only messenger who ever approaches him' – Gaber (Trilogy, 106–7) – 'may suggest Beckett's acquaintance with Kafka's "Before the Law"'. George H. Szanto stresses 'the pattern of the unsuccessful quest' in the work of Kafka and Beckett, but cautions against the assumption that 'each similarity [should] imply specific influence', as this 'is one of the basic motifs in all post-Renaissance European literature' (Szanto, 74; 185); see also Szanto,

184–6. For a very positive assessment of Kafka–Beckett affinity and impact, however, see Adelman.

13 This apparent allusion to *Metamorphosis* is noted by Jean-Jacques Mayoux, 'Samuel Beckett and Universal Parody', in Esslin, *SB*, 77–91 (84). Albright (197) sees Dostoevsky's Underground Man as a precedent for the Unnamable as 'protagonist of a story', concluding, however, that 'one can meet Dostoevskian wretches at many a cocktail party, whereas no one, I hope, has ever been introduced to anyone reminiscent of the Unnamable'. Uhlmann (146) stresses Rimbaud's 'je est un autre' and its impact on French poststructuralism in connection with the 'self', quintessentially displayed as 'Beckett's unnamable'. Tim Parks, as an epigraph to his novel *Cara Massimina* (1990), employs a quotation from Max Stirner: 'The realms of thought, philosophy and the spirit break up and shatter against the unnameable [*sic*], myself'.

14 Beckett started to write seriously in French – a language in which he felt able to write 'without style' – in 1946, commencing with *Suite* (later known as *La Fin* and *The End*: Knowlson, 357–8), although he began some writing and translating in French in 1938 (ibid., 295; 761, notes 159, 160). There had also been the much earlier spoof lecture, 'Le Concentrisme', of 1930 – in itself something of an absurdist exercise (Beckett, *Disjecta*, 35–42; see Knowlson, 121–2; Pilling, 1997, 53–5); he also dabbled in French verse from 1930 (Cohn, *Beckett Canon*, 20; 27). For that matter, *Suite* was in fact begun in English, Beckett switching to French after 29 pages (Knowlson, 358). Beckett had much earlier translated numerous works (mostly poetic) from French into English; among the French authors favoured with such attentions were Apollinaire (and an essay on Apollinaire), Eluard, Jarry, Michaux and Rimbaud (including *Le Bateau ivre*).

15 The rudderless vessel is, of course, an age-old metaphor. Dante, in the *Convivio*, writes of himself, in perpetual exile from Florence, as 'truly a ship without sail or rudder, driven to many ports and straits and shores by the parching wind of grievous poverty' (quoted from Ciaran Carson's 'Introduction' to his translation of *The Inferno of Dante Alighieri*, London: Granta, 2002, xiv).

16 *Io non mori', e non rimasi vivo: / pensa oggimai per te, s' hai fior d' ingegno, / qual io divenni, d'uno e d'altro privo* (*Inferno*, Canto XXXIV, 25–7; Carson's translation: *The Inferno*, 238).

17 Bridgwater, 123–6 (Bridgwater adds Italian *gracchio* to the bird words quoted earlier, as well as the Latin *graecus* ('Greek'), corresponding to Nietzsche's 'Dionysian Greek': 123–4).

18 Knowlson, 681 (referring to 1982); 701 (1988–89). See Calder, 77; and 145, n. 58. In early 1983, Beckett wrote to one correspondent of feeling 'such inertia and void as never before'. He continued: 'I remember an entry in Kafka's diary. "Gardening. No hope for the future." At least he could garden. There must be words for it. I don't expect ever to find them' (Knowlson, 684). In 1940 he had explained to Joyce the apparent lack of interest in *Finnegans Wake* in Dublin by conveying the impression that, in some sense, 'Kafka had preempted him' (Bair, 260). Beckett's earlier reading of Kafka is an assumption made by, among others, Ruby Cohn (1961), George H. Szanto (1972) and Daniel Albright (1981). Cohn (1961, 154) quotes Beckett (in Shenker, 1956)

saying he had read *The Castle* in German ('serious reading') and 'a few things in French and English', though with no indication given as to when. One may expect Beckett to have read the Kafka works printed in *transition*, especially those in issues to which he himself had contributed: 'Three Stories' ('The Married Couple', 'An Everyday Confusion' and 'A Knock at the Farm Gate') in *transition* 21, 1932; the conclusion to *Metamorphosis*, 'The Housefather's Care' and Max Brod's 'Franz Kafka's Letter to his Father' (all in *transition* 27, 1938, together with a sample of sketches by Kafka): for details of the journal's contents (*transition* 11, 1928, had included Eugene Jolas's version of 'The Sentence', the first appearance of Kafka in English) see Dougald McMillan's study of *transition*. The first appearance in English of *The Hunter Gracchus* dates from 1946. It is tempting even to compare Beckett's short *Echo's Bones* poem 'The Vulture' with Kafka's brief story of the same name, though Goethe may be a common source (Beckett, *Collected Poems*, 9; 173; Kafka, CS 442–3; GWC 132); see also Knowlson (239–40), and Cohn (*Beckett Canon*, 62–3) for other 'vulture' associations.

19 Belacqua, who appears in Canto IV of *Purgatorio*, condemned to living through his life again in Antepurgatory for his indolence in having 'put off good sighs to the last', was a Florentine instrument maker, known to Dante (see *Dream Notebook*, 42–5; Cohn, *Beckett Canon*, 29). Incidentally, 'Belacqua', literally meaning 'beautiful water' is also a near-homophone of 'Benàco', the former name of Lake Garda (mentioned in Canto XX of *Inferno*). The lurking presence and significance of Dante throughout Beckett's work would be hard to exaggerate (see Keir Elam, 'Dead Heads': Pilling, 1994, 152–5; and, for further references, 163, n. 15). The full name of Beckett's protagonist, however, is 'Mr Belacqua Shuah' (*More Pricks*, 111), also to be seen as 'a crude approximation of the low Dublin pronunciation of "Bollocky Shore"' (Francis Doherty, *Samuel Beckett*, 1971, 17; see also Ricks, 56). Belacqua is indeed called 'Bollocky' by the narrator of the forerunning *Sedendo et Quiescendo* (CSP, 13, 16). 'Shuah' is seen as (indirectly) based on Genesis, 46:12 (*Dream Notebook*, 60), although the exact name does not occur there (cf. 'Zohar', 'Shaul', Genesis, 46:10).

20 A point seemingly appreciated by Dylan Thomas, who called the novel 'a strange mixture of Sodom and Begorrah' (see *New English Weekly*, XII, 17 March 1938, 454–5; quoted by Kiberd, 1996, 534; 692, n. 19).

21 Although Beckett visited a mental hospital in Beckenham, the statement (still on the back cover of the Calder paperback editions of *Murphy* at least into the 1990s; and a version still propagated by Gordon, 37) that the novel draws on the author's 'experiences as a male nurse' is erroneous. 'This simply never happened' (Knowlson, 209).

22 As Doherty (1971, 29) points out, 'the joke [here] is on Murphy when he leaves via the gas-route' ('The gas went on in the w.c., excellent gas, superfine chaos': *Murphy*, 142). 'It is Chaos', moreover, 'because Murphy decides (rightly) that etymologically "gas" is the same as "chaos"' (Doherty, 1971, 29).

23 The first drafts of *Watt* were begun as early as 1941: for an account of the notebooks see Pilling, 1997, 170–7; and Cohn, *Beckett Canon*, 109–13, on what she calls the 'Ur-*Watt*'. Among others, L.A.C. Dobrez (20) considers that

'*Watt* marks Beckett's turning point' and moreover 'that Deirdre Bair is surely right when she views it as the novel of Beckett's breakdown during the war'. Adelman, indeed, sees much of Beckett's work from the war on as imbued with imagery of occupation, Holocaust and death-camps. The concept of the 'turning point' in Beckett (rapture, vertigo and epiphany – biographical and creative), is also examined by Lawley (2000). The totality of Beckett's earlier work is surveyed in Pilling's *Beckett Before Godot* (1997).

24 See Part 1 of Dobrez's study, entitled 'The Beckett Irreducible' and particularly his first chapter, 'Beckett: the Reduction' (7–49), in which the process is outlined.

25 While Mr Knott is clearly the total opposite of the 'absentee landlord', there may be a suggestion of a colonialising, as well as a class, provenance in the use, for instance, of the phrase 'unmistakable specimen of local indigent [and therefore also 'indigenous'?] proliferation' (*Watt*, 97).

26 Gontarski (in *CSP*, xxiv) writes of 'the four separate narrators (or the single collective narrator called "I")'.

27 Cf. in the same story, *The Calmative*: 'For me now the setting forth, the struggle and perhaps the return, for the old man I am this evening, older than my father ever was, older then I shall ever be' (*CSP*, 64).

28 On the ordering of these novellas see note 5 above. Connor discusses the possible relationship between the novellas and the novels, as to whether the former should be 'gathered together as a group and placed before the Trilogy' or 'rather, interleaved with the Trilogy' (84).

29 'Threshold', according to Amiran (99), one way and another 'is easily one of Beckett's most important concepts' (at least from *Watt* onwards).

30 On this topic see the chapter "Repetition and Self-Translation' (Connor, 88–114); and Ann Beer, 'Beckett's Bilingualism' (in Pilling, 1994, 209–21). This situation is not dissimilar to that pertaining in the instance of Nabokov's self-translations from Russian to English (and occasionally, too, the reverse); however, as Beer points out (214), 'unlike almost all other major bilingual writers of the twentieth century, Beckett's bilingualism was entirely voluntary'. It is of course an entirely different matter with any text of which we have only a unilingual version from Beckett himself (such as *Eleutheria*, in French; and *Worstward Ho*, in English; not to mention the early English fiction). Ricks (1995) quotes all Beckett's texts in both languages (wherever bilingual Beckett versions exist), making many a keen comparison. There appears to be a sense too in which original writing was, for Beckett, a form of translation, as intimated in his *Proust* (Amiran, 68; 68, n. 7, quoting *Proust*, 64).

31 Characteristically, the French title of the later novel contains within itself multiple homophonic puns (*commencer, commencez, commençais, comme on sait* etc.).

32 *CSP*, 182–5. First issued as a separate 'book' (*Imagination Dead Imagine*, London: John Calder, 1965; illustrated edition, 1977), this plotless 'story' achieved exposure too (prior to inclusion in subsequent collections of Beckett's prose) in the *Sunday Times* (7 November 1965, 48); *Evergreen Review* (10.39, February 1966, 48–9); and *The Penguin Book of Modern European Short Stories*, edited by Robert Taubman (Harmondsworth: Penguin, 1969, 329–31).

33 In addition to Dante, Knowlson (536) suggests other possible sources in Beckett's reading. For an analysis of *The Lost Ones* see Knowlson and Pilling (*Frescoes*, 156–67).

34 Collected as *Nohow On*, a title chosen by Beckett (from its last words): see Gontarski's Introduction ('The Conjuring of Something out of Nothing: Samuel Beckett's "Closed Space" Novels': *Nohow On*, vii–xxviii). The subtitle of this '3 in 1' collection (emphatically, it is claimed, *not* a 'trilogy': see xiii–xiv) extends to the formulation 'Three Novels by Samuel Beckett'.

35 Beckett produced autotranslations of the first two works, but gave up on *Worstward Ho*, deeming it 'untranslatable' (a French version was, however, eventually produced by Edith Fournier, as *Cap au pire*: Paris, 1991).

36 See Knowlson, 651–3; O'Leary ('Beckett's *Company*', 111) refers to it as 'his autobiographical novel'. The literary allusions go back to Belacqua and 'figments' beginning with 'M' and 'W', as well as the Unnamable; there could even be said to be a forward allusion, with the use of the phrase 'stirrings still' (*Nohow On*, 16).

37 O'Leary, 83. His 40-page article probably constitutes the most detailed analysis available of this work. See also, however, Dobrez, 45–9.

38 Renton provides a detailed analysis of this last work: '*Worstward Ho* and the End(s) of Representation' (in Pilling and Bryden, 99–135), 113.

39 'The persona is supplied with memories of another world, the world above, in the light, but he has long been cut off from the land of the living. His writing is entirely consigned to the process of dying, and his physicality is now a matter of residual stirrings gradually dying down' (O'Leary, 110).

40 Cf. the comment that 'there is nowhere to go after *Malone Dies* yet Beckett continues to go there for another forty years' (O'Leary, 91). According to O'Leary (98), '*Company* is one of the "residual" texts which constitute a long series of disorienting epilogues to Beckett's earlier longer works'.

41 H. Porter Abbott (77–80) writes of Beckett's repeated elaboration, and parody, of 'the Victorian trope of onwardness' (77).

42 On his earlier abandoned dramatic work in English (of 1937), dealing with Samuel Johnson, see Lionel Kelly, 'Beckett's *Human Wishes*' (Pilling and Bryden, 21–44); Cohn, *Beckett Canon*, 104–7. The only scene actually composed for this play is to be found in Beckett, *Disjecta*, 155–66.

43 According to the Faber edition of Barbara Wright's English translation (1996), performing rights were still not available. The French original was published by Les Éditions de Minuit in 1995. A first English translation by Michael Brodsky was published as *Eleutheria* (New York: Foxrock, 1995).

44 As Knowlson (366) points out, its only already staged predecessor of any note at this point would have been Genet's *Les Bonnes* (1947). One other significant production of that same year, however, was André Gide and Jean-Louis Barrault's staging of Kafka's *The Trial* (noted by Esslin, *Th. Abs.*, 355–6). For a fuller critique of Beckett's first play see Knowlson's chapter in Knowlson and Pilling, *Frescoes*, 23–38.

45 Paul Davies, 'Three Novels and Four *Nouvelles*', in Pilling, 1994, 43–66 (46–7).

46 Quoted from Boxall, 13. Boxall provides a summary with ample quotations of the reception of *Waiting for Godot* and *Endgame* from first productions to the 1990s.

47 Ricks (123–4) makes considerable play with the Unnamable's citing 'a ponderous chronicle of moribunds in their courses' (Trilogy, 310) and Beckett's use elsewhere of 'corse' and 'corpse'. T. Miller (190–5) discusses Beckett's interest in the Russian (and then Soviet) pair of clowns, Bim and Bom, with particular reference to the nursing system in *Murphy*.

48 Abbott (80) sees Pozzo and Lucky as 'an outrageous caricature of the westward course of empire'.

49 For an account of Lucky's tirade as 'a mock account of the history of Western thought concerning the relationship between God and man' see Morrison, 23–5. Dobrez (19) sees Arsene's much longer valedictory peroration in *Watt* as 'anticipating Lucky's speech in its inspired confusion'; the later *Text 12* has been deemed 'a more economical version of Lucky's tirade' (Knowlson and Pilling, *Frescoes*, 57; CSP, 149–51).

50 'Endgame is a game that cannot end, an irresolvable tension between irreconcilable forces' (Kearney, 1988, 81); or 'a typical and to some extent norm-governed situation separated by a caesura from the midgame with its combinations' (Adorno, 270). On Beckett, *Endgame* and chess see also Kenner (in Boxall, 76; 172, n. 51). Beckett's interest in chess (see also the game in *Murphy*, 136–8) may be compared to that of Nabokov, who composed chess problems, as well as the 'chess novel' *Luzhin's Defense* (1930; English version 1964). For another 'chess novel' written by a sometime absurdist see Fernando Arrabal, *The Tower Struck by Lightning*, translated by Anthony Kerrigan, New York: Viking, 1988 (first published as *La torre herida por el rayo*, 1983).

51 'For rehearsal purposes Beckett divided his full-length plays into manageable self-contained sections, which in a more conventional work would be called scenes' (Fletcher, 125): for Ruby Cohn's listing of these in *Endgame*, see ibid., 125–6.

52 The old questions, answers and stories abound in Beckett. 'Stories, stories. I have not been able to tell them. I shall not be able to tell this one', says Moran (*Molloy*, Trilogy, 138). 'The same old mutterings, the same old stories, the same old questions and answers': the narrator of *Texts for Nothing*, 1 is thus 'all ears for the old stories' (CSP, 103). We may care to note, too, that Kafka's Gracchus muses: 'Ah, coherent. The old, old stories. All the books are full of it' (Kafka, *GWC*, 54). One of the main preoccupations of Adelman's study is to trace the 'stories' in (and behind the stories in) Beckett's work.

53 Pilling (1997, 185) calls *Watt* 'a dog of a novel, hence the problem of the dog in it'. Beckett was, of course, fully aware that 'dog' is 'god' (or 'God') backwards and that the reverse of 'Godot' is 'to dog'. As pointed out by Gordon (61), 'Godot is also virtually a contraction of [the] nicknames, Gogo and Didi'.

54 Esslin, *Th. Abs.*, 65 (his emphasis), compares *Endgame* to Nikolai Evreinov's *The Theatre of the Soul. Monodrama* (translated by M. Potapenko and C. St John, London, 1915). 'While it is unlikely that Beckett knew this old and long-forgotten Russian play, the parallels are very striking' (66).

55 The English version (see *CDW*) is subtitled: 'A tragi-comedy in two acts'. No subtitle appears in the French (*Théâtre I*) edition.

56 'The *theatrum mundi* metaphor was derived from the idea that God was the sole spectator of man's actions on the stage of life' (Elizabeth Burns,

Theatricality, 1972; quoted by Fletcher, 20). On Beckett's work as 'late modernism' see Abbott; and T. Miller (169–203).

57 The first editions of George Gibian's translations of Kharms and Vvedensky had, however, been published in the first half of the 1970s (see Bibliography), as had early efforts at Kharms translation by the present author (in the Dublin literary magazine *Atlantis*, 6, Winter 1973/74, 47–52).

58 Wanner, 2003, 25–7 (Baudelaire and Turgenev); 61–2 (Andrei Bely); 94–5 (Aleksei Remizov).

59 Appropriately enough, *Breath* was directed by Damien Hirst in the complete filming of Beckett's stage works (Blue Angel Films, 2001). The figure of Schwitters also comes to mind in this connection.

60 Beckett's musical interests and ability are well documented. In terms of relevance within his work, suffice it to mention Schubert's *Death and the Maiden* and *All That Fall*; and Beethoven's so-called 'The Ghost' trio and Beckett's television play *Ghost Trio* (1975).

61 Anders, 'Being Without Time', in Esslin, *SB*, 140–51 (145). See also Kearney, 1985 (277–88).

62 T. Miller (185) similarly draws attention to Beckett's letter to Axel Kaun (of 1937: see *Disjecta*, 172), in which he favours the (at least gradual) elimination of language, placing himself at this point closer to 'the logographs of Gertrude Stein' than to Joyce.

63 Cf. Kearney (1985, 286) on Watt's '"mystical" conclusion that true knowledge is non-knowledge, that the truth of being is non-being'. On 'inexistence' in Beckett, see Ricks, 137–40.

64 Cohn *Beckett Canon*, 114. See also, for instance: 'Not that Watt was ever to have any direct dealings with Mr. Knott, for he was not' (*Watt*, 64). Jacqueline Hoefer says that Mr Knott 'remains for Watt the Knotty source "Of nought"': see her '*Watt*' (Esslin, *SB*, 62–76), 72 (and *Watt* itself, 164). Pilling (1997) calls his chapter on that novel '*Watt* and *Watt* not'. Mooney (16) remarks that the 'what?' question (of Watt) receives the 'not'/'knot' answers (of Knot): both negation and ensnarement.

65 Doherty, 1991, 199, n. 14. These words, indeed, far from being an afterthought, occurred in the 'Ur-*Watt*' (Cohn, *Beckett Canon*, 111). The Addenda are read by Daniela Caselli as a *mise en abyme* (noted by Cohn, *Beckett Canon*, 395, n. 6).

66 Perhaps the closest to a coherent summary of the novel, in something like this sense at least, is that provided within Cohn, *Beckett Canon*, 113–23.

67 We read of 'the period of Watt's revelation, to me' (*Watt*, 76); and that 'I' heard everything from Watt, 'some years later' (i.e. after the 'events': ibid., 123), and noted down 'in my little notebook' (124; 163). Whoever we take 'Sam' to be, he is presumably not the 'cousin Sam' member of the Lynch family (98; 104) – if for no other reason than that the 'paralysed' condition of that particular Sam would preclude the antics described in part III.

68 One can imagine this, along with certain later texts, as the inspiration for Donald Barthelme's six-page 'Sentence' (*Forty Stories*, 147–53).

69 One is inevitably reminded here of 'Dante's damned, with their faces arsy-versy. Our tears will water our bottoms' (*All That Fall*: *CDW*, 191), one of a number of Beckett's variations, seeming to derive from *Inferno*, XX, 22–4).

70 See T. Miller (252, n. 33) on Beckett's use of the names 'Quin', 'Capper Quin'
   and thence 'Cooper', allegedly derived from 'a Trappist monastery in Munster
   at Cappoquin'.
71 Watt's immortal expletive is repeated as the fourth line from the end of
   (recorded) Voice's monologue in the late work *Rockaby* (written 1980: 'rock
   her off / stop her eyes / fuck life / stop her eyes / rock her off / rock her off',
   CDW, 442). Amiran (193) connects this with a Beckettian sexualisation of the
   Earth (though the French original may slightly undermine this, suggesting
   rather a link with the Beckettian 'quaqua') and notes that it has been called
   'the exasperated cry' summarising 'the existential priorities of Beckett's characters'.
72 'It was while watching him [Malone] pass that I wondered if we cast a
   shadow', muses the Unnamable (Trilogy, 294).
73 See Marjorie Perloff, *Wittgenstein's Ladder* (115–43), 21. The 'mere ladder' in
   question, a reduction from 'Dante's purgatorial staircase' (ibid., xiv), had been
   identified with the notion of 'existence off the ladder', when (mid-monologue)
   Arsene quips: 'Do not come down the ladder, Ifor, I haf taken it away' (*Watt*,
   42). This 'ladder' was said by Beckett to allude to 'a Welsh joke' (rather than
   a German one, let alone a Wittgenstein reference); in any case, Beckett did not
   read Wittgenstein until the late 1950s (Perloff, 134; 8) and his
   'Wittgensteinian' qualities are seen (ibid., 134–5; 140–1) as closer to the
   language games of the *Philosophical Investigations* than to the *Tractatus*
   (which contains the 'famous' ladder metaphor on its final page: ibid., xiv; see
   Tractatus, 49).
74 P.J. Murphy, 'Beckett and the Philosophers', in Pilling, 1994, 222–40 (229).
75 A.J. Leventhal, 'The Beckett Hero', in Esslin, *SB*, 37–51 (46–8); the approval
   comes from Doherty (1971, 45), one of the few commentators to take note of
   Leventhal's suggestion.
76 *Concise Routledge Encyclopedia of Philosophy*, London and New York:
   Routledge, 2000, 323. The 'nihilism of Gorgias' figures amid a range of
   concepts, thinkers and writers (Beckett included) in Barthelme's sketch
   Nothing: A Preliminary Account (*Sixty Stories*, 239–42).
77 On Beckett and Artaud see also Connor, 117–18; 140–1; 156–7; 213, n. 25.

9

Flann O'Brien and the purloined absurd

The riddle of the universe I might solve if I had a mind to, he said, but I prefer the question to the answer. It serves men like us as a bottomless pretext for scholarly dialectic. (Flann O'Brien, *At Swim-Two-Birds*, 1939)

Answers do not matter so much as questions, said the Good Fairy. A good question is very hard to answer. The better the question the harder the answer. There is no answer at all to a very good question. (Flann O'Brien, *At Swim-Two-Birds*, 1939)

'The first beginnings of wisdom,' he said, 'is to ask questions but never to answer any. *You* get wisdom from asking and *I* from not answering'. (Flann O'Brien, *The Third Policeman*, 1940/1967)

I love the old questions. [*With fervour.*] Ah the old questions, the old answers, there's nothing like them! (Samuel Beckett, *Endgame*, 1957/58)

The hydra-headed man

Names are just the foolishness of language, which is a bigger kind of fool-ishness than most.

(Hari Kunzru, *The Impressionist*, 2002)

In the words of one Beckett commentator, reporting a conversation he was fortunate enough to have had with that author, 'Beckett told me that James Joyce saw him as O'Brien's pessimistic twin' (Amiral, 20, n.). This remark would, of course, have derived from the end of the 1930s, when Beckett and Flann O'Brien were, after a fashion at least, making their names as authors of comic, grotesque – or even absurdist – fiction. 'Even Beckett's remorseless hilarity', in Seamus Deane's view, 'cannot quite match the humour of O'Brien's deadpan prose' (Deane, 194). Flann O'Brien (1911–66), born Brian O'Nolan, had published *At Swim-Two-Birds* in March 1939 – a work said to have been the last novel Joyce read in his near-blindness. We shall have to return, in further brief mentions, to Joyce again shortly.

Brian O'Nolan (also at times Brian Nolan and Brian Ó Nualláin), who first 'impinged on Dublin' in his student days in the early 1930s (when he was reported to have had 'the visage of a Satanic cherub')[1] wrote his first two books as 'Flann O'Brien' – a name to which he returned, probably only for commercial reasons, in his second novelistic career, post-1960 (and the reprinting of the neglected At Swim-Two-Birds). Meanwhile he wrote satirical-comic columns for some twenty-five years, mainly for the Irish Times, as 'Myles na Gopaleen' (or, in the earlier stages, 'Myles na gCopaleen': literally 'Myles of the Ponies'), having published a humorous novel, purportedly 'edited' by Myles na Gopaleen (or, rather, 'na gCopaleen'), in Irish – which had in fact been his first language: The Poor Mouth (An Béal Bocht, 1941).[2] He later made what are probably fictitious claims to have written a number of the Sexton Blake detective stories. He certainly did, though, have something of a career in his later years as a television script writer (partly as 'Myles', but mainly as 'Brian Nolan').[3]

In addition to his rather up-down-up again (although his lifetime literary reputation never matched his more recent posthumous one), and largely part-time, literary career, Brian O'Nolan (like Kafka, T.S. Eliot and E.T.A. Hoffmann) followed a bureaucratic occupation – working for eighteen years in the Civil Service. Like Beckett (whom he knew a little, and who had also 'praised At Swim-Two-Birds very highly': Cronin, 55; 93; Clissmann, 310), he wrote in two languages. Indeed, Keith Hopper points out that 'the two post-modernist authors who most resemble O'Brien – Samuel Beckett and Vladimir Nabokov – also wrote in their second language' (Hopper, 35). So, for that matter, did Ionesco. Unlike Beckett (and of course Joyce) O'Brien remained in Ireland. The only trip abroad he is known to have taken was a brief one to Germany in 1933 or 1934 (which he soon subsequently 'extended' and mysteriously embroidered; and in much later life he made even more mysterious claims to have visited Joyce in Paris).[4] As Hopper (57) puts it, O'Nolan was 'a writer whose exile was interior'.

Like a number of other writers treated in this study as probable absurdists, O'Nolan was a talented cartoonist. The 'shadow' of Joyce apart, the young O'Nolan much admired Proust, Kafka and Kierkegaard, as well as 'the 19th-century Russians', although, his biographer Anthony Cronin (58–9) reports, 'his admiration did not prevent him from striking an attitude which was to become familiar in later years in speaking of "layabouts from the slums of Europe poking around in their sickly little psyches"'. Somewhat in the manner of Kharms, he adopted what has been called 'a myriad of pseudonymous personalities in the interests of pure destruction'.[5] From now on, though, if only for the sake of convenience, we shall endeavour to refer to O'Nolan – much of the time at least – as 'Flann O'Brien'.[6]

Among other European layabouts for whom O'Brien also evidently found at least some time were the Čapek brothers, given that he produced his own Irish relocation of *The Insect Play* (*Ze života hmyzu*, 1921; written principally by Karel Čapek). This play – one of three written under Myles's name, and produced at Dublin's Gate Theatre for a week in 1943, as *Rhapsody in Stephen's Green* – was long thought to have been lost (other than for Act I), but a prompt copy was found in an American archive (in Northwestern University) and published only in 1994.[7] In his 'Series Editor's Preface' to this work, W.J. Mc Cormack draws comparative attention to Kafka's novels, with their 'logic as inescapable and elusive as that of *The Third Policeman*', and considers that 'Relations between the various epicentres of literary modernism cannot be measured in miles or kilometres' (O'Brien, *Rhapsody*, vi). Himself writing under another name (as Hugh Maxton), that same commentator had contributed, as an 'Afterword' to an earlier volume in the same series presenting a selection of the briefer stories of Daniil Kharms, a short essay entitled 'Kharms and Myles' (Maxton, 1989).[8] M. Keith Booker comments in more detail on affinities between Kafka and O'Brien, mentioning also shared elements of Menippean satire discerned between O'Brien and writers from Central and Eastern Europe, already familiar to us on absurdist grounds, such as Hašek, Bruno Schulz and Gombrowicz (Booker, 1995, 127–33; 126, n. 6). Furthermore, the same commentator goes on to discuss parallels in twentieth-century Russian literature (bringing in Nabokov and, in more detail, Mikhail Bulgakov), but without mention of Kharms (ibid., 135–9).

Quite how or why O'Brien lit upon *The Insect Play* (which had been translated into English in 1923) is not clear. However, the Chief Engineer's statement that 'The master of Time will be master of all' (Brothers Čapek, 157) must have struck a chord in relation to what was to be the later version of the figure of De Selby (in *The Dalkey Archive*, 1964, in an animated elaboration of this character from being merely the subject of footnotes, as 'de' Selby in *The Third Policeman*, completed by the very beginning of 1940). O'Brien also must have seen a parallel worth drawing between the post-first-World-War ethos of *The Insect Play* (instanced by the Tramp's 'The night we left a thousan' dead – / And keptured two latrines': Brothers Čapek, 163) and a confused Second World War (nominally neutral) situation pertaining in Ireland, twenty years after the Irish civil war. O'Brien clearly saw considerable mileage in the insect formula[9] (though with variations in species: the butterflies of the originals of Act I becoming bees), the episodic structure (with the Tramp as the recurrent commentating figure) and the scope for social and political satire, as well as wordplay (in the Myles manner) – with the added bonus of exploiting a range of Irish accents. The warring ants of Act III introduces 'loyal' Unionist aggression from 'the Prawvince of the

Awnts' (*Rhapsody*, 60), though the leader of the 'Green Ants' (an undis-
guised de Valera figure) ends up equally (and literally) stamped upon. As
Robert Tracy contends, therefore (*Rhapsody*, 7), the resulting play 'is
essentially an original work by Myles himself'.

Another foray into the literary traditions of Europe resulted in the play
Faustus Kelly, which had a slightly longer (two-week) run at the Abbey
Theatre, also in 1943. The Faust legend comes to Ireland. Here the keen
satirical observations of Myles, fuelled by the O'Nolan work experience
in the Department of Local Government and his dim view of the Irish
political scene and its machinations, are penetrated by the
Goethe–Marlowe Faust model. An aspiring politician named Kelly,
seeking venal political and sexual advancement, enlists the help of a
mysterious stranger – dubbed 'Mr Strange' (*Stories and Plays*, 117). This
particular Mephistophelian emissary, who may owe something to the
depiction of his counterpart in Dostoevsky's *The Brothers Karamazov*,
(apparently as 'The Devil') signs Kelly up to 'a diabolical bond' in a brief
silent prologue (ibid., 99). Finally, dismayed at the refusal of the political
powers above to 'sanction' him as a local government employee, and in
desperate reaction to Kelly's tedious speechifying, The Stranger tears up
the contract, declaring (but in capital letters): 'I want nothing more of
Irish public life!' (165). Bureaucracy has defeated the Devil. The first act,
at least, was generally regarded as amusing and successful; however, it
may have been straining credulity to suggest that the Devil would have
gone anywhere near Irish Free State politics in the first place.

Somewhat bizarre references to Russia (whether Soviet or Tsarist)
occur in *The Third Policeman* and *Faustus Kelly* – as well as in the writings of Myles and earlier in a magazine they called *Blather*. Maxton (93)
uses as his epigraph to 'Kharms and Myles', from the former work, the
following gem: '"In Russia," said the Sergeant, "they make teeth out of
old piano-keys for elderly cows …".' Characters in *Faustus Kelly* are
prone to proclaiming Russia the land of 'nothing but trousers' for 'men,
women and children', and of 'the Russian steamroller', as well as nudism,
'vodka and beans' and 'new potatoes in March' (*Stories and Plays*,
100–2). 'Brother Barnabas', the first prominent pseudonym used by
O'Nolan in writings as a student in 1932, had unexpectedly revealed
himself as 'a halfcaste Russian Jew … of good *kulak* stock' (O'Brien,
Myles Before Myles, 72–3). Myles (or, at least, one of his voices – in an
alleged dream) claims that Guinness's 'own nearly all Siberia' (O'Brien, *At
War*, 77).[10] O'Brien himself, however, in 1954 turned down a chance to
join a writers' delegation visiting the USSR, citing his mother's health as
the reason (Cronin, 196).

In addition to the shared propensity for pseudonyms between O'Brien
and Kharms, Maxton (94) advances the theory that one way of register-
ing 'a crucial difference between spiritual and physical terror in the cases

of Kharms and O'Brien' might be to say that 'one died of hunger and the other did not die of thirst'. Indeed, O'Brien wrote a short play entitled *Thirst* (written in the 1940s), combining satire of the absurd operation of licensing laws with tall story-telling of heat in the Mesopotamian desert (O'Brien, *Stories and Plays*, 81–93); this narration, incidentally, forms an interesting shaggy-dog verbal counterpart to Beckett's mime with music, *Act Without Words I* (directions written in French, 1956: Beckett, *CDW*, 201–6). Maxton, however, draws attention to a further 'curious interest' which Kharms and O'Brien share: 'detective fiction or fictional detectives' (ibid., 97). Kharms frequently posed as Sherlock Holmes, while O'Brien (or rather O'Nolan), as we have noted, effected to contribute plots (if not even actual stories) to the Sexton Blake series.[11] Policemen (secret, mystical or otherwise) appear in various of their works. A common projection from Kharms, and for that matter Holmes, assiduously exploited by O'Brien (or at least by Myles), was the (quintessentially Dublin) figure of 'the brother'.[12] What Anne Clissmann (285) describes as O'Brien's 'delight in humour that springs from an apprehension of violence' was emphatically a quality in the work of Kharms (see the sadistic tortures and mutilations purportedly visited upon Trellis in *At Swim-Two-Birds*). Another feature shared in the works of both is the tendency towards destruction of story. A more personal bent in common between O'Brien and Kharms was a propensity for snooker or billiards: the former made much of the billiard room in his student days, while Kharms's prowess at that game earned him the added nickname of 'Mister Twister' around the billiard halls of Leningrad. Yet another shared interest between the two is in extravagant (or mythical) forms of machinery: O'Brien's leanings in this direction are evidenced in the contortions undertaken by de Selby, and displayed in certain of the Myles columns; in the case of Kharms, there are (albeit disputed) accounts that he kept a mysterious (and apparently purposeless) machine in his flat. The 'Myles na Gopaleen Research Bureau', however, which frequently figured in the *Irish Times* columns, is perhaps more reminiscent of the almost contemporaneous Mr Nackybal and the 'research expedition in the County Clare' occurring in Beckett's *Watt*.

While the bulk of the material in the 'Myles-ian' columns (as their author occasionally referred to his efforts: *Best of Myles*, 250),[13] may, in its more parochial aspects, be considered somewhat 'foreign' to the Kharmsian *oeuvre*, it is nevertheless not difficult to find comparable pieces, passages or figures. One might, to take a first instance, consider the protagonist of 'A Knight' (Kharms, *Incidences*, 105–8) alongside the 'elderly man who gave his name as Myles na gCopaleen' in the Dublin court, 'charged with begging, disorderly conduct, using bad language and being in illegal possession of an arm-chair' (*Best of Myles*, 148–53). This particular case in 'The District Court' (and Myles/O'Brien is quite often at his best when broaching legal and police matters) even contains within it a brief explanatory passage than could almost stand alongside Kharms's (non-explanatory) brevities:

> Defendant said he got the chair from a man he met in Poolbeg Street. He did not know the man's name. The man was on his way to pawn the chair and witness agreed to take it off his hands. He bought the chair. (*Best of Myles*, 148)

Other Kharmsian examples have already been quoted in our Kharms chapter; but here is the isolated 'incident' numbered 19 and entitled 'An Encounter' (*Vstrecha*: Kharms, *PSS*, 2, 345; analysed, under the title 'A Meeting', by Wanner, 2003, 129–31):

> On one occasion a man went off to work and on the way he met another man who, having bought a loaf of Polish bread, was wending his way home.
> And that's just about all there is to it. (*Incidences*, 67)

In the case of O'Brien (or certainly of Myles), that would never quite be 'all there is to it'. In fact, though, Myles also has a short piece of half a page entitled 'An Encounter', in which the narrator, dissatisfied at the progress of a horse-drawn cab (hailed to hurry 'to Cabinteely to buy some carpet slippers for the granda'), displaces the horse and gets 'in between the shafts with myself'. 'No trouble to me, of course', concludes Myles: 'I am, as you know, a hack!' (*At War*, 156–7).

Published as a short story entitled 'Two in One' (in *The Bell*, 1954) is a piece that epitomises the interface between absurdity and the fantastic in the writings attributed to Myles, combining too the grotesque and the detective story. The narrator (one Murphy), assistant to a taxidermist (named Kelly), 'a swinish overbearing mean boss, a bully, a sadist', murders his employer. Applying 'the general technique and flaying pattern appropriate to apes', he then expropriates his victim's skin. However, the skin was subsequently found to have 'literally fused with my own' and, in the upshot, the narrator is arrested and convicted of his own murder (O'Brien, *Various Lives*, 160–4). An adaptation for television, under the title *The Dead Spit of Kelly*, was produced by RTE in 1962 (Clissmann, 30).

Cronin (201) speculates that the appeal of Sexton Blake writing for O'Brien may have been 'first, perversity, and secondly because it fitted so well with the idea of the original genius who was also an expert and versatile literary journeyman, prepared, unlike Proust, Kafka and, above all James Joyce, to turn his hand to anything'. O'Brien may, at least in his dreams, have written commercial detective fiction; he certainly wrote journalism and television scripts – as alternatives (and partly for financial reasons) to both the civil service and novel writing. Kharms had just about scratched out a living as a children's writer in 1930s Leningrad, with almost all his 'adult' writing done, perforce, for his 'desk drawer'. Kafka had left instructions for Max Brod to burn his unpublished works. O'Brien, without going that far, nevertheless adopted a perverse attitude to much of his production. His most successful (at least, within his life-time) fictional work, *At Swim-Two-Birds*, he in later life dismissed as 'juvenilia, public nose-picking' (Cronin, 247). *The Hard Life* he hoped would be banned in Ireland – a hope which rested largely, it would seem, on the inclusion of a leading character under the name of 'Father Fahrt, SJ'. His 'gleeful anticipation of the prospect' (ibid., 213) was, however, disappointed, as the book did not have quite the scurrilous qualities required for this fate in the Ireland of the early 1960s (by which time, certainly, 'to be censored was considered something of a mark of distinc-tion': ibid.). As for his masterpiece, *The Third Policeman*: this typescript he frequently pretended to have lost – in fact he 'forgot' it, apparently leaving it exposed (in a manner reminiscent of Poe's 'purloined letter'), to gather dust for more than a quarter of a century on his sideboard (Cronin, 165), after its initial publishing rejection.[14]

We have already referred above to the 'shadow' of Joyce.[15] According to Cronin (176): 'The figure of Joyce hung over [O'Brien's] life like a sort of cloud from which the apocalyptic vision could come or had come'. Deane (194) regards this perception as 'one of the most astonishing exam-ples of the "anxiety of influence" to be found'. Anecdotal evidence apart, O'Brien (or rather Brian Nolan) published, as an editorial contribution, a somewhat tortured 'essay', entitled 'A Bash in the Tunnel', for a Joyce issue of the literary review *Envoy* in 1951 (*Stories and Plays*, 169–75). This curious composition contrives a metaphorical combination of a hilarious tall story of alcoholic excess with snatches of a somewhat resent-ful literary (and religious) criticism of Joyce. Frequent mentions were made of Joyce over the years in the Myles columns.[16] However, the most startling treatment of Joyce was reserved for the late O'Brien work, *The Dalkey Archive*.

'Joyce spent a lifetime establishing himself as a character in fiction', claims Nolan–O'Brien in his Joyce essay (as 'the ageless Stephen'); conversely, 'Thousands of people believe that there once lived a man named Sherlock Holmes' (*Stories and Plays*, 173). Brother Barnabas, for that matter, had claimed to have known Holmes and Dr Watson as students at University College, Dublin (O'Brien, *Myles Before Myles*, 69). He seems intrigued by a suggestion that Joyce might have 'dearly wished to be recalled to Dublin as an ageing man to be crowned with a D Litt. from the National and priest-haunted University' (ibid., 174). A decade later, O'Brien brings the ageing Joyce back to fictitious life – denying authorship of his major works and working as a barman in the coastal town of Skerries. Furthermore, Joyce, who had apparently written pamphlets for the Catholic Truth Society, has 'now' developed a burning ambition to join the Jesuits. As a final (albeit hilarious) indignity, this purported Joyce is offered a job as a repair seamster, darning and sewing patches on to the Jesuits' underwear.[17]

Not for nothing has the subject of this chapter been called 'the three-headed man'.[18] Brian O'Nolan 'talked like a controlled and directed tempest'.[19] Flann O'Brien was the 'novelist and short story writer'. Myles na Gopaleen was the 'author of that column in the *Irish Times* which both S.J. Perelman and James Thurber rated the funniest newspaper feature ever published'. The three heads (or at least four, if we count O'Nolan the civil servant, in addition to the inebriated talker and the solitary drinker) could not easily and indefinitely coexist. The career of the civil servant was eventually destroyed, in large measure by offence eventually taken at certain of the writings of Myles. The camouflage that Myles was purport-edly a composite columnist had been laid bare by the unwise publication of a cover-blowing satirical photograph (see Cronin, 181). It has frequently been conjectured, too, that the journalistic activities of Myles na Gopaleen must have had a deleterious effect on the novelistic career of Flann O'Brien (see Kiberd, 1996, 511–12).[20] Absurdist incursions into real life arising out of the hydra-headedness of this phenomenon were not unknown either. At the first night of *Faustus Kelly*, instead of the custom-ary playwright's bow (and to the annoyance of many in the audience), that honour fell to 'a gentleman, dressed as the traditional stage Irishman with pipe, caubeen and cutaway coat, who did a bit of a jig and then silently vanished' (Cronin, 134). This was an Abbey actor, gnomically 'disguised' as the mythical personage, 'Myles na gCopaleen' – an original 'stage-Irish buffoon' (Kiberd, 1996, 497). O'Nolan, the civil servant, advisedly (given the play's stance and content) kept a low profile, to avoid any public identification with Myles.

There is, however, an alternative view of the mass of Myles material. This has been suggested by John Wyse Jackson, who finds the totality of the *Cruiskeen Lawn* columns to be no mere 'series of humorous squibs, satires and sketches, albeit displayed against a glittering backdrop of verbal prestidigitation', but 'a modernist (or rather a proleptically post-modernist) *coup de maître*, written in two primary and several languages whose boundaries are repeatedly breached and confused' – even perhaps 'a random, episodic, wildly innovative beast of a "novel", in which the novel form itself has been stretched to screaming point and beyond' (Introduction to *At War*, 11).[21] Something of Wyse Jackson's perception is conveyed by his selection of Flann O'Brien *At War*, subtitled 'Myles na gCopaleen 1940–1945', through the chronological ordering and the more restricted timescale of the material, underlying which, we may agree, is a certain 'continuity and fictional progress' (ibid., 12). A more complete judgment of this approach, though, might require (re)publication of a complete *Cruiskeen Lawn* (said to be 'bad Irish for "A Full Jug"': ibid., 7;

or 'Cruiscín Lán' in Irish) which, estimated by Wyse Jackson at 'almost 3,000 more columns in tiny print ... perhaps four million words in all' (ibid., 8), may not be soon in coming.[22] 'Is it modernist epic or mere ephemera?' asks Joseph Brooker (*F O'B*, 107).

It somehow seems curiously apt if some of the mysteries surrounding Brian O'Nolan (such as foreign trips, and the authorship of detective fiction) should remain unresolved. For that matter, his other (and marginally earlier) biographers, Peter Costello and Peter van de Kamp (130), speculate on the possible existence of a further five undiscovered books by O'Nolan under yet further (as yet unknown) pen-names. While sharing, to an extent at least, Hopper's 'incipient mistrust' of 'biographical criticism' (Hopper, 18–19 and passim), and a preference for more Formalist and metacritical approaches, I would suggest that it may already be apparent that in certain cases – and, if such there be, Brian O'Nolan is surely one – certain biographical details, and aspects of the publishing history of writings, can be so bizarre that a blanket omission of all such considerations could be seriously counter-productive.

Reverting from Myles to the prose works of Flann O'Brien, the remaining sections of this chapter will turn to the two main Flann O'Brien novels. *The Hard Life* is rarely considered a great literary success. The somewhat uneven *The Dalkey Archive* has its inspired ideas and moments (including elements of what Brian McHale [17] would call a 'transhistorical party' – mixing characters from different historical eras), but a number of these derive from the rejected earlier novel. 'To list the book's characters and events is to play with absurdity', writes Brooker (80), not entirely admiringly of this work.[23] From what we have of a final unfinished novel, known as *Slattery's Sago Saga* (see *Stories and Plays*, 19–64), it is hard to see that this would have been a very significant addition to the O'Brien canon. It remains, therefore, to consider *At Swim-Two-Birds* and *The Third Policeman*.

At Swim-Two-Birds: juvenile scrivenry as metafictional absurd?

The first Flann O'Brien novel was written through the second half of the 1930s and, to an extent at least, follows from the early writings of that decade: the Brother Barnabas offerings in the student magazine *Comhthrom Féinne* (or 'Fair Play') and the activities in and around the short-lived journal *Blather* (see the selection of early writings presented in O'Brien, *Myles Before Myles*[24]). It appears too that bits of material from O'Nolan's MA thesis on 'Nature in Irish Poetry' (written in Irish, and accepted by UCD in 1935, after rejection the previous year) 'made their way into the book' (Costello and van de Kamp, 60),[25] along with various other opportunistic additions from varying outside sources – somewhat in the spirit of the 'collective' policy of composition advocated by the group around *Blather* and a bevy of spoof correspondents, a little later, to the *Irish Times*. Such plans were afoot to produce by collaborative means 'the Great Irish Novel', which would establish a 'Ready-Made School' of literary composition, analogous to certain of the artistic activities of the Dada and Surrealist movements; in a sense at least, Brooker sees *Cruiskeen Lawn* as a logical consequence of such a process (see his *F O'B*, 43; 102). What now emerged under the name of O'Brien, however, was something that, although deriving in part from such an approach, was rather more extraordinarily individualistic.

While *At Swim-Two-Birds* attracted enthusiastic comment in certain literary circles, its commercial progress was modest; after a reported sale of 244 copies, the Longman's warehouse in London was destroyed by German bombing. This was effectively the end of the novel (and of O'Brien as a published novelist) until the successful reprint of 1960 (an American edition of 1951 having made little impact). Publication at Longman's had been assisted by Graham Greene, in his capacity as publisher's reader. The original dust jacket was thus able to quote Greene's 'continual excitement' on reading the typescript and his apposite summary of the novel's structure:

> We have had books inside books before but O'Nolan [O'Brien's real name here slipped through from the reader's report] takes Pirandello and Gide a long way further. The screw is turned until you have (a) a book about a man called Trellis who is (b) writing a book about certain characters who (c) are turning the tables on Trellis by writing about him. (quoted by Cronin, 89)

As if the intervention of Greene were not fortuitous enough, the novel attracted another (this time not quite accurate) expert comment, within a couple of months of publication, from no less a figure than the Anglophile master of labyrinths, Jorge Luis Borges – writing in the 'Foreign Books and Authors' page which he edited for an Argentinian women's magazine.[26] This mini-review (of which, one assumes, O'Brien was never aware, and which had no impact anyway for at least half a century) is worth quoting at length:

> I have enumerated many verbal labyrinths, but none so complex as the recent book by Flann O'Brien, *At Swim-Two-Birds*. A student in Dublin writes a novel about the proprietor of a Dublin public house, who writes a novel about the habitués of his pub (among them, the student), who in their turn write novels in which proprietor and student figure along with other writers of novels about other novelists. The book consists of the extremely diverse manuscripts of these real or imagined persons, copiously annotated by the student. *At Swim-Two-Birds* is not only a labyrinth: it is a discussion of the many ways to conceive of the Irish novel and a repertory of exercises in prose and verse which illustrate or parody all the styles of Ireland. The magisterial influence of Joyce (also an architect of labyrinths; also a literary

Proteus) is undeniable but not disproportionate in this manifold book. (Borges, *TL*, 162)

The final remark would have irritated O'Brien with its (already inevitable) Joycean comparison, but might have consoled him slightly in its measured tone.

Novels within novels, then, were not unknown. The pre-American fiction of Nabokov (which O'Brien, though, could not have known – even the first English novel, *The Real Life of Sebastian Knight*, was not published until 1941) includes play on the birth of novels, and characters who suspect their status to be a figure in some greater work. The models which can be pointed to, however, are James Branch Cabell's *The Cream of the Jest* (1917) and Aldous Huxley's *Point Counter Point* (1928), which O'Brien certainly knew; Sterne and Joyce, naturally enough, are also considered germane (Clissmann, 93–9). Huxley is indeed even mentioned within the text, taking his place on the narrator's bookshelf (*At Swim*, 11).

A rather more recent, and a tersely effective, summary is provided by Joseph Brooker (29): 'At Swim-Two-Birds is a novel in which a man writes a novel in which another man writes a novel, whose characters take over the writing of the novel and take revenge upon their author'. From the first page, with its 'examples of three separate openings' (introducing an Irish folk devil, the Pooka MacPhellimey; a Dubliner named Furriskey, 'born at the age of twenty-five'; and Finn MacCool, 'legendary hero of old Ireland': *At Swim*, 9), which follow the initial and much more prosaic opening, 'At Swim-Two-Birds is a book which refuses to be one book' (Brooker, 27).[27] Consequently, as this commentator affirms, or predicts for the reader (ibid.), 'the very absurdity of this world ... will undermine its unity'. On the other hand, from this tripled beginning to a matching triple conclusion, Keith Booker (1995, 28) sees, in Bakhtinian terms, 'the polyphonic multiplicity of the entire text'.

Anne Clissmann writes of three books in all (the narrator's about Dermot Trellis, Trellis's book about 'sin', and his ill-conceived son Orlick's book about his father); adding Flann O'Brien's book about the narrator, 'we have four narratives, one within the other' (Clissmann, 84–5). Joan FitzGerald adds on the element of oral story-telling, to bring the narrative levels up to five, and provides a diagram to illustrate her conception of the narrative structure (FitzGerald, 48–9). A farrago of narratives, styles, extracts, poems, parodies and conflations, *At Swim-Two-Birds*, according to Clissmann's count, in what is frequently seen as textual trellis work, presents 'some thirty-six different styles and forty-two extracts' – from a variety of supposed or actual sources (Clissmann, 86). Kiberd (*Irish Classics*, 502) terms the result 'a set of fragmented narratives, drawn from Celtic Studies, cowboy novels, proletarian balladry, racing tipsters, encyclopedias and modernist literature'.[28]

As if this might not be sufficient, the antics of authorship (or 'a series of flickering ontological levels': Hopper, 112) do not quite stop (or rather begin) there. Moving now upwards from the bottom of the pyramid (or perhaps, rather, a two-dimensional triangle), rebellious and interchangeable characters conspire against their despotic creator (or perhaps rather their 'manager'), Trellis as author, a figure who is himself subservient to his own author – the (unnamed) narrator.[29] As Brooker (36) points out, Orlick Trellis's narrative 'throws the structure ... into reverse', as well as imposing a style of 'ornate and circumlocutory prose'.[30] The whole – including of course the narrator's 'biographical reminiscences', given that the narrator is writing a memoir, as well as a novel – is the work of the implied author of this (as it happens, his first) novel, *At Swim-Two-Birds*: Flann O'Brien. However, as we know (and Richard Kearney, lest we forget, reminds us), the author we know as 'Flann O'Brien' is himself 'a fictional creation – a pseudonym – of the "real" author and Dublin civil servant Brian O'Nolan' (Kearney, 86).

The approach to a novel and its character possibilities is laid out by O'Brien in a much quoted passage from the early stages of *At Swim-Two-Birds*. The 'satisfactory novel', here contrasted with the (theatrical) play, a work for public consumption, is 'self-administered in private' – making it sound more like masturbation, or an enema – and 'should be a self-evident sham to which the reader could regulate at will the degree of his credulity' (*At Swim*, 25).[31] 'Characters', O'Brien (or, rather, his narrator) goes on to say, 'should be interchangeable as between one book and another', with 'the entire corpus of existing literature' an open drawer (or 'limbo') at the disposal of 'discerning authors'; creation of a new 'puppet' should be a last resort. 'The modern novel', consequently, 'should be largely a work of reference' (ibid.).[32] 'That is all my bum' is the reply elicited from Brinsley, the narrator's friend. Tongue in cheek, to a certain extent, all this may be, but a sketch entitled 'Scenes in a Novel' (1934), the 'probably posthumous' swansong of Brother Barnabas, had already floated such notions – of rebellious characters conspiring to assassinate their author (O'Brien, *Myles Before Myles*, 77–81). The 'creation' of Furriskey, 'at the age of twenty-five', as pointed out by McHale (211) is really a normal fictional practice, but is here 'laid bare'. Keith Booker (1995, 39–40) suggests 'a Parody of the Virgin Birth'. Characters can change levels (or 'straddle ontological boundaries': ibid.) within a text, as well as jumping books and authors. However, the idea of 'creation of character' when 'carried to its logical conclusion' may seem 'absurd and fantastic' (Clissmann, 92). Furthermore, as FitzGerald (56–7) suggests, 'when characters become, in a Pirandellian way, free of their author', arguably 'literary creation becomes literary destruction', letting in that result which O'Brien's narrator had claimed would not ensue ('It would be incorrect to say that it would lead to chaos', he affirms: *At Swim*, 25).[33]

The 'work of reference' aspect, to be rather more developed over the years (in both real and spoof terms) in the Myles *Cruiskeen Lawn* columns, is itself here parodied by the use made of borrowed or 'hired' characters, whether from mythological or folkloric sources, or from fictitious works of fiction (such as the Dublin cowboys), rather than the blatant plagiarising of 'actual' fiction (though parody, especially of Joyce, is never ruled out: on this see Clissmann, 106–15). Fictionalised reference sources are also highlighted, such as the supposed multi-volume *A Conspectus of the Arts and Natural Sciences* – a work of no little 'deliberate obscurity'.[34]

What then is to be made of this experimental collation of undermined unity? According to Deane (199), O'Brien, 'along with Beckett, had found his way to the anti-novel as the ideal form in which the romantic conception of the artist-as-hero could finally be dismantled'. Clissmann (121) sees the undercutting of 'realism' in *At Swim-Two-Birds* as central to 'the conventions of the anti-novel', in contrast to products of the 'pure' imagination. Such all-consuming imagination, which denotes 'no exit from the process of writing itself', leads Kearney (84) to think in terms of O'Brien's 'post-novels', with narrative becoming, 'for O'Brien, as for Joyce and Beckett, a questioning of its own conditions of possibility'. It might therefore seem to represent an emblematic signature for metafiction. And indeed it serves as such for Patricia Waugh, who considers that 'in its (to quote Flann O'Brien) "self-evident sham", ... metafiction has merely reduced the complex stylistic manoeuvres of modernism to a set of crude statements about the relation of literary fictions to the real world' – or so, at least, it could seem (Waugh, 26). Any further progression along this road might appear destined to connect with the later O'Brien's harsh, yet unchanging, dismissal of this work as 'juvenile scrivenry' (Clissmann, 82).[35]

Brooker (44) sees *At Swim-Two-Birds* as 'radically open-ended and self-consuming'. Kearney's view too is that, in this novel, 'the snake of fiction curls up and swallows its own tail' (Kearney, 88). Indeed, for him, with *At Swim-Two-Birds*, all but drowning in an authorial sea of pseudonyms and narratorial strategies, the 'real' author's vehement denials of his pseudonymous creations provide, in this respect at least, a prime exemplification of 'Roland Barthes's famous account of the "death of the author" in modern literature' (ibid.), a point reinforced too by Hopper (19; 114–15). In point of fact, Trellis is left as an author 'seriously wounded at the hands of his own creations' (Kiberd, *Irish Classics*, 509), ironically enough, saved from ultimate destruction by an unwitting act of literary arson in another ontological slide (see *At Swim*, 215–16).

The Third Policeman: questions, mysteries, answers?

The step made by Flann O'Brien from *At Swim-Two-Birds* to *The Third Policeman*, within such a short time and remaining unknown within his lifetime, was a gigantic one. Many of the elements that went into the first novel were trimmed and recast into a more limited, and a more disciplined, form in the second. According to Brooker (*F O'B*, 46) in *The Third Policeman* 'complexity of form is replaced by complexity of content'. It might be preferable to say that, in *The Third Policeman*, the relationship of form to content achieves something much closer to a perfect match. Hugh Kenner calls *The Third Policeman* 'something not just brilliant but disturbingly coherent'; the content, which is certainly more concentrated, and arguably more 'serious', than that of the preceding novel, has struck many readers, a number of O'Brien critics included, as of itself 'disturbing', or 'appalling'; moreover, there is speculation that such a feeling may have been shared by Brian O'Nolan himself, and that this may, in some measure at least, account for his failure – indeed his refusal – to do anything further after 1940 towards having the work published.[36]

For a working summary of *The Third Policeman*, we can probably do no better than to quote Keith Hopper (47: albeit with minor amendments).

> The novel opens with (another) nameless narrator announcing that he is a murderer. In a rambling, fragmented account he relates how he and his partner, John Divney, had murdered and robbed a farmer, old Phillip Mathers, for the contents of his mysterious black box. The narrator ... tells us he needed the money to publish the definitive work on an eccentric idiot-genius philosopher known as de Selby. The novel is elliptical in design and it is only at the end of it that the reader discovers that [the narrator] has been dead all along as he narrates his tale; killed by a booby-trapped bomb planted in the black box by Divney. The bulk of the tale concerns [his] punishment at the hands of three absurd policemen; supernatural and devilish characters who inhabit and police 'The Parish', a hell-world of [the narrator's] making. At the end both [the narrator] and the reader understand that he must endure this torment for eternity, repeating his macabre odyssey *ad infinitum*: 'Hell goes round and round. In shape it is circular and by nature it is interminable, repetitive and very nearly ... unbearable'.[37]

Just from this synopsis, we learn that the narrator reveals himself as a murderer (indeed he does this in the very first line of the novel – which must of itself count as an unusual ploy). For the narrator eventually to emerge too (almost at the very end of the work: *TP*, 170) as a murder victim (or, as Martin Amis would prefer, a 'murderee') is probably unprecedented. This inevitably begs questions about the provenance of the narrative of what must already be recognised as something, at the very least, of a metaphysical detective story. The motivation indicated above –

for 'my greatest sin' (*TP*, 9), the burning desire to further what purports to be 'de Selby scholarship' – turns the text equally, if not exactly into what would be called an 'academic novel', at least into something of the 'research novel', as is amply illustrated with the academic-style footnoting (referring to writings by and on de Selby); it is also very much a quest novel (the search for the black box and, at the same time, an 'ontological quest').[38] Hopper (229) confirms 'the popular detective mystery, or "whodunnit"' as 'the central ideological dominant' of O'Brien's novel (using Jakobson's term: see Jakobson, 1987, 41–6), and Brooker (*F O'B*, 50) stresses the turn to the ghost story, and thereby the Gothic – though these points do not, of course, remotely exhaust the ways of discussing *The Third Policeman*.

'"The Parish", a hell-world of [the narrator's] making' is a vital component of the novel requiring further elucidation in any reading. 'The parish' is the term felicitously picked up from the text by Hopper[39] for the 'zone' into which the narrator passes when he leaves old Mathers's house after being, so we much later learn, (unknowingly) blown up.[40] The parish is purportedly situated in close proximity to the area in which the narrator has lived most of his life, and close to the Mathers house, yet up a road in an unfamiliar territory which is to display peculiar properties of landscape, buildings, scientific laws and human conduct. It has something of the Carrollian Wonderland about it (Tigges, 1988; Brooker, *F O'B*, 48; 53), yet remains strangely and perhaps anachronistically Irish: 'an Irish hell' deriving in large part from 'the lost world of an Irish country boyhood where policemen were both burly and threatening', in the words of Francis Doherty (1989, 51).[41] Hopper (140; 190) detects a cinematic quality and borrowings from *The Wizard of Oz* (released 1939). Brooker (*F O'B*, 52) refers to 'a parallel universe where few things work the way they did, and many things happen despite being impossible'. Doherty also sees it as 'a world unknowingly created from himself': 'his own hell, ... it is the land of *his* eternal and unchanging youth' – 'generated from himself, from dreams, fantasies, memories, fictions' (Doherty, 1989, 51; 62; 58).

A yet further, or deeper, zone or dimension is entered in Chapter Eight, when the narrator and Sergeant Pluck take 'the road to eternity' (*TP*, 108) for a brief visit to that location – a portal to which is clandestinely situated within the parish. Here, in this 'underground heaven' (*TP*, 156), the laws of physics (of time, space, light, colour, smell, weight and of wishful acquisition) are completely suspended.[42] As if this post-afterworld were not mind-boggling enough, apparently nothing has been seen yet: '"The next time you come here," MacCruiskeen promised, "you will see surprising things"' (*TP*, 120).

'Only someone who was obsessed with the lunacies of the thinker De Selby [*sic*] could conceive the universe in his terms', remarks Doherty (1989, 57), 'and this is partially what is being conceived'. Referring to his earlier residence, back in the 'real' world, the narrator declares: 'I knew that my own work [on de Selby] was more important than myself' (*TP*, 11). The two things, however, are far from mutually exclusive – and even more so once the narrator (and indeed the reader) enters the parish. This is particularly the case should we choose to follow the lead first established by J.C.C. Mays, who 'deconstructed etymologically' the 'oddness of the name "de Selby" ... as a variation of the German "der Selbe"; meaning "the self"' (Hopper, 208–9).[43] As well as reinforcing elements of, among other things, an 'underlying misogyny and sexual unease', the de Selby 'pseudo-footnotes play a vital autocritical function' (Hopper, 91) in their thematic interplay with the primary text, forming 'a critical commentary on how to read that narrative' (ibid., 184), or even '*in toto* constitute a thirteenth chapter' (185).[44] In any case, they indubitably 'present a parody of the narcissism of scholarly commentary that rivals the hobby-horse phenomenon of Sterne's *Tristram Shandy*' (Keith Booker, 1995, 52).

The narrator's transition into this – at times idyllic, at times horrific – otherworld of the parish is marked by the appearance, or rather just the voice, of 'Joe', coming 'from deep inside me, from my soul' (*TP*, 22), and speaking (on the page) in italics. Joe acts as something of the narrator's (at least marginally) better self, his collected thoughts – as Hopper suggests (261), 'his confidant', or Brooker (*F O'B*, 54), his 'caustic companion'. This is similar to the rather ghoulish 'conversation' that the (also nameless) narrator of Kharms's novella *The Old Woman* has with what he terms 'my own thoughts' (Kharms, *Incidences*, 36) – itself reminiscent of a speculative passage on corpses in Gogol's *Nevsky Prospect*. Joe's appearance, and his threatened and actual disappearance, seemingly, are immediately connected with death. '*When I am gone you are dead*', Joe declares; however, having followed this with '*Goodbye!*', uttered in a fit of pique at any suggestion of his having a scaly body (*TP*, 104), Joe soon in fact pipes up again.

However, following musings on what would be a (second?) death, when it appears that the narrator is about to be hanged, Joe delivers pantheistic murmurings of his own and, when the narrator is dragged to 'the middle of the platform where I knew there was a trapdoor which could be collapsed with machinery', Joe cautions: '*Steady now!*' (*TP*, 140).[45] These are the last words we read from him. It may therefore be that the narrator *has* after all been 'stretched' (once again unknowingly, and whatever meaning that might have in 'hell') and that he must proceed soulless, or 'Joeless', into a further gradation of death;[46] after all, when he later tells Policeman Fox (who affects surprise at his 'unexpected corporality after the morning on the scaffold') – 'I escaped', the retort comes: 'Are you sure?' (*TP*, 158).[47] Some such transitional shift may occur too with the narrator's smashing of the window on his return to the Mathers house, when: 'Nothing happened for a time. Probably it was four or five seconds but it seemed an interminable delay of years' (*TP*, 155). It may be that not only the window was smashed, as the aftermath of this incursion into the Mathers house, and the encounter with Policeman Fox, somehow enables some sort of return (albeit as ghost, and visible only to Divney) to the 'real' world of the novel's opening – although an apparent parish-time of three days has been stretched there to sixteen years. The transitional between-world function of the Mathers house in the overall narrative should be noted here, particularly as, in the 'real' world, we are told, this edifice had been 'blown to bits' (*TP*, 170). Yet a further phase appears to have been reached at the end, when the narrator emerges from a state of mind 'completely void' to again 'noticing my own existence and taking account of my surroundings' (*TP*, 171) – back in the parish, this time joined by Divney, to engage again with the weird architecture of the barracks and to encounter again 'an enormous policeman' – and to be greeted again with the question: 'Is it about a bicycle?' (*TP*, 172).

   In both cases, in a sense, it was, or at least it could have been 'about a bicycle'. On the second occasion, as Tigges (1988, 213) points out, the answer should be 'yes', because the narrator has indeed lost a bicycle – the Sergeant's flirtatious 'female' bicycle – 'the one we assume is again now behind lock and key in the police station'. Even on the first occasion the answer could, or perhaps should, have been 'yes' (had bicycles been properly uppermost in mind) – as, for what difference it may have made, the narrator and Divney had 'walked the distance' to the Mathers house, ostensibly to retrieve the black box, as 'my own bicycle was punctured' (*TP*, 18). Moreover, when the interface between these zones, or worlds, is under consideration, interference with bicycles at the instigation of the police barracks, even at this stage, perhaps cannot be ruled out. If bicycles are of some, albeit limited, importance in the 'real' world, and according to Hopper (57) 'the bicycle is also a metonymic discourse of repressed sexuality and Catholic catharsis' in new post-colonial Ireland, by the time we get to the parish, bicycles have in themselves almost become the dominant. 'Bicycles have become not only a constant', declares Doherty (1989, 60); 'they are a monomaniacal obsession'.[48]

   If 'bicycle' may be something of a coded term in *The Third Policeman* (see Hopper, 94–8), it is by no means the only one. We have already encountered such usage of the term 'parish'. In addition, Hopper regards 'house' as 'a recurrent self-reflexive metaphor for the textual frame' or 'a metonymic code-word for "text"' (Hopper, 116; 120). 'Box' he sees as 'a metaphor for book', and 'black box' indeed as a (Faustian) 'book of knowledge, with the power to manipulate all the other puppet-characters of the text, including the other policemen' (ibid., 142; 149)'. 'Hammering' (ostensibly of a carpenter erecting the scaffold) is seen as metafictional hammering at the keys of a typewriter – 'the sound of the invisible author' (ibid., 136).

In addition to coded words, there are (and again in addition to 'bicycle') words which may become textual motifs. One prominent example is the word 'gold' or 'golden', first occurring in the title of de Selby's book *Golden Hours* (*TP*, 8) – of which Brooker (*F O'B*, 58) remarks: 'these ought to be rustic memoirs, not philosophical tracts'. The de Selby project, Divney flatters the narrator, 'might make your name in the world and your golden fortune in copyrights?' (*TP*, 13). The non-possession, or 'loss', of an 'American gold watch' is adopted as a diversionary tactic (from the end of Chapter Two) – and is perhaps the 'lie which was responsible for the bad things that happened to me afterwards' (*TP*, 32). A supposed sovereign (in fact a 'bright penny') is given to the narrator, *en route* to the barracks, by the one-legged Martin Finnucane as 'the golden token of your golden destiny' (*TP*, 42). The gold watch is speculatively transformed into 'a golden bicycle' (*TP*, 54) – a prospect not to be sneezed at, as, by means of the miraculous substance known as 'omnium' (and administered by Policeman Fox), the narrator conjectures: 'I would present every poor labourer in the world with a bicycle made of gold' (*TP*, 163).[49] In the dreary hellish whirligig of the parish, however, such anticipation is presumably no more substantive than the gold bars the narrator can acquire in, but cannot remove from, 'eternity'. There is, however, given the publishing history of *The Third Policeman*, an ironic metafictional note struck, when Policeman MacCruiskeen (whose name is also clearly noteworthy) remarks on 'the no-bicycle' as 'a story that would make your golden fortune if you wrote down in a book where people could pursue it literally' (*TP*, 61).

Hopper (198), as the title of his study suggests, wishes to regard *The Third Policeman* 'as an early post-modernist novel' – indeed, as its 'first great masterpiece' (ibid., 15). The catch-all nature of postmodernism leads him to read this novel largely in terms of metafiction – a category in which he discerns a certain 'shamanism' and 'a self-conscious awareness of its own intertextuality' – and a label he prefers to 'anti-novel' (Hopper, 4; 8–9); however he brings to bear as well the tools of Formalism, such as 'defamiliarisation' (ibid., 23–4), though with particular reference to O'Brien – and, say, bicycles – seeks 'an Irish brand of formalism' (56). This extends to reading the novel as Menippean satire, and discerning a polyphonic composition (the narrator 'interprets language monologically; the reader is invited to read it dialogically': 211), with elements of carnivalisation. Keith Booker (1995, 46–65), in a study published in the same year as Hopper's, also adopts a Menippean approach, noting the Bakhtinian view that 'carnivalesque representations of hell are particularly subversive of religious (especially Catholic) authority' (Booker, 1995, 60, n.).[50]

A Freudian reading, as such, does not appear to have been advanced. However, Doherty (1989) does put forward rudimentary building blocks for at least the inclusion of psychoanalysis among the range of theoretical approaches conceivably applicable to *The Third Policeman*. The 'new world' in which the narrator 'now invents himself as well as finds himself' comes, Doherty stresses (1989, 58), as already noted above, from his dreams, fantasies and memories, and is a reversion to a lost, though now scarred, world of childhood innocence. Furthermore, Doherty suggests (without taking it further): 'the killing of the man with the box, "old Mathers," is the killing of a combined mother and father, the compounded plural "Mathers," not a difficult task for Myles na Gopaleen of *Cruiskeen Lawn*' (ibid., 57). Such an argument may be strengthened if we note the eventual appearance of the elusive third policeman, whose 'great fat body in the uniform did not remind me of anyone I knew' – but *the face at the top of it belonged to old Mathers*' (*TP*, 158: the italics are in the original, but no longer, at this stage, attributable to 'Joe'). Doherty thus summarises the significance of this development:

> Killing Mathers [i.e. his parents] isolates the narrator from all mankind, leaving him only his victim and heavenly-hellish policemen, his conscience, his dreams of success, his obsession with the alternative physical system of de Selby, and neither God nor Devil, Heaven nor conventional Hell. (Doherty, 1989, 58)

The doubling of Mathers and the third policeman, it may be added, may take on a particular significance, given the latter's (perhaps otherwise puzzling) name of 'Policeman Fox': 'Fox' being (normally) neither a comic nor a common Irish name, but plausibly here evoking the Dublin pronunciation of a word O'Brien could not (and would not) have used in print.[51]

As allusions to *Alice in Wonderland* and other details may suggest, *The Third Policeman* has been seen as essentially a nonsense, or a 'non-sense', work (see the commentaries by José Lanters and Wim Tigges).[52] Tigges (1988, 216) places *The Third Policeman* in the nonsense category 'mainly because' of the 'constant shifting and reshifting of perspectives', concluding that 'O'Brien displays just sufficient playfulness in this novel to keep it from crossing over into the absurd, and just enough inconsistency to prevent it from becoming a fantasy'; nevertheless, it is clear to him that 'we have reached the borders of nonsense'. Furthermore he acknowledges 'the policemen's world' to be 'a Sisyphus-like round of punishment (or guilt)' (ibid., 214). Clissmann (354–5, n. 23) compares the circularity of O'Brien's novel with Sartre's *Huis Clos* and quotes Esslin and Hinchliffe to establish affinities with Theatre of the Absurd. This is noted by Doherty (1989, 52) who extends the suggestion to bring in *Nausea* and Beckett's *Watt*, remarking on the proximity of composition between Sartre's novel and the first two novels by both O'Brien and Beckett. Keith Booker (1995, 125) discerns 'an air of absurdity (and of pessimism) that immediately suggests the world of Kafka', proceeding (128 ff) to draw parallels in particular with *The Castle*. Hopper (72) regards O'Brien as 'an exponent of absurdist humour' who is 'firmly implanted within a certain Irish tradition of cruel humour' (the last propensity allying him, as already noted, with Kharms).

A more solid case for considering *The Third Policeman* as a work of the absurd, however, can perhaps be built upon three main foundation blocks: the structure of the novel, its use of language and the work's overall impact. '*The Third Policeman* is a novel in a constant state of internal contradiction', remarks Hopper (170). The novel has 'a structural reflection in the "strange loop" which turns [it] into an endlessly repeating cycle' (ibid., 250–1). The 'loop' may be seen as operating linguistically between the two instances of the question, '"Is it about a bicycle?" he asked' (*TP*, 48; 172), or, perhaps more plausibly, between the 'deaths', or transitions between worlds, occurring with the narrator himself (blown up in Chapter Two) and the demise of Divney (joining him on the last page, leading up to the second asking of the question). Circular as this process is frequently held to be, it is not, as may already be clear, quite as precise, or as simple, as that. As Brooker points out (*F O'B*, 51–2), 'the book does not describe a perfect circle'; the first complication is the second-time-round entrance of Divney into the parish, which must inevitably alter the ensuing progression(s) to some degree; secondly, there is a 'hidden non-sense of its structure', in that the story itself is narrated in the past tense (from somewhere, from some time) by a narrator seemingly deprived of previous experience – a situation, arguably, 'not possible within the novel's own terms'. Similarly, David Cohen remarks that the story must be 'written well after the events described' (viz. the de Selby footnotes, for a start) with a consequent logical 'impossibility of the narrative'.[53]

A narrative with a provenance from the afterlife (whether the 'dead', the 'double-dead' or even the 'completely dead') may be indicative of a work of nonsense, or a work of the absurd (*The Third Policeman* was itself, of course, published posthumously, but that is not quite the same thing). A feeling of the absurd is heightened virtually throughout the novel by the nature of, and the variations in, O'Brien's use of language: whether in dialogue (the eccentric register of the policemen's speech; and the narrator's attempts to approach their wavelength), the narrator's own essentially neutral though variable narrative tone, the mock-scholarly discourse of the de Selby notes, or the description of the indescribable ('at the limits of language': Brooker, *F O'B*, 55) and the invisible – a novelistic world beset with 'deliberately awkward, ceaselessly estranging diction' (ibid., 59), with a content to match. The 'most casual remarks' of the policemen, O'Brien wrote in a letter of 1939, 'create a thousand other mysteries' (cited by Hopper, 260). The writing of O'Brien, as of Kafka and Beckett, arises, according to Keith Booker (1995, 133) from the 'failure of language' to communicate a 'paradoxical perception that the modern world is both hopelessly banal and irreducibly strange'. Booker (131–2) argues that the suggestions of imperialism and patriarchy informing their works, provoke 'problematic communication' within 'the absurd worlds' depicted by O'Brien, Kafka and Beckett (in particular *The Third Policeman*, *The Castle* and *Watt*), alongside the 'overt implication of imperialism' to be found in another novel 'based on a quest for epistemological closure that remains unsolved': namely Conrad's *Heart of Darkness* – a work also discussed earlier in the present book. Incommunicability, and a recognition of 'the infinitely self-referential nature of all knowledge' (ibid., 58–9), whether indicated by peering inside Policeman MacCruiskeen's fantastic boxes (as Policeman Fox is said to have done), or parading a 'brain-destroying bicycle' daubed in MacCruiskeen's ineffable colour of abysmal paint (*TP*, 143) – or just the fathoming of questions that cannot be answered – can lead to immediate insanity.[54]

In terms of impact, *The Third Policeman* strikes on a number of fronts. The 'shamanistic world-view', according to Hopper (9) can affect even 'our belief in "objective" science, itself deconstructed in *The Third Policeman* as a paradigmatic language game'. The result is 'an abstracted poetry of estrangement, adrift in a chaotic universe' (ibid.) – and this in itself provides a very fair description of an artistic work of the absurd. 'The comic *reductio*' in this novel, Clissmann considers (181), 'tends to lead to the world of the absurd'; but, she adds, 'this was a world in which O'Brien was unable to live for very long'. Most O'Brien commentators, such as Clissmann and Cronin, stress his continued Catholicism. 'The book's vision of Eternity', according to Kenner (71), 'was subversive and devoid of hope' – and any hope in the book 'consisted of pantheistic yearnings'.

O'Brien (or at least O'Nolan), as already suggested, had his own difficulties with this. Kenner (ibid.) sees the author's conscience as a 'Fourth Policeman', putting a stop to such trespassings. As almost a final written word (in 1966), he wrote of the quandary of looking 'sanely at the awful human condition' (quoted by Cronin, 248). Critics too, as previously noted, have their difficulties. Kenner (69) confesses to displaying 'the absurdity of any attempt to interpret'; while Hopper (228) talks of the smug ivory-tower triumphalism of 'the critic ... having successfully reduced the novel to an allegorical heap of ashes'.

Finally, let us return to the murder story element already discerned as the 'dominant' of *The Third Policeman*. Hopper (261) remarks that the narrator, as 'the arch-materialist, personifies the eccentric amateur detective, with Joe as his confidant'. Reinforcement for such an emphasis is abundant enough from within the text. In the bicycle recovery expedition, Sergeant Pluck refers to 'our mission of private detection and smart policework' (*TP*, 68), while the successful 'detective-work' is efficiently accomplished through the Sergeant's dual capacity as stealer and detector of bicycles (*TP*, 71). Reporting another non-theft (this time of a bicycle lamp) later to Policeman Fox, the narrator is told: 'what may seem unimportant to yourself might well give a wonderful clue to the trained investigator' (*TP*, 159). The idea of the persona of the sleuth, however, enters too the narrator's own mind. Among the possible names for him put forward by the Sergeant, are the suggestive 'Joseph Poe or Nolan?' (*TP*, 87). These options, like all others, are rejected; however, Joe relaxes at the absence among the proposed names of '*J. Courtney Wain, private investigator and member of the inner bar. Eighteen thousand guineas marked on the brief. The singular case of the red-headed men*' (*TP*, 88).

Regardless of the significance pertaining to the last name (and the allusion to a – relatively absurdist – Sherlock Holmes story referred to in Chapter 6 above), the mooted cluster of 'Joseph' (Joe: the narrator's 'soul'), 'Poe' (as in Edgar Allan) and 'Nolan' (the ultimate author of *The Third Policeman*) assumes particular interest in the present context. What is regarded as 'analytic detective fiction', said to originate with Poe's Dupin tales of the 1840s, may be opposed to subsequent 'adventure' thrillers, seen as a revival of 'quest romance'.[55] *The Third Policeman*, as already observed, would appear to subsume – much else apart – elements from both types. We have already compared the treatment, or abandonment, of the novel's typescript to the tactic employed in Poe's classic Dupin story *The Purloined Letter*; in what by now may seem almost a frame-breaking play on Poe. In terms of art, superficial structural comparisons, at least, can be made between *The Third Policeman* and *The Purloined Letter*: involving an unnamed narrator (though Poe's storyteller is merely that, and not the protagonist), one-upmanship (between Divney and the narrator; and between the policemen), police operations, doubled characters and scenes, lost (purloined or not purloined) objects: be it a (refolded) letter in Poe, or a (tampered with) black box, gold watch or bicycle in O'Brien, and an overall implication of circular, or rather spiral, (potentially eternal) continuation.[56] Poe's precious purloined letter was scrunched into 'a trumpery fillagree card-rack of paste-board' that hung just beneath the mantelpiece – a document 'full in the view of every visitor'.[57] In terms of life, it is as though Brian O'Nolan were deliberately leaving out his supposedly lost novel for eventual purloining, by a *facteur de la vérité* (in this case his widow, Evelyn O'Nolan) – for the purpose of posthumous publication. According to Lacan, 'a letter always arrives at its destination'; however, Derrida reminds us that 'it belongs to the structure of the letter to be capable, always, of not arriving'.[58] The same may go for novels; Keith Booker (1995, 138) notes parallels between the publishing fates of *The Third Policeman* and Bulgakov's *The Master and Margarita* – the novel in which the claim is made that 'manuscripts do not burn'.

Notes

1 Claud Cockburn, 'Introduction' to O'Brien, *Stories and Plays*, 9; Anne Clissmann, *Flann O'Brien*, 10.

2 The English version of *The Poor Mouth* (published London: Hart-Davis, MacGibbon Ltd, 1973), is however attributed to Flann O'Brien, and is translated from the Irish by Patrick C. Power. A number of Irish commentators (including Seamus Deane and Declan Kiberd) count this 'subversive anti-pastoral' (Kiberd, 1996, 498) as one of O'Brien's two, or three, major works. For a note on the originals of 'Myles' see Robert Tracy's introduction to O'Brien, *Rhapsody*, 2; Kiberd, 1996, 497–8.

3 A list of writings for television is included in the bibliography of his works in Anne Clissmann's *Flann O'Brien*, 1975, 359–65 (361–3). See also John Wyse Jackson's 'Primary Bibliography' in Clune and Hurson (1997), 185–6; the fullest 'Secondary Bibliography' is that by Anne Clune [Clissmann] in the same volume (187–230).

4 O'Brien's travels, or their lack, are one of a number of mysteries. On O'Brien in Germany see Cronin, 67–70, who states that it is 'probably the only journey outside Ireland he ever made' (70). See also, though, Costello and van de Kamp, 45–50, who refer to multiple visits to that country. For that matter, Clissmann (24; 80) claims various trips made by O'Brien to England, Europe and New York.

5 Quoted by Cronin, 54. Clissmann (1) gives the main subsidiary pseudonyms as 'John James Doe, George Knowall, Brother Barnabas and Great Count O'Blather' (the latter being also 'Blazes Blather', or more commonly just 'The O'Blather'); there were a number of others. Biographical material is here taken largely from Cronin; O'Brien's principal biographer, Anthony Cronin (a personal friend, though a generation younger) was subsequently to write a biography of Beckett.

6 One sympathises, however, with Joseph Brooker when, early in his study (Brooker, *F O'B*, 4), he declares: 'I shall not . . . refer to him as "O'Brien" throughout, because I want to register the multiplicity of his names, and the elusiveness of the personality that this implies' (on O'Nolan's names see Brooker, 4–6).

7 See Tracy's 'Introduction' to the Lilliput edition, in the 'Essays and Texts in Cultural History' ('ETCH VI'): O'Brien, *Rhapsody*. This production is sometimes said to have taken place at the Gaiety (even by the same commentator: see also Clissmann, 23; 260). According to Costello and van de Kamp (82), it was produced by the Gate Company and ran at the Gaiety Theatre.

8 'Kharms and Myles: An Afterword', Daniil Kharms, *The Plummeting Old Women*, translated by Neil Cornwell, Dublin: Lilliput, 1989 ('ETCH III'), 93–100. The Kharms translations in this volume were subsequently absorbed into the expanded volume: Kharms, *Incidences* (London: Serpent's Tail, 1993).

9 'The chief source for *The Insect Play*, as Karel Čapek acknowledged, was *La Vie des insectes* (1910)', extracted from *Souvenirs etymologiques* (1879–1907) by Jean-Henri Fabre: Tracy (*Rhapsody*, 8). The Irish War of Independence lasted from 1919–1921; this was followed by the Irish Civil War, 1922–23. Brooker (in his *F O'B*, 8–11) provides a concise historical background to the emerging O'Brien.

10 Elsewhere, we are informed: 'Mr Myles na gCopaleen has left town (i.e. Moscow) for two weeks' (O'Brien, *At War*, 168). For that matter, a column also appeared in the *Irish Times* in that (wartime) period (in fact written by the Editor, R.M. Smyllie) under the purported authorship of 'Nichevo' (ibid., 135) – presumably deriving from the Russian word *nichego* (pronounced 'nichevo': meaning 'nothing').

11 On this apparently vexed issue see Cronin, 198–201; and Costello and van de Kamp, 64; 89; 95 (on Stephen Blakesley thrillers).

12 Maxton (97) reminds us of another Kharmsian pose – that of his (fictitious) brother – and of Sherlock's brother, Mycroft Holmes. For a photograph, in which 'D. Kharms depicts his own non-existent brother Ivan Ivanovich Kharms, former *privat-dotsent*, St Petersburg University, 1930s' see Kharms, *Polet v nebesa*, 352. On Kharms and Holmes see Chapter 6. The use of the figure of 'The Brother', especially by Myles in his columns, but also by O'Brien in *The Hard Life* (1961), has become legendary. The story *John Duffy's Brother*, however (1941), while opening with an unusual treatment of the brother theme, is largely concerned with a man's belief that he is a train (*Stories and Plays*, 73–80). For another fraternal variant see Robert Coover's 'The Brother' (*Pricksongs & Descants*, 92–8). Note may also be taken of Willem de Kooning's pencil drawing *Self-Portrait with Imaginary Brother* (1938), cited in Paul Auster's novel *Oracle Night* (2004).

13 In addition to alluding to the culture of the ancient Ionian city of Miletus, 'Milesian', in Irish mythology, refers to 'a member of a group of people from a royal Spanish family who invaded Ireland about 1300 BC and became the ancestors of the modern Irish', named after Milesius, their legendary head (*Encarta World English Dictionary*).

14 Even this, though is not exactly certain. Costello and van de Kamp (115) refer to O'Brien dragging the novel out and having it read again (in 1958 or 1959); cf. Cronin (e.g. 208), who makes no mention of such an action.

15 On O'Brien's ambivalent attitudes to Joyce see Cronin (passim, but particularly 172–6; 247); Clissmann, 220–4; M. Keith Booker, 1991, 79–84; 1995, 11–16 and passim.

16 Selections from the 'Cruiskeen Lawn' columns are to be found in various collections, including Myles na Gopaleen (Flann O'Brien), *The Best of Myles*, edited by Kevin O'Nolan, London: Picador, 1977 (first published 1968); Flann O'Brien, *The Various Lives of Keats and Chapman and The Brother*, London and Dublin: Scribner/Townhouse, 2003 (first published 1976); O'Brien, *At War*.

17 On Joyce in *The Dalkey Archive* see Clissmann, 306–16. Deane (195) also links the 'out of time' conversations of De Selby with the early Church fathers, including notably St Augustine, with James Augustine Joyce. And, indeed, Joyce and St Augustine are mentioned together, in terms of 'side by side monasticism and brothelism', in the first Bloomsday *Cruiskeen Lawn* column (reproduced in Costello and van de Kamp, 16).

18 Benedict Kiely: quoted by Cockburn, in *Stories and Plays*, 13.

19 Ibid. Conversely, he was also held to be a 'poor conversationalist' (quoted in Clissmann, 2).

20 Kiberd (1996, 512) takes this further, to distinguish between 'Myles na

gCopaleen', the 'original' columnist and author of *The Poor Mouth* (in the character of whom 'O'Nolan rescues the buffoon from the Victorian stage and makes him articulate': ibid., 497), and (the subsequent) 'Myles na Gopaleen' – 'the fatal clown, the licensed jester, who lurked within O'Nolan, whom he roundly despised but whom he could never fully suppress'.

21 For a similar view see Steven Young, 'Fact/Fiction: Cruiskeen Lawn, 1945–66', in Clune and Hurson, 111–18.

22 Costello and van de Kamp (71) reprint the words and music of the song 'Cruiskeen Lawn' from Boucicault's play *The Colleen Bawn* (1860), one of the main sources for 'Myles'. For a rounded appreciation of the Myles columns see Brooker's chapter 'Local Unaesthetic: *Cruiskeen Lawn*', in his *F O'B*, 87–108.

23 For a sympathetic and carnivalistic reading of this novel see Keith Booker's chapter, 'O'Brien's Final Critique of Authorities' (Booker, 1995, 105–20). Hopper, however, while also discerning Menippean satire in O'Brien's fiction, regards *The Dalkey Archive* as 'a pilfered pastiche of disparate thematic elements from *The Third Policeman*, re-cast in a new context' – though some elements at least are seen as 'devoid of any context' (Hopper, 40; 50–1).

24 This collection also includes three variant passages originally intended for *At Swim-Two-Birds* (O'Brien, *Myles Before Myles*, 178–85).

25 See O'Brien, *Myles Before Myles*, 253. According to Kiberd (*Irish Classics*, 501), this dissertation, applying 'the fashionable modernist ideas of T.S. Eliot and Ezra Pound' to 'ancient Gaelic verse', is 'a dismal job which would hardly pass muster today', its author 'clearly holding his best energies in check for writing of a more creative kind'.

26 Jorge Luis Borges, 'Cuando la ficción vive en la ficción' ['When Fiction Lives in Fiction'], *El Hogar* [Home], 2 June 1939. Reprinted in *Textos cautivos*, 1986 (see notes to Borges, *TL*, 533). Although 'the student' tells his friend (Brinsley) 'I was talking to a friend of yours last night, I said drily. I mean Mr Trellis' (*At Swim*, 34–5), his intercourse with Trellis is purely through pen and paper; neither the primary narrator nor his student friends (on that story-telling level) make an appearance at the Red Swan Hotel (Trellis's licensed premises).

27 Even before the novel's opening page (*At Swim*, 9), comes the mock disclaimer: 'All characters represented in this book, including the first person singular, are entirely fictitious and bear no relation to any person living or dead'. This is followed by an epigraph in Greek, meaning 'all things naturally draw apart and give place to one another': Euripides, *Heracles*, line 104 (also known as *Heracles Mainomenos*, or *The Madness of Heracles*; referred to as *Hercules Furens* by Kiberd, *Irish Classics*, 502); the Latin formulation is considered 'a solecistic backformation' from the Seneca play of that title. It should perhaps be noted that O'Brien's brother (Kevin O'Nolan) was a classicist, becoming Professor of Greek at University College Dublin. I am grateful to Paul Cartledge for classical advice.

28 The 'Dublin cowboys' had been prefigured in *Blather* (O'Brien, *Myles Before Myles*, 159).

29 Seeing the (non)identification of O'Brien's narrators as potentially confusing, some commentators choose to bestow a label on them: thus, for instance, Borges, FitzGerald and Brooker (reasonably enough, perhaps) refer to the

primary narrator of *At Swim-Two-Birds* as 'the student'; Hopper calls his counterpart of *The Third Policeman* 'Noman' (47 and passim).

30 Like *At Swim-Two-Birds* itself, Orlick's story begins three times; however, in this case, the first two paragraphs are identical each time (*At Swim*, 164, 169–70, 172).

31 Cf. also Kiberd (*Irish Classics*, 507): 'a writing that takes on the quality of furtive, jeopardized masturbation'.

32 Such an at least ostensibly cavalier attitude to literary composition makes one wonder whether an awareness of another 'F. O'Brien' played any part in O'Nolan's choice of pen-name: the Irish-American writer of fantastic tales Fitz-James O'Brien (1828–62) went in for literary 'borrowing' in at least some of his works. On this see the present author's 'Piracy and Higher Realism: The Strange Case of Fitz-James O'Brien and Vladimir Odoevsky' (Neil Cornwell, *Vladimir Odoevsky and Romantic Poetics: Collected Essays*, Providence and Oxford: Berghahn, 1998, 157–67).

33 Such a (what we would now identify as Kharmsian, though at greater length) story destruction is also pointed to by Kearney (85): 'the reader … is witnessing not a story but the problematic creation (and destruction) of a story'.

34 See Sue Asbee, '*At Swim-Two-Birds*: Readers and Literary Reference', in Clune and Hurson, 53–6.

35 Cf. the *Times Literary Supplement* (18 March 1939): 'a schoolboy brand of mild vulgarity', quoted by Hopper (88), who offers a revealing analysis of such traits in *At Swim-Two-Birds* (85–92) and elsewhere in O'Brien. Borges, however, back in 1939 (*TL*, 162), had concluded his observations on *At Swim-Two-Birds* by declaring: 'Arthur Schopenhauer wrote that dreaming and wakefulness are the pages of a single book, and that to read them in order is to live, and to leaf through them at random, to dream. Paintings within paintings and books that branch into other books help us sense this oneness.'

36 Hugh Kenner, 'The Fourth Policeman', in Clune and Hurson, 70–1. Doherty (1989, 51) calls it 'a comic and appalling book'. See too, for instance, Brooker, *F O'B*, 47; and Wyse Jackson (O'Brien, *At War*, 7), on whom the book (while being 'his best and funniest') 'had so strange and disturbing an effect on me that in the end I swore never to read it again'.

37 In fact, the booby-trapping may not be exactly as here stated: what had been planted 'was not the black box but a mine, a bomb' (*TP*, 170); the 'presence' of the black box thus remains unclear, in apparent contradiction of the original account (see *TP*, 20). The excisions in this synopsis are to avoid Hopper's irritating and repeated designation of the narrator as 'Noman'. Brooker (*F O'B*, 49) similarly sees fit to dub him 'Anon'. The final sentence (in quotation marks) comes from the 'Publisher's Note' (*TP*, 173; and in this edition, at least, without an ellipsis) said by Hopper (55, n. 65) to be an 'unpublished excerpt from initial draft manuscript'.

38 See Merivale and Sweeney (18; 20); the 'research novel' is seen as originating with Henry James's *The Aspern Papers* (18). See the essays therein by Sweeney and Jeanne C. Ewart. Indeed, the latter's '"A Thousand Other Mysteries": Metaphysical Detection, Ontological Quest' (179–98) highlights *The Third Policeman* in this regard (179; 189–90).

39 Hopper, 92 and passim. See, for instance *TP*, 58: Policeman MacCruiskeen

'began questioning me about my arrival in the parish'.

40 Cf. Doherty (1989, 56): 'But the "moment" of his death is not known to the narrator.'

41 On Irishness here see also Kenner, 64–5. Clissmann (239) nevertheless sees *The Third Policeman* as 'the least "Irish" of [O'Brien's] books'.

42 For 'scientific' readings of this novel see Charles Kemnitz, 'Beyond the Zone of Middle Dimensions: A Relativistic Reading of *The Third Policeman*', *Irish University Review*, 15:1 (1985), 56–72; and Mary A. O'Toole, 'The Theory of Serialism in *The Third Policeman*', *Irish University Review*, 18:2 (1988), 215–25.

43 Clissmann (352, n. 5) links de Selby with Des Esseintes, the protagonist of *À Rebours* (1884) by J.-K. Huysmans (see also Hopper, 96–7; 127–8). De Selby's 'ideology' is compared with the ideas of J.W. Dunne (Clissmann, 292; Hopper, 248), as is Sergeant Pluck's 'Mollycule Theory' (on O'Brien and Dunne see Hopper, 241–50). Hopper (261) also lists Anaximander, Aristotle, Vico, Wittgenstein, Einstein, Walter Shandy and Slawkenbergius among the philosophical/literary 'suspects' discerned in the 'composite character of de Selby' and/or parodied in the novel. Keith Booker (1995, 51) brings in Zeno, and Bergson's commentaries thereon.

44 The de Selby footnotes, spread over eight of the chapters, from numbers 2 to 11, are subjected to a revealingly close reading by Hopper (179–96).

45 This phrase may be compared with that used to ease Hugh Person into the otherworld, in the final words of Nabokov's *Transparent Things* (1972): 'Easy, you know, does it, son'.

46 The Sergeant's words: 'If you are going to be dead completely . . .' (*TP*, 106: cf. the conjuring with being 'completely dead' noted previously in this book) seem to support the idea of gradations of death and/or afterlife.

47 'Take left turns as much as possible', the Sergeant had instructed the narrator in Dantesque infernal fashion (*TP*, 53); 'it was leftwards that all my troubles were' (and 'to that quarter the next world lay'), the narrator recognises, in his 'escape' from the barracks, and so turns 'resolutely to the right' (*TP*, 150) – in the direction of spectral transition back to the 'real' world.

48 On bicycles in O'Brien and Beckett see Booker, 1991; and 1995 (chapter 2).

49 Policeman Fox, however, appears concerned only with using this substance for the most mundane of 'miracles' – bringing him close to the abstaining miracle-worker of Kharms's *The Old Woman*.

50 As an Appendix, Booker (1995, 143–50) lists Bakhtin's fourteen characteristics of Menippean satire, with brief comments on the display of each in O'Brien's works. Booker (60, n. 19) suggests too a comparison with Dante's *Inferno* 'which is heavily informed with interpretive confusion'.

51 Though O'Nolan was much given to the use of it in Dublin life (Cronin, 186, reports O'Nolan's departure from the Civil Service 'in a final fanfare of fucks'); O'Brien would certainly have known that '*Fuchs*' (German for 'fox') is a surname and may have been aware of its Czech spelling as 'Fuks'. Like Beckett, O'Brien appeared to have a liking for the word 'ineffable' (see for instance *TP*, 21): noted by Doherty (1989, 56). The other policemen's names tend towards the comic: 'Sergeant Pluck'; 'Inspector O'Corky'. 'Policeman MacCruiskeen' by now needs no further comment.

52 José Lanters, '"Still Life" versus Real Life: The English Writings of Brian O'Nolan', in Tigges, 1987, 161–81; and Wim Tigges, 'Flann O'Brien', in Tigges, 1988, 205–16.

53 David Cohen, 'Arranged by Wise Hands: Flann O'Brien's Metafictions', in Clune and Hurson, 57–60 (60).

54 Keith Booker (1995) links such notions to the ideas of Nietzsche and Heisenberg, 'that our access to Truth is belated and indirect, caught in a loop of self-reference' (56); and, with an 'emphasis on questions as opposed to answers', to Richard Rorty's 'hermeneutics' (61).

55 See John T. Irwin, 'Mysteries We Reread, Mysteries of Rereading: Poe, Borges, and the Analytic Detective Story', in Merivale and Sweeney, 27–54 (27).

56 *The Purloined Letter* has an (unidentified and possibly unidentifiable) epigraph from Seneca ('*Nil sapientiae odiosius acumine nimio*': 'Nothing is more hateful to wisdom than excessive cleverness') – a quotation likely to appeal to O'Brien. For a meta-reading of *The Purloined Letter*, as another twirl of the screw previously turned in celebrated essays (of a largely psychoanalytical persuasion) by Lacan, Derrida and Barbara Johnson, see Irwin's discussion (in Merivale and Sweeney, 27–41). See also in the same volume Joel Black's comments (75–80) in his '(De)feats of Detection: The Spurious Key Text from Poe to Eco' (75–98). Irwin (41–52) considers that Borges, in his three detective stories (published almost exactly a century after those of Poe), is to a degree 'rewriting' *The Purloined Letter*.

57 'The Purloined Letter', *Complete Stories and Poems of Edgar Allan Poe*, Garden City, New York: Doubleday, 1966, 125–38 (136; 137).

58 Jacques Derrida, 'Le Facteur de la vérité', in his *The Post Card: From Socrates to Freud and Beyond*, translated by Alan Bass, Chicago and London: University of Chicago Press, 1987, 411–96 (443–4).

IV

In conclusion

10

Beyond the absurd?

It made as much sense as anything else ... (Joseph Heller, *Catch-22*, 1961)

There were answers everywhere you *looked*. There was no question about it ... (Tom Stoppard, *Rosencrantz and Guildenstern Are Dead*, 1967)

The prosaic absurd?

A survey of the absurd in prose writing of the second half of the twentieth century, unless, or until, accorded a full book-length study in itself, is inevitably going to be selective, inadequate and arbitrary. The present concluding chapter to this book can be no exception in that sense – especially as some consideration will then be given to some of the more recent developments in drama, as well as brief reference made to certain popular, theoretical and general areas.

Boris Vian

According to James Sallis, in postwar Paris (just as Theatre of the Absurd was under way, we might add, and Beckett was converting himself into a French writer): 'The lack of meaning in it all, the way events just happen – that zero at the centre – was very much in the air, simmering into existentialism on Left Bank stoves' (Vian, *I Spit*, viii). The jazz trumpeter, actor and writer Boris Vian was then becoming 'a kind of guru sans portfolio, but with clown hat provided – in the College of Pataphysics' (ibid., xi–xii).[1] Vian was indeed a contributor to absurdist theatre, in particular with his play *Les Bâtisseurs d'Empire* (*The Empire Builders*, 1959: see Esslin, *Th. Abs.*, 274–7).

An early novel of Vian's, *I Spit on Your Graves* (*J'irai cracher sur vos tombes*, 1946) is notable as an absurdist work perhaps more for the bizarre circumstances which surround it than for its actual content, which has been aptly described by the comment that it 'borders on trash while fondling literature and winking at pornography' (ibid., xi). Everything about it has been likened to distorting mirrors, in which the image grows increasingly grotesque, but – and more particularly: 'Mirrors too, because we have a white man (Vian) pretending to be a black man (Sullivan) writing a novel about a black man (Lee Anderson) pretending to be white' (x). In a first-person narrative, that eventually turns (perforce) to the third person, the protagonist (the last named figure) seduces and murders two sisters from a wealthy white family in revenge for the lynching of his brother. Vian's rather nasty confessional thriller, written for a bet, was launched as a mock-translation (supposedly the work of a black American called Vernon Sullivan). *I Spit on Your Graves* managed a curious array of achievements: it became a bestseller, it gave rise to protracted legal action, and it appears to have occasioned at least one copycat murder – before being banned. Three more 'Sullivan' novels followed, as well as contracts to do actual translations (from such authors as Raymond Chandler and James M. Cain). Finally, however, Vian died from a heart attack (at the age of thirty-nine) suffered after sneaking in to the preview of a screen version of that very novel – details of the adaptation of which incensed him beyond measure. In 1948 Vian had himself collaborated on the English translation of this 'translated' novel.

A more genuinely absurdist work by Vian, in the textual sense, might be *Heartsnatcher* (*L'Arrache-coeur*, 1953). A 'heartsnatcher', for the gory extraction of that organ, is an implement featured in a previous work, *L'Ecume des jours* (1947: translated both as *Froth on the Daydream* and as *Mood Indigo*), and which supplied the title for Vian's last novel. Set in a less than natural landscape, *Heartsnatcher* deals mainly with an obsessive mother who dismisses her husband for causing her the pain of childbirth and goes to unnatural lengths to protect her three children. These events are witnessed by a psychiatrist named Timortis, 'an individual born at an adult age and without any memories' (*Heartsnatcher*, 195) – in itself a metafictional phenomenon reminiscent of the 'creation' of Furriskey, in Flann O'Brien's *At Swim-Two-Birds*. The town has a 'scapegoat' who absolves the citizens of their guilt by fishing rubbish from the river with his teeth.[2] Timortis can feel 'the piercing pain of the monstrous massacre' of the felling of trees (ibid., 199). The elderly get auctioned off at an 'Old Folks Fair'; horses can be crucified; psychoanalysis is interpreted as a euphemism for sexual intercourse; and there are talking animals and a man who turns into a cat.

One highlight of *Heartsnatcher* is the response of the priest when the townsfolk assail him in church on a Sunday demanding rain. 'Vulgar, vulturous, vulpine villagers!', he storms, 'I am offering you a real, genuine luxury: I am offering you God ... G, O, D, for whom this geodesic jewel, this ritual in architecture, was invented. but God is not interested in rain' (58–9). His rant resumes:

> It will not rain! God is not a utilitarian. God is a birthday present. A free gift. A luncheon voucher. An ingot of platinum. A priceless picture. A French pastry. God is something extra. And he is neither for nor against. God is eleven thousand buckshee trading stamps! (59)

Eventually, however, he submits to a hailstorm of missiles and violent shoving: The crowd burst the doors open: 'Then came a veritable downpour which beat a tattoo with tambourine accompaniment on the black crystalline slates of the roof' ... "Service is over", he said quite simply' (60).

Some American absurdist novels

In his study of *The Absurd Hero in American Fiction*, David Galloway takes Camus as his starting point, before proceeding to examine the main protagonists in works by John Updike, William Styron, Saul Bellow and J.D. Salinger. Galloway therefore concentrates his attention on the reactions, and the intentions, of the 'heroes' of his chosen authors to the surrounding 'reality', which is generally of a recognisable realistic nature. An 'absurd hero', to Galloway (x), is someone who can 'transcend (or promise to transcend) the absurd in terms of the absurd', and who may thus go 'beyond the absurd' in what may then be seen as 'the optimistic literature of the absurd'.

In many ways, such a formula also fits Sebastian Dangerfield, the protagonist of J.P. Donleavy's *The Ginger Man* (1955). Donleavy uses a distinctive style of a mix of first- and third-person narrative, conveyed in terse non-sentences, interspersed with occasional flights of lyricism and (mock-)religious imagery (centred in particular on the Blessed Oliver Plunket – 'B.O.P. ... My patron': *Ginger Man*, 258). Dangerfield has a limitless talent for creating chaos and absurdity out of his everyday life in the admittedly not unpromising – indeed, apparently all but infernal as shown – environment of postwar Dublin. Dangerfield, who can and does say and think anything, opines: 'There must be a lot of steps to heaven. And Ireland is closest of all. But they are ruining Jesus with publicity' (ibid., 202). This anglicized-hibernicized American anti-hero, who alternately goes to town (in various senses) and relapses into squalor, is – Donleavy asserts – 'waiting to come into his estate'.[3] This, in a manner of speaking at least, and in unexpected circumstances, he appears to do by the end of what amounts to the novel's London epilogue (comprising chapters 26 to 31).

Another – perhaps the most famous – American subversive classic of the second half of the twentieth century is Joseph Heller's *Catch-22*

(1961), in which the dominating theme is the bureaucratic (military wartime) absurd emblematized by the title, which has become a catch-phrase in the language. Based, apparently, on its author's experiences in the European 'theatre' of the Second World War, the novel was influen-tial in the Vietnam years and stands as equally applicable in the era of Gulf wars and the 'War on Terrorism'. This is only to be expected in that the military mind-set, at least in certain quarters, never changes, and the novel's philosophy extends, in any case, into corporate thinking and into the basic elements of human existence. Edward Galligan (158) notes that Heller has 'picked up on Eliot's remarks (in his essay on Marlowe) about the possibility of a "serious, even savage" kind of farce', and Marguerite Alexander (151) remarks that, by its closing stages, 'Catch-22 makes the transition from comedy of the absurd towards tragedy of the absurd', and indeed from the absurd to the sinister.

'Catch-22' is the ultimate corrective. It arises first as the counterstroke to any attempts to get out of flying combat missions on the grounds of being 'crazy', as 'a concern for one's own safety in the face of dangers that were real and immediate was the process of a rational mind' (Catch-22, 62). 'That's some catch, that Catch-22', observes the novel's principal protagonist, Yossarian: 'There was an elliptical precision about its perfect pairs of parts that was graceful and shocking, like good modern art' (63). It acts as a countermand even to regulations, as any order has to be obeyed; it extends too to civilians, suffering at the hands of an occupying military force: 'Catch-22 says they have a right to do anything we can't stop them from doing' (514). In supposedly objective, or even legalistic, terms, Yossarian was positive that 'Catch-22 did not exist, ... but it made no difference' (516). The principle here evoked permeates not only mili-tary life, but the human condition. 'Each day [Yossarian] faced was another mission against mortality' (225); in addition to 'a bad persecution complex' (379), he is accused of 'a morbid aversion to dying' (384). 'Death was irreversible', in any case, 'he suspected, and he began to think he was going to lose' (438).

The novel is filled with a galaxy of hapless, comic, grotesque or sinis-ter minor characters, such as Chaplain Shipman, the parade-mad Lieutenant (somehow subsequently promoted to General) Scheisskopf, 'Nately's whore' (who pursues Yossarian manically from Rome), the ('resurrected') 'Soldier in White', and Major Major (who, owing to his first and second names, both 'Major', can only be administratively toler-ated on promotion to 'major'). The initial introducer of the term 'Catch-22' is Doc Daneeka, who himself falls supremely victim to the system by being declared bureaucratically (and therefore irrevocably) dead – his physical presence notwithstanding – owing to his having been included (on paper) in the flight-crew of a plane which crashed. This phenomenon is something of a mirror image to the case of the protagonist of Flann O'Brien's *The Third Policeman*, who realises that 'because I have no name I cannot die' and his would-be executioners cannot be held responsible for his death, even if they kill him (O'Brien, *TP*, 89). It is also a reversal of the situation in Iurii Tynianov's novella *Lieutenant Kizhe* (*Podporuchik Kizhe*, 1928), set in the reign of Tsar Paul I, in which an officer created by a bureaucratic error takes on a life of his own (paralleled by a counterpart who, like Heller's Doc Daneeka, is declared irreversibly dead when patently alive).[4]

One of the central points of *Catch-22*, the death of a young airman named Snowden, is introduced in the early stages (at least within the chronological scrambling and backtracking by which the novel is formed) and mentioned again from time to time, but given full exposition only in the novel's penultimate chapter. '[T]he question that had no answer' is posed by Yossarian: 'Where are the Snowdens of yesteryear?'; '*Où sont les Neigedens d'antan?*', he reiterates, supposedly 'to make it easier' for his interlocutor (49). Heller is here playing with the François Villon line, celebrated by many a ludic modernist writer: '*Où sont les neiges d'antan?*': cf. Sorrentino (see below); and Stoppard, 'Oh the yes-no's of yesteryear' (*Travesties*, 25) – to note but two. 'Snowden's secret', as his entrails – from a second lethal wound – 'spilled all over the messy floor', is finally revealed through a near-quote from *King Lear* (V, ii): 'Ripeness was [is] all' (554). 'Catch-22' and its ramifications, stretching from the comic to the horrific, from the mad military self-promotion of Colonel Cathcart to the limitless free-market mania of Milo Minderbinder, are epitomised in the forlorn plea of a nameless warrant officer: 'Just for once I'd like to see all these things sort of straightened out, with each person getting exactly what he deserves. It might give me some confidence in this universe' (219).

Gilbert Sorrentino's *Mulligan Stew* (1979) is an extravagant *mélange* of metafictional devices and *bricolage*, 'Chinese-box' narratives, multiplex lists, epistolary exchanges, in-house literary tittle-tattle, and intertextual parody. Any attempt at plot summary would almost certainly prove superfluous and, in short, this work exhibits strong claims to exemplifying the postmodernist novel *par excellence*. Dedicated 'to the memory of Brian O'Nolan – his "virtue *hilaritas*"', Sorrentino duly makes numerous 'borrowings' from, among many others, Flann O'Brien – in particular, characters, situations and settings from *At Swim-Two-Birds*: Dermot and Orlick Trellis, Antony and Sheila Lamont, Paul Shanahan, Jem Casey, the phenomenon of the 'Irish western', and the Red Swan Hotel are all prominently present. Also to be found therein are 'a neglected genius, one DaSalvi' who 'maintained that night is simply an insanitary condition of the atmosphere due to accretions of black air' (*MS*, 30; he re-emerges as 'Da Salvi': 150); 'the old Mathers place', complete with 'rusty bicycle' and policemen (139); and references to invented conversations between Keats and Shelley, attributed by 'the slanderous Miles O'Nolan' (245), and

'Myles of the Ponies' (442). The question *'Where are the snows of yester-year?'* is duly posed, and Antony Lamont purports to be engaged in the composition of 'an "absurdist" mystery story – if you can conceive of such a thing' (28).

One author who did conceive of such a thing is Robert Coover, who published a novel which, whatever else it does, parodies the country-house thriller in ludicrous – indeed in absurdist – fashion: *Gerald's Party* (1985).[5] A protracted and seemingly infernal party (the darkroom 'glowed from the inside like hell in a melodrama': *GP*, 206), which features murder, chaos, sadism and diverse (and usually public) sexual mayhem, forms the subject matter of the first-person narrative delivered by the host, Gerald. His wide, albeit (perforce) limited, observation of events is presented in a stream of consciousness that mingles reminiscence, stories and the fragments of conversation emanating from countless guests. Reactions to extreme events are often surprisingly blasé all round (whether from stimulants, callousness, sheer lust or other causes); Gerald's apparently alert perception seems undiminished even while he is barely conscious, having sustained a flesh wound – before he swiftly revives sufficiently to take on the role of mercy killer of his best friend Vic (himself grievously wounded by a trigger-happy cop, while trying to attack Gerald, who had just all but deflowered his teenage daughter).

Theatrical and art metaphor abounds and the events are 'artistically' captured, not only through narrative, but by press photography and video footage, – or grotesquely reinvented for purposes of stage or cinema: 'punch in this torture number to set up the death dance and Last Supper routine: shit, man, it's a fucking *classic!*' (ibid., 266). As for the entire violent scenario – 'it was as though we'd all been dislodged somehow, pushed out of the frame, dropped into some kind of empty dimensionless gap like that between film cuts, between acts ...' (105–6); or else people are 'drifting about without focus', akin to 'an endless intermission' in 'the last play in the world' (192). A ridiculous detective investigation, involving further severe (indeed fatal) bodily harm is conducted by Inspector Pardew into 'some dalliance, as it were – or so I feel – with *oblivion itself!*' (142). 'Holistic criminalistics' are applied through 'the laws of social etiology' (144), to inane (indeed insane) effect. 'The victim is the killer' is one of Pardew's theories (217): a brainwave which may have been taken from a line near the end of Fassbinder's film of *Despair* (see note 18 below).

Events towards the end seem to get even more bizarre, until Ros (the murdered actress and mistress of many) is either (re)discovered or (re)appears: 'Now c'mon, let's try that again! From the beginning!' (336). Either the whole party is to start again, one may assume, or, with narrator and readership alike in a cinematic trance, the filmic reel will turn again from the beginning. Perhaps the whole sequence has been a night-mare (turning wet dream), with the 'real' party still to begin. While there would not appear to be overt allusion to O'Brien's works in *Gerald's Party*, the infernal repetitive cycle may seem reminiscent of *The Third Policeman* – and there *are* three strangely behaving policemen.[6]

Some more English-language absurdist novels

O'Brien is duly recognised, albeit in a more minor vein, in British novels, such as Alasdair Gray's chronologically scrambled (or 'misnumbered', in the order 3, 1, 2, 4; cf. the 2, 1, 3, 4 of Beckett's *Watt*) purgatorial epic of 'Unthank' (a post-Glasgow) epic, *Lanark* (1981), and John Fowles's *Mantissa* (1982).[7] 'The hero's biography after death', Gray acknowledges, 'occurs in Wyndham-Lewis's trilogy *The Human Age*, Flann O'Brien's *The Third Policeman* and Golding's *Pincher Martin*'; however, the hellishly inspired 'smoke-laden grey sky' of *Lanark* essentially came 'From Franz Kafka'.[8]

Fowles uses a 'slightly adapted' quotation from *At Swim-Two Birds* as an epigraph to the fourth part of *Mantissa* (*Mantissa*, 153; cf. O'Brien, *At Swim*, 63), with references at the end to 'Mr O'Brien's frantic cuckoo-clock', and '*Keep the fun clean, said Shanahan*' (*Mantissa*, 189–90; *At Swim*, 64). *Mantissa* is essentially a confrontation, supposedly taking place within his own brain, between a writer (one Miles Green) and a protean female character: muse doubling as protagonist (through the persona of Erato: daughter of Mnemosyne and Greek muse of love poetry, subsequently assigned to prose fiction). Who, ultimately, has created whom? The ontological tables are turned several times (see McHale, 214–15), in keeping with Brian McHale's thesis of an ontological dominant in postmodernism, rather than an epistemological equivalent in modernism. 'The sexual exploitation's nothing beside the ontological one', complains Erato (posing as a 'character' in one of the novel's set-piece set-tos), '[you] can kill me off in five lines if you want to'; 'I feel so terribly conscious I'm only a few pages old' (*Mantissa*, 93; 104). As the metafictional ploy is developed (O'Brien fashion), multiple references occur to the concept of absurdity.[9]

One twenty-first-century novel to make an attempt at a continuation of this tradition is Neil Astley's farrago of folklore, mythology and magic, *The End of My Tether* (2002), which essays a combination of shape-shifting and metafictional text-shifting with the elements of a rural and ecological detective novel. 'Literary theft' is committed from a number of works, in particular from Thackeray's *Vanity Fair* but also from O'Brien: 'And what were you doing in *The Third Policeman* without a warrant?', one officer is asked (*The End*, 480). The suggestion is made of stealing the bicycle from that novel, to hide it in another book, *A Brief History of Time*: 'Every book about time needs a displaced bicycle if it's to answer the big question' (385). 'Yer have to sound Irish to get inside *The Third*

Policeman, or *Oirish, to be sure*', it is declared (386), while more than once the O'Brien question ('Is it about a bicycle?) is asked, instead of the appropriate Astley one ('*Is it about the cattle disease?*': 474; 479; 480). By the end, the figure of the author is being arrested for involvement in the death of a range of his characters, but, being in 'reality' the Green Man (Cernunnos), he is easily able to escape.

European absurdist prose and American minimalism

The Dutch writer Cees Nooteboom is known as a poet, a novelist and a travel writer. His novella *The Following Story* (*Het volgende verhaal*, 1991) is in the first place a circular, and an apparently whimsical, shaggy-dog story, with its final words ('then I told you / the following story': Nooteboom, *FS*, 98) directing the reader (not that 'you' is the reader – or at least assuredly not *only* the reader) back to the first page, serpent's-tail-like. This schema is prefigured early on by the image of 'a dog trying to bite its own tail' (ibid., 7–8). Such a narrative device is not, we need hardly say, of itself original to Nooteboom; however, this only covers the formal structure. The novella is essentially a meditation on life and death, together with a fluidity of time and identity.

The first-person narrator is a classics teacher (nicknamed 'Socrates') at a Dutch *lycée*, who, after dismissal following a playground altercation with a jealous colleague (with whose wife, another colleague, he is having an affair – and with whose teenage pupil-mistress he is becoming 'Platonically' obsessed), has turned his hand, under an assumed name, to travel writing. The first part of *The Following Story* fills in this background, as the protagonist (originally Hermann Mussert) awakes in Lisbon, a city he had visited years earlier with his paramour, although he believes he had gone to bed the night before in Amsterdam. His 'ridiculous feeling' on awakening is that 'I might be dead' (5), while, in any event, he recalls, 'life's a bucket of shit that keeps being added to' (an enunciation supposedly attributable to St Augustine: 38). The Lisbon setting, naturally enough, gives rise to allusions to Pessoa and 'his three alter egos' (39; 50), while 'grating ... carapaces', and a beetle vomiting over 'a pellet of carrion', may suggest Kafka (35).

In the second part (prefaced by an epigraph from the end of Nabokov's *Transparent Things*), Mussert's initial feeling is apparently borne out. He (as teacher, translator of Ovid, lover and travel writer) embarks on a voyage from Lisbon's Belém to the Amazon, an oceanic traversal of the Styx, together with a group of disturbed deceased (or 'travellers in limbo': 91), each with a story to tell, on what may seem to be a steam variant of 'the ship of fools'. The 'endless wanderings' to be embarked upon by Mussert's body, 'never to be ousted from the universe' and taking part in seemingly pointless, but 'the most fantastic metamorphoses' (97), again suggest Kafka, but this time perhaps *The Hunter Gracchus* (reinforced by reference to Orion the Hunter: 66). Each individual in turn tells their (confessional) story, to be led away by the figure of death – appearing to each in an esoteric guise (and to the classicist in 'Persephone mask': 95). Finally, at Mussert's turn, 'you' duly manifests the (Platonic) form of 'my dearest Crito, the girl who was my pupil, so young that one could speak about immortality with her' (98). 'And then I told her, then I told you / the following story' (ibid.).

Roland Topor (1938–97) was a French cartoonist (see examples in his *Stories and Drawings*), a painter, an actor and a designer, as well as an absurdist writer (and founder member of 'Groupe Panique', which included Arrabal). His minimalist short stories are reminiscent of Daniil Kharms, in their featuring of grotesque exaggeration, senseless violence, paranoia, irony and 'what if?' reversals of norms or archetypes. Accused – and not unjustifiably – of 'sick humour', Topor frequently dwells on amputation, cannibalism and acts of medical and mental aggression. Identity is played with, as friends and strangers are suddenly reversed ('My Dear Friends ...'; *Amis très chers* ...) or the acquisition of a telephone brings undesired consequences ('Wrong Number'; *Le Coup du téléphone*). In 'Local Thunderstorms' (*Orages*), the situation familiar to us from Gogol's *Diary of a Madman* (in which the diarist comes to think of himself as the King of Spain) suddenly becomes the accepted norm, as tyrannical figures from history start to abound. 'A sick joke' (an effective translation here of *'une mauvaise plaisanterie'*) is the narrator's literal and figurative conclusion at the end of 'A Father's Sacrifice' (*S and D*, 83–90; *Le Sacrifice d'un père*, in *Lucienne*, 75–86),[10] in which human remains are found in a barrel washed in from the sea, accompanied by a green bottle containing a letter begging that the enclosed organs be restored to the body of the writer's father at Père Lachaise cemetery.

Topor provides examples too of what must be considered 'sci-fi absurd': 'Well Hung' (*À point*) and 'The Liberators' (*Les Libérateurs*) – the latter story might seem to comprise a reversal inspired by Nabokov's recollection of a newspaper story of 'an ape in the Jardin des Plantes' which produced a sketch that 'showed the bars of the poor creature's cage'.[11] The narrator of a brief story called 'Continuous Performance' (*S and D*, 141–3; *Le Spectacle est permanent*, in *Lucienne*, 227–30) is translated from his position in a cinema audience to, in effect, become the cinema screen. Topor's play *Leonardo Was Right* (*Vinci avait raison*, 1976), takes French farce into the scatological absurd, while his novel *The Tenant* (*Le Locataire chimérique*, 1966; filmed as *The Tenant* by Roman Polanski) is a nightmare narrative of paranoia and a Gothic-absurd shift of identity.

We have already discussed in some detail the work of Daniil Kharms and Aleksandr Vvedensky, absurdists of the late 1920s and through the

1930s, and representatives of the OBERIU movement, unpublished and persecuted in their lifetimes and rediscovered over the last three decades of the twentieth century. Another Russian writer to undergo such recent rediscovery (in so far as he had ever been discovered in the first place) is Leonid Dobychin (1896–1936), who published stories unconventional in plotline and darkly satirical in their view of the new society. In 1935 his short novel *The Town of N* (*Gorod En*) appeared; following critical vilification, Dobychin vanished and is presumed to have committed suicide. This work, set in the Latvia of the Russian Empire, is Gogolian in inspiration (being parodically allusive to *Dead Souls*) and plays too with other literary prototypes, including elements from Dostoevsky. Its schoolboy narrator sees the surrounding spiritual wasteland in faintly absurd terms, before discovering, in more than one sense: 'everything I'd seen incorrectly'.[12]

A more comprehensively absurdist figure rediscovered and re-promoted in the later decades of the twentieth century is the Italian writer Achille Campanile (1900–77). Campanile achieved a certain reputation with the prolific writings of his early career (short stories, novels, dialogues and plays) of the 1920s and 1930s, stemming from Italian Futurism and Pirandello, plus affinities with surrealism. He later turned more to journalism and scriptwriting, but was 'rediscovered' in later life as an absurdist and avant-garde writer by a new generation, in the wake of Theatre of the Absurd and other such developments of the second half of the century. He excelled in sketches and scenarios of extraordinary brevity (rivalled only by Kharms and Topor), as demonstrated in his collection *Tragedie in due battute* (*Tragedies in Two Cues*) – any staging of which would seem inconceivable, although 'spectaculars' had been mounted in his early days. These can be described as minute examples of Theatre of the Absurd, and seen as anticipations of Beckett at his most sparse. Campanile claimed to have produced over 2500 'theatrical works' – many of which were tiny in length ('a perhaps insuperable monument to brevity': Masolino d'Amico, introduction to *Tragedie* i–vi). He equally produced collections of short stories, in a somewhat similar vein, of which *Manuale di conversazione* (*Manual of Conversation*) is just one prime example. Notable among Campanile's longer plays is *L'inventore del cavallo* (*The Inventor of the Horse*, 1925), in which a designer is convinced that, through sheer planning power, he has invented the horse – only to commit suicide in despair on learning that horses already exist.

'Minimalism', a quality or a style frequently associated in this book with the absurd, has been seen as 'the postmodern form par excellence' (Wanner, 2003, x). As a term, it spread from the plastic arts to short fiction, where it represented a 'transition from modernist maximalism to postmodernist minimalism', although the more accurate literary term might be 'miniaturism', as 'minimalism' does not always entail a structural smallness (ibid.). As discussed here, very short texts by Kharms and Campanile, and some later prose by Beckett, as well as texts by Topor and Ronshin, fit the minimalist-miniaturist bill. Enoch Brater calls his (1987) study of Beckett's late theatrical style 'Beyond Minimalism', while Sinéad Mooney (83) can see Beckett's late prose as 'minimalist in scope, but not in ambition'. Anyway, perhaps the world's shortest story is 'The Dinosaur' by the Guatemalan writer Augusto Monterroso – so short that it may enjoy the luxury here of being printed in dual text: *Cuando desperto, el dinosaurio todavía estaba allí.* The English translation, at one word longer, reads: 'When he awoke, the dinosaur was still there.'

Short (or very short) fiction in North America, particularly popular in the 1980s, came to be designated 'minimalism'. This phenomenon is often seen as exemplified by the stories of Raymond Carver – though he himself is scarcely to be classed as absurdist. Certain of the short stories by Robert Coover, Walter Abish and Donald Barthelme, who also of course wrote much longer works somewhat in this vein, are quite another matter.

We have earlier (in the Kharms chapter) encountered an example in a comparison made with Coover's 'The Marker' (1963); uncannily close comparisons too can be entertained (also demonstrated in that chapter) with the absurdist fables of Russell Edson. The 'prose poems' of Edson are minimalist in length (ranging from three or four lines to a couple of pages) and amount very often to surrealistic anecdotes or parables. The themes – of sex and violence (often domestic), off-beat slants on life and death, nature and the elements, the local and the cosmic, animals and insects, anthropomorphism or personification and the reverse, philosophical and metaphysical questions – are very similar to what is to be found in the works of other writers of this miniaturist genre: Kharms, Campanile, Topor and Ronshin (on the latter see below). Horses and simians (various) are particular favourites. We even find again the invention of the horse: 'The horse was invented by man after the horseless carriage' (*The Tunnel*, 19); and, when a man straddling the top of his roof cries 'giddyup': 'The house rears up on its back porch and all its bricks fall apart and the house crashes to the ground' (ibid., 18). Wordplay and syntactic jumbling are liable to occur: see 'There Was' (ibid., 44–5); or the mother who is simultaneously 'being borne by him or he [is] being born by her' ('Signs', 61–2). Bodily disintegration and grotesque forms of feeding are a prominent feature. Nevertheless, lyricism is at times the dominant, as in the miniature 'Little Dead Man':

> Onward, little dead man, said a little man passing through a land of butter-flies, purple and white, yellow and black, all in flux; they are not told from the flowers they drink, nor are the wind fluttered flowers from those they host.
>
>   This is a land of vibrating velvet. Eating itself. Forming itself. This is the land of death. Endless. Absurd. (*The Tunnel*, 34)

Not surprisingly, late twentieth-century Russia has produced its own successors to Kharms. One figure who might have been examined here is Vladimir Sorokin, as noted for his 'narrative theatre of cruelty' as for his 'excremental poetics' (see chapters in Epstein *et al.*; and Lipovetsky, 1999, respectively) – and latterly as a controversial opera librettist. Sorokin is regarded as a representative of Russian 'Conceptualism', a tendency which has grown in the post-Communist (postmodernist) period, of which, it is said (Lipovetsky, 2001, 33) that 'a "thing" is substituted not with another "thing" ... but with *nothingness*', thus bringing it close to Baudrillard's concept of 'the hyperreality of simulacra'.[13] Russian Conceptualism, Mark Lipovetsky affirms, 'gravitates toward the tradition of Daniil Kharms and the OBERIU' and therefore comes closer to the avant-garde than to 'high modernism' (ibid., 41).

A notable recent exemplar of this phenomenon, however, is Valery (Valerii) Ronshin, who, like Kharms, is also a children's writer, and who utilises themes analogous not only to those discussed previously in Kharms, but with an equal affinity, one could suggest, to works and devices utilised by Campanile and Topor. Notable among Ronshin's works are grotesque or Gothic-absurdist versions of an afterlife (in which the scatological frequently meets the eschatological) that may be reachable, or returnable from, by train (or metro) journey.[14] Such may be found in 'How Tryapkin the Detective Set Out to Moscow and Arrived in Arsehole' (Ronshin, 79–83; *triapka* in Russian means 'rag', or 'nonentity'), where he finds the earth and the sky to be a dismal brown; or in the avowedly meaningless universe (in which the universe is itself denied) of his longer story 'We're All Long Dead' (ibid., 86–114). Other similar 'destinations' in such of his stories include Amsterdam and (in a Lermontov parody) Taman. Or similar situations can be depicted in a series of lives, as in 'Eternal Return' (183–208). Certain similarities may be seen with Etgar Keret's afterlife for suicides, *Kneller's Happy Campers* (in Keret, *The Bus Driver*, 91–130). Another further reach of weirdness is attained in Ronshin's miniature 'How I Became a Fly' (67–70), in which the narrator, a shopkeeper, is dismembered and metamorphosed at the hands of a 'strange customer'.

Beyond the 'Theatre of the Absurd'?

a world of chaos need not be dreaded ... (William W. Demastes, *Theatre of Chaos*)

A bizarre hybrid specimen of fiction, which would seem to require at least a brief comment here, were it only on the grounds of its title,[15] is Karen Cobb's gay novel *Theatre of the Absurd* (1995), set in San Francisco's theatre world, in which the framing prose fictional plot surrounds, interacts with, influences and is influenced by, the play within this plot – a stylised harlequinade called 'The Struggle for Creation'. 'Theatre of the Absurd' is here used by Cobb as both a metaphorical and a literal device to project the personal obsessions of a bisexual playwright and other self-fixated theatricals, reduced sharply towards, and destructively beyond, the absurd and its theatre. Something of a reverse of this structural model is to be found in Martin McDonagh's *The Pillowman* (2003), in which a number of stories are embedded (and narrated or read) in an extremely black comic play, to which we shall return shortly.

Women's absurd?

There seem to have been few women absurdist writers – a question addressed by Toby Silverman Zinman (in Brater and Cohn, 203–20); one, however (in Zinman's view) is the Cuban-born playwright Maria Irene Fornes. While, to an extent at least, employing absurdist linguistic techniques, women writers are seen as avoiding, or rejecting, the pessimistic and abstract philosophies entailed in absurdism (a strident exception to this, however, to be considered later, is Sarah Kane). Caryl Churchill, who combines the (postmodernist) transhistorical gathering with contemporary social satire (in *Top Girls*, 1982) might also be a case for discussion. Nevertheless, up to this point anyway, 'male exclusivity' is seen as 'a defining feature of absurdism' (Celeste Derksen, 209).

Another figure seen (indeed by Derksen) as developing established absurd theatre into something of a 'feminist absurd' is the Canadian writer Margaret Hollingsworth – particularly in her quartet of short plays, published under the title of *Endangered Species* (1988). In one of these, *The House that Jack Built*, Hollingsworth builds on nursery rhyme, with its accumulative and repetitive structure (rather than, say, the shaggy dog story, or the language learning primer), to elucidate issues of gender roles, marriage and consumerism. Such a developing political awareness, in terms of absurdist subjecthood, is seen to have been foreshadowed even by Esslin (in his second edition of 1969: Derksen 211–12), in his excursions into East European absurdism. In this interrogative play by Hollingsworth, 'the absurd joins feminism in a fraught marriage' (ibid., 227).

In Soviet Russia too, the Brezhnev 'period of stagnation' saw the plays of Liudmila Petrushevskaia extend 'beyond the boundaries of social criticism into the fringes of absurdity', which restricted performances during those years; comparisons are seen this time with the work of Pinter (though subsequently with Ionesco and Beckett: Simmons, 2–3; 18).[16] Petrushevskaia, like most Russian women writers, may prefer to avoid the term 'feminist', but her themes are predominantly of gender and family, with lack of communication to the fore and frequently a disintegration of language. A 'more animal condition' than that found in previous absurdist theatre, along with an 'absurdist joining of mirth, banality and terror', is discerned by another commentator (Dalton-Brown, 11; 16), while a Russian critic (in an essay entitled 'Paradise of Monsters') considers that Petrushevskaia's texts read as though 'written by a member of the Gestapo'.[17] Among the range of genres (dramatic and prose fictional) exploited by Petrushevskaia, and latterly extending to the novel, are the monologue, fairy tale, 'requiem' and urban myth – the latter in the form of the *sluchai* (or 'incident' – although connections with Kharms are played down). References occur to Greek sources, to Shakespeare and to music (with 'characters as puppets dancing above an abyss' [ibid., 92] – as a virtual revival of 'the dance of death'), often in the form of 'Kafkaesque parable' or accompanied by 'Dostoevskian perversity' (180). In the bleak vision of 'destructive darkness' (109) and 'structures of negation' (161) that pervade much of Petrushevskaia's writing, the 'time' is, in one sense or another, predominantly 'night' – emblematically displayed by the title of her most celebrated novella, *The Time: Night* (*Vremia noch'*, 1992).

The chaos of absurdist drama

Giuseppe Manfridi goes beyond Theatre of the Absurd to what he calls 'Theatre of Excess', depicting extremes of horror within the realistic and slapstick setting of a normal apartment, reviving ancient myth through modern shock. In his play *Cuckoos* (*Zozòs*, 1990; English version by Colin Teevan, 2000), two of the three characters spend the dramatic duration locked in anal intercourse under a parachute. Beckettian concepts such as 'deadlock' and 'stalemate' (Manfridi, 23) are bandied in witty exchanges, with the arrival of the gynaecologist-father figure (plus 'endgame': 64), before the sexual farce takes on undertones of Dante and ends in a drastic re-working of the Oedipus myth (in which even the parachute assumes an unexpected significance). Double entendres convert into tragic irony, in the form of 'edifice wrecked' (67). The path which *Cuckoos* follows, through and beyond the surreal and the absurd, as director Peter Hall states (Preface to ibid., 6) 'takes us right back to the Greeks'.

Theatre of the Absurd, or in particular what became accepted as 'British Absurd' assimilated into itself, in the wake of Pinter and Orton, the early plays of Tom Stoppard, beginning with *Rosencrantz and Guildenstern Are Dead* (1967); in addition to his purported British predecessors, Stoppard was seen to display 'echoes of Sartre, Beckett and Kafka' (see Zarhy-Levo, 2003, 67–93, on Stoppard's reception). In a more specifically theatrical European sense, his ancestors, or models, were observed to include Ionesco and Pirandello, as well as Beckett – in addition, of course, to Shakespeare. Stoppard's second play, *The Real Inspector Hound* (1968), has been seen not only to parody the detective genre (in particular Agatha Christie's *The Mousetrap*), but to model itself too on *The Prismatic Bezel* (itself 'a rollicking parody of the setting of a detective tale'), a supposed novel by the supposed subject of Nabokov's novel, *The Real Life of Sebastian Knight*.[18] *Travesties* (1974) makes hay with Wilde's *The Importance of Being Earnest*, James Joyce and Dadaism (not to mention Leninism). In *Dogg's Hamlet* (1979), Stoppard writes dialogue largely in 'Dogg language', a code of verbal substitution, based on the exchanges of building workers, as derived from Wittgensteinian language games in *Philosophical Investigations* – juxtaposed with a greatly compressed version of *Hamlet* – an exercise in reduction repeated in *Cahoot's Macbeth* (1980). Indeed, the second portion of this presumed double-bill amounts to an absurdist *mélange* of reduced *Macbeth*, contagious Dogg-language, detective foolery, English lorry deliveries and post-Dubček Czechoslovak 'normalization'.

Some critics, however, were already seeing Stoppard as a 'post-absurdist' figure; he may have marked 'the beginning of the postabsurdist movement', according to one commentator (who called his 1979 study of Stoppard's work *Beyond Absurdism*); or he may even be seen 'as *starting* "beyond absurdity"' (see Zarhy-Levo, 2003, 89).[19] A rather similar line is further developed by William Demastes, who discusses some later Stoppard plays in his study *Theatre of Chaos* (subtitled 'Beyond Absurdism, into Orderly Disorder'). John Fleming (3) admits that Stoppard's plays 'are open to a multitude of responses'; in the case of *Jumpers* (1972), 'the play's dazzling form' has led to interpretations 'antithetical to Stoppard's professed values' (ibid., 84), and to suggestions that *Jumpers* does not objectively support his supposed position in any case (Fleming 272, n. 3).

However that may be, Stoppard's *Jumpers* may perhaps be regarded as the summit of his absurdist phase, with its metaphorical (and literal) philosophical acrobatics, coupled with further detective shenanigans. Indeed, such a pinnacle is manifested, at the end of the play, by the overt homage to Beckett of the line 'Wham, bam, thank you Sam', following close allusions to *Waiting for Godot* ('one of the thieves was saved'; and 'At the graveside the undertaker doffs his top hat and impregnates the prettiest mourner': *Jumpers*, 87).[20] The main character, George Moore, a professor of moral philosophy, finds himself 'lumbered with this incredible, indescribable and definitely shifty *God*, the trump card of atheism' (ibid., 68), and acknowledges a ludicrous academic reputation, gained largely by his 'aptitude for traducing a complex and logical thesis to a mysticism of staggering banality' (72).

Demastes develops his analysis of 'Theatre of Chaos' from scientific theories elaborated in the later decades of the twentieth century, and popularised in James Gleick's book *Chaos: Making a New Science* (1987), which Stoppard also had studied. The ideas – boiling down to the notion that chaos has had a bad press, at least over the past two millennia – derive philosophically from Lucretius's (first-century BC) confrontation with Aristotelian models, and his insertion of the 'clinamen' (or 'swerve'), a force that disrupts orderliness and introduces diversity, leading to a consequent non-Newtonian escape into nonlinearity (Demastes, 3–5).[21] Science (re)advanced into such realms with the advent of quantum theory, and it is by no means coincidental, suggests Demastes (35), that quantum physics and surrealism both developed in the period around 1925, and that the former frequently expressed itself in theatrical metaphor. The involvement of 'the art world ... in theory' was accompanied by an entanglement of epistemology with ontology, as had been argued by select earlier thinkers (such as Berkeley and Kant: ibid., 41). The polarities in thought and art (especially theatre: 104) are seen as naturalism, and its outright rejection (in favour of a dependence on chance and randomness) in absurdism. 'Unlike the absurdist paradigm arguing that the world is governed by chance', says Demastes (49), 'the quantum paradigm is governed by a belief in free-swinging choice among countless probable options': 'The quantum paradigm subscribes neither to chance nor to linear determinism, but to a system of probability, less secure than determinism/fate but more stable than randomness/absurdism' (50).

Demastes points to the 'higher' degrees of order that overlay 'every actual instance of randomness', according to the new science, discernible already in the work of Beckett (see 57–63); indeed, he maintains, 'Patterns within chaos pervade Beckett's art', amounting to an 'unpredictable determinism' (60), or 'a mitigated absurdism at best' (62).[22] 'Chaotics' (or 'deterministic chaos': see Fleming 192–4) offers a 'controlled anarchy' (Demastes 120) which can be reflected, too, in artistic (and theatrical) regeneration. Such a trend can be pointed to in the overt discussions of what amounts to chaos theory which occur in Stoppard's *Hapgood* (1988) – a spoof-spook farce of 'quantum personalities and double agency' (53) – and in the intricately constructed period-parallel and non-linear histrionics of *Arcadia* (1992).[23] The latter work, in the view of Fleming (3), is 'the play that weds the pre- and post-*Travesties* Stoppard'.

A play to which quantum mechanics is central is *Copenhagen* (1998; revised 2003) by Michael Frayn – himself very much a former humorist (in his journalism, novels and earlier plays, such as the farce *Noises Off*). *Copenhagen* is a highly serious play (filmed for television in 2003), which produced a range of often extreme responses[24] – though by no means without its comic moments, as well as its multi-levelled ironies – treating the mysterious visit of 1941 made by Werner Heisenberg (by then in Nazi employ) to his former mentor Niels Bohr in German-occupied Denmark. Quantum mechanics meets 'uncertainty' amid 'complementarity' on a scientific, a personal and a global strategic level – as the development of the atomic bomb is what is really at issue. The discussions confirm 'the final core of uncertainty at the heart of things' (Frayn 94), from the micro- to the macro-level – not excluding, least of all, world events. Language, as ever, is a suspect and inadequate quality: 'What something means is what it means in mathematics', insists Heisenberg (65), while, as the Copenhagen theorists had discovered, in the mid-1920s, Bohr reminds him (and us) 'that there is no precisely determinable objective universe' (71–2). Neither is anything at all precisely determinable through the memories of the three protagonists; the third is Margarethe Bohr, who – by her presence and her keen participation – provides, not least, the dramatic justification for the delivery of complex discussions in something approximating to an intelligible (not an impenetrably technical) linguistic register.

What is most impressive about *Copenhagen* is the success of the non-linearity of its structure, melding themes of theory with levels of 'reality'. The three personages reconvene as embodied (though absolutely not omniscient) spirits, revisiting their previous meetings, in the Bohrs' (now deserted) Copenhagen house, of 1941 and 1947, cutting with purportedly 'actual' snippets from those times and interspersed with later ruminations. The scenes and discussions are gone over repetitively with subtle differ- ences and developments in what are presented as 'drafts', based on restructured reminiscence, of the crucial conversations (Bohr calls for 'One final draft!': 86). Uncertainty dominates as science and human deportment struggle to assert themselves as 'history' through memory and ironic speculation (from Heisenberg) on needing 'a strange new quantum ethics' (92). As Frayn later argues (148): 'History … is not what happens when it happens, but what seems to people to have happened when they look back on it'.

Martin McDonagh's play *The Pillowman* (the structure of which – stories embedded in a drama – has been mentioned above) may be seen as a literal revival of 'Theatre of Cruelty', given its horrific themes of child (and parental) murder and mental defection, and its on-stage actions of torture and execution. At the same time, it is a grotesque, somewhat Stoppardian, mixture of totalitarian interrogation (Central European, one has to assume), criminal investigation shenanigans and black comic repar- tee, narrating and relating to the gruesome fairy stories composed by the principal character – an arrested writer. 'That's a good story. That's something -esque, What kind of "esque" is it? I can't remember. I don't really go in for that "esque" sort of stuff anyway …', remarks the writer Katurian when the detective has read aloud one of his grim tales (*Pillowman*, 18). The interrogator Tupolski (soon to be executioner) has written a story himself: 'It sort of summed up my world view in some ways. Well, no it didn't really sum up my world view. I don't have a world view. I think the world's a pile of shit. That isn't really a world view, is it? Or is it? Hmmm ...' (ibid., 85). In the end, Katurian's works are preserved (though sealed with his case-file for fifty years).

Sarah Kane

An expressionist nag / Stalling between two fools (Sarah Kane, *4.48 Psychosis*, written 1998–99)

Somwhere beyond the absurd, and beyond even 'Theatre of Cruelty', looking back to the starkest elements of Greek tragedy and on to a nihilism of self-fragmentation, is a territory inhabited by the plays – the characters (when such they can be called), the actions and the increasingly indeterminate voices – of Sarah Kane, whose active production career lasted just three and a half years (from 1995 to 1998) and consisted then of four plays, and a television screenplay (*Skin*, transmitted on Channel 4 in 1997), plus a posthumously produced final dramatic work, *4.48 Psychosis* (staged in 2000). Kane's plays deal with human relations, of a sort, usually involving (either by enacting or recalling) extreme acts of violence and sexuality, amid a background of social strife (almost, if not entirely, uncontextualised) and, to put it mildly, a troubled view of the human condition.

Blasted (1995) begins with what appears to be a routine sexual encounter in a Leeds hotel, which becomes quickly engulfed in personal and civil conflict. The contention that nothing makes sense without the existence of God, or something, receives the retort: 'Don't be fucking stupid, doesn't make sense anyway. No reason for there to be a God just because it would be better if there was' (Kane, 55). *Phaedra's Love* (1996), a revival – or rather an extreme parody – of Euripidean Greek tragedy in a modern setting, surrounded by television and electronic toys, includes the line from Hippolytus: 'I can't sin against a God I don't believe in' (ibid., 95). The play ends with Hippolytus, whose besetting reaction to life has been one of boredom, saying with a smile, as he dies from disembowelment, encircled by vultures: 'If there could have been more moments like this' (103). Artaud looms into view again. *Cleansed* (1998) offers extreme forms of identity and gender anxiety, mutilation, and other varieties of psychotic mayhem in what purports to be a university (rather than an unambiguous madhouse) precinct.

Kane's last two plays contain her most interesting and perhaps her most lasting work. *Crave* (1998) presents four voices (named just C, M, B and A: two male and two female, or one male and three female – according to director's preference), who indulge in conversation at times connected, but often disconnected, involving vague pre-histories of rape and abuse. *Crave*'s theatrical precedents would appear to include Beckett's *Play* (here done in a slower version) and Sartre's *Huis clos* (*In*

Camera, or *No Exit*, 1944). In contrast to her subject matter and nihilistic outlook, Kane can produce surprisingly poetic effects and a rhythmic musicality, as in the dark lyricism of this utterance by C(189):

> Let the day perish in which I was born
> Let the blackness of the night terrify it
> Let the stars of its dawn be dark
> May it not see the eyelids of the morning
> Because it did not shut the door of my mother's womb

The Beckett-like sentiments here expressed may take us back to *Phaedra's Love*, in which the eponymous mother responds to the greeting of her daughter (Strophe): 'Go away fuck off don't touch me don't talk to me stay with me' (69), which seems to echo, in *Waiting for Godot*, Estragon's 'Don't touch me! Don't question me! Don't speak to me! Stay with me!' (Beckett, *CDW*, 54).

Emotional (and physical) contradiction seem to lie at the heart of Kane's world – not least in her powerful *4.48 Psychosis*. Here the voices are undilineated in number and nature (three actors played them in the original Royal Court performance), though much of the text reads as the day-book of a psychotic subject, or conversation between 'patient' and 'psychiatrist'. 'I have become so depressed by the fact of my mortality that I have decided to commit suicide' (Kane, 207), announces the self-styled 'child of negation' (239), who is not lacking in 'gallows humour' (209); one reply given to this is the tragically prophetic: 'Nothing will interfere with your work like suicide' (221). 'There's not a drug on earth can make life meaningful' is countered (or followed, depending on who the speaker is) with: 'You allow this state of desperate absurdity' (220). 'And my mind is the subject of these bewildered fragments', we are told in the early stages (210) of this exploration of the ultimate impatience of the 'patient'. Issues of identity seems to dominate, as often in Kane. This means identity both as self-identity and as that of an absent or non-existent lover (who may be of either sex, or a lover perhaps from a distant epoch); and yet, even at the end: 'It is myself I have never met, whose face is pasted on the underside of my mind'; 'please open the curtains' is the final (personal and metatheatrical) plea (245).

Kane is one dramatist who goes from post-absurdity, already beyond the absurd, to a disturbing psychotic nihilism.[25] As noted already, there appear to have been few women absurdists and perhaps Sarah Kane – somehow – contrives to show us why.

Popular culture

Overy clown has a silver lifeboat (John Lennon, *A Spaniard in the Works,* 1965)

Without here straying very far into the areas of feature film, animation, live performance or other fields of possible interest, a few words should at least be said about the fruitful sequence of inspirationally zany comedy, or satirical absurdism, in British radio and television, stretching from the middle of the twentieth century, and about some of the key personalities involved. These must surely have fed off, and just as surely fed into, what were more strictly the literary activities of the absurd.

The Goon Show – a seminal radio programme of anarchic mania which ran from 1951 to 1960 (and briefly re-featured as *The Tele Goons* in the early 1960s) – may be seen as the first in this line of then unprecedented lunacy (the one analogue that comes to mind would be the Marx Brothers). Of the three stars of this long-running cult series, who went on to what may or may not have been greater things, Peter Sellers became the most versatile international comic actor of his day (in films ranging from *The Pink Panther* to *Dr Strangelove,* both 1963; as well as 'stealing' Kubrick's *Lolita,* 1962); and Spike Milligan (the Goons' main writer), acting apart, wrote absurdist fiction (notably *Puckoon,* 1963) and 'memoirs' (*Adolf Hitler: My Part in his Downfall,* 1972). Another spin-off was the short arch-absurdist *The Running, Jumping, Standing Still Film* (directed by Richard Lester with Sellers in 1959, and featuring Milligan). A comic-nostalgia commemorative show, *Ying Tong – A Walk with the Goons,* opened in London in February 2005.

One writer certainly influenced by the Goons, as equally by Lewis Carroll (and, one must assume, Edward Lear), was John Lennon, whose *In His Own Write* and *A Spaniard in the Works* astonished many on their appearance in 1964 and 1965 (they were reprinted together in 1997).[26] These two volumes of stories, poems and sketches (with Lennon's line drawings also in the absurdist tradition) are notable for their inventive wordplay – punning, inconsistency, 'wrong' words, and the use of sub-standard, juvenile and macaronic forms (often somehow contriving to resemble Old English). Comparisons have even been made with *Finnegans Wake* (Tigges, 1988, 171). In a typological table within his study of nonsense, Tigges places Lennon under the headings 'nursery rhyme' and 'irrational', and close to 'Dada' (ibid., 87). Lennon's occasionally hilarious writings, at their best, can stand comparison with those of the other miniaturists discussed here. 'There once was a man who was partly Dave' (Lennon, 9) is an opening line which should ring bells with those familiar with such writers (whom Lennon could not have known).

Predominantly 'nonsense' Lennon's texts may be, but some have at least a suspicion of a black absurdist edge (for instance 'Randolf's Party';

'Amarinta Ditch'; and 'Last Will and Testicle'). Lennon indulges also in topical and cultural satire amid his extensive paronomasia ('They seemed olivier to the world about them': ibid., 54) and religious parody ('Goody Griff, which artery in HEFFER harold be thy norm!': 142). He must also have known the prep school satires of Willans and Searle (*Down with Skool!* and *How to be Topp*, published in 1953 and 1954), although his own ethos is very different, and he is particularly effective in pastiching other popular forms, including 'The Famous Five through Woenow Abbey', 'Treasure Ivan', Sherlock Holmes (who emerges as 'Shamrock Womlbs', in 'The Singularge Experience of Miss Anne Duffield') and 'Snore Wife and Some Several Dwarts'. Lennon arguably makes miniature contributions to absurd theatre too, through such pieces as 'Scene three Act one' and 'I Believe, Boot ...'. Lennon's writings seem also to have impacted upon his later song lyrics (such as 'I am the Walrus': Jon Savage, in Lennon, viii).

The next significant step in the absurdist comic line came in the early 1960s with *Beyond the Fringe*, which premiered at Edinburgh in 1960. Of its talented squad, Jonathan Miller later turned from medicine to opera and theatre direction, while we have already encountered Alan Bennett as a playwright; Peter Cook and Dudley Moore developed their own television spin-off, *Not Only ... But Always* (1965–70), and Cook was a founder (in 1961) of the satirical magazine *Private Eye*. Supreme admirers of *Beyond the Fringe* were another Oxbridge grouping who, in the late 1960s, formed *Monty Python's Flying Circus*, which enjoyed a cult following among the younger generation with its four television series (from 1969 to 1974) and films (especially the Gospel burlesque, *The Life of Brian*, 1979). Many of these figures (including Miller, Cook and John Cleese) had come through Cambridge 'Footlights' reviews; most of them, along with representatives of a younger comic generation and pop musicians, came together in the Amnesty International shows, *The Secret Policeman's Ball* (1979–89). From the Python team (leaving aside Cleese and *Fawlty Towers*), Michael Palin and Terry Jones wrote the two series of *Ripping Yarns* (starring Palin, 1976–79, mention of which has been made earlier in this book; a BBC DVD was issued in 2004). Palin has more recently achieved a different sort of acclaim as a television traveller, while Jones has emerged as a Chaucerian critic and a popular historian (latterly, at least, with political interests: see *Terry Jones's War on the War on Terror*, 2005).

Perhaps the most notable more recent succession to this line has been the group antics of *The League of Gentlemen* (dating from 1999, title taken from the 1960 Ealing comedy of that name), through three series and a live tour (*The League of Gentlemen Live at Drury Lane*: Universal Video, 2001; a movie, *The League of Gentlemen's Apocalypse*, was relased in 2005). Set in and around the fictional northern town of

Royston Vasey (in reality Hadfield, north Derbyshire, posing by the name of a controversial northern stand-up comic), *The League*, performed predominantly by a trio of highly talented character actors, who are also the writers (along with a fourth, Jeremy Dyson, who restricts himself to minor appearances) remains – as is the case with its predecessors – predominantly a male preserve, with eccentric cross-dressing as consummation of the main (if not quite all) female roles.[27] Indeed, some of the latter are undoubtedly among the most memorable of *The League*'s creations (Tubbs, Pauline and her pens, Mrs Levinson and her cleaner).[28]

Some, at least , would argue for the addition to any such list (of ludicrous comedy with edge) of, say, *The Young Ones* and, from more recent programmes, *The Fast Show* – or even *The Office* – and particularly, perhaps, *Little Britain* (which would seem inconceivable without the precedent of *The League*).

A further absurdist performer to venture somewhat beyond mere performance is *The League*'s Mark Gatiss, who has published a competent spoof Edwardian thriller, *The Vesuvius Club* (2004), written in a largely convincing early twentieth-century brand of English. Gatiss's protagonist, Lucifer Box (resident at Number 9, Downing Street), is a self-acknowledged 'fêted artist [and] dashing dandy', as well as a 'philanderer, sodomite and assassin' (Gatiss, 238); something of a burlesqued James Bond *avant la lettre*, Box can boast of 'artistic licence to kill' (15).

Finally, in the realm of modern art, as in the varied forms of popular culture, the question of what is genuine or absurd (in whatever sense) in any serious artistic terms may be open to wide discussion. There would seem, however, to be little possible doubt over the absurdist credentials of the following art transaction, labelled 'Whiff of cash for Merde d'Artiste' (reported *The Guardian*, 28 June 2003): 'Merde d'Artiste, a tin of 30 grams of human excrement produced by Piero Manzoni, an Italian conceptual artist, was sold for £17,925 at Christie's in London.'

That miscellaneous and ubiquitous absurd

Without stupidity and illusion the world would collapse. (Matthijs van Boxsel, *The Encyclopaedia of Stupidity*, 2003)

Thought

In what amounts to something like a twenty-first century version of *In Praise of Folly*, Matthijs van Boxsel's *The Encyclopaedia of Stupidity* ranges far and wide over its subject and informs us that: 'Research has been done into the effect of side winds on arithmetic sums, into the specific gravity of a kiss, and into the surface of God' (26). Emphasising 'the fictional character of the world', he commends 'the need for ritual follies in which is embedded the idiocy that necessarily lies at the heart of our existence' (161). 'All the strategies aimed at controlling our stupidity combine to form our civilization', he argues, while culture of itself is the product of 'a series of more or less abortive attempts to come to grips with the self-destructive folly found in all countries and at all times' (166). Van Boxsel's precepts regarding stupidity inevitably overlap with the absurd, and can even at times sound as though they had been drawn from Beckett and Kharms:

> Stupidity is unavoidable. Make your stupidity a personal, unique stupidity. If you fail, fail at the highest level. If you fall, fall with elegance and a song in your heart. Be as colourfully and versatilely stupid as you can. That way you avoid blandness and rigidity, the two dangerous sides of stupidity. Make stupidity your most redeeming quality. (van Boxsel, 53)

'Stupidity', van Boxsel proclaims, 'is the ontological condition of human existence': 'Thanks to a catastrophe, there is something rather than nothing. Man is fundamentally unhinged' (189).

One commentator, having lived through almost the whole of the twentieth century, Jacques Barzun (who was born in 1907), made plain a deep distrust of absurdity as concept in his survey (subtitled '500 Years of Western Life: 1500 to the present') – *From Dawn to Decadence* (2000). Barzun's account of the absurd (see 754–60), from a chapter he entitles 'Embracing the Absurd', takes its cue from Theatre of the Absurd and from 'the novels of Albert Camus and a number of other talents' (756). The Dadaists and the Surrealists are also seen as practitioners of the absurd. The absurd, having been developed and reproduced, nevertheless – and seemingly to its discredit – 'set off no spark of positive electricity, no rebellion against the absurdity of the Absurd (757)'. 'Even the Stoics', Barzun considers, 'who did not dance with joy at the idea of being alive, left life and the cosmos their validity'. 'The Absurd', however, marks a failure of nerve' (ibid.).

John Weightman, on the other hand (another veteran critic), 'came out' in his last years as a self-confessed (one might almost say 'born again') 'Absurdist' with two books: the somewhat bathetically entitled *The Cat Sat on the Mat* (though it also has the subtitle 'Language and the Absurd') and the more bravely labelled *Reading the Bible in the Run-up to Death* (2002 and 2003 respectively). Weightman's influences and impulses as well stem largely (though not exclusively), as would be expected, from French literature and thought. Language is seen by him as 'a secular, contingent prosthesis' (*The Cat*, 10) – the latter word representing a concept already applied (rather differently and unbeknown then to Weightman) by Derrida.[29] Language, then, is 'contingent' and 'shifting' (92), of an 'equivocal nature', itself revealing that 'the world is "absurd" from the human point of view, and it is itself part and parcel of that Absurd' (125). Absurdism, to Weightman also, is 'a form of Stoicism' (77) and he draws it from the tradition of Mallarmé and Rimbaud, plus Lautréamont, Jarry, Roussel, Artaud and Georges Bataille, connected too with Theatre of the Absurd (Ionesco and others), and with de Sade and Nietzsche ('two writers who operated on the borders of insanity'), 'but *not* – it is important to note – with the concept of the Absurd, as expounded by Sartre and Camus', as 'their perception of the Absurd depends essentially on their faith in reason' (176; my emphasis). Weightman writes entertainingly of William James 'bombinating in the void' on God's existence (42); for himself, he concludes that doctrinal religions are 'a linguistic mirage' (70) and, from past and present religious conflicts, that 'the vacuous and all-purpose term "God" is a virus that has been present in the linguistic system of civilization throughout recorded history' (*Reading the Bible*, 114).

Not that the Bible itself is necessarily immune from absurdity, even as far as some of its proponents are concerned: a conference was held at the University of Turin in 2005 on 'Laughter and Comedy in Ancient Christianity'. For that matter, heated discussions in the European Union's council of ministers have been ongoing, at least since 2003, as to whether the aforementioned deity, as the figurehead of Christian civilization, should achieve citation in the preamble to the EU's new constitution. Conclusions, at various stages, have seemed to be heading in a negative direction, with fudge or compromise seemingly beyond reach: 'Putting God into the constitution is simply in the "too difficult to agree" category', diplomatic sources have divulged. The controversy, however, drags on – fuelled by the arrival in the EU of a new, largely Catholic populated, membership.

Not that great palliatives are necessarily to be expected from Eastern philosophy. The Kyoto school, whose chief luminary was Nishida Kitaro (1870–1945), now considered proponents of 'a world philosophy', vie with Heidegger in such impenetrable utterances as: 'the individual is mediated by nothingness through a self-negating mediation of the specific'.[30] The Kyoto thinkers take their (greatly pre-Heideggerian) pedigree from the Buddhist notion of 'emptiness' (*kú*), prompting such statements as 'the true absolute is absolute nothingness' and seeing nothingness as 'the ground of reality'. Kyoto philosophy, like Heidegger, shares 'a resolutely anti-transcendent view' of essential nothingness: '"Emptiness is itself empty", declare the sutras, and must not, therefore, be conceived of as a special kind of being – the theists' God, say – that stands above or beyond the world' (seen indeed as 'the characteristic mistake of the West'; and otherwise describable as 'bombinating in the void'?). Rather than either transcendence or nihilistic despair, this school of thought calls, apparently, for 'dying to philosophy', or a non-theistic quietism.

Back in the West, we can even find philosophers behaving badly. An incident lasting apparently only ten minutes or so, at King's College, Cambridge, in 1946, has now become the subject of a book-length study. In *Wittgenstein's Poker* (2001), David Edmonds and John Eidonow contextualise and attempt to reconstruct the meeting of the Moral Science Club at which (visiting speaker) Karl Popper clashed with (chair and resident professor) Ludwig Wittgenstein, in the presence too of Bertrand Russell – in what has been described as 'a "symbolic and in hindsight prophetic" watershed' (see Edmonds and Eidinow, 7); 'inseparable from the story of their times, ... it is the story of the schism in twentieth-century philosophy over the significance of language', with particular regard to the question of philosophical problems (ibid. 4). A titanic clash of rival philosophical approaches, stemming from the one Viennese background, but with wide social and intellectual contrasts, this confrontation had been retold and written up many times – yet no two observers could agree on the exact details or the sequence of events. Wittgenstein brandished aggressively, gesticulated with, or merely fidgeted with, a poker (using it as baton, tool or potential weapon), which may have been red hot, or cool, in the face of, or merely in the presence of, Popper – interrupting (as was his wont) the latter's (apparently provocative) analysis of philosophical problems. Popper's quip, that an example of 'a moral rule' was 'not to threaten visiting lecturers with pokers', rather than causing Wittgenstein to stomp out (or merely leave quietly) may well have been uttered after Wittgenstein's departure – and may therefore not, as such, have been the victorious thrust he subsequently suggested it to have been (Popper, *Unended Quest*, 1974).

The difficult personalities of both philosophers are clearly vital to any assessment of their performances in this piece of philosophical theatre of the absurd – the only occasion on which they met. Wittgenstein, in particular, has been invoked in literary and artistic works going beyond philosophical analysis (see, for instance Terry Eagleton's *Saints and Scholars*, and those detailed in Marjorie Perloff's *Wittgenstein's Ladder*). Edmonds and Eidinow suggest that: 'perhaps the secret is to see Wittgenstein as a literary figure who fits as easily into a discourse on authors – such as Proust, Kafka, Eliot, Beckett – as into a study of philosophers' (18). 'One of the aims of philosophy', for that matter, in Wittgenstein's view, they affirm, 'is to turn latent nonsense into patent nonsense' (184).

Science. And everything else ...

> The more the universe appears comprehensible, the more it also appears pointless. (Steven Weinberg, 1988)

The so-called 'perfect joke' has now been reduced to a mathematical equation (as reported in *The Guardian*: 14 June 2004), according to the 'Comedy Research Project'. The calculation – said to be: '$c = (m + nO) / p$' – reveals that the joke's quality ('c') is determined by 'm', or the 'comic moment' (the punchline's humour rating, multiplied by its build-up time), added to 'nO' (or pratfalls multiplied by 'ouch factor'); the total is divided by 'p' (the number of puns). Shaggy dog stories (including perhaps, for that matter, Barthelme's 'The Falling Dog': *Sixty Stories*, 163–8) thus do not require the funny punchline of a shorter wisecrack. Puns, though, are a dissipating factor, seen as tending to encourage groans rather than mirth.

At another extreme, some cosmologists have recently put forward what Paul Davies terms 'a catch-all argument for cosmic pointlessness' in the form of 'the multiverse concept': the theory that our universe is but one small component in a vast assemblage, or conglomeration, of universes.[31] The relevance of this concept to 'cosmic pointlessness' should not be hard to fathom. A further consequence is that, in a multiverse of millions of universes popping into (albeit incommunicable) existence, one at least should have the precise physical conditions needed for life. For what there is to be said for this proposition, some (such as George Ellis) would argue that it requires as much faith as traditional belief in a God-created universe. At the same time, it is affirmed that, from a scientific viewpoint, it makes as much sense as anything else and it could be right. Davies points out that a 'pointless' universe, existing without reason is 'ultimately arbitrary and absurd'; all scientific 'chains of reasoning' would thus be 'grounded in absurdity'; the 'breathtaking rationality' of the 'order of the world' would therefore 'have to spring, miraculously, from absurdity'. For what enlightenment it may bring, Davies suggests turning Weinberg's (above) dictum on its head: 'the more the universe seems pointless, the more it also seems incomprehensible'.

The universe may reside within a multiverse. Quantum theory may have led to 'string theory', or 'M theory'.[32] From the biggest picture of all, to (for many) the big enough picture of world order (new or otherwise) in international affairs, all the way down to the trivia as reported in the tabloids planet-wide – without going into further and probably here superfluous (not to say tendentious) details and examples[33] – the impression of absurdity at all levels remains depressingly (or perhaps even reassuringly) consistent. In modern media parlance: 'you couldn't make it up!'

Notes

1 'Pataphysics' was a concept invented by Alfred Jarry and taken up by later exponents of absurdism or proto-absurdism (see earlier mentions).

2 This too may be compared to the case of Sitric O'Sanassa, in Flann O'Brien's *The Poor Mouth* (1941), who makes his abode with seals to escape the famine and the abuse of the world, growing in time into 'a tasty fish' containing 'a whole winter's oil' (London: Picador, 1975, 98); and the 'undersea' scenes in *The Dalkey Archive* (1964).

3 James Campbell, 'John Patrick Donleavy: The Spice of Life', *The Guardian: Review*, 26 June 2004, 20–3 (22).

4 Iury Tynyanov, *Lieutenant Kizhe and Young Vitushnikov*, translated by Mirra Ginsburg, Boston, MA.: Eridanos Press, 1990. This work is also known from Prokofiev's orchestral suite of that name.

5 See also the comments on works by Nabokov and Stoppard (in note 18 below).

6 The idea of victim as killer is also to be found in O'Brien: in the story 'Two in One'; the narrator of *The Third Policeman* begins as a murderer and is eventually revealed also to be a murder victim (on both see our Chapter 9).

7 In addition to these two novels, Keith Booker, in his chapter on 'Flann O'Brien in the Twentieth Century' (1995, 121–39), mentions Sorrentino, and works by B.S. Johnson and Anthony Burgess's *Earthly Powers*, among those manifesting an impact from O'Brien.

8 Alasdair Gray, *Lanark: A Life in Four Books*, Edinburgh: Canongate, 2002, 489, n. 6; 569.

9 Metafictional devices continue to evolve, beyond even those exploited by Sorrentino and Fowles in these novels, in the direction of absurdity. José Carlos Somoza, for instance (in his *The Athenian Murders*, translated by Sonia Soto, London: Abacus, 2002) develops what might be called the device of the 'metatranslational'.

10 The short prose works translated in *Stories and Drawings* (1968) represent a selection from the collection published (in the original French) under the title *Four Roses for Lucienne* (1967).

11 Vladimir Nabokov, 'On a Book Entitled *Lolita*', *The Annotated Lolita* (Harmondsworth: Penguin, 1995, 311).

12 Leonid Dobychin, *The Town of N*, translated by Richard C. Borden and Natalia Belova, Evanston, Ill.: Northwestern University Press, 1998, 102. See, for information on Dobychin, Borden's 'Introduction' (vii–xxvi).

13 See also Eco's essay 'Travels in Hyperreality' (1975; in Eco, 1987). These may have contributed to inspiring, in a rather different and sexualised way, the concept of 'hyperdramatism' – so-called 'because it goes *beyond* drama': 'hyperdramatic art consists of putting young women like you naked or semi-naked in "artistic" poses. Young men too, of course. And a lot of adolescents, children even', whereby they become saleable or rentable 'paintings', or 'works of art' ('canvases' or even 'ornaments'): see Somoza's novel *The Art of Murder* (112; 116 and passim). Another inspiration for Somoza's 'hyperdramatic art' – Carroll's *Through the Looking Glass* and aspects of contemporary and conceptual art apart (see 'Author's Note', 469–70) – may have been the frozen pictorial quality in certain later Beckett works (such as *Catastrophe*). In Vanessa Beecroft's *VB55*, a hundred 'nude' women (in transparent tights) posed for three hours at the New National Gallery, Berlin (April 2005).

14 Valery Ronshin, *Living a Life* (Moscow: Glas, 2002), volume 29 in the Glas series. Some of these works may also be found in the earlier *Glas: New Russian*

Writing 7: Booker Winners and Others, edited by Natasha Perova and Arch Tait, Moscow and Birmingham, 1994; and in volume 14 of the same series, *Beyond the Looking Glass (Moscow and Birmingham, 1997)*.

15 Similar reasoning would seem to demand a mention too for Alan Ayckbourn's play *Absurd Person Singular* (1972). However, in his Preface (Ayckbourn, *Three Plays*, London: Chatto and Windus, 1977, 7–9), Ayckbourn admits the title to be 'arbitrary': 'originally intended for a play I didn't write' (7). In his 'first offstage action play' (ibid.), the three acts take place in a domestic kitchen; perhaps the closest it comes to the absurd is the mildly sinister enforced dancing finale (to Act 3) – reminiscent perhaps of Kafka's expostulatory 'Dance on, you pigs; what concern is it of mine?' (*Diaries*, 272).

16 Katy Simmons brings 'Theatre of the Absurd' into the title of her study of Petrushevskaia's plays, while Sally Dalton-Brown calls her study of Petrushevskaia's genres *Voices from the Void*. Dalton-Brown claims: Petrushevskaia's 'true genre is that of a [deliberately] failed carnival narrative, one which denies its own communality' (viii; 16). Slobodanka Vladiv-Glover offers a Wittgensteinian reading of Petrushevskaia's *A Modern Family Robinson* (*Dissonant Voices: The New Russian Fiction*, edited by Oleg Chukhontsev, London: Harvill, 1991, 414–24, translated by George Bird): see Epstein *et al.*, 232–42).

17 D. Bykov (*Ogonek*, 18, 1993), quoted by Dalton-Brown (176).

18 See Priscilla Meyer, 'The Real Hound, The Real Knight', in Jane Grayson *et al.*, *Nabokov's World. Volume 2: Reading Nabokov*, Houndmills and New York: Palgrave, 2002, pp. 204–13. This 'work' by Sebastian Knight is summarised in Chapter 10 of Nabokov's *The Real Life of Sebastian Knight*. Stoppard, Nabokov and the absurd converge again in Fassbinder's film of the Nabokov novel *Despair* (starring Dirk Bogarde; screenplay by Stoppard, 1978), in which the unhinged protagonist schemes a psychological murder on the basis of a 'double' who does not in fact look like him.

19 See, respectively, Victor L. Cahn, *Beyond Absurdity: The Plays of Tom Stoppard*, London: Associated University Presses, 1979, 157; Tim Brassell, *Tom Stoppard: An Assessment*, London: Macmillan, 1985, 61.

20 Esslin, in his chapter 'Beyond the Absurd' (in the third edition), stresses that the play's debt to Beckett 'could not have been more clearly emphasized' (*Th. of Abs.*, 434). Cf. the similar references in Tymoteusz Karpowicz's *Solving Spaces*: 'the number of thieves beside us isn't of significance as we die it's the number as we live' (*New American Writing* [20], 2002, 171); and 'as walking among the spools of galaxies only she the mother of the poet slain obliquely by the general's boomerang is carrying in herself the intra-venous plumb-line of the world as straight as pain in kicked crotches of clock hands amidst which she birthing time astraddle the tombs of all becketts and by means of her loins is straightening out eternity' (ibid., 163; translations by Frank Kujawinski).

21 On Lucretius, the Epicurean author of *De rerum natura* (*On the Nature of Things*) see Latham (in Edwards, 1967, 5:99–101).

22 Cf. however Hersh Zeifman's comments on the 'black hole' to be found in Beckett with the 'trick of light' in Stoppard: 'A Trick of the Light: Tom Stoppard's *Hapgood* and Postabsurdist Theater' (Brater and Cohn, 175–202 (198).

23 For readings of these two plays see respectively Demastes 41–50 and 85–103; and Fleming 175–90 and 191–207.
24 For historical background, variety of responses, post-play developments and the author's considered position see the lengthy Postscript (95–132) and 'Post-Postscript' (133–49) to Frayn, *Copenhagen* (London: Methuen, 2003).
25 A somewhat comparable dramatist may be Philip Ridley, who creates images of extreme shock and violence (Greek themes set in the contemporary world), enacted out of 'love', with a profession of faith in redemption. His *Mercury Fur* (2005) necessitated a change of publisher before even reaching the stage.
26 A third book, published posthumously (John Lennon, *Skywriting by Word of Mouth*, London: Pan Books, 1986), is regarded as less successful.
27 While female, or for that matter feminist, comedy has made great strides over this period, both in sitcom (such as *Absolutely Fabulous*) and in stand-up comedy, it still seems not quite to compete in terms of absurdist edge; the closest approach has perhaps been the double-act of French and Saunders.
28 For an extension of *The League of Gentlemen* into print see '*My Scrapbook*' *by Tubbs: A Local Book for Local People* (or *Armistice Souvenir Scrapbook; Made in Royston Vasey*), London: Fourth Estate (no date).
29 Jacques Derrida, *Le Monolinguisme de l'autre ou la prothèse d'origine* (1996); Weightman engages with this study in an appendix (*The Cat*, 181–6).
30 See David E. Cooper, 'An Honourable Withdrawal' (review of James W. Heisig, *Philosophers of Nothingness*), *TLS*, 28 March 2003, 7–8.
31 Paul Davies, 'Universal Truths', *The Guardian*, 23 January 2003 (Science, p. 10). See also the George Ellis interview: *The Guardian*, 13 May 2004 (Life, p. 6).
32 'Membrane theory': a variation of string theory developed by Michio Kaku and operating out of eleven dimensions; similarly, 'multi-worlds theory' (cf. 'multiverse' above), a new version of quantum theory, predicts possible clones of ourselves with separate lives (John Crace, 'Mr Parallel Universe', *Education Guardian*, 22 February 2005, 20–1).
33 See, for instance, the survey of modern absurdity offered by Barzun (760–71).

Conclusion

Not only is the Universe stranger than we think, it is stranger than we can think. (Werner Heisenberg)

A few final words may be in order first on the four 'special author' representatives of absurdism highlighted in this study as the subjects of individual chapters.

Kharms (any special pleading from the present author apart) has become something of a cult author in Russia, but also – albeit in a minor way – now too in the Western world. Dramatic productions based on his works are staged in Britain and the USA.[1] The Icelandic composer Haflidi Hallgrimsson has created Kharmsian 'music dramas' (his opera *Die Wält der Zwischenfälle*, or 'Whirled of Incidents', premiered in Lübeck and Vienna in 2005). A publication called *Bust Down the Door and Eat All the Chickens* (presenting itself as 'The Journal of the Institute of Advanced Surreal and Absurd Studies' and all but dedicated to Kharms) launched its first issue in 2003.[2] Translations of works by Kharms (and other OBERIU members) have even contrived to appear in *New American Writing* (Number 20, 2002), followed by a new anthology (from the same translators), with an introduction by Susan Sontag, announced for 2005.[3]

The Taganka Theatre in Moscow, for its fortieth anniversary in 2004, premiered a production entitled *Go On, and Stop Progress* (*Idite i ostanovite progress*) about the 'Oberiuty', balletically and acrobatically choreographed in a set based on the Supremacist 'Black Square' of their friend Malevich (from whom also the title is taken). Such traditions have been developed too by the Akhe Theatre (also promoted as 'Russian Engineering Theatre'), an absurdist group from St Petersburg who have brought shows to Western countries (winning an award at the Edinburgh Fringe with their production *White Cabin*, 2003).

With regard to the other three, the name of Kafka is, of course, constantly invoked with reference to grossly excessive paperchains and the tentacles of unseen powers. In addition to novels such as Marc Estrin's *Insect Dreams: The Half Life of Gregor Samsa* (2002), the spirit of Kafka lives on too in further Kafkan dramas (such as Emma Spurgin Hussey's 2003 play, *Axe for the Frozen Sea*, entangling Kafka on the Prague–Berlin overnight train); in Murakami's *Kafka on the Shore* (2002: about Franz Kafka, in any real sense, or not); in Poul Ruders's opera *Proces Kafka* (Copenhagen, 2005 – which certainly is about Kafka); and indeed in 'The Kafka Academy'- a weekly satirical column by Ted Wragg (in *The Guardian*'s education supplement) on the manic bureaucracy inflicted on the English school system. The adjective 'Beckettian' is almost as common as 'Kafkaesque', while 'it's like waiting for God-oh' has even been intoned in the graveyards of *Buffy the Vampire Slayer*. The director of London's South Bank arts complex, calling for a 'world-class park' to adjoin the Royal Festival Hall, has said: 'I do feel that anything called a park should have at least one token Waiting for Godot tree.' Certain of the novels of such a popular author as Paul Auster are frequently compared to the fiction of both Kafka and Beckett (in particular *The New York Trilogy*, 1985–87).[4] Even Flann O'Brien, whose world profile remains somewhat lower than the two last named, despite his well-established literary (and journalistic) influence, has 'starred' (indeed, as Myles na gCopaleen) in Arthur Riordan's absurdist satirical musical *Improbable Frequency* (staged at the Dublin Theatre Festival, 2004; revived at The Abbey, 2005).[5] 'The Franz Kafka Literary Prize' (among others) was awarded in 2005 to Harold Pinter.

In the introductory chapter of this book a number of definitions applied to the absurd were put forward and a number of approaches outlined. As will have become apparent through the body of the following chapters, the term absurd (or 'the Absurd') has become applied to literature in several ways. As has been pointed out, the term 'Theatre of the Absurd' (through which the 'absurd' label first derived its recent literary critical currency) was established by Martin Esslin and it underwent a certain development, as well as an expansion of the proposed theatrical canon, even through the three editions of his book (of 1961; 1968; and 1980); Esslin used the term rather more assertively, having appropriated the concept of the absurd in the first place from Camus and chosen to apply it to what he identified as a new theatrical trend – in the formation of which, arguably, he became himself an active participant (see Zarhy-Levo, 2001, 9–13). It has also – or more notably, perhaps, since – been applied similarly to prose fiction, as well as to other forms of cultural (not to mention worldly) activity.

Yael Zarhy-Levy (2001, 87) can by no means be alone in discerning an 'anarchy governing the usage of the term'. Principally, however (as she suggests: ibid., 2–3), but without again going over the gamut of linguistic effects we have seen to be involved, it is used in three ways. It may be considered a prominent period style, observable in the second half of the twentieth century, or (given the presence of now recognised practitioners from the 1920s and 1930s) perhaps a period running through the two middle quarters of the century, and a little beyond. It may also be regarded as a category with philosophical (latterly usually Existentialist) implications, a timeless disposition or quality, which may be seen to pertain – at the very least here and there – throughout the history of literature, and certainly from some of the works of the Greeks. This application of the term may also be illustrated by modern, usually ludic, reworkings of much older works, such as Tom Stoppard's 'play' on *Hamlet*; or Howard Barker's take from the same source, *Gertrude, The Cry* (2002). Acceptance or application of the tenets of deconstruction, for that matter, has been seen (by Hayden White, writing in 1976) as delivering *any* text ultimately into the arms of absurdity. More narrowly, the absurd can be confined to the 'school category', in the manner developed in theatre by Esslin; this gains acceptance (as and when it does) through what has been called 'the driving force of critical consensus' (ibid., 120).

Exploration of the absurd in literature (close-reading analyses of its poetics apart) is likely to be undertaken diachronically, but may also be carried out rather more synchronically, or perhaps – as has occasionally been the case here – in a fashion that may be regarded as rather more diagonal. In a similar manner, the inclusion of theatrical drama, or related (not necessarily stageable) literary forms, may vary in emphasis amid what again, here at least, is primarily a concentration on prose fiction (although this too has been seen to come in a variety of lengths and subgenres).

The literary (including the theatrical) absurd may be seen to have been taken variously 'beyond' – into 'chaotics', into politics (by, in very different ways, Pinter, Stoppard and, say, Edward Bond), back into nonsense, into nihilism, or into silence. If there be such a thing as the sado-masochistic absurd, it is surely to be found in Robert Coover's *Spanking the Maid* (1982). There is 'Theatre of Excess' (Manfridi) and 'Theatre of Catastrophe' (Barker), to name but two 'categories'. Of theatre companies, Complicité have been alluded to more than once; Ariane Mnouchkine's Le Théâtre du Soleil (of the Bois de Vincennes, Paris) present the adventures of asylum seekers across Europe in *Le Dernier Caravansérail*, a production in which the actors' feet are said never to touch the ground; while Improbable Theatre go to almost any lengths to embrace failure (their catchphrase in rehearsals being: 'get it wrong, fuck it up!').[6] The last named company's show *The Hanging Man* (2003), featuring an architect who hangs himself inside his own unfinished Gothic cathedral but doesn't die, just hanging there rejected by a Death piqued at having his thunder stolen, might be seen in its storyline somehow to counterbalance or reflect the anonymous anecdote featured at the beginning of the Preface to this book.

One might, when all is said and done, wish to part company with Zarhy-Levo (2001, 107), however, in her implicit extension of Brian McHale's assertion that 'there "is" no such "thing" as postmodernism' as an 'identifiable object "out there" in the world' to the category or quality of the absurd.[7] While the absurd undoubtedly – some might well want to say predominantly – 'exists as a cultural artifact rooted in the critical discourse' (ibid.), its apparent validity and permeation as even a fundamental or universal property (intangible though it may appear to be) stretches out into infinity. The absurd seems to have its existence as signified, in addition to its function as signifier. Demastes, however, would wish to maintain that the absurd (at least in philosophical, cultural and theatrical terms) has been overtaken through the phenomenon of chaos theory, which, he emphasises, 'actually has literal (as well as metaphoric) value' (Demastes, 18). This indeed applies – possibly even, one might say, persuasively – on the world stage (to re-use advisedly the age-old metaphor). 'The pre-Cold War delusional security of neo-Newtonianism can no longer be relied upon, nor can the impotent absurdist despair of existentialism', he argues (170). 'Our destinies', he claims, 'lie somewhere in between' (ibid.).

Such a verdict may well, at the present stage of thought, culture and science, appear more acceptable – or even attractive – as a philosophical attitude to dealing with the world. It at least restores a modicum of optimism (although that might also therein have its dangers). On a more individual level, though, with a mind to both the human condition and the playout of the immediate and the intermediate effects of the swings that constantly occur within the incomprehensible patterns of orderly disorder, one might still think that the absurd – verbal, logical twists and all – has a considerable future before it. Enoch Brater, writing in 1990 (Brater and Cohn, 300), stresses that the absurd is still '*all* around, even in unexpected corners. There's no *after* after the absurd.'

Or, as Stoppard's James Joyce has it of his 'Dublin Odyssey' (*Travesties*, 62–3: italics in the original): 'yes by God *there's* a corpse that will dance for some time yet and *leave the world precisely as it finds it*'.

Notes

1 Théâtre de Complicité's 1994 show (*Out of a House Walked a Man*) has already been alluded to; Complicité (a post-absurdist theatre company headed by Simon McBurney, placing a marked emphasis on visual and musical aspects) had also produced *The Street of Crocodiles*, based on the Bruno Schulz collection, in 1992.

2 See www.millstreambooks.com: an animated figure of Kharms serves as logo to the website.

3 *OBERIU: An Anthology of Russian Absurdism*, translated by Eugene Ostashevsky *et al.*, Evanston: Northwestern University Press, 2005.

4 See Stephen Bernstein, '"The Question Is the Story Itself": Postmodernism and Intertextuality in Auster's *New York Trilogy*', in Merivale and Sweeney, 134–53: 'Auster emerges, like the Beckett who asserts in *Watt* that there are "no symbols where none intended" . . . , as a master ironist, a practitioner of the absurd who wants to communicate nothing so much as that communication is impossible' (150).

5 This production features a Dublin wartime gathering which includes Myles na gCopaleen, John Betjeman and quantum physicist Erwin Schrödinger (whom Flann O'Brien may actually have consulted over his 1943 adaptation of *The Insect Play*: see the Dublin Theatre Festival 2004 programme for *Improbable Frequency*).

6 Brian Logan, 'We got it wrong? Great!', *The Guardian*, G2 (28 May 2003, 10–11).

7 Brian McHale, *Constructing Postmodernism*, London: Routledge, 1992, 1.

Bibliography

Primary sources (Philosophy, prose writings and drama)

Abish, Walter, *Minds Meet*, New York: New Directions, 1975

Absurd Drama: Eugène Ionesco, Arthur Adamov, Fernando Arrabal, Edward Albee, introduction by Martin Esslin, Harmondsworth: Penguin, 1965

Apollinaire, Guillaume, *The Poet Assassinated and Other Stories*, translated by Ron Padgett, Manchester: Carcanet, 1985

Apollinaire, Guillaume, *Flesh Unlimited: Two Erotic Novellas*, translated by Alexis Lykiard, London: Velvet, 1995

Aristophanes, *The Complete Plays of Aristophanes*, edited by Moses Habas, New York: Bantam Books, 1971

Artaud, Antonin, *Antonin Artaud. Selected Writings*, edited, with an Introduction, by Susan Sontag, translated by Helen Weaver, Berkeley: University of California Press, 1988 (first published 1976)

Astley, Neil, *The End of My Tether*, London: Scribner, 2003

Auster, Paul, *The New York Trilogy: City of Glass, Ghosts, The Locked Room*, London: Faber, 2004 (first published 1985–87)

Barthelme, Donald, *Paradise*, New York: Putnam, 1986

Barthelme, Donald, *Sixty Stories*, New York and London: Penguin, 2003 (first published 1982)

Barthelme, Donald, *The Dead Father*, New York: Farrar, Straus, 2004 (first published 1975)

Barthelme, Donald, *Forty Stories*, New York and London: Penguin, 2005 (first published 1987)

Beckett, Samuel, *Watt*, London: Calder and Boyars, 1970

Beckett, Samuel, *Théâtre I*, Paris: Les Éditions de Minuit, 1971

Beckett, Samuel, *Molloy, Malone Dies, The Unnamable* [*Molloy*, 1950; *Malone meurt*, 1951; *L'Innommable*, 1952], London: Calder and Boyars, 1973

Beckett, Samuel, *More Pricks Than Kicks*, London: Picador, 1974

Beckett, Samuel, *How It Is* [*Comment c'est*, 1961], London: John Calder, 1977

Beckett, Samuel, *Collected Poems 1930–1978*, London: John Calder, 1986 (reprinted 1999)

Beckett, Samuel, *The Complete Dramatic Works*, London: Faber, 1990

Beckett, Samuel, *Dream of Fair to Middling Women*, Dublin: Black Cat Press, 1992

Beckett, Samuel, *Murphy*, London: Calder Publications, 1993

Beckett, Samuel, *The Complete Short Prose, 1929–1989*, edited by S.E. Gontarski, New York: Grove Press, 1995

Beckett, Samuel, *Eleutheria*, Paris: Les Éditions de Minuit, 1995

Beckett, Samuel, *Eleutheria*, translated by Barbara Wright, London: Faber, 1996

Beckett, Samuel, *Nohow On: Company, Ill Seen Ill Said, Worstward Ho*, New York: Grove Press, 1996

Beckett, Samuel, *Mercier and Camier* [*Mercier et Camier*, 1970], London: John Calder, 1999

Beckett, Samuel, *First Love and other Novellas*, edited by Gerry Dukes, London: Penguin, 2000

Beckett, Samuel, *Disjecta: Miscellaneous Writings and a Dramatic Fragment*, London: John Calder, 2001

Bennett, Alan, *Two Kafka Plays: Kafka's Dick* and *The Insurance Man*, London: Faber, 1987

Bennett, Alan, *Kafka's Dick: A Comedy*, London: Samuel French, 1992 (second revised edition)

Berkoff, Steven, *The Trial, Metamorphosis, In the Penal Colony: Three Theatre Adaptations from Franz Kafka*, Oxford: Amber Lane Press, 1988

['Bonaventura'] *Die Nachtwachen des Bonaventura / The Night Watches of Bonaventura*, edited and translated by Gerald Gillespie, Edinburgh: Edinburgh University Press, 1972

Borges, Jorge Luis, *Labyrinths*, edited by Donald A. Yates and James E. Irby, preface by André Maurois, Harmondsworth: Penguin, 1970

Borges, Jorge Luis, *Collected Fictions*, translated by Andre Hurley, New York: Penguin, 1999

Breton, André, *What is Surrealism? Selected Writings*, edited by Franklin Rosemont, London: Pluto Press, 1978; reprinted 1989

Breton, André, *Nadja*, translated by Richard Howard. Introduction by Mark Polizzotti, Harmondsworth: Penguin, 1999 (published Paris, 1928; translation first published 1960; author's revised edition published Paris, 1963)

Bufalino, Gesualdo, *Tommaso and the Blind Photographer* [*Tomasso e il fotografo cieco*, 1996], translated by Patrick Creagh, London: Harvill, 2000

Campanile, Achille, *The Inventor of the Horse and Two Other Short Plays*, translated by Francesco Loriggio, Toronto and New York: Guernica, 1995

Campanile, Achille, *Manuale di conversazione*, Milan: Bur 5, Rizzoli, 2001

Campanile, Achille, *Tragedie in due battute*, Milan: Bur 11, Rizzoli, 2001

Camus, Albert, *A Happy Death* [*La Mort heureuse*, 1971], translated by Richard Howard, London: Hamish Hamilton, 1972

Camus, Albert, *The Outsider* [*L'Étranger*, 1942], translated by Joseph Laredo, Harmondsworth: Penguin, 1983

Camus, Albert, *The Myth of Sisyphus* [*Le Mythe de Sisyphe*, 1942], translated by Justin O'Brien, Harmondsworth: Penguin, 1975

Camus, Albert, *Caligula and Other Plays*, Harmondsworth: Penguin, 1984

Camus, Albert, *The Rebel* [*L'Homme revolté*, 1951], translated by Anthony

Bower, Harmondsworth: Penguin, 1962; reissued 1971

Camus, Albert, *The Fall* [*La Chute*, 1956], translated by Justin O'Brien, Harmondsworth: Penguin, 1963; reprinted, Introduction by Olivier Todd, 2000

Čapek, The Brothers, *R.U.R. and The Insect Play* [translated by Paul Selver], London: Oxford University Press, 1975 (first published as separate editions, 1923; first issued by Oxford University Press, 1961)

Cardullo, Bert and Knopf, Robert, eds, *Theater of the Avant-Garde 1890–1950: A Critical Anthology*, New Haven and London: Yale University Press, 2001

Carroll, Lewis, *The Annotated Alice: Alice's Adventures in Wonderland* and *Through the Looking Glass*, introduction and Notes by Martin Gardner, Harmondsworth: Penguin, 1970

Chandler, Robert, ed., *Russian Short Stories from Pushkin to Buida*, London: Penguin, 2005

Cobb, Karen, *Theatre of the Absurd*, Montreux, London and New York: Minerva Press, 1995

Conrad, Joseph, *Three Short Novels*, New York: Bantam, 1960

Coover, Robert, *Pricksongs & Descants: Fictions*, New York: Grove Press, 1969

Coover, Robert, *Spanking the Maid*, New York: Grove Press, 1982

Coover, Robert, *Gerald's Party*, London: Paladin, 1988 (first published 1985)

Dada Market, The: An Anthology of Poetry, translated with an Introduction by Willard Bohn, Carbondale: Southern Illinois University Press, 1993

Day, Barbara, ed., *Czech Plays: Modern Czech Drama* [translated by Barbara Day *et al.*], London: Nick Hern Books, 1994

Dickens, Charles, *Great Expectations*, edited by Angus Calder, Harmondsworth: Penguin, 1965

Dickens, Charles, *Bleak House*, edited by Norman Page, introduction by J. Hillis Miller, Harmondsworth: Penguin, 1971

Donleavy, J.P., *The Ginger Man*, London: Abacus, 1996 (first published 1955)

[Dostoevsky] *Great Short Works of Fyodor Dostoevsky*, with an Introduction by Ronald Hingley. New York: Harper and Row, 1968

Dostoevskii, F.M., *Polnoe sobranie sochinenii v tridtsati tomakh* [30 vols], Leningrad: Nauka, 1972–90

Eco, Umberto, *The Name of the Rose* [*Il nome della rosa*, 1980], translated by William Weaver, London: Picador, 1984

Edson, Russell, *The Tunnell: Selected Poems*, Oberlin, OH: Oberlin College Press, 1994

Edson, Russell, *The Tormented Mirror*, Pittsburgh: University of Pittsburgh Press, 2001

Ford, Ford Madox, *The Good Soldier*, edited by Martin Stannard, New York: Norton, 1995

Foscolo, Ugo, *Last Letters of Jacopo Ortis* [*Ultime lettere di Jacopo Ortis*], translated by J.G. Nichols, London: Hesperus Press, 2002

Fowles, John, *Mantissa*, London: Triad/Panther, 1984

Frayn, Michael, *Copenhagen*, London, Methuen Drama, 2003 (first published 1998)

Gatiss, Mark, *The Vesuvius Club*, London: Simon and Schuster, 2004

Gibian, George, ed. and trans., *The Man in the Black Coat. Russia's Literature of the Absurd: Selected Works of Daniil Kharms and Alexander Vvedensky*, Evanston, IL: Northwestern University Press, 1987 (first published as *Russia's Lost Literature of the Absurd: A Literary Discovery*, 1971; 1974)

Gogol, Nikolai, *Plays and Petersburg Tales*, translated by Christopher English, Oxford: Oxford University Press, 1995

Gombrowicz, Witold, *Ferdydurke*, translated by Eric Mosbacher, London: Marion Boyars, 1979 (first published 1961; original published Warsaw, 1937)

Hašek, Jaroslav, *The Good Soldier Švejk and his Fortunes in the World War* [*Osudy dobrého vojáka Švejka za svetové války*, 1921–23], translated by Cecil Parrott. Harmondsworth: Penguin, 1974

Havel, Vaclav, *Largo Desolato*, translated by Tom Stoppard, London: Faber, 1987

Havel, Václav, *Open Letters: Selected Prose, 1965–1990*, edited by Paul Wilson, London: Faber, 1991

Havel, Václav, *The Garden Party and Other Plays* [translated by Vera Blackwell et al.], New York: Grove Press, 1993

Heller, Joseph, *Catch-22*, London: Vintage, 1994 (first published 1961)

Hofmannsthal, Hugo von, *Selected Prose*, translated by Mary Hottinger, and Tania and James Stern. Introduction by Hermann Broch, New York: Pantheon Books ('Bollingen Series XXXIII'), 1952

Hollingsworth, Margaret, *Endangered Species: Four Plays by Margaret Hollingsworth*, Toronto: Act One, 1988

Ionesco, Eugène, *Notes and Counter Notes: Writings on the Theatre* [*Notes et contres-notes*, 1962], translated by Donald Watson, New York: Grove Press, 1964

Ionesco, Eugène, *Four Plays: The Bald Soprano, The Lesson, Jack, or the Submission, The Chairs*, translated by Donald M. Allen, New York: Grove Weidenfeld, 1982 (first published 1958; originally published in French, 1954)

James, Henry, *The Sacred Fount*, edited by John Lyon, Harmondsworth: Penguin, 1994

Kafka, Franz, *The Complete Stories*, edited by Nahum N. Glatzer, New York: Schocken Books, 1971

Kafka, Franz, *Letters to Felice*, edited by Erich Heller and Jürgen Born, translated by James Stern and Elisabeth Duckworth, New York: Schocken Books, 1973

Kafka, Franz, *Amerika* [1927], translated by Willa and Edwin Muir, New York: Schocken Books, 1974

Kafka, Franz, *The Castle; Definitive Edition* [*Das Schloss*, 1926] translated by Willa and Edwin Muir with additional materials transalated by Eithne Wilkins and Ernst Kaiser, New York: Schocken Books, 1974

Kafka, Franz, *The Trial: Definitive Edition* [*Der Prozess*, 1925], translated by Willa and Edwin Muir, New York: Schocken Books, 1974

Kafka, Franz, *The Diaries of Franz Kafka 1910–23*, edited by Max Brod [translated by Joseph Kresh and Martin Greenberg], Harmondsworth: Penguin, 1975

Kafka, Franz, *Letters to Friends, Family, and Editors*, translated by Richard and Clara Winston, New York: Schocken Books, 1977

Kafka, Franz, *Wedding Preparations in the Country and Other Stories* [includes 'Letter to His Father'], Harmondsworth: Penguin, 1978

Kafka, Franz, *Letters to Milena*, edited by Willy Haas, translated by Tania and James Stern, London: Vintage, 1999 (first published 1953)

Kafka, Franz, *The Great Wall of China and Other Short Works*, translated and edited by Malcolm Pasley, London: Penguin, 2002 (first published as *Shorter Works*, Volume 1, 1973)

Kafka, Franz, *Metamorphosis and Other Stories*, translated by Richard Stokes, London: Hesperus, 2002

Kane, Sarah, *Complete Plays*, introduced by David Greig, London: Methuen Drama, 2001

Keret, Etgar, *The Bus Driver Who Wanted to be God* [translated by Miriam Schlesinger *et al.*], New Milford, CT, and London: Toby Press, 2004

Kharms, Daniil, *Incidences*, edited and translated by Neil Cornwell, London: Serpent's Tail, 1993

Kharms, Daniil, *Polnoe sobranie sochinenii*, edited by V. Sazhin, St Petersburg: Akademicheskii proekt, vols 1–3, 1997; *Neizdannyi Kharms*, 2001; plus *Zapisnye knizhki, Dnevnik*, parts 1–2, 2002

[Lautréamont] Isidore Ducasse, Comte de Lautréamont, *Oeuvres complètes: Les Chants de Maldoror. Lettres. Poésies I et II*, Paris: Gallimard, 1973 (copy printed 2001)

Lautréamont, Comte de, *Maldoror* and *Poems*, translated by Paul Knight, Harmondsworth: Penguin, 1978

Lennon, John, *In His Own Write* and *A Spaniard in the Works*, London: Pimlico, 1997 (first published separately 1964; 1965)

McDonagh, Martin, *The Pillowman*, London: Faber, 2003

Malcolm, Noel, *The Origins of English Nonsense*, London: Fontana, 1998

Manfridi, Giuseppe, *Cuckoos* [*Zozòs*, 1990], translated by Colin Teevan, London: Oberon Books, 2000

Marinetti, F.T., *Selected Writings*, edited by R.W. Flint, translated by R.W. Flint and Arthur A. Coppotelli, London: Secker and Warburg, 1972

Michaux, Henri, *Selected Writings: The Space Within*, translated by Richard Ellmann, New York: New Directions, 1968

Nabokov, Vladimir *Invitation to a Beheading* [*Priglashenie na kazn'*, 1935–36], translated by Dmitri Nabokov with the author, London: Penguin, 1963

Nietzsche [Friedrich], *Thus Spoke Zarathustra* [*Also sprach Zarathustra*, 1883–85], translated by R.J. Hollingdale, Harmondsworth: Penguin, 1969

Nietzsche, Friedrich, *Twilight of the Idols and The Anti-Christ* [*Götzen-Dämmerung*, 1889; *Der Antichrist*, 1895], translated by R.J. Hollingdale, Harmondsworth, Penguin, 1990

Nietzsche, Friedrich, *Beyond Good and Evil* [*Jenseits von Gut und Böse*, 1886], translated and edited by Marion Faber, Oxford, Oxford University Press, 1998

Nietzsche, Friedrich, *The Birth of Tragedy and Other Writings* [*Die Geburt der Tragödie aus dem Geiste der Musik*, 1872, etc.], edited by Raymond Guess and Ronald Speirs, translated by Ronald Speirs, Cambridge, Cambridge University Press, 1999

Nooteboom, Cees, *The Following Story* [*Het volgende verhaal*, 1991], translated by Ina Rilke, London: Harvill, 1994

O'Brien, Flann, *At Swim-Two-Birds*, Harmondsworth: Penguin, 1967 (1971 reprint)

O'Brien, Flann, *The Third Policeman*, London: Picador, 1974

O'Brien, Flann, *The Dalkey Archive*, London: Picador, 1976

[O'Brien, Flann] Myles na Gopaleen (Flann O'Brien), *The Best of Myles*, edited by Kevin O'Nolan, London: Picador, 1977

O'Brien, Flann (Myles na Gopaleen), *Myles Before Myles: A Selection of the Earlier Writings of Brian O'Nolan*, edited by John Wyse Jackson, London: Paladin, 1989

O'Brien, Flann, *Stories and Plays*, London: Paladin, 1991

O'Brien, Flann (Myles na gCopaleen), *Rhapsody in Stephen's Green: The Insect Play*, edited by Robert Tracy, Dublin: Lilliput, 1994

O'Brien, Flann, *At War: Myles na gCopaleen 1940–1945*, edited by John Wyse Jackson, London: Duckworth, 1999

O'Brien, Flann, *The Various Lives of Keats and Chapman and The Brother*, London and Dublin: Scribner/Townhouse, 2003 (first published 1976)

Orton, Joe, *The Complete Plays*, New York: Grove Press, 1976

Palin, Michael, and Jones, Terry, *Ripping Yarns*, London: Eyre Methuen, 1978

Pessoa, Fernando, *The Book of Disquiet* [drawn from *Livro do desassossego por Bernardo Soares*, 1982], edited by Maria José de Lancastre, translated by Margaret Jull Costra, London: Serpent's Tail, 1991

Pessoa, Fernando, *The Book of Disquiet* [*Livro do Desassossego*, 1998], edited and translated by Richard Zenith, London: Allen Lane, 2001

Petrushevskaya, Ludmila, *Cinzano: Eleven Plays*, translated by Stephen Mulrine, London: Nick Hern, 1991

Petrushevskaya, Ludmilla, *The Time: Night* [*Vremia noch'*, 1992], translated by Sally Laird, London: Virago, 1994

Petrushevskaya, Ludmilla, *Immortal Love: Stories*, translated by Sally Laird, London; Virago, 1995

Pinter, Harold, *The Trial, adapted from the novel by Franz Kafka*, London: Faber, 1993

Pinter, Harold, *Plays*, 4 vols (*One to Four*), London: Faber, 1996–98

Pinter, Harold, *Various Voices: Prose, Poetry, Politics, 1948–1998*, London: Faber, 1999

Pinter, Harold, *Celebration & The Room*, London: Faber, 2000

Ronshin, Valery, *Living a Life: Totally Absurd Tales* [translated by Joanne Turnbull *et al.*], Moscow: Glas New Russian Writing, vol. 29, 2002

Roth, Joseph, *Rebellion* [*Die Rebellion*, 1924], translated by Michael Hofmann. London: Granta, 2000

[Roth] *Collected Shorter Fiction of Joseph Roth*, translated by Michael Hofmann. London: Granta, 2001

Roussel, Raymond, *How I Wrote Certain of My Books* [*Comment j'ai écrit certains de mes livres*, published 1935], translated by Trevor Winkfield, New York: Sun, 1975

Sartre, Jean-Paul, *La nausée*, Paris: Gallimard, 1972 (first published 1938); translated as *Nausea* by Robert Baldick. Harmondsworth: Penguin, 1965

Schulz, Bruno, *Sanatorium Under the Sign of the Hourglass* [*Sanatorium pod klepsydra*, 1937], translated by Celina Wieniewska, Harmondsworth: Penguin, 1979

Schulz, Bruno, *The Street of Crocodiles*, translated by Celina Wieniewska,

London: Picador, 1980 (first published as *Cinammon Shops*, 1963; Polish original as *Sklepy cynamonowe*, 1934)

Schwitters, Kurt, *PPPPPP: Poems Performance Pieces Proses Plays Poetics*, edited and translated by Jerome Rothenburg and Pierre Joris, Cambridge [Mass.]: Exact Change, 2002

Sebald, W.G. *Vertigo* [*Schwindel. Gefühle*, 1990], translated by Michael Hulse, London: Harvill, 2000

Simpson, N.F., *A Resounding Tinkle*, in *New English Dramatists 2*, Harmondsworth: Penguin [1960]

Somoza, José Carlos, *The Art of Murder* [*Clara y la Penumbra*, 2001], translated by Nick Caistor, London: Abacus, 2004

Sorrentino, Gilbert, *Mulligan Stew*, London: Picador, 1981

Sterne, Laurence, *The Life and Opinions of Tristram Shandy, Gentleman*, edited by Graham Petrie; 'Introduction' by Christopher Ricks, Harmondsworth: Penguin, 1967

Stoppard, Tom, *Rosencrantz and Guildenstern Are Dead*, London: Faber, 1968

Stoppard, Tom, *Jumpers*, London: Faber, 1973

Stoppard, Tom, *Travesties*, London: Faber, 1975

Stoppard, Tom, *Plays 5*, London: Faber, 1999

Topor [Roland], *Stories and Drawings*, translated by Margaret Crosland and David Le Vay, London: Peter Owen, 1968

Topor, Roland, *Leonardo Was Right* [*Vinci avait raison*, 1976], translated by Barbara Wright, London: John Calder, 1978

Topor, Roland, *The Tenant* [*Le Locataire chimérique*, 1966], translated by Francis K. Price, London: Black Spring Press, 1997 (translation first published 1966)

Topor, Roland, *Four Roses for Lucienne*, Paris: Christian Bourgois, 1998 (first published 1967)

Unamuno, Miguel de, *Tragic Sense of Life* [*Del sentimiento trágico de la vida*, 1913], translated by J.E. Crawford Flitch, New York: Dover, 1954 (first published 1921)

Van Ostaijen, Paul, *Patriotism, Inc. and Other Tales*, edited and translated by E.M. Beekman, Amherst: The University of Massachusetts Press, 1971

Vian, Boris, *I Spit on Your Graves* [*J'irai cracher sur vos tombes*, 1946], translated by Boris Vian and Milton Rosenthal. Introduction by James Sallis, Edinburgh: Canongate, 2001 (translation first published 1948)

Vian, Boris, *Heartsnatcher* [*L'Arrache-coeur*, 1953], translated by Stanley Chapman, Chicago: Dalkey Archive Press, 2003 (translation first published 1968)

Willans, Geoffrey, and Searle, Ronald, *Down with Skool!*, London: Max Parrish, 1953 (reprinted in *Molesworth*, Penguin Classics, 1999)

Willans, Geoffrey, and Searle, Ronald, *How to be Topp*, London: Max Parrish, 1954 (reprinted in *Molesworth*, Penguin Classics, 1999)

Witkiewicz, Stanisław Ignacy, *The Madman and the Nun and The Crazy Locomotive: Three Plays (including The Water Hen)*, translated by Daniel Gerould and C.S. Durer. Foreword by Jan Kott. New York: Applause, 1989 (first published 1966)

Witkiewicz, Stanisław Ignacy, *The Mother and Other Unsavory Plays including*

The Shoemakers and They, translated by Daniel Gerould and C.S. Durer. Foreword by Jan Kott. New York: Applause, 1993 (first published 1966)

Wittgenstein, Ludwig, *Philosophical Investigations*, translated by G.E.M. Anscombe, Oxford: Blackwell, 1968

[Wittgenstein, Ludwig], *Wittgenstein's Tractatus*, translated by Daniel Kolak, Mountain View, California: Mayfield, 1998

Secondary sources (Studies of philosophy, theory and criticism)

Abbott, H. Porter, 'Late Modernism: Samuel Beckett and the Art of the Oeuvre', in Brater and Cohn 73–96

Adelman, Gary, *Naming Beckett's Unnamable*, Lewisburg: Bucknell University Press, 2004

Adler, Jeremy, *Franz Kafka*, London: Penguin, 2001

Adorno, Theodor W., 'Trying to Understand *Endgame*', in his *Notes to Literature, Volume One*, edited by Rolf Tiedemann, translated by Shierry Weber Nicholsen, New York: Columbia University Press, 1991, 241–75

Albright, Daniel, *Representation and the Imagination: Beckett, Kafka, Nabokov, and Schoenberg*, Chicago and London: University of Chicago Press, 1981

Alexander, Marguerite, *Flights from Realism: Themes and Strategies in Postmodernist British and American Fiction*, London: Edward Arnold, 1990

Alexandrov, Vladimir E., ed., *The Garland Companion to Vladimir Nabokov*, New York: Garland, 1995

Amiran, Eyal, *Wandering and Home: Beckett's Metaphysical Narrative*, University Park: Pennsylvania State University Press, 1993

Anderson, Mark, ed., *Reading Kafka: Prague, Politics, and the Fin de Siècle*, New York: Schocken Books, 1989

Anderson, Roger B., *Dostoevsky: Myths of Duality*, Gainesville: University of Florida Press, 1986

Apollonio, Umbro, ed., *Futurist Manifestos* [*Futurismo*, 1970], London: Thames and Hudson, 1973

Armstrong, Paul B., *The Challenge of Bewilderment: Understanding and Representation in James, Conrad, and Ford*, Ithaca and London: Cornell University Press, 1987

Armstrong, Raymond, *Kafka and Pinter Shadow-Boxing: The Struggle Between Father and Son*, Basingstoke and London: Macmillan, 1999

Averintsev, Sergei S., 'Bakhtin and the Russian Attitude to Laughter', in David Shepherd, ed., *Bakhtin, Carnival and Other Subjects*, Critical Studies, 3:2–4: 1/2, Amsterdam and Atlanta, GA: Rodopi, 1993, 13–19

Ayer, A.J., *Philosophy in the Twentieth Century*, London: Counterpoint, 1984

Bair, Deirdre, *Samuel Beckett: A Biography*, London: Picador, 1980.

Bakhtin, Mikhail, *Rabelais and his World* [*Tvorchestvo Fransua Rable*, 1965], translated by Helene Iswolsky, Cambridge, MA: MIT Press, 1968

Bakhtin, M., 'Rable i Gogol' (Iskusstvo slova i narodnaia smekhovaia kul'tura)', in his *Voprosy literatury i estetiki*, Moscow: Khudozhestvennaia literatura, 1975, 484–95; as 'The Art of the Word and the Culture of Folk Humor (Rabelais and Gogol)', translated by Henryk Baran, in Henryk Baran, ed.,

Semiotics and Structuralism: Readings from the Soviet Union, White Plains, NY: International Arts and Sciences Press, 1976, 284–96

Bakhtin, Mikhail, *The Dialogic Imagination: Four Essays* [from *Voprosy literatury i estetiki*, 1975], edited by Michael Holquist, translated by Caryl Emerson and Michael Holquist, Austin: University of Texas Press, 1981

Bakhtin, Mikhail, *Problems of Dostoevsky's Poetics* [*Problemy poetiki Dostoevskogo*, 1963], edited and translated by Caryl Emerson, Manchester: Manchester University Press, 1984

Baldick, Chris, *The Concise Oxford Dictionary of Literary Terms*, Oxford: Oxford University Press, 1990

Barabtarlo, Gennady, ed., *Cold Fusion: Aspects of the German Cultural Presence in Russia*, New York and Oxford: Berghahn Books, 2000

Barber, Stephen, *Antonin Artaud: Blows and Bombs*, London: Faber, 1994

Barzun, Jacques, *From Dawn to Decadence. 1500 to the Present: 500 years of Western Cultural Life*, London: HarperCollins, 2001

Bates, Catherine, *Play in a Godless World: The Theory and Practice of Play in Shakespeare, Nietzsche and Freud*, London: Open Gate Press, 1999

Batty, Mark, *Harold Pinter*, Tavistock, Devon: Northcote House, 2001

Baudelaire, Charles, 'De l'essence du rire et généralement du comique dans les arts plastique' [1855], in Baudelaire, *Curiosités esthétiques*, Lausanne: Éditions de L'Oeil, 1956, 232–52

Baudelaire, Charles, *Selected Writings on Art and Literature*, translated by P.E. Charvet, Harmondsworth: Penguin, 1992 (first published as *Selected Writings on Art and Artists*, 1972)

Belsey, Catherine, *Shakespeare and the Loss of Eden: The Construction of Family Values in Early Modern Culture*, Basingstoke and London: Macmillan, 1999

Benjamin, Walter, *Illuminations*, edited by Hannah Arendt, translated by Harry Zohn, London: Fontana, 1973

Berdyaev, Nicholas, *Dostoevsky* [*Mirosozertsanie Dostoevskogo*, 1923], translated by Donald Attwater, New York: New American Library, 1974

Berger, Peter L., *Redeeming Laughter: The Comic Dimension of Human Experience*, Berlin: Walter de Gruyter, 1997

Bergson, Henri, 'Laughter' [*Le Rire*, 1900], in Sypher, 1956, 59–190

Berkoff, Steven, *Meditations on Metamorphosis*, London: Faber, 1995

Billington, Michael, *The Life and Work of Harold Pinter*, London: Faber, 1996

Bloom, Harold, *The Western Canon: The Books and School of the Ages*, London: Papermac, 1995

Bohn, Willard, *The Rise of Surrealism: Cubusm, Dada, and the Pursuit of the Marvelous*, Albany: State University of New York Press, 2002

Bold, Alan, ed., *Harold Pinter: You Never Heard Such Silence*, London and Totowa, NJ: Vision Press, 1984 and Barnes and Noble, 1985

Booker, M. Keith, 'The Bicycle and Descartes: Epistemology in the Fiction of Beckett and O'Brien', *Eire-Ireland*, 26:1 (1991), 76–94

Booker, M. Keith, *Flann O'Brien, Bakhtin, and Menippean Satire*, Syracus, NY: Syracuse University Press, 1995

Borges, Jorge Luis, *The Total Library: Non-Fiction 1922–1986*, edited by Eliot Weinberger, translated by Esther Allen, Suzanne Jill Levine and Eliot Weinberger, Harmondsworth: Penguin, 2001 (first published as *Selected Non-*

Fictions, 1999)

Boxall, Peter, ed., *Samuel Beckett: Waiting for Godot / Endgame: A Reader's Guide to Essential Criticism*, Duxford, Cambridge: Icon Books, 2000

Boxsel, Matthijs van, *The Encyclopaedia of Stupidity* [*De encyclopedie van de domheid*], translated by Arnold and Erica Pomerans, London: Reaktion Books, 2003

Bradbury, Nicola, *Henry James: The Later Novels*, Oxford: Clarendon Press, 1979.

Bradbury, Nicola, *Charles Dickens's 'Great Expectations'*, New York and London: Harvester Wheatsheaf, 1990

Brandist, Craig, *Carnival Culture and the Soviet Modernist Novel*, Basingstoke and London: Macmillan, 1996

Brater, Enoch, *Beyond Minimalism: Beckett's Late Style in the Theatre*, New York and Oxford: Oxford University Press, 1987

Brater, Enoch and Cohn, Ruby, eds, *Around the Absurd: Essays on Modern and Postmodern Drama*, Ann Arbor: University of Michigan Press, 1990

Brée, Germaine, *Twentieth-Century French Literature* [*Le XXe Siècle II: 1920–1970*, 1978], translated by Louise Guiney, Chicago and London: The University of Chicago Press, 1983

Bridgwater, Patrick, *Kafka and Nietzsche*, Bonn: Bouvier Verlag Herbert Grundmann, 1974.

Brink, André, *The Novel: Language and Narrative from Cervantes to Calvino*, Basingstoke and London: Macmillan, 1998

Brod, Max, *Franz Kafka: A Biography* second, enlarged edition [translated by G. Humphreys Roberts and Richard Winston], New York: Da Capo Press, 1995 (German original, Prague, 1937; translation first published 1947; enlarged edition, New York, 1960)

Brodsky, Joseph, *Less Than One: Selected Essays*, Harmondsworth: Penguin, 1987

Brooke, Nicholas, *Horrid Laughter in Jacobean Tragedy*, New York: Barnes and Noble, 1979

Brooker, Joseph, *Flann O'Brien*, Tavistock, Devon: Northcote House, 2005

Brooks, Peter, *Reading for the Plot: Design and intention in Narrative*, Cambridge, MA: Harvard University Press, 1992 (first published 1984)

Burian, Jarka M. *Modern Czech Theatre: Reflector and Conscience of a Nation*, Iowa City: University of Iowa Press, 2000

Burkman, Katherine H., and Kundert-Gibbs, John L., eds, *Pinter at Sixty*, Bloomington and Indianapolis: Indiana University Press, 1993

Caillois, Roger, *Les Jeux et les hommes: Le Masque et le vertige*, revised and expanded edition, Paris: Gallimard, 1967 (first edition published 1958; translated as *Man, Play and Games* by Meyer Barash, New York: Free Press, 1961)

Calasso, Roberto, *Literature and the Gods* [*La letteratura e gli dèi*], translated by Tim Parks, London: Vintage, 2001

Calasso, Roberto, *The Forty-Nine Steps* [*I quarantanove gradini*, 1991], translated by John Shepley, London: Pimlico, 2002

Calasso, Roberto, *K.*, Milan: Adelphi Edizioni, 2002

Calder, John, *The Philosophy of Samuel Beckett*, London: Calder Publications, 2001

Cardinal, Roger, *Breton: Nadja*, London: Grant and Cutler, 1986

Cardullo, Bert, 'En Garde! The Theatrical Avant-Garde in Historical, Intellectual, and Cultural Context', in Cardullo and Knopf, 2001, 1–39

Carlson, Marvin, *Theories of the Theatre: A Historical and Critical Survey, from the Greeks to the Present*, expanded edition, Ithaca and London: Cornell University Press, 1993

Carrick, Neil, *Daniil Kharms: Theologian of the Absurd*, Birmingham: Birmingham Slavonic Monographs No. 28, 1998

Cartledge, Paul, *Aristophanes and his Theatre of the Absurd*, Bristol: Bristol Classical Press, 1990

Caselli, Daniela, *Beckett's Dantes: Intertextuality in the Fiction and Criticism*, Manchester: Manchester University Press, 2005

Caws, Mary Ann, *The Surrealist Look: An Erotics of Encounter*, Cambridge, MA, and London, MIT Press, 1997

Chamberlain, Lesley, *Nietzsche in Turin: An Intimate Biography*, New York: Picador USA, 1998

Clissmann, Anne, *Flann O'Brien: A Critical Introduction to his Writings*, Dublin; Gill and Macmillan, 1975

Clune, Anne and Hurson, Tess, eds, *Conjuring Complexities: Essays on Flann O'Brien*, Belfast: The Institute of Irish Studies, The Queen's University of Belfast, 1997

Cohn, Ruby, '*Watt* in the Light of *The Castle*', *Comparative Literature*, 13:2 (1961), 154–66

Cohn, Ruby, *A Beckett Canon*, Ann Arbor: University of Michigan Press, 2001

Connolly, Julian W., ed., *Nabokov's Invitation to a Beheading: A Critical Companion*, Evanston, IL: Northwestern University Press, 1997

Connor, Steven, *Samuel Beckett: Repetition, Theory and Text*, Oxford: Basil Blackwell, 1988

Conrad, Peter, *Modern Times, Modern Places*, New York: Alfred A. Knopf, 1999

Conradi, Peter, *Fyodor Dostoevsky*, Basingstoke and London: Macmillan, 1988

Cornwell, Neil, ed., *Daniil Kharms and the Poetics of the Absurd*, Basingstoke and London: Macmillan and New York: St Martin's Press, 1991

Cornwell, Neil, 'The Rudiments of Daniil Kharms: In Further Pursuit of the Red-Haired Man', *Modern Language Review*, 93:1 (1998), 1–13

Cornwell, Neil, 'The Absurd in Gogol and Gogol Criticism', *Essays in Poetics*, 29, 2004 (*Gogol 2002: Special Issue, Vol. 2*), Keele: EIP Publications No. 9, 1–16

Costello, Peter, and van de Kamp, Peter, *Flann O'Brien: An Illustrated Bibliography*, London: Bloomsbury, 1989

Craig, Edward, ed., *Routledge Encyclopedia of Philosophy*, London: Routledge, vols 1–10, 1998

Craig, William Lane, *The Cosmological Argument from Plato to Leibniz*, London: Macmillan, 1980

Cronin, Anthony, *No Laughing Matter: The Life and Times of Flann O'Brien*, London: Grafton Books, 1989

Crosby, Donald A., *The Specter of the Absurd: Sources and Criticisms of Modern Nihilism*, Albany: State University of New York Press, 1988

Dalton-Brown, Sally, *Voices from the Void: The Genres of Liudmila Petrushevskaia*, New York and Oxford: Berghahn Books, 2000

Danto, Arthur C., *Sartre*, Glasgow: Fontana/Collins, 1975

Davies, Paul, *The Last Three Minutes: Conjectures about the Ultimate Fate of the Universe*, London: Weidenfeld and Nicolson, 1994

Davison, Ray, *Camus: The Challenge of Dostoevsky*, Exeter: Exeter University Press, 1997

Deane, Seamus, *A Short History of Irish Literature*, London: Hutchinson, 1986

Deleuze, Gilles, *The Logic of Sense* [*Logique du sens*, 1969], translated by Mark Lester with Charles Stivale, edited by Constantin V. Boundas, London: The Athlone Press, 1990

Demastes, William W., *Theatre of Chaos: Beyond Absurdism, into Orderly Disorder*, Cambridge: Cambridge University Press, 1998

Derksen, Celeste, 'A Feminist Absurd: Margaret Hollingsworth's *The House that Jack Built*', *Modern Drama*, 45:1 (2002), 209–30

Derrida, Jacques, *Writing and Difference* [*L'Écriture et la différence*, 1967], translated by Alan Bass, London: Routledge and Kegan Paul, 1981 (first published 1978)

Dobrez, L.A.C., *The Existential and its Exits: Literary and Philosophical Perspectives on the Works of Beckett, Ionesco, Genet and Pinter*, London: The Athlone Press; New York, St Martin's Press, 1986

Dodd, W.J. *Kafka and Dostoyevsky: The Shaping of Influence*, Basingstoke and London: Macmillan, 1992

Doherty, Francis, *Samuel Beckett*, London: Hutchinson, 1971

Doherty, Francis, 'Flann O'Brien's Existentialist Hell', *Canadian Journal of Irish Studies*, 15:2 (1989), 51–67

Doherty, Francis, '*Watt* in an Irish Frame', *Irish University Review*, 21:2 (1991), 187–203

Downie, J.A., *Jonathan Swift: Political Writer*, London: Routledge and Kegan Paul, 1985

Dukes, Gerry, *Samuel Beckett*, Woodstock and New York: Overlook Press, 2002

Dukore, Bernard F. and Gerould, Daniel C., eds, *Avant-Garde Drama: A Casebook*, New York, Thomas Y. Crowell Company, 1976 (first published as *Avant-Garde Drama: Major Plays and Documents Post World War 1*, 1969)

Dunwoodie, Peter, *Une histoire ambivalente: Le dialogue Camus–Dostoïevski*, with Preface by Ernest Sturm, Paris: Librairie Nizet, 1996

Eagleton, Terry, *Sweet Violence: The Idea of the Tragic*, Oxford: Blackwell, 2003

Eco, Umberto, *Travels in Hyperreality*, translated by William Weaver, London: Picador, 1987

Eco, Umberto, *Six Walks in the Fictional Woods*, Cambridge, MA, and London: Harvard University Press, 1995

Eco, Umberto, *Serendipities: Language and Lunacy*, translated by William Weaver, London: Weidenfeld and Nicolson, 1999

Edel, Leon, *Henry James: The Master, 1901–1916*, Philadelphia: J.P. Lippincott, 1972

Edmonds, David and Eidinow, John, *Wittgenstein's Poker: The Story of a Ten-minute Argument between Two Great Philosophers*, London: Faber, 2001

Edwards, Paul, ed., *The Encyclopedia of Philosophy*, New York and London: Collier Macmillan, vols 1–8, 1967; reprinted (as 8 volumes in 4) 1972

Epstein, Mikhail, 'Post-Atheism: from apophatic Philosophy to "Minimal

Religion"', in Mikhail Epstein, Alexander Genis and Slobodanka Vladiv-
Glover, *Russian Postmodernism: New Perspectives on Post-Soviet Culture*,
New York and Oxford: Berghahn Books, 1999, 345–93

Erasmus, Desiderius, *Praise of Folly* [*Moriae encomium*, 1511], translated by
Hoyt Hopewell Hudson, Ware, Hertfordshire: Wordsworth, 1998

Esslin, Martin, 'Introduction' to *Absurd Drama*, Harmondsworth: Penguin, 1965
7–23

Esslin, Martin, ed., *Samuel Beckett: A Collection of Critical Essays*, Englewood
Ciffs, NJ: Prentice-Hall, 1965 (reprinted 1987)

Esslin, Martin, *The Theatre of the Absurd*, 3rd edition. Harmondsworth: Penguin,
1987 (reissued London: Methuen, 2001)

Ferber, Michael, *A Dictionary of Literary Symbols*, Cambridge: Cambridge
University Press, 2000

Ficowski, Jerzy, *Regions of the Great Heresy. Bruno Schulz: A Biographical
Portrait* [*Regiony wielkiei herezi*, 1967; 1992], translated and edited by
Theodosia Robertson, New York and London: Norton, 2003

Fink, Hilary L., *Bergson and Russian Modernism, 1900–1930*, Evanston, IL:
Northwestern University Press, 1999

FitzGerald, Joan, 'After Yeats – Story-Telling in Flann O'Brien's "At Swim-Two-
Birds"', in Carla de Petris, ed., *Yeats oggi: Studi e ricerche*, Rome: Terza
università, 1993, 45–58

Fleming, John, *Stoppard's Theatre: Finding Order amid Chaos*, Austin: University
of Texas Press, 2001

Fletcher, John, *About Beckett: The Playwright and the Work*, London: Faber, 2003

Fotiade, Ramona, *Conceptions of the Absurd: From Surrealism to the Existential
Thought of Chestov and Fondane*, Oxford: Legenda, 2001

Freud, Sigmund, *Jokes and Their Relation to the Unconscious* [*Der Witz und seine
Beziehung zum Unbewussten*, 1905], translated and edited by James Strachey
(The Penguin Freud Library, vol. 6), Harmondsworth: Penguin, 1991

Frye, Northrop, *Anatomy of Criticism: Four Essays*, Princeton, NJ: Princeton
University Press, 1971 (first published 1957)

Fuentes, Carlos, *Myself With Others: Selected Essays*, London: André Deutsch,
1988

Galligan, Edward L., *The Comic Vision in Literature*, Athens: University of
Georgia Press, 1984

Galloway, David, *The Absurd Hero in American Fiction: Updike, Styron, Bellow,
Salinger*, 2nd revised edition, Austin: University of Texas Press, 1981

Geller, Leonid, 'Teoriia kha[o↔rm]sa', *Wiener Slawistischer Almanach*, 44
(1999), 67–123

Gillen, Francis, 'From Novel to Film: Harold Pinter's Adaptation of *The Trial*', in
Burkman and Kundert-Gibbs, 137–48

Gilmore, Robert, *Alice in Quantumland: An Allegory of Quantum Physics*, New
York: Copernicus, 1995

Gleick, James, *Chaos: Making a New Science*, London: Heinemann, 1988

Gordon, Lois, *Reading Godot*, New Haven and London: Yale University Press,
2002

Graffy, Julian [2000a], *Gogol's 'The Overcoat'*, London: Bristol Classical Press,
2000

Graffy Julian [2000b], 'The Devil is in the Detail: Demonic Features of Gogol's Petersburg', in Pamela Davidson, ed., *Russian Literature and its Demons*, New York and Oxford: Berghahn Books, 2000, 241–77

Gray, Ronald, ed., *Kafka: A Collection of Critical Essays*, Englewood Cliffs, NJ: Prentice-Hall, 1962

Grayson, Jane and Faith Wigzell, eds, *Nikolay Gogol: Text and Context*, Basingstoke and London: Macmillan, 1989

Gruner, Charles R. *The Game of Humor: A Comprehensive Theory of Why We Laugh*, New Brunswick and London: Transaction Publishers, 2000 (first published 1997)

Gussow, Mel, *Conversations with Pinter*, London: Nick Hern Books, 1994

Haight, M.R., 'Nonsense', *The British Journal of Aesthetics*, 11 (1971), 247–56

Hammond, B.S., 'Beckett and Pinter: Towards a Grammar of the Absurd', *Journal of Beckett Studies*, 4 (1979), 35–42

Handy, Rollo, 'Vaihinger, Hans (1852–1933)', in Edwards, 1967, 8:221–4

Hardy, Barbara, *Henry James: The Later Writing*, Plymouth: Northcote House, 1996

Hawkes, Terence, *William Shakespeare: 'King Lear'*, Plymouth: Northcote House, 1995

Haynes, John, and James Knowlson, *Images of Beckett*, Cambridge: Cambridge University Press, 2003

Hibberd, John, *Kafka: Die Verwandlung*, London: Grant and Cutler, 1985

Hill, Carl, *The Soul of Wit: Joke Theory from Grimm to Freud*, Lincoln: University of Nebraska Press, 1993

Hinchliffe, Arnold P., *The Absurd*, London: Methuen, 1969

Hofstadter, Douglas R., *Gödel, Escher, Bach: An Eternal Golden Braid*, New York: Vintage, 1980 (first published 1979)

Holquist, Michael, *Dostoevsky and the Novel*, Evanston, IL: Northwestern University Press, 1986 (first published 1977)

Holquist, Michael, *Dialogism: Bakhtin and his World*, London: Routledge, 1990

Holquist, Michael, 'The Tyranny of Difference: Gogol and the Sacred', in Barabtarlo, 2000, 74–101

Holzberg, Niklas, *The Ancient Novel: An Introduction*, translated by Christine Jackson-Holzberg, London: Routledge, 1995

Honderich, Ted, ed., *The Oxford Companion to Philosophy*, Oxford: Oxford University Press, 1995

Hopper, Keith, *Flann O'Brien: A Portrait of the Artist as a Young Post-modernist*, Cork: Cork University Press, 1995

Howarth, W.D., 'Introduction: Theoretical Considerations', in W.D. Howarth, ed., *Comic Drama: The European Heritage*, London: Methuen, 1978, 1–21

Hoyles, John, *The Literary Underground: Writers and the Totalitarian Experience, 1900–1950*, New York and London: Harvester Wheatsheaf, 1991

Hughes, Kenneth, ed. and transl., *Franz Kafka: An Anthology of Marxist Criticism*, Hanover and London: Clark University, by University Press of New England, 1981

Hyde, G.M., 'Melville's *Bartleby* and Gogol's *The Overcoat*', *Essays in Poetics*, 1:1 (1976), 32–47

Hyman, John, 'Language games in earnest', *TLS* (7 January 2000), 7–8

Innes, Brian, *Death and the Afterlife*, London: Brown Partworks, 1999

Jaccard, Jean-Philippe, 'Daniil Kharms in the Context of Russian and European Literature of the Absurd', in Cornwell, 1991, 49–70

Jakobson, Roman, *Language in Literature*, edited by Krystyna Pomorska and Stephen Rudy, Cambridge, MA: Belknap, Harvard University Press, 1987

Jones, John, *Dostoevsksy*, Oxford: Oxford University Press, 1985 (first published 1983)

Jones, Jonathan, 'For Better Perverse', *The Guardian Weekend* (8 September 2001), 34–43

Jones, Malcolm V., *Dostoyevsky After Bakhtin: Readings in Dostoyevsky's Fantastic Realism*, Cambridge: Cambridge University Press, 1990

Jones, Robert Emmet, 'Gogol and the French Dramatists of the Absurd', in Elena Semeka-Pankratov, ed., *Studies in Poetics: Commemorative Volume Krystyna Pomorska (1928–1986)*, Columbus, OH: Slavica Publishers, 1995, 277–84

Jung, C.G., 'On the Psychology of the Trickster-Figure', in his *The Archetypes and The Collective Unconscious*, second edition, translated by R.F.C. Hull [*The Collected Works of C.G. Jung*, vol. 9, part 1], London: Routledge, 1990 (first printed 1968)

Kappeler, Susanne, *Writing and Reading in Henry James*, New York: Columbia University Press, 1980

Karl, Frederick R., 'Comments on Harold Pinter's Adaptation of Franz Kafka's *The Trial*', *The Pinter Review; Annual Essays 1994*, Tampa, FL: University of Tampa Press, 1994, 75–83

Kayser, Wolfgang, *The Grotesque in Art and Literature* [*Das Groteske: seine Gestaltung in Malerei und Dichtung*, 1957], translated by Ulrich Weisstein, New York: Columbia University Press, 1981 (first published 1963)

Kearney, Richard, 'Beckett: The Demythologising Intellect', in Richard Kearney, ed., *The Irish Mind: Exploring Intellectual Traditions*, Dublin: Wolfhound Press, 1985, 267–93; 347–60

Kearney, Richard, *Transitions: Narratives in Modern Irish Culture*, Manchester: Manchester University Press, 1988

Kelly, Aileen M., *Toward Another Shore: Russian Thinkers Between Necessity and Chance*, New Haven and London: Yale University Press, 1998

Kempf, Franz R., *Everyone's Darling: Kafka and the Critics of His Short Fiction*, Columbia, SC: Camden House, 1994

Kerferd, G.B, 'Gorgias of Leontini', in Edwards, 1967, 3:374–5.

Kiberd, Declan, *Inventing Ireland: The Literature of the Modern Nation*, London: Vintage, 1996

Kiberd, Declan, *Irish Classics*, London: Granta, 2001

Killinger, John, *World in Collapse: The Vision of Absurd Drama*, New York: Delta, 1971

Kirkwood, Michael, 'The Algorithm and the Kaleidoscope: Metaphors for the Nightmare Worlds of Franz Kafka and Aleksandr Zinov'ev?', *New Zealand Slavonic Journal: Festschrift in Honour of Arnold McMillin*, vol. 36 (2002), 143–53

Knowles, Ronald, *Understanding Harold Pinter*, Columbia, SC: University of South Carolina Press, 1995

Knowles, Ronald, *Gulliver's Travels: The Politics of Satire*, New York: Twayne, 1996

Knowles, Ronald, ed., *Shakespeare and Carnival: After Bakhtin*, Basingstoke and London: Macmillan, 1998

Knowlson, James, *Damned to Fame: The Life of Samuel Beckett*, London: Bloomsbury, 1997

Knowlson, James and Pilling, John, *Frescoes of the Skull: The Later Prose and Drama of Samuel Beckett*, London: John Calder, 1979

Kołakowski, Leszek, *Metaphysical Horror*, revised edition edited by Agnieszka Kołakowska, Harmondsworth: Penguin, 2001 (original edition published 1988)

Komaromi, Ann, 'Daniil Charms and the Art of Absurd Life-Creation', *Russian Literature*, 52:4 (2002), 419–37

Kott, Jan, *Shakespeare Our Contemporary*, translated by Boleslaw Taborski, London: Methuen, 1964

Kundera, Milan, *The Art of the Novel*, translated by Linda Asher, London: Faber, 1988 (first published in French 1986)

Kundera, Milan, *Testaments Betrayed*, translated by Linda Asher, London: Faber, 1996 (first published in French 1993)

Lary, N.M., *Dostoevsky and Dickens*, London: Routledge and Kegan Paul, 1973

Latham, Ronald E., 'Lucretius (c. 99–55 B.C.)', in Edwards, 1967, 5:99–101

Lawley, Paul, '"The Rapture of Vertigo": Beckett's Turning Point', *Modern Language Review*, 95, 1 (2000), 28–40

Lawton, Anna, ed., *Russian Futurism through its Manifestoes, 1912–1928*, texts translated and edited by Anna Lawton and Herbert Eagle, Ithaca and London: Cornell University Press, 1988

Lecercle, Jean-Jacques, *Philosophy of Nonsense: The Intuitions of Victorian Nonsense Literature*, London: Routledge, 1994

Lentricchia, Frank and McLaughlin, Thomas, eds, *Critical Terms for Literary Study*, 2nd edition, Chicago and London: The University of Chicago Press, 1995

Lipovetsky, Mark, *Russian Postmodernist Fiction: Dialogue with Chaos*, edited by Eliot Borenstein, Armonk, New York: M.E. Sharpe, 1999

Lipovetsky, Mark, 'Russian Literary Posmodernism in the 1990s', *The Slavonic and East European Review*, 79:1 (2001), 31–50

Lipovetsky, Mark, 'Allegoriia pis'ma: "Sluchai" Kharmsa (1933–1939)', *Novoe literaturnoe obozrenie*, 63:5 (2003), 123–52

Listengarten, Julia, *Russian Tragifarce: Its Cultural and Political Roots*, Selinsgrove: Susquehanna University Press; London: Associated University Presses, 2000

Little, Edmund, *The Fantasts*, Amersham: Avebury, 1984

Lodge, David, 'Harold Pinter's *Last to Go*: A Structural Analysis' [1990], in his *The Practice of Writing: Essays, Lectures, Reviews and a Diary*, Harmondsworth: Penguin, 1997 (first published 1996), 270–86

Lomas, David, *The Haunted Self: Surrealism, Psychoanalysis, Subjectivity*, New Haven and London: Yale University Press, 2000

Lotman, Yuri M., *Universe of the Mind: A Semiotic Theory of Culture*, translated by Ann Shukman, London: I.B. Tauris, 1990

Lynch, William F., S.J., *Christ and Apollo: The Dimensions of the Literary Imagination*, New York: Sheed and Ward, 1960

Macintyre, Alasdair, 'Existentialism', in Edwards, 1967, 3:147–54

Mc Cormack, W.J., *From Burke to Beckett: Ascendancy, Tradition and Betrayal in Literary History*, Cork: Cork University Press, 1994

McHale, Brian, *Postmodernist Fiction*, New York and London: Methuen, 1987

McMillan, Dougald, *'transition': The History of a Literary Era 1927–1938*, London: Calder and Boyars, 1975

MacPike, Loralee, *Dostoevsky's Dickens: A Study of Literary Influence*, London: George Prior, 1981

Macquarrie, John, *Existentialism*, Harmondsworth: Penguin, 1973

Maguire, Robert A., *Exploring Gogol*, Stanford: Stanford University Press, 1994

Malcolm, Norman, 'Wittgenstein, Ludwig Josef Johann (1889–1951)', in Edwards, 1967, 8:327–40

Mann, Iu., 'Vstrecha v labirinte (Frants Kafka i Nikolai Gogol')', *Voprosy literatury*, 2 (1999), 162–86

Maxton, Hugh, 'Kharms and Myles: An Afterword', in Daniil Kharms, *The Plummeting Old Women*, translated by Neil Cornwell, Dublin: Lilliput, 1989, 93–100

Meilakh, Mikhail, 'Kharms's Play *Elizaveta Bam*', in Cornwell, 1991, 200–19

Merivale, Patricia and Sweeney, Susan Elizabeth, eds, *Detecting Texts: The Metaphysical Detective Story from Poe to Postmodernism*, Philadelphia: University of Pennsylvania Press, 1999

Merleau-Ponty, Jacques and Morando, Bruno, *The Rebirth of Cosmology* [*Les Trois Étapes de la cosmologie*, 1971], translated by Helen Weaver, New York: Alfred A. Knopf, 1976

Meyer, Priscilla, "Supernatural Doubles: *Vii* and *The Nose*", in Neil Cornwell, ed., *The Gothic-Fantastic in Nineteenth-Century Russian Literature*, Amsterdam and Atlanta, GA: Rodopi, 1999, 189–209

Meyer, Priscilla, "The Fantastic in the Everyday: Gogol's 'Nevsky Prospect' and Hoffmann's 'A New Year's Eve Adventure'", in Barabtarlo, 2000, 62–73

Michelson, Bruce, *Literary Wit*, Amherst: University of Massachusetts Press, 2000

Miller, Karl, *Doubles: Studies in Literary History*, Oxford: Oxford University Press, 1987

Miller, Tyrus, *Late Modernism: Politics, Fiction, and the Arts Between the World Wars*, Berkeley: University of California Press, 1999

Milner-Gulland, Robin, '"Kovarnye stikhi": Notes on Daniil Kharms and Aleksandr Vvedensky', *Essays in Poetics*, 9:1 (1984), 16–37

Milner-Gulland, Robin, 'Beyond the Turning Point: An Afterword', in Cornwell, 1991, 243–67

Milner-Gulland, Robin, '"This Could Have Been Foreseen": Kharms's *The Old Woman (Starukha)* Revisited: A Collective Analysis', *Neo-Formalist Papers: Contributions to the Silver Jubilee Conference to mark 25 years of the Neo-Formalist Circle*, edited by Joe Andrew and Robert Reid, Amsterdam and Atlanta, GA: Rodopi, 1998, 102–22

Mooney, Sinéad, *Samuel Beckett*, Tavistock, Devon: Northcote, 2006

Morrison, Kristin, *Canters and Chronicles: The Use of Narrative in the Plays of Samuel Beckett and Harold Pinter*, Chicago and London: University of Chicago Press, 1986 (first published 1983)

Nabokov, Vladimir, *Lectures on Literature*, edited by Fredson Bowers, London:

Weidenfeld and Nicolson, 1980

Nabokov, Vladimir, *Lectures on Russian Literature*, edited by Fredson Bowers, London: Weidenfeld and Nicolson, 1981

Nakhimovsky, Alice Stone, *Laughter in the Void: An Introduction to the Writings of Daniil Kharms and Alexander Vvedenskii*, Vienna: Wiener Slawisticher Almanach, Sonderband 5, 1982

O'Leary, Joseph S., 'Beckett's *Company*: The Self in Throes', *English Literature and Language*, 28 (1991), 83–124

Palmer, Jerry, *The Logic of the Absurd: On Film and Television Comedy*, London: BFI Publishing, 1987

Parkin, John, *Humour Theorists of the Twentieth Century*, Lewiston: The Edwin Mellen Press, 1997

Passmore, John, *A Hundred Years of Philosophy*, 2nd edition, Harmondsworth: Penguin, 1968

Peace, Richard, *Dostoevsky's 'Notes from Underground'*, London: Bristol Classical Press, 1993

Pears, David, *Wittgenstein*, London: Fontana/Collins, 1971

Penner, Dick, '*Invitation to a Beheading*: Nabokov's Absurdist Initiation', *Critique: Studies in Modern Fiction*, 20:3 (1979), 27–39

Perloff, Marjorie, *Wittgenstein's Ladder: Poetic Language and the Strangeness of the Ordinary*, Chicago and London: University Press of Chicago, 1996

Píchová, Hana, *The Art of Memory in Exile: Vladimir Nabokov and Milan Kundera*, Carbondale: Southern Illinois University Press, 2002

Pilling, John, ed., *The Cambridge Companion to Beckett*, Cambridge: Cambridge University Press, 1994

Pilling, John, *Beckett Before Godot*, Cambridge: Cambridge University Press, 1997

Pilling, John, ed., *Beckett's Dream Notebook*, Reading: Beckett International Foundation, 1999

Pilling, John and Bryden, Mary, eds., *The Ideal Core of the Onion: Reading Beckett Archives*, Reading: Beckett International Foundation, 1992

Pines, Shlomo, 'Maimonides (1135–1204)', in Edwards, 1967, 5:129–34

Popkin, Cathy, *The Pragmatics of Insignificance: Chekhov, Zoshchenko, Gogol*, Stanford, Stanford University Press, 1993

Preece, Julian, ed., *The Cambridge Companion to Kafka*, Cambridge: Cambridge University Press, 2002

Preminger, Alex, ed., *Princeton Encyclopedia of Poetry and Poetics*. Enlarged edition. London: Macmillan, 1975

Purdie, Susan, *Comedy: The Mastery of Discourse*, New York and London: Harvester Wheatsheaf, 1993

Pynsent, R.B. and Kanikova, S.I., eds, *The Everyman Companion to East European Literature*, London: J.M. Dent, 1993

Raby, Peter, ed., *The Cambridge Companion to Harold Pinter*, Cambridge: Cambridge University Press, 2001

Rayfield, Donald, *The Literature of Georgia: A History*, Oxford: Clarendon Press, 1994

Rees, Martin, 'A Brief History of the Future', *The Guardian* (*Saturday Review*, 29 December 2001), 1, 3

Reid, Robert, 'Gogol: A Stoic Approach', *Essays in Poetics*, 29, 2004 (*Gogol 2002: Special Issue, Vol. 2*), Keele: EIP Publications No. 9, 145–68

Richter, Jean Paul, *Horn of Oberon: Jean Paul Richter's School for Aesthetics* [*Vorschule der Aesthetik*], translated by Margaret R. Hale. Detroit: Wayne State University Press, 1973

Ricken, Friedo, *Philosophy of the Ancients* [*Philosophie der Antike*, 1988], translated by Eric Watkins. Notre Dame and London: University of Notre Dame Press, 1991

Ricks, Christopher, *Beckett's Dying Words*, Oxford: Oxford University Press, 1995

Roberts, Graham, 'Of Words and Worlds: Language Games in *Elizaveta Bam* by Daniil Kharms', *Slavonic and East European Review*, 72 (1994), 38–59

Roberts, Graham, 'Poor Liza: The Sexual Politics of *Elizaveta Bam* by Daniil Kharms', in *Gender and Russian Literature: New Perspectives*, edited by Rosalind Marsh, Cambridge: Cambridge University Press, 1996, 244–62

Roberts, Graham, *The Last Soviet Avant-Garde: OBERIU – Fact, Fiction, Metafiction*, Cambridge: Cambridge University Press, 1997

Salkeld, Duncan, *Madness and Drama in the Age of Shakespeare*, Manchester: Manchester University Press, 1993

Sazhin, Valerii, *A. Vvedenskii i D. Kharms v ikh perepiske*, Paris: Izdanie Assotsiatsii 'Russkii Institut v Parizhe', 2004 ('Bibliograf' Vypusk 18)

Schur, David, *The Way of Oblivion: Heraclitus and Kafka*, Cambridge, MA, and London: Harvard University Press, 1998

Screech, M.A., *Laughter at the Foot of the Cross*, Harmondsworth: Penguin, 1999 (first published 1997)

Sebald, W.G. 'The Undiscover'd Country: The Death Motif in Kafka's *Castle*', *Journal of European Studies*, 2 (1972), 22–34

Segal, Erich, *The Death of Comedy*, Cambridge, MA: Harvard University Press, 2001

Shankland, Hugh, 'Futurism in Literature and the Theatre' in *Fururismo 1909–1919: Exhibition of Italian Futurism*, Newcastle upon Tyne and Edinburgh: Northern Arts and Scottish Arts Council, 1972, 69–88

Shapiro, Gavriel, *Nikolai Gogol and the Baroque Cultural Heritage*, University Park: Pennsylvania University Press, 1993

Shenker, Israel, '"Moody Man of Letters": Interview with Samuel Beckett', *New York Times*, 2 (6 May 1956), 1, 3

Shenkman, Ian, 'Logika absurda. Kharms: otechestvennyi tekst i mirovoi kontekst', *Voprosy literatury* (July–August 1998), 54–80

Sheppard, Richard, *Modernism – Dada – Postmodernism*, Evanston, IL, Northwestern University Press, 2000

Shoham, S. Giora, *Society and the Absurd*, Oxford: Basil Blackwell, 1974

Showalter, English, Jr, *The Stranger: Humanity and the Absurd*, Boston: Twayne, 1989

Shukman, Ann, 'Towards a Poetics of the Absurd: The Prose Writings of Daniil Kharms', in Catriona Kelly, Michael Makin and David Shepherd, eds, *Discontinuous Discourses in Modern Russian Literature*, Basingstoke and London: Macmillan, 1989, 60–72

Shukman, Ann, 'Gogol's *The Nose* or the Devil in the Works', in Grayson and

Wigzell, 64–82.

Sicher, Efraim, 'Dialogization and Laughter in the Dark, or How Gogol's Nose Was Made: Parody and Literary Evolution in Bachtin's Theory of the Novel', *Russian Literature*, 28 (1990), 211–33

Simmons, Katy, *Plays for the Period of Stagnation: Lyudmila Petrushevskaya and the Theatre of the Absurd*, Uiversity of Birmingham: Birmingham Slavonic Monographs, No. 21, 1992

Smith, Zadie, '"The Limited Circle is Pure": Franz Kafka versus the Novel', *The New Republic* (3 November, 2003), 33–40

Sperber, Dan and Wilson, Deirdre, *Relevance: Communication and Cognition*, Oxford: Basil Blackwell, 1986 (second edition 1996)

Spieker, Sven, ed., *GØGØL: Exploring Absence. Negativity in 19th-Century Russian Literature*, Bloomington: Slavica, 1999

Spilka, Mark, *Dickens and Kafka: A Mutual Interpretation*, Bloomington: Indiana University Press, 1963

Steiner, George, *Tolstoy or Dostoevsky*, Harmondsworth: Penguin, 1967 (first published 1959)

Steiner, George, *After Babel: Aspects of Language and Translation*, Oxford: Oxford University Press, 1977

Steiner, George, *Grammars of Creation: Originating in the Gifford Lectures for 1990*, London: Faber, 2001

Stelleman, Jenny, *Aspects of Dramatic Communication: Action, Non-Action, Interaction (A.P. Cechov, A. Blok, D. Charms)*, Amsterdam and Atlanta, GA: Rodopi, 1992

Stephan, Halina, *Transcending the Absurd: Drama and Prose of Sławomir Mrożek*, Amsterdam and Atlanta, GA: Rodopi, 1997

Stern, J.P., *Nietzsche*, Glasgow: Fontana/Collins, 1978

Stewart, Susan, *Nonsense: Aspects of Intertextuality in Folklore and Literature*, Baltimore: Johns Hopkins University Press, 1989 (first published 1980)

Strachey, Edmund, 'Nonsense as a Fine Art', *The Quarterly Review*, 167 (1888), 335–65

Strathern, Paul, *Wittgenstein (1889–1951) in 90 Minutes*, London: Constable, 1996

Strawson, Galen, "Luck swallows everything. Can our sense of free will be true?", *TLS* (26 June 1998), 8–10 (full version as "Free Will", in Craig, 1998)

Styan, J.L. *Modern Drama in Theory and Practice. Volume 2: Symbolism, Surrealism and the Absurd*, Cambridge: Cambridge University Press, 1983

Sutherland, John, *Can Jane Eyre Be Happy? More Puzzles in Classic Fiction*, Oxford: Oxford University Press, 1997

Sypher, William, ed., *Comedy*, New York: Doubleday, 1956; reprinted Baltimore: Johns Hopkins University Press, 1980

Szanto, George H., *Narrative Consciousness: Structure and Perception in the Fiction of Kafka, Beckett, and Robbe-Grillet*, Austin and London: University of Texas Press, 1972

Szulkin, Robert, 'Gogol's *The Nose* in Light of Sterne's *Tristram Shandy*', in Elena Semeka-Pankratov, ed., *Studies in Poetics: Commemorative Volume Krystyna Pomorska (1928–1986)*, Columbus, OH: Slavica Publishers, 1995, 403–14

Thody, Philip, *Albert Camus*, Basingstoke and London, 1989

Tigges, Wim, ed., *Explorations in the Field of Nonsense*, Amsterdam: Rodopi, 1987

Tigges, Wim, *An Anatomy of Literary Nonsense* [doctoral dissertation: University of Leiden], Amsterdam: Rodopi, 1988

Tintner, Adeline R., *The Twentieth-Century World of Henry James: Changes in His Work After 1900*, Baton Rouge: Louisiana State University Press, 2000

Todorov, Tzvetan, *The Poetics of Prose* [*La Poétique de la prose*, 1971], translated by Richard Howard, Oxford: Basil Blackwell, 1977

Todorov, Tzvetan, *Theories of the Symbol* [*Théories du symbole*, 1977], translated by Catherine Porter, Ithaca, NY: Cornell University Press, 1982

Todorov, Tzvetan, *Genres in Discourse* [*Genres du discours*, 1978], translated by Catherine Porter, Cambridge, Cambridge University Press, 1990

Tokarev, D.V., 'Sushchestvuet li literatura absurda?', *Russkaia literatura*, 4 (1999), 26–54

Tokarev, D.V., *Kurs na khudshee: Absurd kak kategoriia teksta u Daniila Kharmsa i Semiuelia Bekketa*, Moscow: Novoe literaturnoe obozrenie, 2002

Uhlmann, Anthony, *Beckett and Poststructuralism*, Cambridge: Cambridge University Press, 1999

Uspenskii, Fedor, and Elena Babaeva, 'Grammatika "absurda" i "absurd" grammatiki', *Wiener Slawistischer Almanach*, 29 (1992), 127–58

Valency, Maurice, *Tragedy*, New York: New Amsterdam, 1991

Vladislav, Jan, ed., *Václav Havel or Living in Truth*, London: Faber, 1989

Wanner, Adrian, 'Russian Minimalist Prose: Generic Antecedents to Daniil Kharms's "Sluchai"', *Slavic and East European Journal*, 45 (2001), 451–72

Wanner, Adrian, *Russian Minimalism: From the Prose Poem to the Anti-Story*, Evanston, IL: Northwestern University Press, 2003

Waszink, Paul M, 'The King Knocks: Writers and Readers in Gogol's *Diary of a Madman*', *Russian Literature*, 41 (1997), 61–92

Waugh, Patricia, *Metafiction: The Theory and Practice of Self-Conscious Fiction*, London: Methuen, 1984

Weightman, John, *The Cat Sat on the Mat: Language and the Absurd*, London: Weech Publishing, 2002

Weightman, John, *Reading the Bible in the Run-up to Death*, London: Weech Publishing, 2003

Welsford, Enid, *The Fool: His Social and Literary History*, London: Faber, 1968 (first published 1935)

Weston, Michael, *Kierkegaard and Modern Continental Philsophy: An Introduction*, London, Routledge, 1994

White, Hayden, 'The Absurdist Moment in Contemporary Literary Theory', in White, *Tropics of Discourse: Essays in Cultural Criticism*, Baltimore and London: The Johns Hopkins University Press, 1985, 261–82 (essay first published 1976)

Wilden, Anthony, *The Rules are No Game: The Strategy of Communication*, London: Routledge and Kegan Paul, 1987

Wilson, Colin, *The Outsider*, London: Pan Books, 1971 (first published 1956)

Wood, Michael, 'Cabrera Infante: Unruly Pupil', in Karen R. Lawrence, ed., *Transcultural Joyce*, Cambridge: Cambridge University Press, 1998, 49–62

Wood, Michael, *Franz Kafka*, Tavistock, Devon: Northcote House, 2003

Wright, Elizabeth, *Psychoanalytical Criticism: Theory and Practice*, London: Methuen, 1984

Wright, M.R., *Cosmology in Antiquity*, London: Routledge, 1995

Zarhy-Levo, Yael, 'Pinter and the Critics', in Raby, 212–29

Zarhy-Levo, Yael, *The Theatrical Critic as Cultural Agent: Constructing Pinter, Orton and Stoppard as Absurdist Playwrights*, New York: Peter Lang, 2001

Zeifman, Hersh, 'A Trick of the Light: Tom Stoppard's *Hapgood* and Postabsurdist Theater', in Brater and Cohn, 175–201

Zima, Peter V., *The Philosophy of Modern Literary Theory*, London: Athlone, 1999

Zinman, Toby Silverman, 'Hen in a Foxhouse: The Absurdist Plays of Maria Irene Fornes', in Brater and Cohn, 203–220

Zischler, Hanns, *Kafka Goes to the Movies*, translated by Susan H. Gillespie, Chicago and London: University of Chicago Press, 2003 (published in German 1996)

Index

Note: The idea of an index to a study of 'the absurd' may well itself seem absurd. Any index supplied, obviously at least somewhat arbitrary and selective, will inevitably be to some degree absurd. The manifest absurdity of attempting to index the term 'absurd' itself, however, has been avoided. In addition to writers, most critics used and the main texts discussed, as well as philosophers and theorists, are included. I am not sure whether this brings the book as a whole closer (in Hayden White's terms) to 'Normal' or to 'Absurdist' criticism. Numbers in **bold** indicate pages of more serious examination.

Abbott, H. Porter 241, 247n.41, 248n.48, 249n.56
Abish, Walter 290
abyss, the x, 5, 7, 11, 16, 23, 43, 90, 103, 104, 112, 121n.5, 122n.18, 199, 293
Adamov, Arthur 59n.23, 97, 127, **131–2**, 154n.34
Adelman, Gary x, 215, 220, 242n.5, 244n.12, 246n.23, 248n.52
Adler, Jeremy 68, 74, 95n.36, 201, 203, 204, 206n.3, 208n.18, 212n.50, 213n.56, n.63
Adorno, Theodor 184, 215, 218, 230, 231, 232, 233, 234, 241, 243n.9, n.12, 248n.50
Aeschylus 129, 179n.22, n.24, 180n.44
Aizlewood, Robin 170
Albee, Edward 116, 127, 133
Albright, Daniel 200, 211n.43, 214n.71, 224, 243n.12, 244n.13, n.18
Allen, Woody 31n.37
Alomar, Gabriel 77
Amiran, Eyal 219, 220, 222, 224, 225, 228, 230, 240, 242n.6, 243n.10, 246n.29, n.30,

250n.71
Amis, Martin 56, 264
Anselm, Saint 219
Apollinaire, Guillaume 74, 81, 84, 86–7, 90, 96–7 *passim*, 113, 160, 180n35, 244n.14
Apollonio, Umbro 76, 94n.24, n.26, n.28
apophatic theology *see* negative theology
Apuleius 36, 39
Aragon, Louis 79, 82
Arcesilaus of Pitane 11
Arendt, Hannah 184, 189
Aristophanes 33, 35, 39, 154n.39, 230
Aristotle 3, 10, 11, 15, 16, 19, 31n.42, 147, 166, 241, 277n.43, 295
Armstrong, Raymond 153n.24, n.26, 187, 191–2, 193, 209n.25, 210n.29, n.34, 212n.52
Arrabal, Fernando 127, 132, 248n.50, 288
Artaud, Antonin 8, 35, 55, 67, 82, 92n.3, 99, **107–14**, 116, 121–3 *passim*, 126–7, 131, 132, 133, 144, 151n.11, 155n.44, 166,

170, 180n.37, 195, 211n.43,
241, 250n.77, 297, 303
Theatre and its Double, The 110,
122n.14, 123n.22, 241
Astley, Neil [*The End of My Tether*]
286–7
atheism 7, 12, 38, 170, 294
Augustine, Saint 6, 26, 31n.42, 46,
274n.17, 287
Auster, Paul 274n.12, 310, 313n.4
Avicenna 10
Ayckbourn, Alan [*Absurd Person
Singular*] 307n.15
Ayer, A.J. 9, 12

Bair, Deirdre 244n.18, 246n.23
Bakhtin, Mikhail 17, 20, 30n.33,
31n.34, 36–9 *passim*, 42–3, 45,
47, 48, 51, 53–4, 56, 57–9
passim, 61–2 *passim*, 86, 101,
117, 144, 261, 268, 277n.50
Baldick, Chris 2, 74
Ball, Hugo 80
Balzac, Honoré de 48, 61n.42,
182n.59, 229
Barber, Stephen 107–14 *passim*,
122–3 *passim*
Barker, Howard [*Gertrude, the Cry*]
311
Barthelme, Donald x, 21, 247n.68,
250n.76, 290, 305
Barthes, Roland 162, 263
Barzun, Jacques 302, 308n.33
Bataille, Georges 82–3, 184,
207n.14, 303
Bates, Catherine 6, 7, 10, 14, 15,
20, 24, 30n.24, n.28, 31n.42,
n.43
Batty, Mark 137, 138, 152n.20
Baudelaire, Charles 15, 16, 30n.30,
52, 62n.48, 67, 84, 110,
179n.17, 233, 249n.58
Baudrillard, Jean 291
Bauer, Felice 190, 191, 203,
207n.12, 209n.26
Beattie, James 16, 42

Beaumarchais, P.A. Caron de 68
Beckett, Samuel x, xi, 3, 4, 8,
31n.37, 35, 41, 43, 67, 81,
92n.3, 127, 128, 136, 138, 139,
143, 149, 155n.42, 162, 166,
179n.21, 182n.60, 194, 199,
205, 207n.14, 213n.63, **215–50**,
251, 252, 255, 263, 269,
270–1, 277n.48, 280, 286, 289,
290, 292–5 *passim*, 297–8, 302,
304, 306n.13, 307n.20, n.22,
310, 313n.4
All That Fall 221, 249n.60, n.69
Calmative, The 216, 218, 223,
242n.5, 246n.27
Company 225, 226, 247n.36,
n.40
*Dream of Fair to Middling
Women* 199, 220–1, 242n.6,
245n.19
Eleutheria 226–7, 243n.8,
246n.30, 247n.43
Endgame 35, 218, 219, 228,
230–2, 247n.46, 248n.50,
n.54, 251
How It Is 218, 220, 224, 225
Lost Ones, The 215, 220, 225,
226, 247n.33
Malone Dies 155n.42, 217, 223,
247n.40
Mercier and Camier 224, 228,
238
Molloy 215, 217, 223, 238, 241,
242n.6, 248n.52
More Pricks Than Kicks 220, 221,
245n.19
Murphy 221–2, 233, 234, 238,
239, 240, 245n.21, n.22,
248n.47, n.50
Unnamable, The 215, 217–18,
219, 220, 223, 224, 234, 238,
239, 244n.13, 248n.47,
250n.72
Waiting for Godot 3, 145, 148,
154n.36, 182n.60, 226,
227–30, 232, 234, 247n.46,

294, 298, 310
Watt 215, 222, 232, 234, **235–9**,
    240, 243n.8, 245n.23,
    246n.25, 248–50 *passim*, 255,
    269, 271, 286, 313n.4
Beecroft, Vanessa 306n.13
Beethoven, Ludwig van 249n.60
Benjamin, Walter 20, 184, 188, 201,
    205, 207n.9, n.13
Bennett, Alan [*Kafka's Dick*] 184,
    196–8, 212n.49, n.52, n.55, 300
Berdyaev, Nicolas [Nikolai] 6,
    28n.8, 63n.54
Berger, Peter L. 3, 7, 10, 16, 21, 22,
    23
Bergson, Henri [*Le Rire*] 16, 17, 19,
    20, 22, 31n.34, 68, 79, 95n.30,
    134, 277n.43
Berkeley, George 295
Berkoff, Steven 184, **194–6**,
    211n.40–7 *passim*, 214n.73
Beyond the Fringe 300
Billington, Michael 135, 136, 138,
    139, 140, 141, 151n.9,
    152n.12–20 *passim*, 153n.23,
    n.31, 193, 194, 210n.34
Blanchot, Maurice 184, 186,
    209n.25, 214n.74
Blin, Roger 227, 232, 241
Bloom, Harold 120n.3, 173,
    182n.63, 201
Bohn, Willard 31n.25, 39, 74, 81,
    95n.34, 96n.42, n.43, 100
Bohr, Niels 202, 295–6
'Bonaventura' [*Night Watches of
    Bonavenura, The*] 33, 43–4, 47,
    52, 54, 58n.16–19, 62n.47, 67
Bond, Edward 311
Booker, M. Keith 253, 261, 262,
    266, 268–72 *passim*, 274n.15,
    275n.23, 277n.43, n.48, n.50,
    278n.54, 306n.7
Borges, Jorge Luis 10, 16, 23–4,
    29n.15, 16, 21, 31n.37, 42,
    59n.28, 66, 89, 94n.27, 120n.3,
    162, 174, 183n.67, 184, 196,

201, 202, 205n.2, 207n.16,
    260–1, 275n.26, n.29, 276n.35,
    278n.56
Bosch, Hieronymus 58n.13, 242n.7
Boxsel, Matthijs van 19, 41, 93n.6,
    301–2
Bradbury, Malcolm 184, 207n.9
Bradbury, Nicola 50, 61n.38, 71,
    93n.13
Brandist, Craig 179n.29
Brater, Enoch 120n.1, 290, 312
Brecht, Berthold 88, 94n.23, 113,
    132
Brée, Germaine 81–2, 83, 110, 116
Breton, André 55, 64n.59, 66, 79,
    81–4, 92, 96n.42–4, 97n.50,
    107, 160, 180n.40, 224
    Nadja 82–3, 96n.44, n.48,
    180n.40, 224
Brink, André 184, 207n.16,
    210n.31, 211n.45
Brod, Max 68, 74, 185, 186, 189,
    190, 193, 197, 199, 201,
    208n.19, 211n.45, 212nn.50,
    53, 54, 245n.18, 257
Brodsky, Joseph 30n.25, 63n.55,
    247n.43
Brook, Peter 113
Brooker, Joseph 259–66 *passim*,
    268, 270, 273n.6, n.9, 275n.22,
    276n.37
Brooks, Peter 50–1, 69
Buber, Martin 205, 214n.72
Büchner, Georg 94n.23, 129,
    154n.36
Buddhism 11, 14
Bufalino, Gesualdo [*Tommaso and
    the Blind Photographer*] 23
Buffy the Vampire Slayer 310
Bulgakov, Mikhail 253, 272
Burgess, Anthony 306n.7
Burian, Jarka 149, 150
Burkman, Katherine 137, 138,
    152n.21
Burliuk, David 77
Byron, Lord [Byronism] 54, 63n.58

Cabell, James Branch 261
Caillois, Roger 9, 10, 31n.43
Calasso, Roberto 4, 33, 54, 56n.1,
    57n.3, 63n.57, 66, 110, 184,
    188, 191, 203, 204, 206n.5,
    208n.17, 213n.59, 214n.69,
    216, 242n.4
Calder, John 214n.69, 216, 242n.4
Campanile, Achille **289–90**, 291
Camus, Albert 2, 3, 5, 6–7, 8, 24,
    28n.12, 91, 98n.63, 99, **114–19**,
    124–5n. *passim*, 127, 155n.46,
    184, 185, 186, 196, 206n.8,
    209n.26, 241, 282, 302, 303,
    310
  Caligula **116–17**, 119
  Fall, The 115, 116, **117–18**, 119,
    124n.39, 155n.46
  Myth of Sisyphus, The 3, 5, 6, 8,
    28n.12, 98n.63, 99, 114–19
    passim, 124n.31, 125n.42,
    n.45, n.46, 127, 186, 196,
    206n.8
  Outsider, The 114, 115, 116
  Rebel, The 117, 118, 119,
    124n.32, n.33, n.37, n.38
Canetti, Elias 184, 203, 214n.68
Čapek Brothers [Josef, Karel] 148–9,
    154n.39, 155n.48, 253, 273n.9
  Insect Play, The 149, 154n.39,
    155n.48
  see also O'Brien, Flann
Cardinal, Roger 83, 91n.48
Cardullo, Bert 75, 80, 81, 86, 93n.6,
    94n.22
Carlson, Marvin 96n.41, 131, 132
carnivalesque 20, 22, 36–9, 40, 42,
    45, 48, 51, 52, 53, 57n.11,
    61n.45, 80, 86, 88, 95n.36,
    165, 171, 228, 268, 275n.23
  see also Bakhtin, Mikhail
Carrick, Neil 12, 170, 172, 173,
    177, 179n.22, 181n.46, n.47,
    n.54, n.58
Carroll, Lewis 18, 19, 21, 22, 55–6,
    64n.62, 84, 91, 98n.63, 102,

    106, 113–14, 116, 123n.29,
    134, 162, 170, 179n.19,
    181n.47, 265, 299, 306n.13
Cartledge, Paul 35, 275n.27
Caws, Mary Ann 55, 83, 84,
    96n.43, n.46, 122n.15
Celan, Paul 100
Cervantes, Miguel de 38, 43, 44, 48,
    207n.18
  Don Quixote 10, 207n.16
Chamberlain, Lesley 6, 8, 27n.4,
    28n.10, 31n.37
chaos x, 14, 34, 39, 41, 44, 77, 79,
    80, 104, 105, 110, 112, 121n.5,
    141, 170, 181n.48, 221, 222,
    245n.22, 285, 291, 293–5, 312
Chaplin, Charles 17, 91, 199
Chaucer, Geoffrey 18, 39, 172, 300
Chekhov, A.P. 8, 35, 67, 68, 131,
    142, 146
Chesterton, G.K. 21
Chestov *see* Shestov, Lev
Christ, Jesus 6, 10, 28n.8, 105, 192,
    218
Christianity 7, 10, 15, 16, 21,
    27n.4, 28n.9, 29n.21, 41, 47,
    63n.54, 110, 115, 118, 119,
    125n.40, 170, 303
Churchill, Caryl 292
Cicero 15
circus 20, 35, 80, 128, 146, 161,
    171, 229, 300
Clissmann [Clune], Anne 252, 255,
    261, 262, 263, 269, 271, 273–4
    passim, 277n.41, n.43
Cobb, Karen [*Theatre of the
    Absurd*] 291–2
Cocteau, Jean 96n.41, 107
Cohn, Ruby 120n.1, 215, 218, 222,
    235, 236, 238, 241, 242n.1,
    243–5 *passim*, 248–9 *passim*
comedy
  Old Comedy 33, 34, 35
  see also Greek theatre
commedia dell'arte 37, 44, 128,
    148, 229

communication theory 24, 31n.42, 150, 165, 170

Complicité, Théâtre de 160, 311, 312n.1

Connolly, Jeanne 193, 210n.34, 230n.35, n.36

Connor, Steven 224, 225, 230, 231, 235, 237, 246n.28, n.30, 250n.77

Conrad, Joseph 66, **69–70**, 72, 73, 93n.9, n.14, 166, 271
Heart of Darkness 66, **69–70**

Conrad, Peter 17, 32n.45, 52, 66, 76, 81, 83, 93n.6, n.7, 95n.31, 96n.48

Conradi, Peter 52, 53, 62n.54, 63n.56

Cook, Peter 300

Coover, Robert 175, 176, 183n.69, 274n.12, 285, 290, 311
Gerald's Party **285–6**
'Marker, The' 175–6, 183n.69, 290

Coppa, Francesca 137, 142, 143, 152n.12

Corngold, Stanley 201, 214n.65

Cornwell, Neil 59n.28, 85, 177n.2, 178–9 *passim*, 181n.50, 183n.66, 286n.32

Corpus Dionysiacum [anon.] 10

cosmogony 14, 30

cosmology 14, 20, 21, 30n.27, 31n.37, n.38, 111, 221, 305
cosmological argument, the 4, 27n.3

Costello, Peter 259, 273–4 *passim*, 275n.22

Craig, William Lane 3, 4, 8, 11, 27n.3

Cronin, Anthony 252, 254, 256, 257, 258, 260, 271, 273n.4, n.5, 274n.11, 277n.51

Crosby, Donald A. 4, 5, 7, 9

cruelty 16, 34, 55, 107–14 *passim*, 123n.24, 124n.36, 132, 133, 144, 154n.36, 180n.37

'Cruelty, Theatre of' 35, 107–14 *passim*, 121n.12, 122n.14, 126, 151n.11, 166, 211n.43, 291, 296, 297
see also Artaud, Antonin

Cubism 74, 81

Cubo-Futurism *see* Futurism [Russian]

Dada [Dadaism] 10, 48, 68, 74, 76, **78–81**, 82, 85, 86, 87, 94n.29, 95n.32–4, n.36, 100, 107, 108, 162, 260, 294, 299, 302

Dalí, Salvador 55, 63n.59, 82

Dalton-Brown, Sally 293, 307n.16, n.17

Damascius 11, 29n.17

dance of death, the [*danse macabre*] x, 42, 44, 50, 58n.13, n.19, 67, 70, 71, 76, 116, 132, 133, 148, 155n.47, 217, 293

Dante 45, 118, 152n.15, 211.n.38, 220, 221, 225, 242n.6, 244n.15, 245n.19, 247n.33, 249n.69, 250n.73, 277n.47–50, 293
Divine Comedy, The [*Inferno, The*] x, 45, 70, 94n.20, 220, 244n.15, n.16, 245n.19, 249n.69, 277n.50

Danto, Arthur C. 3, 6

Daumal, René 11, 12, 93n.6

Davies, Paul [critic] 227, 228, 247n.45

Davies, Paul [physicist] 5, 31n.38, 305, 308n.31

Davison, Ray 118–19, 125n.43, n.46, n.47

Deane, Raymond 122n.14

Deane, Seamus 229, 251, 257, 263, 273n.2, 274n.17

deconstruction 7, 10, 95n.31, 162, 240, 311

Deleuze, Gilles 7, 10, 11, 18, 114, 122n.17, 123n.28, n.29, 166,

170, 180n.37, 184, 211n.43, 220

Demastes, William W. 291, 294–5, 308n.23, 312

Democritus 240

Derrida, Jacques 4, 27, 108, 111, 121n.12, 126, 162, 184, 272, 278n.56, n.58, 302, 308n.29

Descartes, René 7, 41, 229, 240, 235, 239

determinism 9, 241, 295

Dickens, Charles 42, **48–51**, 54, 55, 60n.36, 60n.36–8, 61n.41–2, n.45, 119, 172, 184, 186, 187, 188, 199
    Bleak House 48, 49–51
    David Copperfield 50, 187, 207n.12
    Great Expectations 50, 51, 61n.38
    Little Dorrit 49, 187, 207n.12

Dionysus [Dionysius] 6, 8, 12, 34, 57n.3, 244n.17

Dobrez, L.A.C. 13, 94n.23, 129, 131, 134–7 *passim*, 139, 140, 222, 223, 224, 228, 230, 234, 239, 240, 241, 242, 242n.6, 245–6n.23, 246n.24, 248n.49

Dobychin, Leonid [*The Town of N*] 289, 306n.12

Dodd, W.J. 52, 60n.37, 185, 187, 202, 207n.10, 212n.55

Doherty, Francis 221, 222, 224, 235, 243n.7, 245n.19, n.22, 249n.65, 250n.75, 265, 267, 268–9, 276n.36, 277n.40, n.51

Donleavy, J.P. [*The Ginger Man*] 282

Dostoevsky, F.M. 6, 7, 21, 28n.8, 33, 36, 37, **51–4**, 60n.37, 61–3 *passim*, 90, 102, 106, **114–19**, 123n.19, 124–5 *passim*, 131, 154n.39, 155n.46, 162, 165, 170, 183n.71, 184, 186–7, 198, 207n.10, 244n.13, 254, 289, 293

Brothers Karamazov, The 118, 119, 124n.31, n.37, n.38, 254

Crime and Punishment 118, 155n.46, 186, 187, 198

Devils, The [*The Possessed*; *The Demons*] 54, 61n.45, 63n.55, 118, 119, 125n.47, 154n.39, 170, 180n.45

Double, The 51–2, 53, 55, 186, 187

Notes from Underground, The 53–4, 56, 117, 118, 183n.71, 187, 244n.13

Doyle, Arthur Conan 172, 181n.50
    'Red-Headed League, The' 171, 272
    Sherlock Holmes 158, 171, 181n.52, 209n.25, 255, 257, 272, 274n.12, 300

'doubles' 47, 51–2, 61n.45, 111, 153n.21
    see also Dostoevsky, F.M., *Double, The*

Druskin, Yakov [Iakov] 12, 124n.36, 161, 170, 233, 234

Duchamp, Marcel 80, 93n.6

Dukes, Gerry 242n.5

Dunwoodie, Peter 118, 119, 125n.41

Dürer, Albrecht 58n.13, 61n.39, 243n.7

Durrani, Osman 196, 206n.5

Dürrenmatt, Friedrich 186

Eagleton, Terry 3, 5, 11, 17, 22, 31n.37, 35, 57n.4, 67, 69, 98n.59, 149, 153n.27, 304

Eckhart, Meister 6

Eco, Umberto 16, 28n.14, 95n.30, 184, 202, 306n.13

Edel, Leon 72, 93n.12, 94n.17

Edson, Russell 174, 289

Einstein, Albert 14, 277n.43

Eleatic thought [the Eleatics] 11, 240
    see also Zeno of Elea [Zeno's

paradox]
Eliot, T.S. 140, 152n.15, 153n.26, 212n.51, 252, 275n.25, 283, 304
Eluard, Paul 79, 244n.14
Epstein, Michael [Mikhail Epshtein] 11, 12, 29n.21, 170, 181n.49, 183n.70, 291
Erasmus 3, 11, 15, 16, 38, 42
Erigena, John Scotus 29n.15, 59n.28
Ernst, Max 80, 82
Esslin, Martin xi, 2, 3, 7, 8, 33–4, 37–8, 39, 41, 42, 67, 74, 89, 94n.23, 113, 127–35 passim, 143, 149, 151n.1, n.11, 152n.19, 155n.45, 182n.56, 224, 229, 231, 232, 248n.54, 280, 307n.20, 310, 311
Estrin, Marc 189, 208n.23, 309
eternity 31n.37, 112, 153n.27, 264, 265, 268, 271, 307n.20
eternal recurrence [return] 7, 20, 31n.37, 230, 291
Euripides 80, 275n.27
Evreinov, Nikolai 248n.54
existentialism 2–8 passim, 22, 24, 27n.2, 62n.54, 79, 115, 241, 280, 312
Christian existentialism 115
Expressionism 74, 94n.23, 146

faith 3, 7, 10, 21, 23, 28n.7, n.9, 34, 53, 93n.9, 115, 119, 128, 305, 308n.25
Fascism 76, 77, 142
Fassbinder, Werner Maria 285, 307n.18
Felice see Bauer, Felice
Fermat's Theorem 32n.46
Ficowski, Jerzy 89, 199, 206n.3, 207n.14, 213n.63
First Cause, the 13
FitzGerald, Joan 261, 262, 275–6n.29
Flaubert, Gustave 59n.24, 197
Fleming, John 294, 295, 308n.23

Fletcher, John 133, 227, 228, 229, 230, 232, 241, 243n.12, 248n.51
Fondane, Benjamin 6, 8, 10, 28n.9, 35, 62n.52, 128
Fool, the [fools, foolery] 14, 20, 39, 40, 57n.7, 60n.32, 70, 88, 108, 204, 294
see also ship of fools, the [Ship of Fools, The]
Ford, Ford Madox [The Good Soldier] 72–3, 74, 88, 94n.17
Formalism see Russian Formalists / Formalism
Fornes, Maria Irene 292
Foscolo, Ugo 43, 44–5
Fotiade, Ramona 3, 6, 7, 8, 10, 11, 13, 28n.9, 29n.19, 34, 35, 62n.52, 83, 92n.5, 93n.6, 96n.47, 97n.49, 122n.13, 125n.45
Fowles, John [Mantissa] 286, 306n.9
Frayn, Michael [Copenhagen] 295–6
Freud, Sigmund 15, 17, 18, 22, 30n.28, 31n.34, 61n.45, 68, 84, 88, 152n.12. 166, 173, 207n.15, 268
Frye, Northrop 17, 36, 37, 39, 40, 42, 56, 60n.36
Fuentes, Carlos 184, 185, 202, 206n.9, 207n.16
Futurism [Georgian, Italian, Russian] 19, 73, 74–8, 79, 80, 85, 86, 90, 94–5 passim, 100, 108, 109, 147, 151n.4, 159, 162, 233, 289

Galich, Aleksandr 160
Galligan, Edward L. 15, 21, 283
game theory 9–10, 31n.43
see also language games
Gardner, Martin 55, 56, 64n.61, n.62
Gatiss, Mark [The Vesuvius Club] 301
Gautier, Théophile 19, 22

Geller, Leonid 19, 176, 178n.9,
179n.18, 181n.48
Genet, Jean 127, 132–3, 141, 143,
151n.7, 181n.56, 247n.44
Genesis, the Book of 14, 245n.19
Giacometti, Alberto 165
Gide, André 9, 107, 247n.44, 260
Gillen, Francis 193, 210n.34
Gilmore, Robert 18, 56, 64n.60,
202
Glass, Philip 184, 206n.3
Gleick, James 14, 295
Glotser, Vladimir 162, 178n.8,
179n.18, n.19
Gnosticism 12, 21, 91, 98n.65, 111,
145, 173
Gödel's Theorem 14
Gogol, N.V. 12, 25–6, 45–8, 50,
51–2, 55, 58n.20, 59–60
passim, 61n.42, 88, 106, 114,
123n.30, 130, 131, 146, 162,
163, 170, 172, 179n.22,
181n.49, 184, 185–6, 187, 199,
206n.7, n.9, 208n.20, 213n.59,
266, 288, 289
Dead Souls 45, 47, 61n.43, 289
Nevsky Propspect 47, 58n.20,
60n.34, 130, 179n.22, 266
Nose, The 46, 47, 48, 52, 59n.28,
60n.29, n.33, 170, 185
Notes [Diary] of a Madman 46,
52, 146, 288
Goll, Yvan 94n.23
Gombrowicz, Witold [*Ferdydurke*]
89, 90, 148, 253
Gontarski, S.E. 223, 224, 225, 226,
228, 242n.1, n.5, 246n.26
Goodman, Paul 188, 207n.14
Goons, the [*Goon Show, The*] 20,
299
Gordon, Lois 33, 224, 241,
245n.21, 248n.53
Gorgias of Leontini 4, 240, 250n.76
Gothic [Gothic novel, the] 43, 44,
54, 84, 225, 265, 288, 291
Graffy, Julian 60n.33, n.35,

179n.16, 182n.61
Grand Guignol 67, 92n.4
Gray, Alasdair [*Lanark*] 286
Greek theatre 33, 44, 196, 229, 293
Greek tragedy 34–5, 141, 145, 247
Greene, Graham 260
Grossman, Jan 149, 150
Gruner, Charles R. 20, 30n.29, n.31
Grünewald, Hazel 144, 145,
154n.35
Guelincx, Arnold 240
Gussow, Mel 153n.28, 193, 194,
210n.34

Haight, M.R. 22
Hall, Peter 152n.16, 227, 293
Hallgrimsson, Haflidi 309
Hamsun, Knut 160, 162, 172,
179n.21, 181n.50
Hardy, Barbara 72, 93n.16
Hašek, Jaroslav [*The Good Soldier
Švejk*] 88, 97n.55, 175
Havel, Václav 127, 147, 149–50,
155–6 *passim*
Garden Party, The 149, 150,
156n.50
Memorandum, The 149,
155–6n.49, 156n.54
Hawkes, Terence 40
Hegel, G.W.F. 11, 15
Heidegger, Martin 4, 6, 9, 22, 27,
28n.5, 86, 131, 239, 240, 303
Heinonen, Jussi 179n.22, 183n.71
Heisenberg, Werner 14, 72,
278n.54, 295, 296, 309
Heller, Joseph [*Catch-22*] 280,
282–4
Heraclitus 20, 84, 186, 240
Hill, Carl 15, 173
Hinchliffe, Arnold P. xii n.2,
121n.12, 269
Hirst, Damien 247n.59
Hitler, Adolf 17, 107, 198, 299
Hobbes, Thomas 15, 16, 30n.29
Hoefer, Jacqueline 237, 239, 240,
249n.64

Hoffmann, E.T.A. 15, 44, 59n.20, 187, 252
Hofmannsthal, Hugo von [*The Lord Chandos Letter*] 68, 69, 93n.7
Hofstadter, Douglas 9, 11, 14, 22, 29n.20, 93n.16
Hollingsworth, Margaret 292
Holquist, Michael 46, 47, 48, 53–4, 57n.6, 59n.20, n.24, 165–6
Hopper, Keith 252, 259, 262–8 *passim*, 270, 271, 275n.23, 276–7 *passim*
Hoyles, John 62n.54, 184, 187, 195, 199, 201, 202, 204, 209n.26, 210n.37
Huelsenbeck, Richard 79
Hume, David 3
humour **14–18**, 19, 20, 22, 25, 41, 116, 162, 165, 166, 171, 173, 251, 255, 270, 298, 305
    black humour 19, 55, 84, 86, 97n.50, 117, 169
    sick humour 19, 288
    see also jokes, joke theory
Humphries, Barry 95n.36
Hussey, Emma Spurgin 310
Hutcheson, Francis 16
Huysmans, J.-K. 84, 97n.49, 277n.43
Huxley, Aldous 261
Hyde, G.M. 60n.33, 199, 213n.59

Ibsen, Henrik 35, 67, 129, 242
Improbable Theatre 311
incongruity ix, 15, 16, 17, 19, 23, 25, 46, 82, 147, 173, 176
Ionesco, Eugène 3, 4, 8, 13, 25, 34, 41, 60n.32, 93n.6, 98n.63, 125n.42, n.44, 126, 127, **128–31**, 132, 133, 137, 140–50 *passim*, 151n.2–5, 152n.19, 226, 252, 292, 293, 303
    Bald Prima Donna [Soprano], The 25, **129–30**, 133, 144
    Chairs, The 130, 137, 151n.4
    Lesson, The 25, 130, 144

irrational, the 3, 6, 8, 23, 27n.1, 70, 78, 126, 149, 165–6, 185, 222, 239, 299
Iser, Wolfgang 228
Iuvachev, D.I. *see* Kharms, Daniil

Jaccard, Jean-Philippe [Zhakkar, Zhan-Filipp] 98n.66, 144, 154n.34, 170, 173n.13, n.16, 182n.65, 213n.61
Jackson, John Wyse 258, 259, 273n.3, 276n.36
Jacobean tragedy 41, 141
Jakobson, Roman 25–6, 136, 140, 152n.14, 170, 265
James, Henry 69, **70–2**, 73, 74n.17, n.21, 93n.13–16, 94n.17, 124n.34, 172, 189n.59, n.60, 276n.38,
    Sacred Fount, The **70–2**
James, William 303
Jarry, Alfred 67–8, 74, 84, 89, 92n.6, 96n.41, 107, 143, 149, 154n.36, 160, 244n.14, 303, 305n.1
Jaspers, Karl 6, 28n.7
Jean Paul *see* Richter, Jean [Johann] Paul
Jesenská, Milena 191, 201, 203, 207n.9, 208n.19, 209n.25, 214n.66
Johnson, B.S. 306n.7
jokes, joke theory 14–18, 19, 30n.28, n.34, 152n.12, 221, 231
    see also humour; shaggy dog stories
Jones, David 193, 210n.31, n.33
Jones, John 52, 53, 55, 61–3 *passim*, 170, 180–1n.45
Jones, Jonathan 83, 96n.43
Jones, Malcolm 52, 53, 62n.46
Jones, Terry 155n.42, 300
Joyce, James 23, 67, 166, 240, 243n.10, 244n.18, 251–2, 256, 257–8, 260–1, 263, 274n.15,

n.17, 294, 312

Kabbala, The 173, 182n.63
Kafka, Franz x, xi, 2, 4, 20, 46, 48,
    49, 52, 56, 60n.37, 61n.38, 68,
    74, 88, 89, 91, 98n.59, n.63,
    116, 121n.7, 141, 142, 145,
    147, 149, 150, 153n.24, n.27,
    159, 162, 179n.21, **184–214**,
    215–20, 221, 225, 243n.12,
    244n.18, 248n.52, 252, 253,
    256, 257, 269–70, 271, 286,
    287, 288, 293, 304, 307n.15,
    309–10
  'Before the Law' 191, 204,
    243n.12
  Castle, The 56, 61n.38, 186, 187,
    188, 199, 203, 205, 206n.4,
    215, 220, 245n.18, 270, 271
  Give it Up! [Give Up!; A
    Comment] **204**
  Hunter Gracchus, The **190–1**,
    209n.25, 216–18, 220, 233,
    242n.3, n.4, 245n.18,
    248n.52, 288
  Judgement, The [The Sentence;
    The Verdict] 187, 188,
    214n.74
  Metamorphosis [The
    Transformation] x, 59n.28,
    91, 98n.59, 185–9 passim,
    194–5, 206n.7, 207n.14,
    208n.20, n.21, 244n.13
  Trial, The 4, 89, 141, 145, 149,
    186–9, 191–6, 198, 202–3,
    205, 206–14 passim
Kamensky, Vasilii 78
Kandinsky, Vasilii 97n.52
Kane, Sarah 292, **297–8**
Kant, Immanuel 3, 16, 59n.28, 79,
    170, 240, 295
Kappeler, Susanne 71, 72
Karl, Frederick R. 195, 196–7,
    210n.34, n.35
Karpowicz, Tymoteusz 227,
    307n.20

Kayser, Wolfgang 31n.39, 43, 46,
    58n.16
Kearney, Richard 162, 220, 229,
    230, 234, 239, 240, 248n.50,
    249n.63, 262, 263, 276n.33
Kenner, Hugh 229, 231, 239,
    248n.50, 264, 271, 277n.41
Keret, Etgar x, 291
Kermode, Frank 73
Kharms, Daniil [Iuvachev, D.I.] xi,
    12, 25, 29n.22, 31n.34, 70, 81,
    85–6, 88, 90, 91, 92, 93n.11,
    95n.30, 97n.52, 97–8 passim,
    106, 108, 117, 124n.36,
    125n.47, 130, 143–7, 151n.5,
    153–4 passim, **158–83**, 184,
    200, 201, 202, 213n.61, n.63,
    232–4, 241, 249n.57, 252, 253,
    254–5, 266, 270, 273n.8,
    274n.12, 277n.40, 288–91
    passim, 293, 302, 309, 312n.2
  'Blue Notebook No. 10' ['The
    Red-Haired Man'] 166,
    169–74, 175, 180n.42,
    181n.47, 234
  'Carpenter Kushakov, The' **167–8**,
    200
  Incidents 161–2, 163, 167,
    169–70, 177, 180n.37, n.42,
    309
  Old Woman, The 125n.47, 130,
    154n.34, 162, 177, 179n.22,
    183n.71, 234, 266, 279n.49
  Yelizaveta [Elizaveta] Bam 86, 91,
    130, **143–5**, 146, 147,
    154n.32–8, 159, 163,
    213n.61
Khlebnikov, Velimir 77, 94n.29,
    95n.30, n.31, 122n.18, 162
Kiberd, Declan 221, 228, 229, 231,
    258, 261, 263, 273n.2, 274–5
    n.20, 275n.25, 276n.31
Kierkegaard, Søren 3, 6, 7, 10, 12,
    15, 21, 27n.5, 28n.6, 31n.44,
    115, 186, 205n.2, 209n.26,
    252

Killinger, John xii n.2, 60n.31, 110, 111, 116
Kirkwood, Michael 203, 214n.65
Kitaro, Nishida 303
Klíma, Ivan 149
Knowles, Ronald 41, 42, 57n.11, 135–6, 137, 138, 140, 152n.13, n.15, 153n.26, 192–3, 210n.34, n.35, 211n.38
Knowlson, James 215, 220, 222, 224, 226, 227, 229, 230, 231, 240, 241, 242–5 *passim*, 247–8 *passim*
Koestler, Arthur 16, 17, 30n.31
Kołakowski, Leszek 5, 11, 24, 28n.10, 29n.17, n.18, n.20, 32n.46
Komaromi, Ann 159, 171, 176, 177, 234
Kooning, Willem de 274n.12
Kopit, Arthur 127
Kott, Jan 35, 40, 41, 57n.8, 93n.9, 231
Kruchenykh, Aleksei 77–8, 94n.30
Kundera, Milan 153n.27, 164, 184, 186, 188, 189, 199, 200, 201, 206n.6, n.9, 207n.13, n.16, 208n.22, 211n.37, 212n.53
Kunzru, Hari 251
Kyoto philosophy 303

labyrinth 184–214, 220, 260
language games 26–7, 144, 150, 154n.38, 176, 250n.73, 271, 294
Lacan, Jacques 30n.28, 114, 123n.20, 153n.31, 272, 278n.56
Laing, R.D. 134
Lang, Fritz 75
Lautréamont, Comte de [Isidore Ducasse, *Les Chants de Maldoror*] 54–5, 63n.57, 58, 59, 66, 84, 96n.49, 110, 123n.21, 124n.39, 303
Lawley, Paul 216–17, 218, 223, 246n.23
Lawton, Anna 77, 78, 95n.30
League of Gentlemen, The 95n.36, 300, 308n.28
Lear, Edward 18, 21, 22, 162, 179n.23, 299
Lecercle, Jean-Jacques 12, 13, 18, 19, 20, 22
Leibniz, Gottfried Wilhelm 4, 28n.14, 29n.20, 59n.28
Lennon, John [*In His Own Write*] x, **299–300**, 308n.26
Lermontov, Mikhail 54, 63n.58, 291
Leskov, Nikolai 171, 181n.51
Leventhal, A.J. 240, 242n.1, 250n.75
Lewis, (Percy) Wyndham 30n.32, 95n.37, 286
Leyden, Lucas van den 109, 111
Lindsay, David [*A Voyage to Arcturus*] 173, 181n.50, 182n.62
Lipovetsky, Mark 162, 180n.37, 291
Listengarten, Julia 142, 144, 145, 147, 154n.36, 155n.40, n.44
Lodge, David 25, 136, 152n.14, n.18
Lomas, David 55, 63–4n.59, 96n.49
Lotman, Yuri M. 99, 100, 120n.2, 166, 183n.71
Lucian 36, 38, 39, 42
Lucretius 295, 307n.21
Lynch, William F. 12, 21
Lyon, John 70, 71, 72
Lyotard, Jean-François 184

Mc Cormack, W.J. 207n.14, 240, 243n.9, 253
see also Maxton, Hugh
McDonagh, Martin [*The Pillowman*] 292, 296–7
McHale, Brian 219, 259, 262, 286, 312
Macintyre, Alasdair 6, 8, 9, 14

MacPike, Loralee 51, 54, 61n.42, n.45
Macquarrie, John 3, 5, 6, 7, 8
Maddox, Conroy 84, 96n.43
Maeterlinck. Maurice 67, 92n.3
Maguire, Robert 45, 46, 47, 59n.24
Maiakovsky, Vladimir 77, 89
Maimonides 10
Malcolm, Noel 18, 20, 41
Malevich, Kazimir 77, 85, 97n.52, 309
Mallarmé, Stéphane 66, 303
Manfridi, Giuseppe [*Cuckoos*] 293, 311
Manicheanism 12
Mann, Iurii 46, 48, 185, 186, 187
Marinetti, F.T. 74–6, 77, 94n.26, n.28, n.29, 147, 151n.4
Marks, Louis 191, 192, 209n.27, 210n.33, n.34
Marlowe, Christopher 254, 283
Marx Brothers, the 109, 133, 196, 198, 206n.4, 299
Maturin, Charles 15, 54, 255, 274n.12
Maxton, Hugh 253, 254, 255, 274n.12
    see also Mc Cormack, W.J.
Megaric school, the [Megarians, the] 3, 16
Meilakh, Mikhail 97n.54, 144, 145, 154n.32, n.39, n.40, 178n.8
Meinong, Alexius 11
Melville, Herman [*Bartleby*] 60n.33, 199, 213n.59
Menander 35, 36, 68
Menippean satire 36, 37, 42, 45, 56, 57n.5, 61n.45, 179n.24, 253, 268, 275n.23, 277n.50
Mercier, Vivian 228
Merleau-Ponty, Jacques 9, 14, 20, 21
metafiction 59n.26, 67, 86, 98n.65, 106, 133, 162, 223, 237, 238, 259, 263, 267, 268, 281, 284, 286, 306n.9

metatheatre 34, 133, 230, 232, 298
Meyer, Priscilla 46, 47, 59n.20, 60n.30, 307n.18
Meyrink, Gustav 162, 179n.21
Michaux, Henri 91–2, 98n.66, 121n.7, 163, 164, 179n.22, 244n.14
Michelson, Bruce 15, 17, 21, 31n.34
Milena *see* Jesenská, Milena
Miller, Arthur 195
Miller, J. Hillis 49, 50, 51, 55
Miller, Jonathan 16, 300
Miller, Karl 52, 61n.44, n.45
Miller, Tyrus 30n.32, 76, 95n.37, 163, 221, 234, 248n.47, 249n.56, n.62, 250n.70
Milligan, Spike 20, 299
Milne, A.A. 179n.19
Milner-Gulland, Robin 178n.6, 179n.21, n.22, 183n.70, 200, 202, 213n.62
mime 33, 60n.36, 128, 196, 240, 255
minimalism 158, 161–2, 166, 176, 179n.18, 180n.34, 202, 224, 228, 287, 288, 289–90
miniaturism 62n.48, 68, 166, 289–90, 299
Mnouchkine, Ariane 311
modernism 66, 68, 69, 74, 79, 80, 90, 95n.37, 107, 163, 232, 253, 263, 286, 291
Molière [Jean-Baptiste Poquelin] 34, 151n.10
Monterroso, Augusto 179n.25, 290
Monty Python's Flying Circus 20, 300
Mooney, Sinéad 221, 224, 235, 249n.64, 290
Morando, Bruno 14, 20, 21
Morgenstern, Christian 21, 31n.39
Morley, Robert 226
Morrison, Kristin 137, 138, 139, 218, 231, 243n.11, 248n.49
Mrożek, Sławomir 127, 147–8
Murphy, P.J. 240, 250n.74

music hall 35, 37, 80, 128, 153n.26, 228
Musil, Robert 95n.31

Nabokov, Vladimir 49, 50, 51, 60n.35, 62n.49, 63n.54, 70, 89, **90–1**, 93n.10, 98n.63–6, 106, 116, 121n.7, 124n.34, 145, 175, 184, 188–9, 197, 207n.14–16, 208n.20, n.21, 212n.51, 246n.30, 248n.50, 252, 253, 261, 277n.45, 287, 288, 294, 306n.11, 307n.18
Invitation to a Beheading 91, 98n.63, n.66, 145, 175
Lolita 299, 306n.11
Real Life of Sebastian Knight, The 261, 294, 307n.18
Transparent Things 277n.45, 287
Nakhimovsky, Alice Stone 85, 144, 145, 147, 154n.33, 155n.40, 163
negation ix, 6, 7, 10, 11, 29n.21, 97n.49, 105, 170, 171, 181n.45, n.49, 186, 213n.59, 234, 249n.64, 293, 298
see also via negativa
negative theology **10–13**, 29n.16, n.21, 111, 170–1, 176, 181n.49, 183n.71, 233–4, 239
Neoplatonism 225, 240
Nietzsche, Friedrich 4, 5, 6–8, 13, 20, 23, 27, 27n.4, 28n.8, n.10, 30n.24, n.29, 57n.3, 67, 75, 91, 110, 111, 116, 123n.24, 124n.33, 126, 186, 188, 201, 203, 214n.69, 220, 239, 241, 278n.54, 303
Birth of Tragedy, The 20, 57n.3, 123n.24, 241
Thus Spake Zarathustra 20, 208n.18
nihilism 4–5, 9, 27n.4, 42, 43, 50, 54, 59n.24, 76, 79, 103, 104, 115, 117, 119, 126, 160, 193, 224, 235, 240, 241, 250n.76,
297, 298, 303, 311
Noh theatre 225, 226, 229
nonsense [Nonsense] x, 12, 13, 14, 17, 18–23, 35, 39, 41–3, 56, 84, 85, 124n.36, 133, 143, 147, 162, 165, 167–9, 176, 233, 235, 269, 270, 299, 304, 311
Nooteboom, Cees [*The Following Story*] 287–8
Nothingness x, 9, 11, 23, 27n.4, 29n.14, n.18, 43, 130, 131, 173, 234, 239, 291, 303

OBERIU [Oberiuty, the] 12, 60n.31, 85–6, 97n.51, **143–7**, 154n.39–155n.44, 159–61, 167, 177n.6, n.7, 289, 291, 309
O'Brien, Fitz-James 276n.32
O'Brien, Flann [Brian O'Nolan; Myles na Gopaleen] xi, 98n.60, 155n.48, 164, 177, **251–78**, 281, 284, 286–7, 306n.2, n.6, n.7, 310, 313n.5
At Swim-Two Birds 251–2, 255, 257, **259–63**, 264, 275–6 *passim*, 281, 284, 286
Cruiskeen Lawn 258, 260, 263, 265, 268, 269, 274n.16, n.17, 275n.22
Dalkey Archive, The 253, 257, 259, 274n.17, n.23, 306n.2
Insect Play, The 253, 273n.9, 313n.5
see also Čapek Brothers
Third Policeman, The 251, 253, 254, 257, 259, **264–72**, 275n.23, n.29, 276n.38, 277n.41, n.42, 284, 286, 306n.6
Odoevsky, Vladimir 174, 183n.66, 276n.32
O'Leary, Joseph S. 225, 226, 247 *passim*
O'Nolan, Brian *see* O'Brien, Flann
Oleinikov, Nikolai 160, 165
ontology ix, 4, 18, 23, 24, 79, 102,

130, 134, 173, 177, 219, 233,
234, 262, 263, 265, 286, 295,
302
ontological argument, the 27n.3,
219
Orton, Joe 56, 126, **141–2**
What the Butler Saw 126, 142
Orwell, George 169
Ostaijen *see* Van Ostaijen, Paul
Ovid 71, 287
Metamorphoses 71

Palin, Michael 155n.42, 300
see also Ripping Yarns
Panic theatre 132
Parkin, John 16, 17, 20, 38
Parks, Tim 244n.13
Parmenides 11, 59n.28, 240
Pascal, Blaise 6, 7, 23, 115, 174
Pasley, Malcolm 204, 213n.64, n.70
Passmore, John 3, 6, 26
'pataphysics' 68, 92n.6, 280, 305n.1
Peace, Richard 62n.53, n.54
Pears, David 26, 27
Peirce, C.S. 26
Pelagianism 12
Pelevin, Victor 155n.39
Perloff, Marjorie 239, 250n.73, 304
pessimism 6, 9, 28n.6, 73, 100–7,
112, 241, 269
Pessoa, Fernando 98n.61, 99,
100–7, 108, 112, 120–1 *passim*,
160, 241, 287
Book of Disquiet, The 98n.61, 99,
101–7, 120n.4
Petronius 36, 39
Petrushevskaia, Liudmila **292–3**,
207n.16
Picabia, Francis 80, 82
Picasso, Pablo 74, 84, 107
Pilling, John 213n.63, 220, 230,
235, 236, 238, 241, 242n.5,
n.6, 243n.12, 245–6 n.23,
247n.33, 248n.49, n.53,
249n.64
Pinter, Harold 8, 23, 25, 41, 73,

127, 133, **134–41**, 142, 143,
145, 151n.1, n.9, 152–3,
155n.46, 156n.51, 184, 187,
191–4, 195, 209n.27, 210–11
passim, 227, 292, 293, 311
Betrayal 73, 127, 134, 140
Birthday Party, The 134, 137,
142, 145, 191
Caretaker, The 134, 152n.15,
153n.31
Family Voices 137, **139–40**, 141,
153n.24, 191
Homecoming, The 134, 136, 191
Landscape 136, 137, **138–9**
Last to Go 25, 136, 152n.14
Moonlight 23, 136, 137, 140–1,
153n.26, 192
Old Times 134, 140, 153n.21
Slight Ache, A 134, **137–8**, 142,
152n.19, 153n.21
Trial, The [screenplay] **192–4**
Pirandello, Luigi 67, 89, 260, 289,
293
Plato 6, 10, 16, 22, 31n.37, 59n.28,
174, 287, 288
Plautus 35, 151n.10
play theory *see* game theory
Poe, Edgar Allan 59n.28, 63n.58,
110, 123n.19, n.21, 142, 172,
175, 181n.50, 257, 272, 278n.56
'Man That Was Used Up, The'
172, 175
Purloined Letter, The 272,
278n.56
pointlessness 22, 38, 305
Polanski, Roman 211n.42, 288
Popkin, Cathy 45, 47, 58n.20,
59n.21, 60n.31
Popper, Karl 304
Post-Impressionism **69–73**, 74
postmodernism 42, 52, 68, 79,
95n.37, 140, 154n.39, 162,
166, 174, 183n.70, 258, 268,
284, 286, 289, 291, 292, 312
poststructuralism 11, 244n.13
Pound, Ezra 275n.25

pragmatics 24
pre-Socratics, the 20, 22, 174, 240
Proust, Marcel 246n.30, 252, 256, 304
pseudo-Dionyius (the Areopagite) 12, 29n.23
Punter, David 182n.59
Purdie, Susan 16

quantum theory 14, 18, 56, 295–6, 305, 308n.32, 313n.5
Quevedo, Francisco 41
Quintilian 15

Rabelais 15, 36, 38–9, 42, 43, 45, 47, 48, 57n.9, 109
Radcliffe, Ann 63n.58, 84
Rayfield, Donald 78–9
redundancy 24, 45, 130, 135, 150, 181n.48
Rees, Martin 31n.7, n.38
Reid, Robert 46
relevance 24
Renner, Stanly 172, 182n.60
Renton, Andrew 226, 247n.38
Rice, Anne 123n.26
Richter, Jean [Johann] Paul 15, 16, 19, 44, 58n.20
Ricken, Friedo 11, 29n.16, 95n.30
Ricks, Christopher 42, 43, 155n.42, 216, 217, 243n.10, 245n.19, 246n.30, 248n.47, 249m.63
Ridley, Philip 308n.25
Rimbaud, Arthur 55, 84, 97n.49, 216, 244n.13, 303
Riordan, Arthur [Improbable Frequency] 310, 313n.5
Ripping Yarns 155n.42, 300
Roberts, Graham 29n.22, 85, 86, 144, 146, 147, 154n.38, 173
Roche, Anthony 140, 153n.28
Romanticism 26, 44, 84, 126, 173, 174
    German Romanticism 6, 48, 59n.20, 66
Ronshin, Valery [Valerii] 290, 291,
306n.14
Rose, Gillian 184, 206n.3
Roth, Joseph 60n.32, 88, 90, 97n.56, 184
Roth, Philip 184, 185, 189, 206n.4
Roussel, Raymond 84, 303
Różewicz, Tadeusz 127
Russell, Bertrand 13, 21, 304
Russian Formalists/Formalism 31n.41, 42, 59n.29, 159, 236, 259, 268

Sade, Marquis de [sado-masochism] 44, 84, 108, 113, 123n.27, 142, 231, 303, 311
Said, Edward 124n.35
Salacrou, Armand 113
Salkeld, Duncan 39, 41
Saramago, José [The Year of the Death of Ricardo Reis] 107
Sartre, Jean-Paul 2–6 passim, 9, 12, 27n.2, 63n.54, 115, 124n.35, 132, 140, 153n.27, 241, 269, 293, 297, 303
    Huis Clos 140, 269, 297
    Nausea 4, 269
Saussure, F. de 26
Schelling, F.W.J. von 4, 174
Schiller, Friedrich 10, 30n.34, 80
Schubert, Franz 215, 249n.60
Schulz, Bruno 69, 89–90, 160, 184, 194, 201, 206n.3, n.4, 207n.14, 211n.39, 213n.63, 253, 312n.1
    Sanatorium Under the Sign of the Hourglass 89–90
    Street of Crocodiles, The 89–90, 312n.1
Schur, David 186, 209n.25, 213n.59, 214n.74
Schwitters, Kurt 80–1, 96n.40, 249n.59
Schopenhauer, Arthur 5, 9, 16, 28n.6, 29n.15, 201, 239, 241, 276n.35
Screech, M.A. 11, 15, 38, 39, 57n.9
Searle, Ronald see Willans, Geoffrey

Sebald, W.G. 184, 190–1, 194,
    208–9n.24, 215–16
  Vertigo 190–1, 209n.24
Segal, Erich 17, 31n.40, 34, 35, 36,
    58n.13, 68, 96n.41, 129, 130,
    132, 143, 151n.3, 151n.10,
    229–30, 232, 241
Sellers, Peter 299
Sénancourt, Etienne 9
Severianin, Igor 78
shaggy dog stories 15, 88, 130, 133,
    152n.13, 231, 255, 292, 305
Shakespeare, William 18, 33, 34, 35,
    36, 38, **39–41**, 43, 44, 48,
    57n.11, 60n.32, 68, 104, 129,
    153n.23, 232, 243n.8, n.10,
    293, 294
  Hamlet 44, 58n.13, 58n.18,
    243n.10, 294, 311
  King Henry VI, Part 2 39, 57n.11
  King Lear 35, 40–1, 52, 57n.12,
    60n.32, 231, 284
  Macbeth 40, 68, 294
Sheppard, Richard 28n.11, 68, 74,
    79–80, 88, 93n.7, 95n.33, n.36,
    96n.40
Shershenevich, Vadim 77, 78
Shestov, Lev [Chestov, Léon] 6, 8,
    10, 13, 28n.9, n.12, 35, 62n.52,
    63n.54, 115, 125n.45, 128, 186
ship of fools, the [*Ship of Fools,
    The*] x, 42, 58n.13, 147, 217,
    243n.7, 287
Shoham, S. Giora 13, 24
Showalter, English 115, 116
Shukman, Ann 25, 47, 48, 60n.29,
    170
Sicher, Efraim 47, 59n.29, 60n.33,
    n.34
Simmons, Katy 292, 307n.16
Simpson, N.F. [*A Resounding
    Tinkle*] 127, **133–4**, 141, 142,
    151n.8, 197, 226
skaz 47, 52, 59n.29
Smith, Zadie 199, 202, 204, 206n.9
Soares, Bernardo *see* Pessoa,

Fernando
Socrates 4, 6, 11, 22, 36
Somoza, José Carlos v, 306n.9, n.13
Sontag, Susan 107–8, 109, 111,
    122n.13, 123n.26, 309
Sophocles 34, 35, 41, 129, 241
Sorokin, Vladimir 291
Sorrentino, Gilbert [*Mulligan Stew*]
    284–5, 306n.7, n.9
Sperber, Dan 24, 25
Spieker, Sven 12, 46, 123n.30,
    181n.49
Spilka, Mark 60n.37, 186, 187, 188
Stalin, Joseph [Iosif]; Stalinism 77,
    85, 144, 159, 163, 169
Steiner, George 33, 53, 54, 57n.12,
    61n.38, 62n.46, n.54, 74, 80,
    93n.7, 100, 122n.16, 210n.28
Stephan, Halina 147, 148,
    155n.45–7
Stern, J.P. 5, 7, 8
Sterne, Lawrence [*Tristram Shandy*]
    41–3, 47, 48, 58n.15, 59n.21,
    60n.33, 261, 266
Stewart, Susan 18, 19, 20
Stirner, Max 244n.13
Stoics, the 11, 20, 31n.42, 41, 46,
    95n.30, 302, 303
Stokes, John 23, 141, 153n.29
Stoppard, Tom 13, 78, 80, 150,
    155n.45, n.49, 280, 284, **293–5**,
    296, 307n.18, n.22, 311, 312
  Arcadia 295
  Hapgood 295, 307n.22
  Jumpers 13, 294
  Real Inspector Hound, The 294,
    207n.18
  *Rosencrantz and Guildenstern are
    Dead* 280, 293
  Travesties 78, 80, 284, 294, 295,
    312
Strachey, Edmund 18
Strawson, Galen 9
Strindberg, August 67, 129, 131,
    133, 242
string theory 305, 308n.32

Styan, J.L. 68, 92n.3, n.5, n.6, 113,
    127, 128, 133, 153n.29
suicide 3, 91, 112, 114, 115,
    117–19 passim, 181n.45, 190,
    209n.25, 211n.37, 218, 289,
    298
Surrealism [surrealism] 9, 11,
    31n.35, 39, 42, 55, 67, 74, 76,
    79, 81–5, 86, 87, 92, 96–7
    passim, 100, 107, 108, 109,
    110, 112, 121n.13, 123n.23,
    162, 169, 233, 260, 289, 295,
    302
Sutherland, John 50
Swift, Jonathan 39, 41, 42, 56,
    58n.14, 84, 172, 243n.7
    Gulliver's Travels 42, 58n.14, 217
Symbolism 15, 74, 77, 78, 84,
    94n.24, 96n.45
Szanto, George H. 206n.3, 243n.12,
    244n.18

Tabucchi, Antonio 107, 121n.8, n.9
Tardieu, Jean 181n.56
Terence 35, 229
Terent'ev, Igor 78, 85
Tertullian 10, 12, 21, 104, 111, 115
Tertz [Terts], Abram [Siniavsky,
    Andrei] 162
theology ix, 6, 7, 18, 29n.15
    see also negative theology
Thomas, Dylan 23, 245n.20
Tigges, Wim 18, 19, 20–2, 167,
    179n.23, 265, 267, 269, 299
Tintner, Adeline 72, 93n.15
Todorov, Tzvetan 31n.42, 59n.28,
    62n.51, 69, 107, 110, 111, 127
Tokarev, D.V. 179n.21, 232, 233,
    234, 241
Topol, Josef 149
Topor, Roland 288, 289, 290, 291
Tracy, Robert 254, 273n.2, n.7, n.9
Turgenev, Ivan 4, 61n.42, 158,
    179n.17
Tynan, Kenneth 8
Tynianov, Iurii 284

Tzara, Tristan 10, 80, 82, 95n.32

Uhlmann, Anthony 223, 228, 241,
    242n.6, 243n.7, 244n.13
Unamuno, Miguel de [The Tragic
    Sense of Life] 4, 5, 6, 9, 10, 12,
    13, 21, 22, 23, 29n.24, 64n.62
uncertainty principle 14, 72, 93n.16
    see also Heisenberg, Werner
Updike, John 89, 282

Vaché, Jacques 84, 97n.50, 160
Vaginov, Konstantin 86, 97n.53,
    177n.6
Vaihinger, Hans 9, 28n.13
Valency, Maurice 34, 35
Valle-Inclán, Ramón del 67
van de Kamp, Peter 259, 273n.4,
    n.7, n.11, 274n.14, n.17,
    275n.22
Van Ostaijen, Paul 87–8, 98n.66,
    106, 121n.7, 160
Varro 36, 42, 61n.45
via negativa 10, 234
Vian, Boris 127, 280–2
    Heartsnatcher 281–2
    I Spit on Your Graves 280–1
Vigny, Alfred de 103
Villon, François 110, 284
Vitrac, Roger 155n.44
void, the x, 11, 12, 23, 43, 46, 50,
    58n.16, 59n.26, 64n.62, 68, 69,
    90, 91, 96n.47, 101, 110, 112,
    113, 119, 130, 204, 214n.69,
    221, 224, 225, 226, 239,
    244n.18, 267, 303, 307n.16
Voinovich, Vladimir 97n.57, 162
Voltaire [F.M. Arouet] 42
Vvedensky, Aleksandr 12, 29n.22,
    85–6, 97n.54, 124n.36, 143,
    145–7, 155n.40–4, 158, 159,
    177n.5, n.6, 232, 249n.57, 288
    Christmas at the Ivanovs' 86,
    146–7, 155n.40–4

Walser, Robert 213n.59

Wanner, Adrian 62n.48, 97n.52, 159, 161, 170, 176, 179n.17, n.23, 180n.25, n.34, 183n.71, 233, 256, 289
Wardle, Irving 136
Warner, Marina 208n.21
Waugh, Patricia 237, 263
Wedekind, Frank 67
Weightman, John 302–3, 308n.29
Weinberg, Steven 304, 305
Weiss, Peter 113
Welles, Orson [*The Trial*] 184, 189, 192, 206n.3
Wells, H.G. 59n.28, 94n.29, 172
Welsford, Edith 14, 37, 38, 39, 40, 57n.7, n.8
Weston, Michael 4, 10, 15, 26, 27n.5, 28n.6, 31–2n.44
Wilde, Oscar 142, 294
Wilden, Anthony 11, 12, 24
Willans, Geoffrey [*Molesworth*] 19, 300
Wilson, Angus 54
Wilson, Colin [*The Outsider*] 27n.2, 62n.49, 124n.35
Wilson, Deirdre 24, 25
Winterson, Jeannette 2
Witkiewicz, Stanisław ['Witkacy'] 57n.11, 89, 97n.58, 107, 108, 124n.36, 143, 148
Wittgenstein, Ludwig 13, 14, 26, 30n.26, 32n.45, 86, 144, 150, 181n.49, 201, 239, 250n.73, 277n.43, 294, 304, 307n.16
   Philosophical Investigations, The 26, 32n.45, 250n.73, 294
   Tractatus, The 181n.49, 250n.73
Wood, Michael 23, 193, 194, 203, 206n.3
Worton, Michael 230
Wragg, Ted 310
Wright, M.R. 11, 20, 30n.27, 33, 57n.2

Xenophanes of Colophon 29n.16

Yeats, W.B. 153n.28

Zabolotsky, Nikolai 85, 158–9, 160, 178n.6
Zarhy-Levo, Yael 136, 141, 152n.12, 293, 294, 310, 312
Zatonsky, Dmitri 205, 205n.1
zaum' [trans-sense language] 19, 77, 78, 85, 109, 143
Zdanevich, Il'ia 78, 99
Zeifman, Hersh 153n.23, 215, 307n.22
Zen *see* Buddhism
Zenith, Richard 101, 120n.3, 120–1n.4
Zeno of Elea [Zeno's paradox] 205n.2, 240, 247n.3
Zinman, Toby Silverman 292
Zinoviev, Aleksandr 214n.65
Žižek, Slavoj 184